SPECIFICATIONS FOR COMMERCIAL INTERIORS

SPECIFICATIONS FOR COMMERCIAL INTERIORS

S.C. REZNIKOFF

WHITNEY LIBRARY OF DESIGN
an imprint of Watson-Guptill Publications/New York

First published in New York by Whitney Library of Design
an imprint of Watson-Guptill Publications
a division of Billboard Publications, Inc.
1515 Broadway, New York, NY 10036

Library of Congress Cataloging-in-Publication Data
Reznikoff, S. C.
    Specifications for commercial interiors : professional
liabilities, regulations, and performance criteria / S. C. Reznikoff.
  —Rev. ed.
        p.   cm.
    Bibliography: p.
    Includes index.
    ISBN 0-8230-4893-4
    1. Building laws—United States. 2. Architects—Malpractice—
United States. 3. Building—Contracts and specifications—United
States. 4. Interior decoration. I. Title.
KF5701.R49   1989
343.73'07869—dc19
[347.3037869]   88-38890
                                                                       CIP

Manufactured in U.S.A.
First printing of this edition, 1989

2 3 4 5 6 7 8 9 / 94 93 92 91 90

For my Mother, Husband, Son, and Daughter

ACKNOWLEDGMENTS

The interior architectural students at Arizona State University provided the stimulus for this book and gave continued suggestions and encouragement throughout the research and development stages.

A book of this scope would not have been possible without the assistance of many people. I am especially indebted to Erma Striner, director of the General Services Administration Design Action Center, for valuable research directives. Among the many federal agencies that supplied information and data are the National Institute of Standards and Technology (formerly Bureau of Standards), the National Fire Academy, the Consumers Product Safety Commission, the Federal Supply Services, the Department of Health and Human Services, and the General Services Administration.

Richard Hopper, Carpet and Rug Institute; Hank Roux, Armstrong Cork Company; John Galloway, Dupont Company; Don Henning, IBD; Cliff Avery, ASID; Diane Bramman Worth, ADID; Richard E. Stevens, NFPA; Professors Mary Shipley and Richard Perrell, FCSI, are among the people who reviewed portions of the manuscript and made helpful suggestions. Fire Engineers Donald Belles and Edward Prendergast also offered expert guidance.

The National Fire Protection Association, the American Society for Testing and Materials, the Construction Specifications Institute, the Architectural Woodwork Institute, the Carpet and Rug Institute, the Carpet Cushion Council, the Wallcovering Manufacturers Association, the Hardwood Plywood Manufacturers Association, and the Business and Institutional Furniture Manufacturer's Association are a few of the organizations that generously supplied information.

The scope of this book was greatly enhanced by people in private industry and those design firms that gave permission for the inclusion of their photographs, drawings, and specifications.

Michael Byun, Andrew Goodman, Barbara and Gary Powell, Bambi Wesche, and Lu Schildmeyer worked many evenings and weekends to prepare the typed manuscript, drawings, and charts.

Without the enthusiasm and encouragement provided by the editors and staff of The Whitney Library of Design, this book would not have been possible. Special thanks to Sarah Bodine who visualized the timeliness and importance of the material and gave invaluable editorial guidance. I am particularly grateful to Susan Davis whose editorial expertise guided the original work to completion. This second edition was started under the guidance of Julia Moore. Cornelia Guest, Senior Editor, worked many hours to fine tune every detail of this second edition.

CONTENTS

LIST OF ABBREVIATIONS

AATCC   American Association of Textile Chemists and Colorists
AHA   American Hardboard Association
AHLI   American Home Lighting Institute
AIA   American Institute of Architects
ALSC   American Lumber Standards Committee
ANSI   American National Standards Institute
APA   American Plywood Association
ASAHC   American Society of Architectural Hardware Consultants
ASHRAE   American Society of Heating, Refrigerating, and Air Conditioning Engineers, Inc.
ASID   American Society of Interior Designers
ASTM   American Society for Testing and Materials
ASI   American Specification Institute
AWI   Architectural Woodwork Institute
BHMA   Builders Hardware Manufacturers Association
BIFMA   Business and Institutional Furniture Manufacturers Association
BOCA   Building Officials Conference of America
BRAB   Building Research Advisory Board
BRI   Building Research Institute
CCC   Carpet Cushion Council
CIA   Cork Institute of America
CPSC   Consumer Product Safety Commission
CRI   Carpet and Rug Institute
CS   Commercial Standards
CSI   Construction Specifications Institute
CTI   Ceramic Tile Institute
DOC   Department of Commerce
DOL   Department of Labor
DOT   Department of Transportation
DWI   Durable Woods Institute
EPA   Environmental Protection Agency
FAA   Federal Aviation Administration
FHA   Federal Housing Administration
FPL   Forest Products Laboratory
FPRS   Forest Products Research Society
FRA   Federal Railroad Administration
FS   Federal Specifications
FSPT   Federation of Societies for Paint Technology
FSS   Federal Supply Service
FTC   Federal Trade Commission
FTI   Facing Tile Institute
FTMS   Federal Test Method Standard
GSA   General Services Administration
HHS   Department of Health and Human Services
HMMA   Hardware Merchants and Manufacturers Association
HPMA   Hardwood Plywood Manufacturers Association
HPSC   Home Products Safety Council
HUD   Department of Housing and Urban Development
IBD   Institute of Business Designers
ICBO   International Conference of Building Officials
IDEC   Interior Designer Educators Council
IES   Illuminating Engineering Society

LCC   Life Cycle Costing
MA   Mahogany Association, Inc.
MCSC   Model Codes Standardization Council
MFMA   Maple Flooring Manufacturers Association
MIA   Marble Institute of America
MIL   Military Specifications
MPS   Minimum Property Standards
NADAF   National Association of Decorative Architectural Finishes
NAMD   National Association of Marble Dealers
NAMM   National Association of Mirror Manufacturers
NAMP   National Association of Marble Producers
NBC   National Basic Building Code
NBHA   National Builders Hardware Association
NCIDQ   National Council for Interior Design Qualification
NEC   National Electrical Code
NFPA   National Fire Protection Association
NHLA   National Hardwood Lumber Association
NIBS   National Institute of Building Sciences
NIST   National Institute of Standards and Technology
NKCA   National Kitchen Cabinet Association
NOFMA   National Oak Flooring Manufacturers Association
NPDA   National Plywood Distributors Association
NPVLA   National Paint, Varnish, and Lacquer Association
NTMA   National Terrazzo and Mosaic Association
NWMA   National Woodwork Manufacturers Association
OSHA   Occupational Safety and Health Administration
PBS   Public Building Service
PHS   Public Health Service
PLIB   Pacific Lumber Inspection Bureau
PMA   Philippine Mahogany Association
PPW   Ponderosa Pine Woodwork
PRF   Plywood Research Foundation
PS   Product Standards
SBC   Standard Building Code
SGA   Stained Glass Association of America
SPA   Southern Pine Association
SPI   Society of the Plastics Industry, Inc.
SSA   Social Security Administration
SSBC   Southern Standard Building Code
TC   Tile Council of America
UBC   Uniform Building Code
UL   Underwriters Laboratories, Inc.
ULC   Underwriters Laboratories of Canada
USCS   United States Department of Commerce, Commercial Standards
USFA   United States Fire Administration
VA   Veterans Administration
WCLIB   West Coast Lumber Inspection Bureau
WFIA   Wood Flooring Institute of America

Mathematical Symbols
$>$ Greater than
$<$ Less than
Σ Summation of

INTRODUCTION

It may prove unsettling to take a backward look at some of the events that have brought the interior designer to this era of liabilities and regulations. Until the mid-1960s, interior design had been a profession rooted in aesthetics and involved almost exclusively in residential work. *Contract design*, a term meaning the design of commercial and institutional spaces, evolved during the late fifties and early sixties. The prosperity of these years brought about a surge of commercial construction. Small and large corporations turned to designers for assistance in planning and furnishing interior spaces that would project a corporate image. An editorial by Harry Anderson in *Interior Design* magazine in 1961 proudly announced "the interior designer's role as sculptor of the corporate image through the interior environment that he creates for business is now well established and respected . . . the finest non-residential interiors are created by professionals trained in residential work because of their *instinctive sensitivity* to the requirements of the individual."[1]

Apparently the transition from the personalized residential role to the corporate image-maker was not too difficult for the interior designer. And it soon became evident that there were two major advantages in commercial work: One was economic gain and the other was professional status. Sherman Emery's 1965 editorial in *Interior Design* magazine expressed the professional identity problems of that period: "The tremendous growth in contract work in recent years can be measured in more than dollars and cents. For in addition to becoming a multi-million dollar business, it has greatly increased *the professional standing* of the designer. Designing a non-residential installation also carries with it the connotation of *professionalism* . . . it frequently requires working with an architect, and this helps to further the *professional image*."[2]

The past three decades have witnessed the dynamic evolution of the interior design profession. The formation of the *American Society of Interior Designers* (ASID) in 1974, resulting from the merger of the American Institute of Designers and the National Society of Interior Designers, created the largest single organization of professional designers in the United States. The *Institute of Business Designers* (IBD) was organized in the mid-1960s to meet the needs of the increasing number of designers specializing in commercial design work. Professional membership in these major national organizations requires that design competence be measured by the successful completion of a qualifying examination. The *National Council of Interior Design Qualification* (NCIDQ), composed of members from concerned organizations, developed and administers the examination. During the late 1980s, ASID, IBD, and other interior design professional organizations worked together to gain legal registration in many states. In 1989, the American Institute of Architects (AIA) joined with ASID and IBD to reach a consensus regarding a unified approach to title registration of interior designers.

Commercial and institutional design currently represents a $15 billion industry and involves more than the creation of a corporate image. More is required of a designer than "instinctive sensitivity." The increase in federal regulations and the liability-lawsuit trend have resulted in an increasing professional sense of responsibility and a concern for acquiring more information about the technical and behavioral sciences. With this new emphasis, designers have become better equipped to deal with critical commercial and institutional spatial needs. It has, however, become increasingly difficult for the practicing designer to maintain a working knowledge of the technical advances in performance testing and the accompanying federal regulations. The primary purpose of this book is to provide this needed information that will allow designers to establish a systematic approach to making responsible specification decisions and thereby to minimize the possibility of professional liability. The contents of the book are divided into three parts:

Part 1 established the bases for specification decisions. Chapters 1 and 2 provide information on current professional and product liability problems facing designers today. Chapter 3 compiles information from many diverse sources to present a summary of federal and state regulations. Chapter 4 deals with potential fire hazards in interior spaces and Chapter 5 covers fire test methods used to evaluate and establish code regulations for a major number of interior finishes. Chapter 6 examines the extensive research that has provided the link between interior furnishings and upholstery to the early stages of a fire scenario. The codes and regulations specifically dealing with this aspect are explained.

Part 2 provides the designer with a survey of interior subsystems and materials. Specification guidelines for each subsystem include information on construction and quality control, performance standards and regulations, installation, maintenance, and methods of life cycle costing.

Part 3 deals with the format and contents of specification documents. The importance of coordinating working drawings, schedules, and specification documents is clarified.

Chapter 18 explains the use of the Master Format developed by the Construction Specifications Institute as a means of data management.

Part 1

LIABILITIES AND REGULATIONS

PROFESSIONAL LIABILITIES

The last three decades in America have been called the "golden age of consumerism." During the seventies, Ralph Nader became the consumer's advocate. In a 10-year period, 20 pieces of consumer legislation were presented to Congress; of them, 16 were passed into law.

Because the professional designer of commercial spaces may not actually sell products to an individual consumer, the designer may think that consumer legislation has little effect on his or her practice. Actually the commercial designer has created a new type of consumer—a *captive consumer*. A captive consumer is a person or persons using offices and public spaces such as hospitals, stores, airports, and other non-live-in institutional space. They are considered "captive" because they have not been directly involved in the selection of the interior materials, furniture, and furnishings they are forced to use.

Each time a designer enters into a contractual agreement and specifies furnishings, floor, and wallcoverings, or any other subsystem of a commercial or institutional space, he or she becomes liable, or *responsible*, for the performance of that system. The system should perform well under normal usage and under critical conditions that might occur. As in the case of fire, the material should not contribute excessively to flame spread or smoke development.

In a study prepared by the Office of Professional Liability Research, a division of the Victor O. Schinnerer Company, it was found that malpractice suits against architects were increasing at a rate of 20 percent a year. The report also stated that the average value of claims against architects for alleged design and construction failure had tripled from 1960 to 1978. By the mid-seventies almost 30 percent of insured architectural firms had been sued. In the 1980s it was not uncommon for insurance premiums to increase from 100 to 400 percent. These increased premiums frequently accounted for almost 6 percent of a small design firm's total income.

DIFFERING VIEWS ON THE LIABILITY PROBLEM

During this decade of increasing liability lawsuits, we have witnessed the development of many differing views on the advantages and disadvantages of this trend. Justin Sweet, professor of law at the University of California and an authority on professional liability, observed that "Those who support such a trend argue that it is long overdue. They contend that professional persons have enjoyed a type of immunity from responsibility for their acts which is not accorded others. Those who favor such a trend content that it has made professional persons exercise a higher degree of care than they would have without such legal accountability. They also argue that professionals often operate through highly organized and profitable associations which can and should respond for losses caused by their conduct in furnishing professional services. This trend can also be supported as a method of eliminating incompetent professionals who somehow manage to continue to practice because of the laxity of enforcement of licensing and registration laws."

Many professional groups feel that such increased liability in the long run hampers proper professional practice. Opponents of increased professional liability state that it has forced professionals into large organizations which have not always produced imaginative professional work. They agree that increased liability has caused the rates for professional liability insurance to soar astronomically and places an unreasonable burden on the younger professional. They also contend that increased professional liability will inhibit professionals from using new or unconventional techniques for fear that they will be held liable if things go wrong. While some professionals are willing to accept legal responsibility for their negligence, they feel that in reality they will be held to a standard of perfection by judges and juries. If anything goes wrong, they fear they will be held responsible.[1]

BASES FOR MOST LIABILITY SUITS

The legal bases for most liability suits are professional negligence, implied warranty or misrepresentation, implied fitness warranty, breach of contract, joint and several liability, and liability without fault for design defects. In many circumstances, these legal bases overlap. For example, a designer's failure to condemn or reject defective work by a supplier or contractor may be classified as professional negligence and breach of contract.

Professional Negligence. The concept of professional negligence is based on the ability of the client to prove one or more of the following:

1. That the designer exposed the client to unreasonable risk

2. That the designer did not conform to a certain *standard of professional conduct*

3. That a reasonably close or casual connection existed between the designer's conduct and the client's injury (whether physical or monetary)

4. That a legally protected right was involved (this can include personal, economic, or emotional injuries)

Many liability suits involve simple errors of omission; however, whenever a designer exposes others to unreasonable risks because of defective design, selection of inadequate or improper materials or equipment, and/or failure to condemn defective work, he or she can be sued for professional negligence. Many disputes have involved the performance failure of a certain product or material. In other cases, the problem stems not from product failure, but from negligence on the part of the designer to determine the right material for a particular use. A hospital forced to replace carpeting a few months after installation because the designer was unaware of static buildup in critical areas should rightfully seek retribution.

Negligence in tort law is frequently defined in degrees.

1. Slight negligence is failure to use great care.

2. Ordinary negligence is failure to use ordinary care.

3. Gross negligence is failure to use even slight care.

Other types of negligence are listed in the Glossary at the end of Chapter 2.

Implied Warranty or Misrepresentation. A designer's ability to perform design work is not directly stated in a contractual agreement, but it is *implied*, and therefore warrants, or promises, professional competence. Verbal opinions expressed by a designer can also be construed as implied warranties. The definiteness with which the designer's professional opinion is stated may be the deciding factor in a legal judgment. It should be noted that compliance with building and fire codes is usually an implied warranty in a professional design contract. Failure to comply with state and local codes may also be considered professional negligence.

Implied Fitness Warranty. This warranty involves the specification of a product or material that later proves unfit for the intended use. If the designer knew of the specific intended use and the client relied on the designer's knowledge and skill, then the designer is responsible. However, if the client ordered the use of a certain product or material, based on the specification of a third party, the designer would not be held responsible. The American Society of Interior Designers advises that the designer "refrain from procuring furniture, furnishings, and equipment in any capacity other than as an agent for the owner. If the Designer is considered to have purchased and RESOLD FF&E, then the Designer may incur liability under an express warranty, under implied warranties of merchantability and fitness for a particular use, as well as under strict products liability (liability regardless of fault or negligence) for any defects in the FF&E, as part of the 'chain of distribution.'"[2]

Breach of Contract. Breach of contract requires proof that the "breach" or failure to perform the design contract has caused actual loss to the client. This usually involves monetary loss for which the client seeks retribution. Designers should be aware that, in addition to the stated written content of the contract, there may also be many *implied* responsibilities. In some cases, this may involve design errors that are responsible for additional construction costs, depreciation of property values, or loss of the owner's business profit. If a retail store is scheduled to open on a certain date and the opening is delayed because an area is unfinished or a counter was built according to inaccurate measurements specified by the designer, then the designer is responsible for the owner's loss of income caused by the delayed opening.

Although it is not common in breach-of-contract cases, a client may seek restitution for "emotional distress" or "mental concern." This can involve the general satisfaction of the client regarding subjective decisions, such as color choice. While color selections may be approved at every phase of the design work, the client's inability to visualize the final installation may result in disagreement.

Lawsuits have also been based on mental anguish. For example, if a section of a mirrored wall begins to crack, the clients may suffer mental anguish concerning their safety. In addition, if the client can prove undue "aggravation and inconvenience," the designer will be ordered to pay restitution.[3] Legal judgments regarding mechanical performance are usually objective, but decisions involving aesthetics are often necessarily subjective.

Joint and Several Liability. This legal concept is based on the sharing of rights and *liabilities* among a group of people individually and collectively. The injured party may collect equal or unequal amounts from each party found guilty of negligence. The client cannot, however, collect in total more than the amount of damages. (See the "deep pockets concept" in the Glossary at the end of Chapter 2.)

Liability without Fault for Design Defects. Most professional contracts attempt to clearly define the limits of responsibility for both the designer and involved contractors. If, however, any injury or damage does occur that is the direct result of the designer's drawings, design, or specification, the designer will be held responsible. If the designer or his or her employees gave instructions or directions that can be proven to have been the primary cause of the injury or damage, the design firm will be held responsible.

Although liability suits have increased against interior designers, no formal study has been made to determine the exact number of claims. A random sampling of the types of suits incurred by designers in the early 1980s indicates that the majority of claims involved three major areas:

1. Professional negligence
   a. Defective design
   b. Inaccurate measurements
   c. Noncompliance with codes

2. Breach of contract
   a. Defective design delaying job completion
   b. Inadequate supervision of installations

3. Implied warranty
   a. Specification of materials unsuitable for intended use

The two most frequent causes for claims were *inaccurate measurements* and the *specification of chairs unsuitable for intended use*.

HOW TO LESSEN THE POSSIBILITY OF LIABILITY SUITS

There are six specific ways that you can protect yourself from the possibility of liability suits: perform within your area of expertise, use concise contracts and specifications, comply with codes and regulations, secure the services of reputable contractors and/or workrooms, keep accurate records, and secure legal counsel and liability insurance.

Perform within Your Area of Expertise. Many designers undertake project responsibilities that fall outside the acceptable area of practice generally understood by courts of law to be the prerogative of the interior designer. Structural alterations, rewiring, heating, and air-conditioning changes do not fall within the realm of interior design practice. Designers must comply with the legally established definitions of architecture and interior design. Each state has different laws governing design practice. Designers in each profession are legally responsible to seek the assistance of other professionals licensed to practice the design of lighting, acoustics, interior plant landscaping, and other specialized areas. Legally, designers are not able to collect fees for services performed outside their area of expertise.

Use Concise Contracts and Specifications. Contracts should carefully list all the areas of responsibility, both of the designer and of the owner/client. Although the law does not hold designers to a standard of perfection in the performance of professional services, applicable legal standards can be unintentionally, but dramatically, altered by the terms of the professional's contract. Courts will construe common words and phrases in contracts according to their common meaning. Therefore, every word in a contract should be read and interpreted literally and not according to the custom usage, or slang, of the construction or design profession. When a contract contains provisions which connote a standard of perfection, the successful defense of a professional liability claim arising out of those provisions becomes very difficult, if not impossible.

The following is a common example of a contract provision which seems to indicate that the designer's performance must reach unrealistic levels of attainment:

The Design Professional shall prepare complete drawings and specifications for the project.[4]

According to various dictionary definitions for the word "complete," this contract requirement would obligate the designer to prepare drawings and specifications that were not lacking or incomplete in any respect; i.e., they must be perfect. Even though the law only requires design professionals to prepare drawings and specifications in accordance with the ordinary standard of care of the profession, i.e., without negligence, a court could interpret the above contract provision to hold that a substantially higher standard of performance had been agreed to by the parties. To avoid this problem, the use of substitute language patterned after the following would be helpful:

The Design Professional shall prepare drawings and specifications setting forth in sufficient detail the requirements for constructing the Project.[5]

In fact, the above statement is all that the parties normally intend since the drawings and specifications are not an end in themselves. They are the documents by which the designer conveys the design requirements to the contractor so that the project can be constructed. Therefore, designers should avoid contract terms which are absolute in their meaning unless that result is exactly what is intended by the parties.

Professional contracts should also clarify the meaning of estimated costs and project completion dates in regard to unforeseen circumstances beyond the control of the designer.

Comply with Codes and Regulations. Compliance with codes does not provide an absolute defense, but helps in proving that the designer was aware of *standards of professional conduct.* Determine the authorities who have jurisdiction to regulate a particular project.

A designer who specifies upholstery or drapery fabric that does not comply with local fire codes may face a legal suit if the installation fails to pass a fire safety inspection that results in delaying completion of the project. Ignorance of a code or regulation is not a legal defense. Refer to Chapter 3 for more information on code compliance.

Secure the Services of Reputable Contractors and/or Workrooms. Be familiar with previous work of consultants and contractors; their skill and expertise should be consistently evident. Reliability in regard to meeting installation and job deadlines is an important aspect to consider.

Keep Accurate Records. There are many complicated details that demand attention during the course of a project. The areas of concern where the designer's responsibility is most frequently in question are changes of orders, directive instructions given during the course of the project, and rejection of defective work. Verbal discussions with clients and verbal instructions given to contractors should be subsequently recorded in written form.

Secure Legal Counsel and Liability Insurance. Two professional organizations, the American Society of Interior Designers and the Institute of Business Designers, have provided their memberships with a group professional liability insurance policy. Many policies cover errors, omissions, and negligent acts as a result of drawings, plans, specifications, schedules, and shop drawings. The coverage may not include implied warranties and inaccurate estimates of probable cost or cost estimates being exceeded. Coverage is usually extended only to work performed within the "customary" area of interior design performance; i.e., no structural alterations or other work normally performed by other professions. Legal counsel should be obtained on all contractual and insurance matters.

Note: A glossary of terms for Chapters 1 and 2 appears at the end of Chapter 2.

PRODUCT LIABILITY

A major problem affecting manufacturers, retailers, wholesalers, and distributors is the abundance of product liability lawsuits. Although designers may consider this an exclusive concern of manufacturers, evidence points to the fact that designers and specifiers not infrequently become involved in product liability suits because of *strict liability* tort laws which extend responsibility to those outside the chain of distribution. It is therefore important to understand current product liability laws and the ensuing product liability insurance problems which directly affect the availability and cost of interior systems.

Product liability is primarily concerned with negligence. It is considered the "duty" of the manufacturer to provide products that will not expose the consumer to undue risk, bodily injury, death, or property damage as a result of the construction, design, installation, and assembly of the product. Also included in product liability actions is the manufacturer's failure to warn against a danger or hazard in the use or misuse of the product and failure to provide adequate instructions for the use of the product. Violation of *express warranty* may also be involved. An express warranty is a guaranty of performance and includes all advertising claims made by the manufacturer.

PRODUCT-RELATED INJURIES

Each year the U.S. Consumer Product Safety Comission publishes a list of product-related accidents. The list is long and includes everything from carpet to sporting and recreational equipment. A sampling from a recent survey indicates the large number of reported injuries involving chairs and other furnishings (see Table 2.1).

In a recent survey, published in *Human Behavior Magazine©, it was found that 40 percent of the consumers questioned expressed a caveat emptor* (buyer beware) attitude.[1]

  50% believed manufacturers shirked their responsibility to buyers
  75% thought manufacturers were more interested in making a profit than in serving the customer
  55% concluded the quality of products was not being improved
  32% favored the federal government testing of competitive brands and the establishment of standards
  75% favored a federal Consumer Protection Agency

These opinions undoubtedly contributed to the large increase in product liability claims.

BASES FOR EVALUATING PRODUCT LIABILITY ACTIONS

Courts of law attempt to determine the contents and validity of the complaint against a product by examination of the following areas of concern: statute of limitations, foreseeable events, useful life of the product, misuse or subsequent product modification, state of the art, duty to warn, punitive damages, and strict liability.

Statute of Limitations. Statutes of limitations establish prescribed time periods during which certain types of claims must be filed. These limitations vary from state to state. A typical

TABLE 2.1 PRODUCT-RELATED INJURIES

	Estimated Injuries
Chairs, not upholstered	105,977
Chairs, upholstered	1,897
Couches/sofas	17,324
Bars and bar stools	6,430
Tables	85,592
Glass tables	4,421
Furniture, not otherwise specified	11,781
Carpeting	1,184
Window shades/blinds	2,933

The Administrative Office of the U.S. Courts statistics show the continuing increase in product-liability cases. Source: Consumer Product Safety Commission.

situation involving a 12-year-old hotel will serve to illustrate the problem. When the hotel was new an interior designer for the project specified 200 chairs for the dining area. The chairs were used consistently for the 12 years, perhaps 7 to 100 times a day. One evening during routine cleaning, an employee dropped one of the chairs, which imperceptibly weakened the structure of the chair. The next morning a customer sat on the chair, which collapsed, and the customer was injured. The legal suit that followed provoked many perplexing problems. How long is a manufacturer or a designer responsible for the performance of a product? Research has found that 4 percent of all product liability claims involve products 25 years old. Insurance sources report that every decade produces claims on products manufactured 50 years prior to the injury. There are also many claims against products 20 years or older. Products in use for approximately 6 years account for the largest number of claims.

Many current statutes allow product-related claims to be filed against the manufacturer at the time of the injury, regardless of the age of the product involved. This procedure has provoked much concern for statute of limitations reform. If the mechanisms of statutes of limitations are to be changed from a time-of-injury to a time-of-sale basis, the best approach may involve making the statute applicable only to certain types of products. Product-related injuries are rare after 10 years have elapsed from the time of sale. However, capital goods, such as furniture, which frequently lasts a long time, seem more susceptible to such claims. Consideration should be given to allow the statute to regulate only durable industrial goods or to assign different lengths of time to different categories of products.

Another approach that has been suggested would allow the statute to run from the date of sale only if the product had been used without problems in the intervening period. Suggested limitation periods have ranged from 4 to 12 years. If this approach were to be adopted, certain claims, such as those resulting from long periods of improper maintenance and use, rather than from the defective condition of the product when sold, would be eliminated. However, where the evidence indicates that improper maintenance was the cause of the injury, courts have for the most part refused to impose liability upon the manufacturer.

Limiting the duration of time for which a manufacturer could be liable for its products would undoubtedly reduce the number of claims, eliminate much of the current uncertainty, and perhaps allow manufacturers to price their products more accurately. However, such results could also be accomplished by the use of the "useful life" approach.

Useful Life. To some extent the courts have recognized the concept of *useful life*, citing the adage that "a manufacturer or seller is not required, under the law, to produce or sell a product that will never wear out."[2] The courts have also refused to impose liability where the evidence indicates that the accident in question was caused by normal wear and tear of the product. Thus the institution of useful life defense has been suggested. Under such a defense, a manufacturer would incur no liability after the product's useful life had expired.

Misuse or Subsequent Modification. Misuse is often cited as a defense by the manufacturer. If the seller or the consumer made alterations or modifications to a product and these subsequently became the substantial cause of the incident giving rise to the claim, then the manufacturer is not held responsible. This also applies to the installation of a product that was not operated in compliance with the directions or specifications of the manufacturer. Misuse of a given product may involve the injured party or a third party. Manufacturers claim that misuse is considered "unforeseeable" at the time that the product is manufactured.

Foreseeable Events. Based on fire statistics, fire in public places is considered a *foreseeable* event. Designers and manufacturers may legally be expected to conform to the general rules of foreseeability that are applied in many product-injury cases. A 1973 ruling made in the case of *Raymond v. Reigel Textiles* states that manufacturers must "anticipate the environment which is normal for the use of their product and must anticipate the reasonable foreseeable risk of the use of their product."

State of the Art. Many groups of manufacturers have complained that groups have judged the danger of their products according to the current state of technology and knowledge, even if the product was as safe as others at the time of sale. Although courts admit evidence known as *industry custom* with respect to a product, it is not a final determinant of the issue of proper design, since the entire industry may be remiss in its design.

Duty to Warn.
Products. Manufacturers feel that duty to warn should apply only to products that are dangerous beyond what the ordinary consumer would expect. The courts consider what is known as "common knowledge"; i.e., a manufacturer of shoes that become slippery when wet is not liable because it is common knowledge that shoes tend to become slippery when wet. This, combined with unrealistic consumer expectations of product performance, plays a large part in product liability.

Environment. The duty to warn must be in ratio to the risks that are perceived in the environment in which the product is used. Warning must be adequate to provide safety

1. for people in public buildings at any given time;

2. for use in immediate surroundings and in remote areas of a building. For example, toxic gases and smoke from products burning on the first floor in the 1980 MGM Grand Hotel fire contributed to the death of hotel guests twenty floors above.

Punitive Damages. Punitive damages are awarded as an additional remedy to supplement compensatory damages in actions where the defendant's conduct shows intentional or reckless disregard of the rights of the consumer. The basic purposes behind the doctrine are to punish manufacturers for their misconduct and to deter them and others from engaging in such conduct in the future. Punitive damages must be proven with clear and convincing evidence. Some states are placing a monetary limit on punitive damage claims. Other states do not allow punitive damages to be awarded in actions for property damages.

Strict Liability. Strict liability was initiated to alleviate problems of the consumer's burden of proof. It shifts the focus from the conduct of the manufacturer to the performance of the product. In design defect cases, the alleged defective design is considered the result of a conscious choice, whether the problem developed through the manufacturing process or was the result of a design defect. The difference between negligence and strict liability, in either a design or manufactured defect, is the element of conscious choice or knowledge on the part of the manufacturer or designer that the product was potentially dangerous. Strict liability is a much more serious charge than simple negligence, which may only involve a worker omitting a bolt during the assembly of a product.

HOW DESIGNERS CAN MINIMIZE PRODUCT LIABILITY ACTIONS

Specify Products Manufactured for the Intended Use. Manufacturers of commercial and institutional interior systems claim that a large percentage of product liability actions result from designers' specification of products that are unsuitable for the intended use. Some manufacturers have become actively engaged in educating designers about their role in preventive measures to lessen the number of product liability claims. In some cases manufacturers insist on supplying the designer with a written statement relieving the manufacturer from responsibility for the life of the product if improper specifications are made. They point out that their product liability insurance rates, which have increased dramatically in the last decade, are reflected in increased wholesale prices to designers and clients.[3]

Figure 2.1 illustrates the rapid increase of product-related cases in federal district courts from 1975–1985. Increased insurance rates are a reflection of the erratic but continued growth in jury-awarded settlements (see Figure 2.2).

GLOSSARY FOR CHAPTERS 1 AND 2

Code violation: A violation of the building code. While code violation does not provide conclusive evidence of negligence, it does make it easy to establish a designer's liability.

Culpable negligence: Criminal negligence that is more than the slight negligence found in civil law. In criminal law, culpable negligence is recklessness or carelessness resulting in injury or death. Headless disregard and indifference to the safety or rights of others.

Damages: The monetary compensation that the law awards to one who has been injured by the actions of another. This can include a legal wrong such as breach of contract.

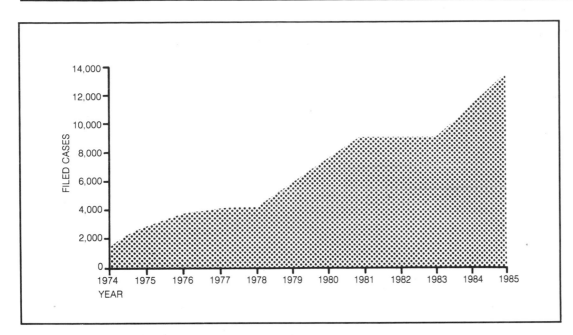

Figure 2.1 Product liability case filed in federal district court. Source: Administrative Office of the United States Courts.

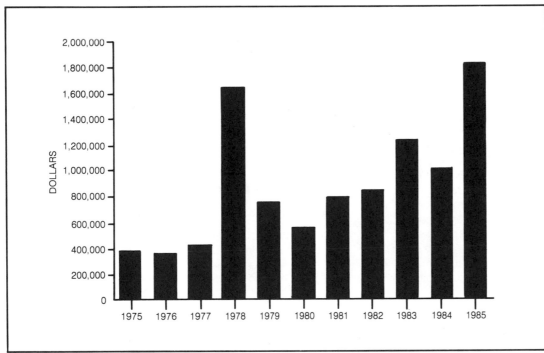

Figure 2.2 Average product liability jury verdict. Source: Administrative Office of the United States Courts.

Deep pocket concept: A concept that a plaintiff is allowed to collect large monetary awards from a rich defendent, regardless of blame.

Fault-based liability: Liability often based on standards of professional care, such as charges of negligence.

Frivolous suits: Claims not supported by fact or clearly lacking in substance.

Injury: Any wrong or damage done to another, either to that individual's person, rights, reputation, or property. Not to be confused with the ordinary meaning of "injury," which refers to damages to the body. Legal injury refers to a violation of a legal right.

Joint and several liability: Liability in which more than one person or official may be held responsible.

Standard of care: A uniform standard of behavior or care requiring a person to do what is expected of a reasonable person. The theory of "negligence" is based on this. The professional designer would be expected to do what other professionals would have done.

Tort: A wrong, either private or civil, or an injury resulting from a breach of a legal duty that exists because of society's expectation regarding interpersonal conduct. Does not refer to obligations established by a contract or other private relationship. Torts include wrongs, such as assault and slander.

Tort reform: Efforts to limit the monetary amounts of claims; i.e., to put a "cap" on maximum claims.

Wanton negligence: An intentional act of an unreasonable character in disregard of a known risk. "Wanton" has the same meaning as "willful" and "reckless."

REGULATIONS AND STANDARDS

Just as in all other aspects of life, government regulations and standards have become necessary to protect people from unsafe living and working conditions. This chapter will survey federal, state, and local legislation; detail building codes as well as the authorities with jurisdiction; and discuss risk management procedures for compliance.

FEDERAL REGULATIONS

Though many people consider federal regulations an intrusion on the rights of individuals and private enterprise, few of us understand that the origin of those regulations dealing with product performance and fire safety is the result of the federal government's power to regulate commerce among the states. The rationale of this approach is the need to protect the safety of the general public and maintain a steady flow of interstate commerce. For example, if the practices of the petroleum industry are unsafe, tragic accidents could result that would close down operations of a major part of that industry. This shutdown could trigger an economic chain reaction affecting transportation, employment, and the building industry, which might jeopardize the nation's entire economic structure.

Laws are passed periodically, as Congress sees the need for uniform regulations in certain areas of industry. The enforcement of these laws is delegated to various federal agencies and departments. Each agency is authorized to develop further regulations within the limits of authority granted it by a specific act of Congress. Even though the regulations may not be actual congressional legislation, they have the binding force of law. Violation of a regulation can result in criminal penalties ranging from sizable fines to incarceration.

Table 3.1 summarizes the various federal agencies and departments that regulate areas pertinent to professional designers. The agencies and departments that *enforce* standards and regulations are noted. The identities and functions of these agencies can change without notice. Their function depends on current need.

STATE AND LOCAL LEGISLATION

State laws dealing with public safety represent an exercise of the powers that are "reserved to the states" in the Tenth Amendment of the federal Constitution. Local authority to enact ordinances and laws is based on powers granted by the constitution of each state. Over the past few years the increasing federal concern for public safety has resulted in preempting certain areas of state and local regulatory authority. The general areas of state and local regulatory atuhority. The general policy concerning overlapping areas of concern has been handled in the following manner:

State laws on the same subject are superseded by federal law.
State laws not conflicting with federal laws remain valid.
State law does prevail if the state law is more stringent than the federal law. This often occurs in the area of fire protection.[1]

CODES

Many federal, state, and local regulations result in systematized bodies of law known as "codes." Adequate standards of practice and uniformity of workmanship are ensured by code enforcement; however, it should be noted that codes only provide for minimum levels of performance. Although codes represent the experience and knowledge of many professionals and are continually evolving through the consensus of many groups, codes often cause resentment among designers. Such regulations are considered interference, harassment, and, above all, time-consuming trivia. We all lose sight of the fact that the major concept of code development is safety. Most codes have come into existence after the fact—after a major tragedy involving the loss of human life. Modern investigative methods attempt to determine the cause of the product or structure failure, and the data gained is incorporated into codes that hopefully will prevent similar tragedies.

STANDARDS AND MODEL CODES

Standards establish criteria of excellence, or "models," that provide a means of comparison for measuring quality. Safety standards can be classified as "mandatory" or "voluntary." Some mandatory standards are established by government and enforced by law; others are enacted as statutes. Voluntary standards, or "model codes," are recommended but not enforced as law, unless adopted by federal, state, or local authorities. The major model building codes listed below have each developed accompanying fire prevention codes. More complete information on code agencies can be found at the end of this chapter.

MODEL BUILDING CODES

Sponsoring Group		Building Code	
BOCA	Building Officials Code Administrators International	NBC	Basic/National Building Code
ICBO	International Conference of Building Officials	UBC	Uniform Building Code
SBCCI	Southern Building Code Congress International	SBC	Standard Building Code

In addition to these major model codes there are approximately four hundred nonprofit organizations that produce voluntary standards. The best-known organizations that produce many fire-related standards are the following:

AATCC: American Association of Textile Chemists and Colorists
AHLA: American Home Lighting Association
ANSI: American National Standards Institute
ASTM: American Society for Testing and Materials
BHMA: Builders Hardware Manufacturer's Association
BIFMA: The Business and Institutional Furniture Manufacturer's Association
CRI: Carpet and Rug Institute
FM: Factory Mutual
NFPA: National Fire Protection Association
RFCI: Resilient Floor Covering Institute
UFAC: Upholstered Furniture Action Council
UL: Underwriters Laboratories

TABLE 3.1 FEDERAL AGENCIES

Federal Departments		Duties	Acts of Congress	Date
DOC	Department of Commerce			
NIST	Institute of Standards and Technology (formerly National Bureau of Standards)	Testing of materials. Promotes enforcement and adoption of uniform building codes.	Public Law 177 Act to establish NBS	1901
FEMA	Federal Emergency Management Agency	Includes Civil Defense and Federal Disaster Administration and U.S. Fire Administration.	Reorganization Plan No. 3	1978
USFA	United States Fire Administration	Service, education and training. Supports state and local fire safety training (National Fire Academy). Maintains a fire data system.	Federal Fire Prevention and Control Act	1974
HHS	Department of Health and Human Services	Fire safety standards for health-care facilities.		
PHS	Public Health Service	Sets Standards for private and public nonprofit hospitals/nursing homes.	Hill Burton Act Title IV of Public Health Service Act	1974
SSA	Social Security Administration	Medicare and Medicaid. Requires compliance with fire safety standards.	Social Security Act Title 18-19	1965
HUD	Department of Housing and Urban Development	*Enforces* standards for one- and two- family dwellings and nursing care-type housing.		
FHA	Federal Housing Administration	Establishes and *enforces* minimum building standards.	Housing and Community Development Act	1974
DOL	Department of Labor	*Enforces* mandatory standards for safety and health of employees.		
OSHA	Occupational Safety and Health Administration	Established 1970. Develops and *enforces* mandatory standards for safety, educational, and training programs for state and federal programs.	Title 29—USC Section 651	1970
DOT	Department of Transportation	*Enforces* standards and regulates construction of private and commercial vehicles. Conducts research.	National Traffic & Motor Vehicle Safety Act	1966
			Transportation Safety Act	1974

Federal	Departments	Duties	Acts of Congress	Date
FAA	Federal Aviation Administration	*Enforces* standards for safety in aircrafts and airports.	Federal Aviation Act	1958
FRA	Federal Railroad Administration	Sets standards for equipment and operations of trains/railroads.		
CPSC	Consumer Product Safety Commission	*Enforces* and regulates standards for products sold to consumers. Collects injury data. Conducts public educational programs. Administers the Flammable Fabrics Act.	Consumer Product Safety Act Public Law 92-573	1972
			Flammable Fabrics Act	1967
EPA	Environmental Protection Agency	*Enforces* and regulates standards in regard to air, water, and noise pollution. Publishes reports on criteria for noise levels.	Noise Control Act PL 92-574-HL-11021	1972
FTC	Federal Trade Commission	*Enforces* standards for: 1. Misleading advertising of products	Wool Products Labeling Act	1939
		2. Misleading labeling of goods	Textile Fabric Products Identification Act	1951
		3. Assists CPSC in enforcing the Flammable Fabrics Act.	Fur Products Labeling Act	1951
GSA	General Services Administration	Provides supplies and buildings for federal agencies. Performance Standards. Systems approach to design.	Federal Property and Administrative Services Act	1949
			Section 206	
FSS	Federal Supply Service	Buys supplies and contracts for services for federal agencies.		
PBS	Public Building Services	Responsible for supervising the design, construction, operation, and maintenance of federal buildings.		
VA	Veterans Administration	Regulates and sets standards for VA hospitals and health-care facilities. Conducts research on flammable fabrics. Sets standards for tests methods.		

Note: The identities and functions of federal agencies can change without notice. Their function depends on current need.

Federal, City and State Agencies that Produce Standards

The following agencies produce the most frequently adopted standards:

Boston Fire Department
California Bureau of Home Furnishing
California State Fire Marshal's Office
The Commonwealth of Massachusetts Department of Public Safety
City of New York Board of Standards and Appeals
New York State Department of State, Office of Fire Prevention and Control
Port Authority of New York and New Jersey
U.S. Consumer Product Safety Commission
General Services Administration
Federal Aviation Administration
Federal Motor Vehicle Administration
Urban Mass Transportation Administration
National Bureau of Standards
Bay Area Rapid Transit
Coast Guard

Others are listed in Table 3.1.

Frequently local authorities will adopt one of the major model building codes and, in addition, all or parts of the codes and standards of the three groups listed on page 20.

Codes and standards may be classified as either "descriptive" or "performance" in character. Many are a combination of both approaches. Descriptive standards define exact materials or forms, whereas performance standards describe what a system should accomplish, regardless of its form or material content. The incorporation of standards into specifications is discussed in Chapter Sixteen.

Building codes are primarily concerned with (1) the construction requirements of building and (2) hazardous materials or equipment used in the building.

Fire codes and standards are an integral part of building codes. It has been estimated that 75 percent of all codes deal with fire protection. Fire protection codes are concerned with minimizing fire hazards and may be classified as follows:

Fire prevention: Concerned with occupancy hazards, sources of ignition, and combustible fuel loads in buildings. Interior designers are most often involved with preventive-type fire codes which classify furnishings and interior finishes as potential fuels that contribute to the spread of fire.

Fire control: *Active:* Installation and maintenance of sprinklers, alarms, and extinguishing systems.
Passive: Construction elements that control the spread of fire, i.e., fire doors and fire walls.

Building codes:

Building space
Doors and windows
Design loads
Structural elements
Wood systems
Masonry systems
Steel systems
Concrete systems
Site and foundation
Roof construction

**Fire codes
(within building codes)**

Exit signage
Fire and smoke control
Human life safety
Egress from building
Exit design
Exit components
Methods of fire protection
Accessibility
Occupancy concerns
Fire protection of structural elements
Site requirements

Mechanical codes: HVAC

Electrical codes: Electrical

**Plumbing codes
(within building codes):** Plumbing

Classification of Buildings

Because building classification is the basis of most fire prevention regulations, interior designers should be aware of the various established categories.

1. *Occupancy classification.* Occupancy classifications are based on the purpose for which a building or portion of a building is used or intended to be used.

   Assembly   Industrial
   Business   Mercantile
   Detention & correctional Mixed
   Educational   Residential
   Health Care   Storage
         Unusual

2. *Fuel load classification.* Based on the amount of combustibles in a building (per square feet of floor space):
   a. *Low hazard*
   Apartments Museums
   Churches   Nursing care facilities
   Dormitories Office buildings
   Hospitals   Prisons
   Hotels   Residences
   Institutions Schools
   Libraries   Theaters
   b. *Moderate hazard (ordinary)*
   Auto parking
   Retail shops

   c. *High hazard.* Occupancy involving processing, mixing, storage, and/or dispensing of flammable or combustible liquids, and/or poisonous or explosive gases.
   Airport hangars
   Paint shops
   Service stations
   Varnish and paint works
   Warehouses
   Woodworking shops
   d. *Unusual structures.* This class includes buildings or structures that do not fit into the above categories:
   Mobile homes
   Towers
   Underground structures
   Windowless buildings

Surveying the above list, designers might assume they are, for the most part, concerned with low- and moderate-hazard classifications. It should be noted, however, that regardless of the fuel load, a building classified as low hazard could easily be reclassified as high hazard because of variances in occupancy load.

Variances in Occupancy Load Classifications

Classifications vary depending on occupancy load and type of occupancy.

Occupancy Load. This refers to the total number of people expected to be in a building at any given time. As the occupancy load increases, the fire prevention requirements increase.

PLACES OF ASSEMBLY	
Capacity	**Classification**
50–300	Low risk
300–1000	Moderate risk
1000+	High risk

Type of Occupancy. This is another classification factor. Safety standards increase when the occupants are children or elderly people; higher standards are also applied to physically disabled people.

LACK OF CODE UNIFORMITY

One of the most confusing aspects of codes and standards is the lack of uniformity between federal agencies, states, counties, and municipalities. The feasibility of ever attaining complete and total uniformity seems unlikely. There have been major efforts to unify codes on the national level. Approximately 85 percent of the states now have accepted model codes. Federal agencies such as the Department of Health and Human Services (HHS) and the Department of Housing and Urban Development (HUD) have adopted the Uniform Building Code, and all the standards and codes of the National Fire Protection Association (NFPA) and the American National Standards Institute (ANSI).

Counties and municipalities present quite a different problem. Some cities, such as Houston, have large oil refineries, which create particular hazards. Chicago, New York, and other large cities require special codes and standards that relate to high-rise buildings and population density. A small Mid-western town in the path of tornadoes may require special storm-protection standards. The fact that codes have evolved through modification for particular geographic and population needs is understandable. Figure 3.1 shows the overlapping code structures and the authorities with jurisdiction that may be encountered at the local level.

Authorities with Jurisdiction

The authority with jurisdiction may be the individual who represents an organization or government office, that is, the person having statutory authority to enforce a code, and approve equipment or installation procedures. In projects involving high risk, with expensive insurance coverage, the insurance company representative may become the authority with jurisdiction. The following list clarifies the jurisdictional areas of the major codes and standards authorities that designers may encounter.

Federal. Federal laws, codes, and standards apply to federal buildings or structures built with the assistance of federal funds, such as hospitals, schools, and nursing homes. In some cases the federal agency will be required to obtain a local building permit and comply with additional state, county, or city standards. This occurs only when the local standards are more stringent than the federal standards.

State. State codes and standards regulate state-owned buildings, state hospitals, schools, and occasionally large places of assembly such as coliseums and exhibition centers. States rarely impose regulations on incorporated municipalities. Counties or small towns without codes or standards may be governed by state standards.

County. County building and fire safety regulations usually apply only to unincorporated rural areas.

Municipality. Municipality building and fire safety codes may be administered through one planning office or through several agencies such as the office of the city fire marshal, health department, or zoning commission.

Zoning. Zoning ordinances exist at the county and city levels. Zoning ordinances usually involve land use, type of building, occupancy, as well as building and fire safety standards.

Health Departments. Health departments primarily enforce code regulations involving sanitation, levels of occupancy, health, and safety. Their areas of concern include the food preparation facilities of restaurants, hospitals, schools, prisons, nursing homes, and day care centers. Floor, wall, and ceiling finishes are expected to perform well under heavy sanitation maintenance requirements. Many states divide enforcement responsibilities between state, county, and city health departments.

Insurance. Insurance interest should always be consulted by the designer. Having plans reviewed in the early design phase may reduce not only fire-hazard problems, but also insurance rates on the building. Consultation may involve an individual insurance company already insuring the building or an insurance group such as Factory Insurance Association or Factory Mutual Insurance Association. Because insurance is subject to state regulations requiring standardized fire rating, many insurance agents rely on the rating bureaus. The most

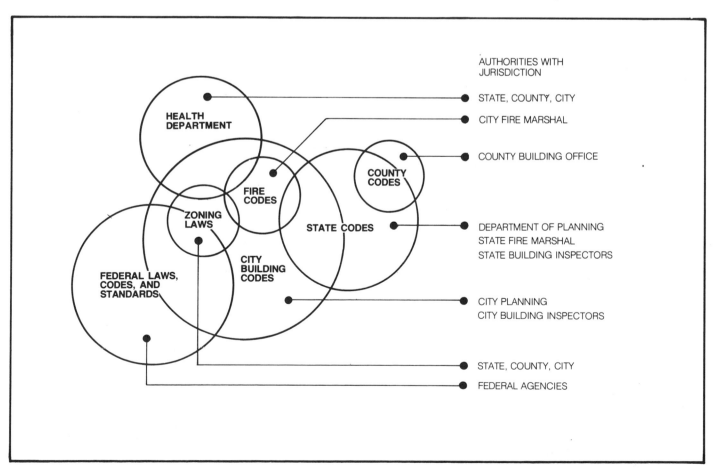

Figure 3.1 Overlapping code structures.

important insurance-supported rating bureau is the Insurance Services Office.

RISK MANAGEMENT: PROCEDURES FOR CODE COMPLIANCE

In the programming phase of the design project, when studies are being made to determine the feasibility of achieving the stated requirements of the project, it would be advisable to evaluate the fire-safety factors of the proposed or existing building. Experts in the building fire safety from the local fire department or insurance agencies should be consulted if any major deficiencies are discovered.

General Checklist for Fire Safety

1. What is the occupancy classification of the building?

2. What is the accepted occupancy load?

3. What types of occupancy are allowed?

4. Has a structural fire resistance rating been established?
   a. Floors
   b. Walls: interior and exterior
   c. Ceilings

5. Is the electrical wiring adequate for the proposed use?

6. What are the existing fire control and prevention methods in the building?
   a. Alarms
   b. Extinguishers
   c. Smoke detectors
   d. Sprinklers

Seek Interpretation on Levels of Compliance

To prevent costly changes in completed project plans, designers should contact the offices of the authorities with jurisdiction early in the design phase. After having the proposed project checked for compliance, designers may wish to seek interpretations on levels of compliance. *Levels of compliance* are alternate methods of achieving fire safety. The alternatives are based on infinite variances. Two variances on occupancy loading have already been discussed in this chapter. Other variances may include the use of sprinklers. A lower flame-spread rating may be allowed on a particular wall finish if sprinklers have been installed in that area of the building (see interior finish requirements in the 101 Life Safety Model Code on page 44). The same may apply to floor coverings in critical areas such as corridors that serve as access to exits. In another case, a special feature, such as a raised dance floor, may be allowed if seating capacity is reduced.

Clarify Terminology

Terms such as "finishes" and "furnishings" may take on different meanings depending on the project installation and on the particular code in use. In some jurisdictions, carpet is considered a furnishing if it is installed over a finished floor. If installed directly over concrete, it is classified as interior finish (see definition of interior finishes in Glossary, under Chapter Five). If a regulation defines carpet as a floor-covering finish with no mention of its use as a wallcovering, do not specify carpet as a wallcovering without clarification. Because something is *not* mentioned in a code *does not mean that it is permitted*.

Another area of confusing terminology involves movable partitions that are an integral part of office landscape systems.

In some jurisdictions these partitions may be classified as furnishings, while in other jurisdictions they may be considered temporary walls.

Seek Clarification on Questionable Regulations

Designers generally shirk from questioning regulations or they totally avoid areas of uncertainty. Here are two suggested approaches:

1. Check on current regulations that have been adopted by the authorities in your jurisdiction. Do not assume that the current editions of codes and standards that are in your office are the same as those adopted by the local authorities.

2. Seek variances when outdated regulations are identified and try to initiate interest in modifying outdated regulations.

Proof of Compliance

Although professional contracts usually hold the owner/client responsible for filing documents required for the approval of authorities, the implied (and actual) responsibility for compliance rests with the designer.

Proof of Compliance Checklist. There are four points that should be considered on every job:

1. Submit a complete set of project working drawings, schedules, and specifications in duplicate to the various authorities involved. The number of sets needed for submittal will depend on the complexity of the project and local regulations. Every design firm should have a staff member knowledgeable about code requirements and regulations who can answer questions posed by the authorities with jurisdiction. If changes are required, an addendum should be attached to the contract docuents.

2. Seek information on approved or qualified laboratories recommended by the authorities with jurisdiction. Some cities and states have established their own testing facilities. Federal agencies provide a listing of approved testing laboratories that are located throughout the United States. The National Fire Protection Association (NFPA) also provides a listing of laboratories that perform flammability testing.

3. If a particular material must be tested to prove compliance with safety performance requirements, always require written proof of the test results. Some jurisdictions require photographic documentation of the test results. More information on documenting test results is discussed in Chapters Fifteen and Sixteen. It should be noted that even though a material has been tested and rated, the authority does not have to accept the use of the material in your project. Factors that influence these decisions may involve total fuel loads, occupancy loads, and any number of variances.

4. Keep records on the approval from on-site inspectors. After building permits are issued, field inspectors visit the project site to make sure that all work is being executed according to the approved drawings and specifications. The inspections are coordinated with each phase of the work; i.e., after electrical wiring has been installed, after interior finishes are completed, and a final inspection prior to occupancy. Inspection record cards are usually provided by building permit departments.

Risk Management Summary

1. Evaluate the building and project area for fire safety.

2. Seek interpretation on levels of compliance.

3. Clarify code terminology.

4. Seek clarification on questionable regulations.

5. Secure proof of compliance on all materials testing and on-site inspections.

6. Whenever possible, specify safety performance beyond code requirements.

GLOSSARY

Automatic door-closing device: A device that is activated only by smoke or heat. It will close a door only when needed to protect occupants.

Building model code: A code developed by consensus vote of persons concerned with human safety within buildings. These persons may be manufacturers of building materials, fire and structural engineers, interior designers and architects, fire officials, building owners, insurance companies, and any concerned citizen.

Combustible: Capable of undergoing combustion.

Combustion: A chemical process that involves sufficient oxidation to produce heat or light.

Common path of travel: That portion of exit excess that must be traversed before two separate or distinct paths of travel to two exits are available. Paths where persons merge on common paths of travel are measured in same manner as travel distance.

Existing building: Any structure erected prior to an existing code. A building built according to standards enforced by the code previously in effect. (See *Plan approval.*)

Fire barrier: A continuous membrane such as a wall, ceiling, or floor assembly that is designed and constructed with a specified fire-resistant rating to limit the spread of fire and smoke. This resistant rating is based on a time factor. Only fire-rated doors may be used in these barriers.

Fire compartment: A space within a building that is enclosed by a fire barrier on all sides, including top and bottom. Note that the outside walls or doors need not be fire rated unless required by existing code.

Fire-resistant rating: The time in minutes or hours that materials or assemblies have withstood a laboratory-controlled fire exposure prescribed in accordance with test procedures.

Hazardous areas: Multiple-occupancy buildings or portions of structures that contain materials or house activities that present a hazard greater than normal to the general building occupancy.

Occupancy: The purpose or intended use for which a building or portion thereof is built.

Plan approval: Approval by the authorities with jurisdiction based on codes in effect at the time. All codes in effect at the time of plan approval will regulate the building structure and interiors regardless of construction delays and occupancy.

Plenum space: An air compartment or chamber above the ceiling that contains HVAC duct work.

Pressurized stairs: Stairs that provide protection to occupants from fire and smoke through pressurization and ventilation. Pressurization is accomplished through pressure and ventilation control. Buildings containing pressurized stairs are often required by code to be fully sprinklered.

Self-closing: Equipped with a code-approved device that will ensure immediate closure after each use. Note: An *automatic* closing device is one that is smoke- or heat-activated to ensure closing when *needed.*

Smoke barrier: A wall, ceiling, or floor constructed to restrict the movement of smoke. It may or may not have a fire-resistant rating.

Vertical exit: A protected stair that will not admit smoke and fire.

Vertical opening: An opening through the floor or roof.

INTERIOR FIRE HAZARDS

The National Institute of Standards and Technology (formerly National Bureau of Standards) estimates that there are 12,000 fire-related deaths annually in the United States. A large percentage of these deaths have been the direct result of design and construction deficiencies. Research has shown that decorative materials, furnishings, and interior finishes have also been a contributing factor in many fires. (See more details about fabric and upholstery flammability in Chapter 6.)

RESIDENTIAL FIRES STILL DOMINATE

Table 4.1 shows the multiple-death fires from 1980 to 1984. During this four-year period, the cost of fire safety was approximately equal to the national debt.

In the late 1980s, the National Fire Protection Association Fire Analysis Division used the term "catastrophic" to classify residential fires that take the lives of five or more people as "momentous, tragic events." Fire statistics reveal that a major number of fire deaths in the United States involved two age groups: the very young under the age of six and the elderly over the age of sixty-five.

In 1987 there were 60 catastrophic fires:

1) 23 nonresidential fires resulted in 89 deaths.

2) A total of 37 residential fires resulted in 210 deaths. Of the 210 deaths, 89 were children under the age of six. Nine of those residential fires took the lives of 46 children.

In 22 of these fires smoke detectors were absent or nonoperable, and most of the children were unattended by adults at the time of the fire.

Property losses in one- and two-family dwellings between 1981 and 1985 accounted for 89 percent of all property loss. Other losses were:

$3,774 billion—Loss in residential fires
$ 476 million—Loss in apartments
$ 462 million—Loss in places of assembly

Table 4.2 lists only the major fire fatalities during the last two decades.

TABLE 4.1 MULTIPLE-DEATH FIRES 1980–1984

Year	Number of Multiple-Death Fires	Number of Deaths in Multiple-Death Fires*	Fires Causing 10 or More Deaths	Deaths in Fires Killing 10 or More
1984	244	1,007	5	84
1983	259	986	2	34
1982	266	1,111	7	116
1981	296	1,179	6	95
1980	326	1,356†	6	168†

* Includes both civilian and fire-fighter deaths.
† Includes 85 deaths in the MGM Grand Hotel Fire.
   Note: The information presented in this table for 1980 to 1984 may differ from previously published statistics because of additional information which has become available to the NFPA.
   Reprinted with permission from the Fire Protection Handbook, 16th Edition, Copyright © 1986, National Fire Protection Association, Quincy, MA 02269.

TABLE 4.2 MAJOR FIRE FATALITIES

Location	Year	Facility Type	Death Toll
Marietta, Ohio	1970	Nursing home	32
Minneapolis, Minn.	1970	Apartment house	12
Tucson, Arizona	1970	Hotel	28
Texas Twins, Pa.	1971	Nursing home	15
Rosecrans, Wisc.	1972	Home for aged	10
Springfield, Ill.	1972	Nursing home	10
Pleasantville, N.Y.	1973	Retirement home	10
New Orleans, La.	1973	Cocktail lounge	32
Wayne, Pa.	1973	Nursing home	15
Brookhaven, Miss.	1974	Nursing home	15
Columbia, Tenn.	1977	Prison	42
Danbury, Conn.	1977	Prison	5
Southgate, Ky.	1977	Supper club	164
Las Vegas, Nev.	1980	Hotel	85
Harrison, N.Y.	1980	Hotel meeting facility	26
Bradley Beach, N.J.	1980	Boarding home facility	24
Salt Lake City, Utah	1980	Apartment building	12
Brooklyn, N.Y.	1980	Metal manufacturing plant	11
Chicago, Ill.	1980	Apartment building	10
Morganville, N.J.	1981	Boarding home facility	31
Chicago, Ill.	1981	Residential hotel	19
Whitwell, Tenn.	1981	Coal mine	13
East Saint Louis, Ill.	1981	Single-family dwelling	11
Hoboken, N.J.	1981	Apartment building	11
San Bernardino, Calif.	1981	Motor home	10
Biloxi, Miss.	1982	Jail	29
Los Angeles, Calif.	1982	Residential hotel	24
Waterbury, Ct.	1982	Apartment building	14
Bakersfield, Calif.	1982	Aircraft post-crash fire	14
Hoboken, N.J.	1982	Residential hotel	13
Houston, Tex.	1982	Hotel	12
Baltimore, Md.	1982	Single-family dwelling	10
Cincinnati, Ohio	1983	Passenger aircraft	23
Benton, Tenn.	1983	Fireworks factory	11
Orangeville, Utah	1984	Coal mine	27
Romeoville, Ill.	1984	Refinery	17
Beverly, Mass.	1984	Rooming house	15
Paterson, N.J.	1984	Hotel	15
Philadelphia, Pa.	1984	Single-family dwelling	10
San Juan, P.R.	1986	Hotel	96

Source: National Fire Protection Association.

Do not use terms of fire proof

Instead, use:
flame retardant
flame resistant

Designers' Role in Fire Protection

Fire protection experts agree that the first 5 or 10 minutes of a fire are the most critical. The initial materials ignited can either contribute to the growth of the fire or prevent its spread to other areas of the building. All the interior components specified by the designer become crucial elements in the early phase of a fire. Floor and wallcoverings, drapery, and furnishings are the primary elements providing fuel to sustain the growing fire. It is important for designers to acquaint themselves with all available knowledge concerning the nature of *potential fire hazards* and to apply this information effectively in the specification of materials and systems.

Interior Finishes

Little research was directed to interior finishes as potential fire hazards until three major hotel fires in 1946 claimed the lives of 199 people. The fires ocurred in Chicago, Illinois; Dubuque, Iowa; and Atlanta, Georgia. Evidence gathered from the fires indicated combustible interior finishes were definitely one of the contributing factors in the rapid flame spread. Prior to that time little was known about the potential hazards of interior finishes and furnishings.[1]

During the last 10 years that evidence has been verified in many other fires throughout the country (see Table 4.2).[2]

The Fire System

Fire performance testing is based on knowledge gained from the study of fire systems. In order to understand the unique problems of flammability testing, it is important to review the stages in the development of a fire system. Figure 4.1 illustrates three major fire stages:

1. *Stage 1:* Fire engineers refer to the time of *ignition* and the initial fire growth as the first stage of a fire. Fire-suppression methods seek to extinguish fire in Stage I while it is either confined to the trash basket (as shown above) or to the room of origin. Smoke produced during this stage can travel many feet from the room of origin and pose a threat to human life.

2. *Stage II:* This is considered the growth stage, the time when the fire starts to ignite material in the immediate area and proceeds to consume a major part of the room finishes and furnishings. During Stage II, generated heat may cause the fire to *flashover* (see Glossary at the end of this chapter) to surrounding areas of the building such as the corridors and open stairs.

3. *Stage III:* During this stage, the *fully developed* postflashover fire causes the building to quickly become untenable for persons who remain within range of the smoke, heat, and possible toxic gases.[3]

Time-Temperature Curve

The standard time-temperature curve was developed as an engineering test standard against which the burning and heat release of materials and products could be measured. The table in Figure 4.2 illustrated how quickly heat can develop in a fire. In relation to a Stage I fire, note how much heat can be generated in the room of origin within the first 5 minutes after ignition. This clearly illustrates why life safety codes address problems involved in the removal of all persons from a building fire zone within the first 5 minutes following fire ignition.

POTENTIAL FIRE HAZARDS

Many factors contribute to the definition of the term "fire hazard." Table 4.3 points out some of the hazards that normally occur during the major stages of a building fire. The preflashover fire poses a major threat to human life in the immediate area. The flashover and postflashover fire can threaten human life in remote building areas. For example, the MGM Grand Hotel street-level fire transported smoke to the highrise guest rooms located twenty floors above. Codes addressing the flashover and postflashover fire focus on smoke and fire control to prevent building collapse and possible involvement of surrounding structures.

"Risk assessment" and "fire-hazard evaluations" are terms that should not be used interchangeably. Fire risk has been

SIDE ELEVATION (ROOM)   SIDE ELEVATION (ROOM)   SIDE ELEVATION (CORRIDOR)

FLOOR PLAN (ROOM)   FLOOR PLAN (ROOM)   FLOOR PLAN (BUILDING)

1   2   3

Figure 4.1 Stages of fire development. Source: National Institute of Standards and Technology (formerly National Bureau of Standards), NBSIR 78-1436.

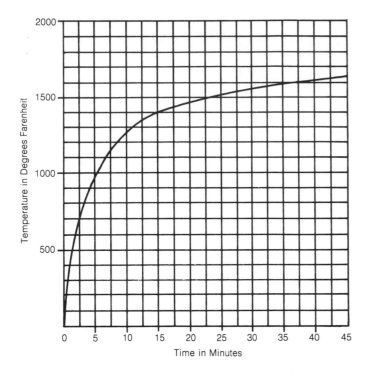

1000° F (538° C) at 5 minutes   1550° F (843° C) at 30 minutes
1300° F (704° C) at 10 minutes   1584° F (868° C) at 35 minutes
1399° F (760° C) at 15 minutes   1613° F (878° C) at 40 minutes
1462° F (795° C) at 20 minutes   1638° F (892° C) at 45 minutes
1510° F (821° C) at 25 minutes

Figure 4.2 Standard time-temperature curve. Reprinted with permission from the Fire Protection Handbook, 16th Edition, Copyright © 1986, National Fire Protection Association, Quincy, MA 02269.

defined as the probability that a fire will occur with the accompanying potential for harm to human life and property damage. Used in this context, the concept of risk is based on a sliding scale of culturally tolerated risks. Those who are frequent airline passengers tolerate the risk of flying as an acceptable alternative to slow ground travel. Most people accept the fact that a totally risk-free environment is beyond reasonable expectation. Based on state-of-the-art technology, codes seek to provide building occupants with reasonable odds of survival.

After many decades of advancement in fire-technology research, the ability to conduct hazard assessment is based on sophisticated applications of collective knowledge pertaining to material performance, fire behavior, and psychological studies based on human response to fire conditions.

The tragic Dupont Plaza Hotel and Casino fire on New Year's Eve 1987 took the lives of 96 people. Figure 4.3 illustrates the lobby casino level and the 14-foot-wide (2.3 m) open stairway down to the ballrooms on the lower level. The casino was a U-shaped, 4,800-square-foot space. The main entry to the casino, located on the east side of the lobby, was constructed of two glass doors that opened in both directions. The west exit door was a single 36-inch-wide wooden door that opened inward.

The fire originated in the ballroom areas located on the lower level and connected to the lobby by a two-story-high lobby shown on the left of the drawings. Following flashover, fire spread rapidly across the lobby and crowded casino area. Flames extended out the lobby and casino areas into the outdoor pool and patio area. Fire alarms located in the empty ballrooms did not activate. The building did not contain sprinklers or smoke detectors because the existing code did not require their use.

Figure 4.4 is an elevation drawing showing the location of the ballrooms in relation to the second-level lobby and the

TABLE 4.3   EFFECTS OF COMBUSTION

Pyrolysis	Movement: Causes/Materials	Effects	Prevention
1. Fire origin			
a. Combustion; simultaneous ignition	Ignition, flash-over. Heat flux. Paper, interior finishes	Heat-produced smoke and flame	Codes—Regulations Fixed heat 165°F sprinklers
b. Smoldering	Wiring, paint rags or cans in confined space	Heat-produced gases and smoke	Central shutdown fans
2. Fully developed fire			
a. Heat	Products of combustion spread fire	Increased heart rate, dehydration, blockage of respiratory track	Holding rooms or areas within the building
b. Flame	Burning of materials in presence of oxygen	1st, 2nd, 3rd degree burns from heat	Sprinklers
c. Oxygen depletion	Oxygen depleted by fire	Diminished muscular skill, faulty judgment	
d. Smoke	Produced by materials burning— plastics, wood, etc.	Obscuration, panic, irritation of eyes. Death in areas remote from fire.	Compartmentalization to control combustion, dilution, exhaust fans
e. Toxic gases	All material and combined materials—plastics	Asphyxiation and death from CO, NO_2, HCN	Codes on combined use of materials—fuel loads
f. Volatile gases	High temperature "back drafts" when fed by oxygen	Asphyxiation—death	135°F sprinklers
3. Spread of fire			
a. Horizontal	Through ducts, ceiling, plenums and doors	Means of escape blocked by smoke and fire	Code-rated materials Vertical divisions
b. Vertical	Duct risers, shafts, stairs, elevators and open windows		Compartmentalization
4. Expansion of contained fire			
a. Explosion	Breakage of containing members— windows and doors	Expansion of fire	Fire rating of building structure
b. Deformation and collapse of structure			

guest rooms located in the highrise tower.

This detailed drawing in Figure 4.5 illustrates the relationship of the north and south ballrooms, which were separated by a movable partition. The 2,304-square-foot south ballroom had a ceiling height of 10 feet (3 m). The ceiling height in the north ballroom was 23 feet (7 m). The arsonist ignited a Sterno can near a large stack of shipping cartons that contained new furniture for the hotel (shaded area on left). The cartons were stacked across a 15-foot (4.6 m) width, 6 feet (1.9 m) high, and extended 30 feet (9.1 m) along the east wall. About 20 percent of these cartons contained sofa beds with foam mattresses. The remaining cartons contained various types of hotel fur-

nishings such as dressers made of wood and particle board. In addition, the ballroom contained 50 stacking chairs stored along the south wall. Both ballroom walls were covered with a fabric wallcovering.[4]

The report on pages 31–34 (Figures 4.6 through 4.13) documented the ability of the Center for Fire Research at the National Institute of Standards and Technology (NIST) to use quantitative computerized engineering tools to construct a description of fire conditions that occurred in the Dupont Hotel fire. Based on the Center for Fire Research's documented heat-release data, this report also points out how sprinklers and smoke detectors could have prevented the large loss of life.

Figure 4.3 DuPont Plaza Hotel and Casino, casino level. Reprinted with permission from NFPA Interim Investigation Report of the DuPont Plaza Hotel and Casino Fire, Copyright © 1987, National Fire Protection Association, Quincy, MA 02269.

Figure 4.4 South-side elevation of DuPont Plaza Hotel and Casino.

Figure 4.5 Ballroom area level of DuPont Plaza Hotel and Casino.

NORTH
BALLROOM

OPEN STAIRS
UP TO
CASINO LEVEL

LINE OF BALCONY ABOVE

PORTABLE
COMBUSTIBLE
PARTITION

STORED
FURNITURE
ITEMS

WINDOW
WALL
PANELS

SOUTH
BALLROOM

	North Ballroom	South Ballroom
Flame Height	None	4.5 ft (1.5 m)
Smoke Layer	22.5 ft (6.9 m)	8 ft (2.4 m)
Smoke Temperature	70° F (22° C)	102° F (39° C)
Vision Distance	1000 ft (305 m)	58 ft (17.7 m)
Oxygen Concentration	21%	21%

Note: No smoke detectors or sprinklers were located in the ballrooms. Within one minute any smoke detector located within 40 feet (12.2 m) of the fire source would have responded. A quick-response sprinkler located directly over the fire would have operated at this time.

Figure 4.6 Situation in ballroom complex at time + 60 seconds (1 minute). From the U.S. Department of Commerce, National Institute of Standards and Technology (formerly National Bureau of Standards), National Center for Fire Research, NBSIR 87-3560.

	North Ballroom	South Ballroom
Flame Height	13 ft (4 m)	12 ft (3.7 m)
Smoke Layer	19 ft (5.8 m)	6 ft (1.8 m)
Smoke Temperature	82° F (22° C)	354° F (179° C)
Vision Distance	72 ft (21.9 m)	18 ft (5.5 m)
Oxygen Concentration	21%	20%

Note: At this time the calculations assume that at least 12 additional feet of panel partitions (located between the south and north ballrooms) failed. Depending on sprinkler programmed-response time, heads located within 7 to 15 feet (2.1–4.6 m) would have actuated at this time.

Figure 4.7 Situation in ballroom complex at time + 180 seconds (3 minutes).

	North Ballroom	South Ballroom
Flame Height	18 ft (5.5 m)	23 ft (7 m)
Smoke Layer	10 ft (3 m)	6 ft (1.8 m)
Smoke Temperature	256° F (125° C)	365° F (185° C)
Vision Distance	6 ft (1.8 m)	15 ft (4.6 m)
Oxygen Concentration	13%	12%

Note: At this point smoke starts to flow under the soffit of the open 10-foot-high door between the north and south ballrooms.

Figure 4.8 Situation in ballroom complex at time +420 seconds (7 minutes).

	North Ballroom	South Ballroom
Smoke Layer	6 ft (1.8 m)	7 ft (2.1 m)
Smoke Temperature	500° F (310° C)	1112° F (600° C)
Vision Distance	4 ft (1.2 m)	3 ft (.9 m)
Oxygen Concentration	7%	7%

Note: With flashover at about time + 583 seconds, the following occurs:

- Smoke temperature rises to above 1500° F (815° C) in the south ballroom.
- Smoke levels drop almost to the floor level.
- Vision drops to *zero*.
- At flashover, the glass two-story partition between the south ballroom and foyer fails.

Figure 4.9 Situation in ballroom complex just prior to flashover, time +580 seconds (9.7 minutes).

Smoke Layer: 21 ft (6.4 m)

Smoke Temperature: 92° F (33° C)

Vision Distance: 80 ft (24.3 m)

Oxygen Content: 21%

Note: Hot gases flow from the door between the north ballroom and the foyer.
The smoke layer at this time is not deep enough to pass under the doorway
soffit to the casino.

Figure 4.10 Situation in foyer and lobby from time + 420–580 seconds (7–9 minutes).

Flame Height/Extension: Flame laps ½ to ¾ the width of timber ceiling.

Smoke Layer: 10–12 ft (3–3.7 m) above floor

Smoke Temperature: 900° F (480° C)

Vision Distance: *nil*

Oxygen Concentration: *near zero*

Note: 1) Fire enters the foyer through the collapsed glass partition between
the south ballroom and the foyer. 2) A 36-foot-wide sheet of fire rises and
spreads across the foyer timber ceiling.

Figure 4.11 Situation in foyer following flashover of south ballroom, time + 600 seconds (10 minutes).

1. Smoke flows through the lobby at about *2.2 ft (.7 m) per second.*

2. Smoke enters from foyer at about *1000° F (540° C).*

3. Smoke temperature drops as it moves across the lobby, but is still intolerable as it exits at the far end of the lobby.

4. Smoke has *lethal concentration of carbon monoxide* and is opaque.

5. Smoke blocks east casino door *almost immediately.*

6. Smoke blocks west casino door in about *40 seconds.*

Figure 4.12 Situation in lobby from flashover of south ballroom, about time + 590 seconds to about time + 630 seconds (9.8 to 10.5 minutes).

1. Flame and fuel-rich smoke are discharged from the foyer into the casino.

2. A flame front crosses the casino at a speed of *6 ft (1.8 m) per second.*

3. Flame crosses casino in about *20 seconds.*

4. Flame breaks out west casino windows

5. Flame eddies lap tongues of flame down to pool-deck level.

Figure 4.13 Situation in casino following breakage of glass partition between casino and foyer from time + 720 seconds to time + 740 seconds (12–12.3 minutes).

Release of Toxic Gases

One of the most disastrous fires in recent years took place in 1977 at the Beverly Hills Supper Club in Southgate, Kentucky. Designed to accommodate approximately 500 occupants, the facilities were crowded with over 1,000 occupants when the fire erupted. Witnesses to the blaze described the "pungent odor of burning plastic." Medical reports showed that the majority of victims died of smoke inhalation. Authorities requested toxicity tests on plastic chairs used in the supper club. Figure 4.14 illustrates the spread of the fire and the intensity of dense black smoke.[5]

Although it is known that plastics represent a potential hazard in the event of fire, plastics have become a way of life. The first commercial use of plastics dates back to the nineteenth century when in 1868 eyeglass frames were made of cellulose nitrate. Today any person reaching out in any direction would most likely find within arm's length a product containing plastics. In the event that plastics were removed from the market, the plastics industry estimates over 500,000 workers would be unemployed. In addition, 1 billion acres, which includes all the agricultural land in the United States, would be needed to graze wool-producing sheep to produce the synthetics the textile industry now uses. Another 40 million acres would be needed for cotton crops. Fire hazards notwithstanding, the only solution apparently seems to be to rely on improved testing methods and responsible use, based on knowledge of potential dangers.

Research has determined that plastics present three major hazards in a fire exposure situation:

1. *Heat:* A comparison of heat release data shows that plastics produce more intense heat than cellulose, resulting

MAKING OF A HOLOCAUST

1 When fire breaks out in the Zebra Room, employees try to extinguish it. Fire department not called for about fifteen minutes.

2 Corridors and air ducts spread smoke through the building, and fire travels through airspace between ceiling and roof.

3 Patrons panic, stampede and fight their way through pitch-black smoky corridors. Scores suffocate.

4 In the crowded Cabaret Room, many guests are overcome by toxic smoke as they struggle to reach the exits. A few die while still seated at their tables.

Figure 4.14 Beverly Hills Supper Club fire. Reproduced with permission of Newsweek/Ib Ohlsson.

in a greater fire severity. One pound of polystyrene releases 18,000 BTU; one pound of pine wood releases 8,000 BTU.

2. *Smoke:* Plastics produce great amounts of dense black smoke. The toxic or flammable gas contents are released quickly at various stages of the combustion process.

3. *Rapid combustion:* Plastics burn more rapidly than natural products and thereby cause a more rapid flame spread.

A fire that occurred in the New York British Overseas Airways Corporation (BOAC) Terminal in 1970 has been termed the "shortest large-loss fire in the history of mankind." The fire started in the west gallery of the new BOAC terminal and within 30 minutes had spread the entire length of the 330-ft (100-m)) area, resulting in $2½ million damage. The only combustible materials in the all steel and glass structure were 600 seats near the gate entrances. The area was totally carpeted with a blend of 80 percent wool and 20 percent nylon installed over a felt pad. Investigations showed that the fire did not start in the seating, but evidence clearly indicated that the foam-plastic seat cushions were the major fuel source and were responsible for the rapid flame spread. The carpet, probably because of the large wool content, did not play a major role in the flame spread.

In the past several years industry has made tremendous strides in reducing the potential fire hazards of foam upholstery. Flame-retardant upholstery components are discussed on pages 59–61.

Designers should remember that all burning substances emit some degree of toxic gases. The primary cause of death in most fires is carbon monoxide, which is the principal toxic substance emitted from any burning material used in furnishings and finishes. Table 4.4 illustrates the principal toxic combustiton products (other than carbon monoxide) emitted from a few nonplastic materials.

While it is possible to measure the exact amount of toxic gases emitted by a particular material in a controlled laboratory condition, the combination of many materials and furnishings in a building often makes accurate analysis impossible. Because of this factor, engineers predict it will be many years before a solution is found to the problem of toxic gas release.

TABLE 4.4   TOXIC GASES FROM COMMON MATERIALS

Substance	Pulmonary Irritants	Other Toxic Gases
Wood/cotton	Acetacdehyde	Acetic acid
Newspaper	Formaldehyde	Methane, formic acid
Wood/silk	Ammonia	Hydrogen sulphide Hydrogen cyanide

Relative Toxic Hazard

Designers should be aware that all burning substances emit some degree of toxic gases. Because of this factor, engineers predict it will take some time before an ultimate solution is found to the problem of exposure to toxic hazards in a structure fire.

Research emphasis from the late 1970s through the 1980s expanded beyond the identification of toxic gases released from burning materials and products to include the biological effects on victims trapped in fires. Scientists from Germany, Japan, and the United States focused on bioassay test methods using rats and mice. Animal subjects were exposed to

smoke from burning material samples to determine the physical effect of potentially toxic products of combustion.

The toxicity index method used in most of the first-generation tests was based on the lethal concentration of smoke (grams) necessary to cause death in 50 percent of the animals in thirty minutes (LC 50 g).

Some test methods, such as the University of Pittsburgh test developed by Dr. Y. Alarie, use a relative classification system based on Douglas fir as the reference material. In the Pittsburgh test, fir produced on LC 50 g of 64. The fir LC 50 g rating was placed at the middle of an order of magnitude on a logarithmic scale. Based on the LC 50 g assigned in the Pitt test, materials were assigned a position on the scale.

1. LC 50 = 0.2–2 = Much more toxic than fir

2. LC 50 = 2–20 = More toxic than fir

3. LC 50 = 20–200 = As toxic as fir

4. LC 50 = more than 200 = Less toxic than fir[6]

(Note: Codes frequently require a *"more–than"* logarithmic scale evaluation for materials. The criteria may involve flame spread or any combustion products, such as smoke or heat release. For example, New York City Code Article 5, C, 26-504-.10 (e), "Interior Finish, Toxicity," states: "No material shall be used in any interior location that upon exposure to fire will produce products of decomposition or combustion that are *more* toxic in concentration *than* those given off by wood or paper when decomposing or burning under *comparable conditions.*" [Italics by author.])

Attempts to rank or compare the toxic potential of materials based on small-scale laboratory screening tests are frequently subject to controversy for the following reasons:

1. The tests are based on generic materials, not products. Designers normally specify complex product systems such as carpet composed of a primary and secondary backing. An upholstered chair presents a very complex system of fabric, liners, padding, cushions, springs, frame, and so forth.

2. The tests do not include information on total hazard.

3. It is difficult to translate irritant data from rodents to humans.

4. The tests are difficult to use in regulatory situations.

New York State Article 15   In December 1986, the New York State Office of Fire Prevention and Control adopted Article 15, Part 1120 (9NYCRR–1120): "Combustion Toxicity Testing and Regulations for Implementing Building Materials and Finishes Fire Gas Toxicity Data File."

The data file also contains information on the flame spread (ASTM E-84) for interior finishes. When carpet is to be installed in corridors, manufacturers must test and provide results from the Flooring Radiant Panel Test (NFPA 253). This data file is a public record available to any interested person. Release of data reports on all test results is required to contain the following statement:

This test is a measure of acute toxicity of the thermal decomposition by-products of the test material using a specified procedure under controlled laboratory conditions. The test results alone do not constitute a characterization of the hazard, safety, or risk of materials, products, or assemblies under actual fire conditions. The results of this test if used in any assessment of hazard or risk, should be considered in conjunction with all of the factors which are pertinent to an evaluation of the fire hazard of a particular end use.

The test required by this code is conducted in accordance with the "Procedure for Evaluation of Acute Toxicity Resulting from Exposure of Mice to Thermal Decomposition Products Using a Modification of the Protocol Developed at the University of Pittsburgh."

Although extensive toxicity research cannot provide a complete answer to the hazards and liabilities of fire, manufacturers, facility managers, and designers of interior products and spaces can exercise greater concern in the following ways:

1. Using smaller percentages of materials that are known to be potentially toxic

2. Using less toxic materials in critical occupancies such as nursing homes, schools, and institutional facilities

3. When specifying materials that are significantly toxic, providing an outer shield that can prevent early ignition

4. Considering the total potential for hazard. Investigating materials with reduced heat-release and burning rates. This could also reduce the amount of smoke produced

5. Staying informed on state-of-the-art combustion testing and supporting manufacturers that incorporate fire-safe materials in their products

GLOSSARY

Combustible: A material or structure which can burn. Combustible is a relative term; many materials which will burn under one set of conditions will not burn under others; e.g., structural steel is noncombustible, but fine steel wool is combustible. Does not indicate ease of ignition, burning intensity, or rate of burning, except when used with the word "higher."

Fire damage: The duration of a fully developed fire and the average fire temperature of the gases generated. The more ventilation the higher the fire temperatures.

Fire hazard (hazardous): Materials of more than average combustibility or materials that are dangerous because of their fire potential, instability, or toxicity. Also may describe the fire vulnerability of a property based on the fireload or fuel in the occupied space.

Fireload: Amount of combustibles present in a given situation, usually expressed in terms of weight of materials per square foot.

Fire prevention: Refers primarily to measures directed toward avoiding the inception of fire.

Fireproof: Officially *discontinued* in NFPA publications. No material is immune to the effects of fire of sufficient intensity and duration.

Fire protection: In the general sense this term includes everything related to the prevention, detection, and extinguishment of fire. In its specific sense, fire protection refers to the methods of providing for fire control or fire extinguishment.

Fire resistance: See listing under Chapter 6.

Fire retardant: See listing under Chapter 6.

Flameproof: A misleading term. The use of this term is discouraged in favor of "flame retardant" or "flame resistant."

Flame resistant: See listing under Chapter 6.

Flammable: A combustible material that ignites very easily, burns intensely, or has a rapid rate of flamespread. Flammable is used in a general sense without reference to specific limits.

Flashover: The phenomenon of a developing fire (or radiant heat source) producing radiant energy at wall and ceiling surfaces. The radiant feedback from those surfaces gradually heats the contents of the fire area, and when all the combustibles in the space have become heated to their ignition temperature, simultaneous ignition occurs.

Fuel: The amount of combustibles present in a fire situation.

Highrise buildings: Classified on the basis of height differences and correlated with the degree of life safety hazard present. Group 1: buildings of 6 stories or less with a height of up to 80 ft (24 m). These buildings can be completely evacuated within five minutes. Group 2: buildings with at least 6 stories but not exceeding 25 stories, with a height between 80 and 264 ft (24 and 83 m). These buildings have stack-effect potential and are beyond the reach of the fire department aerial ladders, but could be evacuated within a reasonable amount of time. Group 3: buildings exceeding 25 stories or 264 ft (83 m). These buildings fit all the classic parameters of a highrise building as set forth in the General Services Administration definition.

General Services Administration definition: (1) beyond the reach of fire department aerial ladder equipment; (2) requiring unreasonable evacuation time; (3) capable of creating significant stack effect; (4) requiring the fire suppression efforts to be executed internally.

It should be noted that these classifications do not account for special cases where immobile occupants are present, e.g., hospitals.

Sprinkler systems: The objective of a life-safety sprinkler system is not necessarily to effect final extinguishment of a fire, but to allow time for the occupants to escape by confining the fire to the room of origin. The system is composed of relatively small diameter copper pipe. The weight of this system is only one-third that of a conventional system. The sprinkler heads require a water pressure of approximately 30 psi and protect an area ranging from 160 to 225 sq ft (15 to 21 sq m). Automatic sprinkler systems are the most effective method that can be used to reduce the loss of life by fire. In a study of 661 highrise fires, sprinklers controlled 654 of the fires. This would mean a 98.9 percent satisfactory performance. When sprinkler systems are used in a commercial building, there is often a waiver of certain code requirements, resulting in more liberal interior materials standards, e.g., lower flame-spread rating for floor- and wallcoverings.

Toxic gases: The gases produced as a result of combustion. Toxic gases account for more fire death than all other causes combined. Gases produced by fire depend on many variables such as the chemical composition of the burning material, the amount of oxygen available for combustion, and temperature. The most common toxic gases are carbon monoxide, carbon dioxide, hydrogen sulfide, sulfur dioxide, ammonia, hydrogen cyanide, hydrogen chloride, nitrogen dioxide, acrolein, and phosgene. The concentration of these gases in smoke is measured in PPM (parts per million).

Ventilation: In a fire situation, refers to insufficient air being provided to the involved room or area to fully burn the gases that are being generated. This results in excess distillation of the gases being driven off the "fuels." When air does enter the space, combustion of the gases occurs.

INTERIOR FINISHES: FIRE PERFORMANCE TESTING

A representative of the Federal Trade Commission once remarked that no single test could predict the reaction of materials when exposed to the wide range of fire conditions. This comment only hints at the broad range of problems involved in the field of fire research.

TRENDS IN FIRE PERFORMANCE TESTING METHODS

Of concern to many fire engineers are the inherent limitations of conventional laboratory testing methods. Testing one sample under one condition does not adequately predict performance in fire exposure. *Fire exposure* implies that materials will be exposed not only to the variety of temperatures that occur in a fire, but also to the heat released from all the other components contained in a compartment fire. Figure 5.1a shows the time-temperature profiles that frequently occur from the growth phase to the fully developed phase of a fire system.[1] Contrast this to the standard time curve that is employed in laboratory testing (see Figure 5.1b and Figure 4.2). There appears to be a large variance between furnace-generated heat and actual fire conditions.

Millions of dollars are spent each year evaluating performance test methods. To assure that tests will have validity and provide results, the following criteria have been established:

1. The test methods should simulate, as much as possible, conditions typical of real use.

2. The test should provide reliable and quantitative results.

3. Results should be repeatable and reproducable. Tests conducted on a given material in the same laboratory, under the same conditions, should not vary widely but provide a continuous scale of measure.

4. The test method should be economically suited to wide use. The size and cost of some testing equipment, as well as the time required for the test, must be considered, as well as the sample size or quantity required for testing.

5. The test results should be reported in terms that can be understood by groups of people who will make use of the test findings. Architects, interior designers, and code officials must be able to apply test results in their practices.

Flammability Testing

Flammability testing may be broadly classified according to the stage of the fire system which the test seeks to evaluate:

Ignition/Growth Stages. Ideal fire performance testing involved with the first two stages of the fire development should measure material characteristics that *contribute* to the development and spread of fire. Combustibility (i.e., the ease of ignition, flame-spread qualities, and the amount of heat and smoke released by a material) is of major importance.

Fully Developed Fire Stages. Testing that deals with the fully developed fire is concerned with (1) the endurance of the building structure and (2) the physical endurance of humans exposed to the heat, flame, oxygen depletion, smoke, and toxic gases.

Flammability testing methods used to evaluate materials in the various stages of fire development may be classified as follows:

Calculation prediction methods. These performance tests are based on known release-rate data. The amount of heat and smoke released by materials under varied fire exposure conditions is documented and used as a basis for testing. The test method is employed in controlled laboratory conditions.

Full-scale simulation methods. This test method measures material performance under simulated fire exposure. Efforts to simulate fire conditions range from "room burns" to full-scale burn-outs in buildings slated for demolition. The full-scale burn-out of a building offers valuable reference points for predicting what might happen in a similar circumstance. The probability, however, of a similar condition occurring is highly

Figure 5.1 Time-temperature profiles. Reprinted from Progressive Architecture, *copyright Reinhold Publishing Company.*

unlikely. Since weather conditions such as temperature and wind direction are factors in a full-scale fire, accurate evaluations are difficult.

Combination laboratory and full-scale methods. The National Institute of Standards and Technology (formerly the National Bureau of Standards) constructed a fire research building in 1974, which incorporates a 40-ft (14-m) corridor lined with full-sized burn rooms. This facility has been successfully used to develop new data on the potential hazards of flame spread in corridors.

CURRENT FLAMMABILITY TESTING: INTERIOR FINISHES

Designers are often puzzled by the long lists of flammability performance tests shown on many interior finish products. An illustration of this point, taken from a typical product sample, is shown in Table 5.1. The remainder of this chapter will survey the tests listed in Table 5.1 and explain the application of tests index rating systems.

TABLE 5.1 PRODUCT FLAMMABILITY PERFORMANCE

Test	Number	Measurement
Federal standard	DOC. FF-1-70	Pass
Steiner Tunnel Test	ASTM E-84	
Flame spread		Under 75
Fuel contribution	UL 992	Under 4
Smoke density	NBS 708/NFPA 258	Under 200
Radiant panel	NBS IR 75-950	
Radiant flux	NFPA 253	.45 watts/sq cm

Methenamine Pill Test

DOC. FF-1-70

DOC. FF-2-70

This test (Figure 5.2) was developed by the National Bureau of Standards and adopted by the Department of Commerce in 1970.

Purpose. This test seeks to prevent the use of highly flammable fiber floorcoverings capable of spreading flame in Stage I fire exposure. The ease of surface ignition and surface flammability are evaluated. Some authorities require tests on both the front and back carpet surfaces and occasionally on carpet padding. DOC. FF-1-70 applies to carpet. DOC. FF-2-70 applies to rugs.

Test Procedure. A carpet sample 9 in. (22.9 cm) square is placed on the bottom of a 1 ft (30.5 cm) draft-protected square enclosed cube, which is open at the top. The sample is held in place by a 9-in. metal plate which has an 8-in. (20.3-cm) hole in the center. A timed methenamine pill is placed in the center of the carpet and lighted. The surface flame should not show considerable spread. If the sample burns to within 1 in. (2.5 cm) of the metal plate, it fails the test. The test is repeated 8 times, and 7 out of 8 samples must pass to qualify for test approval.

Rating System. The samples are given a pass/fail rating.

Official Adoption. Since 1971 this test is required by law for all carpet produced in the United States. DOC. FF-2-70 is required on domestic and imported rugs.

SIDE VIEW

TOP VIEW

METHENAMINE PILL

9″ (23 CM) DIAMETER CARPET SAMPLE

STEEL PLATE WITH 8″ (20 1/2 CM) DIAMETER HOLE

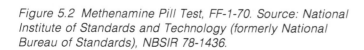

Figure 5.2 Methenamine Pill Test, FF-1-70. Source: National Institute of Standards and Technology (formerly National Bureau of Standards), NBSIR 78-1436.

Figure 5.3 Steiner Tunnel Test, ASTM E-84. Source: National Institute of Standards and Technology (formerly National Bureau of Standards), NBSIR 78-1436.

Steiner Tunnel Test

ASTM E-84

NFPA 255

UL 723

Developed by A. J. Steiner for the Underwriters Laboratories, Inc. after World War I, this test (Figure 5.3) was adopted by ASTM and NFPA as official standards in 1958.

Purpose. The test was devised to test the comparative surface burning characteristics of *building materials* and interior finishes. The test is designed to simulate a Stage II, or fully developed fire exposure, and provides data on flame spread, fuel contribution, and smoke density.

Test Procedure. A sample 24 ft (7.5 m) long and 20 in. (50.8 cm) wide is placed on the ceiling of a 25-ft (7.6-m) long tunnel. A double-jet gas burner at the end of the tunnel provides about 5,000 BTU per minute during the test, which is 10 minutes in duration. Air is induced into the tunnel to pull the gas flame upstream for about 4 ft (121.9 cm). The distance of the burn along the test sample is measured to determine the flame-spread rating.

Rating System. All materials are rated on a scale ranging from 0 to 100. Cement-asbestos board, which will not burn, is arbitrarily given a rating of zero (0) and red oak flooring is rated at 100 (moderate burning rate).

Classification	Flame-Spread Range
A	0–25
B	26–75
C	76–200

Official Adoption. This test method is currently required in most states. It is used in the ASTM model code and the NFPA 101 Life Safety Code. Among federal agencies adopting this test method are HHS, GSA, and FHA, and the test is required to meet the standards of the Hill-Burton Act that regulates fire safety in health-care facilities.

Objections to Test. The carpet industry has long opposed the application of the ASTM E-84 test method for carpet for the following reasons: (1) the test was primarily designed for wall and ceiling finish materials. The tunnel test requires carpet to be tested in an upside-down position, wich causes many fibers to melt and drip at an early stage in the test process. (2) Research has proven that temperatures during a fire are much higher at the ceiling level than at the floor level. (3) It has been difficult to establish repeatable data when testing carpets in this method.

The Chamber Test

UL 992

This test method was developed as an alternative to the Steiner Tunnel Test.

Purpose. This test seeks to determine the flame spread and flame propagation of carpet.

Testing Procedure. A carpet sample 2 by 8 ft (.6 by 2.4 m) is installed on the floor of the chamber. A gas flame is then applied to the carpet for 12 minutes with a controlled air draft of 100 ft (30 m) per minute.

Rating System. Calculations are based on the length of the flame spread and time of flame travel. A rating index from 0 to 25 is used.

Class B	0–4
Class C	5–8

Objections. The rating index divides material into two groups, which makes a continuous classification scale difficult, and the index has not been proven relevant to fire hazards.

Official Adoption. Used by several states and some federal agencies, such as HHS and FHA.

SIDE ELEVATION

Figure 5.4 Flooring Radiant Panel Test. Source: National Institute of Standards and Technology (formerly National Bureau of Standards), NBSIR 78-1436.

WATTS—CM²

Figure 5.5 Flooring Radiant Panel Test Index. Source: National Institute of Standards and Technology (formerly National Bureau of Standards), NBSIR 78-1436.

Flooring Radiant Panel Test
ASTM E648

NBS IR 75-950

NFPA 253

The first research on this test method (Figure 5.4) was conducted by the Armstrong Cork Company in 1966. The National Institute of Standards and Technology (formerly National Bureau of Standards) had considerable influence on the development of the test and the establishment of the Critical Radiant Flux Index rating. Many early tests were conducted at the NIST facilities, which allowed full-scale corridor testing. The test is highly recommended for testing floorcovering systems for the following reasons:

1. It measures radiant exposures, which are very important in full-scale corridor tests.

2. The total flooring system is tested, as used and on a horizontal plane.

3. Reproducibility and repeatability are excellent.

4. The test apparatus is simple and compact; the test sample is small.

5. The test procedure is simple and provides a continuous scale of performance in the range of 0.1 to 1.0 watts/cm² radiant exposure.

Purpose. In the past decade many lives have been lost in hotel and nursing home fires. Both building types use corridors as a means of egrese. This test specifically deals with the measurement of flame spread in a corridor or exitway which is under the influence of a fully developed fire in an adjacent room. The fully developed fire within the room transmits heat and radiant energy to the ceilings and walls of the corridor, which ignite the carpet, thus blocking the only means of escape.

Test Procedure. Sample size is 39 in. (99.1 cm) long by 8 in. (20.3 cm) wide and is mounted horizontally. The sample receives radiant energy from an air gas-fueled radiant panel mounted above the sample at an angle of 30°. After the sample is preheated, a gas-fired pilot burner ignites the flooring system.

Rating System. The radiant energy flux decreases along the length of the carpet (REF vs. distance profile); therefore, the pilot flame is placed at the end closest to the source of the radiant energy. Once the carpet sample is ignited, the flame is allowed to travel along the carpet until it is no longer reinforced by the radiant energy force and self-extinguishes. The point where the burning carpet self-extinguishes is called the point of critical radiant flux. Critical radiant flux is defined as the minimum amount of radiant energy needed to sustain flame. The test is indexed in watts per square centimeter. In the test, the higher the number of watts per square centimeter, the more resistant the carpet to flame propagation. The lower the number, the greater the tendency of the carpet to spread flame (Figure 5.5).

Critical Radiant Flux Recommended Limits. The National Institute of Standards and Technology (formerly National Bureau of Standards) recommends the following:

Class I = 0.45 watts/cm² within corridors and exitways of hospitals and nursing homes

TABLE 5.2 MAJOR FLAMMABILITY TESTING OF INTERIOR FINISHES

	ASTM E-84 Steiner Tunnel	FF 1-70 FF 2-70	NFPA 253 Flooring Radiant	NFPA 258 Smoke Density
Purpose of Test	Flame spread Fuel contribution Smoke contribution	Ease of ignition Surface flammability	Flame spread in corridors	Smoke density

Procedure
  Sample size
	20″ × 25′ on ceiling of
	  chamber
		9″ × 9″ placed under
		  9″ × 9″ steel plate
			39″ × 8″ mounted in
			  holding frame
				3″ × 3″ flaming or
				  smoldering condition

Test chamber	25′ long chamber	Draft controlled, hooded-
		  mirror
			Radiant panel at 30° angle	Chamber: 2′ D
				                3′ W
				                3′ H

Heat applied	Pilot source at one end.
	Standard draft condition
		Methenamine pill lighted by
		  match
			Chamber preheated. Pilot
			  heat source. No forced air
				2.2 BTU per ft²
				(2.5 w/cm²)

How results measured	Based on red oak standard
	  flame spread of 100.
		7 out of 8 samples must
		  pass
			Class I = 0.45 w/cm²–
			  Nursing Homes
			Class II = 0.22 w/cm²–
			  Commercial
				Photometric light measures
				  optical density of smoke

	Flame spread: Class A = 0–25 Class B = 26–75 Class C = 76–200	Rated: pass/fail	Measured in watts per square cm	Smoke particles (EPM) Optical density

Federal agencies adoption	HHS, Hill-Burton
	GSA, FHA
		Federal law 1971—all carpet
		  produced in USA must
		  pass FF1-70
			HHS, VA, DOT, GSA	NIST, HHS, GSA, FHA

Class II = 0.22 watts/cm² within corridors and exitways of all commercial buildings and hotels

Official Adoption. All major federal agencies have adopted the test. This includes HHS, Veterans Administration, Public Building Service, Department of Defense, and the Department of Transportation. NFPA adopted the test as a standard in 1978.

Smoke Generation of Solid Materials
NFPA 258-1987

Purpose. This test was devised to measure the smoke potential of solid materials. Because the density of smoke often prevents escape in a fire situation, the light obscuration characteristic of generated smoke is also measured.

Test Procedure. The chamber is a closed cabinet 2 by 3 by 3 ft (61 by 91.4 by 91.4 cm). A sample 3 in. (7.6 cm) square is supported vertically in a holder while exposed to heat under two conditions: flaming and nonflaming (smoldering). A photometric meter measures light density.

Rating System. Smoke quality is reported in terms of maximum optical density. The index range is between 0 and 800 units, which covers most building finish materials. Most federal agencies require a smoke density rate of 450 or less (flaming).

Official Adoption. Many states and federal agencies have adopted this method, including HHS.

Corner Test
This test has been used occasionally over the last 20 years and may be gaining in use for the testing of wallcoverings. Recent testing by fire engineers Belles, Fisher, and Williamson has demonstrated the test's importance in collecting heat-release data on wallcoverings.[2] A small-scale test that could possibly simulate this test is under investigation.

Purpose. This test simulates real use conditions of interior finishes on walls and ceilings (Figure 5.6).

Test Procedure. This test method makes use of a corner construction, usually 8 ft (2.4 m) tall. Extensions on either side

of the corner may extend from 4 to 8 ft (1.4 to 2.4 m) and a ceiling may also be attached. Material to be tested is applied to the walls and ceiling. A wooden "crib" placed on the floor close to the corner walls is used as an ignition source. The 2-ft-square wood slat box filled with excelsior simulates a small trash-basket fire.

Rating System. Materials are allowed to burn out and efforts are made to determine the extent of flame spread. No formal index has been published.

Official Adoption. Some cities have evolved their own version of the corner test, such as the Phoenix Corner Test. A corner test has not yet been officially adopted by the National Fire Protection Association.

Table 5.2 summarizes the major test methods used to evaluate interior finishes.

Figure 5.6 Corner test.

TABLE 5.3　COMPARATIVE TEST INDEX RATINGS

ASTM E-84 Steiner Tunnel Test	UL 992 Chamber Test	NFPA 253 Flooring Radiant Panel
Class A = 0–25		Class I = 0.45 w/cm²— Nursing homes
Class B = 26–75	Class B = 0–4	Class II = 0.22 w/cm²— Commercial
Class C = 76–200	Class C = 5–8	
The higher the index rating, the greater the hazard.	The higher the index, the greater the hazard.	The higher the index rating, the *less* the hazard.

TABLE 5.4　NFPA INTERIOR FINISH REQUIREMENTS.

Occupany	Exits	Access to Exits	Other Spaces
Assembly—New Class A or B Class C	A A	A or B A or B	A or B A, B, or C
Assembly—Existing Class A or B Class C	A A	A or B A or B	A or B A, B, or C
Educational—New	A	A or B	A or B C on low partitions
Educational—Existing	A	A or B	A, B, or C
Day-Care Centers—New	A I or II	A I or II	A or B
Day-Care Centers—Existing	A or B	A or B	A or B
Group Day-Care Homes	A or B	A, B, or C	A, B, or C
Family Day-Care Homes	A or B	A or B	A, B, or C
Health Care—New	A I	A B lower portion of corridor wall I	A B in small individual rooms
Health Care—Existing	A or B	A or B	A or B
Detention & Correctional—New	A I	A I	A, B, or C
Detention & Correctional—Existing	A or B I or II	A or B I or II	A, B, or C
Residential, Hotels & Dormitories—New	A I or II	A or B I or II	A, B, or C
Residential, Hotels & Dormitories—Existing	A or B I or II	A or B I or II	A, B, or C
Residential, Apartment Buildings—New	A I or II	A or B I or II	A, B, or C
Residential, Apartment Buildings—Existing	A or B I or II	A or B I or II	A, B, or C
Residential, Board and Care			
Residential, 1- and 2-family, Lodging or Rooming Houses	A, B, or C	A, B, or C	A, B, or C
Mercantile—New	A or B	A or B	A or B
Mercantile—Existing Class A or B	A or B	A or B	ceilings—A or B existing on walls— A, B, or C
Mercantile—Existing Class C	A, B, or C	A, B, or C	A, B, or C
Office—New	A or B I or II	A or B I or II	A, B, or C
Office—Existing	A or B	A or B	A, B, or C
Industrial	A or B	A, B, or C	A, B, or C
Storage	A or B	A, B, or C	A, B, or C
Unusual Structures	A or B	A, B, or C	A, B, or C

Notes:
　Class A Interior Wall and Ceiling Finish—flame spread 0–25, smoke developed 0–450.
　Class B Interior Wall and Ceiling Finish—flame spread 26–75, smoke developed 0–450.
　Class C Interior Wall and Ceiling Finish—flame spread 76–200, smoke developed 0–450.
　Class I Interior Floor Finish—minimum 0.45 watts per sq cm.
　Class II Interior Floor Finish—minimum 0.22 watts per sq cm.
　Automatic Sprinklers—where a complete standard system of automatic sprinklers is installed, interior wall and ceiling finish with flame spread rating not over Class C may be used in any location where Class B is required and with rating of Class A in any location where Class A is required; similarly, Class II interior floor finish may be used in any location where Class I is required and no critical radiant flux radiant flux rating is required where Class II is required.
　Exposed portions of structural members complying with the requirements for heavy timber construction may be permitted.
Source: Reprinted by permission from NFPA 101, *Life Safety Code*, copyright © 1988, National Fire Protection Association, Boston, Mass.

APPLICATION OF FIRE TESTING

Fire tests are valuable in determining the potential hazards of materials. It should be noted that many test methods establish different index ratings for the particular fire characteristic being evaluated. In some tests a high index rating indicates a greater hazard; in others it represents a lower hazard. The three tests presented in Table 5.3 illustrate the differences.

Codes and Standards Application

When referring to codes and standards, designers should also be aware that the same index rating may be used by more than one test method. Tunnel tests, such as NFPA 255, UL 723, and ASTM E-84, classify the flame spread of interior finishes in the following manner:

Class A	0–25
Class B	26–75
Class C	76–200

The 101 Life Safety Code published by the National Fire Protection Association classifies the flame-spread requirements for interior finishes according to occupancy and the index rating of the NFPA 255, "Method of Test of Surface Burning Characteristics of Building Materials" (see Table 5.4).

In an example from the Veterans Administration requirements (UM-44c) for floorcoverings, the flame-spread ratings of both the ASTM E-84 and the UL 992 are listed in Table 5.5.

Code Officials' Application

When a code official informs a designer that an interior finish or a component presents a fire hazard and cannot be used in a particular project, the designer often finds it difficult to understand the reason for the product rejection.

A researcher, interested in understanding the decision-making process used by code officials, devised a hypothetical situation in which a designer submitted the fire performance test results, shown in Table 5.6, to a code official for approval of a panel system to be used in an open office plan. On the basis of the tests submitted, officials were asked to evaluate the panel systems.

The presentation of this problem to code officials produced some interesting insights about the decision-making process

used in evaluating fire safety factors. The majority of officials began by selecting the test methods thought to be the most appropriate for evaluating the office panels. Many chose the flame-spread factor (ASTM E-84) while others chose the ease of ignition (FF 1-70). Some were concerned with the heat potential (ASTM STP 464), although many would have preferred more information on rate of heat produced, rather than the total heat potential.

Another important criteria in the decision process involved the size and use of the panel, i.e., how the panel would interface with other materials in the space.[3]

This simple experiment can perhaps help designers to identify with code officials who are faced with many complex decisions regarding the approval of products.

Designers' Application

Making fire safety decisions is perhaps even more complicated for designers because of the additional concerns about function, costs, and aesthetics. As a result of research in the area of fire safety systems, the U.S. Department of Housing and Urban Development projected the need for a designers'

TABLE 5.5 VETERANS ADMINISTRATION (UM 44C) FLOORCOVERING REQUIREMENTS

Location within Building	Surface Flame-Spread Rating— Maximum Range, Floors
Enclosed stairways and other vertical openings	0-75 (4)
Corridors or hallways and other exits	0-200 (8)
Public rooms and entrance spaces	0-200 (8)
Lobbies and corridors between exit stairway and exterior	0-200 (8)
Service rooms, enclosing heat-producing or other mechanical equipment, and all other fire hazardous areas	0-75 (4)

Notes: 0-75; 0-200 = ASTM E 84 limits. ( ) = Index number for UL Standard No. 992.

TABLE 5.6 PANELS FOR USE IN OPEN OFFICE PLAN

Panel No.	Surface Area, ft^2	Product Material	Ease of Ignition*	Fire Characteristics of Product			
				Flame-Spread Rating†	Potential Heat,‡ BTU/ft^2	Smoke Density,§ D_m	Carbon Monoxide Max., ppm¶
1	8	A	1	100	8,000	100	3,000
2	18	B	2	75	4,000	300	5,000
3	6	C	4	25	10,000	350	2,000
4	6	D	1	200	16,000	450	5,000
5	12	E	3	50	6,000	200	6,000

Notes: All panels are of the same design, except for the surface area.
Fire characteristic test methods:
*Fictitious: number of combined methenamine tablets needed to cause sustained burning.
†ASTM E-84 (25' tunnel).
‡ASTM STP 464, pp. 127-52, per ft^2 of surface area.
§NBS Smoke Density Chamber, flaming mode.
¶Measured in NBS Smoke Density Chamber, flaming mode.

TABLE 5.7   FLAME-SPREAD RATING OF INTERIOR FINISHES (ASTM E-84)

Alternative	Walls	Ceiling	Cabinets
1	200	200	200
2	200	200	25

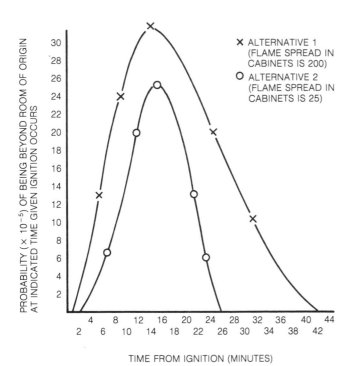

Figure 5.7 Distribution for two types of kitchen wallcovering, given ignition in kitchen.

"application handbook."[4] This handbook would assist designers by providing information on evaluating the alternatives and probabilities involved in fire safety decisions. For example, a designer planning a kitchen interior may establish two sets of kitchen interior finish parameters (Table 5.7). Having selected the wall and ceiling finish, the designer would then have to decide between cabinets 1 and 2. Cabinet 1 has a flame-spread rating of 200 and costs $1,500. Cabinet 2 has a flame-spread rating of 25 and will cost $2,500.

The less expensive cabinet would meet the minimum requirements for the particular project, but in the event of fire would present a high probability of spreading the fire beyond the kitchen. Figure 5.7 illustrates that a fire occurring in the kitchen with cabinet 2 would only present a small probability of spreading beyond the kitchen.

Before making a decision between increased fire safety and cost factors, designers may also consider the possibility of other alternatives. There are often unspecified combinations of factors that may achieve equivalent levels of fire safety such as:

1.   Smoke density potential versus use of smoke detectors.

2.   Flame spread versus amount of fuel loading in the area.

3.   Flame spread versus availability of public fire protection.

4.   Heat content of materials versus use of sprinklers.

In order to make alternate decisions, it is evident that designers must be familiar with product test results indicating the smoke density potential, rate of heat release, and heat content of a particular material. It is also evident that designers making *responsible design decisions* is no less difficult than code officials making product approval decisions.

RISK MANAGEMENT CHECKLIST

1.   Early in the design process try to determine the fire hazard potential of the project.

2.   Determine the performance test method that will provide the level of fire protection required for the project.

3.   Keep informed of new test methods as they are developed.

4.   Make every effort to use concise fire terminology in specifications. ASTM has established guidelines regarding the use of certain terms as adjectives and nouns (see *Flame resistant* and *Flame resistance* in the Glossary for Chapter 6).

GLOSSARY

Full-scale test: A test that may involve the use of an entire building donated for research. Also refers to a full-scale room constructed to simulate actual fire conditions.

Interior finish.   Defined by National Fire Protection Association as those materials that form the exterior/interior surfaces of wall, ceiling, and floors. Variations of this basic definition are found in some building regulations where countertops, built-in cabinets, and even doors are included in the definition. Many codes, such as NFPA 101, Life Safety Code, exclude trim and incidental finish on the basis that it comprises less than 10 percent of the wall and ceiling areas. Free-hanging drapery that covers most or all of a wall surface may be considered interior finish. Surface coatings such as paint or varnish may also be included. Some authorities include the lining or coverings of ducts, shafts, and plenum spaces, as well as batt and blanket insulation, if the back faces a stud space through which fire might spread.

Nonflaming (NF): This rating indicates that a test has been conducted on a material without the use of a flame as a source of ignition. For example, NFPA 260 B, which tests for resistance to cigarette ignition, tries to ignite a material with a "nonflaming" or smoldering cigarette (see Chapter 6).

Pyrolysis: Decomposition as a result of heat.

Radiant flux: The minimum energy necessary to sustain flame propagation (see *Flashover*, p. 37).

Research and development test: A test that has not firmly established an index rating or has not fully answered all the questions that prompted the research.

Room burns test: A type of test that simulates a portion of a burning building. The "mock" room may contain furniture, drapery, wallcoverings, or any objects scheduled for testing.

Simulated full-scale test: A test conducted in an effort to simulate an actual burning building or interior space.

Smoke load: The total smoke which could be liberated by the combustion of furnishings and interior finishes in a compartment under prescribed exposure conditions.

Specific optical density (DS): Optical density measured by the percent of light transmission passed through the smoke. A photometric device is used to measure the light transmission. DM means the maximum optical density.

Test index: This usually explains how the product or material is being evaluated in the test. The index may be a pass/fail or it may provide a rating based on letters or numbers. For example: ASTM E-84 provides an index such as Class A = 0–25. See pages 40–44 for more details.

UPHOLSTERY AND FURNITURE FLAMMABILITY

Designers have traditionally specified upholstered furniture on the following basis:

1. Style

2. Comfort, based on knowledge of human factors

3. Functional and spatial needs

4. Construction performance: strength and durability

5. Cost factors

In recent years another consideration has been brought to the attention of designers; the potential flammability hazard of fabrics and filling materials used in upholstered furniture. Though a great deal of research had been done on the problem, little effort has been made to aid designers in applying the research findings to actual specification decisions.

This chapter will provide a review of research and new terminology that has resulted from efforts to establish a uniform national standard for producing more flame-resistant upholstered furniture. Prior to the 1972 adoption of the federal standard for the Flammability of Mattresses (FF 4-72) [reprinted in Appendix C], there had been no regulations of interior furniture. Table 6.1 lists the mandatory standards that became effective during the 1970s. With the adoption of each standard, designers have expressed concern about federal intervention in design areas previously free of regulations. The proposed flammability standard for upholstered furniture, first announced in 1972, provoked headlines in major city newspapers and many articles in professional magazines. The subject of death by fire is a highly charged subject, especially when linked to the antismoking campaigns of the late seventies and eighties.

The process involved in the development of a federal standard is complicated and often controversial. With the passage of the Consumer Product Safety Act in 1973, Congress also formed the Consumer Product Safety Commission (CPSC) to (1) protect the public against unreasonable risks of injury associated with consumer products; (2) assist consumers in evaluating the comparative safety of consumer products; (3) develop uniform safety standards for consumer products and minimize conflicting state and local regulations; (4) promote research and investigation into the causes of product-related deaths and injuries.[1] The goal of the CPSC is to encourage industry self-regulation that can prevent the necessity of a federal regulation. With these responsibilities and very carefully regulated procedures, the commission must establish priorities before taking action on a particular product by evaluating the frequency and severity of injuries associated with a product and projecting future injuries, deaths, and property loss.

BASIS FOR CONCERN: INJURY AND FIRE FATALITIES

Information on injuries and deaths from upholstered furniture fires is not all contained in computer banks. Some is never reported, while much comes to the public through the daily news media. Examples can be found in many local newspapers:

FIRE KILLS RESIDENT; HOUSE IS DAMAGED
A 54-year-old man died Monday in a fire that heavily damaged his north Phoenix home. The man was found in the den of his home. Fire investigators said the blaze started in a love seat in the den and was apparently caused by careless disposal of smoking material . . . the fire apparently smoldered for some time before spreading through the den, firemen said. The den and kitchen suffered fire damage, and the remainder of the house was heavily damaged by intense heat and smoke. The loss was estimated at $38,000.[2]

The Consumer Product Safety Commission gathers information on injuries and fatalities from many different sources:

National Fire Protection Association (NFPA)

United States Fire Administration

National Household Fire Survey

Maryland State Fatality Study

TABLE 6.1 FEDERAL FLAMMABILITY STANDARDS

End Use	Agency	Finding That Standard May Be Needed	Publication of Proposed Standard with Test Method	Adoption of Proposed Standard	Effective Compliance Date
Large carpets and rugs Larger than 24 sq ft	CPSC	Dec. 1968	Dec. 1968	April 1970	April 1971
Small carpets and rugs Less than 24 sq ft	CPSC	Dec. 1968	April 1970	Dec. 1970	Dec. 1971
Airplane carpet and upholstery	DOT	—	—	—	May 1972
Automobile upholstery and carpet	DOT	—	Dec. 1969, June 1970	Dec. 1970	Sept. 1972
Mattresses	CPSC	June 1970	Sept. 1971	May 1972	July 1973
Furniture upholstery	CPSC	Nov. 1972	Dec. 1976	NA	

Source: Frost and Sullivan, New York.

Flammable Fabrics Accident Case and Testing System (FFACTS)

CPSC In-Depth Investigations

Death Certificates

National Electronic Injury Surveillance System (NEISS)

National Center for Health Statistics (NCHS)

From these sources, the CPSC estimated that 45,000 residential upholstered furniture fires occur each year in the United States. It was also estimated that an annual rate of 3,200 injuries and 800 deaths (from a range of 544 to 1,038 deaths) occur from residential upholstered furniture fires. It was found that approximately 1,700 of the injuries and 500 of the deaths were related to cigarette ignition of the upholstery. These estimates are based on data gathered from 1971 through 1976.

The CPSC further reports that economic losses due to the ignition of upholstered furniture are estimated to be about $540 million annually. These losses are the sum of estimated losses from deaths, injuries, and property damage. The estimates include hospital costs, rehabilitation costs, and losses in earnings. These figures do not include the total annual losses from pain and suffering.[3]

From a tabulation of all these figures, certain similarities began to appear in the fire incidents:

1. *Location and time of incidents.* The majority of fires occurred in the living room areas during the early morning hours between midnight and 6 A.M.

2. *Activity leading to ignition.* It appeared that most people became involved in these fire incidents after (a) falling asleep on the upholstered furniture while smoking a cigarette or (b) leaving a lit cigarette smoldering on the furniture.

3. *Age of victims.* People directly involved in these upholstered furniture fires were mostly adults between the ages of 21 and 64.

4. *Involvement of intoxicants and disabilities.* Evidence strongly indicated that alcohol, drugs, and physical and/or mental disabilities sometimes played a part in these incidents, although not in the majority of cases. When intoxicants or disabilities were present, they involved adults in the above age range.

5. *Number of victims per incident.* Situations in which victims fell asleep with smoking materials tended to be single victim incidents; i.e., these adults were the victims of their own actions. Incidents in which cigarettes were left smoldering on the furniture tended to result in multiple victims. This involved injuries and deaths of children and elderly people, as well as the person responsible for leaving the cigarette on the furniture.

6. *Causes of injuries and deaths.* Burns, closely followed by smoke inhalation, caused the majority of injuries. Inhalation caused the majority of deaths.

7. *Property losses.* In situations where the victim fell asleep on the upholstered furniture with smoking materials, the property-loss values were usually low ($300 or less). When the smoking material was left smoldering on the furniture, the property losses were usually extensive ($10,000 to $3,000,000).

8. *Material components of furniture involved.* In incidents where textile remnants were available after the fire for laboratory analysis, the results indicated that cellulosics predominated as the outer layer upholstery fabric. Cotton, rayon, and blends of these two fibers were most frequently involved. Research also found the fabric weight of the outer layer of upholstery averaged over 20 oz/sq yd. Cotton batting and combinations of urethane foam/cotton batting predominated as the inner layer of upholstery.[4]

If the commission, after carefully reviewing the data, decides that a standard or regulation is needed to protect the public from further unreasonable risks, they have been authorized to proceed in the following manner:

1. The commission publishes a "notice of proceedings" in the *Federal Register.* This notice serves as a public announcement to all concerned parties that a regulation is needed for a particular product and that research will begin on the development of a standard.

2. The commission is also authorized to publish a proposed standard. This proposed standard may be one that has previously been issued or adopted by a qualified public or private agency or organization.

3. The commission may also accept offers from agencies, organizations, or individuals who wish to propose a standard. Congress specifies that these must be submitted within 150 days after the "notice of proceedings" is published in the *Federal Register.*

4. The commission also encourages the general public and all interested people to participate in the development of a standard.[5]

5. If after considering the feasibility of all proposals submitted, the commission determines that no proposals have met the established criteria, the "development proceedings" may be terminated and the commission may then independently develop a standard.

EXISTING REGULATIONS ON THE FLAMMABILITY OF UPHOLSTERED FURNITURE

Prior to the "notice of proceedings" issued in 1972 by CPSC indicating the need for a flammability standard, several states and cities had issued regulatory standards on upholstered furniture and had already prompted many areas of industry to improve the flammability resistance of furniture components, such as fabric and substrate.

The federal, state, city, industry association, and testing society regulations exerting the most influence are listed in Tables 6.2 and 6.3. Surveying these regulations indicates that the majority require component testing using an open-flame source of ignition with components being rated by distance of flame spread or ability to self-extinguish within 0 to 15 seconds. The State of California Standard requires mandatory testing of furniture, both with open-flame and cigarette ignition sources.

Because of the Coconut Grove Night Club fire that claimed 492 lives in 1942, Boston has established many regulations dealing with interior finishes and furnishings. The voluntary industry standards established by the Business and Institutional Furniture Manufacturers Association (BIFMA) and the

Upholstered Furniture Action Council (UFAC) are a direct result of concerns expressed by the CPSC.

Designers should note that the majority of tests on Table 6.3 use a small flame as the source of ignition and are rated on a pass/fail basis. Most of the other test criteria is based on the following:

1. *Seconds* allowed for completion of any afterflame or afterglow phase. Seconds allowed for self-extinguishment are also regulated. (See term definitions in the Glossary at the end of this chapter.)

2. *Inches* allowed for the size or length of burn or char area.

TABLE 6.2 FLAMMABILITY STANDARDS AND TEST METHODS

STATES AND CITIES

Boston Fire Department
General Requirements
Fire Prevention Code
Classification Fire Test BFD IX-1, 5/16/86
Procedure for Approval of Upholstered Furniture IX-10, 5/19/86
Boston Fire Dept. Chair Test, Draft Jan. 1986
Tentative Performance Criteria: Foam Cellular Plastic Padding for
  Regulated Upholstered Furnishing, 5/20/82
Approved Upholstery Foam Products, 3/1/86
Approved Barriers for Foam Padding, 3/1/86
Application for Installation of Floor Coverings
State Regulations for Soft Coverings for Corridors and Exitways
  (Stairways and Lobbies)
Application for Installation of Wallcoverings
Fire Prevention Regulations (Flameproofing Certificates)

California Bureau of Home Funishing
Technical Information Bulletin 116
  Requirements, Test Procedures, and Apparatus for Testing the Flame-
    Retardance of Upholstered Furniture, Jan. 1980
Technical Information Bulletin 117
  Section A through E Inclusive: Requirements, Test Procedure, and
    Apparatus for Testing the Flame-Retardance of Resilient Filling
    Materials Used in Upholstered Furniture, Jan. 1980
      Section A—Foams and Polystyrene Beads
      Section B—Natural Filling Material
      Section C—Synthetic Filling Material (Other Than Foam)
      Section D—Filling Material Cigarette Test
      Section E—Fabric
      California Labeling Requirements
Technical Information Bulletin 121
  Flammability Test Procedures for Mattresses Used in High-Risk
    Occupancies, April 1980
Technical Information Bulletin 133
  Transmittal Page
  Test: Flammability Test Procedures for Seating Furniture for Use in
    High-Risk and Public Occupancies, May 1984
Flammability Law
  Provisions of State Code with Mandate the Requirement for Bulletins
    116, 117, and 121 including Labeling of Upholstered Furniture and
    Mattresses

California State Fire Marshal's Office
Draperies, Curtains, Decorative Materials
  Laws and Regulations Relating to Flame-Retardant Chemicals,
    Fabrics, and Application Concerns Extracted from the Health and
    Safety Code, Regulations from the California Administrative Code
    Title 19—Public Safety through 1979

Massachusetts
Flammable Decorations Form FPR 20, May 1975
Amendment to FPR 20, Feb. 20, 1976

New York City
Draperies and Decorative Materials Bulletin #44 of the Board of Standards
  and Appeals, City of New York, Oct. 29, 1964

New York State
Fire Gas Toxicity Update
Article 15 of the Uniform Fire Prevention & Building Code Effective Dec.
  16, 1986, Part 1120, Combustion Toxicity Testing
Regulations for Implementing Building Materials & Finishes—Fire Gas
  Toxicity Data File

Port Authority of New York and New Jersey (Revised April 1981)
Specifications Governing the Flammability of Upholstered Materials and
  Plastic Furniture
Specifications Governing the Flammability of Plastic Laminate and Wood
  Veneer Furniture
Specifications Governing the Flammability of Carpets
Specifications Governing the Flammability of Drapery and Curtain
  Materials

U.S. GOVERNMENT

Consumer Product Safety Commission
Code of Federal Regulations Title 16
  FF 1-70   Part 1630
              Standard for the Surface Flammability of Carpets and
              Rugs
  FF 2-70   Part 1631
              Standard for the Surface Flammability of Carpets and
              Rugs
  FF 4-72   Part 1632
              Standard for the Flammability of Mattresses and Mattress
              Pads (Includes Classification Test for Tickings)

General Services Administration
GSA Handbook: Accident and Fire Prevention—General PBS P5900.2B,
  Oct. 31, 1985
    Chapter 14—Building Fire Safety Standards
    Chapter 15—Special Building Fire Safety Standards
    Chapter 16—Exit Arrangement and Interior Construction

ASTM (American Society for Testing and Materials)
E 84 (1986) Standard Test Method for Surface Burning Characteristics
              of Building Materials
E 162 (1983) Standard Test Method for Surface Flammability of
              Materials Using a Radiant-Heat Energy Source
E 603 (1977) Standard Guide for Room-Fire Experiments (reapproved
              1983 without change)
E 648 (1986) Standard Test Method for Critical Radiant Flux of Floor
              Covering Systems Using a Radiant-Heat Energy Source
E 662 (1983) Standard Test Method for Specific Optical Density of
              Smoke Generated by Solid Materials
E 906 (1983) Standard Test Method for Heat and Visible Smoke Release
              Rates for Materials and Products
D3675 (1983) Surface Flammability of Flexible Cellular Materials Using a
              Radiant-Heat Energy Source

**BIFMA (The Business and Institutional Furniture Manufacturer's
  Association)**
First Generation Voluntary Upholstered Furniture
Flammability Standard for Business and Institutional Markets F-1-1978
  (Rev. A80)

UFAC (Upholstered Furniture Action Council)
UFAC Program Explained "An Ounce of Prevention"—revised through
  1983
Barrier Test Method—1983
Decking Materials Test Method—1983
Fabric Classification Test Method—1983
Filling/Padding Component Test Method—1983
Interior Fabric Test Method—1983
Welt Cord Test Method—1983
Standard Method of Laundering—1983

Underwriters Laboratories
UL 214   Standard for Tests for Flame Propagation of Fabrics

TABLE 6.3 CITY AND STATE UPHOLSTERY AND DRAPERY FLAMMABILITY REGULATIONS

Jurisdiction	End Use	Test Number	Method	P/F	Criteria
The Port Authority of New York and New Jersey	Upholstery Padding/cushions over ½" thick Plastic laminate Wood veneer	191-5906	(F)	P/F	Burn length max. 8". Afterflame max. 15". Drip burn less than 5 sec.
	Plastic	ASTM D 635	(F)	P/F	Self-extinguish
	Drapery	FAA 25.853 b Vertical	(F)	P/F	Char <8" Afterflame <15 sec.
	Upholstery	Horizontal			Burn rate 4" per min.
City of Boston	Curtains/decor	BFD 11	(F)	P/F	Afterflame <2 sec.
	Drapery/decor.	BFD 11-3	(F)	P/F	No flaming drop off. Char 7.0" max.
	Drapery/uph.	IX-1	(F)	P/F	Flame spread
	Uph. cover Padding	IX-10	(F)	P/F	6" max. Afterglow <80 sec.
	Chair test	CA.133	(F)	P/F	See CA.133
	Upholstery	NFPA 260	(Sm)	P/F	Class I/II (See standard)
Commonwealth of Massachusetts	Decorative covers Curtains/drapery Coverings in places of assembly	FPR 20	(F)	P/F	Afterflame <2 sec. Afterglow <40 sec.
State of New York	Drapery/Decor	Bulletin #44	(F)	P/F	Afterflame <3 sec. Afterflow <20 sec.
	All Upholstery	CCC-T 191b Method 5903	(F)	P/F	Burn length 8" max.
State of California, Bureau of Home Furnishings	Uph. fabric	116	(Cig)	P/F	Char dia. <2.0"
	PU beads	117-A	(F)	P/F	Char <6". Afterflame <5 sec. Afterglow <10 sec.
	Natural fill	117-B	(F)	P/F	Flame spread <7 sec.
	Synthetic fill	117-C	(F)	P/F	Flame spread <7 sec.
	Nonfoam fill	117-D-I	(Cig)	P/F	Char <2.0" beyond
	Cellular fill	117-D-II	(Cig)	P/F	<20% weight loss.
	Fabric—raised Fabric—flat	117-E	(F)	P/F	Burn rate <7 sec. Burn rate <3.5 sec.
	Uph. seating, high-risk occupancy	133	(F)	P/F	Ceiling: <300°F Smoke: <75% opacity 4' above floor. CO <1,000 PPM Weight loss <10% in <10 min.
	Mattress	121	(F)	P/F	Weight loss <10%. Heat <500° F. CO <1,000 PPM
California State Fire Marshal	Natural fibers Drapery/Wall hangings	Title 19 1237.1 Small scale	(F)	P/F	Char <6" Afterflame <1 sec.
	Inherent FR Synthetics	Title 19 1237.3 Intermed.*	(F)	P/F	Afterflame <2.0 sec. Flame front shall not reach top.

(F) = Flame; (Cig) = Cigarette ignition; CO = Carbon Monoxide; P/F = Pass/fail; PPM = Parts per million; F/N = Flaming and nonflaming ignition.
* Based on NFPA 701;

TABLE 6.4 FABRIC FLAMMABILITY CHARACTERISTICS

Fabric	Temperature °F			Comments
	Melting	Ignition	Burning	
Natural				
Cellulose	N/A	490–750	1,560	Does not shrink away.
Linen				
Manmade				Chars.
Cellulose		790	1,560	Continuous burning.
Rayon				Afterglow.
Protein				
Silk	N/A	1,060	1,720	Curls away from flame.
Wool				Self-extinguishes.
Fibrous				Chars.
Leather	N/A	1,060	1,700	Curls away from flame.
Synthetics				
Nylon	420/490	840/1,060	1,600	Melts.
Polyester	480/570	840/1,060	1,290	Shrinks away from flame.
Olefin	330	935/1,060	1,540	Melts and burns.
Acrylics	450/572	860/1,040	1,560	Chars. Self-extinguishes.
Cellulose acetate	500	840/1,000	1,760	Melts and/or burns.

Thermoplastics tend to resist low temperatures.

TABLE 6.5 FLAME-RETARDANT (FR) FIBERS

Fiber Type	LOI	Ignit. Temp. °C/°F	Burning Behavior	Trade Names
PVC	37	500/930	chars, shrinks at low temps.	*Rhovyl, Leavyl, Teviron*
FR Rayon	31	—	chars	*PFR*
Matrix	29–32	500–600/ 930–1,100	chars at 220/430, shrinks	*Kohjin, Cordelan*
Modacrylic	27–30	315/600	chars, shrinks at 140–180/ 280–360	*SCF, Verel, Dynel*
FR Polyester	28		melts at 250/480	*Trevira 271, Heim*
FR wool	32–34	570–600/ 1,060–1,100	chars, intumesces	—
FR cotton	28–32	290/450	chars	—

Source: Natural Fire Protection Association, Inc.

TEXTILES: USE IN AMERICAN HOMES AND COMMERCIAL INTERIORS

The use of interior decorative fabrics increased from 11.5 billion pounds in 1980 to 13.5 billion pounds in 1985. The most popular fibers are evident in the following figures.

1982 to 1983	Wool	28% increase
	Cotton	19% increase
	Manmade	22% increase
1983 to 1984	Wool	21% increase
	Cotton	7% increase
	Manmade	No increase
1984 to 1985	Wool	10% increase
	Cotton	6% increase
	Manmade	6% increase

Regardless of style trends, the contrast between demand for natural and manmade fibers remained constant during the eighties.

Attempts to regulate flammability testing of textiles have been based on a knowledge of the flammability characteristics of natural and manmade fibers. Table 6.4 lists the ignition and burning temperatures of the most popular fibers.

Blends and Special Finishes

When one or more fibers are blended together, their flame-resistant qualities can be changed. For example, when a thermoplastic such as polyester is blended with a char-forming fiber such as cotton, the untreated textile will ignite with the characteristics of the cotton. As a general rule, blended fibers tend to adopt the ignition temperature of the fiber with the lowest temperature.[6] Table 6.5 lists flame-retardant fibers.

Flame-Retardant Treatments. The terminology associated with the burning behavior of textiles can be confusing because the terms are frequently misused. For example, "flame retardant" should only be used as a noun to define a chemical used to impart flame resistance. A fabric may be described by an adjective as "flame-retardant-treated," which means the fabric received a flame retardant. The term "flame-retardant-treated" does not apply to fabrics that are *inherently* flame resistant due to intrinsic properties of the material or the fiber-forming polymer. (See additional definitions in the Glossary for this chapter.)

Flame retardants are usually classified according to their permanence and effectiveness in providing resistance to open-flame ignition. The majority of flame retardants provide the following degrees of durability:

1. Nondurable: a water-based chemical compound which is removed with water and requires frequent reapplication.

2. Semidurable: an applied chemical compound that will make the fabric flame resistant and will resist water, but will not withstand dry-cleaning solutions.

3. Durable: chemical retardants that will withstand dry cleaning and usually last the lifetime of the fabric.

Basis of flame-retardant treatments. Knowledge of how fibers respond to heat has produced several major theories of flame retardancy.

1. The *chemical flame retardant theory* is based on the fact that certain chemicals can alter the decomposition of some fabrics. Cellulose, for example, can be treated to reduce the release of flammable gases.

2. The *flame-retardant-coating* concept is frequently used. Fibers are coated with flame retardant to increase flame resistance. Because of their nitrogen content, natural protein-based fibers such as wool and silk resist ignition; synthetic fibers may be coated with nitrogen to raise their ignition temperature.

3. The *gas theory* or the Limiting Oxygen Index (LOI) is the basis for some resistant treatments. The ability of all fabrics to sustain combustion is based on their oxygen content. Fabrics assigned a high Limiting Oxygen Index have a greater probability of self-extinguishing after the ignition source is removed. For example, the LOI of cotton is 19 percent; therefore, if its oxygen were reduced below 19 percent, cotton would not continue to burn after the removal of the flame source. The LOI rates fabrics according to the established parameters shown below.

LOI	Self-Sustained Combustion
0 to 22	Will sustain combustion
22 to 28	Sustain combustion under certain conditions
29 or more	Will not sustain combustion

Some materials in the 0-to-22 LOI range are cotton, polyethylene, polystyrene, and Douglas fir. Table 6.5 list the LOI of various flame-resistant materials. Note that the oxygen content of cotton is increased by the flame-retardant treatment. Materials having a high LOI rating in combination with a high ignition temperature, such as modacrylic, are considered safe for use in upholstery.

Smolder Resistance Treatments. Manufacturers have developed several methods of producing smolder resistance (SR). Though most flame retardants offer resistance to open flame ignition, many do not provide protection from smoldering combustion, which is a major problem in upholstered furniture. The cotton industry has been conducting extensive research on means of providing smoldering resistance. Although phosphates and borates have been successfully used to retard flame and afterglow factors in cotton fibers, these chemical compounds were not effective in inhibiting smoldering.[7] The Southern Regional Research Center has developed a methyl borate system which appears to be effective on cellulosic fabrics. This process involves bringing the fabric into contact with the methyl borate vapors in an enclosed chamber. The vapors react with the moisture content of the cellulose fibers and form boric acid, which becomes deposited on and within the fibers being treated.[8] This process shows great promise because of the availability of borax as a raw material, but further research is needed to determine how this treatment will interact with soil-resistant chemicals, colorfastness, and dye changes.

Changes in Fiber Content. Another method of achieving flame resistance is to blend thermoplastics with cellulosic fibers. When fabric weights contain at least 35 percent thermoplastic content, it has been found that the smolder potential is greatly decreased. Many fabric styles and looks formerly achieved only with cellulosics are now being produced with thermoplastics: Examples include velvets, brocades, matélasse, and bulky Haitian-style fabrics.

Fabric Backcoating. In the past several years approximately 40 to 60 percent of upholstery-weight fabrics have been backcoated to increase dimensional stability, promote wear, and provide resistance to seam slippage. Increased research in the field of flame retardancy has prompted an interest in the application of flame retardants to backcoatings. The addition of sulfur to latex polymer backcoatings has proven successful in upgrading heavy-weight cellulosics, but industry anticipates some problems in the application of backcoatings to lighter-weight cottons because of the high application required per unit weight.

DEVELOPMENT OF UPHOLSTERY FLAMMABILITY TESTING METHODS

When research began on methods of testing individual furniture components, several approaches were proposed. Since data indicated that the cigarette was a major source of ignition, many felt that this should be the ignition source used. Other authorities felt that a variety of sources should be considered, such as crumpled newspaper, matches, flaming trash basket contents, radiant heaters, and other flaming furniture in the same room. Other than differing opinions on the source of the ignition, the ultimate purpose of the test was considered, and the following alternatives were discussed:

Prevention of ignition	Ignition test
Prevention of flame spread	Flame-spread test
Prevention of heat contribution to growth of fire	Heat-release test
Prevention of smoke development	Smoke-generation and obscuration test

In all these approaches several methods are employed; the testing of an individual material (component testing); mock-up testing (simulated combination of materials as used in the total furniture unit); and a full-scale test that simulates the full range of fire growth and development.

The test method developed for a standard must be practical; i.e., it must be possible to produce a piece of upholstered furniture that will meet the test criteria. It must also relate to the hazard of the product tested and be reproducible and repeatable. In addition, the test must be simple, easy to understand, and inexpensive to perform.

The National Institute of Standards and Technology (formerly National Bureau of Standards), working with CPSC, determined the following hazards and products were involved:

1. Product: upholstered furniture (fabric and filling materials)

2. Hazard: smoldering combustion (fire, smoke, and heat)

3. Primary ignition source: nonflaming (cigarettes)

Component Testing: Fabric Classification

To make the early testing procedure economically feasible, a fabric classification system was developed. Upholstery manufacturers may handle as many as 70 to 100 kind of fabrics, and find it impossible to test each type. The proposed standards classify fabrics on the basis of their resistance to ignition by a cigarette. Two tests were devised to determine fabric classification. The first series of tests determines whether a fabric will ignite and support ignition without the influence of upholstery filling material. An individual fabric sample is placed on glass fiberboard (a nonflammable material) and tested by placing lighted cigarettes on the fabric surface. Fabrics are classified by the char length produced. See the BIFMA classification system shown in Figure 6.1. Figures 6.2 and 6.3 illustrate the device developed for fabric component testing.

Mock-up Testing of Furniture

Based on information from the injury data, it was evident that upholstery ignited by cigarettes tended to smolder; therefore, researchers determined it would be necessary to test finished products to accurately predict performance in a smoldering fire.[9] Previous testing experience with mattresses showed that individual components, such as fabrics and filling, may perform well when tested separately, but often display different burning characteristics when tested as a total unit.

A mock-up must simulate the particular furniture being produced by the manufacturer doing the testing. In other words, it must be constructed with upholstery filling and a specific fabric assembled in the same configuration as the actual production furniture (see Figure 6.4). Mock-up testing allows for various critical surface areas to be evaluated, as well as the fabric and filling combinations. The number of surfaces that should be evaluated depends on the furniture design. Critical areas/surfaces may include (1) side cushion and crevice, (2) top of the armrest, (3) back cushion and crevice, (4) seat support system or deck supporting the loose seat cushions, and (5) the seat cushion surface and welt edges. If a sofa is manufactured with surface treatments such as quilting or tufting, each cushion type should be tested in a separate mock-up assembly.[10]

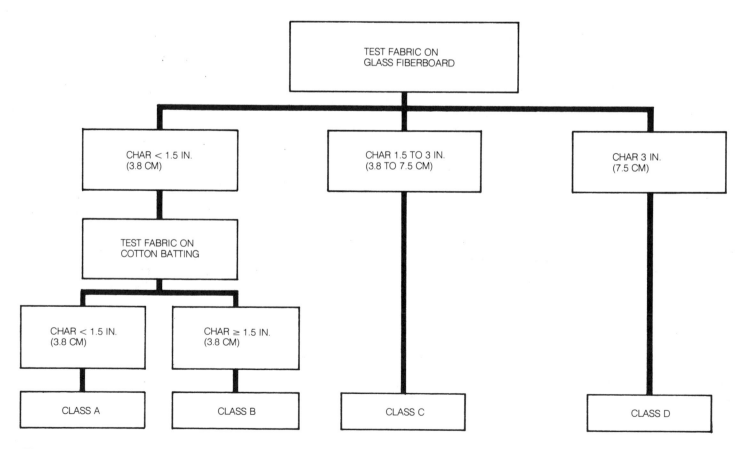

Figure 6.1 Upholstery fabric classification test. Source: Business and Institutional Furniture Manufacturers Association.

1" (2.5 CM) GLASS FIBERBOARD
8" X 8" (20.3 X 20.3 CM)

FABRIC 8" X 12"
(20.3 X 30.5 CM)

FABRIC 8" X 8"
(20.3 X 20.3 CM)

1" (2.5 CM) GLASS
FIBERBOARD
5" X 8" (12.7 X 20.3 CM)

1/8" (3.2 MM)
ADJUSTMENT PIN

8"
(20.3 CM)

3"
(7.6 CM)

3 3/4"
(9.5 CM)

8" (20.3 CM)

8 3/4" (22.2 CM)

Figure 6.2 Upholstery fabric flammability test: glass fiberboard. Source: Engineering Standards Committee of BIFMA.

Figure 6.3 Upholstery fabric flammability test: cotton batting. Source: Engineering Standards Committee of BIFMA.

FABRIC 12" X 12"
(30.5 X 30.5 CM)

MACHINE DIRECTION
FABRIC 8" X 8"
(20.3 X 20.3 CM)

PLYWOOD 8" X 8"
(20.3 X 20.3 CM)

COTTON BATTING
2" (5.1 CM)

GLASS FIBERBOARD

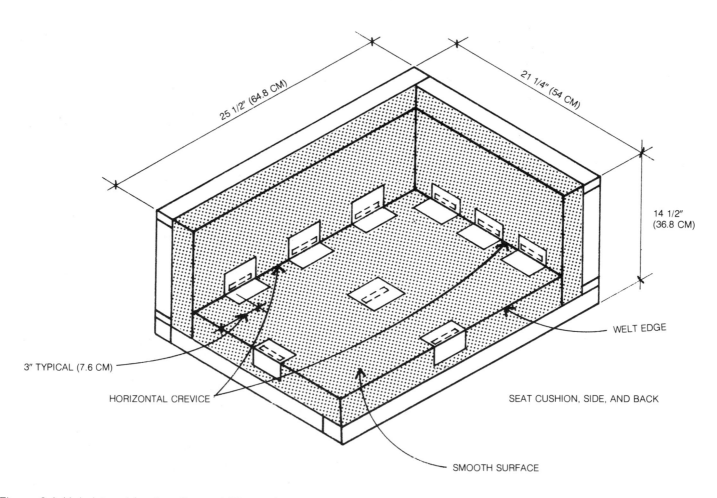

Figure 6.4 Upholstered furniture flammability mock-up test.
Source: Engineering Standards Committee of BIFMA.

Cigarette Smolder Ignition

The differences between tests that evaluate smolder resistance are shown on Table 6.6, "Comparative Table of Test Methods for Smolder Resistance of Upholstered Furniture."

All of the tests have the following factors in common:

1. All are evaluated on the furniture's ability to resist flaming ignition.

2. All are evaluated by char size.

Upholstery Filling Material

Having confirmed that filling materials used beneath the fabric were a critical factor in controlling smoldering potential, the industry became concerned with the means of creating smolder resistance in the most commonly used fillers, such as cotton batting, polyester batting, polyurethane foam, and neoprene latex foam.

Batting. Boric acid is widely known as an effective means of controlling smoldering in cotton batting, but the increased cost and shortages of boric acid in recent years have forced researchers to try to find other methods of control. The methyl borate vapor process is one suggested alternative to using powdered boric acid. Another alternative under consideration is the substitution of polyester fiberfill for cotton batting.

Barriers. Various types of liners have been developed that serve as heat barriers between the upholstery fabric and the filling material. Liners have been produced from polyester/cotton materials, aluminum foil, and carboxylated chloroprene latex. The aluminum foil liner is made from a very thin layer of hole-punched aluminum, which has one side coated with a woven fiberglass and the other side covered with spun fiberglass.[11] This liner does not create undue stiffness when placed between the fabric and the filling.

The carboxylated chloroprene latex[12] is similar to neoprene cushioning foam and is produced in various thicknesses for use as a liner, a fabric backcoating, or a complete encasement around the filling material. This interliner serves as more than a simple heat barrier by providing three types of retardant action when subjected to a heat source: (1) During the early stages of combustion this liner heats and releases water vapor, which serves to cool the fabric and filling material; (2) if the heat source continues, the liner releases chemical flame retardants; and (3) in a final stage of decomposition, the liner forms a char layer, which helps to insulate the cushioning material from the heat and limits the flow of oxygen into the cushion. DuPont, the manufacturer of this liner, does not recommend it for use in installations that may be subjected to vandalism, such as public transit systems, public assembly seating, or institutional bedding.

Welt Cords. Numerous tests indicated that welt cording used at seam edges presented a flammability hazard because cigarettes dropped on upholstery became lodged against the welt cord.[13] Traditionally, welt cords have been constructed of untreated paper twist or cotton, but in 1978 many manufacturers began specifying smolder-resistant cords.

Foams. It has been found that foam can be effectively treated with flame retardants to reduce the risk of open-flame ignition, but research has shown that some chemicals that modify the open-flame burning process may in fact compound the smol-

TABLE 6.6 COMPARATIVE TABLE OF TEST METHODS FOR SMOLDER RESISTANCE OF UPHOLSTERED FURNITURE

Test	Function of Material	Test Index	Ignite No	Ignite Yes	Performance Criteria
NFPA 260	Cover fabric 3 samples	Class I	X		Char <1.75"
		Class II		X	Char >1.75"
	Interior fabric 3 samples	Class I	X		Char <1.5"
		Class II		X	Char >1.5"
	Welt cords 3 samples	Class I	X		Char <1.5"
		Class II		X	Char >1.5"
	Filling/padding	Class I	X		Char <1.5"
		Class II		X	Char >1.5"
	Decking material 3 cigarettes	Class I	X		Char <1.5"
		Class II		X	Char >1.5"
	Barrier material	Class I	X		Char <2.0"
		Class II		X	Char >2.0"
UFAC	PU substrate	Pass	X		Char <2.0"
		Fail		X	Char >2.0"
	Barriers	Pass	X		Char <2.0"
		Fail		X	Char >2.0"
	Cover fabric	Pass	X		Char <1.75"
		Fail		X	Char >1.75"
	Filling/padding	Pass	X		Char <1.5"
		Fail		X	Char >1.5"
	Interior fabric	Pass	X		Char <1.5"
		Fail		X	Char >1.5"
	Welt cord	Pass	X		Char <1.5"
		Fail		X	Char >1.5"
	Decking	Pass	X		Char <1.5"
		Fail		X	Char >1.5"
Calif. 116	Upholstered fur. Mock-up	Pass	X		Char <2.0"
		Fail		X	Char >2.0"
Calif. 117 D-1	Filling material not foam	Pass	X		Char <2.0"
		Fail		X	Char >2.0"
BIFMA	191-53	P/F			
	Fabric over cotton batting	Class A	X		Char <1.5"
		Class B	X		Char >1.5"
	Fabric over glass fiberboard	Class C	X		Char ≤1.5–3"
		Class D	X		Char > 3.0"
	Mock-up Char in any direction	Pass	X		Char <3.0"
		Fail		X	Char >3.0"

dering process in some foams. Highly flammable polyurethane treated with retardant functions well in open-flame ignition tests, but tends to smolder. Without the retardant, the same foam displayed a resistance to smoldering. With or without a retardant, urethane produces large amounts of smoke.[14]

Federal Trade Commission Warnings

Care should be taken to use correct terminology when specifying for flammability resistance. In 1974 the Federal Trade Commission warned that certain cellular plastic products may present serious hazards in case of fire. These products were identified as polyurethane foam, polystyrene foam, polyvinyl chloride foam, ABS foam, cellulose acetate foam, epxoy foam, phenolic foam, polyethylene foam, polypropylene foam, urea foam, inomer foam, silicone foam, and foamed latex.

The commission warned the manufacturers of these products to "cease and desist from using, publishing or encouraging others to use, publish or disseminate directly or indirectly, orally or in writing with reference to any test or standard, such descriptive terminology or expressions as 'Non-Burning.' 'Self-Extinguishing,' 'Non-Combustible,' or any other term, expression, product designation or trade name of substantially the same meaning." Manufacturers were also warned that any reference made to a numerical flame-spread rating must be accompanied by the following statement:

This numerical flame spread rating is not intended to reflect hazards presented by this or any other material under actual fire conditions.[15]

In the opinion of the FTC, cellular plastics will produce a significantly higher flame spread in an actual fire condition. Therefore designers should be cautious about specifying these materials as furniture components. The manufacturer should be consulted regarding the intended use.

Private industry, as well as NBS, have conducted tests to determine the heat, smoke, and ignition characteristics of neoprene and polyurethene foams. Many of these tests have focused on rapid transit and public theater seating, using an open-flame ignition source on the trash and litter that is frequently found in public areas. In two tests conducted at the Factory Mutual Burn and Test Center, the test environment was carefully constructed to simulate the conditions found in theaters and rapid transit systems.[16] (See Figures 6.5 and 6.6.)

The testing of seats normally used in buses and rapid transit systems indicated a vast flammability difference between urethene (poly) and neoprene foam. Table 6.7 lists the seat construction, flame time, smoke peak (percentage of obstruction), and peak temperature.

Early in 1979 a fatal fire forced the closure of the underwater rapid transit system between San Francisco and Oakland, California. Sparks from an unknown source ignited one of the train cars, and victims described thick smoke and toxic fumes coming from the blazing plastic seats. One fireman died from smoke inhalation and 35 were hospitalized. This tragic accident confirms test findings that the standard polyurethane foam vinyl-covered seat ignites easily, burns rapidly at a high temperature, and produces a high level of smoke obscuration.

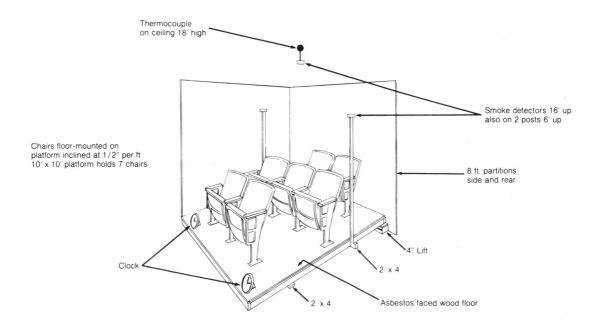

Figure 6.5 Theater seat test facility. Reproduced with permission of E. I. du Pont de Nemours & Company, Incorporated, Elastomer Chemical Department.

TABLE 6.7 INGNITION OF BUS SEATS (WITHOUT LINER)

Test	Seat Construction	Flame Time	Comments	Smoke Peak, % of Obscuration	Temperature Peak
1	Vinyl upholstery Urethene foam	13 minutes, 20 seconds	Seats totally consumed	100% at 10 minutes, 30 seconds	1000°F
5	Vinyl upholstery Neoprene	4 minutes, 30 seconds	Vinyl on back burned. Neoprene only slightly burned	67% at 8 minutes	250°F

Source: E.I. du Pont de Nemours and Company, Incorporated, Elastomer Chemicals Department.

DESIGNERS' GUIDELINES FOR THE SPECIFICATIONS OF UPHOLSTERED FURNITURE

The upholstery flammability standards discussed in this chapter have produced extensive research and information that can be applied by the designer in making specifications decisions.

Cigarette-ignition testing confirmed that flammability was influenced by the following factors:

1. Cellulosic fiber content (cotton, rayon, linen) tends to present a smoldering ignition hazard.

2. Smoldering potential increases as the fiber weight is increased.

3. The content of the filling used in the upholstery has an important effect on the smoldering potential of the entire furniture unit.

4. Thermoplastics (vinyl plastics, heavy-weight nylons, olefins, polyesters, and acrylics) rarely present a smoldering hazard.[17]

Table 6.8 illustrates how the same materials respond to different sources of ignition. The upholstery components are arranged in an approximate order of descending resistance to cigarette and small-flame ignition.

The extensive research conducted during the 1980s has provided designers with important information on which to base specifications for smolder-resistant upholstered furniture.

1. The specification of upholstered furniture for commercial and institutional use requires that designers be aware of particular installations that may present special fire hazards:
   a. Areas where smoking is permitted.
   b. Installations that may accommodate seating for extended periods of time (one hour or more):
      (1) Transportation seating: planes, buses, rapid transit systems.
      (2) Transportation terminals.
      (3) Cocktail lounges.
      (4) Restaurants.
      (5) Lounge areas in public buildings such as dormitories and hotels.
   c. Areas where the lighting level is low, such as cocktail lounges and many restaurants.
   d. Live-in accommodations that include bedding as well as seating, such as hotels, motels, dormitories, nursing or retirement homes.

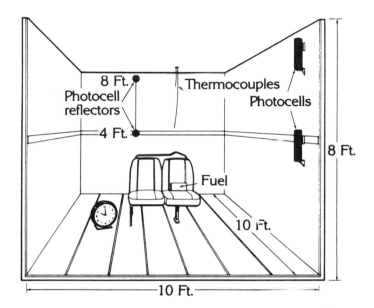

Figure 6.6 Bus seat test facility. Reproduced with permission of E. I. du Pont de Nemours & Company, Incorporated, Elastomer Chemical Department.

TABLE 6.8 UPHOLSTERED FURNITURE COMPONENTS LISTED IN APPROXIMATE ORDER OF DESCENDING IGNITION RESISTANCE

Resistance	Cover Fabric[a]	Padding	Interliners	Welt Cords	Construction Parameters
A. Cigarette ignition resistance					

HIGH ↑ ↓ LOW	Wool, PVC
	Heavy thermoplastics
	
	Cellulose/thermoplastics
	  blends (depending on
	  thermoplastic percentages)
	Light thermoplastics
	Light cellulosics
	Heavy cellulosics
		Specialty foams[b]
		Polyester batting
		
		SR PU
		SR cellulosic batting
		Untreated PU
		Mixed fiber batting
		Cellulosic batting
			Aluminized fabrics
			Neoprene sheets
			Vinyl coated glass fab.
			Novoloid felts
			Thermoplastic fabrics
			Cellulosic fabrics
				Aluminized
				PVC
				
				Thermoplastics
				SR treated cellulosics
				Cellulosics
					Flat areas
					Flat areas near
					  welt cord
					
					Tufts
					Crevices

B. Small flame ignition resistance and fire growth					

HIGH ↑ ↓ LOW	FR wool
	Wool, PVC coated
	  cellulosics[c]
	Cellulosics[c]
	
	Thermoplastics
		Specialty foams[c]
		FR cellulosic batting
		FR PU
		Cellulosic batting
		Polyester batting
		Untreated PU
		Latex foam
			Aluminized, gas
			  impermeable fabrics
			Neoprene sheets[c]
			Novoloid fabrics[c,d]
			
			Aramid fabrics[c,d]
			Vinyl coated glass
			  fabrics[c]
			FR cellulosic fabrics[c,d]
			  cellulosic fabrics[b,d]
			  thermoplastic
			  fabrics
				Effect of welt cord
				has not been
				investigated,
				believed minor
					Flat areas
					Vertical areas
					Corner areas

SR—smoulder resistant; FR—flame resistant; PU—polyurethane foam.
[a] Data on the behavior of acrylic are sparse but it seems to act more like cellulosics (smolder) than thermoplastics.
[b] Neoprene; combustion modified, high resiliency PU.
[c] Heavier materials have higher ignition resistance and generally higher heat release and lower flame spread rate.
[d] Fabrics here includes woven, knitted and rewoven structures.
Source: National Institute of Standards and Technology (formerly National Bureau of Standards)

2. Any of these commercial and institutional situations or a combination of all four factors (smoking, extended periods of seating, live-in, and low lighting levels) should require special upholstery-flammability considerations:

    a. Fabric should be specified with a high thermoplastic content or a form of flame-retardant or heat barrier.

    b. Tufting or other decorative surface treatment should be limited to vertical surfaces. Tufting used on a horizontal seat and arm provides a critical area where a cigarette may lodge and burn unnoticed in a dimly lighted area (cocktail lounge or restaurant).

    c. Welt cording should be composed of a treated material or PVC because it also provides a crevice in which a cigarette may lodge. Specify welt cording only where necessary.

    d. Seams that are used across the horizontal seat area as a decorative treatment (square or diamond shapes) should be avoided because these seams tend to pull loose under heavy wear. This exposes the inner filling material to possible ignition from a cigarette.

    e. When possible, specify seating in which the back area and horizontal seat area are separated by 1 in. (2.5 cm). This will provide one less area or crevice in which a cigarette may lodge.

    f. Upholstery filling materials should be considered in relation to the fabric selected as the outer covering. Heat barriers, such as liners, should not be specified in seating that may be subject to vandalism (slashing or cutting) because this will render the liner ineffective.

SPECIFICATION CHECKLIST FOR FLAME-RESISTANT UPHOLSTERED FURNITURE

When specifying furniture from a particular manufacturer, request the following information:

1. The fiber content of the upholstery covering.

2. When the fabric is labeled as "flame resistant," request information on the type of flame retardant used.
    _____ Chemical (semidurable or durable)
    _____ Fiber blend
    _____ Backcoating
    _____ Other

3. What material is used in the welt cording?
    _____ Paper (treated or untreated)
    _____ Cotton cord (treated or untreated)
    _____ PVC
    _____ Other

4. When fabric is to be specified COM, determine the following:
    _____ Will the fabric accept a chemical retardant treatment?
    _____ Will the treatment adversely affect the soil resistance of the fabric?
    _____ Will any shrinkage occur?
    _____ Does the flame-retardant chemical meet the required standards of the authority with jurisdiction? Currently, some states and local authorities only approve certain chemicals applied in approved laboratories.

5. What filling materials are used in the following areas?
   _____ Horizontal areas (seats, arms, and top back)
   _____ Vertical areas
   _____ Deck area
   _____ Loose cushions

6. Will any of the above materials be treated with a flame retardant?

7. If a heat barrier is to be used, request information on the type and how it will be applied.
   _____ Type
   _____ Liner
   _____ Backcoating
   _____ Encased around filling

8. What will the addition of a flame retardant to the following components cost?
   _____ Upholstery fabric
   _____ Filling material
   _____ Welt cording

GLOSSARY

Ablate: To evade flame by melting.

Abutment: The horizontal crevice formed when the vertical side or back panels meet horizontal panel or seat cushions in upholstered furniture.

Afterflame: The time a sample material continues to flame after the ignition source (burner flame) has been extinguished.

Afterglow: Glow in a material after the removal of an external ignition source or after the cessation (natural or induced) of flaming of the material. (See also *Flame, Glow,* and *Smoldering.*)

Backcoating: A finishing technique that involves coating the underside of a fabric with a layer of polymeric or other material to improve dimensional stability, wearing quality, and resistance to seam slippage and raveling. Some backcoatings may serve as a heat barrier.

Barrier (heat): A liner used immediately below a fabric to prevent flaming or smoldering heat from igniting the upholstery filling below. This liner or heat barrier may be neoprene, polyester/cotton blend, polyester fiberfill, or aluminized liner. May be applied as a backcoating.

Burnout: Test terminology meaning that a cigarette has burned its entire length.

Butt end: The unlighted end of a cigarette.

Cellulosics: Fabrics made from natural plant fibers. Examples: cotton, linen, hemp, jute, and ramie. Manufactured cellulose is made from wood pulp and cotton linters. Example: rayon.

Char: The material remaining from incomplete combustion.

Contract fabric: A fabric engineered to withstand heavy use in commercial and institutional installations. Characterized by a tight weave construction, high yarn count, and large percentage of thermoplastic-fiber content. Frequently backcoated and treated for soil and flame resistance. Performance tested for abrasion, fading, and flame resistance. Colors are usually intense primaries or darker shades and neutrals (limited amount of tints and pastels). Patterns are usually limited to stripes, plaids, and geometric shapes.

Convertable sofa: An upholstered sofa that converts into an adult-size bed. The mattress unfolds out and up from under the seat cushion.

Deck: See *Seat support system.*

FR: Flame resistant, when referring to textiles and many interior finishes. When applied to building materials, FR may indicate that the material is either fire resistant or fire rated.

Fabric classification: In flammability testing, the classification may be based on the ability of a fabric or group of fabrics to withstand ignition from either (1) a nonflaming source or (2) an open flame. Classification may also be based on specific construction, finish application, fiber content, and nominal weight per unit area. Coated fabrics with different chemical formulas and methods of application are usually considered fabric types in testing situations.

Fire: As related to textile flammability, destruction of materials by burning, in which the associated flames are not constant in size and shape and which results in a relatively high heat flux. (Compare with *Flame.*)

Fire rated: Refers to the amount of time a material will withstand a particular heat level. Interior materials are not normally fire rated.

Flame: As related to textile flammability, a hot luminous zone of gas or matter in gaseous suspension, or both, that is undergoing combustion, that is relatively constant in size and shape, and that produces a relatively *low heat* flux. (Compare with *Fire.*) Examples are a match flame, candle flame, or a Bunsen burner gas flame.

Flame resistance: The property of a material whereby flaming combustion is prevented, terminated, or inhibited following application of a flaming or nonflaming source of ignition, with or without subsequent removal of the ignition source. Note: (1) Flame resistance can be an inherent property of the basic material or product, or it may be imparted by specific treatment; (2) the degree of flame resistance exhibited by a specific material during testing may vary with different test conditions.

Flame resistant (adj.): Having flame resistance. Note: (1) "Flame resistant" is the government-mandated description for certain products that meet established governmental conformance standards or specifications when the product is tested by a specific method; (2) where no conformance standards exist, "flame resistant" is a relative term and is used to compare one material to another.

Flame retardant (adj.): Undefined. This term should not be used as an adjective except in the terms "flame-retardant-treated" and "flame-retardant treatment."

Flame-retardant treatment: A process for incorporating or adding flame retardant(s) to a material or product. Note: The term "flame-retardant treatment" does not apply to textiles that are inherently *flame resistant*.

Furniture mockup: A representation of production furniture that utilizes the same upholstery fabric and upholstery filling assembled in the order used in the finished production furniture. Fabric representing the same fabric class (type) may be substituted, if permitted in the test standard.

Glow: Visible, flameless combustion of the solid phase of a material. (See also *Afterglow* and *Smoldering*.) Note: A solid may both glow and give all combustibles that burn in the gas phase (i.e., flame), but the two are not necessarily interdependent.

Inflatable furniture: Gas- or liquid-filled furniture which may be a chair, lounger, or other type of furniture used for seating or sleeping.

Intumescent: The ability of a material to swell and char when exposed to heat.

Limiting Oxygen Index (LOI): A means of measuring the tendency of a burning fabric to continue burning after the ignition source is removed.

Loose seat cushion: A removable or interchangeable, attached or unattached, part of an upholstered furniture item upon which one sits.

Main support system: The frame or other supporting structures in the furniture item. Usually constructed of wood, plastic, or metal.

Mock-up testing: See *Furniture mock-up*.

Noncombustible textile: Fabrics made entirely from inorganic material, i.e., fibers. This may include glass, quartz, carbon, graphite, and stainless steel.

PU: Polyurethane.

PVC: Polyvinyl chloride.

Production furniture: All upholstered furniture manufactured or reupholstered for sale.

Reupholstered furniture: Furniture that has been reworked to replace any material such as upholstery fabric, cushioning, or upholstery filling and is intended for sale by the reupholsterer or person contracting with the reupholsterer. This does not include minor repairs to the surface or frame.

SR: Smolder resistant.

Seat support system: The supporting medium for loose seat cushions.

Slipcover: A removable, fitted cover (fabric or related material) used on upholstered furniture.

Smoldering: Combustion without flame that may burn for a relatively long time while generating smoke, toxic gases, and heat.

Smolder resistance: The property of materials in which nonflaming combustion is prevented, terminated, or inhibited following the application of a flaming or nonflaming source of ignition.

Standard fabric: A term designating fabrics that represent the minimum performance characteristics of their respective type (classification).

Surface location: The designated area used for placement o the ignition source (cigarette) in mock-up furniture flammability testing. Surface locations include horizontal crevices seat cushions, tops of armrests, the top of back cushions, and loose-seat support systems.

Thermoplastic fabrics: Materials that tend to become soft o moldable when heat is applied. Examples: vinyl, nylon, olefin polyester.

Tight seat: Any fixed or integrated part of the upholstered furniture item upon which one sits.

Tufted: An upholstery term referring to a surface treatment created by buttons which are laced through the upholstery fabric or upholstery filling.

Upholstery fabric: The outer layer of fabric or related material used to enclose the main support system and upholstery filling used in the furniture item. (Slipcovers are not included in this definition.)

Upholstery filling: Padding, stuffing, or filling material used in a furniture item. May either be loose or attached, enclosed by an upholstery fabric, or located between the upholstery fabric and support system.

Upholstered furniture: A unit of interior furniture with a resilient surface, in whole or part, with a fabric or related material, that is intended for use in homes, offices, or other places of assembly and is intended for seating or reclining. Upholstered furniture not normally included in flammability regulations are inflatable furniture; ottomans not intended or promoted for use in modular seating groups; any chair or stool that has an upholstered seat and upholstered back (and/or sides) that are separated by 1 in. (2.5 cm) or more. Example: secretarial posture chair.

Welt edge: The seam or border edge of a cushion, pillow, arm, or back of a furniture component.

Part 2

INTERIOR SYSTEMS/ MATERIALS

FLOOR SYSTEMS: RUGS AND CARPETS

On the federal, state, and local levels carpeting is one of the most heavily regulated interior floor systems. The carpet industry, in addition, has established many self-regulatory standards of performance which have led to a wider acceptance of carpeting, not only in offices, but in schools and hospitals. Because of the many performance guidelines' that have been established, one would assume that designers would have little difficulty in writing specifications for carpeting. On the contrary, the number of liability suits involving carpet seems to be increasing. In most instances, it is not the quality of the carpet that is questioned, but the fact that the carpet specified was not suited to a particular use. Such specifications often indicate scanty knowledge regarding the performance quality of various fibers, carpet construction, installation methods, and padding requirements. Maintenance and life cycle costing factors are frequently ignored.

The fact that designers are supplied with an overwhelming amount of carpet statistics perhaps accounts for the problem. Lacking the time to sort and study the material, designers are inclined to place their confidence in one particular fiber or carpet construction that proved successful in previous installations. This failsafe method of repeatedly specifying the same type of carpet for all projects without analyzing the particular variances in each installation can result in costly errors.

To discuss this broad subject in a clear and organized manner, this chapter is divided into three sections. The first deals with rugs, the second with woven and tufted carpet, and the third establishes specification programming for carpet.

RUGS

Rugs receive heavy scrutiny from the federal government in regard to flammability factors. The federal *Standard for the Surface Flammability of Small Carpets or Rugs* (FF 2-70) (see Chapter Five for a detailed description of flammability test FF 2-70) defines a rug, or small carpet, in the following manner:

> any type of finished product made in whole or part of fabric or related material and intended for use or which may reasonably be expected to be used as a floor covering which is exposed to traffic in homes, offices or other places of assembly or accommodation, which may or may not be fastened to the floor by mechanical means such as nails, tacks, barbs, staples, adhesives, and which have no dimension greater than 1.83 m (6 ft) and an area not greater than 2.23 m^3 (24 ft^2).

Products such as "carpet squares," which have dimensions smaller than these but are intended to be assembled upon installation into assemblies that may have dimensions greater than these, are excluded from this definition. They are, however, included in this standard. Mats and hides with natural or synthetic fibers and other similar products are also included in this definition if they are within the defined dimensions, but resilient floorcoverings such as linoleum, asphalt tile, and vinyl tile are not included.

This standard applies not only to goods exported from the United States, but also to all goods imported into this country. One-of-a-kind rugs such as antique Orientals or hides are excluded from this regulation.

Failure of the Flammability Test. Any rug that fails to pass the FF 2-70 test criteria must be labeled: "Flammable (fails the U.S. Department of Commerce Standard FF 2-70): Should not be used near sources of ignition."[1]

Use of Fire Retardant. A fire-retardant treatment, as defined in the FF 2-70 standard, is any process to which a rug has been exposed which significantly decreases the flammability of that rug and enables it to meet the acceptance criterion of the standard. When a rug has received a fire-retardant treatment, it is washed prior to undergoing the FF 2-70 test. This is done to determine if the retardant will remain effective for a reasonable length of time. A rug successfully meeting the test requirements must display "a conspicuous, legible and permanent label containing the following the following information: DO NOT WASH IN HOME MACHINE OR DRY CLEAN—AVOID RUBBING OR BRUSHING WHILE DAMP."[2] Additional instructions on the label explain acceptable cleaning methods. More detailed information on flame retardants is presented in Chapter Eleven.

Oriental Rugs

The use of Oriental rugs in commercial installations is recommended only on a *very limited basis*. Executive offices, conference rooms, special reception areas, or private clubs are examples of semiprivate spaces where the specification of an Oriental rug may be feasible. The Oriental Rug Retailers of America offers this description of an Oriental rug: "a rug made of either wool or silk knotted entirely by hand by native craftsmen in some parts of Asia—from the shores of the Persian Gulf, north to the Caspian Sea and eastward through Iran, the Soviet Union, Afghanistan, Pakistan, India, China, and Japan." To become completely knowledgeable concerning Oriental rugs would require years of intensive study; therefore designers would be well advised to consult with an expert on the subject. When consulting with a dealer the designer should be aware of the various classifications of Oriental rugs.

1. Age
   a. Antique: over 75 years old
   b. Semiantique: below 75 years and used in native land
   c. New: made in the last 10 or 15 years

2. Country of Origin
   Near and Middle Eastern countries have produced large numbers of Orientals, which are classified into four major groups:
   a. Persian
   b. Turkish
   c. Turkoman
   d. Caucasian
   Only a few of the many rug types found in these four categories would prove suitable for commercial installations because of size and construction limitations.

3. Size
   The intended use of the rug dictates the size, i.e., a prayer rug, camel cover, or floorcovering. It should be noted that Orientals rarely are made in what we would consider "stan-

dard sizes." Oriental rug measurements are usually uneven, such as 4'5" (1.4 m × 1.7 m) or 11'5" × 14'5" (3.5 m × 4.4 m).

4. Design Style
Two main design styles characterize Oriental rugs. One group is primarily based on geometric motifs, while the other major style is largely curvilinear and floral in character. Nomadic tribal movements account for the widely overlapping styles found in various provinces.

5. Construction
   a. Kelims: smooth surface with no pile and having the same appearance on both sides. Kelims are common in the Persian style.
   b. Sumak: Woven into a herringbone effect on the front surface without knotted pile. There are usually many loose yarn ends on the back.
   c. Knotted: The most popular production method, which features pile on the front surface while the reverse side is smooth. The knots most frequently used are Persian and Turkish.

Specification Guidelines. Table 7.1 provides an overview of the major style characteristics of rugs from the Near and Far East. Recommendations concerning usage of particular types are based on sizes currently available.

Installation. Installation of Oriental rugs is not a complicated matter. Orientals may be placed over rigid floor surfaces or placed over smooth-surfaced wall-to-wall carpet. A felt or foam padding that is thin and firm should be used under Oriental rugs to prevent slippage, wrinkling, and excessive wear.

Maintenance. Maintenance is an important factor in preserving the beauty of an Oriental rug. The following maintenance procedures are recommended:

1. Spot clean as needed.
2. Vacuum weekly in a crosswise direction.
3. Professionally clean only when absolutely needed. Excessive cleaning removes the natural oils from the wools.
4. Rotate and reverse at least once a year to distribute wear evenly.

Machine-Made Domestic Oriental Style Rugs. A designer may choose to specify a machine-made or contemporary hand-tufted rug that closely resembles an authentic Oriental style. Not only do they cost less, but the designer can also specify the exact size and color and can order duplicates if needed.

Dhurries

These flat, woven cotten or wool rugs have been produced in northeastern India for hundreds of years. Most of the very old dhurries were made in striped or geometric patterns. More recent rugs have also been produced with stylized flowers or small animals in pastel colors. Popular colors include red, brown, blue, yellow, and soft gray. Sizes range from 2' × 3' (0.609 m × 0.914 m), to 4' × 6' (1.21 m × 1.82 m), 6' × 9' (1.82 × 2.74 m), and room size.

Specification Guidelines. Depending on their size, dhurries may be used a floorcoverings, accent rugs, or wall hangings.

Quality assurance. Colors shall be clear in quality. Subject details should exhibit clear outlines. Colors and details should not show excessive fading. The rug must be square and lie flat.

Maintenance. When a dhurrie is to be used on a hard-surface floor, specify a lightweight rubber or felt pad. Clients should be urged to reverse the rug and vacuum it frequently.

TABLE 7.1 ORIENTAL RUGS: INDEX AND SPECIFICATION GUIDE

Place of Origin	Persian	Turkish	Caucasian	Turkoman	Chinese
General style					
Design motifs	Curvilinear floral design. Vases, birds. Medallion in center	Many prayer rugs. Mihrab altar design. Tulips. Reds, greens	Geometric figures of men, birds and animals. Dark reds	Rows of rectilinear octagons (guls). Dark reddish browns.	Typical Chinese symbols. Yang-yin. Cloud bands. Flowers, birds
Sizes: (In., mm not shown)	10' × 15' (3 × 4m) 13' × 24' (4 × 7.31 m)	3' × 5' (.91 × 1.5 m) 6' × 10' (1.82 × 3.04 m) 5' × 7' (1.5 × 2.13 m)	5' × 7' (1.5 × 2.13 m) 6' × 10' (1.82 × 3.04 m) Most are small	6' × 10' (4.87 × 3.04 m) 15' × 24' (4.57 × 7.31 m) Most are small	9' × 12' (2.74 × 3.65 m) 8' × 5' (2.43 × 1.52 m)
Usage: Floor H M L	Saruk—Bijar Herez Kerman/Tabriz X			Bokhara	Peking style
AC		X	X	X	
Wall		X	X	X	

Notes: H—Heavy traffic; M—Medium traffic; L—Light traffic; AC—Accent rug; Wall—Wall hangings; X—Majority of style types.

CARPETS

Carpets can be categorized as either woven or tufted.

Woven Carpet

Reviewing the list of mills that produce woven carpet in the United States (Table 7.2) clearly indicates that velvets and Wiltons are the most available and most frequently used woven carpets in commercial work. Although woven carpets represent perhaps only 10 percent of the commercial carpet market, they are frequently specified for large commercial installations that require an extremely dense pile and tightly woven construction. The construction of woven carpets also allows the designer to specify custom-designed, intricaté patterns.

Originally most woven carpets were made of wool, but today a large percentage are produced in nylon, acrylics, and a variety of blends that are somewhat lower in price and provide an equally beautiful long-wearing carpet.

TABLE 7.2   DOMESTIC MILLS PRODUCING WOVEN CARPETS

Manufacturer	Axminster	Wilton	Velvet
Bigelow-Sanford		X	X
Burlington		X	
Bloomsburg Carpet			X
Commercial Carpet Corp.			X
Couristan, Inc.	X	X	X
Downs Carpet Co.		X	
Firth Carpets*	X	X	X
Gulistan Carpets			X
Harding Corp.			X
Karastan Rug Mills	X		
Lees Carpets		X	X
Magee Carpet Co.			X
Mohawk Carpet Mills*	X		X
Philadelphia Carpet Co.		X	X
Sabre Carpet Co.		X	X
Seamloc-Loma-Loom Carpet Co.			X
Alexander Smith Carpet*	X		X

*Division of Mohasco, Inc.

TABLE 7.3   CONSTRUCTION FEATURES: WOVEN CARPETS

	Axminster	Wilton/Velvet
Fibers	Wool/nylon/acrylics	Nylon/wool/acrylics
Dye method	Skein dyed	Skein dyed
Backing	Jute/manmade/cotton	Jute/manmade/cotton
Texture	Cut pile	Varied
Pitch	189*	216*
Face weight (oz/sq yd)	23 to 33*	18 to 64*
Widths	27" (6.87 mm) to 12' (3.65 m)* Some 15' (4.57 m)	4'6" to 12'* (6.37 m to 3.65 m)
Flame spread ASTM E-84	75	75

*These figures represent averages. Construction may vary according to designer specification.

Axminster.   The production of Axminster carpet requires a very sophisticated loom. There are perhaps not more than three or four such looms in the United States. The weaving process entails long spools of various colored yarns, carefully preset in a desired sequence and delivered to the weaving section of the loom at a precise moment in the pattern design sequence. The process of changing pattern production is very costly and time-consuming. The Axminster carpet has a smooth cut-pile surface and can be woven in limitless colors and patterns. An identifying feature is the heavy ribbed backing that only allows the carpet to be rolled lengthwise.

Wiltons.   The Jacquard loom used to produce Wiltons was developed in England. The process makes use of preprogrammed pattern cards that are perforated and used to regulate the feeding of the colored yarn into the carpet surface. Although color ranges are sometimes limited, the surface texture of Wiltons can vary from level cut pile to multilevel loop construction.

Velvets.   Velvets are produced on a relatively uncomplicated loom. This carpet is available in many color combinations and textures. The simplicity of the loom does not allow for patterned designs, but beautiful color combinations are used to produce tweed effects that are frequently used in commercial installations.

Table 7.3 further explains construction differences between woven carpets.

Tufted Carpet

The tufting process has been responsible for the tremendous growth of the carpet industry in America. This fast and relatively inexpensive process, combined with the use of synthetic yarns that have been developed in the last 20 years, has made carpet a standard floorcovering in most commercial and institutional installations. It has been estimated that tufted goods represent over 95 percent of the carpet produced in the United States. European countries are now also beginning to produce tufted carpet.

Figure 7.1 illustrates the basic construction differences between tufted and woven carpet. Tufting is basically a sewing process. Needles, threaded with yarn, punch back and forth through a premade backing material and produce a looped or cut tufted surface. Tufting machines, averaging 12 ft (3.6 m) in width, can produce hundreds of yards per day. After the yarn is punched through the primary backing, latex is applied to the underside, securely binding the tufts in place. A secondary backing of either jute or a manufactured fiber is applied to give better dimensional stability.

Fusion-bonded Carpet Tiles

Fusion-bonding is a process of implanting yarn *without* needles into a liquid vinyl and heat-fusing it to a fiberglass-reinforced vinyl backing material. The process produces two identical carpets by slicing through a "sandwich" of fibers implanted between two backings. Fusion-bonded carpets are made in 6-ft widths; the process is mainly used for the production of carpet tiles.

Carpet tiles are primarily specified in commercial, institutional, and public-assembly installations because they offer a solution to the following problems:

1. Heavy traffic prohibiting the use of separate cushioning.

2. High maintenance and replacement costs.

3. Computer and other heavily wired facilities with access floors that may require tile.

TUFTED

WILTON

VELVET

AXMINISTER

FUSE-BONDED

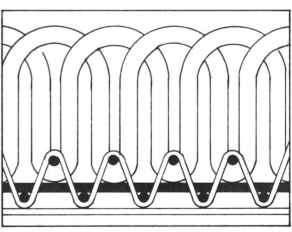

KNITTED

Figure 7.1 Types of currently manufactured carpet.

CARPET SPECIFICATION PROGRAMMING

The remainder of this chapter on carpeting will provide a systematic approach to the specification of commercial and institutional carpet.

Phase 1. Evaluation of Performance Criteria (Questionnaire)[3]

Phase 2. Selection of Generic Fibers

Phase 3. Analysis of Yarn Construction and Weight

Phase 4. Selection of Carpet Construction

Phase 5. Determinating Coloration Factors

Phase 6. Evaluating Durability Factors

Phase 7. Specification of Appearance Retention

Phase 8. Criteria for Health, Safety, and Comfort Factors

Phase 9. Traffic Classification

Phase 10. Criteria for Padding Selection

Phase 11. Estimating Yardage Requirements

Phase 12. Installation Criteria

Phase 13. Maintenance Programming

Phase 14. Life Cycle Costing

Phase 1: Evaluation of Performance Criteria

The following questionnaire will aid designers in assembling information to formulate specification criteria:

General

1. Type of traffic expected:
   Light_____ Medium_____ Heavy_____

2. Will carpet be used on stairs?
   Yes_____ No_____

3. Will there be concentrated traffic patterns?
   Yes_____ No_____

4. One-way traffic?
   Yes_____ No_____

5. Is plushness desired?
   Yes_____ No_____

   Degree:
   Minimum_____ Moderate_____ Extreme_____

6. Are employees walking on floors as part of daily work (i.e., retail, manufacturing, showroom, hospital)?
   Yes_____ No_____

7. Will carpet be exposed to direct sunlight?
   Yes_____ No_____

8. What kind of lighting will be used in the area?
   Incandescent_____ Fluorescent_____ Natural_____

9. Has a budget been established?
   Yes_____ No_____

Health, safety, and comfort factors

Flammability

1. Will carpet be used on walls?
   Yes_____ No_____

2. Will carpet be used in stair wells?
   Yes_____ No_____

3. Will carpet be used in exit ramps?
   Yes_____ No_____

4. Will carpet be used in a medical facility?
   Yes_____ No_____

5. Is Hill-Burton federal funding to be used?
   Yes_____ No_____

6. Will a fireplace or other open flame source be nearby?
   Yes_____ No_____

7. What is the occupancy load of the building?_____

8. Will sprinklers or other fire-prevention equipment be used in the area?
   Yes_____ No_____

Static

1. Is static control a necessity?
   Yes_____ No_____

2. Is static control for human comfort_____, computer tape _____, memory transmission machines_____, heart monitoring equipment_____ required?
   Yes_____ No_____

3. Will there be some method of controlling humidity above 20 percent at 70°F?
   Yes_____ No_____

4. Will electric typewriters and metallic office equipment be used?
   Yes_____ No_____

Acoustics

1. Are airborne noises important to consider, i.e., talking, machinery, typewriters, trays and dishes, cash registers, etc.?
   Yes_____ No_____

2. Will impact noise reduction be important, i.e., walking, rolling carts, dropping objects?
   Yes_____ No_____

3. Will area be used for public events or speeches?
   Yes_____ No_____

4. Will music listening be involved?
   Yes_____ No_____

5. Will a concentration of seating be prevalent?
   Yes_____ No_____

Installation

1. Type of floor: Wood_____ Concrete_____ Terrazzo_____ Other_____

2. Grade level: Below_____ Ground level_____ Above_____

3. Does the floor contain utilities? Access_____, Cellular _____, Flat cable_____, Under floor duct_____, Power poles_____, Poke-through hardware_____

4. Type of building: New_____ Old_____

5. Is carpet presently on floor? Yes_____ No_____
    If yes, a. How old is it?_____
          b. Type of carpet?_____
          c. Type of backing (rubber, jute)?_____
          d. Installation method (direct-glue, tackless)?
          _____

6. Will old carpet be removed?
    Yes_____ No_____

7. Will this disrupt operations?
    Yes_____ No_____

8. Could a direct cement (no pad) installation be used?
    Yes_____ No_____

9. Is pattern an important feature in the design criteria?
    Yes_____ No_____

10. Will mechanical access to trench header ducts be required?
    Yes_____ No_____

11. Will partitions be fastened to the floor?
    Yes_____ No_____

    Will they be movable?
    Yes_____ No_____

12. Will there be wheeled traffic?
    Yes_____ No_____
    If yes, a. Average weight of vehicle_____
          b. Number of wheels_____
          c. Size of wheels_____

13. Will wheeled traffic move directly from street to carpet (airport baggage carts, etc.)?
    Yes_____ No_____

14. In office areas, will chairs have casters?
    Yes_____ No_____

    If yes, what type?
    Regular_____ Carpet_____

Maintenance

1. Is there a daily maintenance program?
    Yes_____ No_____

    Other? Weekly_____ Biweekly_____ Bimonthly_____

2. Will maintenance program include emergency spot removal or daily stain removal?
    Yes_____ No_____

3. Will smoking be permitted in carpeted area?
    Yes_____ No_____

4. Will carpet be installed on street level?
    Yes_____ No_____

5. Will carpet be exposed to "walk-off" from adjacent street areas, gutters, i.e., mud, snow, etc.?
    Yes_____ No_____

Spillage

1. Are surroundings exposed to moisture?
    Yes_____ No_____

2. Will food service be available in or directly adjacent to carpeted areas?
    Yes_____ No_____

3. Will beverages be consumed in carpeted area?
    Yes_____ No_____

    If yes, hard drinks_____, soft drinks_____, coffee/tea _____?

4. Will carpet be used in a medical or clinical complex?
    Yes_____ No_____

5. Will the area be exposed to possible flood situations?
    Yes_____ No_____

Phase 2: Selection of Generic Fibers

Reviewing the project evaluation will reveal the major performance requirements, i.e., traffic and static levels, spillage, and so forth. For example, if spillage will be a problem in certain carpet areas, a carpet fiber should be selected that would have a low moisture-absorption rate. Table 7.4 provides information on the generic qualities of the fibers most frequently used in carpets today. After determining which fiber will best fulfill the majority of the project requirements, the designer can then proceed to evaluate the yarn construction of that particular fiber.

Phase 3: Analysis of Yarn Construction and Weight

Yarn weight and construction are determined in the following manner:

1. *Yarn count* refers to the fineness or coarseness of the finished yarn.
    a. Woolen count: This refers to the number of running yarns in 1 ounce of finished yarn. This count system includes the number of piles of a yarn. Example: 3/60 count = 60 yards of 3-ply yarn per ounce.
    b. Denier count: This system makes use of metric measurements. The yarn weight is measured in grams based on a standard 9,000-meter length of yarn. Example: a yarn denier of 1,225 means that 9,000 meters of the yarn weighs 1,225 grams.

2. *Yarn plies* refers to the number of single yarns that are plied or twisted together (see Figure 7.2). Simply ply yarns may be composed of three or more yarns. Manufactured fiber yarns such as nylon may be composed of long, unbroken lengths twisted together (continuous filament). Yarns, such as bulked continuous filament (BFC) nylon, may also be given added fullness in the finishing process.

Figure 7.2 Carpet yarn ply.

TABLE 7.4 COMPARATIVE FIBER PERFORMANCE FEATURES

	WOOL	ACRYLICS	NYLON	OLEFIN
SPOTTING & SPECIAL CLEANING				
Removes discolorations and soil thereby giving added visible acceptability wear-life	May be cleaned on location. avoid alkaline detergents	VERY GOOD. Responds to standard methods. Usually complete on most acrylics	May be wet or dry cleaned. Readily spot cleans for stains. Cleans as for wool carpeting.	May be wet or dry cleaned. Readily spot cleans for stains. Cleans as for wool carpeting
STATIC ELECTRICITY	POOR	VERY GOOD	EXCELLENT With static control.	VERY GOOD
MOISTURE REGAIN				
At the standard relative humidity 70° F + 2. Wet cleaning is more effective on rapid drying fibers than on high moisture regain fibers. Fibers with a low moisture regain are more resistant to stains and have good texture retention.	POOR 16% absorption	EXCELLENT 1.3 to 2.5% absorption	EXCELLENT 4% to 5% absorption	EXCELLENT Less than 1% absorption
TOUGHNESS, FLEXIBILITY & ABRASION RESISTANCE				
Wear resistance determines the durability of a carpet and reduces fiber loss and damage during use.	VERY GOOD	VERY GOOD TO EXCELLENT	EXCEPTIONAL	OUTSTANDING FOR HEAVY DUTY
SOIL RESISTANCE				
Smooth fiber and filament surfaces eliminate crevices or indentations which entrap difficult-to-remove soil. Staple and textured yarns are less soil resistant than filament or smooth yarns.	GOOD TO EXCELLENT	GOOD TO EXCELLENT, CLEANS EASILY	GOOD TO EXCELLENT	GOOD TO EXCELLENT

Source: Interface Flooring Systems.

	WOOL	ACRYLICS	NYLON	OLEFIN
FLAME & HEAT RESISTANCE When a fiber is subjected to heat it will either burn and scorch or therm-melt. Cigarette burns fall in the category of "glow" burn damage. Flame resistance fibers will not support combusion and are termed safe fibers.	EXCELLENT Harsh at 212°F Scorches at 400°	FAIR Flame travel depends upon texture and construction sticks at 450° to 497° depending on type. Often blended with PVC to offer better resistence.	GOOD, melt burns. Melts at 428°	GOOD, melt burn Melts at 325°
SMOKE DENSITY	FAIR TO POOR	FAIR TO POOR	GOOD	GOOD
SURFACE FIBER COVERAGE Fine smooth fibers and filaments give least coverage. Any filament may be textured to produce loft so that yarn made from the fiber has more bulk or coverage for the same weight. Specific gravity fiber weight.	GOOD	VERY GOOD, EQUAL OR BETTER THAN WOOL	GOOD, EQUAL TO WOOL, depends on fiber cross section and textured finish.	GOOD
RESILIENCE OF PILE Elasticity of fiber permits rapid recovery from short term crushing, and recovery after 24 to 48 hours from large deformation from weighty objects or long term crushing	EXCELLENT	EXCELLENT Closely packed pile gives best service	GOOD TO EXCELLENT depends upon type and construction. Dense cut pile best	FAIR TO POOR

Figure 7.3 Carpet construction terms.

Figure 7.4 Contrast in pile heights.

Phase 4: Selection of Carpet Construction

The quality of carpet construction is based on density factors, such as stitched per square inch and gauge and/or pitch; pile height; and yarn weight or average pile density (see Figure 7.3):

1. Density factors
   a. *Stitches or tufts per square inch* refers to the number of tufts within 1 sq in. (6.5 sq cm) of carpet. The more stitches per square inch the denser the carpet.
   b. *Gauge* represents the distance between rows of tufts across the width of a *tufted* carpet. If the gauge is listed as 5/32, tufts would be applied by 6.4 needles per inch.
   c. *Pitch* is the method used to determine the density factor in *woven* carpet. It refers to the distance between rows of tufts, but is counted on a 27-in. (68.6-cm) width of finished carpet. Therefore if the pitch listed is 316, it means that there are 316 rows of tufts in every 27-in. width.

      Table 7.5 defines the relationship between gauge and pitch.

2. Pile height
   This is an important consideration in the overall evaluation of carpet construction. *Pile height* refers to the distance from the top of the yarn to the backing. When a carpet has a multilevel construction, the overall height is averaged. A lower pile height requires an increase in the stitches per inch. Pile height in woven carpets is referred to as "wire size" (see Figure 7.4).

3. Yarn weight or average pile density
   Yarn weight is measured in ounces per square yard. Average pile weight refers to the amount of yarn in the *surface pile* of the carpet (face weight). This measurement does not include the primary backing, latex, or secondary backing. A carpet may have a total weight of 59.3 oz/sq yd and only have a face weight of 28 oz/sq yd. It is the face weight or actual surface yarn that is important. The average pile density is obtained with the following formula:

$$\frac{36 \times \text{face weight (oz/yd)}}{\text{Finished average pile height}} = \text{Pile density}$$

TABLE 7.5 GAUGE-PITCH RELATIONSHIP

Pitch (Woven)	Needle Ends per in. (2.54 cm)	Gauge (Tufted)
108	4.0	1/4
144	5.3	3/16*
173	6.4	5/32
180	6.6	—
189	7.0	9/64
216	8.0	1/8*
243	9.0	1/9
252	9.3	—
256	9.5	—
270	10.0	1/10*
356	12.8	5/64*

*Gauge density frequently used in commercial carpet.

a. Example: Information supplied by manufacturer on a particular carpet:

Yarn size and ply: (1225, 1245)/2
Machine gauge: 3/16 in. (144 pitch)
Stitches per inch: 5.3
Face weight: 29.5 oz/sq yd (pile weight)
Finished pile height: 12/32 (.375) in.
Total finished weight: 68.8 oz/sq yd (includes face weight + latex + backing)

Using this information a designer can calculate the average pile density:

$$\frac{36 \times 29.5 \text{ oz/sq yd}}{.375} = 2832 \text{ average pile density}$$

Many federal specifications extend the density figures to include "weight density" (WD).

b. Example

Textures	Oz/sq yd	Average Pile Density (D)	Weight Density (WD)
Level loop	35	3600	126,000
Multilevel	40	3200	128,000
Plush	40	3000	120,000

The mathematical formula for calculating WD is:

$$\frac{\text{Face weight} \times \text{face weight} \times 36}{\text{Pile height}} = WD$$

Unless a designer is dealing with a federal specification, the Carpet and Rug Institute recommends that primary emphasis be placed on the average pile density factor.

Phase 5: Determining Coloration Factors

In selecting the dye method best suited to a particular specification crtieria the designer will normally be concerned with the economy, soil-hiding factors, fade resistance, and aesthetics. Because some coloration methods may not be effective on all fibers, it would be advisable to consult with a textile expert. The following methods are commonly used to dye carpet. Dyeing is the process of coloring materials by impregnating fabric with dyestuff. Different dyeing terms include the following:

1. *Solution dyeing:* a process in which synthetic yarn is spun from a colored solution; the filament is thus impregnated with the pigment.

2. *Stock dyeing:* a process in which fibers are dyed before spinning.

3. *Yarn (or skein) dyeing:* a method in which yarn is dyed before being fabricated into carpet.

4. *Piece dyeing unfinished carpet:* a process whereby carpet is dyed "in a piece" after tufting or weaving but before other finishing processes such as latexing or foaming.

5. *Cross dyeing:* method of dyeing fabrics with dyestuffs which have different affinities for different types of yarns.

6. *Space dyeing:* process whereby different colors are "printed" along the length of yarn before it is manufactured into carpet.

7. *Continuous dyeing:* the process of dyeing carpet in a continuous production line, rather than piece dyeing separate lots. Most often done on Kusters continuous dyeing

equipment, which flows on dyestuffs, as distinguished from submerging carpet in separate dye bocks.

8. *Print dyeing:* roller printing employing embossed cylinders to deposit the design on the face of the carpet. Several rollers in tandem, each printing a different color, produce multicolored patterns. Screen printing employs flat templates, or screens, through which dyes are forced on the carpet pile. Each color in a multicolor design requires a separate screen.

9. *Random multicolor dyeing:* a dyeing process achieved with a random dye applicator, or TAK random pattern machine. The TAK machine disperses regulated amounts of dye on carpet already dyed in a single ground color, or even on totally undyed goods. Several TAK dyers in tandem can apply several different colors at preset intervals to achieve pattern effects.

10. *Controlled color spacing:* a process in which yarn is fed through the needle, while dye is applied along its length in different colors. Color sequence is carefully controlled. Carpet produced with this method of dyeing looks woven instead of tufted.

11. *Jet dyeing:* a dyeing process in which a continuous carpet roll feeds under jet-dye heads at 24 ft (7 m) per minute. A computer programs a sequence of jet dye squirts. This system is also known as the Millitron system. Carpets can be printed in patterns with little waste. See Table 7.6.

Fade Resistance. When specifying carpet that will be exposed to direct sunlight or extensive wet cleaning processes, it is important to require that tests be performed to determine colorfastness under the following conditions:

1. Intense sunlight

2. Atmospheric (ozone) fading

3. Wet cleaning

4. Abrasion (crocking) fading

Tests which determine textile colorfastness make use of the "Gray Scale" rating system. The amount of color change is

TABLE 7.6 COMPARATIVE DYE SYSTEM EVALUATIONS

	Large Dye Lots	Small Dye Lots	Color-fastness	Color Clarity	Multi-Color Capability
Fiber Dyeing					
Solution	1	NA	1	2	2
Stock	2	NA	2	1	2
Yarn Dyeing					
Skein	NA	2	2	1	2
Package	NA	2	2	1	2
Space	2	3	2	3	3
Carpet Dyeing					
Piece	NA	1	3	1	NA
Continuous (TAK)	2	NA	3	2	3
Printing	1	2	3	2	2

This table lists the major carpet-dyeing methods and the quality obtained from each.

1—Excellent   2—Very Good   3—Good   NA—Not Applicable

Source: Monsanto

determined visually and given the following rating (the term "break" refers to the amount of color change or fading):

5 No break
4 Slight break
3 Moderate break
2 Poor break
1 Severe break   See Table 7.7.

Phase 6: Evaluating Durability Factors
Durability factors involve the physical strength of the carpet structure. It is advisable that designers require test results on the following components: tuft bind, delamination, dry breaking strength, and shrinkage (see Table 7.8).

Phase 7: Specification of Appearance Retention
The specification of factors that will *maintain the appearance level* of carpeting is as important as the actual construction qualities. A carpet may have to be replaced long before it has reached the end of its "useful life" because of the appearance level, i.e., the inability of the fiber to resist crushing, stains, and abrasion (see Table 7.9).

Crush and Abrasion Resistance. Designers should be aware that many factors other than foot traffic affect the ability of a fiber to withstand crushing and abrasion. The level at which a carpet is maintained (regular cleaning), the carpet density, and surface texture are all factors to consider in relation to crush and abrasion resistance (Table 7.10 and Figure 7.5).

Modular Carpet Tiles. The specification of modular tile units allows for individual tile replacement or rotation in areas of extreme traffic or high spillage (see Figure 7.6).

TABLE 7.7   SPECIFICATION GUIDE TO COLORFASTNESS TESTING METHODS

Performance Quality	Test Method	Rating Index
Light	1. Actual sunlight condition 2. Xenon arc weatherometer (AATCC 16 E test method)	Synthetics not below 4.0 on gray scale
Atmospheric ozone fading	Sample exposed to high ozone in high humidity condition. (AATCC 129/109 test methods)	Carpet should not have a shade change rating below 3.0
Wet cleaning	Test method described in DDD-C-0095A, Section 111-E-4. Sample put through cleaning process and rated. (AATCC 138-1972)	Carpet should show no change below 4.0
Crocking (abrasion fading)	Sample submitted to 20 friction cycles with a test cloth. Amount of color transferred from sample to test cloth is evaluated. (AATCC 8)	Results should not be below 4.0

TABLE 7.8   SPECIFICATION GUIDE TO DURABILITY TESTING METHODS

Performance Quality	Test Method	Rating Index
Tuft bind	Test for tuft permanent attachment to carpet back. Tuft pulled with minimum of 100 lb (45.36 kg). (ASTM D 1335) (DDD-C-0095A)	Test measured in pounds of pull tuft withstands. High rating 6-8 lb (2.72-3.63 kg)
Delamination strength	Measures permanent attachment of secondary backing to primary backing. Force used to determine if any separation will occur. (FTMS 191-5100)	Delamination strength should be a minimum of 2.5 lb per in. (warp direction) and withstand wheel load of 1500 lb
Dry breaking strength	4" x 6" (10.1 cm x 15.2 cm) sample subjected to pull force to determine breaking point. (FTMS 191-5100)	Sample should withstand 100 lb (45.36 kg)
Shrinkage	Sample is measured and then shampooed and dried to determine shrinkage. (FTMS 191-5100) (DDD-C-0095A)	Sample should not shrink beyond 5% in any direction

TABLE 7.9   SPECIFICATION GUIDE TO APPEARANCE-RETENTION TESTING METHODS

Performance Quality	Test Method	Rating Index
Abrasion resistance	Test determines the amount of abrasion carpet will withstand. Taber abrader wheel is used. (ASTM D-1175)	Sample should withstand 6000 to 8000 cycles without showing excessive wear
Crush resistance	Test determines ability of carpet to recover thickness after subjected to heavy weight (furniture) or constant traffic. 50 lb/sq in. for period of 48 hr placed on carpet. (FTMS 501 A-3231)	Carpet should show an 85% recovery rate
Stain resistance	1. Ten major staining compounds are applied and cleaned immediately 2. Ten major staining compounds applied and left for 24 hr. (NBS-F 2)	Carpet should resist discoloration and show no noticeable staining (visual evaluation)
Pilling/fuzzing resistance	Carpet is placed in a cylinder and tumbled to determine amount of pilling and fuzzing that will occur in use. (DuPont Random Tumble Test 609)	Rated on scale between 5 to 1. Filament yarns should not rate below 4.0, staple yarns not below 3.0 (5 is highest rate = negligible)

TABLE 7.10 ABRASION RESISTANCE OF SURFACE TEXTURES

Surface Textures	Recommended Use

1. Loop construction
  a. Level loop
  b. Cut and loop
  c. Ribbed loop
	Usually high density. Good crush and abrasion resistance. Heavy traffic classification.

2. Cut pile construction
  a. Single level (plush)
  b. Shag
  c. Multilevel
  d. Saxony*
	Moderate-high to light density. Moderate to light traffic classification depending on density.

*Saxony refers to carpet constructed of plied heat-set yarns.

A. Level loop

B. Velvet plush

C. Frieze tightly twisted yarn

D. Multilevel loop

E. Saxony plush

F. Cut and loop

Figure 7.5 Carpet surface finishes.

Face yarn
Primary backing
Latex
Secondary backing

Figure 7.6 Tufted carpet construction.

Phase 8: Criteria for Health, Safety, and Comfort Factors

Flammability. The federal regulations involving carpet flammability are concerned with flame spread, surface flammability, ignition, radiant heat flux, and smoke development. The following testing methods are required in some jurisdictions. Refer to Chapter Five for detailed descriptions of each test method.

ASTM E-84	Steiner Tunnel Test
UL 992	Chamber Test
DOC FF 1-70	Methenamine Pill Test
NBS IR 75-950 NFPA 253	Flooring Radiant Panel Test
NBS 708	Smoke Density Chamber

A summary of all carpet performance testing is provided in Table 7.11.

Acoustics. Test results released by the Carpet and Rug Institute have shown that carpet provides valuable interior acoustic qualities in three major areas of concern:

1. Airborne sound absorption (NRC)

2. Impact Noise Reduction (INR) or Impact Insulation Class (IIC)

3. Surface noise reduction (NRC)

Airborne sound. Airborne sound is defined as noise that radiates directly from machines, voices, radios, and other sources. Control of airborne sound is measured in terms of NRC (Noise Reduction Coefficient).

Impact noise. This is the result of an object having impact on the structural surface of the building, such as footsteps on the floor above or furniture being dragged across the floor.

Surface noise. Such noise is usually generated within the same room or area by objects scraping against the surface of

TABLE 7.11 TESTS SUMMARY OF CARPET PERFORMANCE ATTRIBUTES

Attribute	Tests	Minimal Federal Performance Requirements*
1. Flammability		
a. Flame spread	ASTM E 84 NFPA 255 UL 992	Flame spread <75 unsprinklered Flame spread ≤200 sprinklered Flame spread 4.0 unsprinklered Flame spread 8.0 sprinklered
b. Surface flammability ignition	DCC-FF1-70 DDD-C-95(Rev) ASTM 2859-70T DOC-FF 2-70	Charred portion not to exceed within 2.54 cm (1.0") of frame edge
c. Flooring radiant panel test	ASTM E-162-67 NBS IR-75-950 NFPA 253	Health care: Class I = 0.45W/cm^2 (unsp) 0.22 w/cm(w/sp) Commercial: Class II = 0.22W/cm^2 (unsp) FF-1 70 (w/sp)
d. Smoke	NBS 708 NFPA A 258/1976	Specific op density = 450/critical 16 @ 90 sec
2. Acoustics		
a. Airborne sound	ASTM C 423 PBS C.1	SPP ≥60 in OPP/SPP ≥70 in RM NIC' + (NC 40) ≥60 in OPP NIC' + (NC ≤35) ≥70 in RM
b. Impact sound	ASTM C 423-66 PBS C.2	Mask vertical footfall with NC ≤40
3. Colorfastness		
a. To light	AATCC 16E-1982	Rating of 4.0
b. To gas	AATCC 23-1975	Rating of 4.0
c. To ozone	AATCC 109-1975	Rating of 3.0
d. Crocking (W/D)	AATCC 8-1981	Rating of 4.0
e. Shampooing	AATCC 107-1975	Rating of 4.0
4. Electrostatic	AATCC 134-1979	Static level 3KV
5. Light reflectance	ASTM E 97 IES transaction 33. P .378-1938	No more than 5% Not to exceed 15%
6. Azotic control	AATCC 112/30/90 100/103	High antibacterial level
7. Durability (physical strength)		
a. Tuft bind	ASTM D 1335 DD C 0095A	7 lb
b. Delamination	FTMS 191-5100†	Withstand wheel load of 1500 lb
c. Breaking	FTMS 191-5100	Withstand at least 100 lb
d. Shrinkage	DOC C 0095 A	Not to exceed 5% in any direction
8. Appearance		
a. Pilling/fuzz	Dupont TRL 609	≥4.0
b. Stain resistant	PBS-F.2	No noticeable stain
c. Crush resistant	FTMS 501A/3231	85% recovery
d. Abrasion	ASTM D 1175 641 (Taber)	6000–8000 cycles

* Required by majority of federal agencies.
† FTMS—Federal Test Method Standard.

a desk or the floor (Table 7.12).

The following test was conducted to determine how the various weights and types of cushions increased the NRC of carpet. The carpet used in each case was a 40-oz [1.1-kilogram (kg)] loop pile construction with a .390-in. (9.9-mm) pile height (Tables 7.13 and 7.14).

Based on test results that show bare concrete to have a .05 NRC, the acoustic advantages of carpet cushion revealed outstanding results. This test showed that a sponge rubber cushion bonded to carpeting produced an NRC of only .30, but a ⅜-in., 31-oz (9.5-mm, 9-kg) foam rubber cushion installed separately produced a .60 NRC. It was found that hair-jute cushions coated with foam on one side produced a better NRC rating when installed with the foam side facing the floor. Hair-jute 56-oz (1.6-kg) cushion foam, coated on both sides, has produced ratings as high as .70 NRC.

Because the direct glue-down installation method is so frequently used in commercial installations, tests were conducted to determine the NRC rating of carpet installed directly over bare concrete without cushion (see Table 7.14).

Tables 7.14 and 7.15 illustrate the ability of carpet installed directly over concrete to control airborne sound. Although many factors affect on NRC rating, such as ceiling, walls and other room components, the Carpet and Rug Institute was able to reach the following conclusions:

1. Variations in pile yarn fiber had little or no influence on sound-absorption factors.

2. Cut pile seemed to achieve a higher NRC than loop pile construction. Increased pile height and weight also resulted in better sound absorption.

TABLE 7.12 ACOUSTICS TESTING METHODS OF AIRBORNE AND IMPACT SOUND

Performance Quality	Test Method and Purpose
Airborne sound	Reverberation room is used to test for floor sound absorption. Carpet installed with and without pad directly over concrete floor. ASTM C-423-60T. NRC rating system used.

TABLE 7.13 NOISE REDUCTION PROVIDED BY CARPET PADDING

Pad Wt.	Pad Material	NRC
	None	.35
32 oz.	hair	.50
40 oz.	hair	.55
54 oz.	hair	.55
86 oz.	hair	.60
32 oz.	hair jute	.55
40 oz.	hair jute	.60
86 oz.	hair jute	.65
31 oz.	⅜″ foam rubber	.60
40 oz.	hair jute* foam rubber	.50
42 oz.	hair jute ⅛″* foam rubber latex	.60
44 oz.	sponge rubber	.45
86 oz.	sponge rubber ⅜″	.50

* Tested foam side down.   Source: Carpet and Rug Institute.

TABLE 7.14 NRCs OF VARIOUS CARPET INSTALLED DIRECTLY OVER CONCRETE

		Pile Wt.	Pile Ht.	Surface	NRC
Test carpet: identical construction, different manufacturers	a.	44 oz.	.25″	loop	.30
	b.	44 oz.	.25″	loop	.30
	c.	44 oz.	.25″	loop	.30
Identical constructions, different surfaces	a.	35 oz.	.175″	loop	.30
	b.	35 oz.	.175″	cut	.35
Pile weight/height relationship in Cut Pile Carpet	a.	32 oz.	.562″	cut	.50 *(lighter wt., higher pile)*
	b.	36.5 oz.	.43″	cut	.50 *(heavier wt., lower pile)*
	c.	43 oz.	.50″	cut	.55 *(heavier wt., higher pile)*
Increasing pile weight/height relationships in loop pile carpet	a.	44 oz.	.25″	loop	.30
	b.	66 oz.	.375″	loop	.40
	c.	88 oz.	.50″	loop	.40
Increasing pile weight (height constant) in loop pile carpet	a.	15 oz.	.25″	loop	.25
	b.	40 oz.	.25″	loop	.35
	c.	60 oz.	.25″	loop	.30 *(added weight actually reduced NRC, possibly because of incrased pile density)*

- Specialized acoustic materials   .50 to .95 NRC
- Bare concrete floor   .05 NRC
- Tile or linoleum over concrete   .05 NRC

Source: Carpet and Rug Institute.

3. Carpet having a loop pile construction did not produce a higher NRC rating when the weight was held constant and the height increased (see Table 7.15).

Tests (Tables 7.15 and 7.16) were made to determine the impact noise rating of carpeting installed over concrete, both with and without carpet cushion. These tests indicate that the impact noise reduction was greatly increased in carpets having a heavier pile weight. Carpet cushion produced the following results:

1. Foam rubber cushions (weight for weight) produce the best impact noise reduction.

2. A mixture of hair and jute proved superior to all-hair cushions.

3. Cushions installed separately provided better impact noise reduction than cushion bonded to the carpet back.

4. Sponge rubber cushions that were generally not effective in reducing airborne noise performed well in the impact noise reduction tests.

The Kondaras Acoustical Laboratories (KAL) in Elmhurst, New York, advise that a rating (INR) of +10 to +15 should be about 80 to 90 percent satisfactory. Impact noise reduction ratings above +20 may or may not provide increased comfort, depending on the noise factors involved.

It should be noted that the Impact Insulation Class (IIC) is also listed in Table 7.17. The Federal Housing Administration (FHA) makes use of this numerical rating scale. To transpose INR to IIC, simply add 51 to the INR plus or minus number (INR +5 +51 = IIC 56).

Static Electricity.[4] The increased use of carpet combined with the increased use of electronic equipment in the contemporary commercial and institutional environment has been responsible for an increased awareness of electrostatic problems in the following areas: (1) hospitals: patient rooms and other areas where oxygen is used, and areas where heart monitors are in use; (2) commercial and industrial facilities: computer input terminals, data processing facilities.

Operating and service personnel in computer facilities are aware of problems arising from static. Apart from personal discomfort, computer users have commonly experienced static-caused operating troubles ranging from a transient malfunction to system shutdown. A static spark can have many different consequences because of the tremendous number of variables involved. Some of the more significant factors are the nature of the spark, its location, the path followed by the current, the machine state at the instant of discharge, and the susceptibility of the computer and its peripherals.

Although static problems are well recognized, their causes are not widely understood. Floorcoverings, particularly carpeting, and relative humidity are known generally to play an important role. However, the significance of shoe-sole materials, furniture, and clothing is realized by very few, even among designers, specifiers, and managers who must make important decisions. As a consequence, situations come about in which carpeting is not used because it is believed to be the cause of the static electricity problems. A hard surface floor, although noisy, is specified because it is believed to be non-static.

Generation of static electricity. Static electricity generation in textile systems is primarily frictional or triboelectric in nature. This simply means that when two dissimilar materials which are in contact are separated, there is a tendency for a redistribution of charge between the two contacting surfaces; i.e., one surface becomes negatively charged and the other becomes positively charged. Determining which material will become negatively or positively charged is based on knowledge of the molecular structure of the two surfaces and on the

---

TABLE 7.15   MEAN VALUE NRCs OF TYPICAL COMMERCIAL CARPET INSTALLED ON CONCRETE

Pile Height	NRC (mean)
1/8" (.125)	.15
3/16" (.187)	.20
1/4" (.250)	.25
7/16" (.437)	.40

Source: Carpet and Rug Institute.

TABLE 7.16   IMPACT SOUND

Performance Quality	Test Method and Purpose
Impact sound	ISO R-140 Tapping Machine "Field and Laboratory Measurements of Airborne and Impact Sound Transmission." Machine set placed on floor above room. Microphone in room below measures sound transmitted. INR rating system used (−0 termed unsatisfactory; + number considered superior).

TABLE 7.17   TEST FINDINGS: IMPACT NOISE RATINGS (INR)—ON CONCRETE SLAB

Fabric No.	Pad Description	Impact Noise Rating (INR)	Impact Insulation Class (IIC)
	No carpet or pad	−17	34
#1	None	+2	53
#2	None	+4	55
#3	None	+6	57
#5	None	+9	60
#6	None	+14	65
#8	3/16" sponge rubber attached	+17	68
#6	40 oz. hair & jute	+22	73
#6	Urethane foam pad	+24	75
#6	44 oz. sponge rubber	+25	76
#6	31 oz. 3/8" foam rubber	+28	79
#8	80 oz. sponge	+29	80

Rating improves as pile weight increases

CARPET FABRIC KEY

CARPET	PILE WEIGHT, OZ	PILE HEIGHT, IN.
#1	20	.35-.15
#2	27	.20
#3	32	.56
#5	44	.25
#6	60	.25
#8	44 OZ WITH ATTACHED 3/16" SPONGE RUBBER PAD	

Source: Carpet and Rug Institute.

relative position each holds in the triboelectric series. Figure 7.7 illustrates a typical triboelectric series. This table offers a basic ranking of materials in a dry condition without the addition of antistatic materials. Other common variances such as humidity, frictional speed and pressure, and temperature are not a consideration of the triboelectric series., The series simply points out that certain materials are positively or negatively charged. For example, if a person wearing shoes with PVC soles walked across a polyester or acrylic carpet, very little static electricity would be produced. If the carpeting was constructed of wool or nylon (which is positively charged), the negatively charged PVC soles would produce static electricity.

The same situation occurs when a person wearing a nylon shirt is seated in a chair upholstered in an acrylic fabric. Arising from the chair will cause static electricity if the shirt has been in direct contact with the upholstery. These surface charges induce a potential on the conductive human body, which can produce a spark when brought close to ground potential (finger to elevator button or doorknob). The potential becomes even higher as the person walks away from the chair or floor area where the charging took place.

Conductors and insulators. To understand performance testing for static potential and the application of static control methods used by the carpet industry, some basic terms should be clarified:

1. *Conductors* are the substances that do not offer undue resistance to the flow of electrical current. Conductors vary in the amount of resistance they produce.

2. *Insulator,* or nonconductor, is a term applied to substances that offer a very high resistance to the flow of electricity. Because all conductors offer some resistance and all insulators allow some flow of electrical current, the terms "conductor" and "insulator" are relative.

3. *Resistance* of a particular substance to the flow of electricity is measured in units known as "ohms." Substances with a resistance over 10^{13} ohms are usually considered insulators. At 10^8 ohms a 250-volt system would produce a current of only 2.5 microamperes, which is far below the normal level of perception. This relation between ohms and volts is universally considered safe, and the NFPA minimum standard for conductive flooring is stated in this way:

$$\text{Voltage} = \text{current} \times \text{resistance}$$
$$250 = 2.5 \times 10^4 \text{ ohms}$$

Safety criteria established by the IBM Corporation ranges from 1.5×10^5 ohms to 2×10^{10} ohms. This range provides safety from electrical shock hazards involving flooring, furniture, and carts used in computer facilities.

The most commonly accepted carpet static test used in this country is the AATCC 134, 1975, which is entitled the "Electrostatic Propensity of Carpets." This test measures static voltage levels of people walking on a carpet in a prescribed manner, wearing prescribed shoes, and with a prescribed 20 percent relative humidity (RH) and 70°F temperature. These testing criteria represent some of the common conditions under which carpet will be used.

Human sensitivity to static shock varies widely, but 2,500 to 3,000 electrostatic volts [2.5 to 3 kilovolts (kv)] is considered a safe level (1,000 volts = 1 kilovolts). Figure 7.8 illustrates typical static voltages generated by walking on common floor-

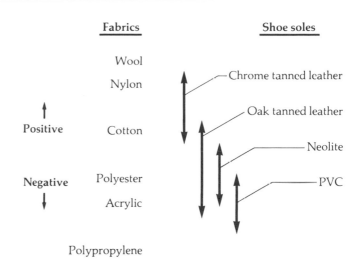

Figure 7.7 Typical tribolectric series. Reproduced with permission of W. G. Klein.

covering materials at 50 percent relative humidity and 20 percent relative humidity. (It should be noted that as the humidity lowers the static voltage increases.) These test conditions were measured by the AATCC 134 test method with Neolite shoe soles.

Computer sensitivity. Although the sensitivity varies according to the type of equipment, many problems occur with inadequately shielded devices. Trouble can be caused by a relatively distant spark from across the room or by static discharges that occur directly on the frame of the equipment. Many undesirable consequences can result from static sparks, such as erroneous keyboard entries, change of data in MOS memory equipment, and upsets to terminal displays. Testing has established the critical voltage levels which may affect computer systems (see Table 7.18).

Referring to Figure 7.7 one can see the importance of maintaining the temperature and relative humidity levels in computer facilities. Many computer facilities have completely self-contained environmental systems which do not circulate air from the exterior and have a separate power source in the event of a general power failure. But the problem of smaller, "mini" computer systems that are used in general office situations remains difficult to control.

TABLE 7.18   VOLTAGE EFFECTS ON COMPUTER SYSTEMS

Voltage	Effects on Computer Systems
Below 2500	Usually none
2500-4000	Occasionally
4000-6000	Frequently
Above 6000	Almost always
Above 8000	Some equipment will have physical damage
Above 10,000	Common physical damage

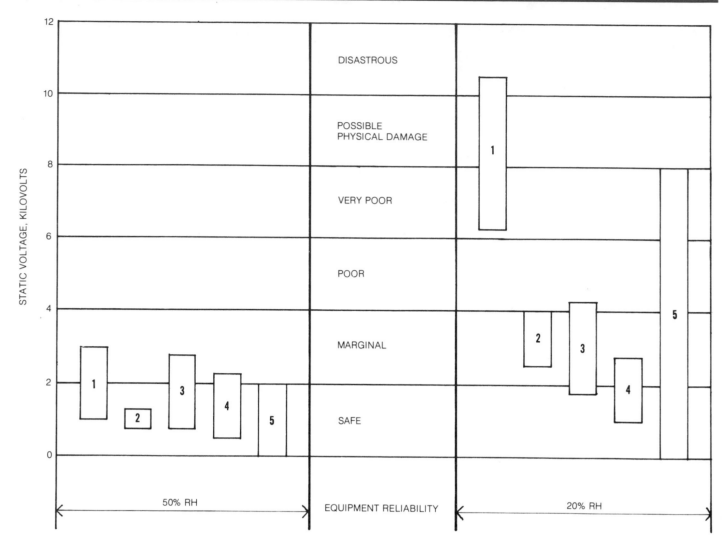

MATERIAL KEY; 1 REGULAR NYLON, 2 COMMERCIAL ANTISTATIC NYLON, 3 VINYL ASBESTOS TILE, 4 HIGH-PRESSURE LAMINATE, 5 ACRYLIC AND POLYESTER.

Figure 7.8 Typical static voltage generated by walking on common floorcovering materials.

Carpet static control methods. Many methods are available for the control of static levels in carpeting, but the designer must determine which method will best meet the needs of a particular installation. When reviewing these various methods, designers should consider the following factors:

1. Is the control method durable?

2. Will the control method function at all relative humidity levels?

3. Will the treatment attract or increase soiling?

The available methods are described below:

1. *Provide a Conductive Path from Body to Ground:* In highly critical areas, for example, where explosives are being handled, a ground for the body is often provided by ankle or wrist grounding straps, but these would not be practical in office environments. It is possible, however, to make floorcoverings electrostatically conductive. This, together with many shoe soles currently in use, can provide a reasonable means of control.

2. *Select Material with the Smallest Triboelectric Propensity:* Figure 7.6 shows that polypropylene furniture upholstery and nylon clothing are far apart on the scale and could generate high static electricity. Ideally, all contacting materials should be basically the same, as in hospital operating rooms where traditionally everyone wears cotton. This is not practical in commercial situations, but the concept should be understood in relation to carpet specification. For example, the triboelectric scale illustrates that Neolite, oak-tanned leather, and PVC soles, which constitute a large part of the shoe market, are all on the negative end of the scale. Since carpet fibers, such as polyesters, acrylic, and polypropylene, are also on the same negative end of the scale, they are thought to be inherently static-free. If nylon was a commonly used shoe sole material, nylon would be considered inherently static-free.

3. *Coat Surface with a Triboelectric Shifter:* A common form of antistatic protection for nylon carpet consists of treating the nylon carpet with chemical materials whose triboelectric position is close to that of common shoe sole materials. This approach is effective if properly done, and the effect can be enhanced by a contamination of the shoe soles with some of the chemical treatment which makes the shoe sole and the carpet even more similar electrically. These chemicals are not very durable, but are suitable for light commercial and residential use. Almost any antistatic treatment that coats the fibers will rub off on shoe soles and result in increased soiling of the carpet.

4. *Apply Electrostatically Conductive Finishes:* These finishes are generally ionic-humectant materials which attract and absorb moisture from the air and thus reduce the static electricity that is produced. This system has not proven terribly effective in very low humidity, but it tends to increase the soiling rate of carpet.

5. *Provide a Permanent Electrostatic Conductivity:* All relatively permanent antistatic systems used in carpets today employ elements in which the conductivity depends on metals or carbons. These elements may be metal fibers or polymeric fibers which have been made conductive by metal plating or carbon infusing. Metals such as copper, aluminum, and stainless steel have been successfully tufted with the fibers and woven into the backing. Carbon is infused into the core of the carpet fiber, and these carbon-infused fibers are spaced through the carpet. Each of these methods has its own particular advantage in terms of cost, manufacturing versatility, degree of static suppression, aesthetic effects, and longevity. For the exacting requirements of computer facilities and other static-sensitive areas, the carbon-infused polymeric fiber has distinct advantages. Predetermined spacing of these conductive elements throughout the carpet can be very effective. For example, a carpet with 10 conductive elements per inch, each with a resistance of 10^8 ohms/cm, will give much better static performance than a carpet with one conductive element per inch and a resistance of 1 ohm/cm. There are carpets on the market today that also employ a conductive backing in addition to the carbon-infused fibers on the surface and keep static electricity in the 2 kv range.

6. *Provide Adequate Humidity:* Static is not usually a problem in areas having a relative humidity of 50 percent or greater. Most floorcoverings generate voltage under 3 kv (regardless of shoe soles) in relative humidity of 50 percent. But it is not always possible to maintain the humidity at or near this ideal percentage. Many office areas housing personal computers frequently drop to 20 percent relative humidity. Without the installation of expensive humidification equipment, the control of humidity factors is not very reliable.

Furniture-generated static. The upholstery used on furniture does create electrostatic problems, but it appears that very few antistatic fabrics are specified because most designers are not aware of triboelectric factors. Authorities in the field of static control recommend that vinyls not be used on furnishings where static concerns are important.

Metal furniture is also not recommended. Wooden desks having metal trim and metal legs can be used safely with the addition of carbon on the base of the desk legs. Carbon coatings should also be specified for casters on chairs and carts that will be used in computer areas.

In summary, furniture-associated static in static-sensitive areas is a problem for which there is no foolproof solution, but the problem can be minimized by avoiding plastic-coated furniture, keeping chairs as far away as possible from sensitive equipment, and removing any piece of furniture known to be generating static electricity.

Antistatic specification guidelines

1. Specify carpet with a permanent method of static control. The specification should clearly state the required voltage level and the relative humidity and temperature factors.

   2,500 volts at 20% relative humidity and 70°F

   These same requirements may also be stated in terms of kilovolts:

   2.5 kv at 20% RH and 70°F

   Many federal agencies specify a higher voltage level of 3000 volts, or 3 kv, which is considered the minimum safety level.

2. Carpet tiles are frequently specified for computer areas because they offer accessibility to in-floor electrical distribution systems.

3. Evaluate all ambient conditions, such as humidity, temperature controls, and type of furnishings that will be used in computer areas.

Sanitation Aspects of Carpeted Health-Care Facilities.[5]
For more than a decade the use of carpet in health-care facilities has been a controversial subject. There have been
many studies made in hospitals to establish the precise mi-
crobiological effects of carpet on the hospital environment.
The results of these studies have been enlightening in terms
of the tendency for carpet to serve as a dust trap and at the
same time to lower bacterial counts.

Since the results of these investigations have been so universally positive in favor of carpet, the use of carpet in hospitals and nursing homes has increased significantly over the
years and currently has attained an important status in the
American contract market. By the mid-1970s, roughly 6 percent
of the total commercial carpet produced was utilized by hospitals and nursing homes.

But before carpet was adopted, some unique problems had
to be confronted: the determination of bacteria counts in carpet, estimating the probability of increased bacteria growth in
carpet, and the establishment of optimum cleaning and dis-
infecting cycles that would be required.

Bacterial testing.   Since tests were to compare the bacterial
growth between resilient flooring and carpet, it was important
to establish identical contamination potentials. The hospital
areas to be used as test sites were carefully selected to offer
varied levels of contamination. Both new and used carpet were
seeded with bacteria. After an incubation period, it was found
that the bacteria count had actually dropped in the first twenty-
four-hour period after seeding. In all investigations where the
bacteria mortality rate was categorized, it was found that carpet induced a higher mortality rate for bacteria than other surfaces such as resilient, cement, and wood flooring. Some
researchers have attributed this to the catalyst containing for-
maldehyde used in the adhesive bonding of the carpet. While
many studies found tthat vacuuming carpet reduced the number of bacteria present in the pile, it was found that the wet
mopping process used on tile floors actually fostered patho-
genic growth in dirt-clogged seams.[6]

Maintenance factors.   The fact that dust and soil are trapped
in the pile of carpet would appear to be a negative factor, but
because carpet serves as a dust trap it actually lowers the rate
of airborne dust and bacteria. But carpet does present a unique
maintenance situation in hospitals. Aside from having a porous, flexible surface, the three-dimensional construction necessitates a cleaning process for both the top and bottom
levels of the pile. It has been found that carpet can be effectively disinfected by any aldehyde-containing disinfectant
chemical compound when applied as a shampoo. The fact that
carpet must be thoroughly saturated with this liquid compound
can create problems such as drying time and carpet shrinkage,
however.

Other benefits of carpet.   There are several other reasons to
choose carpet for hospital use:

1. The danger of slipping and falling in patient rooms and in
    corridors is greatly reduced. One study, conducted over
    an extended period of time, found that there were 17 per-
    cent fewer injuries after the installation of carpet. The di-
    rect glue-down method of installation has eliminated
    problems associated with the movement of wheeled carts
    and stretchers.

2. Research on the acoustic qualities of carpet in hospitals
    found that patients showed faster rates of recovery in areas

free from noisy corridors, scraping chairs in adjoining
rooms, and impact noise from other floors.

3. Carpet creates a noninstitutional atmosphere that pro-
    motes patient relaxation and eases tension. When patients
    are given the choice of a carpeted or uncarpeted room,
    the vast majority choose a carpeted room.

Conclusions.   Summarizing the findings of the combined research indicates that the following advantages of carpet were
substantiated by the majority of researchers:

1. Lower bacterial counts

2. Increased patient safety

3. Reduction in noise levels

4. Lower maintenance costs

5. Greater thermal qualities

6. Improved appearance

In spite of the merits of carpet in hospital environments, there
is general agreement that several hospital areas *should not*
be carpeted. These areas include operating rooms. All these
areas are subject to heavy spillage, staining, and unusual soilage.

Specification recommendations.   The following critical factors should be considered when specifying carpet for health-
care facilities:

1. *Flammability*
    Specify that carpet has the following ratings:
    ASTM E-84, Steiner Tunnel Test, Class A
    Corridors: NFPA 253, Flooring Radiant Panel Test
    0.45 watts/cm^2 (unsprinklered)
    0.22 watts/cm^2 (sprinklered)
    Patient rooms: FF 1-70, Methenamine Pill Test

2. *Static Electricity*
    3 kv at 70°F and 20% RH

For more details on carpet construction, fibers, and installation
suggestions, refer to the specification guidelines in Table 7.24.

Phase 9: Traffic Classification
Before designers proceed to specify carpet padding, installation, or a maintenance program, the concept of traffic classification should be considered. The amount of wear that a
floor surface will receive is calculated in the following ways:

1. The number of people who will *enter* or *leave* a given space
    per day following the same path as they enter or leave the
    space. For example, the foyers and halls of hospitals,
    schools, hotels, terminals, and commercial buildings re-
    ceive *heavy* traffic. If this traffic is *constant*, night and day,
    and in addition, objects are wheeled across the floor sur-
    face, such as in hospitals and airports, then this would be
    considered *extra heavy* traffic.

2. The location of a space within the building also plays a
    part in the traffic classification. Aside from a foyer receiv-
    ing heavy foot traffic, the floorcovering will be exposed to
    heavy soilage from tracked in dirt, mud, or water. Heavy
    traffic classifications should therefore include soilage and
    spillage factors. For example, a restaurant may not have
    the same amount of foot traffic as a hotel lobby, but the
    spillage factors would necessitate a classification in the
    heavy category.

Traffic classification is, to a large extent, judgmental on the part of the designer. Figure 7.9, provided by Monsanto Textiles Company, illustrates traffic classifications used to determine carpet requirements.

Phase 10: Criteria for Padding Selection

There are many reasons for specifying carpet cushioning.

1. *Acoustic qualities:* The Noise Reduction Coefficiencies which were discussed in Phase 8 illustrate that carpet padding is effective in substantially reducing airborne and impact noise. An evaluation of the other acoustic components that will be used in the space will indicate the amount of NRC the carpet padding should produce.

2. *Service life requirements:* The lifespan of a carpet can be extended by the addition of a padding underlay which may prevent (a) loss of thickness due to abrasion, (b) fraying and cutting of fibers by grinding action of embedded dirt, (c) pile crushing and packing. Carpet padding also increases the effectiveness of vacuuming processes by providing air circulation throughout the entire carpet structure.

3. *Thermal qualities:* The overall thermal environment will be improved by the heat transfer and insulating qualities of carpet padding.

4. *Installation factors:* Padding can often make installation less costly because it allows carpet to be installed over less than perfect surfaces without extensive repairs. Cracks, blow holes, and trowel marks will not be evident on the surface of the carpet that has a padding underlay.

There are four major categories of carpet padding available for use by designers.[7] Each type may present slightly different qualities in regard to the amount of firmness provided, and the acoustic factors may also vary. For example, sponge rubber was found to have better acoustic qualities than a hair-jute pad when tested for impact sound transmission. Though installation requirements will vary, one of the four padding types will probably meet specification needs.

Felt. There are four types of felt padding:

1. *Hair felt,* made of 100 percent hair.

2. *Combination felt,* made of animal hair mixed with other fibers.

3. *Fiber felt,* composed of 100 percent fibers.

4. *Rubberized felt,* which refers to any of the above which has a rubberized coating on one or both sides.

Performance qualities. Felt offers a very firm, dense cushion which performs well in heavy, moderate, and light traffic classifications.

Figure 7.9 Traffic classification. Reproduced with permission of Monsanto Textiles Co.

(L-M) denotes light-medium traffic
(H) denotes heavy traffic

CARPETED AREAS	TRAFFIC RATING
EDUCATIONAL+	
1. Schools & Colleges	
a. administration	L-M
b. classroom	H
c. dormitory	H
d. corridor	H*
e. cafeteria	H
f. libraries	L-M
2. Museums & Art Galleries	
a. display room	H
b. executive	L-M
c. lobby	H
MEDICAL+	
1. Health Care	
a. executive	L-M
b. patients room	H
c. lounge	H
d. nurses station	H
e. corridor	H*
f. lobby	H
COMMERCIAL+	
1. Banks	
a. executive	L-M
b. lobby	H
c. teller windows	H
d. corridors	H*
2. Retail Establishments	
a. aisle	H*
b. check-out	H
c. sales counter	H
d. smaller boutiques, etc.	H
e. window & display area	L-M
3. Office Buildings	
a. executive	L-M
b. clerical	H
c. corridor	H*
d. cafeteria	H
4. Supermarkets	H
5. Food Services	H
RECREATIONAL+	
1. Recreation Areas	H
a. club house	H
b. locker room	H
c. swimming pool	H
d. recreational vehicles	H
e. boats	H
2. Theaters & Stadiums (Indoors)	H
3. Convention Centers	
a. auditorium	H
b. corridor	H*
c. lobby	H
TRANSPORTATION+	
1. Terminals	
a. corridor	H*
b. administration	L-M
c. ticket counter	H
MULTI-RESIDENTIAL+	
1. Apartments, Hotels & Motels	
a. lobby/public areas	H*
b. corridors	H
c. rooms	L-M
RELIGIOUS+	
1. Churches/Temples	
a. worship	L-M
b. meeting room	H
c. lobby	H

+Major Construction Categories
*If objects are to be rolled over an area of carpet, the carpet should be of maximum density to provide minimum resistance to rollers. For safety, select only level loop or low, level dense cut pile.

Manufacturing process. Felt cushion is manufactured by garnetting the material, lapping, and needle punching through a substrate to form a dense heavy cushioning. Many federal specifications require that the animal hair shall be predominantly from washed cattlle hair, which shall be the main fiber of the felt, but not to the exclusion of other fibers. The fiber content of all felt shall not be less than 90 percent cattle hair, except for the core material. Up to 9 percent adhesive is permitted for binding the interliner material. The animal hair shall be cleaned, washed, and sterilized by thorough drying and shall be free of loading materials and foreign matter. Rubberized jute and rubberized animal-hair cushions shall be of needle-punched construction. A rubber coating shall be applied to both faces of the cushion. The rubber used may be either foamed or unfoamed rubber made from natural, reclaimed, or synthetic rubber. Rubber should not readily peel off when rubbed with fingers at a normal pressure.[8]

Widths. Available in widths up to 12 ft (3.7 m).

Weights. The grade of the carpet cushion is determined by weight per square yard. Felt is available in weights from 32 oz (995 g) to 86 oz (2,674 g) per square yard.

Sponge Rubber. Two types of sponge rubber padding will be discussed:

1. *Flat sponge* with a smooth or flat surface.

2. *Waffled sponge* with a rippled or waffle surface.

Performance qualities. Sponge rubber will provide a degree of firmness depending on the formulation of the sponge and waffle pattern. Flat sponge is recommended for heavy traffic classification.

Manufacturing process. Sponge rubber cushions are manufactured by combining natural and/or synthetic rubber with other chemicals, oils, and fillers in a pulverizing operation. Blowing and curing agents are then added to the compound. Flat sponge rubber is formed and expanded into a continuous sheet. Waffled sponge rubber is allowed to form and expand on a chain belt to achieve the desired waffled configuration. Both types have a synthetic fiber facing material laminated to the top side so conventional carpet products may readily slide across the rubber surface and allow stretching of the carpet during installation.

Widths. Sponge rubber is available in widths to 12 ft (3.7 m) in various wall lengths.

Weights/Thickness. Flat sponge rubber is available in thicknesses from $\frac{1}{16}$ in. (1.6 mm) to $\frac{1}{8}$ in. (3 mm) to $\frac{5}{16}$ in. (8 mm). Weights range from 41 oz (1,275 g) to 120 oz (3,732 g) per square yard. Waffled sponge is normally specified in terms of thickness.

Urethane Foam. Three types of urethane foam padding will be considered:

1. *Prime urethane foam*

2. *Densified prime urethane foam*

3. *Bonded urethane foam*

Performance Qualities. This is a light-weight cushion which can provide a degree of firmness depending on the resiliency achieved in manufacturing. It may be used in heavy-, medium-, or light-weight traffic.

Manufacturing process. Each type of urethane foam discussed below is manufactured differently:

1. *Prime urethane foam* is manufactured by a chemical mixing process of polymeric materials. The foam is cut into continuous sheets of cushion and a facing is applied to one side.

2. *Densified prime urethane foam* is produced through a modified cell structure. Density is varied by controlling the cellular configuration. The foam is poured in large bins of devised density and slit into desired thicknesses to produce continuous rolls. A facing material is applied to one side.

3. *Bonded urethane foam* is manufactured from trimmed waste material left over from the manufacture of prime urethane. It is then granulated and bonded together through a compression and curing process into blocks, sheets, or rolls. Federal specifications will not allow fillers other than prime urethane. Designers should be aware that some quality of bonded foam may be composed of additives such as impregnated vinyl, fabric-backed foams, and foreign materials such as dirt, wood chips, and paper. No more than 1 percent debris should be permitted. The prime urethane should be ground or shredded to a particle size not exceeding $\frac{1}{2}$ in. (12.7 mm). Coloring matter may be added, but the color should not bleed or cause any unsatisfactory performance of the padding or the carpet.

Widths. Urethane foams are available in 12 ft (3.7 m) widths and various roll lengths.

Weights/thickness. Each type of urethane foam is specified by a different density and thickness:

1. Prime: Specified by density (pounds per cubic foot or ounces per square yard [kilograms per cubic meters or grams per square meters]). Available in densities from 1.3 lb (.6 kg) to 6 lb (2.8 kg) per cu ft. Thickness varies from $\frac{1}{4}$ in. (6.4 mm) to $\frac{3}{4}$ in. (19.1 mm).

2. Densified prime: Specified by density averaging from 2.7 lb (1.2 kg) to 6 lb (2.8 kg) per cu ft. Thickness varies from .250 to .750 in. (6.4 to 19.1 mm).

3. Bonded: Density from 4 lb (1.8 kg) to 10 lb (4.6 kg) per cu ft. Thickness varies from $\frac{5}{16}$ in., (7.9 mm) to $\frac{3}{4}$ in. (19.1 mm).

Performance Testing for Carpet Padding. Designers should be aware that carpet padding is subject to standard flammability testing; several federal test methods standards have been established to evaluate physical performance.

Flammability. There are two tests to measure the flammability of carpet padding:

DOC FF 1-70 or DOC FF 2-70

ASTM E-84

Physical performance tests. These tests are covered under Federal Test Method Standards. The exact test methods used can be obtained in HUD and FHA Standard UM 72, 1979.

Weight	FTMS 191, Method 5040, 5041
Thickness	FTMS 601, Method 12031 FTMS 191, Method 5030
Deflection	FTMS 601, Method 12151 ASTM D-3574 LC 001369
Compression	FTMS 601, Method 12131
Tensile strength	FTMS 601, Method 5100

Performance terminology.

1. Gauge—Thickness
   a. Definition: The overall thickness of a cushion expressed in fractions of an inch or their decimal equivalent.
   b. Typical Ranges:

Felt	$\frac{5}{16}''$ to $\frac{9}{16}''$ (2.38–1.43 cm)
Flat Sponge	$\frac{3}{16}''$ to $\frac{3}{8}''$ (0.48–0.95 cm)
Ripple Sponge	$\frac{1}{4}''$ to $\frac{9}{16}''$ (0.64–1.43 cm)
Rebonded Urethane	$\frac{3}{8}''$ to $\frac{5}{8}''$ (0.95–1.59 cm)
Prime Urethane	$\frac{3}{8}''$ to $\frac{5}{8}''$ (0.95–1.59 cm)

2. Weight
   a. Definition: The weight of a cushion expressed in ounces per square yard.
   b. Typical Ranges:

Felt	32 oz. to 56 oz. (907.2 g–1,587 g)
Flat Sponge	48 oz. to 100 oz. (1,360 g–2,835 g)
Ripple Sponge	36 oz. to 100 oz. (1,020 g–2,835 g)
Rebonded Urethane	16 oz. to 75 oz. (453 g–2,126 g)
Prime Urethane	4.5 oz. to 38 oz. (127.5 g–1,077 g)

3. Density
   a. Definition: The weight of a cubic foot of a cushion expressed in pounds.
   b. Typical Ranges:

Felt	not a common criterion
Flat Sponge Rubber	not a common criterion
Ripple Sponge Rubber	not a common criterion
Rebonded Urethane	3.75 to 10 lbs. per cubic foot (1.7 to 4.53 kg. per cubic meter)
Prime Urethane	1.1 to 5 lbs. per cubic foot (0.45 to 2.26 kg. per cubic meter)

   c. Special Note: GSA specifies polymer density rather than apparent density. To determine the actual density of a "loaded" or "filled" urethane foam, the weight of the "ash" has to be deducted from the actual weight.
      Example:
      Apparent Density: 3 lbs per cubic foot (1.36 kg. per cubic meter)
      Ash: 20 percent
      Polymer Density: 3 less 20 percent = 2.4 lbs. per cubic foot (1.09 kg. per cubic meter).

4. CLD (Compression Load Deflection)
   a. Definition: The amount of force in PSI required to achieve a 25 percent, 65 percent or 75 percent compression of a square sample of the cushion.
   b. Typical Ranges at 25% Deflection:

Felt	not an applicable measurement
Flat Sponge	1 to 9 psi
Ripple Sponge	0.125 to 1.25 psi
Rebonded Urethane	0.125 to 5.00 psi
Prime Urethane	0.10 to 5.00 psi

   c. *Special note:* Prime and rebonded urethane are commonly tested for compression load deflection at 25 percent deflection, 65 percent deflection, and 75 percent deflection. To properly test these products they should be piled up to a maximum thickness of 1 in. (2.5 cm).

5. IFD (Indentation Force Deflection)
   a. Definition: The number of pounds required to achieve a 25 percent, 65 percent, or 75 percent compression of a 4″ × 15″ (10.1 cm × 3.81 cm) piece of foam using a 50 sq. inch—8″ diameter (322.5 cm² —20.32 cm diameter) indenter.
   b. Typical Ranges at 25 percent Deflection:

Felt	not a criterion
Flat Sponge	not a criterion
Ripple Sponge	not a criterion
Rebonded Urethane	not a criterion
Prime Urethane	5 to 50 psi

6. Compression Modulus (sometimes referred to as Sag or Comfort Factor)
   a. Definition: The ratio of the ILD or CLD at 65 percent deflection to the ILD or CLD at 25 percent deflection.

   Example: CLD at 25 percent deflection = 0.42 psi
   CLD at 65 percent deflection = 0.90 psi
   $$\text{Compression Modulus} = \frac{0.90}{0.42} = 2.14$$

   b. Typical Values:

Felt	not a criterion
Flat Sponge	4.0 to 10.0
Ripple Sponge	4.0 to 8.0
Rebonded Urethane	4.0 to 10.0
Prime Urethane	1.0 to 5.0

7. Resilience
   a. Definition: The percent rebound of a steel ball dropped from a height of three feet on a specified thickness of foam.
   b. Typical Ranges:

Conventional Foam	40 to 60 percent
HR Foam	60 to 70 percent

8. Loaded Prime Foam
   a. Definition: A foam which contains inert inorganic fillers.
   b. Effects: Increases the density. Increases the load-bearing properties at high deflections, thus providing additional support. Reduces tensile strength, tear, and elongation.

9. HR (High Resilience) Foam
   a. Definition: A foam with a special additional ingredient that changes the cell structure (the shape of the cell) giving a much higher resiliency.
   b. Advantages:
      1. Higher resiliency and higher compression modulus.
      2. Higher compression modulus, which means: softer at 25 percent deflection and firmer at 65 percent deflection.

Federal specifications. The following are commonly referenced federal specifications used for carpet cushion.

1. Federal Housing Administration (FHA) UM 72 shown in Table 7.19 establishes three types:
    Type I   Felt
    Type II   Cellular Sponge Rubber
    Type III Urethane Foam
    Further classification establishes two classes for each of the three types:
    Class I   Moderate Traffic
    Class II Heavy Traffic

2. General Services Administration (GSA) makes use of the following federal specifications and purchase descriptions:
    a. Rubber cushion
        Federal Specification ZZ-C-00811b
            Class 1   Firm
            Class 2   Medium
            Class 3   Soft
    b. Ripple rubber
        GSA Purchase Description FEHS 77–96
            Class 1   48 ounce (1360 g)
            Class 2   60 ounce (1701 g)
    c. Felt
        Federal Specification DDD-C-001023
            Type I   Hair felt
            Type II   Rubber coated hair and jute
    d. Bounded urethane
        Federal Specification L-C-001369
            Class 1   Firm
            Class 2   Medium
    e. Prime urethane
        Federal Specification L-C-001676
            Class 1   Firm
            Class 2   Medium

Carpet Padding Specification Checklist. When specifying carpet padding the following physical aspects should be required:

1. Length	When definite length is specified, the delivered cushion shall not vary more than 1 percent.
2. Width	Width shall not vary more than 1 in. (2.5 cm).
3. Weight	Weight shall be as stated by manufacturer (within 5 percent). If weight exceeds 5 percent, it is not considered a defect.
4. Cuts/holes/tears	Holes and tears shall not exceed ½ in. (1.3 cm).
5. Lumps/high spots	The padding shall be free of lumps or high spots.
6. Thin or weak spots	The padding shall be free of these defects.
7. Imbedded or protruding foreign matter	This is considered a defect.
8. Seams	Seams shall be intact and smooth.
9. Edges	Padding edges shall be straight, parallel, and square.
10. Surfaces	All padding surfaces shall be flat and parallel.
11. Facing	Facing shall be as specified. Facing shall cover 98 percent of the surface area and not be tacky, nor have any loose areas. Facing shall be nonpeeling.

Padding installation. Carpet cushion should be installed in the largest possible lengths with a minimum number of sections. Cushion should be placed flush with the edges of the tackless strips and installed with the scrim side facing upward. A slight stretch is required to flatten the wrinkles from the cushion.

Subfloors. When cushion is installed over concrete subfloors, it must be securely adhered to the subfloor with a cushion cement to prevent shifting. Cushion installed over wood floors may be stapled in place.

Seams. Cushion seams should be planned to prevent them from occurring directly under carpet seams. Sponge or foam cushion seams should be taped with a 4-in. (10-cm) wide nonpaper tape.

Recommended carpet cushion weight. Designers frequently overspecify carpet cushion weights in commercial and institutional installations. Unlike residential installations that stress plushness, commercial carpet usually requires a firm cushion foundation because of the intense wear the carpet will receive. A cushion with excessive vertical displacement, such as waffled or rippled sponge rubber, places a strain on the carpet backing. This can result in accelerated wear and may necessitate restretching the carpet in areas that receive heavy traffic. Table 7.19 lists recommended cushion weights for medium and heavy traffic.

Phase II: Estimating Yardage Requirements
Estimating the initial cost of carpet often involves a preliminary cost estimate before the project drawings are finalized. This can be accomplished by totaling the square feet of floor space to be carpeted. Because carpet is sold by the square yard, the square footage must be converted to square yards. Table 7.20 presents conversions in even numbers as a quick reference. Uneven amounts may also be determined from this table. Square feet may be converted to square meters by following the process shown in Table 7.21.

Any estimate based on project drawings must be considered preliminary because of the variances that may occur during the building process. Accurate measurements of the actual spaces must be made immediately prior to installation.

Measurement Techniques. Although designers frequently rely on the carpet contractor's expertise in matters of measurements and yardage estimates, the designer should understand measurement techniques and other factors that influence the total yardage requirements, such as carpet width, nap direction, and placement of seams.

Carpet measurements require that careful notations be made regarding projections, doorways, columns, and risers that will involve carpet cutting or seaming. To prevent miscalculations

TABLE 7.19 DETACHED CARPET PADDING PERFORMANCE

Type	Class	Characteristics	Class 1[‡]	Class 2[§]	Test Method
1. Felt	a. Uncoated animal hair	Weight, oz/sq yd, min.	40.0 −5%	50.0 −5%	FTMS 191, Method 5040 or 5041
		Thickness, in., min.	0.25	0.375	FTMS 191, Method 5030
		Compression set, %, max.	15	15	FTMS 601, Method 12131
		CLD, 25% defl., psi, min.	30	30	FTMS 191, Method 5100
		Flammability*	Pass	Pass	DOC FF 1-70
			75 or less	75 or less	ASTM E-84
	b. Rubberized animal hair/jute	Weight, oz/sq yd, min.	40.0 −5%	50.0 −5%	FTMS 191, Method 5040 or 5041
		Thickness, in., min.	0.27	0.375	FTMS 191, Method 5030
		Compression set, %, max.	15	15	FTMS 601, Method 12131
		CLD, 25% defl., psi, min.	30	30	FTMS 191, Method 5100
		Flammability*	Pass	Pass	DOC FF 1-70
			75 or less	75 or less	ASTM E-84
2. Cellular sponge rubber	a. Rippled	Weight, oz/sq yd, min.	48.0 −5%	64.0 −5%	FTMS 191, Method 5040 or 5041
		Thickness, in., min.	0.30	0.40	FTMS 601, Method 12031
		CLD, 25% defl., psi, min.	0.615	0.875	FTMS 601, Method 12151
		Compression set, %, max. @ 50% deflection	15	15	FTMS 601, Method 12131
		Tensile strength, psi, min.	8	8	FTMS 191, Method 5100
		Flammability*	Pass	Pass	DOC FF 1-70
			75 or less	75 or less	ASTM E-84
	b. Flat sponge	Weight, oz/sq yd, min.	56.0 −5%	64.0 −5%	FTMS 191, Method 5040 or 5041
		Thickness, in., min.	0.250	0.250	FTMS 601, Method 12031
		CLD, 25% defl., psi, min.	0.75	1.5	FTMS 601, Method 12131
		Compression set, %, max. @ 50% deflection	10	10	FTMS 601, Method 12131
		Tensile strength, psi, min.	8	8	FTMS 191, Method 5100
		Flammability*	Pass	Pass	DOC FF 1-70
			75 or less	75 or less	ASTM E-84
	c. Latex foam	Weight, oz/sq yd, min.	38.0 −5%	46.0 −5%	FTMS 191, Method 5040 or 5041
		Thickness, in., min.	0.25	0.25	FTMS 601, Method 12031
		CLD, 25% defl., psi, min.	1.0	2.0	ASTM D 1564
		Compression set, %, max. @ 50% deflection	15	15	FTMS 601, Method 12131
		Tensile strength, psi, min.	8	8	FTMS 191, Method 5100
		Flammability*	Pass	Pass	DOC FF 1-70
			75 or less	75 or less	ASTM E-84
3. Urethane foam	a. Prime	Density, lb/ft³, min.[†]	2.2 −5%	3.0 −5%	ASTM D 3574
		Thickness, in., min.	0.375	0.375	ASTM D 3574
		CLD, 65% defl., psi, min.	0.7	1.0	ASTM D 3574
		Compression set, %, max. @ 50% deflection	15	15	ASTM D 3574
		Tensile strength, psi, min.	10	10	ASTM D 3574
		Fatigue height loss, max.	5.0	5.0	ASTM 1564
		Load deflection loss & max.	25.0	25.0	ASTM 1564
		Elongation, %, min.	100	100	ASTM D 3574
		Flammability*	Pass	Pass	DOC F 1-70
			75 or less	75 or less	ASTM E-84
	b. Densified	Density, lb/ft³, min.[†]	2.2 −5%	3.0 −5%	ASTM D 3574
		Thickness, in., min.	0.313	0.25	ASTM D 3574
		CLD, 65% defl., psi, min.	0.85	1.30	ASTM D 3574
		Compression set, %, max. @ 50% deflection	10	10	ASTM D 3574
		Tensile strength, psi, min.	17	20	ASTM D 3574
		Elongation, %, min.	100	100	ASTM D 3574
		Flammability*	Pass	Pass	DOC F 1-70
			75 or less	75 or less	ASTM E-84
	c. Grafted and modified	Density, lb/ft³, min.[†]	2.2 −5%	2.7 −5%	ASTM D 3574
		Thickness, in., min.	0.375	0.25	ASTM D 3574
		CLD, 65% defl., psi, min.	0.85	1.30	ASTM D 3574
		Compression set, %, max. @ 50% defelction	15	15	ASTM D 3574
		Tensile strength, psi, min.	12	17	ASTM D 3574
		Elongation, %, min.	100	100	ASTM D 3574
		Flammability*	Pass	Pass	DOC FF 1-70
			75 or less	75 or less	ASTM E-84
	d. Bonded	Density, lb/ft³, min.[†]	5.0 −5%	6.5 −5%	L-C-001369
		Thickness, in., min.	0.375	0.375	L-C-001369
		CLD, 65% defl., psi, min.	4.0	5.0	L-C-001369
		Compression set, %, max. @ 50% deflection	15	15	L-C-001369
		Tensile strength, psi, min.	5	7	L-C-001369
		Elongation, %, min.	45	45	L-C-001369
		Particle size, in., max.	0.50	0.50	L-C-001369
		Debris	1%	1%	See Section 4, Type III d
		Flammability*	Pass	Pass	DOC FF 1-70
			75 or less	75 or less	ASTM E-84

*Either test may be used for compliance; in DOC FF 1-70 the laundering requirement does not apply.

†Apparent density will be corrected to urethane polymer density by performing the following test: Ash content, %, as determined in ASTM D 297, subtracted from 100%, and multiplied by apparent density, shall equal the minimum values listed in the above table.

‡Medium-light traffic.

§ Heavy traffic.

Source: FHA Standard for Detached Carpet Padding UM 72.

TABLE 7.20   CARPET: SQUARE FEET TO SQUARE METERS CONVERSION TABLE

Ft²	Yd²	M²	Ft²	Yd²	M²	Ft²	Yd²	M²
50	5.6	4.5	310	34.4	27.9	570	63.3	51.3
60	6.7	5.4	320	35.6	28.8	580	64.4	52.2
70	7.8	6.3	330	36.7	29.7	590	65.6	53.1
80	8.9	7.2	340	37.8	30.6	600	66.7	54.0
90	10.0	8.1	350	38.9	31.5	700	77.8	63.0
100	11.1	9.0	360	40.0	32.4	800	88.9	72.0
110	12.2	9.9	370	41.1	33.3	900	100.0	81.0
120	13.3	10.8	380	42.2	34.2	1,000	111.1	90.0
130	14.4	11.7	390	43.3	35.1	2,000	222.2	180.0
140	15.6	12.6	400	44.4	36.0	3,000	333.3	270.0
150	16.7	13.5	410	45.6	36.9	4,000	444.4	360.0
160	17.8	14.4	420	46.7	37.8	5,000	555.5	450.0
170	18.9	15.3	430	47.8	38.7	6,000	666.7	540.0
180	20.0	16.2	440	48.9	39.6	7,000	777.8	630.0
190	21.1	17.1	450	50.0	40.5	8,000	888.9	720.0
200	22.2	18.0	460	51.1	41.4	9,000	1,000.0	810.0
210	23.3	18.9	470	52.2	42.3	10,000	1,111.1	900.0
220	24.4	19.8	480	53.3	43.2	20,000	2,222.2	1,800.0
230	25.6	20.7	490	54.4	44.1	30,000	3,333.3	2,700.0
240	26.7	21.6	500	55.6	45.0	40,000	4,444.4	3,600.0
250	27.8	22.5	510	56.7	45.9	50,000	5,555.5	4,500.0
260	28.9	23.4	520	57.8	46.8	60,000	6,666.7	5,400.0
270	30.0	24.3	530	58.9	47.7	70,000	7,777.8	6,300.0
280	31.1	25.2	540	60.0	48.6	80,000	8,888.9	7,200.0
290	32.2	26.1	550	61.1	49.5	90,000	10,000.0	8,100.0
300	33.3	27.0	560	62.2	50.4	100,000	11,111.1	9,000.0

TABLE 7.21   CARPET SQUARE FEET CONVERSION

Ft²		Yd²		M²
5000	=	555.5	=	450.0
600	=	66.7	=	54.0
50	=	5.6	=	4.5
5650	=	627.8	=	508.5

during installation, measurements are written without the foot (') or inch (") symbols, i.e., 4'6" is written 4^6. Carpet measurements should extend 3 to 4 in. within each doorway to allow seam placement directly beneath the closed door. All doorways or openings leading to adjoining areas that may or may not be carpeted should be clearly labeled (see Figure 7.10).

Even during the most careful construction procedures, areas may not be squared; i.e., parallel walls may not be parallel. To check the squareness of a room the following method may be used:

Step 1:   Starting at one corner of the room, point A, measure 3 ft along wall AB and mark this distance X (Figure 7.11a).

Step 2:   Attach a chalkline at point X and extend it 5 ft and attach it to wall AD. Mark the point at which it intercepts with a Y (Figure 7.11b).

Step 3:   If the point between A and Y measures 4 ft in length, the corner may be considered square. If this measurement is more or less than the required 4 ft, then it can be assumed that one or both adjoining walls are not right-angled. This is commonly known as the "3-4-5 geometric method"[9] (Figure 7.11c).

Irregular-Shaped Areas.   Many commercial installations involve complicated irregular shapes. To determine the required carpet yardage the area must be squared. The 3-4-5 method may be used to establish a right angle.

Starting in one angled corner, attach a chalkline from A through F to the opposite wall BC, establishing point G (Figure 7.12a). This results in a right angle between DAG.

The accuracy of the right angle DAG can be further verified by the use of a multiple such as 6-8-10 to establish point J on the AG line (Figure 7.12b).

To establish two additional right angle corners, the same 3-4-5 method is used from point G to point M along line CD. These corners may also be verified by the 6-8-10 method.

The remaining triangles of space may then be measured to determine the additional carpet needed for these irregular shapes.[10] (Figure 7.12c).

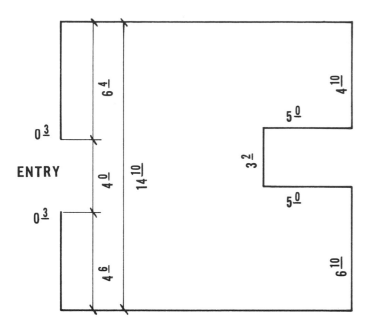

Figure 7.10 Carpet measurement diagram.

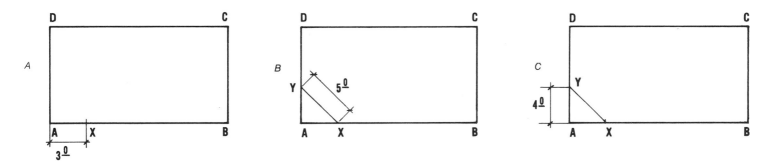

Figure 7.11 Measuring for squareness.

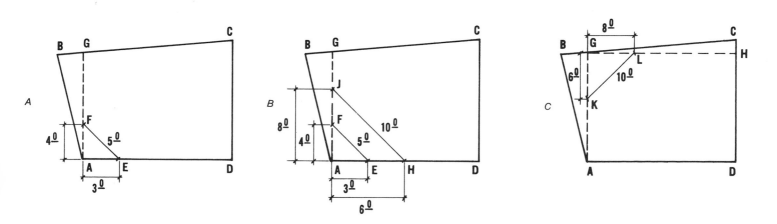

Figure 7.12 Measurement of irregular rooms.

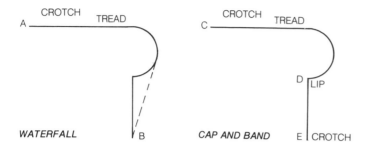

Figure 7.13 Stair installation methods.

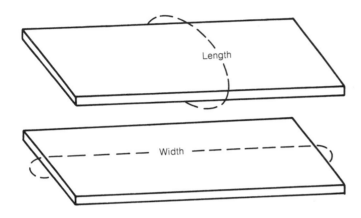

Figure 7.14 Suspended stair measurement.

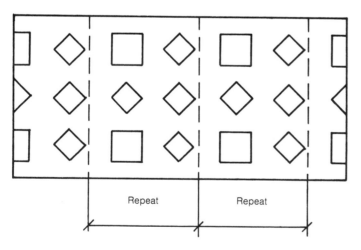

Figure 7.15 Set match pattern

Stairs. Two methods are used to carpet stairs. The cap-and-band method uses one piece of carpet for the riser area (D to E) and another carpet piece from the crotch (C) over the tread and lip (D). The second method employs one continuous piece of carpet and is known as the "waterfall" installation. The carpet is attached in the crotch area of the stairs (points A and B). (See Figure 7.13.)

Hanging or suspended stairs are usually carpeted completely around both sides. A wraparound measurement is made to determine the carpet yardage. An additional 3 in. should be allowed on the length and width measurements for seaming (Figure 7.14).

1. To calculate the length:
   a. Multiply the number of risers times the height of each riser (in inches).
   b. Multiply the number of treads times the width of each tread (in inches).
   c. Add the two results (A and B) together (in inches).
   d. Add a full inch to each step (tread and riser) and an additional 12 inches to overall length.
   e. Divide by 12 inches = total length in feet.

2. To calculate square yardage:
   a. Multiply the length (in feet) times the width of the stairs (in feet) = square feet.
   b. Divide the square feet by 9 = square yards.

Patterned Carpets. Patterned carpets are composed of designs that are repeated at regular intervals in the length and width of the carpet. When the carpet is installed it must be side matched for perfect pattern continuity. Estimating the yardage needed for patterned carpets requires an understanding of the process of matching pattern repeats. A *repeat* is the distance from one design pattern motif to the next identical design pattern motif along the length of the carpet. Repeats may vary from 3 in. to 6 ft in length, and the size of the repeat determines the additional amount of carpet that will be required to match the repeats when carpet cut lengths are installed side by side.

The three major types of patterns produced in carpet today are the set match, the drop match, and the quarter drop match:

Set match pattern. This is composed of designs that are positioned or *set* side by side on the same level to form a straight line across the width of the carpet (see Figure 7.15). In estimating for a set match pattern always measure the matching pieces to be cut at the next highest multiple of the repeat length. For example, estimate for carpet 12' in width with a set match pattern repeat measuring 3' in length to be used in an area 24' × 33' (cut A) and a second area measuring 12' × 33' (cut B). A length of 33' is the next highest multiple of 3' over the required 30' length that will allow for matching the pattern (Figure 7.16).

Drop match patterns. These patterns are such that every other repeat is dropped down one half its length to produce a diagonal match of patterns across the width of the carpet (see Figure 7.17). This design matches diagonally either up or down on half the length of the repeat or may be matched on the multiple of the repeat. This means that the carpet may be matched in the following ways:

1. Multiples of the repeat plus one-half of one repeat. Example: A drop match with a 3' repeat could be side matched every 4'6" (one repeat plus one-half repeat).

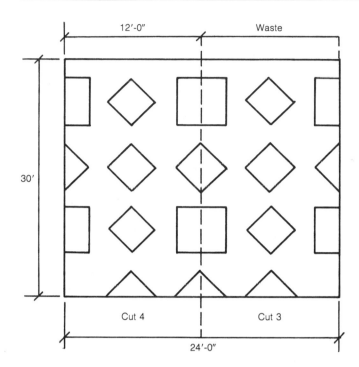

Figure 7.16 Estimating repeat length.

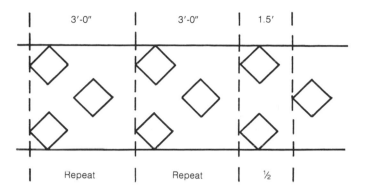

Figure 7.17 Drop match pattern.

2. Multiples of the repeat only (depending on the length of the carpet and the number of widths required). Example: A drop match with a 3' repeat could be matched every 9' (three multiples) or every 10'6" which would be three multiples plus one-half repeat.[11]

Quarter drop match patterns. These are usually found in 27-in-width woven carpets. This pattern is made up of four blocks in every length repeat. Each repeat drops one block or one-quarter block of the repeat as shown in Figure 7.18. There are three methods used to accomplish a side match.

1. Multiples of the repeat plus one-quarter of a repeat. Example: If the repeat is 3' in length, you would estimate a side match in one multiple (3') plus one-quarter of the repeat (9") for a total of 3'9".

2. Based on the same 3' repeat, a second method would employ one multiple plus one-half of a repeat (3' plus 18").

3. A third method makes use of one multiple plus three-quarters of the 3' repeat (3' plus 27").[12]

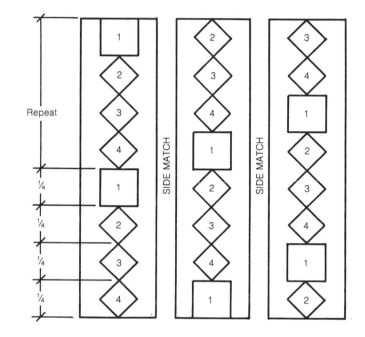

Figure 7.18 Quarter drop match.

General Guidelines for Estimating and Specifying Patterned Carpet. The following points should be considered:

1. Obtain manufacturer's recommendations for the installation of patterned carpet.

2. When designing a custom patterned carpet, consult with the manufacturer regarding the pattern and repeat size that would be feasible in the proposed installation space.

3. Obtain the services of a carpet contractor who is experienced in the installation of patterned carpet. Visit several installations that have been completed by the contractor under consideration.

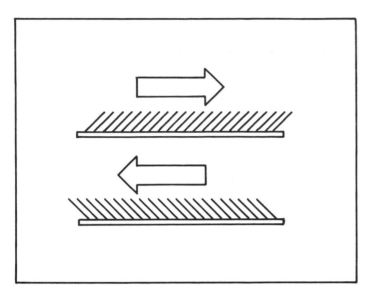

Figure 7.19 Carpet nap direction.

PLAN A

NAP DIRECTION

— — — CARPET SEAM

PLAN B

Figure 7.20 Carpet seaming diagram.

Carpet Nap. Carpet refers to the carpet pile and the direction the pile tends to slant or lie (see Figure 7.19). The direction from which the nap is viewed affects the way in which the color is perceived (i.e., nap direction tends to produce shading effects). Looking into the nap tends to make the carpet look darker. Nap should be considered on stair and floor installations as follows:

Stairs. Carpet should always be installed with the nap running downward on the stairs. Aside from providing a more pleasing visual effect, this also provides longer wear. An exception is when a patterned carpet has an upward directional design, in which case the pattern should point up the stairs.

Floors. Pile nap should run in the same direction; i.e., carpet cuts and side matches should be installed with the nap running in the same direction. If a carpet section is installed at a right angle to another section, the directional change and the seam will be obvious. When contractors submit seaming charts, the nap direction of each carpet section should be indicated.

Carpet Seam Placement. The placement of the carpet seams is perhaps one of the most important factors to consider in measuring and installation. The following guidelines should be followed in seam placement:

1. Avoid seam placement at pivot points where people using the space will change walking directions, e.g., in front of office equipment such as copy machines or near elevators.

2. Avoid seams that run across areas that receive heavy foot traffic, such as halls, meeting rooms, and reception rooms.

3. Do not plan seams that will run directly into a doorway, although seams placed horizontally across a doorway are sometimes unavoidable.

4. Request that carpet contractors submit a seaming diagram prior to installation. Seaming plan A shown in Figure 7.20 illustrates a good seam placement between cut A and B, but the nap direction of cut B will not create a good installation. The placement of the carpet seam between cut A and B in plan B runs directly into the doorway and also cuts across a direct traffic area.

5. Do not attempt to save on seaming or carpet by allowing carpet widths to be mixed. Carpet from a different roll width may also be from a different dye lot and vary in color.

Carpet padding is usually estimated in the same quantity as the carpet.

Phase 12: Installation Criteria

Each carpet manufacturer provides specific installation recommendations for his particular products; therefore, the information contained in this section is based on general recommendations provided by authorities in the industry.[13] Because carpet specification documents contain installation instructions, designers should be familiar with installation terminology regarding the two basic methods of installation in use today: (1) carpet stretched over padding (tackless strip) and (2) direct glue-down.

Tackless Strip Installation. This method of installation involves *stretching* a carpet over a large area and attaching it with tackless strips. Tackless strips are made of water-resistant 3-ply plywood strips varying in thickness from 9/32 in. (7.1 mm) to 3/8 in. (9.5 mm). Strips are usually 1½ in. (38.1 mm) wide and available in 4-ft (1.22-mm) lengths. These plywood strips contain two or three rows of angular rust-resistant pins positioned at a 60° angle and are long enough to penetrate through the carpet backing and rovide a firm attachment. In commercial installations involving over 500 sq ft (46.5 m²), three rows of pins are usually specified (see Figure 7.21).

Tackless strips are installed around the perimeter of the area to be covered by carpet and are fastened to the floor a distance from the wall that is equivalent to about two-thirds of the carpet's thickness. Methods of securing the tackless strips to the floor surface depend, to a large extent, on the type of flooring involved:

Wood Floors   Strips may be attached with nails spaced close enough to assure holding power.

Cement Floors   Three methods may be used:
1. Adhesive applied according to the manufacturer's recommendations.
2. Drill and plug method
3. Nailing

Radiant-Heated Floors   Tackless strips usually attached with adhesive. Drill and plug or nailing method should only be used if pipe locations are known.

Tackless strip estimation is usually calculated at 2½ linear feet of tackless strip for each square yard of carpet. Ten percent should be added for waste.

Seaming Methods. Although most carpets are produced in 12-ft (3.6-m) widths, almost every installation will involve seams. Three methods may be used to obtain a tight seam that will withstand the forces of stretching during the installation process as well as normal wear during the life of the carpet. It is recommended that carpet seams have a breaking strength of not less than 100 lb (46 kg).

Hand sewing. This method requires skill and special equipment, such as curved needles for certain types of seams. Sewing should be done with a suitable carpet thread, such as a number 18 linen, and the completed seams should be ironed and coated with a latex adhesive to assure a flat seam. Hand sewing may not be feasible on some types of carpet construction, i.e., heavily sized backings, tightly woven carpets, and carpets having a double jute backing. Because this is a rather slow process, it is not used as frequently now as in the past.

Hot melt tape. A taped seam produces a flat, almost invisible seam that is very strong. This method makes use of a tape that is surfaced with an adhesive that bonds the carpet seams together when activated by heat. A small heating device (an iron) capable of reaching 425°F (218°C) is used to apply the tape. The Technical Services Department of Burlington's Carpet Division makes the following recommendations regarding the use of the hot melt tape method:

1. This method should only be used on fabrics for which it is recommended.

2. Seams should always be pretacked and fitted before the tape is applied.

3. The seam should be allowed to cool for at least 10 minutes prior to stretching.

4. Tape should not be used on carpets containing yarns with a low melting point, a rubber or heavily latexed back, or

Figure 7.21 Tackless strip installation.

a double-backed carpet where the secondary backing adhesion is not known.

5. This method is not recommended for use in conjunction with foam or sponge rubber underlays because they do not "accept" the tape; i.e., the seams become noticeable. Felt padding is recommended for a flat, less visible seam.[14]

Latex tape. This method is very similar to the hot melt tape method except that latex becomes the binding agent that holds the seams together. A tape 2.5 in. (6.4 cm) wide is used at the back of the seam.

Carpet Stretching Methods. Occasionally designers are faced with a complaint about a carpet installation that may involve a stretching problem; i.e., the carpet is puckering or buckling due to expansion. A few weeks after completing a hotel lobby installation, one designer concluded that if the carpet expanded any further he would have enough extra carpet for an additional lobby. Improper stretching and changes in the temperature and humidity are all possible causes of the problem. The use of a carpet with a very heavy and dimensionally sound backing will not ensure against expansion, nor will the apparent tautness at the time of installation. Only stretching to the recommended "percent of stretch" in the warp (length) and filling (width) directions will prevent excessive expansion.

When specifying carpet, the designer should require the manufacturer to supply information on the amount of stretch in both the warp and filling directions. Because the carpet construction and the amount of lamination applied to the backing vary with each manufcturer and each carpet type, a different percent of stretch will be required for each carpet specified. For example, carpet with synthetic secondary backings usually requires extra taut stretching when installed over padding and the amount of stretch is usually 1½ to 3 in. per every 12 ft (3.8 cm to 7.6 cm per every 3.6 m).

The information and percentage conversions in Table 7.22 were compiled by the Technical Services Department of Burlington's Carpet Division. The amount of stretch prescribed for each carpet is stated as a percentage, which must be converted into inches for the purpose of installation. Here is the procedure for using the conversion table:

1. Secure the specific stretch information from the manufacturer.

2. Refer to the chart for the percentage conversion. Start with the warp stretch and then the filling directional stretch.

TABLE 7.22 CONVERSION TABLE: PERCENTAGE OF STRETCH TO INCHES PER FOOT OF CARPET

	¼%	½%	¾%	1%	1¼%	1½%	1¾%	2%	2¼%	2½%	2¾%	3%	3¼%	3½%	3¾%	4%
1 ft.	1/32	1/16	1/8	1/8	3/16	3/16	3/16	1/4	1/4	5/16	5/16	3/8	3/8	7/16	7/16	1/2
2'	1/16	1/8	3/16	1/4	5/16	3/8	7/16	1/2	9/16	5/8	11/16	3/4	3/4	13/16	7/8	15/16
3'	1/16	3/16	5/16	3/8	7/16	9/16	5/8	11/16	13/16	7/8	1.	1 1/16	1 3/16	1 1/4	1 3/8	1 7/16
4'	1/8	1/4	3/8	1/2	5/8	3/4	13/16	15/16	1 1/16	1 3/16	1 5/16	1 7/16	1 9/16	1 11/16	1 13/16	1 15/16
5'	1/8	5/16	7/16	5/8	3/4	7/8	1 1/16	1 3/16	1 3/8	1 1/2	1 5/8	1 13/16	1 15/16	2 1/8	2 1/4	2 3/8
6'	3/16	3/8	9/16	3/4	7.8	1 1/16	1 1/4	1 7/16	1 5/8	1 13/16	2.	2 3/16	2 5/16	2 1/2	2 11/16	2 7/8
7'	3/16	7/16	5/8	13/16	1 1/16	1 1/4	1 1/2	1 11/16	1 7/8	2 1/8	2 5/16	2 1/2	2 3/4	2 15/16	3 1/8	3 3/8
8'	1/4	1/2	3/4	15/16	1 3/16	1 7/16	1 11/16	1 15/16	2 3/16	2 3/8	2 5/8	2 7/8	3 1/8	3 3/8	3 5/8	3 13/16
9'	1/4	9/16	13/16	1 1/16	1 3/8	1 5/8	1 7/8	2 3/16	2 7/16	2 11/16	3.	3 1/4	3 1/2	3 3/4	4 1/16	4 5/16
10'	5/16	5/8	7/8	1 1/8	1 1/2	1 13/16	2 1/8	2 3/8	2 11/16	3.	3 5/16	3 5/8	3 7/8	4 3/16	4 1/2	4 13/16
20'	5/8	1 1/8	1 13/16	2 3/8	3.	3 5/8	4 3/16	4 13/16	5 3/8	6.	6 5/8	7 3/16	7 13/16	8 3/8	9.	9 5/8
30'	7/8	1 13/16	2 11/16	3 5/8	4 1/2	5 5/8	6 5/16	7 3/16	8 1/8	9.	9 7/8	.10 13/16	11 11/16	12 5/8	13 1/2	14 3/8
40'	1 3/16	2 3/8	3 5/8	4 13/16	6.	7 3/16	8 3/8	9 5/8	10 13/16	12.	13 3/16	14 3/8	15 5/8	16 13/16	18.	19 3/16
50'	1 1/2	3.	4 1/2	6.	7 1/2	9.	10 1/2	12.	13 1/2	15.	16 1/2	18.	19 1/2	21.	22 1/2	24.
60'	1 13/16	3 5/8	5 3/8	7 3/16	9.	10 13/16	12 5/8	14 3/8	16 1/8	18.	19 13/16	21 5/8	23 3/8	25 3/16	27.	28 13/16
70'	2 1/8	4 3/16	6 5/16	8 3/8	10 1/2	12 5/8	14 11/16	16 13/16	18 7/8	21.	23 1/8	25 3/16	27 5/16	29 3/8	31 1/2	33 5/8
80'	2 3/8	4 13/16	7 3/16	9 5/8	12.	14 3/8	16 13/16	19 3/16	21 5/8	24.	26 3/8	28 13/16	31 3/16	33 5/8	36.	38 3/8
90'	2 11/16	5 3/8	8 1/8	10 13/16	13 1/2	16 3/16	18 7/8	21 5/8	24 5/16	27.	29 11/16	32 3/8	35 1/8	37 13/16	40 1/2	43 3/16
100'	3.	6.	9.	12.	15.	18.	21.	24.	27.	30.	33.	36.	39.	42.	45.	48.

Source: Technical Services Department, Burlington Carpet Division, Burlington Industries, Inc.

Example. "A fabric [carpet] that has a recommended stretch of ¾ percent in warp and 1 percent in the filling direction is to be installed in an area that measures 23′ × 47′4″ [7 m × 14.3 m]. The carpet should be installed with the warp of the carpet running in the longer direction. Consequently the warp measures 47′ in length (disregard the 4″) and the filling 23′.

"Referring to the chart, ¾ percent stretch for 40′ [12 m] equals 3⅝″ [9.2 cm]; ¾ percent for 7′ [2.1 m] is about ⅝″ [16 mm], making the total required stretch 4¼″ [10.8 cm] in the warp direction. Referring to the chart for the filling stretch, 1 percent for 20′ [6.1 m] is 2⅜″ [6 cm] and 1 percent for 3′ [.9 m] is about ⅜″ [9.5 mm], making a total of 2¾″ [6.9 cm] of stretch to be obtained across the width. The recommended stretches should be obtained in each direction because ease of stretch in just one direction can be gained at the expense of stretch in the other direction. The percent stretch is particularly useful when working on an unfamiliar fabric [carpet]."[15]

Carpet Molding Installation. The edges of carpet ending at doorways or connecting with resilient or hard-surface flooring should be anchored with metal binders (commonly known by their trade name: "Z" bars or "Gripperedge"). These metal binders should be specified on plans prior to installation.

Direct Glue-Down Installation. Direct glue-down installation involves three basic types of carpet products: (1) carpets with high-density foam backings, (2) carpets with a jute or nonwoven synthetic secondary backing, and (3) carpets with a unitary backing, i.e., finished with latex, polyvinyl chloride, or polyurethane compounds.

This installation method evolved during the mid-1960s when carpet reached full acceptance as a floorcovering in large public areas receiving heavy traffic loads. Previously, tackless strip installations had proven unsatisfactory in some of these areas because heavy traffic had caused the carpet to shift and pull the seams apart.

Before reaching a specification decision regarding this method of installation, one should review the advantages and disadvantages of direct glue-down application.

Disadvantages. There are four disadvantages to direct glue-down installation:

1. Direct glue-down installation makes no use of a separate carpet cushion, which could tend to increase the abrasion factor on carpet fibers and thereby shorten the useful life of the carpet.

2. The lack of a separate carpet cushion reduces the acoustic advantages normally associated with the use of a carpet.

3. The luxury factor normally associated with a soft carpet tread is lost.

4. Installation necessitates the use of a tight, low-surface carpet construction; therefore the variety of textures that may be specified is limited.

Advantages. There are three advantages to this method of installation:

1. Carpet is held firmly to the floor and does not shift or flex under heavy traffic. This has been particularly successful in areas where wheeled traffic is a factor, such as airports, hospitals, and food service centers.

2. This installation method allows access to floor areas containing electrical wiring. Total floor areas are often elevated to accommodate computer requirements.

3. Delamination and mildew problems are often eliminated.

Direct glue-down specification requirements. Important factors that must be considered in the specification of direct glue-down installations include: (1) carpet construction, (2) abrasion resistance of fibers, (3) seaming, (4) preparation of subflooring, (5) adhesives, and (6) environmental conditions.

1. The carpet construction must provide a surface that will withstand the use of wheeled traffic and direct pressure against the subfloor without cushioning. The tightness of construction and the face weight of the tufted or woven carpet is very important. A low, level loop surface treatment will permit wheel traffic to move easily across the surface. The following are suggested face weights and gauges for use in direct glue-down installations (Figure 7.26).

   The backing applied to the carpet should be one that will remain stable and provide a secure bond with the adhesive. Both jute and nonwoven synthetic backings have proven successful in this type of installation.

2. Fiber selection for this type of installation is very important. The abrasion resistance of a particular fiber should be carefully considered. Fiber blends are often used in direct glue-down applications. For example, a wool will offer better performance qualities when blended with a nylon. The fibers listed in Table 7.23 have been successfully used in direct glue-down installation.

3. Secure seaming is usually provided through the specification of a tight tuft bind construction that will prevent tufts from pulling loose at the seam edges. Prior to installation, seams are sealed with a latex-type glue.

4. Preparation of the subflooring assumes a greater importance in this type of installation because of adhesive application requirements. Surface irregularities, which normally would be concealed by the use of the cushion underlay, must also be corrected prior to installation. Listed below are some typical subfloor conditions that may be encountered:

   a. Concrete floors are classed as suspended (above ground), on-grade (directly in contact with the ground), and below-grade floors (slabs poured below ground level), (See Figure 7.22.) Moisture presents a major problem in dealing with concrete floors. On-grade and below-grade floors may have moisture continually rising through the slab. As the water passes through the slab, it mixes with the salts in the concrete and forms an alkaline mixture which can completely

TABLE 7.23 SPECIFICATION GUIDELINES: DIRECT GLUE-DOWN

Fiber	Face Weight	Gauge
Nylon	28 oz/yd²	1/10
Acrylic	42 oz/yd²	1/10
Wool	42 oz/yd²	1/10
Olefin		
Spun yarn	33 oz/yd²	1/10
Continuous fiber	28 oz/yd²	1/10

Safe for resilient flooring
with proper cross ventilation

Suspended

Inadequate
ventilation

On grade

Alkaline solution rises to surface

Below
grade

Moist air   Moisture   Moisture

Figure 7.22 Ground moisture through concrete. Reproduced with permission of Armstrong Cork Co.

destroy the bonding ability of the adhesive. If the installed carpet has a synthetic backing that will not permit the moisture to evaporate, the carpet would gradually be destroyed by the alkaline solutions. Latex emulsion-type adhesives have been developed that may withstand a major portion of the alkaline solution. Various tests have been developed to determine the moisture level in concrete subfloors. One simple test method makes use of a rubber mat which is placed on the floor and left in the same position for several hours. If moisture collects under the mat, it indicates that a potential problem exists.

    b.   Painted concrete floors will necessitate the removal of oil-base paint prior to application of the adhesive.

    c.   Radiant-heated floors must be maintained at a temperature level that will permit proper drying rates for the specified adhesive.

    d.   Existing resilient floors are often encountered in building renovation or remodeling projects. In some cases only minor repairs and a thorough cleaning may be necessary. If an asphalt floor must be removed by sanding, safety precautions should be taken to prevent inhaling the asphalt dust. Adhesive compatibility with various types of tiles should be verified.

    e.   Nonporous floors, such as terrazzo, ceramic, and quarry tile, usually require that the carpet have a porous-type backing, such as jute, that will allow the evaporation of the adhesive solvents. It may be necessary to fill grout lines and remove old wax and sealers. Manufacturers of the adhesives will provide detailed information on necessary floor preparation.[16]

5. Adhesives used for direct glue-down installations are grouped into four categories. Each type has different characteristics and application procedures.
    a.   Natural latex
    b.   Synthetic latex
    c.   Solvent base rubber adhesive
    d.   Alcohol solvent resins
    Some latex-type adhesives have been specially developed for the installation of vinyl-backed carpets.

6. Environmental conditions may have an important effect on the success of the installation. The temperature of the carpet and the floor as well as the relative humidity are factors that can affect the stretch of the carpet and the drying rate of the adhesive. If the building has a central heating and cooling system, it should be in working order prior to the installation. Temperature in the areas to be carpeted should be maintained at between 70 and 80°F (21 and 27°C) for at least twenty-four hours before installation. Space heaters will not serve as a substitute because they will not heat the floors evenly. All the carpet should be spread in the area at least twenty-four hours before installation, and the temperature and humidity should be maintained at the same level for at least forty-eight hours after installation. Schools, churches, and similar institutions that shut down their heating or air conditioning for periods of time should be warned that the carpet may buckle due to the change in temperature.

Other Installation Considerations. The following factors should be included in a written carpet specification. The responsibilities of the contractor, owner, and designer must be clearly stated in contractual language (see Chapter Sixteen) that prevents misunderstanding. A complete carpet specification example is included in Chapter Sixteen. (The word "shall" is used in this section to designate a definite responsibility of the particular person involved.)

Delivery and storage. The carpet contractor is usually responsible for the shipping instructions, receiving, and placement of the carpet on the job site. Carpet should be delivered to the job site or designated workroom in the manufacturer's bundles, and the size, dye lot, and material content shall be clearly marked on each bundle. The contractor shall keep a written record of the carpet received.

In the event that special equipment is needed to lift carpet bundles to a highrise building installation, the contractor shall only be responsible for delivery to the first floor.

The owner of the building should provide locked storage for the carpet, padding, and necessary tools while the work is in progress. In addition, the owner should provide containers for scrap material. The owner should make access to the building and use of the elevators available for carpet installation during the normal working hours to prevent overtime charges. The owner should contact the general contractor regarding doors that should be trimmed and rehung prior to the carpet installation.

Excess carpet. All carpet remnants 1 sq yd (.9 sq m) or larger should be left at the job site or packaged in appropriate wrapping, labeled, and delivered to the owner. These excess pieces are useful for replacement and repairs.

Responsibility of the contractor. Aside from receiving and installing the carpet at the job site, the contractor shall be responsible for the following:

1. The contractor shall provide records that will verify his training and experience in carpet installation. This should include a list of previous work that is similar in scope. Names of people to contact for references should also be included. A minimum of five years' experience is required.

2. The contractor shall provide names of carpet manufacturers with whom he has worked in the past.

3. The contractor shall provide evidence that the work shall be performed by skilled installers and that the number of installers assigned to the job site will be adequate to complete the installation.

4. The contractor shall physically recheck all measurements provided in the specification. After completing the inspection and measurements, the contractor may make suggestions regarding another carpet width or type of installation that may eliminate unnecessary seams and yardage. This recommendation should be submitted to the designer for approval. A complete seaming diagram should also be submitted. No request for extra carpet will be considered when measurement or takeoff errors have been made by the installation contractor.

5. The contractor shall inspect all subfloors and test for moisture content. After inspection, the contractor should submit a written report on any conditions that would prevent the proper installation of the carpet. Once the carpet has been installed, it shall be understood that the contractor assumes responsibility for any unacceptable condition in the subfloor.

6. The contractor shall install all carpet as recommended by the manufacturer's installation manual. Carpet shall be installed wall to wall, using continuous lengths and as broad widths as possible. Cut edges shall be trued and appropriately treated to form nonraveling joints where exposed.

7. The contractor shall be fully responsible for the condition of the carpet until it has been finally approved. Upon completion of each floor, the installation shall be inspected by representatives of the owner and installer prior to approval by the owner. All dirt and carpet scraps must be removed from the surface of the carpet. All soiled spots or excessive adhesive on the carpet shall be removed with the proper spot remover. All pieces of loose face yarn must be removed with sharp scissors. The entire surface should be vacuumed with a heavy-duty machine.

8. The installation contractor shall guarantee in writing to relay or restretch the carpet, repair seams, joints, and edges one time if required after the original installation is completed. The guarantee shall be in effect for one year after the final approval of the installation. The owner shall provide the contractor with a two-week notice regarding the needed repairs.

9. The contractor shall be responsible for repair of any damage to wall surfaces, doors, or woodwork.

Responsibilities of the designer. The designer shall be responsible for providing the contractor with drawings and specifications which clearly detail the location of the carpeted areas within the project and provide installation instructions. The time of the installation and the necessary completion date should be included in the contract specification. The designer should plan a preinstallation and postinstallation inspection.

Preinstallation checklist. Four points need to be checked:

1. Has the carpet installation been properly scheduled? Be sure that all painting of doors and woodwork is completed, and that all wall finishes and adjoining resilient or hard-surfaced floors have been installed prior to the carpet installation.

2. Is the heating and/or air conditioning equipment in operating condition so that proper temperature and humidity can be maintained during installation?

3. Has adequate storage been provided for the carpet and tools prior to installation?

4. Will the carpet installation take place on the prearranged date?

Postinstallation checklist: Eight items need to be considered:

1. Check the carpet for wrinkles and buckling.

2. Check that all seams run with the flow of traffic and not counter to the traffic flow.

3. Check that seams do not appear to have been pulled too taut in the stretching process.

4. Check the nap direction of the carpet. All carpet should be installed in the same direction unless specified otherwise.

5. Check the nap direction on the stairs. Does the nap run downward on the stairs? Carpet backing should not show through tufting when curving over the stair structure.

6. Check the installation for any evidence of patching.

7. If the direct glue-down method was used, check for adhesive spots along the seam lines and be sure that the seams are tightly sealed.

8. Check that the carpet is securely attached to the metal moldings at doors and other areas where the carpet adjoins another floor surface.

Phase 13: Maintenance Programming

In the past carpet maintenance was regarded as a semiannual or annual cleaning after the carpet had become very badly soiled. Extensive research and the development of new chemicals by those involved in the carpet industry have changed the whole approach to carpet maintenance. Carpet maintenance is now programmed on a regular basis to prevent abrasive soil particles from collecting between carpet fibers. Spills and spots are removed regularly to maintain the overall appearance of the carpet.

Level of Appearance.

The level of appearance at which a carpet is maintained is based on the owner's requirements. Figure 7.23 illustrates how regular maintenance relates to the concept of appearance level. Figure 7.24 demonstrates how appearance level drops when carpet is allowed to become heavily soiled prior to cleaning. A 100 percent appearance level is considered "brand new" or in original installation condition. A maintenance level of 85 to 80 percent is considered excellent, and levels between 80 and 70 percent are considered good. The majority of commercial and institutional installations are maintained at an 85 percent level of appearance.

Several specification factors may result in a lower carpet appearance level and increased maintenance costs:

1. *Color selection* should be carefully considered, not only for aesthetic reasons, but because of maintenance factors. Generally, carpets selected in the midvalue range will show less soil than those of very dark or very light colors. Carpet color selection should take into consideration the regional soil color. If the geographic area has a yellowish, sandy soil and the area to be carpeted will receive traffic directly from the exterior, a dark carpet would be difficult to maintain. Patterned or multicolored carpets often provide a good floorcovering for heavily traveled areas such as hotels, hospitals, theaters, and restaurants.

2. *Carpet construction* is also a serious factor to consider in

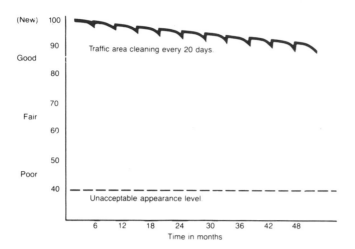

Figure 7.23 Appearance level, 20-day maintenance plan. Reproduced with permission of Host/Racine Industries, Inc.

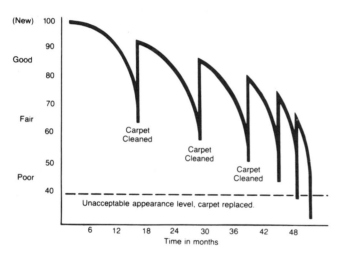

Figure 7.24 Appearance level, old-fashioned wet method. Reproduced with permission of Host/Racine Industries, Inc.

relation to maintenance. A loosely constructed carpet with a low-fiber density allows soil and dirt to collect between the fibers and filter to the base of the carpet. The deeply embedded soil is difficult to remove and promotes carpet damage. Carpet specified for commercial installations should be tightly constructed with a high yarn density.

3. *Fiber selection* should be based on the traffic load and location of the carpet within the building. Where high spillage is expected, a fiber with a low moisture content should be specified. Many new so-called soil-hiding carpet fibers, though highly popular, may also produce maintenance problems. Maintenance experts caution against allowing long periods of time to elapse between cleaning these soil-hiding fibers because the soil, though not noticeable, is actually accumulating and causing carpet damage.

4. *Placement of the carpet* within the building may also be responsible for unnecessary maintenance expense. The installation of "islands" of carpet surrounded by large areas of hard-surfaced flooring will result in wax and dust being tracked onto the carpet from the hard-surfaced floor (see Figure 7.25). In the maintenance process there is also the danger of wax and cleaning solutions being splashed on the carpet.

Figure 7.25 Carpet island.

Preventive Maintenance. Adequate preventive maintenance planning is based on knowledge of soil sources and the areas that will receive the major soilage. Three common sources of carpet soilage are (1) airborne soil, (2) spillage, and (3) shoe surfaces. Maintenance authorities further classify soil into two categories:

1. Water-soluble soil, such as sugars and other food contents that can be dissolved by water and detergents.

2. Solvent-soluble soil, such as oils and airborne cooking grease, that can be dissolved by dry cleaning solvents and detergents.[17]

As soils build up in the carpet the oily content in these soils sticks or binds to the carpet fibers and is impossible to remove through the normal vacuuming process. At this point chemical and mechanical cleaning methods are required to break the oil bond and pull the soil away from the carpet fibers. This loosened soil must then be removed to prevent its being dispersed farther into the pile and becoming a source of resoiling. Effective carpet maintenance involves not only dissolving the soil, but completely removing all soil (other than permanent stains).

Major areas that require frequent or daily maintenance are defined as track-off and funnel areas:

Track-off areas. These exist where carpet collects foot soil tracked in from outdoors or from hard-surfaced floors. Track-off areas at most building entrances average 90 sq ft (6′ × 15′). Internal doorways average 10 sq ft (2′ × 5′), and corridors 6 ft in width average about 40 sq ft (5′ × 8′) of track-off area. Preventive maintenance for track-off areas includes daily vacuuming, walk-off mats (both inside and outside), and regular spot and overall cleaning. The important objective is to prevent accumulated soil from being carried farther onto the remaining carpet areas.

Funnel areas. These exist where foot traffic is squeezed into or through a concentrated area, such as elevators, doorways, stairways, corridors, and areas in front of drinking fountains and vending machines or counters. Funnel areas are estimated to be 12 sq ft (2′ × 3′) on either side of a door jamb and 2′ × 6′ in front of drinking fountains and vending machines. These area estimates are used to calculate necessary maintenance time and equipment used in the following 20-day maintenance plan.

An outstanding preventive maintenance plan shown in Figures 7.26 and 7.27 was developed by the Racine Industrial Plant, Inc. and schedules a 20-day cycle for regular maintenance. The schedule covers 20 working days (excluding Saturdays and Sundays). It repeats 13 times per year, assuming 52 weeks' usage of the carpeting. Annual labor is shown per 1,000 sq ft (92.9 m²). Rates or production for the activities are based on several years of experience in many types of installations and in a broad range of geographic locations. "Odd" and "even" days refer to the day of the schedule not to the calendar date.

Preventive Maintenance Activities and Equipment. There are three areas of concern here:

1. Vacuuming is usually performed with a heavy-duty upright-type machine equipped with brush agitators. Direct glue-down installations require a special "carpet groomer" agitator with two rows of brushes, rather than a brush and beater bar normally used on carpet installed over padding. Vacuuming equipment should be properly maintained and vacuum bags emptied frequently.

2. Spot removal should be accomplished as soon as possible after spills and spots occur. In very large carpet installations a special maintenance person may be required to handle only spot removal. Commercial spot cleaning kits are available and contain the chemical compounds necessary to remove most common causes of spotting.

3. Traffic lane maintenance involves daily vacuuming, spot removal, and corrective or restorative cleaning. Because traffic lanes receive heavy wear, corrective overall cleaning is required to maintain a level of appearance that will equal the surrounding areas of carpet.

Corrective Maintenance. The accumulation of oily soils on carpet fibers is one of the major reasons that corrective or overall cleaning must be performed. Prior to cleaning, carpeting should be preconditioned; i.e., carpet fibers should be carefully vacuumed to separate and loosen packed pile to allow the penetration of the cleaning agents.

There are several cleaning methods used for corrective maintenance, and selection of a particular method should be based on the manufacturer's recommendations, plus an understanding of the client's needs. For example, a wet method that requires several hours to dry before the area can be restored to use would be feasible in an office or school that is closed in the evenings and on weekends. In a hospital or other public facility that remains in operation day and night a wet cleaning method would be found to be impractical. The following cleaning methods are the most frequently used.

1. *Detergent solutions* should be selected with caution because some may contain harsh chemicals that could adversely affect carpet dyes. Unless recommended by the carpet manufacturer, detergent solutions should be tested on a small portion of the carpet. The following characteristics would be desirable in a detergent-type cleaning method:
   a. Ability to clean the soiled carpet
   b. Prevents dulling of the carpet appearance
   c. Prevents rapid resoiling
   d. Avoids fading of the carpet dye
   e. Provides a disinfectant
   f. Avoids creating static electricity
   g. Provides a reasonable drying time

2. *Dry-foam cleaning methods* provide a simultaneous vacuum pick-up to remove soil and the dry-foam detergent. The detergents are contained in the dry foam that is deposited just ahead of the brush. Soil particles are loosened from the carpet fibers by agitation of the reel-type brush, suspended in the foam, and vacuumed back into the machine in one operation. This method prevents overwetting of the carpet, and cleaned areas are usually ready for use within one hour.

3. *Liquid dry cleaners* contain synthetic detergents and solvents that are sprayed over the carpet in a fine mist by a pressurized sprayer. The solution is allowed to penetrate into the carpet for about 10 minutes before a single-disk floor machine lifts the soil from the carpet. The cleaned area may be ready for use within less than an hour.

Figure 7.26 The 20-day carpet maintenance plan.

ACTIVITY	FREQUENCY	PRODUCTION RATE	EQUIPMENT
Trash pickup	Daily	2.2 minutes/1000 sq. ft.	Upright vacuum. Broom and dustpan optional
Vacuum track-off & funnel areas	Odd days	30 minutes/1000 sq. ft.	Upright vacuum
Vacuum corridors	Even days	15 minutes/1000 sq. ft.	Upright vacuum
*Vacuum office areas or other rooms	10th day	30 minutes/1000 sq. ft.	Upright vacuum
*Spot removal	10th day	43.3 minutes/1000 sq. ft.	Spot remover Chewing gum freezer Dry cleaning machine Absorbent compound
*Traffic area cleaning	20th day	11.4 minutes/1000 sq. ft.	Traffic lane cleaner Dry cleaning machine Absorbent compound
Overall cleaning	Only as needed	80 minutes/1000 sq. ft. does not include the moving of furniture	Traffic lane cleaner Dry cleaning machines Absorbent compound

The schedule covers 20 working days (exclude Saturdays and Sundays). It repeats 13 times per year, assuming 52 weeks usage of carpeting. Annual labor and material costs are shown per 1000 square feet. Rates of production for the activities are based on several years of experience in many types of installations and in a broad range of geographical locations. ODD and EVEN days refer to the day of the schedule not to the calendar date.

*The PLAN indicates that once in every 20 days specific time is scheduled for each of these vital activities.

Carpet Maintenance Calendar

If carpeting is new, begin the 20 Day Plan immediately.
If it is not new, first give it a thorough overall wall-to-wall cleaning, then begin the 20 Day Plan.   From _____ To _____

SUNDAY	MONDAY	TUESDAY	WEDNESDAY	THURSDAY	FRIDAY	SATURDAY
	1 Vac track-off and funnel areas only — Trash Pick-Up	**2** Vac corridors only — Trash Pick-Up	**3** Vac track-off and funnel areas only — Trash Pick-Up	**4** Vac corridors only — Trash Pick-Up	**5** Vac track-off and funnel areas only — Trash Pick-Up	
6 Vac corridors only — Trash Pick-Up	**7** Vac track-off and funnel areas only — Trash Pick-Up	**8** Vac corridors only — Trash Pick-Up	**9** Vac track-off and funnel areas only — Trash Pick-Up	**10** Remove stains Vac offices Vac corridors — Trash Pick-Up		
11 Vac track-off and funnel areas only — Trash Pick-Up	**12** Vac corridors only — Trash Pick-Up	**13** Vac track-off and funnel areas only — Trash Pick-Up	**14** Vac corridors only — Trash Pick-Up	**15** Vac track-off and funnel areas only — Trash Pick-Up		
16 Vac corridors only — Trash Pick-Up	**17** Vac track-off and funnel areas only — Trash Pick-Up	**18** Vac corridors only — Trash Pick-Up	**19** Vac track-off and funnel areas only — Trash Pick-Up	**20** Traffic area cleaning by Dry Cleaning track-off and funnel areas — Vac corridors Trash Pick-Up		

REPEAT 20 Day Schedule (13 times per year).

Figure 7.27 Carpet maintenance calendar.

4. *Hot-water extraction cleaning* injects the pile with a hot detergent solution under pressure. The solution is immediately extracted along with the soil. This process is time-consuming, and it may overwet the carpet and result in prolonged drying periods.

5. *Powder cleaners* are absorbent compounds consisting of an organic powder impregnated with detergents, solvents, and phenolic inhibitors. The powder is sprinkled over the carpet and brushed into the pile. These powders may be left on the carpet for a short period, during which the soil is attracted to the powder, and later the soil and the power are vacuumed away. This method is ideal for interim cleaning and overall cleaning of areas that must remain in constant use, such as hospitals and hotels.[18]

Improper Cleaning Methods. There are two major problems that can result from improper cleaning:

1. Fading and shrinking may result from carpet fibers being overwet for prolonged periods of time.

2. Carpet shading, or "pooling"—sometimes referred to as "browning"—may result from several factors. This problem usually occurs in dense cut pile carpet that may begin to pack and lie flat under pressure of constant foot traffic. Large spots or pools may also result from wet cleaning solutions not being adequately removed from the carpet.

Maintenance Manuals. Operational and maintenance instructions for products and components specified by the designer should be assembled into a manual and presented to the owner. Details concerning the development of a maintenance manual will be discussed in Chapter Sixteen. Specification requirements for maintenance information from the manufacturer should include recommended brand names of cleaning solutions, spot removers, and equipment.

Phase 14: Life Cycle Costing
Estimating the life cycle cost of carpet involves establishing the initial cost factors as explained in Chapter Six. Recurring maintenance costs make up a major portion of total life cycle considerations. The cost schedule for 1,000 sq ft (92.9 m²) of carpet in Figure 7.28 is based on the time factors established in the 20-day maintenance plan (frequency and production rate).

The worksheet in Figure 7.29 developed by the Racine Industrial Plant, Inc. provides an effective method for arriving at the total yearly maintenance cost for 1,000 sq ft of carpeting based on an appearance level of 85 percent.

General Specifications Guidelines
Table 7.24 provides general guidelines for carpet specifications in various types of commercial occupancies. The recommended carpet weights are minimum and the maintenance levels will vary according to the actual use and maintenance provided. Figure 7.30 illustrates an additional type of carpet specification checklist that may be developed to aid designers in making decisions on performance requirements. Figures 7.31 and 7.32 illustrate sample specifications.

ACTIVITY	ANNUAL HOURS	×	HOURLY RATE	=	ANNUAL LABOR COST	+	ANNUAL MATERIALS COST*	=	ANNUAL TOTAL 1000 sq. ft.
Daily trash pickup	9.53		$8.00		$76.24		NA		$76.24
Vacuuming**	12.72		$8.00		$101.76		NA		$101.76
Spot removal***	9.39		$8.00		$75.12		$5.94		$80.52
Traffic area cleaning	2.28		$8.00		$18.24		$16.69		$35.21
ANNUAL TOTALS	**33.92**				**$271.36**		**$22.63**		**$293.99**

Some custodial personnel are required to cover 2400 square feet per hour for all maintenance. This equals 108.34 hours per year spent on each 1000 square feet. Industry figures show that about 52% of a custodian's time, or 56.3 hours, should be allowed for floor care. The 20 DAY PLAN requires only 33.98 hours per 1000 square feet vs. the 56.3 hours of time allowed by the industry formula.

If a higher appearance level is desired, additional time should be scheduled for vacuuming and traffic area cleaning, since these activities will produce noticeable results.

* Original equipment cost and depreciation not included.

** Assumes that 10% of carpeted area is in corridors, and also that TRACK-OFF and FUNNEL AREAS average 64 square feet.

*** Spots are easier to remove while they are fresh. However, prompt action is not always possible. It is more practical to schedule a specific time for spotting procedure. *Most spots can be removed quickly by using a dry cleaning machine, an absorbent compound, plus a general-purpose spotting agent.*

Figure 7.28 Cost schedule per 1000 square feet.

A. Vacuuming

   1. Vacuuming of track-off areas.

       a) _____ track-off areas at internal doorways × 10 sq. ft. = _____ sq. ft. per vacuuming

       b) _____ track-off areas in corridors × 40 sq. ft. = _____ sq. ft. per vacuuming

       c) _____ track-off areas at outside entrances × 90 sq. ft. = _____ sq. ft.

       d) _____ total of a, b and c above × 129 times per year = _____ sq. ft. per year

       e) _____ sq. ft. per year ÷ 2000 sq. ft. per hour = _____ hours

       f) _____ hours × $ _____ per hour labor rate = $ _____ yearly track-off area vacuuming cost

   2. Vacuuming of funnel areas:

       a) _____ internal funnel areas at doorways × 12 sq. ft. = _____ sq. ft. per vacuuming

       b) _____ funnel areas at fountains, vending machines, etc., × 12 sq. ft. = _____ sq. ft. per vacuuming

       c) _____ total of a and b above × 129 times per year = _____ sq. ft. per year

       d) _____ sq. ft. per year ÷ 2000 sq. ft. per hour = _____ hours

       e) _____ hours × $ _____ per hour labor rate = $ _____ yearly funnel area vacuuming cost

   3. Vacuuming of corridors:

       a) _____ corridors × _____ sq. ft. per corridor = _____ sq. ft. per vacuuming

       b) _____ sq. ft. per vacuuming × 129 vacuumings = _____ sq. ft. per year

       c) _____ sq. ft. per year ÷ 4000 sq. ft. per hour = _____ hours

       d) _____ hours × $ _____ per hour labor rate = $ _____ yearly corridor vacuuming cost

   4. Vacuuming offices:

       a) _____ total sq. ft. of offices × 13 vacuumings = _____ sq. ft. per year

       b) _____ sq. ft. per year ÷ 2000 sq. ft. per hour = _____ hours

       c) _____ hours × $ _____ per hour labor rate = $ _____ yearly office vacuuming cost

   5. Sum of 1, 2, 3 and 4 above = _____ total yearly vacuuming cost

       a) _____ total sq. ft. of carpeting ÷ 1000 = _____ areas

       b) $ _____ total yearly vacuuming cost ÷ _____ areas = $ _____ yearly vacuuming cost per 1000 sq. ft.

B. Spot removal

   1) 43.3 minutes per 1000 sq. ft. × 13 times per year = 562.9 minutes ÷ 60 = 9.39 hours × $ _____ labor rate = $ _____ yearly labor cost per 1000 sq. ft.

   2) Spot remover $.92 + chewing gum remover $.25 + dry cleaning compound $4.77 = $5.94 yearly material cost per 1000 sq. ft.

   3) $ _____ labor (#1 above) + $5.94 materials = $ _____ yearly spot removal cost per 1000 sq. ft.

C. Daily trash pick-up

   1) 2.2 minutes per 1000 sq. ft. × 260 times per year = 572 minutes ÷ 60 = 9.53 hours.

   2) 9.53 hours × $ _____ labor rate = $ _____ yearly trash pick-up cost per 1000 sq. ft.

D. Traffic area cleaning

   1) 11.4 minutes per 1000 sq. ft. × 12 times per year = 136.8 minutes ÷ 60 = 2.28 hours × $ _____ labor rate = $ _____ yearly labor cost per 1000 sq. ft.

   2) Absorbent compound 21.5 lbs. × 57.8/lb. = $13.66 + traffic lane cleaner $3.03 = $16.69 materials + $ _____ yearly labor cost = $ _____ yearly area maintenance cost per 1000 sq. ft.

E. Total

   Totals from:

   A. $ _____

   B. $ _____

   C. $ _____

   D. $ _____

   $ _____ Total yearly maintenance cost per 1000 sq. ft.

Figure 7.29 Estimating time and cost totals.

TABLE 7.24 CARPET SPECIFICATION GUIDELINES: OCCUPANCY INDEX*

Occupancy Type	Traffic Class	Carpet Construction	Carpet Fiber	Carpet Face Weight oz	Density	Maintenance Level, %	Installation Method	Installation Padding	Maintenance Program
Schools									
Corridors Exits	Heavy	WO/TU LL/PA	Nyl/OL BLD	28/46	4600 6600	85	DG	None	VAD/SP 20 DP
Classrooms	Mod. heavy	TU/LL 12 lb tuft/BLD	Nyl/Acy BLD	28	3800 4600	85	DG	None	VAD/SP/20 DP
Offices	Light	WO/TU CP/LL	Nyl/Acy	22/28	3800 4600	85	ST	60/80 oz SPR	SP/20 DP
Cafeteria	Heavy	TU/WO LL/C&L	Nyl/OL/BLD	22/28	3800 4600	85-90	DG	None	VAD/SP/20 DP
Hospitals									
Corridors	Heavy	TU/WO/PA LL/C&L	Nyl/Acy W/BLD	28/32	4600 6600	85-90	DG	None	VAD/SP/CN
Lobby	Heavy	TU/WO/PA LL/CP	Nyl/Acy W/BLD	28/32	4600 6600	85-90	DG	None	VAD/SP/CN
Nurses Stations	Heavy	TU/WO LL	Nyl/OL Acy	22/28	4600 6600	90	DG	None	VAD/SP/CN
Patient Rooms	Mod. Heavy	TU/WO LL	Nyl/OL	22/28	3800 4600	90	DG	None	VAD/SP/CN
Offices	Light	TU/WO LL/CP/C&L	Nyl/Acy W/BLD	22/32	3800 4600	85	ST	60/80 FL .250 SPR	SP/20 DP
Hotels/Motels									
Corridors	Heavy	WO/TU LL/CP/PA C&L	Nyl/Acy W/BLD	28/36	3800 4600	85	ST	44/50 oz .275 FL SPR	SP/20 DP
Lobby	Heavy	WO/TU/PA LL/C&L	Nyl/Acy W/BLD	28/42	4600 6600	90	DG		VAD/SP/CN
Guest Rooms	Mod.	TU/CP	Nyl/Acy W/BLD	28/32	3800 4600	85	ST	40 oz FL 80 oz SPR	SP/CN
Meeting Rooms	Mod. heavy	WO/TU/PA CP/LL/C&L	Nyl/Acy W/BLD	28/32	3800 4600	85	ST	40 oz FL .275 SPR	SP/CN
Transportation									
Terminal	Extra heavy	WO/TU LL/PA	Nyl/W/BLD	28/36	4600 6600	85	DG	None	VAD/SP/CN
Corridors	Heavy	WO/TU LL/PA	Nyl/Acy W/BLD	28/46	4600 6600	85	DG	None	VAD/SP/CN
Office Buildings									
Executive	Light	WO/TU CP/C&L	Nyl/Acy W/BLD	32/46	3800 4600	90	ST	.325/.525 FL SPR	SP/20 DP
Clerical	Mod. heavy	WO/TU LL/CP/C&L	Nyl/Acy W/BLD	22/32	3800 4600	85	DG/ST	44-50 oz FL 60-80 oz SPR	SP/20 DP
Corridors	Mod. heavy	WO/TU/LL CP/PA	Nyl/Acy W/BLD	22/32	3800 5500	85	DG/ST	44-50 oz 60-80 oz FLAT SPR	VAD/SP/20 DP
Cafeteria	Heavy	WO/TU/LL PA	Nyl/OL Acy/BLD	22/28	3800 5500	85	DG	None	VAD/SP/CN
Banks									
Executive	Light	WO/TU/CP C&L	Nyl/Acy W/BLD	32/46	3800 4600	90	ST	.325 FL SPR 44-50 oz FL	SP/20 DP
Lobby	Heavy	WO/TU/CP LL/PA/C&L	Nyl/Acy W/BLD	28/32	3800 5500	90	ST	.325 FL SPR 44-55 oz FL	VAD/SP/20 DP
Tellers	Heavy	WO/TU/LL	Nyl/Acy W/BLD	22/28	3800 5500	85	DG/ST	44-50 oz FL	SP/20 DP
Computer Facilities	Mod. heavy	WO/TU/LL	Nyl/OL BLD	28/32	3800 4600	85-90	DG	None	VAD/SP/20 DP

*Abbreviations: Carpet construction: WO = woven; LL = level loop; CP = cut pile; PA = patterned; TU = tufted; C&L = cut & loop.
Fibers: Acy = Acrylic; Nyl = Nylon; W = wool; OL = Olfin; BLD = blend.
Installation: DG = direct glue; ST = stretched.
Carpet padding: FL = felt; SPR = sponge rubber.
Maintenance: VAD = vacuum daily; SP = spot clean; 20 DP = 20-day plan; CN = clean as needed.

Note: This table represents suggested *minimum* levels.

Job No. _____

Date _____

CARPET PERFORMANCE SPECIFICATION CHECKLIST

MATERIAL	PROPOSED USE	PERFORMANCE REQUIREMENTS								MAINTENANCE LEVEL		INSTALLATION METHOD	BUDGET
	Location	Local Codes	Fed. Regs.	Ozone Cond.	Static Control	Soil Color	Traffic Amount	Spills	Other	Prevent:	Correct:		
Fiber: Const:	Area:												
Fiber: Const:	Area:												

Figure 7.30 Carpet performance specification checklist.

Figure 7.31 Guide specification for carpets.

SECTION 09680

CARPET

PART 1 GENERAL

1.01 SCOPE

A. This Section covers furnishing of all labor, materials, tools, equipment, and performing all work and services for all carpeting as shown on drawings and as specified, in accordance with provisions of the Contract Documents, and completely coordinated with work of all other trades.

B. Although such work is not specifically indicated, furnish and install all supplementary or miscellaneous items, appurtenances and devices incidental to or necessary for a sound, secure and complete installation.

****
Specifier: These manufacturers are only ones who comply with this spec at the time of writing. Before adding names, verify with interiors department regarding color and pattern. Verify that "or equal" carpets have same type construction and yarn face weights. Verify that flame and smoke ratings comply with State laws.
****

1.02 SUBMITTALS

A. Written approval by Federal, State and local fire authorities, building officials, and other authorities having jurisdiction. Use tests approved by these authorities. In event that authorities require other tests, test carpet by such tests, in addition to test method specified. Submit certificates or letters of approval from authorities having ultimate jurisdiction.

B. Certified copies of test reports to Owner.

C. Samples, shop drawings and seaming diagrams for approval before starting work.

D. Guarantee.

1.03 PRODUCT DELIVERY, STORAGE AND HANDLING

A. Deliver when areas of building are ready for carpet. Provide protection from loss or damage. Deliver with mill register numbers attached. Tag and mark accessory items for identification.

1.04 JOB CONDITIONS

A. Install after all other firnishing operations are completed in area to be carpeted. Verify suitability of substrate to accept carpeting.

B. Check moisture content by sealing an inverted glass tumbler to floor with putty for 24 hours. If moisture condenses inside glass, moisture content is too high. Delay installation until moisture is within acceptable limits.

1.05 GUARANTEE

A. Guarantee entire carpet installation complies with specifications and that damaged, defective, wrinkled, shrunken, or stained carped will be removed and replaced. Guarantee carpet will not shrink or show excessive wear for a period of five years from date of acceptance. Excessive wear is defined as wearing away of face yarns which reduces pile height by more than 10 percent in any area, seam separation and/or pulling out of nap.

B. Guarantee to cover entire cost of carpet replacement, including removal and disposal of defective carpet.

C. Written guarantee to be jointly signed by Contractor, Installer and Manufacturer.

****
Specifier: This carpet is current office standard for institutions per fire and other codes, where 25 Class A flame spread is required. Modify if necessary for other projects. Verify smoke rating. Edit as required. See State Requirements for smoke. If no State Requirements, use Federal Requirements.
****

1.06 FIRE, SMOKE, STATIC, AND HANDICAP REQUIREMENTS

A. All carpet (and padding) shall comply with applicable State and local codes regarding flame spread, fuel contributed and smoke developed as tested by ASTM E-84. Flame spread not exceeding 75 and smoke not exceeding 450.

****
Specifier: In health care facilities specify minimum critical flux of 0.45 watts. In facilities other than health care specify minimum critical flux of 0.22 watts.
****

B. Provide carpet with minimum critical flux of (0.45) (0.22) per square centimeter as determined by Flooring Radiant Panel Test (NBS) in all corridors and means of egress.

C. In other areas, provide carpet which meets requirements of Standard for Surface Flammability of Carpets and Rugs, DOC FF-1-70.

D. Smoke developed for all facilities not exceeding 450 when tested by NFPA Standard 258-76.

E. To meet handicap requirements, provide only carpet of high density, low uncut pile, nonabsorbent fiber with total height of carpet and pad not exceeding 3/8 in. (0.95 cm).

F. Static requirements, for all carpet, not exceeding 3.5 KV per AATCC Test 134-1975.

PART 2 MATERIALS

2.01 ACCEPTABLE MANUFACTURERS

A. Subject to compliance with specifications, products of following manufacturers are approved for use:

Alexander Smith
Bigelow-Sanford
Mohawk
Lees

B. Other manufacturers desiring approval comply with Section 01640. Furnish samples, technical data and laboratory test reports to show flame, smoke, static and handicap requirements.

****
Specifier: Modify manufacturers when other types of carpet are specified.
****

2.02 QUALITY ASSURANCE

A. Carpet: First quality, no seconds or imperfects. Colors as selected by designer.

B. Construction: Face yarns 3 or 4 ply anti-soiling 100 percent solution dyed Acrilan. Static control of copper filament, Zefstat or integral static control. Carpet velvet, woven thru back.

Rows per centimeters:	Minimum of 3.15
Rows per inch:	Minimum of 8
Pitch:	216
Wire size:	.200
Face yarn weight:	Minimum of 35 oz/sq. yd. (0.83 kg/sq. m)
Warp:	Rayon
Stuffer & Backer:	Preshrunk cotton, jute or polyester
Filler:	Jute
Total weight	Minimum of 68 oz/sq. yd. (1.61 kg/sq. M)
Colors:	Base manufacturer's standard line
Width:	12 ft. (3.66 m)

C. Carpet edging: Where carpeting terminates at other types of floor finishes Carpet Transition Reducer No. 101 of thickness to match carpet, as manufactured by Mercer Plastics, Inc., Newark, N.J. Color as selected by designer.

D. Joint filler: Noncrumbling, nonstaining type approved by carpeting manufacturer.

E. Adhesive: Nonstaining, nonbleeding strippable type as recommended by carpet manufacturer.

Figure 7.31 continued

PART 3 EXECUTION

3.01   PREPARATION

A. Check conditions of areas to receive carpet. Fill and level, thoroughly clean, free of foreign matter. Fill all cracks, joints, holes, or uneven areas with noncrumbling latex base floor filler, remove excess.

B. Before commencing work, test an area with glue and carpet to determine "open-time" and bond. Test for moisture.

C. Install using trained, skilled mechanics, with work supervised by an experienced superintendent. Install with minimum of cross seams or visible side seams. Lay so pile and pattern of adjacent pieces have same direction.

D. Where carpet terminates at a noncarpeted floor surface, install edge stripping.

E. Carefully check all dimensions and carefully fit and install carpet. Use a minimum number of seams located where indicated on approved seaming drawings. Do not piece carpeting. Install in longest practicable lengths with seams arranged symmetrically about centerline of room or space.

F. In corridors, install carpet lengthwise.

3.02   INSTALLATION

A. Installation instructions stated herein are based on Bigelow-Sanford installation data. Carpet manufacturer shall submit complete written installation data prior to start of work.

B. Prime all floor areas to receive carpet.

C. Use contact adhesive about 6 in. (15.24 cm) wide along carpet edges where they butt to a wall, where carpet terminates, and along all cross seams, to minimize possibility of later shrinkage from overwetting. Wherever contact adhesive is used, hold glue back at least one inch. Apply carpet glue over all remaining areas where carpet is applied. Apply both contact adhesive and glue at rate, and using tools, recommended by manufacturer.

D. Unroll carpet face up and cut to lengths required, making sure that pile direction is the same in all cuts. Check starting wall for squareness. Allow for off-square wall. Chalk line entire length of area where seam falls. Place two lengths in proper position for installing and trim selvedge. Line up seam edge with chalk line. Make sure that carpet lays perfectly flat and tension-free. Fold or roll both widths back 3 feet (0.91 m) from seam area for entire length of carpet. Do not crease.

E. Apply contact adhesive along seam edges. Spread carpet glue from approximate center toward each end.

F. When sufficient area has been covered with glue, drop or roll first width into place. Apply coating of edge sealer to seam edge of first width. Follow procedure on each succeeding seam. Brush or roll looseness and air bubbles away from seam, then fold over remaining portion of first width. Apply glue to floor and carpet. Drop and roll carpet into place. Place within allowable open time of adhesive.

G. Roll back dry portion of second width toward seam, spread glue, and place carpet to 3 feet (0.91 m) from where next seam will fall. Drop or roll second width into position, and fit seam in tightly.

H. Brush or roll out looseness and air bubbles as carpet is placed, repeat procedure on continuing widths. Use suitable trimmer for trimming carpet.

I. Bind all seams with seam cement.

J. Remove any spillage of glue or adhesive from carpet face or seam using remover provided by manufacturer.

3.03   MAINTENANCE INSTRUCTIONS

A. Provide Owner with 3 copies of carpet care and maintenance instructions. Advise maintenance personnel regarding care and maintenance if Owner so requests.

B. Mill to demonstrate cleaning methods on job site after carpet installation to instruct Owner's personnel.

3.04   CLEANUP

A. After installation is complete, clean up all dirt and debris. Clean carpet of all spots, remove all loose threads with sharp scissors. Completely and thoroughly vacuum.

B. At completion of work, review with Owner all pieces or remnants of carpet. Turn over to Owner all such pieces that he may require for repair. Remove all other scraps from site.

3.05   EXTRA MATERIAL

A. Furnish Owner with minimum of 10 square yards (8.36 square meters) of each type, pattern and color for maintenance purposes.

END OF SECTION

Figure 7.32 Guide specification for carpet cushions.

SECTION 09681

CARPET CUSHION

PART 1 GENERAL

1.01 DESCRIPTION

A. Related Work Specified Elsewhere:
1. Carpet: Section 09685
2. Paving and Surfacing: Section 02500

B. Work Installed but Furnished by Others:
1. Tackless Strips.

1.02 QUALITY ASSURANCE

A. Tests:
1. Ignition Resistance: FF-1-70-Pass
2. Flammability: ASTM E-84 (FS 75 or less)
3. Smoke Generation: Not exceeding 450
4. Compression Load Deflection: 25% deflection
   (require for flat or ripple sponge and rebonded or prime urethane)
5. Indentation Force Deflection: 25% Deflection
   (require for prime urethane)
6. Density: FHA UM-72. Min. 1b/ft^3
   (require for urethanes)
7. Resilience: FHA UM-72. Min. percentage

B. Submittals:
1. Product data. Written test verification.
2. Product samples 6" x 6" for inspection.

C. Product Delivery:
1. Rolled and wrapped cushion to be delivered and stored in horizontal flat area that will provide protection from tears and punctures.

D. Job Conditions:
1. Area is to be cleared of all discarded items left by other trades.
2. All painting and other interior finishes shall be completed prior to cushion installation.

E. Guarantee:
1. The carpet cushion manufacturer shall warrant that the cushion is free from defects in material and workmanship.

PART 2 PRODUCTS

2.01 MATERIALS

A. Tackless carpet stripping shall be standard water-resistant plywood stripping with angular pins protruding from the top. Pins shall grip and hold stretched carpet from below the edges. Provide two rows of pins when carpet width is less than 20 feet and provide three rows of pins when carpet width is 20 feet (6.09m) or more.

B. Adhesive used in installation to conform to manufacturer's recommendation.

C. Manufacturers of carpet cushion:

1. [_____] Type [_____]
2. [_____] Type [_____]
3. [_____] Type [_____]

(Use this format when specification is "or Equal" open bid)

[List type of cushion specified for project. Delete others.]

D. Felt: Composed of a mixture of jute fiber and animal hair or 100% animal hair, needle punched and coated on top and bottom surfaces with latex. Ounces per square yard shall be [_____] and conform to FHA UM 72-79 Class I [_____] or Class II [_____].

E. Cellular Sponge Rubber: Ripple/waffle [_____] or flat [_____] construction manufactured with synthetic rubber with nonwoven synthetic fabric scrim applied to back. Weight and other performance criteria to comply with FHA UM 72-79 Class I [_____] or Class II [_____].

F. Urethane Foam: Based on FHA UM 72-79
1. Prime density [_____to_____] of an inch (2.54 cm).
2. Bonded [_____to_____] of an inch.
3. Densified [_____to_____] of an inch.
4. Modified [_____to_____] of an inch.

PART 3 EXECUTION

3.01 INSPECTION

A. Contractor to confirm acceptable condition of subfloor prior to installation.

B. Inspect cushion to confirm acceptable condition for installation.

3.02 PREPARATION

A. All areas to receive cushion shall be cleared and free of dust, dirt and moisture.

3.03 INSTALLATION

A. Comply with manufacturer's instructions and recommendations for application of tackless stripping using nails or other approved means of attachment.

B. Place cushion scrim side up with seams midway between the carpet seams shown on carpet seaming diagram. Install in longest possible lengths with minimum number of sections.

C. Provide cut-outs for removable electrical access devices in the substrate. Tightly secure cushion edges around the cut-out areas.

D. Install cushion over entire area to be carpeted. Butt cushion tight against tackless edge stripping. Hold cushion back one inch (2.54 cm) from terminal edge of carpeting only where carpet edge is not to be secured by edge of stripping or binder bar.

E. Tape cushion seams with manufacturer-recommended 4-inch (10.16 cm) tape.

F. Provide for safe traffic on stairs and similar substrates; install cushion in a manufacturer-recommended secure manner.

G. In ramped areas, adhere cushion to substrate with partial application of adhesive or two-sided tape, covering 10% to 20% of substrate ramped surface.

3.04 FIELD CONTROL

A. Seams shall be intact and smooth. All cushion surfaces shall be flat with edges straight, parallel and square.

B. No holes or tears shall exceed one-half inch (1.3 cm).

C. Cushion shall be free from lumps or high spots and have no thin or weak spots. No protruding or embedded foreign matter shall be allowed.

3.05 ADJUST AND CLEAN

A. Remove debris from installation site.

B. Advise Contractor that area covered with cushion shall be protected during the remainder of the construction period.

3.06 SCHEDULES

A. Carpet seaming diagram shall be provided to cushion installation Contractor.

B. Schedule of related work to be conducted in the cushion area.

END OF SECTION

GLOSSARY*

Abraded yarns: Continuous filament yarns in which filaments have been cut or abraded at intervals and given additional twist to produce a certain degree of hairiness. Abraded yarns are usually plied or twisted with other yarns before using.

Absorption: The ability of a fiber, yarn, or fabric to attract and hold gases or liquids within its pores.

Acrylics: In the carpet industry, refers to acrylic and modacrylic fibers. Acrylic fiber is a polymer composed of at least 85 percent by weight of acrylonitrile units. Modacrylic fiber is a polymer composed of less than 85 percent but at least 35 percent by weight of acrylonitrile units. Acrylics come only in staple form and are noted for their high durability, stain-resistance, and wool-like appearance.

American Oriental: A term applied to loommade American carpets of the Axminster or Wilton weave which have been manufactured in the color and pattern designs of Oriental rugs. Being without sizing, these American-made carpets are soft and pliable and can therefore be folded like an Oriental. The sheen or lustre distinguishes this type of American carpet from the other weaves.

Antimicrobial: A property or treatment applied topically or fused into carpet fiber. The process resists the growth of odor-causing bacteria and mildew.

Antistatic: Ability of a fabric to disperse electrostatic charges to prevent the build-up of static electricity.

Average stiffness: Average weight in grams per denier that will stretch fiber 1 percent.

Axminster: One of the basic weaves used in making carpets. The pile tufts in this weave are mechanically inserted and bound to the back in a manner similar to the hand knotting of Oriental rugs, making possible almost unlimited combinations of colors and patterns.

BCF: Bulked continuous filament nylon. The highly bulked fibers have a trilobular or triskelion cross section, which gives them greater covering power than round, cross-section fibers possess.

Backing: Material that forms the back of the carpet, regardless of the type of construction. (1) Primary back: in a tufted carpet, the material to which surface yarns are attached. May be made of jute, kraftcord, cotton, woven, or nonwoven synthetics. (2) Secondary back: also called "double backing." Any material (jute, woven, or nonwoven synthetics, scrim, foam, or cushion) laminated to the primary back.

Back seams: While all carpet seams are located on the back or underside of the carpet, those made when the carpet is turned over or face-down are called "back seams," while those made with the carpet face-up are called "face seams."

Bank: A setting-machine yarn creel.

Beam: Large, horizontal cylinders or spools. The warp yarns are wound on beams located back of the line of weave. The woven fabric is wound on a beam located usually in front, just below the line of weave.

* Provided by the Carpet and Rug Institute.

Bearding: Long fiber fuzz on loop-pile fabrics. Caused by fiber snagging and inadequate anchorage.

Beat-up: (1) The action of the lay and reed when forcing the filling to fall off the cloth. (2) The point in the timing cycle of the above operation. (3) The number of tufts per inch of length in a warp row of pile. Used in connection with Axminster, chenille, and other carpets not woven over wires. Synonymous with "wire" in Wilton, velvet, etc.

Bent needles: (1) Needles in the tufting machine permanently pushed out of place causing a streak or grinning; they run lengthwise because of off-standard tuft spacing across the width. (2) A needle in the Jacquard that is out of alignment with punched holes in pattern cards.

Binding: A strip sewed over a carpet edge to protect against unraveling and/or to change its appearance.

Binding yarn: Cotton or rayon yarn running lengthwise of the woven fabric, used "to bind" the pile tufts firmly; often called "crimp warp" or "binder warp."

Bleeding: Loss of color when wet due to improper dyeing or from the use of poor dyestuffs. Fabrics that bleed will stain fabrics in contact with them when wet.

Blend: A fabric containing a mixture of two or more fibers or yarns, or a combination of two or more fibers spun ito a yarn.

Breaking strength: Ability of a fabric to resist rupture by evenly applied tension. Expressed as pounds of force applied to 1 in. width in warpwise or fillingwise direction.

Brussels: A term formerly, but now rarely, used to describe a loop pile or round-wire carpet woven on the Wilton loom.

Brussels pitch: From 252 to 256 dents per 27 in. (68.6 cm) in width.

Buckling: A carpet that does not lay flat on the floor and contains ridges. Can be caused by uneven beam tension, dimensional instability, and putting together mismatched carpet. Failure to stretch wall-to-wall installations sufficiently will also contribute buckles. (See also *Puckering.*)

Bulking: Processing yarn, usually by mechanical means, to fluff it up and give more coverage with the same weight. Also known as texturizing and lofting.

Burling: An inspection process following carpet construction to correct loose tufts, etc.; also the process of replacing missing tufts by hand.

Cam loom: A loom in which the shedding is performed by means of cams. A velvet loom.

Carpet: The general designation for fabric used as a floor-covering. It is occasionally used incorrectly in plural as "carpets" or "carpeting." The preferred usage today is "carpet" in both singular and plural form. It may be used as an adjective, as in "carpeted floors."

Carpet cushion: Any kind of material placed under carpet to provide softness when it is walked on. Not only does it provide a softer feel underfoot, it usually provides added acoustical benefits and longer wear life for the carpet. In some cases the cushion may be attached to the carpet when it is manufactured. Also referred to as "lining," "padding," or "underlay," "carpet cushion" is the preferred term.

Catcher threads: Warp threads in chenille Axminster carpets which attach the chenille fur to the carpet backing structure.

Chain: (1) The binder warp yarn that works over and under the filling shots of the carpet., (2) Axminster loom: the endless chain that carries the tube frames. (3) Dobby loom: the endless chain of pattern selector bars.

Chain binders: Yarns running warpwise (lengthwise) in the back of a woven carpet, binding construction yarns together in a woven construction.

Chenille: A pile fabric woven by the insertion of a prepared weft row of surface yarn tufts in a "fur" or "catepillar" form through very fine but strong cotton "catcher" warp yarns and over a heavy woolen backing yarn.

Cockling: A curliness or crimpiness appearing in the cut face pile as a result of a yarn condition.

Commercial matching: Matching of colors within acceptable tolerances or with a color variation that is barely detectable to the naked eye.

Construction: The methods by which carpet is made, combining the pile fibers to the backing materials. The term is applied to woven, tufted, and knitted carpet.

Continuous filament: Continuous strand of synthetic fiber extruded in yarn form, without the need for spinning, which all natural fibers require.

Count: (1) A number for identifying yarn size or weight per unit of length or vice versa, depending on the particular system being used. (2) Count of fabric is indicated by the number of warp ends and filling ends per inch.

Crab: A hand device usually used for stretching carpet in a small area where a power stretcher or knee kicker cannot be used.

Crimping: Processing of yarns, usually by heat, steam, or pressure, to introduce and/or set a wavy texture and give increased bulk.

Crocking: The excess color rubbing off as the result of improper dye penetration, fixation, or selection.

Cropping: The passage of carpet under a revolving cylinder fitted with cutting blades to obtain a level surface and a uniform height of pile.

Cross-seams: Seams made by joining the ends of carpet together.

Cushion-back carpet: A carpet having a cushioning lining, padding, or underlay material as an integral part of its backing.

Dead: The pile yarn in a Wilton carpet (usually figured) which remains hidden in the backing structure when not forming a pile tuft.

Deep-dyed: Dye penetration in carpet fibers which permits clear, true carpet colors that retain their brilliance for the life of the carpet.

Delustered nylon: Nylon whose normally high sheen is reduced by surface treatment.

Denier: Unit of weight for the size of a single filament. The higher the denier, the heavier the yarn. Denier is equivalent to the number of grams per 9,000 m (30,000 ft).

Density: The amount of pile packed into a given volume of carpet, usually measured in ounces of pile yarn per unit volume.

Density height: The square of the density multiplied by the pile height; a criterion by which the potential wear life of different carpet grades can be compared theoretically. The assumption is made in the use of this criterion that the fibers in the materials being compared are of equal quality and all other factors are constant. For example, if a carpet has a density of 32 and a pile height of .25 in. (6.4 mm), a 25 percent increase in the pile height would mean a corresponding 25 percent increase in the durability of the carpet. However, if the density of the carpet were increased by 25 percent, the durability would be increased by 66 percent.

Differential dyeing fibers (dye-variant fibers): Fibers, natural or manufactured, so treated or modified in composition that their affinity for dyes becomes changed, i.e., some treated fibers will dye lighter or darker than others, depending upon the particular dyes and methods of application employed.

Dimensional stability: Tendency of a fabric to retain its size and shape; may be brought about by chemical treatment or mechanical means: e.g., a secondary backing adds dimensional stability to carpet.

Dope dyed: Same as spun dyed and solution dyed, this applies to synthetic fibers only. The coloring materials are added to the solution before it is extruded through a spinneret to form the filament.

Double back: A woven or nonwoven material adhered to the backing of some carpet as additional reinforcement to provide greater dimensional stability and improved tuft bind. Also known as scrim back.

Drop match: When the design in a carpet must be dropped in the next combining width of carpet to maintain the pattern.

Drugget: A coarse, heavy imported fabric, felted or plain woven, usually of all wool. The designs are either woven into a fabric or printed.

Dye beck: A large vat into which roll lengths are submerged for piece dyeing.

Electrostatic flocking: The process used for the majority of flocked commercial carpets. Specially treated fibers are charged by an electrostatic field. When the charged fibers encounter the object to be coated, they are moving vertically at a high speed and they become firmly embedded in the adhesive.

Embossed: In carpet, the type of pattern formed when heavy twisted tufts are used in a ground of straight yarns to create an engraved appearance. Both the straight and twisted yarns are often of the same color.

Face seams: Seams, either sewed or cemented, that are made without turning the entire carpet over or face-down. They are made during installation where it is not possible to make back seams.

Filament: A single strand of any kind of fiber, natural or synthetic. In textile use, filaments of natural fiber must be spun into yarns, and synthetic filaments are extruded as yarns.

Filler: Fuller's earth or clay, or similar material, used in the mix of latex and attached cushion.

Finishing: A final process through which fabrics are put in order to prepare them for the market; such as bleaching, scouring, calendering, embossing, rapping, mercerizing, waterproofing, or mothproofing.

Foam rotary shampooing: A shampooing method which reduces drying time to 30 to 60 minutes. The new equipment consists of a foamer attachment (a self-contained solution tank and foam builder) which fits on any rotary machine. One man does the shampooing and another removes the heavy dirty suds with a wet vacuum.

Full roll: An unbound cut of carpet, described in the carpet industry as being over 30 ft (9 m) in length and by the width of the production run from which it was cut.

Fusion bonded: Makes use of two backing fabrics that run parallel with a small space between the two. The backing has an adhesive on the facing sides. By implanting a multifold fiber between the backings, a sandwich is formed. At the end of production line, a blade slices through the middle fiber web, producing two identical carpets. Most of the fusion-bonded carpet has a special backing applied, and then it is cut into carpet tiles.

Fuzzing: Hairy effect on fabric surface caused by wild fibers or slack yarn twist or by fibers slipping out of yarn or contour in either service or wet cleaning. It is corrected by shearing in manufacturing and by the professional cleaner. Carpet of continuous filament yarn is fuzzed by filament snagging and breaking.

Gauge/pitch: The number of ends of surface yarn counting across the width of carpet. In woven carpet, pitch is the number of ends of yarn in 27 in. of width; e.g., 216 divided by 27 is 8 ends per inch. In tufted carpet, gauge also means the number of ends of surface yarn per inch counting across the carpet; e.g., ⅛ gauge equals 8 ends per inch. To convert gauge to pitch, multiply ends per inch by 27; e.g., ⅒ gauge is equivalent to 270 pitch, or 10 ends per inch × 27. One-eighth gauge is 8 ends of yarn per inch × 27, or 216 pitch.

Greige goods (Pronounced "gray goods"): Term designating carpet just off the tufting machine and in an undyed or unfinished state.

Grin: A term used to indicate the condition where the backing of the carpet shows between the rows of pile tuft; e.g., some carpet may show the backing when laid over the nosing of a step.

Ground color: The background color against which the top colors create the pattern or figure in the design.

Hair: Animal fiber other than wool or silk.

Hand: The "feel" of a carpet in the hand, determined by such factors as pile height, quality and kind of fibers, type of construction, type of backing, and dimensional stability.

Heather: A multicolored effect provided by intimately blending fibers of different colors prior to spinning carpet yarn.

Heat set: Stabilization of yarns to ensure no change in size or shape; the process of heat-setting in an autoclave, using super-heated steam under pressure.

Heddle frame: The frame on which the heddles are mounted.

Hessian: Plain cloth, usually of jute, containing single yarns of approximately the same count in warp and weft.

High density: A term to describe a material with heavier than normal weight-per-unit volume.

High-density foam: Rubber product applied as a liquid foam, then cured, to form an integral part of the carpet back. The minimum standards are weight of 38 oz/sq yd, thickness of ⅛ in. (3.2 mm), density of 25 lb/cu ft.

High low: A multilevel pile, sometimes combining cut and looped surface yarns.

Hooked rugs: Yarn or strips of cloth inserted into a prewoven cloth stenciled with a pattern. Usually a hand or single needle process. Modern tufting is mechanized hooking.

Hopper: The assembly that engages the pile wire head, drawing it from the front of the wire set and returning it under the pile shed.

Hot melt: A blend of polymer and filling applied in a heated state to a carpet back in order to lock in surface yarns and provide lamination.

Indoor/outdoor: Obsolete term, see *Outdoor carpet.* The first carpet produced for outdoor use was named indoor/outdoor carpet. Over a period of time this term was erroneously thought, by retailers and consumers, to indicate "that if it is okay for outdoor use it has superior qualities indoors." Since this statement is generally incorrect, the carpet industry wants to avoid perpetuating this term.

Ingrain carpet: A double-faced pileless carpet using colored filling yarns to make the design. The fabric is reversible, and the designs and colors on the face and back will also be in reverse positions. This type was also called Scotch or Kidderminster.

Jacquard: The pattern control on a Wilton loom. A chain of perforated cardboard "cards" punched according to the design elements, which when brought into position activates this mechanism by causing it to select the desired color of yarn to form the design on the pile surface. The unselected colors are woven "dormant" through the body of the fabric.

Jacquard cards: Punched cards (usually laced together) which are presented to the Jacquard in sequence, for the selection of lifting of the pile ends as required for patterning.

Jaspe: Irregular stripes of two hues, shades, or values of the same color used to produce a particular effect on the pile yarn of plain or even designed fabrics. Various jaspe effects can be produced by varying the twist of the yarn.

Jerker bar (tufting): The guide or thread jerker which takes up slack tufting yarn during the upstroke of the needle and controls the amount supplied for the backstroke.

Jute: A fibrous skin between the bark and stalk of a plant native to India and the Far East. Shredded and spun, it forms a strong and durable yarn used in carpet backing to add strength, weight, and stiffness.

Kemp: Coarse, brittle white fiber occurring frequently in "non-blooded" carpet wools. These fibers do not accept dye, and consequently an excess could be prominent and undesirable.

Knee kicker: A short tool with gripping teeth at one end and a padded cushion at the other, used in making small stretches during carpet installation.

Knitting: A method of fabricating a carpet in one operation, as in weaving. Surface and backing yarns are looped together with a stitching yarn on machines with three sets of needles.

Laminated: Fabric composed of layers of cloth joined together.

Latex: A milky, rubbery fluid found in several seed plants and used to seal the back of carpet and provide lamination. May be used on tufted or woven carpet.

Latexing: The application of a natural or synthetic latex compound to the back of carpet.

Leno weave: Weave in which warp yarns, arranged in pairs, are twisted around one another between "picks" of weft yarn.

Level loop: A construction in which the carpet face yarns are tufted or woven into loops of the same pile height.

Lip: The chain and/or stuffer left on the edge of carpet after it has been cut.

Loopers: The thin, flat, steep components that move beside the inserted needles and hook the tufting yarn into loops.

Lustering: Finishing process that produces luster on yarns and cloth.

Match, set or drop: In a set-match carpet pattern, the figure matches straight across on each side of the carpet width; in a drop-match, the figure matches the design midway; in a quarter drop-match, the figure matches one-quarter of the length of the repeat on the opposite side.

Mending (picking): A hand operation carried out on carpet before finishing to remove any knots and loose ends of yarn, to insert pile tufts where missing, and to replace and repair backing yarns as required.

Metallic fiber: A manufactured fiber composed of metal, plastic-coated metal, metal-coated plastic, or a core completely covered by metal. The most important characteristic of metallic fiber in carpet is that it reduces build-up of static electricity.

Mil: A unit commonly used for measuring the diameter of textile monofilaments—1/1,000 in.

Mill end: The remainder of a roll carpet, generally described in the carpet industry as being over 9 ft (2.8 m) in length, but under 21 ft (6.5 m) in length, by the width of the roll from which it was cut.

Modacrylics: Refer to *Acrylics.*

Molded rubber back: A new kind of carpet backing. Liquid rubber is coated on the carpet back and then rolled out with an embossed roller.

Monofilament: A filament large and strong enough to be used directly as a yarn for making textiles through any established process.

Moresque: Single strands of different colors of yarn twisted or plied together to form one multicolored yarn.

Multifilament: Yarns made of many filaments plied or spun together. The finer the filaments spun together, the softer and more luxurious the yarn and textiles made from it.

Nap: The pile on the surface of a carpet or rug.

Narrow carpet: Fabric woven 27 in. (68.6 cm) and 36 in. (9.4 cm) in width.

Needle: (1) *Jacquard loom:* the horizontal wires, rods, or plungers, the forward and backward movement of which is controlled by the pattern punch cards. One end is placed into a needle board and the ends extend slightly beyond the board surface. The other end projects into a leveling board, padder, needle box, or spring box. The forward and backward movements position the last cord knots to be picked up by the last board, lifting board, or comberboard, or the hooks to be picked up by the griff remain in the grate. (2) *Axminster loom:* refers to the metal rod used to insert a short filling yarn. (3) *Knitting:* the hooks that make the loops. (4) *Tufting:* the needle with an eye to punch the pile yarn through the backing material. (5) *Needlepunching:* the needle that stitches the fibers to a base fabric.

Needlepunching: A process in which layers or batts of loose fiber are needled into a core, or scrim, fabric to form a felted or flat-textured material. A needlepunched fabric can be embossed, printed, or laminated to a cushion, or otherwise finished.

Noil: A by-product in worsted yarn manufacture consisting of short wool fibers, less than a determined length, which are combed out.

Nonwoven: A fabric made up of a web of fibers held together by a chemical or fibrous bonding agent.

Nosing: The front dividing line of a step, where the top of a riser joins the front of a tread.

Olefin: Any long-chain synthetic polymer composed of at least 85 percent by weight of ethylene, propylene, or other olefin units.

Outdoor carpet: Carpet that has been specially engineered so that all elements of the product will resist the ravages of the sun, rain, and snow. Outdoor carpet is generally made of all synthetic material. Special attention has been paid to sun-fade degradation of the pile fiber.

Padding: See *Carpet cushion.*

Piece-dyed: Dyed by a process in which the entire carpet immersed in a dye bath. Used for dyeing tufted carpet.

Pigmented yarn: A dull or colored yarn spun from a solution to which a pigment has been added.

Pile: The upright ends of yarn, whether cut or looped, that form the wearing surface of carpet or rugs.

Pile crush: Bending of pile by constant walking or the pressure of furniture.

Pile density: The number of tufts both across and lengthwise the carpet. In tufted carpet the measure across the carpet is called needless per inch, or gauge. The lengthwise measurement is called stitches per inch.

Pile height: The height of pile measured from the surface of the back to the top of the pile.

Pile setting: Brushing done after shampooing to restore the damp pile to its original height. A pile-lifting machine or a pile brush is used.

Pile wire: A metal strip or rod over which yarn is woven to produce a pile.

Pilling: A condition in certain fibers in which strands of the fiber separate and become knotted with other strands, causing a rough, spotty appearance. Pilled tufts should never be pulled from carpet, but may be cut off with sharp scissors at the pile surface.

Pitch: See *Gauge.*

Plain or flat weave: A fabric with a flat surface in plain, twill, or fancy weaves, having a printed, stenciled, or "woven in" design, that is generally reversible.

Plied yarns: Two or more strands, ends, or plys either twisted or otherwise cohesively entwined, intermingled, or entangled into a heavier yarn.

Plush finish: A dense cut pile carpet in which the surface has a solid "mirrorlike" appearance. The ends of each tuft tend to merge into a common surface.

Ply: The number of strands of yarn twisted together to form a single yarn, as in "2-ply" or "3-ply."

Polyester: A manufactured fiber in which the fiber-forming substance is any long-chain synthetic plymer composed of at least 85 percent by weight of an ester of a dihydric alcohol and terephthalic acid (p-HOOC-C_6H_4—COOH).

Polymer: In synthetics, the basic chemical unit from which fibers are made. Polymer is made of large complex molecules formed by uniting molecules (monomers).

Polypropylene: High-molecular-weight paraffin fiber made by the polymerization of propylene (FTC classification Olefin).

Power stretcher: An extension-type version of the knee kicker, with more teeth arranged in a head which can be adjusted for depth of bite, or used to stretch larger areas of carpet that cannot be handled by the knee kicker.

Primary backing: The material on which the carpet is constructed. The material to which the visible secondary backing is anchored. Usually jute or polypropylene.

Prime urethane cushion: A carpet cushion made from virgin polyether urethane foam slab stacks.

Printed carpet: Carpet with surface patterns applied by means of dyes used on engraved rollers, wood blocks, or screens.

Printing: The process of producing a pattern with dyestuffs on carpet and rugs. May be done by several methods, such as screen printing (e.g., on Zimmer equipment, which may be flat-bed or rotary-screen printing), or on roller equipment operating on the relief-printing principle (e.g., Stalwart equipment).

Puckering: A condition in a carpet seam, usually due to poor layout or unequal stretching, wherein the carpet on one side of the seam is longer or shorter than that on the other side, causing the long side to wrinkle or develop a pleated effect.

Quarter drop match: See *Match.*

Random-sheared: Textured pattern created by shearing some of the top or higher loops and leaving others looped.

Repeat: The distance from a point in a pattern figure to the same point where it occurs again, measuring the fabric lengthwise.

Residual shrinkage: Amount of shrinkage remaining in a fabric after the decrease in dimensions has been determined by preshrinking; decrease in dimensions of a fabric after washing or dry cleaning.

Resilience: The ability of a carpet fabric or padding to spring back to its original shape or thickness after being crushed or walked upon.

Reverse coloring: The process whereby the dominant background colors and the top colors of a fabric are reversed. It can be done in Wilton weaves by changing the yarn colors of each frame.

Rows or wires: The number of lengthwise yarn tufts in 1 in. (2.5 cm) of carpet. In Axminster or chenille, they are called "rows"; in Wilton and velvet, they are known as "wires."

Rug: Soft floorcoverings laid on the floor but not fastened to it. As a rule, a rug does not cover the entire floor.

Saxony finish: A dense cut pile carpet, usually made of heavy yarns that have been plied and heat set, so that each tuft end has a distinguishable appearance.

Scrim back: A double back made of light, coarse fabric, cemented to a jute, kraftcord, or synthetic back in tufted construction. (See *Double back.*)

Sculptured: In carpet, this refers to a type of pattern formed when certain tufts are eliminated or pile yarns are drawn tightly to the back to form a specific design in the face of the carpet. The resulting pattern simulates the effect of hand carving.

Secondary backing: The extra layer of material laminated to the underside of the carpet for additional dimensional stability and body. Usually latex foam, jute, polypropylene, or vinyl.

Seconds: Carpets or rugs rejected for having certain imperfections, flaws, or deviations of weave and marked as "seconds" or "imperfect" by the manufacturer.

Self-tone: A pattern of two or more shades of the same color. When two shades are used in a pattern or design, it is called "two-tone."

Selvage: The edge of a carpet so finished that it will not ravel or require binding or hemming.

Serging: Also known as "oversewing," this is a method of finishing the edge of carpet. It is customary to serge the side and bind the end.

Set or drop match: In a set-match carpet pattern, the figure matches straight across on each side of the narrow carpet width; in a drop-match, the figure matches half the length of the design; in a quarter drop-match, the figure matches one-quarter of the length of the repeat on the opposite side.

Shading: An apparent change of color in carpet pile caused as light is reflected in different ways when pile fibers are bent; not a defect, but a characteristic, especially of cut pile fabrics, including upholstery and clothing.

Shag: A low-density type of carpet of cut- and/or loop-pile construction wherein the pile surface texture has a random tumbled appearance. This effect is created in use by the random layover of the pile yarn in all directions, as distinguished from the normal upright position of the pile in plush carpet.

Shearing: The process in manufacture in which the fabric is drawn under revolving cutting blades as in a lawn mower, in order to produce a smooth face on the fabric.

Shooting or sprouting: Individual strands of yarn protruding above the surface of the pile. These may be extra long ends of tufts which were not sheared at the mill, pieces of backing material which have risen above the surface, loose ends which were not secured firmly, or occasionally the untwisting of the

tightly twisted tufts in a twist-weave carpet. This condition of sprouting or shooting does not mean that the fabric is coming apart, for it does no damage. It is only necessary to clip or shear these loose ends even with pile surface. The sprouting yarns should not be pulled out.

Short roll: An unbound cut of carpet, generally described in the carpet industry as being over 21 ft (6.5 m) in length, but under 30 ft (9 m), by the width of the roll from which it was cut.

Shot: The number of weft yarns in relation to each row of pile tufts crosswise in the loom. A 2-shot fabric is one having two weft yarns for each row of pile tufts; a 3-shot fabric has three weft yarns for each row of tufts.

Shuttle: In weaving, a boat-shaped, wooden instrument which holds the bobbin from which the weft yarns unwind as the shuttle passes through the warp shed.

Side seams: Seams running the length of the carpet, adding to the width. Also called "length seams."

Sizing: Operation consisting of applying starch, gelatin, oil, wax, or any other ingredient onto yarn to aid the process of fabrication or to control fabric characteristics. Warp sizing is usually referred to as "slashing."

Smyrna: A reversible, double-plied rug, woven from chenille fur strips without the backing characteristic of the chenille weave. The binding yarns are wool, cotton, jute, or paper.

Soil retardant: Agent applied to carpet pile yarns to resist soiling.

Specific gravity: Ratio of the weight of a given volume of the fiber to an equal volume of water taken as standard at stated temperatures.

Spinning: (1) *Chemical spinning:* the process of producing manufactured fibers, including the extrusion of the spinning liquid through a spinneret into a coagulating medium and the winding of the filaments onto bobbins or in cake form. (2) *Mechanical spinning:* twisting together and drawing out short fibers into continuous strands of yarn.

Splush finish: A term used to describe a semidense cut pile carpet, about halfway in appearance between a shag and a plush. The tufts lay less irregularly than a shag, but not as regularly as a plush.

Sponge cushion: A carpet cushion made of chemically blown sponge, including both waffle or flat surfaces.

Sprouting: See *Shooting.*

Stabilizing: Treating a fabric so that it will not shrink or stretch more than a certain percentage.

Staple: Fiber in the natural, unprocessed state, usually in short lengths, which must be spun or twisted into yarn, as opposed to continuous filament.

Staple fiber: The short lengths into which filament yarns are cut to enable them to be spun on conventional-type spinning machinery.

Staple nylon: Nylon composed of specially engineered fibers cut into short staple for spinning yarns.

Stop marks: A mark across the width of tufted carpet caused by an off-standard feed relationship of either yarn or cloth feed or both on the startup of the machine.

Stria or striped: A striped effect obtained by loosely twisting two strands of one shade of yarn with one strand of a lighter or darker shade. The single yarn appears like irregular stripes.

Stuffers: Extra yarns running lengthwise through a woven fabric to increase weight and strength.

Tabby weave: A type of weaving used to give a staggered diagonal pattern across the weft yarns. Most commonly used in loomed carpet construction.

Tak dyeing: A process in which dye is applied over a continuous dyed fabric by a controlled "sprinkle" technique. This allows more color and pattern interest in tufted carpet.

Take up: The difference in distance between two points of a yarn as it lies in the fabric and the same two points when the yarn has been removed and straightened, expressed as a percent of the extended length. Similar to extended length used in tufting except that extended length is linear and the base is 1 in. (2.5 cm) of carpet.

$$\frac{\text{Extended length—woven length} \times 100}{\text{Exended length}} = \% \text{ take up}$$

(See also *Crimping*.)

Tenacity: Stress applied to produce a particular elongation in a fiber. The breaking tenacity is the stress required to elongate a fiber to the breaking point.

Tensile strength: Breaking strain of yarns or fabrics. High tensile strength indicates strong yarns or fabrics.

Thermal conductivity: The measurement of heat flow through a material.

Thick and thin yarns: Specialty yarns of varying thickness.

Tip-shearing: A texture pattern created in the same way as random-shearing, but generally less definite than random-sheared patterns.

Tone on tone: A carpet pattern made by using two or more shades of the same hue.

Top colors: Colors of the yarn used to form the design, as distinguished from ground color.

Total weight: Weight per square yard of the total carpet pile, yarn, primary and secondary backings, and coatings.

Tuft bind: The force required to pull a tuft from a cut pile floorcovering or to pull free one leg of a loop from a looped pile floorcovering.

Tufted carpet: Carpet or rug fabric that is not woven in the usual manner, but formed by the insertion of thousands of needles that punch tufts through a fabric backing on the principle of the sewing machine.

Velvet finish: The surface of a dense cut pile carpet, produced usually on a tufting machine or velvet loom. See also *Plush*, *Splush*, and *Saxony finish*.

Vinyl: A synthetic carpet back which may be applied in either a hard or cushioned form.

Vinyl foam cushioning: A new kind of carpet cushioning made from a combination of solids and liquids. It is claimed that vinyl foam cushioning will not decompose.

Warp: A series of threads or yarns (usually delivered from a beam) running lengthwise in the carpet. Usually consists of chain, stuffer, and pile warp.

Warp pile: An extra set of warp yarns woven into a fabric to form an upright pile.

Weft or woof: The threads running across a woven fabric from selvage edge to selvage edge, binding in the pile and weaving in the warp threads.

Weighting: Finishing materials applied to a fabric to give increased weight.

Woolen yarn: A rather soft, bulky yarn spun from both long and short fibers that are not combed out straight but lie in all directions so that they interlock and produce a feltlike texture.

Worsted yarn: Yarn made of long-staple carpet combed to parallel the fiber and remove the extremely short fibers.

Woven backing: Backing produced by a weaving process using natural fiber, such as jute, cotton duck, or synthetic yarns.

Yarn: A continuous strand for tufting, weaving, or knitting: (1) *Continuous filament yarn:* yarn formed into a continuous strand from two or more continuous filaments. (2) *Spring yarn:* yarn formed from staple by spinning or twisting into a single continuous strand or yarn.

RESILIENT AND HARD-SURFACE FLOORING

Increased concerns about life cycle costing and the length of service provided by interior components have resulted in more frequent specification of resilient and hard-surface flooring in commercial interiors. With many new technical innovations in the resilient-flooring industry, designers have a wide range of surface textures, colors, and materials from which to select.

RESILIENT FLOORING

Although some areas, such as open offices, may require a fiber floorcovering to aid in controlling acoustic factors, other commercial areas are well served by resilient flooring. Numerous performance criteria have been established to assure quality control in the areas of (1) health and safety, (2) construction, (3) physical strength, and (4) appearance. Table 8.1 provides a survey of some of the major physical characteristics and recommended uses for resilient materials.

Health and Safety Criteria

These criteria include such factors as flammability, light reflectance, and slipperiness.

Flammability. Resilient flooring is tested for flame spread and smoke obscuration in the following test procedures:

ASTM E-84

NFPA Standard 258

UL 992

NBS Smoke Chamber

Most federal specifications require a flame spread of 75 in unsprinklered areas and a 200 flame spread in sprinklered areas. Recommended optical density for smoke is 450 in both flaming and nonflaming conditions.

Light Reflectance. This affects the brightness and quality of light in an interior. Too much reflectance can be a source of glare and discomfort in areas where critical work is taking place, such as offices and schools. A person seated at a desk looking downward toward the task will view the floor as a secondary background. Research has established that the task surface (book or papers) should not exceed a reflectance factor of 30 to 50 percent, and the floor should not exceed a 50 percent reflectance level.

Other areas of concern are long hallways in hospitals or nursing homes where the reflectance level and the glare can distort the length or shape of the space and create difficulty for an ill or elderly person. A very glossy surface also creates special subfloor preparation problems; i.e., the surface must be very smooth to prevent any irregularities from showing on the tile surface.

Slipperiness. This is another health and safety factor that has been the subject of research by private industry, shoe manufacturers, insurance companies, and the National Bureau of Standards. National safety statistics have shown that falls in the home kill as many as 12,000 people and injure 6 million a year in the United States. Although the precise causes of the falls are not recorded, slippery floors are listed as a large contributor to these casualty rates.[1] Several laboratory tests have been developed to determine the factors that contribute to slipperiness, i.e., skid resistance or coefficient of friction between flooring and other materials such as footwear sole and heel materials. The coefficient of friction between two surfaces is defined as the ratio of the force required to move one surface over the other to the total force pressing the two surfaces together. Thus:

$$\text{Coefficient of friction} = \frac{\text{horizontal force}}{\text{vertical force}}$$

TABLE 8.1 GENERAL PHYSICAL CHARACTERISTICS OF RESILIENT FLOORING

Material	Size	Gauges	Federal Specification	Load Limit (psi)	Construction and Recommended Use
Rubber tile	9″ × 19″ 12″ × 12″	1/8″ (0.125)	SS-T-312 Type II	200	Rubber compounds of synthetic butadiene-styrene type. Similar to vinyls in quality, but less durable and less resistant to grease and alkalis.
Vinyl sheet	6′ side 90′	.090	L-F-00450 A L-F-475a Type II	100	Vinyl resin surface with a backing of filled fibrous comp. resin-saturated rag fiber. Install all grades. Use only in light or moderate traffic. Low resistance to cigarette burns. Very resilient.
Vinyl tile	9″ × 9″ 12″ × 12″	.080 1/16″ 3.36″ 1/8″	L-F-475 a Type II SS-T-312 B Type IV, Comp. I	200	Blended composition of thermoplastic binders, fillers, and pigments. Binders are polyvinyl chloride. Expensive in translucent type. Very resilient, but low resistance to cigarette burns.
Cork tile	6″ × 6″ 9″ × 9″ 12″ × 12″	1/8″ 3/16″ 5/16″		75	Pure cork particle bonded by baking process and thermosetting binders. May be finished. Light to moderate traffic. Install on grade or suspended grade.
Vinyl cork tile	9″ × 12″	1/8″ (0.125)		150	Same as above, but may have thermoplastic binders and plastic film finishes.
Back sheet vinyl, contract weight	6′ wide × 90′ long	.080″	L-F-475A (3) Type II, Grade A	125	Vinyl resin surface with a backing providing a heavier weight material to use in heavy traffic.

The two types of friction that are considered in these test methods are static and dynamic (kinetic). *Static* friction is the amount of friction between two surfaces at the moment that one begins to move across the other. *Dynamic* friction occurs between two surfaces when movement is in progress without interruption. Laboratory equipment is designed to test flooring materials in a horizontal position, with the application of static friction or the use of dynamic friction in the form of a swinging pendulum. The test results are recorded as an "index of slipperiness" or a "skid resistance index." The specification of flooring that may result in falls is especially critical in lobby or vestibule areas (see barrier-free requirements in Chapter 14). The GSA specification for office buildings requires that resilient flooring be tested according to the ASTM D-2047 and have a slip resistance coefficient of greater than or equal to 0.5.[2]

Asbestos Health Hazards. The Environmental Protection Agency (EPA) estimates that 733,000 commercial buildings constructed prior to 1980 are contaminated with asbestos. This figure does not include approximately 45,000 schools and thousands of buildings built for military use.

In 1973, as evidence of health-related asbestos problems mounted, the EPA banned the use of asbestos in decorative interior finish products. Subsequently, asbestos was banned from all U.S. building materials in 1978. By the early eighties almost 90,000 health-related liability suits had been filed against asbestos manufacturers.

Impact on real estate values. The 1988 Securities and Exchange Commission ruling that full disclosure of true valuation of asbestos affected real estate has resulted in discounts of 8 percent to 20 percent from property market values. More than 95 percent of U.S. industry will be forced to bear the estimated 250-billion-dollar cost of building evaluation and asbestos removal by experts, either before or after a real-estate transfer. Federal law also requires that all asbestos be removed from condemned buildings scheduled for demolition.

Designer liability concerns. Unless absolutely positive beyond any doubt, designers are urged to accept the fact that all buildings constructed between 1960 and 1973 do contain asbestos. Although designers may not envision being involved with asbestos, this material can be encountered in many unexpected places. For example, a residential designer is currently facing a legal suit because a client no longer wanted the textured ceiling in her apartment. The designer instructed the painter to sand the ceiling. When the client later discovered the ceiling was made of asbestos, she filed charges of professional negligence against the designer for having exposed the entire family to unreasonable risk.

Where asbestos is located. Asbestos found within buildings is classified as *friable* or *encapsulated*.

1. *Friable* products contain asbestos fibers that tend to be easily broken down and remain airborn for weeks. Transported through entire buildings through ventilation systems, these fibers are half a micron long (human hair is 80 microns in diameter) and have been found to lodge in the lungs and intestinal tract. Examples include sprayed-on asbestos applications intended to texture a ceiling or make a steel beam fire resistant.

2. *Encapsulated* asbestos products are those composed of asbestos fibers securely embedded in binders. Products such as resilient floor tiles produced during the sixties do

not readily release asbestos fibers unless sanded or improperly removed.

The following types of buildings were found to have exposed asbestos in areas used by the building occupants:

1. Commerical privately owned buildings:
   14% Contained sprayed or troweled-on asbestos
   12% Contained asbestos insulation
   16% Contained some asbestos in soundproofing, floor tiles, and other interior finishes
   5% Contained asbestos ceiling tiles

2. Federal Buildings:
   39% Contained some form of asbestos
   25% Contained asbestos pipe and boiler insulation
   16% Contained sprayed- or troweled-on asbestos
   2% Contained asbestos ceiling tiles

3. Residential Rental Buildings:
   59% Contained asbestos decorative interior finishes and floor tiles
   44% Contained asbestos insulation
   18% Contained sprayed- or troweled-on asbestos
   5% Contained asbestos ceiling tiles

Asbestos abatement specification. Asbestos-safety experts advise that designers develop abatement specifications separately from actual renovation or demolition work. Specifications should be procedural in nature and spell out the detailed abatement requirements that must be imposed on the contractor. The designers should require that the contractor have extensive experience and show evidence of training in an EPA-certified program.

The specification guide shown in Figure 8.4 on page 123 must be edited to adapt it to each individual project. It is a guide for removal of resilient sheet, tile, and cushion-backed flooring. Information for this specification was provided by the Resilient Floor Covering Institute.

Installation

The most important environmental factors to consider in the specification of resilient flooring are:

1. Moisture conditions in concrete subfloors and wooden on-grade floors and surface moisture that may occur in public baths, showers, and laundry rooms can create serious installation problems. The danger of moisture in concrete subflooring is discussed in Chapter 7. Table 8.2 lists the density classification of concrete slabs and recommended resilient floor application. Light-weight concrete may be

TABLE 8.2 DENSITY CLASSIFICATION OF CONCRETE SLABS BY WEIGHT

Density	Type of Concrete	Lb per Cu Ft	Recommendations
Light	Expanded perlite vermiculite and others	200–40	Top with 1″ thickness of standard concrete mix
Medium	Expanded slag, shale and clay	60–90 90–120	Follow above recommendation or that given below
Heavy	Standard concrete of sand, gravel or stone	120–150	Approved for use of resilient flooring if troweled smooth and even

Source: Armstrong Cork Company.

structurally weak on the surface level and not support the adhesive bonding for resilient flooring. Serious problems can occur in wooden on-grade floors because the wood can absorb moisture through the sleepers, and if resilient flooring is installed over the wood, moisture can be trapped between the sleepers and the resilient material, causing the wooden floor to deteriorate. Thus, resilient flooring is not recommended for this type of installation. If, however, the wooden floor is constructed over a crawl space (at least 18 in. [45.7 cm] high) with good cross ventilation, the resilient flooring could be successfully installed.

Surface moisture from spillage can best be counteracted by the selection of a resilient flooring with few seams, such as sheet material.

2. If direct sunlight is expected in areas having resilient flooring, designers should be aware that intense sunlight can blister, fade, and shrink flooring, and even make tile very brittle. Certain pigments, such as yellows and reds, tend to fade rapidly. In situations that present problems of this nature, designers should specify more neutral colors, such as tans and grays, which will resist fading.

3. Stain-producing chemicals may also present problems in making a specification decision. If very sanitary and clean conditions are required, the designer may consider sheet vinyl that is especially engineered for commercial use. Resilient floor tiles may also provide a very tight seam through precision factory cutting.

Underlayments. Many types of subfloors require an underlayment to provide a smooth undersurface and prevent expansion and contraction of wood subfloors. There are two major types of underlayments:

1. Mastic types are made of a binder containing latex or polyvinylacetate resins. These should not be applied in thicknesses exceeding ⅛ in. (3.2 mm) and the subfloor should be free from paint, oil, and varnish.

2. Board-type underlayments may be hardboard, plywood, or particle board. Generally, hardboard is used on renovation projects, and plywood or particle board is used on new construction. Plywood should be specified in ¼ in. (6.4 mm) thickness or heavier, interior type APA Underlayment Grade or exterior type APA CC (plugged). Particle-board underlayments are not recommended by all resilient flooring manufacturers. In fact, some manufacturers will not accept responsibility for flooring performance in the event of underlayment failure.

Adhesives. The specification of adhesives should be based on the manufacturer's recommendations. There are special types of adhesives used for resilient flooring.

Asphaltic. Used for the installation of asphalt and vinyl asbestos tile, these adhesives usually remain soft and tacky for long periods of time. Asphaltic adhesives are divided into two types:

1. Emulsion types are water-based and contain from 50 to 60 percent asphalt with no flammability or toxicity hazards. Standards of performance are established by federal specification MMM-A-115A. This adhesive may be used on suspended, above- and below-grade concrete flooring. Curing time required prior to installation is usually 30 minutes to 1 hour. Estimated coverage per gallon is between 150 to 200 sq ft (14 to 18.5 sq m).

2. Cut-back adhesives are solutions of asphalt in hydrocarbon solvents. Standards of performance are established by federal specification MMM-A-110A. This adhesive is trowel-applied and requires about 30 minutes' drying time prior to installation. Superior to emulsions for vinyl asbestos tiles, it may be used on all concrete grades and plywood or hardwood suspended floors.

Brushable. These are higher viscosity adhesives that can be applied with a brush, roller, or trowel.

Resinous waterproof. These adhesives usually contain alcohol as a solvent and have the same characteristics as linoleum paste. Although this type of adhesive is insoluble in ordinary water, it may be attacked by alkaline solutions. This makes it impractical for concrete surfaces on or below grade levels. Estimated coverage per gallon is about 150 sq ft (14 sq m).

Installation Inspection Checklist. Designers should not neglect to make adequate inspections before, during, and after installation. The following checklist is based on Construction Specifications Institute (CSI) recommendations.

Before:

1. Verify that proper provisions have been made for maintaining installation temperatures [70° F (21° C)].

2. Verify that conditions for storage of materials are satisfactory and that provisions for materials requiring acclimatization have been made.

3. Verify that substrate surfaces are dry, clean, sound, level, and conform with specified requirements.

4. Check that wood subfloors have been securely fastened with nonrising fasteners, and surfaces and joints have been treated to prevent "telegraphing" (when irregularities in a subsurface are noticeable on the surface of an applied finish).

5. Verify that all items scheduled to penetrate the flooring have been installed and that the area will be free from other work and traffic during the period required to complete installation.

During:

1. Check that joints and seams are tight, even, and aligned.

2. Verify that special inset patterns or borders are laid and that the desired laying pattern is followed.

3. See that materials requiring cutting and fitting are prepared in a neat, workmanlike manner.

4. See that materials requiring rolling are properly rolled and that their surfaces are free of air pockets, ripples, bubbles, and unevenness (asphalt and vinyl asbestos tiles do not require rolling).

After:

1. Check that the floor surface is smooth and level with all tile joints tight, flush, and aligned.

2. Check that seams are sealed and matched in sheet material.

3. Witness conductivity tests and verify performance with requirements.

4. Check to see that base coverings are securely installed with sealed joints and properly aligned.

5. Verify that the area is clean and all excess adhesive, scraps, soil, and stains have been removed.

6. See that final finishings, waxing, and polishing are accomplished.

7. After the work is checked, see that it is protected from damage until accepted by owner.

8. Receive maintenance instructions and materials (if required); transmit to owner.[3]

Maintenance

Newly installed flooring should only be damp mopped without the use of excessive water until the adhesive has had time to thoroughly set (four to five days). The floor should be immediately protected with a light coating of water-based polish or finish.

Daily maintenance usually involves sweeping with a soft broom, treated cloths, or treated mops which will remove dirt and dust buildup. Washing of resilient floors may be required every two weeks in light traffic areas and more often in areas that receive heavy spillage, such as refreshment centers. This light-duty cleaning does not require the removal of the polish finish. Alkaline cleaners should not be used because the residue may dull the glossy finish.

Recommended polishes include water-resistant resin or polymer types. Polymeric floor finishes should not, however, be applied over waxy finishes because a streaky film may result, but waxy finishes can be applied over polymerics. Polymer finishes should be removed after every three or four applications to prevent excessive buildup. Paste waxes or liquid-solvent waxes, which contain solvents such as naphtha or turpentine, should not be used on resilient flooring. This flooring should also never be treated with lacquers, varnishes, or similar finishes because they will discolor and be difficult to remove.[4]

Protection against Indentation. Floor protectors are necessary to retain the beauty of resilient flooring. The concentrated weight of furniture legs can be more evenly distributed over the surface by using flat composite cups under the legs. Furniture that is frequently moved should be equipped with casters 2 in. (5.1 cm) in diameter with soft rubber treads at least ¾ in. (19.1 mm) wide. Glides should have a smooth, flat base with rounded edges and a flexible shank. These should be 1¼ to 2½ in. (3.1 to 6.3 cm) in diameter. The Resilient Tile Institute recommends a maximum loading of 75 lb per square inch (psi) for vinyl asbestos tile and 40 lb psi for asphalt tile. To prevent scratch-producing dirt buildup, protectors should be cleaned each time the flooring is washed.

Estimating Initial Costs

The initial cost must include cost of materials, such as adhesive, flooring material, and underlayments. In addition, the labor costs will be dependent on the preinstallation time needed for subfloor preparation. Installation labor costs are usually based on the number of square feet involved. To all these costs, the designed should add 15 to 20 percent for labor overhead and a profit surcharge of 10 to 15 percent.

Drawings and Specifications

The CSI recomends that the following be indicated on the working drawings:

1. The areas to be covered in resilient flooring should be clearly marked.

2. The type of flooring material and location of each different type must be shown on the drawings.

3. If two or more tile types or colors abut or if a resilient floor joins another floor finish, the joints between materials should be carefully shown. When the joining materials involve a difference in thickness, special design treatment, or trim, the details should be clearly shown.

4. In the event that areas are to receive a custom-pattern design or special insert material, the design must be clearly indicated. Figures 8.1 and 8.2 illustrate detailed drawings for a patterned resilient floor.

5. The locations and extent of any required base trim materials or special items, such as edge termination and saddles (insets as interior openings), should be shown.

6. Coverings for stair treads, nosings, risers, runners, and stringers should be noted on the drawings.

The written specifications for resilient tile in Figure 8.5 on page 125 and resilient sheet flooring in Figure 8.6 on page 126 provide examples of the information that should be carefully specified.[5]

HARD-SURFACE FLOORING

The second major type of flooring is composed of hard surfaces, such as marble, quarry tile, brick, and wood, both standard and acrylic. Because acrylic wood involves a relatively new manufacturing process, it will be discussed in detail.

Marble

Marble is very expensive and requires special care, such as buffing and polishing. It is available in squares 11.7″ × 11.7″ (29.7 × 29.7 cm) and strips 3.9″ × 11.7″ × 0.36″ (9.9 × 29.7 × .9 cm). Larger sizes are also available, but because of the weight factor they become very difficult to install. See the written specification in Figure 8.7 on page 127 for more details.

Quarry Tile and Brick

These materials are relatively expensive. Both are usually set within mortars and finished with grouted seams. Brick sizes are normally 2″ × 4″ × 8″ (5.1 × 10.2 × 20.3 cm), which are sliced thin for floor application. Quarry tiles range in size and shape from ½″ (1.3 cm) to 12″ (30.5 cm), in rectangular, square, hexagonal, and other shapes. The written specifications in Figures 8.8 and 8.9 on pages 129–130 give information on installation procedures.

Wood

Wood flooring is available in strips, as well as parquet, which can be set into many intricate patterns (see the specification data in Table 8.3). Standard wood floorings require refinishing and polishing to maintain surface qualities. These maintenance factors have a definite effect on the total life cycle cost.

Acrylic Wood

Acrylic wood flooring has many of the same qualities of resilient flooring. This wood product was developed in the mid-1950s when experimentation was conducted with peace-time use of radiation. This process was developed as an alternative to using natural wood as a flooring material because of its vulnerability to stains, scratches, mechanical damage, and chemical deterioration.

Figure 8.1 Working drawing for patterned resilient corridor
flooring. Source: Architectural Interiors, Inc., Phoenix, AZ.

Figure 8.2 Detail drawing for patterned resilient flooring.
Source: Architectural Interiors, Inc., Phoenix, AZ.

TABLE 8.3   SPECIFICATION DATA FOR WOOD FLOORING

	PRODUCT DESCRIPTION AND PATTERN	PANEL SIZE	GRADE	SPECIES	APPROX. WT. (lbs. per m. sq. ft.)
	STANDARD Pattern Unfinished—Paper-Faced	5/16" x 19" x 19" 16 equal alternating squares	Premium Select Rustic	Cherry—Maple Red Oak—White Oak—Cedar—Pecan—Walnut Rhodesian Teak Angelique (Guiana Teak) Panga-Panga	1250
		5/16" x 12" x 12" 4 equal alternating squares			1250
	STANDARD Pattern Unfinished—WebBack or Mesh-Back	5/16" x 19" x 19" 16 equal alternating squares	Premium Select Rustic	Red Oak—White Oak Pecan	1250
		5/16" x 11" x 11" 4 equal alternating squares	Select & Better (Par & Better) Rustic	Red and White Oak	1250
	STANDARD Pattern Unfinished—WebBack (For Industrial Use)	5/16" x 19" x 19" 16 equal alternating squares	Select & Better (Par & Better) Select	Maple—Red Oak White Oak Pecan	1250 to 2650
		9/16" x 19" x 19" 16 equal alternating squares	Rustic & Better Rustic		
	STANDARD Pattern Unfinished WebBack (For Industrial Use)	11/16" x 11" x 11" 4 equal alternating squares	Select & Better (Par & Better) Industrial & Better (Rustic & Better)	Red Oak—Maple	1250
		¾" x 12-11/16" x 12-11/16" 4 equal alternating squares			
	STANDARD Pattern Factory-Finished (Available in various colors)	5/16" x 6⅜" x 6⅜" 5/16" x 6½" x 6½" individual unit	Choice Natural & Better Natural Cabin	Oak—Walnut Pecan—Maple	1300
	STANDARD Pattern Factory-Finished Foam-Back Tile	5/16" x 6½" x 6½" individual units . . . ⅛" foam, 2 lb. density	Natural & Better Natural Cabin	Oak—Pecan Maple	1300
	ANTIQUE TEXTURED (Factory-finished and Unfinished)—Kerfsawn Various colors available	5/16" x 6⅜" x 6⅜" individual squares 5/16" x 6½" x 6½" individual squares 5/16" x 11" x 11" 4 equal alternating squares	Select Natural & Better Select & Better (Par & Better)	Red Oak & White Oak Red Oak & White Oak	1250
	ANTIQUE TEXTURED (Factory-finished and Unfinished)—Wire brushed Various colors available	5/16" x 6⅜" x 6⅜" 5/16" x 6½" x 6½" individual squares	Natural & Better	Oak	1300
	MONTICELLO Pattern Unfinished—Paper-Faced	5/16" x 13¼" x 13¼" 4 equal alternating squares	Select & Better (Par & Better)	Angelique (Guiana Teak) Red Oak—White Oak Panga-Panga—Black Walnut	1250
	HADDON HALL Pattern Unfinished—Paper-Faced	5/16" x 13¼" x 13¼" 4 equal squares	Select & Better (Par & Better)	Angelique (Guiana Teak) Red Oak—White Oak Panga-Panga—Black Walnut	1250
	HERRINGBONE Pattern Unfinished—Paper-Faced	5/16" x 14⅛" x 18⅛" (Approximate overall) 2 - "V" shape courses wide and 11 slats long	Select & Better (Par & Better)	Angelique (Guiana Teak) Red Oak—White Oak Panga-Panga—Black Walnut	1250
	SAXONY Pattern Unfinished—Paper-Faced	5/16" x 19" x 19" 4 equal squares on diagonal and 8 equal half squares	Select & Better (Par & Better)	Angelique (Guiana Teak) Red Oak—White Oak Panga-Panga—Black Walnut	1250
	CANTERBURY Pattern Unfinished—Paper-Faced	5/16" x 13¼" x 13¼" 4 equal alternating squares with diagonal center slats	Select & Better (Par & Better)	Angelique (Guiana Teak) Red Oak—White Oak Panga-Panga—Black Walnut	1250
	RHOMBS Pattern Unfinished—Paper-Faced	Hexagonal Shape 5/16" x 15⅛" x 15⅛" 12 equal Rhomboids	Select & Better (Par & Better)	Red Oak & White Oak	1250
	BASKET WEAVE Pattern Unfinished—Paper-Faced	5/16" x 15-1/5" x 19" 4 runs of 3 slats and 5 slats alternating	Select & Better (Par & Better)	Angelique (Guiana Teak) Red Oak—White Oak Panga-Panga—Black Walnut	1250
	ITALIAN & DOMINO Pattern Unfinished—Paper-Faced	5/16" x 19" x 19" 400 equal size pieces butt-jointed	Premium Par & Select	Black Walnut Angelique (Guiana Teak) Maple—Red Oak White Oak	1250

Reproduced with permission of the American Parquet Association.

Manufacturing Process. The wood (slates 6″ × ⁵⁄₁₆″ × 1″ [15.2 × .8 × 2.5 cm]) is first vacuumed in a large canister to remove air trapped within the pore network of the wood. A liquid containing plastic, dyes, and fire retardants is then forced into the pores by pressure. When the wood emerges soaked in this liquid, it is then transferred to another canister and lowered into a 20-ft (6-m) pool of water with Cobalt 60, the radiation source, at the bottom of the canister. The water serves to cool and reduce the heat reaction and provides a biological shield which absorbs the radiation. The canister moves along a track at the bottom of the pool, passing the ray of the cobalt. When the product is taken from the canister, it is warm and dry. It is then polymerized by radiation, trimmed, and made into blocks for flooring.[6] Figure 8.3 illustrates the process.

The process can be used successfully on most domestic woods, but is not effective on some exotic foreign woods. Acrylic wood is available in various sizes, ranging from square blocks to random planks.

Physical Properties. Eight qualities characterize acrylic wood flooring:

1. The coloration of the surface cannot be worn off because the plastic contains dyes which permeate the entire wood.

2. The grains and wood tones are enhanced.

3. The surface has a very high abrasion resistance.

4. The wood has a very high density. That of oak, for example, can increase from 35 to 60 percent.

5. The compression strength of the wood is also increased, which decreases, but does not eliminate, the natural tendency of wood to contract and expand.

6. It gains a high degree of fire resistance.

7. It has a high resistance to bacterial growth.

8. The wood has added acoustic qualities.

Installation. Designers should specify that installation be according to the manufacturer's recommendations. The following information is provided to acquaint the designer with typical installation factors that must be considered prior to specification.[7]

On concrete subfloors. Designers should require that concrete subfloors meet the following criteria:

1. Concrete subfloor shall be of good workmanship, structurally sound, and finished to proper elevation to accept the acrylic wood floor. Finish shall be by wood or mechanical float to a true level approved by the manufacturer.

2. Use of concrete curing compounds or surface sealers is prohibited. If used, these must be removed by sanding.

3. In cases where the subfloor is not level or is otherwise unacceptable, the contractor may use corrective measures, such as machine grinding or leveling with material recommended by the manufacturer for such corrective work, and the contractor shall assume full responsibility for proper and permanent bonding of fill and leveling methods.

4. All grime, dirt, oil, or grease shall be removed by thorough scouring and grinding, if necessary.

5. The floor shall be mechanically scarified prior to installation, especially if the slab has been steel-troweled to a smooth finish.

Acrylic/wood conversion process

Thoroughly dried wood is sealed in an evacuation chamber, and vacuumed to remove air trapped within the pore network of the wood (1).

A liquid substance containing the acrylic monomer, methyl methacrylate, dyes, and fire retardants, is then forced into the voids (2) of the pore structure until the wood is impregnated (3).

The canister and its contents are then irradiated by controlled exposure to Cobalt 60 gamma ray source (4). This causes the liquid plastic to polymerize into a solid substance, resulting in the hard, dense acrylic/wood composite (5).

Figure 8.3 Acrylic/wood conversion process. Reproduced with permission of Interiors *magazine.*

6. Moisture in the floor must be controlled as follows: Drying time may vary depending on climatic and site conditions, but the minimum shall not be less than one week per 1-in. (2.5-cm) thickness for suspended slabs and two weeks per 1-in. thickness for on-grade or below-grade installations, under favorable conditions such as free air circulation in temperate weather and heat and ventilation in colder weather. Floors with moisture membranes under the tiles are recommended and may require longer drying times.

7. Moisture-content testing may be accomplished by:
   a. Using a commercial moisture meter designed for such testing.
   b. Using calcium chloride sealed under glass at 10 or 12 well-distributed locations.
   c. Test drilling ¼ in.- (6.4-mm-) diameter holes to ¾ in. (19.1 mm) the thickness of the slab.

8. Concrete floors on-grade or below-grade shall be on washed gravel fill and a membrane of waterproof and fungus-resistant reinforced kraft paper coated with a layer of polyethylene, and 1-in.-thick fiberglass edge insulation shall be installed in accordance with the manufacturer's instructions.

On wood subfloors.   These subfloors must meet the following criteria:

1. Wood subfloors shall be plugged and sanded exterior-grade plywood. When placed over sheathing, ½ in. (2.7-mm) plywood shall be used. When placed over wood joist, 3.4-in. (19.1-mm) plywood shall be used with all sides supported by joists or cripples.

2. All irregularities of joints in the plywood shall be sanded smooth.

3. The plywood shall be nailed on 6-in. (15.2-cm) centers.

Working conditions.   The following conditions must be considered:

1. Flooring work shall not be installed until all masonry, plastering, tile, marble, and terrazzo work is completed and overhead work is finished.

2. The subfloor shall be dry, free from foreign materials, and broom clean. Temperature shall be maintained at 65° F (18° C) or higher for at least one week before, during, and 72 hours following installation.

3. When laying in-line flooring, it is recommended that the strips be laid with individual fillets butting end-to-end, offset by one-half fillet width.

Materials.   The following conditions must be considered:

1. All materials shall be stored at the job site for enough time so that they can come up to equilibrium with site conditions. Cartons shall be opened at least 48 hours prior to installation. In installations where the air conditioning can be expected to be turned on and off, it is important that the material be properly acclimated so as to minimize humidity stress effects after installation.

2. The adhesive shall be recommended by the manufacturer. An epoxy type shall be used on concrete slabs on-grade or below-grade. A latex type shall be used for installations on wood subfloors or on concrete suspended slabs. Since plank flooring has a tendency to cup, it is recommended that the strongest mastic be utilized for these installations. Extra care should be taken to make sure of proper mastic coverage and to roll the strip and plank flooring properly into the mastic to assure good bonding so that the material will be able to resist stresses that might be encountered due to high humidity conditions and water expansion.

3. The adhesive shall be spread uniformly in accordance with the manufacturer's instructions. Flooring shall be installed within the allowable time as specified.

4. Individual parquet blocks shall be placed to match adjoining blocks, properly seated in the adhesive by tamping or rolling with a 100-lb (46-kg) roller. In-line flooring and strip flooring shall be butted together, but not too tightly, and tamped or rolled as described above.

5. An expansion void of ¼ to ½ in. (6.3 to 12.7 mm) shall be provided at the walls to allow for expansion.

After installation.   Cleaning and buffing should include the following points:

1. It is recommended that the newly installed floor, after a 12-hour setting time, be cleaned and buffed before use to enhance its appearance.

2. Clean floor of all dust, grit, and abrasive particles by general sweeping, followed by a dry mop-type sweeper.

3. For a richer, deeper appearance, it is recommended that a coat of liquid buff be applied. Apply it lightly, approximately 1,000 sq ft (95 sq m) per gallon, and remove the excess with dry rags. The floor may be buffed immediately; however, for best results, it is recommended that buffing be delayed for 8 hours.

4. Buff as follows:
   a. Buff with standard green pad.
   b. Buff with standard tan pad to produce a long-lasting, lustrous finish.
   c. To produce a high-gloss finish, buff with standard white pad after completing above steps.

5. Upon completion of work, all materials, tools, equipment, and rubbish shall be removed from the site.

Figure 8.4 Specifications for asbestos abatement. Based in part on information from the Resilient Floor Covering Institute.

SECTION 02080

ASBESTOS ABATEMENT*

PART 1 GENERAL

1.01   WORK INCLUDED

A. The safe removal and disposal of resilient flooring containing encapsulated asbestos fibers.

1.02   QUALITY ASSURANCE

A. Contractor shall ensure that workers concerned with abatement work have completed a state sponsored or Environmental Protection Agency (EPA) approved training course.

1.03   SUBMITTALS

A. Submit written verification of the following:
   1. Provisions to assure safety to occupants in areas of the building outside of the abatement zone.
   2. Provisions for safety of workers on the abatement project. Provide description of protective clothing and approved respirators.
   3. Listing of all tools required for safe completion of the abatement project.
   4. Description of final cleaning procedures.
   5. Description of abatement procedures.
   6. Requirements for containment and final disposal of asbestos materials.
   7. Procedures for verification of building safety after abatement is completed.

1.04   PRODUCT DELIVERY/STORAGE

****
Provide information that applies to project.
****

1.05   JOB CONDITIONS

****
Describe requirements for resilient floor removal. Projects involving removal of friable ceiling and asbestos duct material are not included in this guide.
****

A. The job site is to be clean and cleared of occupants not involved in the abatement procedures.

B. Work area must be secured at all times.

C. A separate exhaust system shall be provided for the abatement area.

D. Temperature shall at no time fall below 55 degrees Fahrenheit. During periods of occupancy temperature shall be maintained at 65 degrees Fahrenheit.

E. All workers shall wear respirators approved for work with asbestos.

F. Portable shower shall be provided for workers.

G. Provide abatement tools required by state and federal agencies.

1.06   GUARANTEE

A. Contractor shall guarantee that the building environment has been made safe for human habitation.

PART 2 PRODUCTS

2.01   MATERIALS

****
Specifier's Note: Supplies required by federal agencies to perform the work may be specified here. If Specifier does not have that information, require that necessary materials be furnished by the Contractor.
****

2.02   MIXES

A. Wet scraping solution to be used in removal of felt backing of adhered sheet flooring shall be mixed on the project site. To one gallon of water add one oz. of liquid dishwashing detergent and one oz. of liquid wallpaper remover. This diluted solution is to be applied in a spray form.

PART 3 EXECUTION

3.01   INSPECTION

A. The area is to remain clean at all times. Asbestos containing material that has been removed from a building surface shall be immediately placed in bags or other EPA-approved containers.

3.02   PREPARATION

A. For the duration of the project the abatement work area shall be isolated from the remainder of the building.

B. Two layers of 6-mil fire-retardant polyethylene sheeting shall be used to seal off all openings, windows, skylights, nonremovable cabinets and equipment.

****
Specifier's Note: 3.04-3.05-3.06 REMOVAL information for three different types of resilient floorcoverings. DELETE nonapplicable floorcovering types.
****

3.03   REMOVAL TOOLS

A. Tools recommended for use:
   1. Heavy-duty wall scraper with 4" (10.16 cm) blade and 6" to 8" (15 to 20 cm) handle.
   2. Impermeable minimum 6-mil-thick polyethylene bags with ties and labels.
   3. Utility or hook knife.
   4. Hand sprayer or sprinkling can.
   5. Hammer.
   6. Commercial type hand-held hot air blower for use in removal of adhesive-adhered tile.
   7. High Efficiency Particulate Air (HEPA) filter vacuum cleaner with disposable dust bag.

3.04   REMOVAL OF NONADHERED SHEET FLOORCOVERINGS

A. Remove binding strips or other restrictive molding from doorways and walls.

B. Cut a strip of sheet flooring 18" (45.7 cm) wide along one wall.

C. Remove strip by gently turning over and rolling face out into a tight roll. Tie or tape securely to prevent unrolling. Repeat this procedure, disposing of each roll immediately in impermeable container large enough to accommodate several rolls. Double bag, tie securely and label.

D. Remove all double-faced tape that may have been used on seams or door openings. Immediately place tape in impermeable bags; tape and label.

3.05   REMOVAL OF ADHERED SHEET FLOORCOVERING

A. Remove any binding strips or other restrictive molding from doorways and walls.

B. Make a series of parallel cuts 4" to 8" (10.1 to 20 cm) apart parallel to a wall.

C. Starting at the end of the room farthest from the entrance door, pry up a corner of the first strip, separating the backing layer.

D. Pull the top layer back on itself slowly and evenly at an angle that permits the best separation of the backing and top layers. Remove this strip, gently turn it over, and roll face out and place in an impermeable container; tie and label.

E. Proceed to remove the next two strips in the same manner.

F. No more than three strips are to be removed prior to the wet scraping removal of the felt fragments that have remained adhered to the floor.

G. Thoroughly spray the felt with a detergent solution. Allow the solution to be completely absorbed by the felt.

H. Remove the felt by wet scraping with a stiff-bladed scraper. The felt shall not be allowed to dry at any time during the scraping process.

I. Larger pieces of felt are to be picked up by hand and immediately placed in an impermeable container.

Figure 8.4 continued

3.06   REMOVAL OF ADHERED TILE FLOORCOVERINGS

A. Begin removal of floor tiles that have a weak floor adhesion. These will normally be found in room areas that have received light foot traffic.

B. Remove tiles by wedging the wall scraper in the seam of two adjoining tiles. A forward pressure and twisting action on the blade should promote tile release.

C. Tiles extremely difficult to remove may require the following procedures:
    1. Apply hammer blows to the scraper handle to remove tiles embedded in hardened or heavily spread adhesive. Slant the scraper handle at a 25- to 30-degree angle to the floor. Protect eyes from possible damage with goggles.
    2. Apply a hot air blower to the tile surface until heat penetrates through the tiles and softens the adhesive.
    3. Scrape the remaining adhesive with a 4" (10.16 cm) blade until a thin, smooth film remains.
    4. Deposit scrapings in an impermeable container.

D. Dispose of the tile immediately as each is removed.

E. Tiles are not to be broken while in the impermeable container.

3.07   FIELD QUALITY CONTROL

A. Site is to be monitored by the Contractor for one year. Air samples shall demonstrate the building is safe for occupancy.

3.08   CLEANUP AND DISPOSAL OF ASBESTOS

A. Cleaning shall take place throughout the removal process. All waste from scrapings and other removal shall immediately be placed in approved containers.

B. Containers shall be marked "CONTAINS ASBESTOS - DISPOSE IN AN APPROVED LANDFILL ONLY."

C. Bags shall not be overloaded.

D. No dry sweeping shall be allowed on the abatement site.

E. Clean all surfaces with water. All scraped areas shall be wet-sponged and kept wet during the cleaning process.

```
***************************************************************
```
Specifier's Note: The following requirement may not be required in every abatement project. Check with EPA or local authorities.
```
***************************************************************
```

F. After completion of wet cleaning apply a single tack coat of penetrating encapsulant. This application shall follow manufacturers' recommendation.

G. Felt shall be removed with HEPA filtered vacuum equipment

H. Operator of vacuum equipment shall stand in vacuumed areas as work proceeds across the floor. Vacuum shall be positioned to prevent discharge air from blowing on the floor area being cleaned.

I. Remove dust bag from vacuum and place in an impermeable container.

J. Workers are to dispose of all contaminated clothing in steel drums and thoroughly wash themselves.

END OF SECTION

*Based in part on information from the Resilient Floor Covering Institute.

Figure 8.5 Specifications for resilient tile. Reproduced with permission of PAGS.

SECTION 09650

RESILIENT FLOORING - TILE

PART 1 GENERAL

1.01 WORK SPECIFIED HEREIN

A. All labor, materials, equipment and services necessary to furnish and install all resilient flooring and related items as indicated or specified.

1.02 SUBSTITUTIONS

A. In accordance with Section 01600.

1.03 SUBMITTALS

A. Submit samples of resilient tile, base, and nosings to Designer for review.

1.04 QUALITY ASSURANCE

A. Manufacturers:

1.05 PRODUCT DELIVERY, STORAGE AND HANDLING

A. Store all materials off the ground under watertight cover and away from sweating walls and other damp surfaces until ready for use. All rooms, subfloors, tiles and adhesives shall be maintained at a minimum temperature of 70 degrees F for at least 48 hours before commencing work. Temperature shall be maintained during installation and for at least 48 hours after completion. Remove damaged or deteriorated material from the premises.

1.06 PROTECTION

A. Protect finished work installed by other trades prior to work under this Section. Any work damaged by workers of this trade shall be replaced without cost to the Owner.

1.07 EXTRA MATERIAL

A. Provide 2 unopened cartons of resilient tile for Owner's future use.

B. Provide 40 lineal feet of resilient base for Owner's future use.

PART 2 PRODUCTS

2.01 MATERIALS

A. Vinyl Asbestos Tile: FS SS-T-312, Type IV, 12" x 12", 1/8" thick. Colors as selected from standard patterns and colors.

B. Rubber Base: Molded rubber cove base (top set) or carpet as manufactured by _____ or approved equal, 4" high x 1/8" thick. Colors as selected from decorator price category. Use matching preformed corners and end-caps.

C. Vinyl Base: Vinyl cove base (top set) or carpet manufacturers as specified above, 4" high x 1/8" thick. Colors as selected from full color range of manufacturer.

D. Flooring Adhesives: As per flooring manufacturer's recommendations.

E. Edging Strips: 1/8" thick, vinyl or rubber, tapered or bullnose edge, color to match tile or as selected from manufacturer's standard colors.

F. Base Adhesive:

G. Underlayment:

H. Molded rubber stair nosings shall be as manufactured by _____. Units to be 1/4" thick, square nose, double lock type, color as selected.

I. Nosing Adhesive:

PART 3 EXECUTION

3.01 PREPARATION

A. Inspect all surfaces to receive tile base and treads and report all defects that will affect the installation. Fill low areas with underlayment. The work under this Section includes filling of all joints, cracks and chips in subfloor with crack filler or underlayment as required to provide a true, even surface to receive tile, and smoothing of walls with underlayment as required to receive cove base. Concrete surfaces to receive tile or base shall be dry, free of paint and oil, and swept clean before work commences. Contractor shall be held responsible for any defects in the subfloor which appear in the flooring surface after completion.

3.02 INSTALLATION

A. After preparation of surfaces, apply adhesive in a thin film and spread evenly with a serrated trowel with notches 1/16" x 1/16", 1/8" apart. Lay tile in a square pattern, without special borders, symmetrical about the axis of the room or space.

B. Direction of graining shall be as directed. Lay out work so that, as far as practicable, no piece of tile shall be less than 5" wide, particularly at doors.

C. All joints shall be tight, in true alignment, and as inconspicuous as possible. Where two colors meet at door openings or where tile terminates at doors to rooms having exposed concrete floors, provide a 1"-wide feature strip directly under the door. Architect shall have the option of selecting different colors in different areas or rooms.

D. Cut and fit tile sufficiently close to walls, columns, etc., so that joint will be covered by the base, where installed. At other fixed surfaces, including thresholds, pipes, removable covers, floor outlets and permanent built-in cabinets and equipment, scribe and accurately fit tile as required. Provide tile inserts at removable floor outlet covers. Remove excess adhesive from all surfaces immediately. Seal joints at pipes with waterproof cement.

E. Provide underlayment as required to bring resilient tile surface to the same level as abutting ceramic tile, or other flooring.

F. Install rubber stair nosings per manufacturer's instructions.

3.03 BASE

A. After preparation of wall surfaces, apply adhesive to back of base, leaving top 1/4" free of adhesive. Press base firmly against the walls sliding horizontally into place, making sure toe is tight to the floor and against the wall. Roll the entire surface of the base with a hand roller, and press the top of the base against the wall with a straightedge. Remove excess adhesive immediately. Install preformed corners at all outside corners. Cope at internal corners. Where base terminates at projections install end-caps.

3.04 CLEANING AND WAXING

A. Clean floors by a method recommended by the manufacturer of the flooring. Wax the tile after the adhesive has had an opportunity to reach its final, firm set. This period of time shall be at least two days after laying the flooring in the summertime and at least five days after laying the flooring in the heated building in the wintertime.

B. Apply one coat of Carnauba wax to the tile according to the manufacturer's instructions at the rate of at least one gallon of undiluted wax for each 3,000 square feet of tile surface.

C. After the cleaning and waxing operation, polish the floor with an electric polisher to a smooth, even and highly reflective finish. Protect the flooring with heavy paper until acceptance of the work.

END OF SECTION

*Figure 8.6 Proprietary (base bid) specification: resilient
sheet flooring. Reproduced with permission of PAGS.*

SECTION 09665

RESILIENT FLOORING - SHEET

PART 1 GENERAL

1.01 WORK SPECIFIED HEREIN

A. All labor, materials, equipment and services necessary to provide
the sheet resilient flooring and related items as indicated or
specified.

1.02 SUBSTITUTIONS

A. In accordance with Section 01600.

1.03 SUBMITTALS

A. Submit samples of sheet vinyl flooring for review in accordance
with Section 01340.

1.04 PRODUCT DELIVERY, STORAGE AND HANDLING

A. Storage of Materials: Store all materials off the ground under
watertight cover and away from sweating walls and other damp
surfaces until ready for use. Store materials for at least 24
hours before commencing work, at a temperature of at least 70
degrees F. Maintain temperature during installation and for at
least 24 hours after completion. Remove damaged or deteriorated
materials from the premises.

1.05 QUALITY ASSURANCE

A. Installer shall be trained and approved by the manufacturer as
competent in the Perimiflor installation technique including the
use of the "Seam-Master" machine.

1.06 GUARANTEE

A. Guarantee in writing that seams will not separate.

1.07 EXTRA MATERIAL

A. Deliver to the Owner leftover remnants of sheet vinyl for use in
future repairs to the floor.

PART 2 PRODUCTS

2.01 MATERIALS

A. Manufacturer: Armstrong

B. Pattern:

C. Color:

D. Gauge: .090

E. Backing: Hydrocord

F. Grade: Perfects

G. Adhesive: Perimiflor adhesive S-200

H. Underlayment: S-235 Latex filler

PART 3 EXECUTION

3.01 PREPARATION

A. Inspect all surfaces to receive sheet vinyl and report all defects
that will affect the installation. Fill low areas with
underlayment. The scope of this Section includes filling of all
joints, cracks and chips in subfloor with crack filler or
underlayment as required to provide a true, even surface to
receive sheet vinyl. Concrete surfaces shall be dry, free of
paint and oil, and swept clean before work commences. Contractor
shall be held responsible for any defects in the subfloor which
appear in the flooring surface after completion.

3.02 INSTALLATION

A. Prime the floors for permanent adhesion in accordance with the
directions of the manufacturer of the floorcovering. Subfloor
shall be completely dry before application of adhesive. Make
moisture tests in accordance with flooring manufacturer's
recommendations. Install sheet vinyl flooring by the Perimiflor
system. Cut seams with "Seam-Master" electric cutting tool. Bond
the seams and perimeter of all sheets to the subfloor with a 4" to
6" band of adhesive, and roll a band of cement into all seam edges.
Remove excess adhesive from the surface before it has set, in
accordance with the manufacturer's instructions. Where indicated,
cove material to form integral base. Terminate with J trim.

3.03 CLEANING

A. Clean floors by a method recommended by the manufacturer of the
flooring. Seal the sheet vinyl floors and base with two coats of
Armstrong C-460 Polymeric Sealer in accordance with manufacturer's
recommendations. After the cleaning operation, the flooring shall
be protected with heavy paper until acceptance of the work.

3.04 PROTECTION

A. Protect finished work installed by other trades prior to work
under this section. Any work damaged by workers of this trade
shall be replaced without cost to the Owner.

END OF SECTION

Figure 8.7 Specifications for marble floors. Reproduced with permission of the Construction Specifications Institute.

SECTION 09615

MARBLE FLOORS

PART 1 GENERAL

1.01   WORK INCLUDED

A. Marble tile floor.

B. Thinset mortar setting bed or thinset adhesive.

C. Thresholds.

1.02   QUALITY ASSURANCE

A. References:
ANSI/TCA A108.3 - Quarry Tile and Paver Tile Installed with
Portland Cement Mortar.

ANSI/TCA A108.5 - Ceramic Tile Installed with Dry-Set Portland
Cement Mortar or Latex Portland Cement Mortar.

ANSI/TCA A108.6 - Ceramic Tile Installed with Chemical Resistant,
Water-Cleanable Tile-Setting and Grouting Epoxy.

ANSI/TCA A118.1 - Dry-Set Portland Cement Mortar.

ANSI/TCA A118.3 - Chemical-Resistant, Water-Cleanable Tile-Setting
and Grouting Epoxy.

ANSI/TCA A118.4 - Latex-Portland Cement Mortar.

ANSI/TCA A136.1 - Organic Adhesives for Installation of Ceramic
Tile, Type 1 and Type 2.

ASTM C615 - Granite Building Stone.

B. Fabricator: Company specializing in stone floor installation shall
have minimum [_____] years documented experience.

1.03   SUBMITTALS

****
Specifier Note: If drawings adequately describe the products of
this section or if this is written as a proprietary specification,
do not request submittals. Review of submittals increases
possibility of unintended variance from the drawings.
****

A. Submit shop drawings illustrating layout and important dimensions
for Interior Designer approval.

B. Submit product data containing specifications, safety factors, and
suggested installation.

C. Submit two _____ samples _____ x _____ and _____ x _____ in
size illustrating color, color range, veining typical of stone.
Samples to be supplied in specified finish texture.

D. Submit samples of mortar colors.

E. Submit maintenance data and recommended cleaning methods. Include
stain-removal, polish and wax information.

1.04   DELIVERY, STORAGE and HANDLING

A. Accept packaged stone materials on site and inspect from damage.
Protect stone from stains prior to installation sealing process.

B. Protect mortar from moisture.

1.05   SITE CONDITIONS

A. Job environment maintained at a minimum 50° F (10° C) prior to,
during and 48 hours after installation.

1.06   EXTRA MATERIAL

A. Provide Owner with 5 percent of total marble provided or 20 tiles
of each stone and color used.

PART 2 PRODUCTS

2.01   STONE FABRICATORS

A. [_____]

B. [_____]

C. [_____]

2.02   STONE MATERIALS

A. Marble: ASTM C503, Classification [I - Calcite] or [II -
Dolomite]; [III - Serpentine]; [IV - Travertine] with [filled]
[unfilled] surface.

****
Specifier Note: If selecting travertine indicate filled or
unfilled.
****

2.03   ADHESIVE MANUFACTURERS

A. [_____] Product [_____]

B. [_____] Product [_____]

C. [_____] Product [_____]

2.04   ADHESIVE MATERIALS

A. Organic Adhesive [ANSI A 136.1, Type [1] [2]]

[_____] thinset bond type.

*********** OR ***********

A. Epoxy Adhesive [ANSI A 118.3, 1] [ANSI A 108.6]

[_____] thinset type.

2.05   MORTAR AND GROUT MANUFACTURERS

A. [_____] Product [_____]

B. [_____] Product [_____]

C. [_____] Product [_____]

2.06   MORTAR MATERIALS

A. Materials: [ANSI/TCA A118.1] [ANSI/TCA A118.3] [_____],
portland cement, sand, [latex additive], [_____],
amd water.

B. Color Admixture: [_____] type, [_____] color [as
selected], manufactured by [_____].

2.07   GROUT MATERIALS

A. Grout: Cementitious type; resistant to shrinking.

****** [OR] ******

A. Grout: Cementitious type with latex additive.

B. Color Admixture: [_____] type, [_____] color [as
selected], [_____] manufactured by [_____].

2.08   STONE FABRICATION

A. Cut stone into required sizes and shapes.

B. Flooring: Conform to the following:

Thickness: [_____] inch ([_____] mm).

Unit Shape: [Square]. [Rectangular]. [_____].

Unit Size: [[_____ x _____] inch ([_____ x _____] mm)]. [Variable
from [_____] to [_____] inches ([_____] to [_____] mm)].
[_____.]

C. Base: Conform to the following:

Thickness: [_____] inch ([_____] mm).

Unit Shape: [Square]. [Rectangular]. [_____].

Unit Size: [[_____ x _____] inch ([_____ x _____] mm)]. [_____].

D. Threshold: Conform to the following:

Thickness: [_____] inch ([_____] mm).

Unit Size: [_____] inches ([_____] mm) deep x width of door frame
opening [ ]. [notched for door stop].

E. Stair Treads: Conform to the following:

Thickness: [_____] inch ([_____] mm).

Unit Shape: [Square]. [Rectangular]. [_____].

Unit Size: [[_____ x _____] inch ([_____ x _____] mm)]. [_____].

F. Stair Risers: Conform to the following:

Thickness: [_____] inch ([_____] mm).

Unit Shape: [Square]. [Rectangular]. [_____].

Unit Size: [[_____ x _____] inch ([_____ x _____] mm)]. [_____].

Figure 8.7 continued

PART 3 EXECUTION

3.01   INSPECTION

    A. Verify that surfaces are ready to receive work.

    B. Verify that field measurements are as [shown on (drawings). (shop drawings)]. [instructed by the stone fabricator].

    C. Beginning of installation means acceptance of [existing surfaces]. [substrate].

3.02   PREPARATION

    A. Establish lines, levels, and pattern. Protect from disturbance.

    B. Clean stone prior to installation.

    C. Seal substrate surface cracks with filler. [Level existing substrate surfaces to acceptable flatness tolerances.]

    D. [Apply (sealer) (conditioner) to surfaces as recommended by adhesive manufacturer.]

3.03   INSTALLATION - THINSET METHOD

    A. Install flooring in accordance with stone fabricator's instructions.

        ****
        Include in the following Paragraph the reference number to TCA Handbook (if that option is selected). If more than one number applies to the Work, consider scheduling the numbers and locations in a Schedule at the end of this Section.
        ****

    B. Install adhesive and grout [in accordance with manufacturer's instructions] [to TCA Handbook for Ceramic Tile Installation, Handbook Number (_____)] to achieve bond to full bearing surface of stone unit and to establish joint dimensions.

    C. Place units in [square] [running bond] [herringbone] [ashlar] [_____] pattern.

        ****** [OR] ******

    C. [Lay units to pattern indicated on (shop drawings). (drawings).] [Request tile pattern from the Architect/Engineer.] Do not interrupt tile pattern around openings.

    D. Place minimum half units at edges and interruptions.

    E. [Place thresholds at door and wall openings where floor finish changes to dissimilar material.]

        ****
        When specifying dissimilar unit sizes, indicate how joint patterns and sizes are to align or form a pattern.
        ****

    F. Cut and fit units tight to penetrations. Form corners [and bases] neatly. [Align floor, base (and wall) joints.]

    G. Maintain uniform joint width of [1/4] [___] inch ([6] [___] mm). Maintain unit joints uniform in width, subject to variance in tolerance allowed in unit size. Rake out joints 1/4 to 3/8 inch (6 to 9 mm) and fill with pointing mortar. Pack and work into voids. Neatly tool surface to [concave] [flush] joint.

        ****** [OR] ******

    G. Place units tight without joint.

    H. Sound units after setting. Replace hollow sounding units.

    I. Allow tile to set for a minumum of [48] [___] hours prior to grouting.

    J. Construct control [and expansion] joints [as detailed] [with joint width of (1/2)(___) inch ([12] [___] mm) by depth of stone unit and setting bed]. [_____]. Caulk joint with sealant, tool to [concave] [flush] joint.

    K. Apply sealant to junction of tile and dissimilar materials and junction of dissimilar plane.

3.04   CLEANING

    A. Clean soiled surfaces with cleaning solution.

    B. Use nonmetallic tools in the cleaning process.

    C. Apply sealer as directed by fabricator.

3.05   PROTECTION OF FINISHED WORK

    A. Protect marble from scratches and staining until occupancy.

    B. Do not permit traffic over unprotected floor.

3.06   SCHEDULE

    A. Provide a schedule of installation locations when more than one type of marble is specified.

        END OF SECTION

Figure 8.8 Specifications for quarry tile. Reproduced with permission of PAGS.

SECTION 09330

QUARRY TILE

PART 1 GENERAL

1.01 WORK SPECIFIED HEREIN

A. All labor, materials, equipment and services necessary to furnish and install all quarry tile as indicated or specified.

1.02 SUBSTITUTIONS

A. In accordance with Section 01600.

1.03 QUALITY ASSURANCE

A. Standards: Materials, preparation and installation shall conform to ANSI standards as listed and the detailed installation instructions of the material manufacturer insofar as applicable.

1. Installation of quarry tile with water-resistant organic adhesives -- ANSI A-108.4.
2. Installation of quarry tile with portland cement mortar -- ANSI A-108.1.
3. Installation of quarry tile with dry-set portland cement mortar or latex portland cement mortar -- ANSI A-108.5.

B. Acceptable manufacturers of quarry tile are:

[_____]

[_____]

1.04 SUBMITTALS

A. Submit samples in accordance with Section 01340 for all work under this section. Submit samples of all materials specified herein of the size specified.

B. Furnish master grade certificate for all tile, before installation, bearing the certification mark of the TCA, signed by the manufacturer stating the type and quality of the material.

C. Furnish manufacturer's printed instructions for use of latex portland cement and mortar.

D. Extra stock: Provide 2 cartons of quarry tile for Owner's future use.

1.05 PRODUCT DELIVERY, STORAGE, AND HANDLING

A. Deliver tile to the job in unopened cartons sealed with a grade seal bearing name of manufacturer and the words "Standard Grade" printed thereon.

B. Manufactured mortars and grouts shall contain hallmark certifying compliance with referenced standards and be types recommended by tile manufacturer for specific applications.

C. Adhesives shall be in containers labeled with hallmark certifying compliance with referenced standards.

D. Organic adhesive containers to bear hallmark of either adhesive and sealant council or TCA certifying compliance with ANSI 1-136.1.

E. Deliver mastic grout ready for use.

F. Deliver dry-set mortar in sealed, moistureproof containers.

G. Store materials under cover in manner to prevent damage or contamination.

1.06 JOB CONDITIONS

A. Set and grout tile in portland cement mortar when ambient temperature is at least 50° F and rising.

B. Comply with minimum temperature recommendations of manufacturer's for bonding and grouting materials in other than portland cement mortar.

C. Protect adjoining work surfaces before tile work begins.

PART 2 PRODUCTS

2.01 MATERIALS

A. All tile shall be of domestic manufacture, standard grade meeting the requirements of SPR R-61 of the U.S. Department of Commerce and shall comply with ANS A-137.1. TCA certification mark shall appear on each carton label.

B. Quarry tile shall be color as selected. Size of tiles shall be 6" x 6" x ½". Base shall be 5" high, covered with bull-nose top. Where shown, furnish tile with abrasive grain surface.

C. Grout material shall be hydroment, color as selected.

D. Portland cement shall conform to ASTM C-150, Type I.

E. Sand shall conform to ASTM C-144.

F. Mortar shall be one part portland cement, 6 parts damp sand by volume.

G. Bond coat shall be portland cement paste on a plastic bed, or dry-set mortar on a cured bed or latex portland cement mortar on a cured bed.

H. Latex portland cement mortar shall conform to ANSI A-118.4.

I. Dry-set mortar shall conform to ANSI A-118.1.

J. Organic adhesive shall be floor type conforming to ANSI A-136.1.

K. Expansion Joints:

L. Sealant: Two component complying with FS TT-S-0227; Type II for joints in vertical surfaces; Type I for joints in horizontal surfaces.

M. Back-up: Flexible and compressible type of closed-cell foam polyethylene or butyl rubber, rounded at surface to contact sealant, as shown in TCA details, and as recommended by sealant manufacturer. It shall fit neatly into the joint without compacting and to such a height to allow a sealant depth of ½ the width of the joint. Sealant shall not bond to the back-up material.

PART 3 EXECUTION

3.01 INSTALLATION

A. Install all quarry tile in portland cement mortar in accordance with ANS A-108.1, and TCA Method F-112-78.

B. Install all quarry tile using water-resistant organic adhesives in accordance with ANS A-108.4 and TCA Method F-116-78.

C. Install all quarry tile in dry-set mortar or latex portland cement mortar in accordance with ANS A-108.5 and TCA Method F-113.78.

D. These specifications, insofar as any portions are applicable, are hereby made a direct part of this specification as though repeated herein.

E. Lay out floors so that no tile less than one-half size occurs. Align all joints in both directions.

F. Grout tile joints flush with face of tiles making a neatly finished, smooth surface. Install specified grout in strict accordance with manufacturer's printed instructions.

3.02 EXPANSION JOINTS

A. Provide expansion joints in all ceramic tile surfaces in accordance with TCA Method EJ-411-78.

B. Expansion joint width shall be 1/4" minimum. Joints through tile and mortar directly over structural joints in the backing must be at least the width of the structural joint.

3.03 PREPARATION

A. Tile edges to which the sealant will bond must be clean and dry. Sand or grind as necessary to obtain optimum sealant bond.

B. Prime tile edges when recommended by the sealant manufacturer. Take care to keep primer off tile faces.

3.04 INSTALLATION

A. Set back-up when mortar is placed or utilize removable wood strip to provide space for backup after mortar has cured.

B. Install sealant after tilework and grout are dry. Follow sealant manufacturer's recommendations.

3.05 CLEANING AND PROTECTION

A. Clean tile after grouting and protect from other trades. Cure all quarry tile floors for a minimum of 3 days.

END OF SECTION

Figure 8.9 Specifications for brick flooring. Reproduced with permission of Henningson, Durham, and Richardson, Phoenix, AZ.

SECTION 09630

BRICK FLOORING

PART 1 GENERAL

1.01   WORK INCLUDED

A. The Contractor shall furnish all labor, materials, tools, equipment, and perform all work and services for all interior brick flooring as shown on drawings and as specified, in accordance with provisions of the Contract Documents, and completely coordinated with work of all other trades.

B. Although such work is not specifically indicated, furnish and install all supplementary or miscellaneous items, appurtenances and devices incidental to or necessary for a sound, secure and complete installation.

****
Specifier: Delete or modify as necessary.
****

1.02   QUALITY STANDARDS

A. ASTM C-62 and C-216 for brick.

B. ANSI and TCA standards for setting and grouting.

C. Other manufacturers desiring approval comply with Section 01640.

1.03   SUBMITTALS

A. Brick samples for color selection.

B. Test reports verifying compliance with ASTM standards.

1.04   PRODUCT DELIVERY, STORAGE AND HANDLING

A. Deliver to site on covered pallets.

B. Store cementitious materials protected from wetting.

1.05   JOB CONDITIONS

A. Verify suitability of substrate to accept installation.

B. Installation of materials constitutes acceptance of substrate and responsibility for performance.

PART 2 PRODUCTS

2.01   MATERIALS

A. Brick Pavers: Comply with ASTM C-62 grade SW for all physical properties. In addition, units to comply with ASTM C-216, Type FBS regarding appearance.

****
Specifier: Insert type, size.
****

B. Colors and finishes as selected by designer.

C. Setting Adhesives: Thinset mortar or adhesive by UPCO or other TCA licensed manufacturer.

D. Grout: Premixed water-resistant type for grouting of brick pavers, by UPCO or other TCA licensed manufacturer. Grout color as selected.

E. Sealant: Gungrade or self-leveling polyurethane, minimum shore A Durometer of 40. Color as selected.

F. Surface Sealer: (Specifier selection).

PART 3 EXECUTION

3.01   INSTALLATION

A. Install in accord with ANSI and TCA recommendations. Cut and drill without marring surfaces. Grind, cut and joint carefully around or against trim or penetrations. Lay so fields or patterns center in areas. Avoid pieces smaller than ½ brick. Install with caulked joints not over 20 ft (6 m) o.c.

B. Clean surfaces as required to remove materials which will adversely affect installation. Fill depressions, cracks or holes with latex mortar or grout.

C. Mix mortar or adhesive in accord with manufacturer's instruction. Spread skim coating and comb with notched trowel. Coat paver backs with mortar or adhesive. Set into place and tap to assure adhesion. Set with nominal ¼ inch (6 mm) joints.

D. Force grout between units to assure complete filling of joints. Remove surplus grout and leave faces clean.

3.02   SEALING

A. Provide sealant joints where pavers abut vertical surfaces and over substrate expansion or control joints. Apply surface sealer.

3.03   PROTECTION

A. Protect with taped-in-place polyethylene.

B. Provide additional protection where traffic may damage pavers.

3.04   FINAL CLEANING

A. Remove protective coverings and rubbish. Clean entire surface. Protect adjacent surfaces from damage due to cleaning operations.

B. Leave installation clean. Do not wax.

END OF SECTION

INTERIOR WALL FINISHES

Most building codes classify interior finishes as the materials used on the surface of walls, partitions, or ceilings. This chapter will survey the finishes most commonly specified by the designer, such as pliant wallcoverings and surface coating systems.

PLIANT WALLCOVERINGS

Pliant wallcoverings are flexible materials such as papers, vinyls, foils, fabric, felt, cork, carpet, and thin wood veneers. Table 9.1 provides a summary of these finishes, their recommended use, their advantages, and their disadvantages.

Vinyl wallcoverings are designed for extreme serviceability and durability and are therefore frequently specified for commercial and institutional interiors. Vinyl wallcoverings are rated for flammability both by the Underwriters Laboratories and by other testing agencies. The ASTM E-84 Steiner Tunnel Test is used to determine the flame-spread and smoke-development factors. Other performance criteria have been established by federal specifications and a voluntary standard.

1. *Federal Specification CCC-W-408A* establishes minimum performance requirements and classifies these coverings into three types:
   a. Type I: Light duty with a total weight of 7 oz/sq yd (minimum 5 oz face coating weight).
   b. Type II: Medium duty with total weights of 13 oz/sq yd (minimum 7 oz face coating weight).
   c. Type III: Heavy duty with a total weight of 22 oz/sq yd (minimum 12 oz face coating weight).

   These three types are further classified:
   d. Class 1: Regular support backing not normally treated to prevent mildew.
   e. Class 2: Mildew resistant.

      Most vinyl-coated products are manufactured with mildew-resistant backings (class 2). This federal specification also establishes criteria for (1) abrasion resistance, (2) crocking, (3) colorfastness, (4) cold cracking, (5) heat aging, and (6) hydrostatic resistance and shrinkage.

2. *Federal Specification CC-T-191b* establishes requirements for abrasion, break and tear strength, and adhesion of the backing.

3. *ASTM Standard D-1308, Standard Method for Test for Effect of Household Chemicals on Clear and Pigmented Organic Finishes.*

4. *ASTM Standard D-751, Standard Methods of Testing Coated Fabrics.*

5. *CCFA-W-101-A, Quality Standard for Vinyl-Coated Fabric Wallcovering.* The voluntary standard developed by the Chemical Fabrics and Film Association establishes three types of wallcovering based on low, medium, and heavy wear. A series of specific physical criteria shown in Table 9.2 serve as the basis for the Types I, II, and III. Table 9.3 lists the test methods. This standard also establishes two classes of fabric wallcoverings based on the ASTM E 84:
   Class A: Flame spread index 0–25 inclusive. Smoke development 0–50 inclusive.
   Class B: Flame spread index 26–75 inclusive. Smoke development 0–100 inclusive.

6. *Voluntary Standard CFFA-W-101A,* developed in 1984 by the Chemical Fabrics and Film Association, establishes a nationally recognized performance criteria for all wallcovering. Recognizing that certain wallcoverings are designed primarily for decorative effects, while others are designed to achieve a high degree of serviceability, the six proposed classes are based on serviceability and performance in the following areas:

Colorfastness	Tear resistance
Washability	Block resistance
Scrubability	Coating adhesion
Stain resistance	Cold cracking resistance
Crocking resistance	Heat aging resistance
Abrasion resistance	Shrinkage
Breaking strength	

Table 9.2 lists the performance criteria for each. Table 9.3 lists the test methods used in CFFA-W-101A (1984). The current

TABLE 9.1 PLIANT WALLCOVERINGS

Covering	Use	Advantages	Disadvantages
Paper	Decorative	Many different patterns and colors. Moderate cost.	Subject to soiling, abrasion and fading. No flammability criteria.
Vinyl	Light, medium or heavy	Can be cleaned, resistant to fading, abrasion and tested for flammability. Many textures available.	No major disadvantages. Installation cost varies according to surface preparation.
Foils	Decorative	Add high reflectance levels, unusual decorative effects.	May create glare in certain areas. Conductor of electricity. Surface subject to abrasion and scratches; expensive installation costs.
Fabric	Decorative	Available in wide sizes and unlimited lengths. Can be installed over wide range of surfaces. Moderate cost.	Must be treated for soil resistance, may require extra backing.
Felt	Decorative, acoustic	Large widths available. Good for acoustic control.	Must be backed with paper. Tends to fade and difficult to spot clean.
Wood veneers	Moderate, heavy	Fire resistant, may be finished on site to desired finish, easy maintenance.	Expensive, special installation requirements.

TABLE 9.2 PHYSICAL TEST REQUIREMENTS

	Type I	Type II	Type III
Total wt., oz/yd^2 (kg/m^2), min.	7 (0.237)	13 (0.442)	22 (.748)
Coating wt., oz/yd^2 (kg/m^2), min.	5 (0.170)	7 (0.237)	12 (0.407)
Breaking Strength, Pounds Newtons Min.			
Machine Direction	40 (178)	50 (222)	100 (445)
Cross Machine Direction	30 (133)	55 (245)	95 (423)
Tearing Strength, Scale Reading Min.			
Machine Direction	14	25	50
Cross Machine Direction	12	25	50
Coating Adhesion, Pounds for 2″ Width, (Newtons for 5 cm Width)	4 (17.8)	6 (26.7)	6 (26.7)
Abrasion Resistance	Note 1	Note 2	Note 3
Colorfastness to Light	Note 4	Note 4	Note 4
Blocking, Scale Rating Max.	2	2	2
Crocking, Scale Rating Min.	Good	Good	Good
Cold-Cracking Resistance	Note 5	Note 5	Note 5
Heat-Aging Resistance	Note 6	Note 6	Note 6
Shrinkage, Percent Max.			
Machine Direction	2.0	2.0	2.0
Cross Machine Direction	1.0	1.0	1.5
Stain Resistance	Note 7	Note 7	Note 7

Note 1: Supporting material shall not be exposed after 200 double rubs.
Note 2: Supporting material shall not be exposed after 300 double rubs.
Note 3: Supporting material shall not be exposed after 1,000 double rubs.
Note 4: There shall be no change in color or shade, discoloration, exudation, development of tackiness, or stiffness.
Note 5: There shall be no evidence of cracking or flaking.
Note 6: Shall not become stiff, brittle, discolored, or show loss of grain.
Note 7: Shall show no appreciable effect of staining.

TABLE 9.3 TEST METHODS

Test	Test Method
Total Weight	Federal Standard No. 191b, Method 5041
Coating Weight	Paragraph 7.1.1
Breaking Strength	ASTM D-751, Grab Method
Tear Strength (1)	ASTM D-751. Pendulum Impulse Method
Coating Adhesion	ASTM D-751
Abrasion Resistance (2)	Federal Standard No. 191b, Method 5304
Colorfastness to Light (3)	Federal Standard No. 191b, Method 5660
Blocking	Federal Standard No. 191b, Method 5872
Crocking	Federal Standard No. 191b, Method 5651-b
Cold-Cracking Resistance	Paragraph 7.1.2
Heat-Aging Resistance (4)	Federal Standard No. 191b, Method 5850
Shrinkage	Paragraph 7.1.3
Stain Resistance (5)	ASTM D-1308b

Note 1. Type I to be tested without the augmenting weight. Type II and Type III to be tested with the augmenting weight.
Note 2. Use #220 grit. Pressure to be 3 pounds, tension to be 6 pounds.
Note 3. Exposure to be 200 hours.
Note 4. Exposure conditions to be 158° F ± 3° F (70° ± 2° C) for seven days.
Note 5. Test period to be 24 hours. Each of the following reagents shall be included:

Distilled water, 1 mL	Detergent solution, 1 mL (mild)
Ethyl alcohol, 1 mL (50 volume %)	Pure orange juice, 1 mL
Acetic acid, 1 mL (5% solution)	Butter, 1 mg
Alkali solution, 1 mL (1% sodium hydroxide)	Catsup, 1 g
Soap solution, 1 mL	Tea, 1 mL

Water, anhydrous isopropyl alcohol, or mild detergent may be used to wipe the spot before examining for staining.

TABLE 9.4 WALLCOVERING INSTALLATION PROCEDURES

Covering	Sizes	Adhesives	Seams	Surface Preparation and Installation
Papers	18-27″ wide. Single or double roll 30-36 sq ft per roll.	Wheat paste or cellulose paste. Apply to paper back	Butted or wired	Clean and smooth surface. Wash to prevent bacteria growth after paper application. Apply with soft, wide brush working from center of panel outward. Matching patterns should be cut from alternating rolls.
Vinyls	54″ wide by 30 yd in length. 405 sq ft per bolt.	Apply paste to fabric back	Overlap and double cut	Prime and seal all surfaces. Apply panels in exact order as cut from roll, using rolls in consecutive order. Use stiff bristle brush or flexible broad knife to eliminate air pockets. Wrap covering 6 in. beyond outside corners and 3 in. at inside corners.
Foils	18-27″ wide. Double and triple rolls.	Premixed vinyls with low water content. Apply to wall	Butted smooth with oval seam roller	Wall surfaces must be painted with oil base enamel undercoat or wall primer. Prewash walls to remove bacteria. Surface must be very smooth. Apply with soft brush. Work from center out to edges. Puncture air bubbles and press down immediately. Wash finished panels with warm, clean water and soft cloth to avoid scratching. Avoid contact with electrical sources. When matching random patterns, reverse every other strip.
Fabric	36-54″ any length. Sold by yard.	Wheat or cellulose. Apply paste to wall	Butted or wired	Clean and smooth surface. Apply antibacteria primer. Staple fabric along top as hanging to handle weight of wet fabric. Staples may be removed later. If not paper backed, do not stretch too tightly or pull out of shape. Use same corner installation as vinyl.
Felt	54-72″ wide. Sold by yard.	Wheat paste applied to wall	Butted or wired	Felt should be paper backed for later removal. Wall should be clean and smooth and washed with antibacteria solution. Apply nap in same direction. Do not overstretch when applying.
Cork	Up to 36″ wide. 36-45 ft lengths.	Wheat or vinyl	Butted	Clean and smooth surface. May require lining paper. Cork does not require matching. Follow manufacturers' installation recommendations.
Wood veneer	10-24″ wide, up to 12 ft long.	Recommended by material supplier	Butted	Follow manufacturers' recommendations. Wood may be pre-finished or finished on site. Temperature control usually necessary prior to and during installation.

classification method that is based on federal specification CC-W-408 (types I, II, and III).

Vinyl Wallcovering Backing Support Materials

The backing used on vinyl wallcoverings is a major factor to consider when strength and dimensional stability are important criteria.

1. *Type I: Woven Backings (scrim).* Contains a weight ranging from 1.3 to 1.6 ounces (36.8 g to 45.3 g) per square yard. Recommended for use in areas of low traffic where minimum strength is required. This would include homes and apartments.

2. *Type II: Osnaburg.* For normal traffic areas and abrasion areas such as office corridors. New polyester cotton osnaburg of 2.5 ounces (70.87 g) per square yard results in increased strength without added production cost.

3. *Types II and III: Polyester Cotton Drill.* Polyester cotton drill of 3.6 oz. (102.06 g) per square yard provides a very strong backing for heavy-duty installation such as hospital and nursing home corridors. These areas often receive damage from food carts, beds, and wheel chairs.

4. *Nonwoven Backings.* The use of new or second-generation substrates, including spun bonded polyester, has maintained the desirable quality of fabric backings while producing greater strength-to-weight ratios. In addition, these synthetic blends can have lower production costs.

Installation

Important considerations in the installation of wallcoverings involve the following factors:

1. Type and condition of wall surface

2. Type of adhesive

3. Environmental conditions

4. Installation procedures
    Seams
    Adhesive application
    Panel sequence

Table 9.4 provides information on wall preparation, types of adhesives, installation procedures, and recommended seams. Figure 9.1 illustrates the three types of seams most frequently used. The lapped seam is commonly used for vinyl wallcoverings and is double cut through both thicknesses, leaving a perfectly fitted seam. The exact procedure is described in the wallcovering specification guide (PAGS),[1] which is given later in this chapter in Figure 9.2. This specification guide also provides the designer with information on all areas of concern that should be included in a vinyl wallcovering specification.

Specification for other types of wallcoverings should follow this general guide. Designers may also require that the contractor install test panels (at least three) that can serve as a standard of required quality for the remainder of the work. Estimates and specifications should also include instructions about providing extra rolls or bolts of wallcovering for the owner's use in the event that repairs are required.

Estimation

The formula for estimating the quantity of wallcovering material needed for a given project is based on the number of square feet on the roll. Many wallcoverings are packaged in single rolls of 36 sq ft (3.4 sq m) or double rolls of 72 sq ft (6.7 sq m).

Measurements of the interior space are made in feet, noting

Figure 9.1 Wallcovering seams

the number of windows, doors, and other major architectural features, such as bookcases. For example, in estimating the wallcovering needed for a 12′ × 12′ (3.6 × 3.6 m) room with 8-ft (2.4-m) ceilings, two windows, and a door, proceed in this manner:

1. Measure the length of each wall and total.

$$12' + 12' + 12' + 12' = 48'$$

2. Multiply the distance around the room by the ceiling height to determine the total number of square feet.

$$48' \times 8' = 384 \text{ sq ft}$$

3. Allow a 20 percent margin for waste.

$$384 \text{ sq ft} + 20\% = 460.8 \text{ sq ft}$$

4. Calculate the actual areas for doors, windows, and other architectural features. Allow 15 ft as an average size per door and for every two windows.

$$2 \times 15 \text{ sq ft} = 30 \text{ sq ft}$$

5. Subtract the area for doors, windows, and other architectural features.

$$460.8 \text{ sq ft} - 30 \text{ sq ft} = 430.8 \text{ sq ft}$$

This last figure represents the total number of square feet of wallcovering that is required to complete the space, and from it the number of rolls of wallcovering that will be needed can be determined.

If the selected wallcovering is packaged in standard rolls containing 36 sq ft:

$$430.8 \div 36 \text{ sq ft/roll} = 11.97, \text{ or } 12 \text{ single rolls}$$

The amount needed would be 12 single rolls, or 6 double rolls. In the event that the wallcovering is packaged in rolls containing 30 sq ft (2.8 sq m), the project would require more wallcovering.

$$430.8 \div 30 \text{ sq ft/roll} = 14.4, \text{ or } 15 \text{ single rolls}$$

In this case the project would require 15 single rolls, or 7 double rolls plus 1 single roll.

Designers should remember that non-integers should always be increased to the next highest whole number. If the wallcovering is only packaged in double rolls, the figures may have to be increased to the next highest even number; i.e., 6.4 rolls would be increased to 8 double rolls.[2]

Vinyl Wallcovering. Because commercial vinyls are packaged in 30-yd (28-m) bolts, which range from 52 to 54 in. (132.1 to 137.2 cm) in width, the estimation may be made in square feet, linear feet, or yards. The most common method used to calculate yardage is explained below in regard to fabric wallcoverings, but if the designer wishes to make the calculation in square feet, the square footage of a bolt can be determined in the following manner:

$$13.5 \text{ sq ft/yd} \times 30 \text{ yd} = 405 \text{ sq ft/bolt}$$

Using the same square footage requirements from the previous problem:

$$430.8 \div 405 \text{ sq ft/bolt} = 1.06 \text{ bolts, or 2 bolts}$$

See the specifications for vinyl wallcovering in Figure 9.2 on page 139 for more details.

Fabric Wallcovering. Estimating the fabric yardage for wallcoverings involves the following procedures:

1. Measure the width of each wall in feet and transpose to inches.

2. Number of widths = wall width (inches) ÷ width of fabric (inches)

3. Length of panels = height of wall (inches) + 3 in. for adjustment

4. Inches of fabric needed = length of panel × number of panels

5. Total yards needed = inches of fabric needed ÷ 36 in.

For example, if fabric was to be applied to one wall of a foyer and the wall was 18 ft wide and 9 ft tall, the designer should determine the number of fabric widths (48 in. wide) needed to cover the wall. After transposing the wall width to inches (18 ft = 216 in.), proceed in this manner:

$$216 \div 48'' = 4.5 \text{ widths of fabric, or 5 widths}$$

The length of each panel or width is determined by transposing the wall height to inches and adding the needed 3 in. for adjustment.

$$9' = 108'' + 3'' = 111''$$

To calculate the total inches of fabric required:

$$111'' \times 5 \text{ (widths)} = 555''$$

To transpose the inches into the required yardage, simply divide by 36 in.

$$555'' \div 36'' = 15.41 \text{ or 16 yd}$$

If the fabric had a pattern, the length of the repeat would have to be considered because this would increase the required yardage. Methods of calculating pattern repeats are discussed in Chapter Ten.

Designer Installation Checklist

After Material Delivery to Project Site

1. Inspect in order to determine that all painting and other work has been completed prior to installation of interior wallcovering.

2. Verify that the delivered wallcovering material is the pattern and colors ordered. Material should be in the original containers with seals unbroken and labels intact.

3. Adhesives delivered to site should comply with those specified.

4. Adequate storage should be provided in a dry area with temperatures above 40°F

5. Wallcovering bolts must be stored flat.

6. Verify that walls to receive material are properly prepared. Cracks, seams, holes, and rough spots must be sanded or filled.

7. Drywall or plaster walls must be cured and free from moisture.

During Installation

1. Repeat patterns must be matched.

2. Verify that all seams are plum and are not closer than 6 inches from the outside corners.

3. Verify that contractor has not overlooked cutouts for all electrical outlets.

4. Verify that wallcoverings are being installed on the walls indicated on your schedule.

After Installation

1. Confirm that finished wall surfaces are smooth and free from wrinkles and air bubbles and that all seams are flat and secure.

2. Check all baseboards and door and window frames for remaining adhesive or damage.

3. Check that all smudges and finger marks have been removed from the surface of the wallcovering.

4. Verify that extra wallcovering has been retained for the owner.

Estimating Labor Costs

Labor costs will vary depending on the preinstallation wall preparation that may be required; the complication of the installation, such as openings, projections, or an intricate patterned material; and the total number of square feet involved.

Labor is charged by the square foot. For example, the labor cost may be $.50/sq ft, or $18 per single roll. The labor charges for vinyl and foils are always higher than those for standard wallcovering. Labor for installing wood veneers can run as high as $3 to $4/sq ft because of the meticulous work involved.

The time involved in the installation depends on the project requirements, but it has been estimated, for example, that the experienced paperhanger may reasonably be expected to install about 250 sq ft, or 7 single rolls, per day.

In addition to the materials and labor cost, designers should remember to add an average of 10 to 20 percent overhead on the materials and labor.

Maintenance

Maintenance requirements vary according to the materials used and the abuse received by the wall surfaces. Table 9.5 summarizes recommended maintenance procedures.

Examples of Specification Guides

The PAGS specification guide for vinyl wallcovering (Figure 9.2) may be easily adapted for use by adding or deleting lines.

For example, lines 29 through 30 can state a more specific flammability requirement. If more than one pattern of wallcovering is to be used, lines 51 through 59 can be altered to include further instructions.

Other examples of specifications are provided for cork (Figure 9.3) and flexible wood (Figure 9.4) wallcoverings on page 140.

Drawings Required for Specification Coordination:

1. Interior elevations should indicate wall surfaces to receive vinyl wallcovering. Elevations are important when a portion of the wall area may be finished with another material such as paneling or paint. (See Chapter 15 for types of interior schedules.)

2. Indicate on drawings the substrate material.

3. Show all horizontal and vertical terminal edges.

COATING SYSTEMS

Designers frequently specify paint by color and finish without consideration for the total coating system, i.e., the surface material, surface condition, method of application, curing process, and projected durability under varied use. To understand the complicated selection of paint coating systems, it is necessary to understand the generic classification of interior paint materials and their recommended application.

Coating systems are classified according to the vehicle or binder used to manufacture the coating, or classification can be based on the recommended use and finish provided.

1. *Vehicles and binders* determine the content and consistency of coating systems. Vehicles form the liquid portion of a paint, and binders are the film-forming oils or resins.

2. *Primers* are classified as wall, wood, or masonry-type primers that are applied as a first coat of a paint, varnish, or lacquer system in order to improve the bond of the finish coats.

3. *Finish coats* provide the final protective coating to the surface. The finish is described as gloss, semigloss (eggshell), or flat.

4. *Transparent finishes* provide protection for wood or other surfaces that do not require an opaque finish. Transparent finishes may include varnishes, shellacs, stains, and lacquers.

Table 9.6 to 9.9 provide a survey of the types of coatings and finishes formulated for interior use.

Estimating Coverage Capacity

The coverage capacity of paint is dependent on factors, such as "hiding power," percentage of volume solids, application methods, and type of surface receiving the coating.

Hiding Power. This refers to the ability of the coating system to cover or conceal the previous surface color. Some colors contain pigments that have little hiding power, and designers may have to specify more coats to compensate for this fact. Table 9.10 lists the pigments frequently having low hiding power. The recommended number of coats will depend on the surface texture and may vary when applying a light color over a dark color. Designers should remember that a series of thin coats is much more effective than one thick coat, which may result in improper drying or curing.

TABLE 9.5 WALLCOVERING MAINTENANCE

Material	Recommended Procedures
Papers	Wipe with soft cloth. Do not apply water, which may cause some inks to run.
Vinyls	Ordinary soilage may be removed with mild soap and water. A soft bristle brush may be used to remove soilage from deeply textured surfaces. Do not use abrasive cleaners, steel wool or solvent-type cleaners. In areas of moderate use, a general cleaning of the surface once or twice a year should be sufficient to maintain original condition. Some difficult stains can be removed with rubbing alcohol or naphtha.
Foils	Wipe with very soft cloth. May be washed with warm water. Care should be taken not to scratch the surface.
Fabrics	Should be treated with soil-resistant chemicals prior to installation. Surface may be vacuumed to remove collected dust. Stains may be removed with dry-cleaning fluids or mild soap and water if the fabric is washable.
Felts	May be vacuumed. Do not apply water or any cleaning solutions which may cause spotting or removal of color. Felts may fade if installed near direct source of light.
Carpet	Requires very little maintenance. May be vacuumed to remove collected dust. If stained, use cleaning method recommended by the manufacturer.
Leather	May be polished with paste floor wax. Some stains can be removed by brushing. Do not use water. Follow directions of supplier.
Cork	Should be vacuumed. May be washed with mild soap and water.
Wood veneers	May be polished to maintain luster. Hard paste wax is recommended.

TABLE 9.6 VEHICLE AND BINDER CLASSIFICATION

Vehicles/Binders	Description	Frequent Use
1. Alkyds	This binder is made from oil-modified resins. Good color retention, easy to apply and moderately priced.	Fast-drying enamels. Should not be used on masonry without alkali-resistant primer.
2. Latex emulsions	Made from synthetics that can be varied to produce various degrees of hardness, gloss and flexibility. Odorless, fast drying, easy to apply, blister and peel resistant.	Walls and masonry
3. Urethanes	Plastic binder used to produce hard-wearing varnishes.	Floor surfaces
4. Vinyl	Plasticized copolymers of vinyl chloride and vinyl acetate used for making varnishes. Usually applied with spray process.	Wooden furniture, paneling
5. Epoxy	Used to produce gloss enamels which offer excellent resistance to chemicals.	Brick, wood and metal
6. Oleoresinous	Composed of oils that are modified with various resins. Produce a hard, glossy finish.	Gym floors
7. Phenolic resins	Modified with oils. Produce hard-wearing sealers and varnishes.	Floors

TABLE 9.7   CLASSIFICATION OF INTERIOR PRIMERS

Primer	Description	Frequent Use
Wall Primers		
Latex	Quick drying, offers excellent alkali resistance. Provides for ease of equipment cleaning.	Drywall, brick, metal
Alkyd	Made from odorless alkyd, somewhat slow drying.	May be applied over partially cured plaster and metal.
Alkali	Alkali-resistant content based on butadine-styrene copolymer or chlorinated rubber.	Masonry, but do not use on below grade.
Wood Primers		
Enamel undercoat	Provides a low gloss and hard film which prevents penetration of the enamel paints that may be applied as top coats.	Excellent on surfaces which require smooth finish.
Paste wood fillers	Made from transparent and coarse pigment held together with a binder.	Used on open-grain woods. Provides added color and smoothness.
Clear wood sealer	Transparent pigment often added to reduce penetration and improve sealing.	Often used under clear wood finishes.
Masonry primers		
Cement grout	A thin mortar applied with a brush or trowel.	Used to provide a smooth surface to rough masonry.
Block fillers	Composed of either latex or a solvent-thinned epoxy-ester. Relatively thick and applied with a brush or roller.	May be applied to damp surfaces. Provides resistance to alkali.

TABLE 9.8   CLASSIFICATION OF INTERIOR FINISH COATINGS

Finishes	Descriptions	Frequent Use
Gloss Enamels		
Enamels	Usually alkyd enamels which are very resistant to yellowing and alkaline cleaners.	Brick, wood, particle board, metal, plywood
Floor enamels	Alkyd enamels that are abrasion resistant, but will blister and peel if wet.	Masonry and wooden floors
	Alkali-resistant enamels that are abrasion resistant, but provide poor resistance to solvents.	
	Epoxy or urethane enamels are abrasion resistant, not affected by water or solvents.	
	Latex floor paint provides good abrasion resistance.	
Dry fallout spray gloss	Similar to gloss enamels, but dries very rapidly.	Walls
Semigloss		
Semigloss enamel	Alkyd-based product with good gloss retention, also grease and alkali resistance.	Drywall, brick, wood, particle board, metal, plywood
Semigloss latex	Has moderate hiding power, ease of application and clean-up, rapid cleaning, low odor.	Drywall, plaster, wood, plywood
Dry fallout spray semi-gloss	Provides a moderate gloss level.	Walls and ceilings
Flat Finishes		
Alkyd flat	Superior to latex paints in hiding power and washability. Odorless, but should be used in well-ventilated areas.	Drywall, brick, wood, metal, plywood
Latex flat	Good hiding power, spreadability, odorless. Requires special primers prior to application on porous surfaces. Do not apply during temperature extremes.	Plaster, drywall, brick, masonry

TABLE 9.9 CLASSIFICATION OF TRANSPARENT FINISHES

Finishes	Description	Frequent Use
Varnishes		
Flat or satin	Flatting agent added which makes it less glossy in finish than glossy varnishes. Mar resistance is inferior to gloss varnish.	All types of wood surfaces
Counter or bar varnish	Dries very hard and is resistant to alcohols. Made from polyurethanes and polyesters.	Bar tops
Penetrating sealers	Very thin varnishes that are applied and removed while the surface is still wet. Fair resistance to marring.	All types of open-grained woods
Conversion varnish	Produced with alkyd and urea formaldehyde resins. Has good resistance to abrasion and allows a higher gloss buildup because of its solid content.	
Shellac	Often termed a "wash" coat on wood surfaces before final sanding. Fast drying, light colored, but has a poor resistance to abrasion, water or alcohols.	Wood, plaster, drywall, brick, plywood
Lacquers		
Standard	A coating material with high nitro-cellulose content that is modified with resins and plasticizers. Good durability, but little resistance to chemicals. Dries quickly and is easy to repair. Increases flammability of surfaces.	Wood furniture and paneling
Catalyzed	Superior to standard lacquer in resistance to chemicals.	Wood furniture and paneling
Vinyls		
Catalyzed	This is a clear converting catalyst vinyl coating. Fast drying and highly resistant to abrasion.	Wood furniture and paneling

TABLE 9.10 PIGMENT HIDING POWER

Pigment	Hiding Power	Coats	
		Semigloss	Flat
Gold	Fair	2	2
Yellow	Poor	3	3+
Green	Fair	2	2
Blue	Fair	2	2
Pink	Poor	3	3+
Off-white	Fair	2	2

TABLE 9.11 AVERAGE COAT REQUIREMENTS FOR INTERIOR SURFACES

Woodwork	Oil gloss paint	2-3 coats
	Semigloss paint	2-3 coats
Plaster	Alkyd flat	2-3 coats
Drywall	Alkyd flat	3 coats
	Vinyl latex	3 coats
Masonry	Vinyl latex	3 coats
Wood floor	Enamel	3 coats

Volume Solids. Paints having 100 percent volume solids (no thinners) will cover more surface and provide a thicker film. This film (when dry) is referred to as the "dry film thickness" (DFT) and the measurement is expressed in mils (1/1000 in.). When reference is made to the dry film thickness, the measurement always refers to the total coating system, not the thickness of one coat.

Because federal and industrial specifications frequently require a dry film thickness measurement (usually 5 mils), designers should be familiar with the terminology involved. Manufacturers usually list the amount of volume solids contained in each gallon and provide information on the number of DFT mils that can be obtained from the particular coating system. The mils, however, can vary depending on the amount of square feet that will be covered by the paint. For example, if the paint is 100 percent volume solid, the DFT mils may be listed in this manner:

Coverage per Gallon

1,200 sq ft = 1 mil DFT

600 sq ft = 2 mils DFT

300 sq ft = 4 mils DFT

If the paint is 50 percent volume solid (thinned 50 percent), the mils of dry film thickness will be considerably altered:

Coverage per Gallon

600 sq ft = 1 mil DFT

300 sq ft = 2 mils DFT

In the event that a designer wishes to specify the dry film thickness, the required mils should be specified as the total thickness. For example, if the surface requires a primer, two coats of paint, and a dry film thickness of 5 mils, do not specify $2\frac{1}{2}$ mils per coat. The specification should state "5 mils dry film thickness applied in two coats."

Application Methods and Type of Surface. These also play a large part in estimating the coverage capacity. The spreadability and the coverage can vary considerably among spray, roller, and brush application methods. Rough textures and porous surfaces usually increase the amount of coating material required. Table 9.11 shows some *average* coat requirements for new interior paint work on various types of surfaces.

The spreading capacity of paint is difficult to calculate because of the variances in surfaces and particular products; therefore, manufacturers' specifications regarding the estimated coverage per square foot (per gallon) should be consulted.

Estimating Labor and Material Costs

To determine the labor cost and materials needed, designers should calculate the amount of surface to be covered. Major interior surfaces are measured in the following manner:

Square Feet	Linear Feet
Floors	Trim length
Walls and ceilings	Piping length
Doors (number, kind)	
Windows (do not deduct for glass)	

After the square and linear feet are determined, it is necessary to calculate the labor cost per square foot. The time required to paint 1 sq ft varies, depending on the location of the surface (floor, ceiling, walls) and the intricacy of the work. In addition, surface preparation, such as sanding, sealing, priming, or patching, will add to the total labor cost. Research has shown that the amount of surface that a painter can cover is also affected by the method of application. For example:

Brush = 50–200 sq ft/hr

Roller = 100–300 sq ft/hr

Sprayer = 300–500 sq ft/hr

Table 9.12 shows the *average* labor hours required for the brushwork application (one coat) of various coating systems. These figures should be doubled if two coats are required.

Painting Inspection Checklist

Careful inspection before, during, and after painting application can result in quality control and prevent project delays caused by improper color matching or application.

Upon Delivery

1. Verify that the specified paints (brands) have been delivered and that the containers are properly labeled and undamaged.

2. Check the area designated for paint and materials storage. Be sure that there is adequate ventilation and fire protection equipment in the immediate vicinity. If possible, the paint workshop (mixing or thinning area) should be located outside the main building.

TABLE 9.12 LABOR HOURS REQUIRED FOR BRUSHWORK APPLICATION

Paint	Sq Ft per Hour per Coat
Calcimining (ceilings)	200-250
Enameling	100-150
Flat painting	120-180
Shellacking	120-180
Staining	120-180
Varnishing	120-180
Trim: filling, spackling (given in linear ft)	50-75
Floors, filling, putting	120-180
Floor staining	150-200
Floor shellacking	150-200
Floor varnishing	140-200
Floor waxing	140-200
Floor polishing	100-150
Machine sanding	100-200

Before Application

1. Verify that the areas to be painted are completed and the general area is free from dust-generating conditions; i.e., other workers will not be sawing or creating other sources of dust.

2. Before work proceeds, require that the painting contractor clean, prepare, and paint a sample 5′ × 5′ area that can serve as a standard of performance for the entire job.

3. Clarify and review the color selections and means of application with the contractor.

During Application

1. Inspect each surface prior to the installation of *each* coat. This assures that the proper curing time has been allowed and the surface textures meet specification requirements.

2. Verify that color schedules are being followed; i.e., colors are being applied in designated areas.

3. Verify that temperature and relative humidity are within the limits recommended by the manufacturer.

4. Be sure that surrounding areas, which are not to receive paint, are protected.

After Application

1. Be sure that the cleanup of the painted area includes removal of all empty paint cans, drop cloths, and other equipment.

2. Make certain that touch-up and restoration of areas damaged during the installation or cleanup are competently completed.

3. Check that storage areas are cleared and cleaned.

Drawings and Specifications

Methods of showing finish locations on drawings and schedules are discussed in Chapter 15. Drawings must show the designated areas that are to receive specific colors and finish coats. This information is also contained in the color and finish schedules, which accompany the drawings and are also attached to the written specifications.

The written specifications contain instructions on the following:

1. Storage and protection of equipment, materials, and surfaces

2. Surface preparation

3. Quality assurance

4. Methods of application

5. Color and finish schedules

6. Products or substitutions

7. Cleaning and final inspection

The painting specification guideline in Figure 9.5 on page 141 is general in scope and allows the designer to substitute or provide additional requirements.

Figure 9.2 Specifications for vinyl wallcovering.
Reproduced with permission of PAGS.

SECTION 09950

VINYL WALLCOVERING

PART 1 GENERAL

1.01 WORK SPECIFIED HEREIN

A. All labor, material, equipment and services necessary to provide the vinyl wallcovering and related items as indicated or specified.

1.02 SUBSTITUTIONS

A. In accordance with Section 01600.

1.03 SUBMITTALS

A. Submit samples of each color and type of vinyl wall fabric in accordance with Section 01340. Samples to be one-half yard, full width of mill run of each pattern and color.

B. Submit affidavits certifying that materials provided and installed on the project are exactly as tested.

1.04 QUALITY ASSURANCE

A. Certification. Vinyl fabric and adhesive shall have been tested to provide a UL Class "B" fire hazard classification.

1.05 PRODUCT DELIVERY, STORAGE AND HANDLING

A. Deliver and store all wallcovering in undamaged condition as packaged by the manufacturer, with manufacturer's seals and labels intact. Exercise care to prevent damage during delivery, handling and storage. Store all materials flat in a clean, dry area with maintained temperature above 40° F. Maintain areas to receive wallcovering at a constant temperature of 45° to 50° F for at least 3 days before, and all during, the application period.

PART 2 PRODUCTS

2.01 MATERIALS

A. Vinyl Wallcovering: Manufacturer: L.E. Carpenter Co.

B. Total Weight/Lin. Yd.:
Fabric/Sq. Yard:
Vinyl/Sq. Yd.:
Thickness (Average):
Fuel Contributed:
Smoke Developed:

C. Adhesive: As recommended by the fabric manufacturer, strippable type.

D. Primer: As recommended by the fabric manufacturer.

E. Sealer: As recommended by the fabric manufacturer.

PART 3 EXECUTION

3.01 INSPECTION

A. Surface to receive wallcovering shall meet the minimum requirements established by the wallcovering manufacturer.

B. Gypsum wallboard shall have all fasteners recessed, with all joints and fastener depressions taped and spackled and sanded.

3.02 INSTALLATION

A. Prime and seal substrates per fabric manufacturer's recommendations for the type of substrate to be covered.

B. Follow the adhesive manufacturer's directions for mixing and applying adhesive.

C. Use fabric panels in exact order as they are cut from rolls; use rolls in consecutive order. Apply paste to the fabric back using a roller or paste brush.

D. Hang smooth, nonmatch patterns by pasting strips on the wall, overlapping the edges, and "double-cutting" through both thicknesses. Use a 0.04 or 0.06" zinc or aluminum strip between wall and material when cutting, to avoid gouging the wall.

E. Use stiff-bristled brush or flexible broad knife to eliminate air pockets and to secure the wallcovering to the wall surface.

F. Fill spaces above and below doors and similar areas in sequence from the roll, not later when all full-length pieces have been installed.

G. Remove excess paste from each seam as it is made and before proceeding to next seam. Use sponge dampened with plain warm water, but not wringing wet. Wipe seam clean with dry cloth towel.

H. Examine each seam carefully when completed. Trim additional selvage where required to achieve a color and pattern match at seams.

I. Remove hardware, accessories, plates, and similar items to allow fabric to be installed. Upon completion of each space, replace the above items.

J. Installed fabric shall be secure, smoth, clean, without wrinkles, gaps or overlaps.

K. Wrap wallcovering 6" beyond outside corners and 3" at inside corners. Cutting at corners will not be accepted, nor will horizontal seams be acceptable other than as indicated or required for pattern change.

3.03 PROTECTION

A. Protect finished work installed by other trades prior to work under this Section. Replace any work damaged by workers of this trade without cost to the Owner.

END OF SECTION

Figure 9.3 Specifications for cork wallcovering. Reproduced with permission of Henningson, Durham, and Richardson, Phoenix, AZ.

SECTION 09953

CORK WALLCOVERING

PART 1 GENERAL

1.01   WORK SPECIFIED HEREIN

A. The Contractor shall furnish all labor, materials, tools, equipment, and perform all work and services necessary for all cork wallcovering work as shown on drawings and as specified in accordance with provisions of the Contract Documents, and completely coordinated with work of all other trades.

B. Although such work is not specifically indicated, furnish and install all supplementary or miscellaneous items incidental to or necessary for a sound, secure and complete installation.

C. Materials must have Class A (under 25) flame, fuel, and smoke ratings.

PART 2 ACCEPTABLE MANUFACTURERS (QUALITY STANDARDS)

A. Manufactured by Laminating Services, Inc.

B. Other manufacturers desiring approval comply with Section 01640.

2.01   SUBMITTALS

A. Samples: 12 in. sq. sample of cork.

B. Certificates: Verifying flame-spread rating.

2.02   JOB CONDITIONS

A. Verify acceptability of substrate to accept installation.

B. Install a test section with adhesive to verify compatibility and adhesion.

    ****
    Specifier: Change type and color as required.
    ****

PART 3 MATERIALS

A. Cork: Cordova, No. 409 Eban, laminated to cloth, with acrylic surface coating. Class A flame spread rated.

B. Adhesive: Vin-L-Fab 415 or Pliant Wood 460.

3.01   INSTALLATION

A. In accordance with manufacturers' recommendations.

END OF SECTION

Figure 9.4 Specifications for flexible wood wallcovering. Reproduced with permission of Henningson, Durham, and Richardson, Phoenix, AZ.

SECTION 09960

FLEXIBLE WOOD WALLCOVERING

PART 1 GENERAL

1.01   WORK SPECIFIED HEREIN

A. The Contractor shall furnish all labor, materials, tools, equipment, and perform all work and services for all flexible wood wallcovering as shown on drawings and as specified,in accordance with provisions of the Contract Documents, and completely coordinated with work of all other trades.

B. Although such work is not specifically indicated, furnish and install all supplementary or miscellaneous items, appurtenances and devices incidental to or necessary for a sound, secure and complete installation.

PART 2 ACCEPTABLE MANUFACTURERS

A. Material specified is manufactured by U.S. Plywood.

B. Other manufacturers desiring approval comply with Section 01640.

2.01   SUBMITTALS

A. Samples of materials, with finish, for Designer selection.

B. Shop drawings of blueprint layout of flitch to show pattern and placement around penetrations.

C. U/L certificate of flame spread, certifying Class A rating and fuel and smoke ratings.

2.02   PRODUCT DELIVERY, STORAGE AND HANDLING

A. Deliver in unopened packages, plainly marked with identifying labels. Store and handle to preclude damage.

2.03   JOB CONDITIONS

A. Verify suitability of substrate to accept installation. Installation assumes responsibility for performance.

PART 3 MATERIALS

A. Weld Wood Architectural Flexwood.

B. U/L Class A flame-spread rating. (Specifier: Insert types and locations)

C. Adhesive: U.S. Plywood No. 710.

D. Wall Primer: As recommended by material supplier.

E. Finish Materials: As recommended by material supplier.

3.01   INSTALLATION

A. Prime wall surfaces. Test wall for moisture and smoothness, fill and sand as required.

3.02   FINISHING

A. Sand surface, with grain, using 00 sandpaper.

B. Apply finish to achieve desired finish.

C. After finish is dry, apply paste wax.

D. Protect until acceptance of building.

END OF SECTION

Figure 9.5 Painting specification guidelines. Reproduced with permission of PAGS.

SECTION 09900

PAINTING

PART 1 GENERAL

1.01 WORK SPECIFIED HEREIN

A. All labor, materials, equipment and services necessary to complete all painting and finishing required for surfaces as indicated or specified.

1.02 SUBSTITUTIONS

A. In accordance with Section 01600.

1.03 SUBMITTALS

A. Prepare samples at the job as required until colors are satisfactory. Paint colors will be as specified by the Designer who, before any work is done, will furnish color chips and a schedule showing where the various colors shall go.

B. Before supplying any material to site, the Painting Subcontractor and the paint manufacturer's area representative shall prepare a complete schedule showing the materials proposed to be used for each treatment specified, and submit same to Designer for review/approval.

1.04 PRODUCT DELIVERY, STORAGE AND HANDLING

A. Deliver all paint to site in manufacturer's labeled and sealed containers. Labels shall give manufacturer's name, brand, type, batch number, color of paint and instructions for reducing. Thin only in accordance with printed directions of manufacturer.

B. Store all material used on the job in a single designated space. Such storage place shall be kept clean. Make good any damage to it or to its surroundings. Remove any oily rags, waste, etc., from the building every night and take every precaution to avoid any danger of fire. In no case shall amount of materials stored exceed that permitted by local ordinances, state laws, or fire underwriter regulations.

1.05 ENVIRONMENTAL CONDITIONS

A. Do not apply exterior paint in damp, rainy weather or until the surface has dried thoroughly from the effects of such weather. Do not apply varnish or paint when temperature is below 50° F. Avoid painting surfaces when exposed to hot sunlight.

1.06 PROTECTION

A. Before painting, remove hardware, accessories, plates, lighting fixtures and similar items or provide ample protection of such items. On completion of each space, replace above items. Use only skilled mechanics for removing and connecting above items. Protect adjacent surfaces as required or directed. Any damage done shall be repaired by the Painting Contractor at his expense. A sufficient supply of clean drop cloths and other protective covering shall be properly distributed and maintained.

B. Finishing of the Following Listed Items and Materials will not be Required and Shall be Protected:
1. Stainless steel, brass, bronze, copper, monel, chromium, anodized aluminum; specially finished articles such as porcelain enamel, plastic-coated fabrics, and baked enamel.
2. Finished products such as ceramic tile, windows, glass, brick, resilient flooring, acoustical tiles, board and metal tees; other architectural features, such as "finish" hardware, finished in aluminum, bronze or plated ferrous metal, prefinished panels, or other items that are installed prefinished.

1.07 COLOR SCHEDULE

A. The Designer will provide a complete schedule of colors. Colors may be selected from various manufacturers' standards. The paint manufacturer supplying this project shall match these colors. Well in advance of commencing work, the painting contractor shall obtain the schedule from the Designer, and proceed to prepare duplicate set of samples of treatments for all major surfaces.

PART 2 PRODUCTS

2.01 PAINT MATERIALS

A. Brands of paint, varnishes and stains are specified herein. Basic painting materials such as linseed oil, shellac, turpentine, thinners, driers, etc. shall be of highest quality, made by reputable manufacturers as specified, have identifying labels on containers and shall be approved by Designer. All paint materials shall be factory fresh.

B. As part of the list of proposed subcontractors, the Painting Subcontractor shall indicate the name of the manufacturer whose material he or she proposes to use.

PART 3 EXECUTION

3.01 PREPARATION OF SURFACES

A. Inspection of Surfaces: Do not begin painting on any surface until it has been inspected and is in proper condition to receive the paint as specified. Should any surface be found unsuitable to produce a proper paint finish, notify the General Contractor in writing. Apply no material until the unsuitable surfaces have been made satisfactory. After acceptance of surface, by application of first coat of paint, assume responsibility for and rectify any unsatisfactory finish resulting.

B. If, after treatment, the completed finish (or any portion thereof) blisters, checks, peels, or otherwise shows indication of dampness or other irregular condition of surface, the Painting Contractor shall, at his own expense, remove the applied treatment and refinish the part affected to the satisfaction of the Designer. (The Painting Contractor should determine dryness of all moisture-holding materials by use of a reliable electronic moisture meter.)

C. Wood: Sandpaper to smooth and even surface and then dust off. After priming or stain coat has been applied, thoroughly fill all nail holes and other surface imperfections with putty tinted with primer or stain to match wood color. Sand all woodwork between coats to a smooth surface. Cover knots and sap streaks with a thin coat of shellac.

D. Steel and Iron: Remove grease, rust and rust scale and touch up any chipped or abraded places on items that have been shop coated. Where steel or iron have a heavy coating of scale, remove by descaling, or wire brushing, as necessary, to produce a satisfactory surface for painting. When area will be exposed to view, sandpaper the entire treated area smooth, feather the edge of surrounding undamaged prime coat and spot prime in a manner to eliminate evidence of repair.

E. Galvanized Metal: Thoroughly clean by wiping surfaces with surface conditioner and prime with galvanized iron primer as recommended by paint manufacturer.

F. Concrete and Concrete Masonry: Prepare surfaces to be painted by removing all dirt, dust, oil and grease stains and efflorescence. The method of surface preparation shall be left to the discretion of the painter, provided the results are satisfactory to the Designer. Before first paint coat is applied, spot prime any nails and other exposed metal occurring in the surfaces with an oil-base masonry primer as recommended by paint manufacturer.

G. Plaster Surfaces: Fill cracks, holes or imperfections in plaster with patching plaster and smooth off to match adjoining surfaces. Before painting any plaster, surfaces shall be first tested for dryness with a moisture testing device. Apply no paint or sealer on plaster when the moisture content exceeds 12% as determined by the testing device. Test sufficient areas in each space and as often as necessary to determine the proper moisture content for painting. If the moisture content is between 8% and 12%, prime with alkali-resistant primer. If 8% or less, prime with specified primer. Remove the dry salt deposits from all plaster surfaces by brushing with a stiff brush before painting.

3.02 WORKMANSHIP

A. Perform all work using only experienced, competent painters in accordance with the best standards of practice in the trade. Hand brush or roll work except where otherwise permitted or directed. Olympia products are to be brush applied. When completed, the painting shall represent a first-class workmanlike appearance. Apply all paint materials under adequate illumination.

B. Tint all primers and undercoats to approximately the color of the finish coat with each coat being sufficiently different from the work in place to permit easy identification.

C. Finish edges, tops and bottoms of all doors same as door faces. Both sides and all edges of doors to be finished simultaneously.

D. Prime coats specified herein will not be required on items delivered with prime or shop coats already applied, unless otherwise specified.

3.03 APPLICATION

A. Stain or paint only when surfaces are clean, dry, smooth and adequately protected from dampness. Each coat of paint shall be well brushed on, worked out evenly and allowed to dry at least 24 hours before the subsequent coat is applied.

B. Finished work shall be uniform, of approved color, smooth and free from runs, sags, clogging or excessive flooding. Make edges of paint adjoining other materials or colors sharp and clean, without overlapping. Where high gloss enamel is used, lightly sand undercoats to obtain a smooth finish coat.

Figure 9.5 continued

C. Each coat of material applied must be inspected and approved by
the Designer before the application of the succeeding specified
coat; otherwise no credit for the concealed coat will be given,
and the Contractor shall assume the responsibility to recoat the
work in question. Painting Contractor shall notify the Designer
when each coat is completed.

D. At completion, touch up and restore finish where damaged and leave
finish surfaces in good condition.

PART 4 SCHEDULES

4.01   SCHEDULE OF FINISHES

A. Refer to the "Finish Schedule" on the drawing for designated
finishes of areas, which are listed in accordance with schedule
following. Items listed are acceptable products of some major
manufacturers. Responsibility for recommending, scheduling
and using the proper paint for the job conditions rests with the
manufacturer and Painting Subcontractor.

                        END OF SECTION

GLOSSARY

Abrasion resistance: A quality of withstanding mechanical action, such as rubbing, scraping, or scrubbing, which may tend to remove material progressively from a surface.

Alkali: A caustic substance such as lye soda or lime. Alkalies or strong alkali solutions are highly destructive to oil paint films.

Appreciable change: A change that is noticeable in comparing the tested specimen with a sample of the original specimen under standard viewing conditions.

Area: The length multiplied by the width determines the area.

Back priming: Applying a coat of paint to the backside and edges of woodwork and exterior siding to prevent moisture absorption.

Binder: A film-forming oil or resin.

Blocking resistance: A quality of resisting adhesion or sticking between any surfaces which touch under uniform loading and temperature conditions for a specified time.

Bolt: A rolled length of wallcovering containing an area specified by the wallcovering manufacturer.

Breaking strength: A measure of the force necessary to break a web when subjected to a pulling force in the plane of the web.

Chalking: Powdering of the paint film on the film surface. Mild chalking may be desirable. Heavy chalking should be removed prior to repainting.

Clear finish: A material that is transparent in nature. Usually referred to if and when an application of the material is applied overall on a finished surface.

Cloth-backed: Wallcovering having a backing of woven or knitted yarns.

Coating adhesion: A measure of the strength of the bond between the surface coating and the backing or substrate of a wallcovering.

Coating system: A combination of specific coating materials and their sequential application to an appropriately prepared surface to impart color or protect the surface.

Cold-cracking resistance: A quality of resisting cracking of the coated or decorative surface when a wallcovering is folded while exposed to temperatures as prescribed in the test method.

Colorfastness: A quality of resisting change or loss of color resulting from exposure to light.

Crocking resistance: A quality of resisting transfer of color from a wallcovering surface by rubbing with a dry cloth of contrasting color.

Dry film thickness: Thickness of applied coating or coatings when dry. Thickness is usually expressed in mils (1/1000 in.).

Eggshell: A luster between semigloss and flat which resembles that of an eggshell.

Embossed: Wallcovering having a three-dimensional design impressed in the surface by pressure with or without heat.

Emulsion paint: A paint, the vehicle of which is an emulsion of binder in water. The binder may be oil, oleoresinous varnish, resin, or other emulsifiable binders.

Enamel: A paint made with varnish or lacquer for a vehicle. The paint is characterized by an ability to form an especially smooth film.

Epoxy resins: A synthetic resin usually made from bisephenol A and epichlorhydrin.

Fabric-backed: Wallcovering having a backing of woven or knitted yarns or a nonwoven structure of randomly distributed textile fibers.

Filler: A pigmented composition for filling the pores or irregularities in a surface preparatory to application of other finishes.

Flat: A finish having no luster or gloss.

Flammability: A quality of resisting the propagation of flame under prescribed test conditions.

Flexographic: A process by which the decorative surface of a wallcovering is machine printed by the transfer of images from raised portions of a flat plate or roll.

Flocked: Wallcovering in which a part or all of the design results from short textile fibers standing more or less on end and bonded by adhesive to the wallcovering.

Fungicide: A substance poisonous to fungi; retards or prevents fungus growth.

Grain: An embossed design impressed on a wallcovering.

Hand printed, hand screened: Wallcovering upon which the decorative surface is applied by hand rather than machine.

Heat-aging resistance: A quality of resisting deterioration of the coated or decorative surface when a wallcovering is exposed to elevated temperatures over an extended period.

Latex paint: A paint containing a synthetic resin used as a binder for emulsion (water-thinned) paints.

Length: The linear measurement of a roll.

Lining: Wallcovering used to prepare a wall or ceiling surface for hanging a patterned wallcovering or for other decorative treatment.

Lot: A designation to indicate similarity of production.

Mildew resistance: A quality of resisting microbial colonization either on the back of the wallcovering while drying after hanging or on the decorative surface when exposed to moisture under use conditions.

Oil stain: A coating material with an oil binder plus dyes or pigments, but formulated so that normal applications do not deposit an opaque film.

Oil varnish: A varnish which contains resin and drying oil as the basic film-forming ingredients and is converted into a solid film primarily by oxidation.

Oleoresin: A vehicle for varnishes and paints consisting of drying oils and resins.

Paint: A pigmented liquid composition which is converted to an opaque solid after application of a thin layer. Generally considered as all coating materials used in the act of painting.

Peelability: A quality which describes a wallcovering from which the decorative surface may be dry-peeled from the substrate, leaving a continuous layer of the substrate on the wall, when the wallcovering has been installed and peeled according to the manufacturer's instructions.

Piece roll: A bolt of wallcovering containing more than one continuous length.

Pigments: Solid coloring agents used in the preparation of paint and substantially insoluble in the vehicle.

Prepasted: Wallcovering having a factory-applied adhesive on the back surface for adherence to a hanging surface after the adhesive has been activated.

Resin: A material, usually a solid or viscous liquid, used as part or all of the film-forming phase of paints, varnishes, and lacquers.

Rotogravure: A process by which the decorative surface of a wallcovering is machine printed by the transfer of images from the valleys of an engraved or etched cylinder.

Run: Sometimes called a making or batch. The collective rollage produced at one time on a single machine, all of which would be expected to have the same overall appearance and physical characteristics.

Sealer: A paint, varnish, or resinous product used to prevent excessive absorption of finish coats by the substrate; also applied to prevent bleeding or bonding chalked masonry surface before painting.

Semigloss: The glossiness of a finish that is between eggshell and a high or full gloss.

Screen printed: Wallcovering upon which the decorative surface is machine printed by a flat or rotary screen process.

Scrubbability: A quality of withstanding scrubbing with a brush and a prescribed detergent solution.

Shellac: A purified lac resin dissolved in an organic solvent (usually alcohol) and used to seal (fill) wood or as a varnish.

Shop coat or shop painting: Coating applied in the fabricating shop or plant before shipment.

Shrinkage: A decrease in dimensions occurring when a wallcovering is exposed to moisture.

Stain: A thin liquid composition, usually transparent, used to change the color of a surface without leaving a film of significant thickness.

Stain resistance: A quality of showing no appreciable change in appearance after application and removal of certain specified materials.

Standard roll: A standard roll as a unit of measure is 36 sq ft (3.3 sq m).

Strippability: A quality that describes a wallcovering which can be dry-stripped after having been installed and striped according to manufacturer's instructions, leaving a minimum of product residue on the wall, without damage to the wall surface.

Tear strength: A quality of resisting the propagation of an existing tear.

Undercoat: In a multicoat system, any intermediate coat or a first or primer coat.

Varnish: A liquid composition which is converted to a transparent or translucent solid film after application as a thin layer. When a varnish is pigmented, it is usually called an "enamel."

Vehicle: The liquid portion of a paint. Anything dissolved in the liquid portion of the paint is part of the vehicle.

Wallcovering: A flexible product designed to cover walls and ceilings for decorative and/or functional purposes.

Washability: A quality of withstanding occasional sponging with a prescribed detergent solution to remove surface soil.

Width: The cross-direction measurement after trimming for hanging.

PANELING

Because there are over 150 varieties of wood veneers available on the commercial market and because these veneers can be provided in a variety of cuts (rotary, plain sliced, or quartered), designers may find that there are approximately 450 different surface veneers available for consideration. In addition, there are 3 basic varieties of core construction and about 10 varieties of panel finishes.

The following guidelines based on information from the Hardwood Plywood Manufacturers Association (HPMA) and the Architectural Woodwork Institute (AWI) should help to clarify and simplify specification decisions regarding wall paneling.

Specification of hardwood plywood paneling involves consideration of the following factors:

1. Flitch selection

2. Species selection

3. Matching of veneer

4. Panel construction

5. Panel finish

6. Flame resistance

7. Acoustical treatment

8. Panel selection

9. Installation

FLITCH SELECTION

The term *flitch* refers to a given section or piece of a log. All the slices or cuts taken from this log are kept in sequence and this entire sequence is referred to as a "flitch" (Figure 10.1). The flitch for any given wall-paneling project is selected by the designer, or the selection may be made by the manufacturer of the paneling. If the manufacturer is to make the flitch selection, based on the designer's requirements, the designer must supply information on the (1) general color range desired, (2) the grain characteristics, such as swirl or straight, (3) the height and approximate linear footage required, (4) the type of wood, and (5) the desired method of matching. See the comparative table of wood species in Table 10.1.

One of the advantages of allowing the manufacturer to make the final flitch selection is the fact that the manufacturer can predict the flitch yield and therefore more accurately adhere to a proposed budget. If a designer wishes to visit a local veneer supplier and make a selection from the showroom floor, the supplier should be questioned regarding the flitch yield. The manufacturer and supplier may not always agree on the amount of yield; i.e., the supplier may quote a 3 to 1 ratio (3,000 sq ft of flitch will be required to produce 1,000 sq ft of panel) and the manufacturer may quote a 4 to 1 ratio.

SPECIES SELECTION

To simplify species selection for the designer, the comparative table of wood species in Table 10.1 has been prepared showing pertinent characteristics of some 34 species of domestic and foreign woods used in the Architectural Woodwork Industry. The table can quickly confirm or deny the wisdom of a species selection by the designer or conversely lead him or her to a proper selection after study of the characteristics.

The key to the table is the column listing *Principal Uses*— both exterior and interior. Careful analysis of this list will immediately narrow the selection appreciably for each type of application.

From this point, consideration is given to *Appearance*, which should be compared with *Finishing* characteristics for both paint and transparent finishes. These two columns have been prepared to assist in the area of aesthetics by describing, as briefly as possible, the appearance of the wood in its natural state.

Relative Cost has been broken into both *Lumber* and *Plywood* headings. The reason for cost variations in the two products is obvious when the physical differences are considered. Generally, the prices of veneered products reflect the high labor and equipment cost and relatively low material cost in their manufacture. However, the price of lumber in most species may not reflect similar cost factors. In spite of their physical differences, the two products are always compatible, and both are essential to complete design freedom in contemporary buildings.

Practical Size Limitations schedules the maximum practical dimensions (not mean or average) of each of the species in thickness, width, and length, considering reasonable quantity

TYPES OF VENEER CUTS

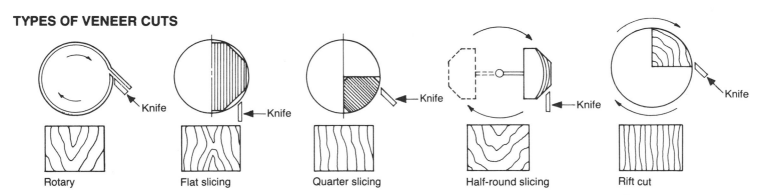

| Rotary | Flat slicing | Quarter slicing | Half-round slicing | Rift cut |

Figure 10.1 Types of veneer cuts.

TABLE 10.1 COMPARATIVE TABLE OF WOOD SPECIES

SPECIES	BOTANICAL NAME	PRINCIPAL USES	APPEARANCE COLOR	FIGURE	GRAIN	RELATIVE COST Lumber	RELATIVE COST Plywood
ASH, White	Fraxinus, American	Trim, Frames & Cabinets	Creamy White to Light Brown	High	Open	100	175
BASSWOOD	Tilia, American	Decorative Molds Carving turnery	Creamy White	No figure	Closed	85	—
BEECH	Fagus grandifolia	Semi-exposed Cabinet Parts	Light to Pinkish	Medium	Closed	80	Not Gen. Available
BIRCH, Yellow, "Natural"	Betula alleghaniensis	Trim, Frames Panelling & Cabinets	White to Dark Red	Medium	Closed	100	100
BIRCH, Yellow, "Select Red" (Heartwood)	Betula alleghaniensis	Trim, Frames Panelling & Cabinets	Dark Red	Medium	Closed	150	150
BIRCH, Yellow, "Select White" (Sapwood)	Betula alleghaniensis	Trim, Frames Panelling & Cabinets	Creamy White	Medium	Closed	130	120
BUTTERNUT	Juglans cinerea	Trim, Frames Panelling & Cabinets	Pale Brown	High	Open	300	500
CEDAR, Western Red	Thuja plicata	Trim, Panelling Exterior & Interior	Reddish to Pinkish Brown nearly White Sapwood	Medium	Closed	100	100
CHERRY, Black	Prunus serotina	Trim, Frames Trim	Reddish Brown	High	Closed	160	200
CHESTNUT, Wormy	Castanea dentata	Panelling and Panelling & Cabinets	Greyish Brown	High	Open with Worm Holes	150	NA
FIRE, Douglas Flat Grain	Pseudolsugu menziesii	Trim, Frames Panelling	Reddish Tan	High	Closed	100	80
FIR, Douglas Vertical Grain	Pseudolsugu menziesii	Trim, Frames Panelling	Reddish Tan	Low	Closed	100	NA
MAHOGANY, African Plain Sawn	Khaya ivornsis	Trim, Frames Panelling & Cabinets	Reddish Brown	Medium	Open	250	250
MAHOGANY, African Quarter Sawn	Khaya ivornsis	Trim, Frames Panelling & Cabinets	Reddish Brown	Low	Open	350	350
MAHOGANY, Tropical American, "Honduras"	Sweitenia macrophylla	Trim, Frames Panelling cabinets & Bar tops	Rich Golden Brown	Medium	Open	200	300
MAPLE, Hard "Natural"	Acer saccharum	Trim, Frames Paneling & Cabinets	White to Reddish Brown	Medium	Closed	75	150
MAPLE, Hard, "Select White" (Sapwood)	Acer saccharum	Trim, Frames Panelling & Cabinets	White	Medium	Closed	90	150
MAPLE, Soft "Natural"	Acer saccharum	Trim, semi-exposed Cabinet parts	White to Reddish Brown	Low	Closed	75	Not Gen. Available
OAK, Red Plain Sawn	Quercus ruba	Trim, Frames Panelling & Cabinets	Reddish Tan to Brown	High	Open	90	130
OAK, Red Rift Sawn	Quercus ruba	Trim, Frames Panelling & Cabinets	Reddish Tan to Brown	Low	Open	200	250
OAK, Red Quarter Sawn	Quercus ruba	Trim, Frames Panelling & Cabinets	Reddish Tan to Brown	Low	Open	200	250
OAK, White Plain Sawn	Quercus alba	Trim, Frames Panelling & Cabinets	Greyish Tan	High	Open	100	165
OAK, White Rift Sawn	Quercus alba	Trim, Frames Panelling & Cabinets	Greyish Tan	Low	Open	200	250
OAK, White Quarter Sawn	Quercus alba	Trim, Frames Panelling & Cabinets	Greyish Tan	Low figure accented with flakes	Open	200	250
PECAN	Carya species	Trim, Panelling & Cabinets	Reddish Brown with Dark Brown stripes	Medium	Open	100	200
PINE, Eastern or Northern White	Pinus strobus	Trim, Frames Panelling & Cabinets	Creamy White to Pink	Medium	Closed	100	NA
PINE, Idaho	Pinus monticola	Trim, Frames Panelling & Cabinets	Creamy White	Low	Closed	100	Not Gen. Available
PINE, Ponderosa	Pinus ponderosa	Trim, Frames Panelling & Cabinets	Light to Medium Pink	Medium	Closed	100	125
PINE, Sugar	Pinus lambertiana	Trim, Frames Panelling & Cabinets	Creamy White	Low	Closed	110	Not Gen. Available
PINE, Southern Yellow	Pinus echinata	Trim, Frames Panelling & Flooring Cabinets	Pale Yellow	High	Closed	65	Not Gen. Available
POPLAR, Yellow	Lirodendron Tulipifern	Trim, Frames Panelling & Cabinets	Pale Yellow to Brown with Green Cast	Medium	Closed	85	NA
REDWOOD, Flat Grain (Heartwood)	Sequoia Sempervirens	Trim, Frames Panelling	Deep Red	High	Closed	110	NA
REDWOOD, Vertical Grain (Heartwood)	Sequoia Sempervirens	Trim, Frames Panelling	Deep Red	Low	Closed	120	NA
ROSEWOOD, Brazilian	Dalbergia nigra	Solid Trim Incidental to Veneered Panelling	Intermingled Reds Browns, and Blacks	High	Open	NGA	780
SPRUCE, Sitka	Tideland spruce Picea sitchensis	Trim, Frames	Light Yellowish Tan	High	Closed	100	NA
TEAK	Techtona grandis	Trim, Frames Panelling & Cabinets	Tawny Yellow to Dark Brown	High	Open	400	400
WALNUT, Black	Juglans nigra	Trim, Frames Panelling & Cabinets	Chocolate Brown	High	Open	300	300
WALNUT, Nogal	Juglans nigra neotropica	Trim, Frames Panelling & Cabinets	Chocolate Brown	High	Open	200	NA

NOTE: Regional distribution differences may affect availability and cost relationship.

(A) Rated from 1 to 4 as follows:
1. In warehouse stock in good quantities and fair assortment of thicknesses and lengths.

PRACTICAL SIZE LIMITATIONS			AVAILIBILITY OF MATCHING PLYWOOD (A)	HARDNESS	DIMENSIONAL STABILITY (B)	FINISHING		REMARKS
Thick	Width	Length				Paint	Transparent	
1½"	7½"	12'	3	Hard	10/64	Not normally used	Excellent	Excellent where strength is required bold grain.
1½"	7½"	10'	4	Soft	10/64	Excellent	Excellent	Best for mouldings no grain.
1½"	7½"	12'	4	Hard	14/64	Excellent	Good	North American Beech not generally used as show wood.
1½"	7½"	12'	1	Hard	12/64	Excellent	Good	One of the most common used.
1½"	5½"	11'	2	Hard	12/64	Not normally used	Excellent	Rich Colour.
1½"	5"	11'	2	Hard	12/64	Not normally used	Excellent	Uniform Appearance.
1½"	5½"	8'	3	Medium	8/64	Not normally used	Excellent	Beautiful and Rich.
3¼"	11"	16'	1 & 3	Soft	10/64	Not normally used	Good	Decay resistant, rough texture favorite.
1½"	5½"	7'	2	Hard	9/64	Not normally used	Excellent	Rich Colour.
¾"	7½"	10'	4	Medium	9/64	Not normally used	Excellent	Very limited supply.
3¼"	11"	16'	1	Medium	10/64	Fair	Fair	Good supply.
1½"	11"	16'	4	Medium	6/64	Good	Good	Very limited supply.
2½"	11"	15'	3	Medium	7/64	Good	Excellent	Fine hardwood.
2½"	7½"	15'	3	Medium	5/64	Not normally used	Excellent	Limited supply.
2½"	11"	15'	3	Medium	6/64	Not normally used	Excellent	One of the world's finest cabinet woods.
3½"	9½"	12'	3	Very Hard	12/64	Excellent	Good	Plentiful supply, excellent properties.
2½"	9½"	12'	3	Very Hard	12/64	Not normally used	Excellent	Uniform appearance.
3¼"	9½"	12'	4	Medium	9/64	Excellent	Not normally used	Good utility hardwood.
1½"	7¼"	12'	1	Hard	11/64	Not normally used	Excellent	Excellent architectural wood, low cost widely used.
1¹⁄₁₆"	5½"	10'	3	Hard	7/64	Not normally used	Excellent	Excellent architectural wood, limited supply.
1¹⁄₁₆"	5½"	8'	1	Hard	7/64	Not normally used	Excellent	Excellent architectural wood, limited supply.
1½"	5½"	10'	2	Hard	11/64	Not normally used	Excellent	Wide Range of grain patterns and colour.
¾"	4½"	10'	3	Hard	7/64	Not normally used	Excellent	Limited availability.
¾"	4½"	10'	3	Hard	8/64	Not normally used	Excellent	Pronounced flake, very limited use and supply.
1½"	5½"	12'	3	Hard	11/64	Not normally used	Good	Subject to regional availability, attractive.
1½"	9½"	14'	3	Soft	7/64	Good	Good	True white pine, wide range of applications for general usage.
1½"	9½"	14'	4	Soft	8/64	Good	Good	True white pine, wide range of applications for general usage.
1½"	9½"	16'	3	Soft	8/64	Good	Good	Most widely used pine, wide range of applications for general usage.
3¼"	11"	16'	4	Soft	7/64	Good	Good	True white pine, wide range of applications for general usage.
1½"	7½"	16'	4	Medium	10/64	Fair	Good	An economical hard pine.
2½"	7½"	12'	3	Medium	9/64	Excellent	Good	Ideal interior hardwood excellent paintability.
2½"	11"	16'	1 & 3	Soft	6/64	Good	Good	Superior exterior wood high natural decay resistance.
2½"	11"	16'	3	Soft	3/64	Excellent	Excellent	Superior exterior wood high natural decay resistance.
—	—	—	3	Very Hard	7/64	Not normally used	Excellent	Exotice figure, high cost.
3¼"	9½"	16'	4	Soft	10/64	Fair	Fair	Limited general available.
1½"	7½"	10'	2	Hard	6/64	Not normally used	Excellent	Outstanding wood for most applications, high cost.
1½"	4½"	6'	1	Hard	10/64	Paint not normally used	Excellent	Fine domestic hardwood extremely limited widths and lengths more readily available in veneer.
¾"	9½"	9'	4	Medium	12/64	Not normally used	Good	Good substitute for juglans nigra where better widths and lengths required.

2. In warehouse stock in fair quantity but not in thicknesses other than ¼" and ¾"; or sizes other than 4'-0" x 8'-0".
3. Produced on a special order only.
4. Not generally available.

(B) These figures represent possible width change in a 12" board when moisture content is reduced from 10% to 5%. Figures are for plain sawn unless indicated otherwise in species column.

Figure 10.2 Veneer matching. Source: Hardwood Plywood Manufacturers Association.

requirements. The thickness and width can be increased by laminating or edge bonding at the mill, while the length restrictions are handled by either a scarf or butt joint in the field. Where significant quantities of hardwoods are to be used, with constant dimensions in both width and length, such as vertical board paneling, consideration should be given to the use of more narrow members in order to reduce the cost of waste. However, the lead time afforded in the construction of a new building is usually adequate to procure quality materials in the quantity needed to satisfy the largest projects.

The *Availability of Matching Plywood* is relatively expressed from 1 (most readily available) to 4 (unavailable).

End use determines the importance of *Hardness* in selecting a species for each particular type of application. Counters, door frames, and wall treatments in high-traffic areas are obvious uses of wood products where hardness and resistance to abrasion must be considered. In many other applications these factors generally are not of great importance.

Dimensional Stability is of much value in helping to select woods for use where humidity conditions may vary widely and where design or fabrication of a wood product does not allow free movement or the use of plywood. The column figures indicate extreme conditions and show the maximum amount of movement possible in a 12″ (30.5 cm) wide piece of unfinished wood where its moisture content changes from 10 to 5 percent, or vice versa. The possible change in dimension demonstrates that unfinished interior woodwork must be carefully protected prior to finishing by keeping it in rooms where relative humidities are between 25 and 55 percent. The column also shows the variation between species and between flat grain and edge grain, where such cuts are available commercially.

Remarks is a general information-type column that could either reinforce or weaken the reasons for a tentative selection. By the time this comes into play, the choice will probably be down to two or three species, and information contained under this heading will surely simplify the final decision.[1]

MATCHING OF VENEER

Veneers are matched twice—once in production and again during installation. Matching is accomplished within each panel and from panel to panel. Within individual panels, the process of matching or arranging the veneer sheets involves alternating and turning over the sheets (like pages of a book), hence the name "book matched" or "book leaf." This production method produces three types of match:

1. *Balance match* is composed of any number (odd or even) of veneer sheets clipped to an equal width for balanced arrangement within each panel.

2. *Running match* is when each panel face is arranged from as many veneer sheets as necessary for the specified panel width. When a portion of a veneer sheet is left over, it is used to start the next panel face.

3. *Center match* is composed of an even number of veneer sheets that are equal in width (approximate), arranged so that a veneer point occurs in the center of the panel. This tends to reduce the usable veneer and increases the cost.

Other methods may be specified for the arrangement of veneer sheets, such as a random effect (no match), diamonds, herringbone, checkerboard, or any other pattern the designer may desire (see Figure 10.2).

Three basic methods are used to match panel to panel:

1. *Blueprint match* is accomplished by making an elevation drawing of the walls or wall to be paneled and numbering in sequence the desired number of panels. Panels are then fabricated in the required sizes and the proper sequence for the entire space. This includes all spaces above and below windows, doors, and bookcases. This produces a perfectly matched room.

2. *Sequence match* is produced by securing as many panels of the same size as are required. These panels are then numbered in sequence from left to right. Doors, if specified, may be furnished from the same flitch, but will not be matched in sequence with the panels.

3. *Warehouse matched sets* are premanufactured sets which are numbered in sequence. Sizes are usually 48" × 96" (121.9 × 243.8 cm) or 48" × 120" (121.9 × 304.8 cm). The sets vary from 6 to 12 panels. If more than one set is required, no match can be expected. Doors cannot be matched and it may be necessary to make wall adjustments near corners or wall ends.

PANEL CONSTRUCTION

Paneling construction is composed of three components: thickness, core, and size.

1. Thickness usually recommended for paneling ranges from ¾ in. (19.1 mm) to ¼ in. (6.4 mm) for installations that may require curving of the wood.

2. There are three basic core types used for paneling and each has a distinct difference (see Figure 10.3). Table 10.2 points out the advantages and disadvantages of each.

Core types are given for the purpose of general comparisons; however, it should be remembered that panel cores can be altered to meet special project requirements. There are other core materials or combination of materials which can be used to achieve special properties. For example:

Treatment Desired	Material
Acoustics	Lead sheet
	Asbestos sheet
	Manufacturer's standard
	Acoustical panel
	Particle-board panel
Fire resistance	Chemically impregnated core
	Mineral core
	Asbestos sheet
Light weight	Aluminum honeycomb
	Kraft paper honeycomb
	Wood coils and grids

Panel Sizes.

Plywoods can be obtained in any length, depending on the length of the flitch available and manufacturers' facilities. Small or long lengths can be ordered, when required. Through the processes of progressive and scarf-joint gluing, unlimited lengths and widths or panels may often be obtained by careful surface matching and joining of selected flitches. The tolerance for width dimension and length dimension should be plus or minus 1/32" (0.8 mm). The tolerance for thickness for

Figure 10.3 Plywood panel cores. Source: Hardwood Plywood Manufacturers Association.

TABLE 10.2   HARDWOOD PLYWOOD PANELING CORE TYPES

Core Type	Thickness	Advantages	Disadvantages
Veneer (all inner plies of hardwood/ wood veneer)	1/4" (3 ply or less)	Inexpensive	Core imperfections may photograph through face veneer
	5/16"-1/2"	Inexpensive	
	Over 1/2" (7 ply)	Best screw-hold power	Difficult to machine. Exposed edge shows core voids and imperfections. Most susceptible to warpage (doors)
Particle board (wood composition, also known as chipboard, chipcore)	1/4" (infrequent) through 2" (usually 3 plies)	Most stable. No core photographing. Least expensive (generally)	Poor edge screw-holding. Heaviest core
Lumber core (consists of strips of lumber 1 1/2" to 4" wide)	5/8" through 2" (usually 5 plies)	Easiest machined. Exposed edges are solid. Stable construction	Highest priced

Source: Hardwood Plywood Manufacturers Association.

TABLE 10.3　SELECTION GUIDE TO THE ARCHITECTURAL WOODWORK INSTITUTE'S FINISH SYSTEMS

	TRANSPARENT										OPAQUE					
	1 Standard Lacquer		**2** Catalyzed Lacquer		**3** Conversion Varnish Alkyd-Urea		**4** Vinyl Catalyzed		**5** Penetrating Oil Synthetic		**6** Opaque Lacquer Standard		**7** Opaque Enamel Synthetic		**8** Opaque Vinyl Catalyzed	
SHEEN	C	P	C	P	C	P	C	P	C	P	C	P	C	P	C	P
Dull Rubbed Effect 16°-24°	X		X	X	X	X	X	X	X							
Medium Rubbed Effect 28°-36°	X		X	X	X	X	X	X								
Full Gloss　88°-96°	X		X	X	X	X	X	X			X		X		X	X
Semi-Gloss 28°-36°											X		X		X	X
Flat　　　16°-24°											X		X		X	X
EFFECT																
Open Grain	X		X	X	X	X	X	X								
Closed Grain	X		X	X	X	X	X	X								
Oil Finish									X							
Oil Finish (Simulated)							X									
PERFORMANCE																
Wear Resistance																
Water & Moisture Resistance	3		2	1	3	3	2	1	4		3		2		2	1
Print Resistance (8 oz. Duck) 2 PSI at room temperature	1		1	1	1	1	1	1	4		1		1		1	1
Abrasion Resistance Tabor Abrasor	3		3	2	3	2	2	1	5		3		2		2	1
Adhesion (Crosshatch)	2		2	2	2	2	1	1	2		2		2		1	1
Cold Check Resistance ASTM D1211-60	1		1	1	2	2	1	1	1		1		2		1	1
Impact Resistance (1 lb. steel ball — 17 inches)	2		2	1	2	3	1	1	1		2		3		1	1
Repairability	1		2	2	3	3	3	3	1		1		3		3	3
Chemical Resistance																
2% Caustic Solution	4		2	2	2	1	2	1	4		4		2		1	1
10% Sodium Hydroxide	4		3	2	4	3	3	2	4		4		4		3	2
10% Trisodium Phosphate	4		3	2	3	2	2	1	4		4		3		2	1
Glacial Acetic Acid	4		3	3	3	2	2	2	5		4		4		2	2
50% Sulphuric Acid	3		2	2	4	3	2	1	5		3		4		2	1
28% Ammonium Hydroxide	4		3	3	3	2	2	1	5		4		4		2	1
95% Ethyl Alcohol	4		3	2	3	2	2	1	5		4		3		2	1
Household Chemical Resistance																
Grease (Cooking Oil)	3		2	1	2	1	1	1	5		3		2		1	1
Hot Coffee	3		1	1	2	1	1	1	5		3		1		1	1
Orange Juice	3		1	1	1	1	1	1	4		3		1		1	1
Tomato Juice	3		1	1	1	1	1	1	4		3		1		1	1
Mustard	3		1	1	1	1	2	1	4		3		2		1	1
Nail Polish & Remover	5		4	3	3	2	2	1	5		5		5		1	1
Detergent (Soap)	4		2	1	2	1	1	1	5		4		2		1	1
Flame Spread																
Substantially affects (increases) Flame Spread	Yes		Yes	Yes	No	No	No	No	No		Yes		No		No	No

KEY

C = Custom　　1 = Excellent
P = Premium　　2 = Very Good
X = Availability　3 = Good
　　　　　　　4 = Fair
　　　　　　　5 = Poor

"DO NOT OVERSPECIFY" The esthetic considerations are generally the same for both Premium and Custom Grades. *The Performance of the finish constitutes the difference between Premium and Custom Grade.*

EXAMPLE 1 — Paneling on the walls of a high traffic corridor may be specified as Premium in view of the resistances required by nature of its location.

EXAMPLE 2 — Paneling on the walls of a Board of Directors Room may be specified as Custom since the need for resistance to wear and chemicals would probably be non-existent.

sanded panels should be plus or minus 3.64" (1.2 mm). However, in architectural (premium) and other specially constructed grades, the tolerances may be kept to plus or minus 0".[2] In some cases, panel sizes and thicknesses may be limited due to the availability of flame-retardant-treated core sizes.

PANEL FINISH

It is usually advised that the designer have panels finished by the manufacturer because greater control is possible and the panels will be protected against moisture during transportation and storage prior to installation. If the project will involve a large amount of cutting and fitting, it may be necessary to finish on the site, but the designer then has to write very specific finishing instructions. In either case, the designer should request a sample of the finished panel before final specification. Table 10.3 lists types of transparent and opaque finishes recommended for paneling. This table also provides information on flammability and performance specification criteria.

FLAME RESISTANCE

Paneling is classified as an interior finish and must therefore be treated for flame-spread characteristics. Many species of wood have been tested, and it has been found that some untreated (without added flame retardant) woods produce a rather low flame spread. Table 10.4 lists approximate flame-spread ratings of some typical veneer species. A more precise rating is dependent on core type (wood density) and manufacturing process.[3]

It has been found that the specific density of wood affects the flame-spread rating; i.e., the lower the density, the lower the flame spread. The following guideline may be used in the specification of wood paneling.

Flame Spread	Hardwood Plywood Paneling
25	1. Treated veneer core with a veneer density of 31.2 lb (14 kg) or less.
	2. Treated particle-board core with veneer density of 42.7 lb (19.5 kg) or less.
25–50	1. Treated veneer core with a veneer density of 43.7 lb (20 kg) or less.
	2. Treated particle-board core with a veneer density of 58.6 lb (27 kg) or less.
50–75	1. Treated (veneer, particle-board, or lumber) cores without species density limitations.

Fire-resistance treatments are applied through impregnation of the cores and crossbands with waterborne salts of varying composition. (The treatment should never be applied to the panel surface because it makes proper finishing very difficult.) The impregnation method requires that the core be bonded with a waterproof-type adhesive.

Designers should order fire-resistant panels factory-finished or factory-sealed. When a complete finish is ordered, make certain that the Underwriters Laboratories allows the panel to be labeled as "finished." Only experienced workers should install these panels because the edges, if cut, must be immediately resealed so that atmospheric humidity will not leach the salts from the core and leave a white deposit on the surface.

TABLE 10.4   FLAME-SPREAD RATING OF TYPICAL VENEER SPECIES

Flame Spread 25	Flame Spread 50	Flame Spread 75
Butternut	White Ash	White Oak
Chestnut	Avodire	Pecan
Cypress	Birch	Rosewood
African Mahogany	Cherry	Ebony
Prima Vera	Red Gum	East Indian Laurel
Redwood	Honduras Mahogany	
Fir	Lauan	
Limba	Tanguile	
	Hard Maple	
	Red Oak	
	Teak	
	Walnut	
	English Brown Oak	

Reproduced with permission of the Architectural Woodwork Institute.

Edges should be sealed with tung oil phenolic primers, tung oil phenolic spar varnish, or shellac.

Fire-retardant paneling does cost more than standard paneling, but savings may be realized on fire-insurance reductions. In addition, it has been found that the treatment for fire resistance also provides resistance to decay from water, humidity, and termites.

ACOUSTICAL TREATMENT

The acoustic quality of hardwood plywood paneling can be increased by (1) modifying the panel construction or (2) selecting an appropriate method of installation.

Designers may specify panel modification in the following manner:

1. Require that face veneers be laid up in random 4-in. (10.2 cm) wide strips with a ⅛" × ⅛" (3.2 × 3.2 mm) routed grove 4 in. on center (oc). Edges should be shiplapped and groves either accented or colored to blend with the face veneer.

2. Require that panels be perforated with holes of varying dimensions, spaces as specified (³⁄₁₆-in. [4.8-mm] holes spaced 1.2 in [12.7 mm] on center.) These perforations, if kept to a minimum size, will absorb high-frequency sound and not disturb the overall grain or surface effect.

The following installation techniques may be effective in reducing noise (see Figure 10.4).

1. Placement of recessed or protruding battens between panels provides good sound diffusers.

2. Alternation of floating panels is also very effective.

PANEL SELECTION

Grades of paneling are usually limited to "architectural," or premium grade, and custom grade. Custom grade assumes the use of standard or stock manufactured panels that are not sequence matched. The specification of premium grade allows the designer to select face veneers by species, specific grain and color, core construction, and matching within the panel and between panels.

1. PANEL PLACEMENT

A. FLOATING PANELS

B. RAISED PANELS

2. BATTEN MOLDINGS

A. METAL (MANY VARIATIONS)

B. WOOD MOLDINGS (MANY VARIATIONS)

C. SPLINE APPLICATION (ON METAL, PLYWOOD, OR PLASTICS)

D. RECESSED METAL MOLDING

Figure 10.4 Panel installation for acoustic control. Source: Hardwood Plywood Manufacturers Association.

INSTALLATION

Installation requires a series of steps that include the following considerations:

Wall Subsurfaces

These fall into the following four categories:

1. *Stud walls* may require the addition of furring strips applied horizontally or vertically. If studs are straight and well seasoned, paneling may be applied directly to the studs.

2. *Plasterboard subwalls* may require an installation which combines adhesives and nailing. The nails must be long enough to penetrate both surfaces.

3. *Plaster walls* will receive a paneling application if the surface is not too rough or badly damaged. If the surface is damaged, furring strips should be applied horizontally.

4. *Concrete block walls* should be carefully checked for moisture prior to installation. Furring strips may be applied to the concrete wall either vertically or horizontally.

Storage and Handling

The Hardwood Plywood Manufacturers Association recommends the following procedures to assure safe handling and storage.

1. Panels should be allowed to remain in the room or in the place of application long enough to adjust to the temperature and humidity of the workroom in which the job is being assembled.

2. During periods of extreme humidity, it is best to wait until the panels have had a chance to dry out before attempting to install them.

3. Never erect a panel installation over fresh plaster. Wood is hygroscopic and will take on moisture from the plaster.

4. Never stand panels on end against a wall for any length of time. If it is not convenient to lay them flat, they should stand on their sides, with care taken not to chip the edges.

5. To prevent moisture from penetrating through the panel to the face, back prime all panels erected over exterior plaster walls with one coat of pure white lead and linseed oil (three white to one linseed oil mixture) before applying to furring. Avoid getting any of the primer on the face of the panels as this will interfere with the finishing of the face.

6. Allow for expansion and contraction of panels. A great deal depends upon the extent of the paneled area, climate, and variables such as air conditioning and exposure to sunlight.

7. Panels stacked flat must not be placed directly on the floor, but should be placed on leveled 2 × 4s spaced not more than 16″ (40.6 cm) on center. An inexpensive cover sheet should be placed on top of the stack to keep the top panel from warping and to protect it from dust and natural or artificial light. Care must be taken that the panels are evenly stacked so as not to expose the face veneer along the edges at any point, since exposed faces are subject to color change.

Paneling may be installed by the use of adhesives, nails, or splints and molding.

Adhesive Applications

These may be made with (1) contact cement, (2) plastic resin, and (3) reclaimed rubber adhesive:

Contact Cement. This is applied to the back of the panel and permitted to partially set before application is made to the wall surface. This method of installation is suggested when nailing is not desirable.

Plastic Resins. These are usually supplied in powder form and are mixed with water to the consistency of heavy cream. This adhesive combined with nailing provides an extremely secure application. If nails are not desired, an electronic machine may be used to speed the drying process of the resins.

Reclaimed Rubber Adhesives. These are applied in thick beads directly to the wall surface by a caulking gun. This method serves to fill in slight imperfections on the wall surface and allows a one-step installation.

Splines and molding methods of application are illustrated in Figure 10.5. Other mechanical devices are recommended for use with adhesives to assure a secure bond. These devices include metal "Z" clips and metal inserts (see Figure 10.6).

TABLE 10.5 PANELING EDGE TREATMENTS

Type	Advantage	Cost
1. Exposed edge lumber core	May be stained to match	Inexpensive
2. Wood trim of matching species	Applied on job site and finished with panel	Inexpensive
3. Edge routed by mill and hardwood strip of matching species glued and inserted (variations)	Facilitates job cutting and conditions	Expensive
4. Matching veneer applied at edge of panel by manufacturer with edge-banding equipment	Can be finished with face veneer	Moderate
5. Matching hardwood lumber edge band inserted by manufacturer prior to application of face veneer	Edges may be routed, trimmed, etc.	Expensive

PLAN MOLDING AND FURRING THICKNESS TO
ACCOMMODATE EXISTING TRIM

SPLINES OR MOLDINGS

Figure 10.5 Splines and moldings. Source: Hardwood
Plywood Manufacturers Association.

Edge Treatment

When an installation requires that ends be left exposed, several methods may be used to finish the edges, Table 10.5 illustrates edge treatments along with the advantages and comparative cost factors.

Inspection

The project must be inspected before, during, and after installation.

Before. Be sure to verify the following four points:

1. Check that architectural hardwood plywood paneling is of the required species and that the finish matches the reviewed samples.

2. Verify that panels are acclimated to building environment for a minimum of 48 hours prior to installation.

3. Check that panel surfaces are free of damage.

4. Check that panels match both in and among panels specified.

During. The following three points must be checked during installation:

1. Check that panels are aligned plumb and true.

2. Assure that panels are installed according to manufacturer's instructions.

3. Make sure that field cuts on flame-retardant-treated cores are sealed.

After. Be sure to check the following points:

1. Make sure that damaged surfaces are restored to original condition.

2. Verify that the job site is left clean.

GUIDELINES FOR SPECIFYING ARCHITECTURAL PANELING

The guidelines developed by the Architectural Woodwork Institute (Figure 10.7) include specification information on panel fire retardancy, flitch selection, and panel finish.[4]

NAILED OR MECHANICAL APPLICATION

"Z" METAL CLIPS STABILIZE
CENTER OF PANEL

SLIP PANEL IN PLACE   CORNER PANEL NAILED

"Z" CLIP MAY BE
USED TO DROP
PANEL AS WELL AS SIDE   OR WOOD MAY BE UTILIZED

ROUTE PANEL TO RECEIVE
METAL MOLDING. SCREW
MOLDING TO WALL AND
SNAP ON COVER

NOTE: IN MECHANICAL FASTENING, IT IS IMPORTANT THAT THE
BASE AND CROWN MOLD ARE UTILIZED TO GIVE ADDITIONAL SUP-
PORT TO THE PANEL.

Figure 10.6 Mechanical devices used to install paneling.
Source: Hardwood Plywood Manufacturers Association.

Figure 10.7 Guidelines for specifying architectural paneling. Reproduced with permission of the Architectural Woodwork Institute.

The many important requirements of an architectural paneling installation are most easily obtained with the use of the AWI Guide Specification.

This specification is a part of the AWI Quality Standards, and its use assures to the specifier the following operations and requirements that will help guarantee a completely satisfactory and well executed installation. Among the many items of work that are required by reference to the AWI Quality Standards, these are of major importance:

Moisture content of the wood, requirements for the appearance of exposed surfaces, the grades of lumber to be used, requirements for the treatment of joints and exposed edges in flush paneling, requirements for the treatment of exterior corners and applied mouldings, adhesive performance requirements, exacting tolerances for all workmanship, ratio requirement of 3 to 1 for raw veneer to finish wall paneling, compatibility of grain and color, requirements for backing or balancing sheets and edge treatment of High Pressure Laminate Paneling, shop assembly, sanding requirements, and specific requirements on how panels are to be raised. These and many other quality insuring factors are automatically required by the use of the AWI Guide Specification.

It is important to specify requirements for Fire Retardancy treating. Code requirements vary in different areas of the country and the extent of treating for each project must be carefully determined. *The following is the AWI Specification for Fire Retardancy treating.*

1.3 Requirements of Regulatory Agencies

A. Treat the following listed items as required by the _____(applicable building code) to obtain spread classifications noted:

Item	Location	Flame spread classification

Note to Specifier: If more than one flame spread classification is required, identify by item or area. Casework and trim are usually exempted from these requirements. Up to ten percent of the combined ceiling and wall surface area is also normally exempted, for unlabeled doors, interior trim and interior finish. Since fire retardant treatments will increase costs substantially and can affect the appearance of architectural woodwork, the applicable code should be studied thoroughly to make sure which, if any, items require the treatment.

The following is the recommended AWI specification for stile and rail panel work and all kinds of flush panel work made of lumber, plywood and high pressure laminate.

2.3 Panelwork

Note to Specifier: Include stile and rail panel work and all kinds of flush panel work made of lumber, plywood and high pressure laminates.

A. Flush Paneling, Wood Veneer

1. AWI quality grade: _____ (Premium grade or Custom grade)

2. Panel shall be: _____ thickness, using _____ core. (Particleboard, Veneer or Lumber)

3. Face veneers: _____ (Species), _____ (Cut).
Note to specifier: Disregard following items 4 through 6 unless premium grade **was selected in 2.3A.1 above.**

4. Matching of adjacent pieces of veneer: _____ (Book match, Slip match or Random match)

5. Panel face assembly: _____ (Running match, Balance match or Center match)

6. Matching of adjacent panels: _____ (Specify one of the following: warehouse sets used full width, warehouse sets selectively reduced in width, sequence matched sets or blueprint matched.)

Note to specifier: Warehouse sets are usually available in 4' x 8' or 10' sheets, in sets of 6 to 12 pieces. Veneers are normally book matched and assembled in a running match. If blueprint matched panels and doors have been selected in paragraph 6 above and the architect either desires to or has already selected the flitch, then paragraph 7 below must be filled out accordingly.

7. Flitch selection: Allow _____ cents per square foot for face veneer - OR - Flitch _____ (Identification number) has been selected from _____ (Name of veneer company) at _____ (Address) containing _____ (Quantity) square feet of _____ (Length) veneer. The ratio of raw face veneer required to panel surface area shall be 3 to 1, unless otherwise specified.

Note to specifier: To determine the approximate amount of face veneer required, multiply the panel surface area by 3. The monetary allowance is for the cost of face veneer only, not the paneling. The above ratio may have to be increased to accommodate exacting requirements of appearance when the flitch contains a wide range of grain characteristics. *It is suggested that the selection be reviewed with someone competent to advise regarding adaptability of the flitch to specific job requirements.*

B. Flush Paneling, High Pressure Laminate.

1. AWI quality grade:_____ (Premium grade or Custom grade)
Note to specifier: AWI grade selection includes quality of workmanship and materials.

2. Laminate selection: _____ (High pressure laminate selection)
Note to specifier: Specify laminate manufacturer, pattern or color by name and number, and texture. If this is not possible, give woodworker choice of manufacturers and specify whether selection will be from solid colors, wood grains or patterns and also texture desired.

C. Stile and Rail Paneling: for Transparent Finish.

1. AWI quality grade:_____ (Premium grade or Custom grade).
Note to specifier: AWI grade selection determines quality of workmanship and material.

2. Solid wood:_____ (Species),_____ (Cut).

3. Plywood:_____ (Species), _____ (Cut).

4. Type of moulding: _____ (Solid or Applied).

5. Type of panel: _____ (Flat or Raised).

D. Stile and Rail Paneling: for Opaque Finish.

1. AWI quality grade:_____ (Premium grade or Custom grade).
Note to specifier: AWI grade selection determines quality of workmanship and material.

2. Solid wood: _____ (Species),

3. Plywood: _____ (Species),

4. Type of moulding: _____ (Solid or Applied).

5. Type of panel: _____ (Flat or Raised).

The following is the recommended AWI Specification for solid wood paneling.

Interior for Transparent Finish

Note to specifier: If both transparent and opaque finish are required for interior standing and running trim, the spaces to receive transparent finish should be listed here or scheduled on drawings and referred to here.

1. AWI quality grade:_____ (Premium grade, Custom grade or Economy grade).
Note to specifier: AWI grade selection includes quality of machining, sanding and materials.

2. Solid wood: _____ (Species),_____ (Cut).

3. Plywood: _____ (Species), _____ (Cut).

Note to specifier: If more than one specie is required for solid wood or plywood, they must be specified here and the spaces in which used noted.

Interior for Opaque Finish

Note to specifier: If both opaque and transparent finish are required for interior standing and running trim the spaces to receive opaque finish should be listed here or scheduled on drawings and referred to here.

1. AWI quality grade: _____ (Premium grade, Custom grade or Economy grade).
Note to specifier: AWI grade selection includes quality of machining, sanding and materials.

2. Solid wood: _____ (Species),

3. Plywood: _____ (Species),

Note to specifier: AWI Premium and Custom grades require particleboard, overlay plywood or hardwood plywood. Fir plywood is allowed only in Economy grade.

In the vast majority of paneling installations, it is desirable to have the paneling factory finished at the woodworker's plant. Wood in its dry unprotected state is hygroscopic and absorbs moisture when subject to dampness. The result is dimensional change and raised grain. Designing to allow free movement of the various parts, plus priming, sealing and finishing at the earliest possible time after the woodwork has been fabricated, results in the most satisfactory installation.

The following is the recommended AWI Specification for Factory Finishing of architectural paneling.

2.12 Factory Finishing

Note to specifier: Includes factory finishing of any and all architectural paneling items specified in this section. The advantages of factory finishing are most apparent for doors, paneling and casework, however, it may be desirable to have other woodwork items adjacent to these factory finished to maintain color and finish match.

A. Transparent Finish

1. Items: _____
Note to specifier: List here those architectural paneling and adjacent items and their locations which are to receive transparent factory finish.

2. AWI Factory Finish System # _____.
Note to specifier: Choose system and quality grade from selection guide for AWI Finish Systems Table (Test 1500-5). If more than one transparent type of finish is to be used on this project, use a separate subsection for each.

3. AWI quality grade: _____ (Premium grade or Custom grade).

4. Stain: _____ (None, Dark, Medium or Light).

5. Degree of Sheen: _____ (Dull rubbed, Medium rubbed, Full gloss).

6. Effect: _____ (Open or Close grain effect).

B. Opaque Finish

1. Items: _____
Note to specifier: List here the architectural paneling and adjacent items and their locations which are to receive an opaque factory finish.

2. AWI Factory Finish System # _____.
Note to specifier: Choose system and quality grade from selection guide for AWI Finish Systems Table (Test 1500-5). If more than one opaque type of finish is to be used on this project, use a separate subsection for each.

3. AWI quality grade: _____ (Premium grade or Custom grade).

4. Degree of Sheen:_____ (Full gloss, Semi gloss or Flat).

C. Field Touch-up

Field touch-up shall be the responsibility of the installing contractor and shall include the filling and touch-up of exposed job made nail or screw holes, refinishing of raw surfaces resulting from job fitting, repair of job inflicted scratches and mars, and final cleaning up of the finished surfaces.

The AWI Guide Specification assures the owner of accurate costs as they are based upon exacting Standards which the industry recognizes and accepts as true Hallmarks of Quality.

WINDOW SYSTEMS

Designers can no longer consider interior window systems, such as blinds, shutters, shades, and drapery, as purely decorative treatments. With increasing concerns about energy conservation, light, and acoustic control, window systems assume an added importance in planning commercial interiors. This chapter will survey performance requirements, fabrication, estimation, installation, maintenance, and other factors that must be considered prior to making specification decisions.

PERFORMANCE CRITERIA

The majority of window components are not regulated by codes, but drapery fabrics that cover large expanses of wall are frequently required to meet certain flammability standards. For example, if drapery covers more than 10 percent of wall area, it is considered an interior finish by many codes.

Drapery Flammability Regulations

Drapery flammability regulations primarily involve fabric used in commercial, health-care, and institutional installations. There are numerous state and city regulations in existence, but the most frequently quoted standards are those required in the City of New York, the City of Boston, and the State of California.

1. *The City of New York* requires that all flame-retardant chemicals used in the city be approved by a Board of Standards and Appeals. After the approval of the chemical is granted, a number is issued which must later appear on a notarized affidavit stating that the fabric has been treated with the approved flame retardant.

2. *The City of Boston* requires that a certificate of flame retardancy add a 15″ × 15″ (38.1 × 38.1 cm) sample of the treated fabric be sent to the Boston Fire Department. Complete details on the intended use must be provided along with a filing fee.

3. *The State of California* requires that all flame-retardant chemicals be approved by the State Fire Marshal. The state also requires that the treatments be applied in approved, licensed finishing companies. Certificates of flame resistance and a 12″ × 12″ (30.5 × 30.5 cm) sample must be submitted to the office of the State Fire Marshal. Designers may obtain a listing of approved pretreated fabrics, finishing companies, and chemicals recommended for particular fibers from the California State Fire Marshal's Office. Figure 11.1 illustrates a typical flame-retardance certificate.

Chapter 12 contains more detailed information on fabric flammability terminology and flame retardants. Fabrics that are considered inherently flame resistant, such as fiberglass, wools, and some modacrylics, do not require flame-retardant treatments. Some fabrics made for health-care facilities contain a blend of saran, verel-modacrylic, and rayon, which is mildew-, rot-, and vermin-proof. This fabric blend will melt rather than support flame when a source of ignition is applied. Fiberglass will neither ignite nor melt. Designers, however, should be aware that some dyes used on the surface of the fiberglass may burn and spread flame across the entire sur-

Certificate of Flame Resistance
ISSUED BY
KIESLING-HESS FABRIC SERVICE COMPANY, INC.
1011 WOOD ST., PHILA., PA. 19107
519 W. 38th ST., NEW YORK, N. Y. 10018

This is to certify that the following materials, delivered to us by

were flameproofed on

The Fire Retardant result of said fabric is in accordance with Federal Specification CCC–t–191b Method 5906 (Flame Retardancy of Textiles, Horizontal).

Tests made on fabrics which have been treated as indicated above have demonstrated that their Fire Resistance will withstand up to 20 solvent dry cleanings. Thus, no routine annual re-treating of such fabrics is necessary.

KIESLING-HESS FABRIC SERVICE COMPANY, INC.

Form 109

Figure 11.1 Certificate of flame resistance. Reproduced with permission of Kiesling-Hess Fabric Service Company, Inc.

face. Designers should require tests to ensure that the fire performance has not been altered by methods of fabrication, weaving, or application of finishes.

Construction and Quality Control

Construction and quality control of interior window components is based on federal specifications that establish standards for a limited number of window coverings.

1. FS DDD-S251d *Shade, Roller, Window; Roller, Slat, Cord, and Accessories* describes performance requirements for one type of cloth window shade in stock widths up to 77 in. (195.6 cm) and lengths to 12 ft (3.6 m). Criteria are established for materials, such as cords, ring pull, rollers, roller diameter, slats, springs, brackets, and thread cotton. Dimensional criteria are established for length, hems, width, and roller coverage.

2. FS L-S-001787 (GSA-FSS) *Interim Federal Specification Shade, Window (Vinyl) with Roller, Slat, Ring Pull and Accessories and Vinyl Film (in Piece Goods)*, 1973, covers requirements for vinyl window shades and vinyl film in piece goods form. Criteria are established for tensile strength, elongation, tear strength, weight, volatility, spe-

cific gravity, color fastness, heat sealing, flame resistance, and resistance to cracking.

3. FS AA-V-00200B (GSA-FSS) *Interim Federal Specification Venetian Blinds*, 1973, covers two types of venetian blinds: type I, 2-in. (5.1-cm) slats; and type II, 1-in. (2.5-cm) slats. This specification establishes requirements for the slats, rails, head rails and braces, bottom rails and tape fittings, end caps, ladder tapes, breaking strength, colorfastness, and dimensional stability, cords, operating hardware, tilting devices, installation hardware, and head rail intermediate supports.

Energy Conservation

Energy conservation can be substantially affected by the use and design of interior window coverings. Windows have six energy functions:

1. Provision of winter solar heat

2. Provision of year-round daylighting

3. Rejection of summer solar heat

4. Provision of air tightness during periods of heating and air conditioning

5. Provision of insulation

6. Provision of natural ventilation during temperate weather[1]

Specification of design components to save energy should be based on the importance of each window's function, the local climate, and the requirements imposed by the activities that will take place in the interior space. Evaluating the effectiveness of a particular installation must take the total window system into consideration:

1. *The site*, which includes shade trees, ground surfaces, orientation to the sun and wind.

2. *Exterior appendages*, such as sun screens, roll blinds, exterior shutters, awnings and architectural projections.

3. *The window framing components*, such as weather-stripping, type of operation, size, and window tilt.

4. *Window glazing methods*, which include applied films, multiple glazing, reflecting glass, and glass block.

5. *Interior window components*, such as blinds, drapery, film shades, interior sun screens, opaque roll shades, and insulating shutters.

6. *The building interior components*, such as task lighting, colors and reflectance levels of interior surfaces, automatic switching, and fixture circulating (see Chapter 13 for more information on task lighting in relation to energy conservation).

Table 11.1 summarizes the advantages and disadvantages of various interior window components. The two most popular window treatments are blinds and drapery. Drapery is often favored because it adds textural contrast and is an excellent method for controlling noise in the interior environment.

Drapery Fenestration Data. An increasing number of contract fabric manufacturers are including fenestration data on fabrics designed for drapery. These data refer to the transmission of solar energy through glass to a building interior. The information provided by these data can be used to determine the heating and air-conditioning needs of an interior.

The selection of decorative fabrics to screen glass walls and wide glass areas requires a knowledge of how weaves, patterns, fabric weights, colors, and luster can influence the transmission of solar energy. When direct sunlight strikes a draped window, the fabric and glass act in combination to:

1. Transmit a portion of light and heat to the interior.

2. Reflect a part of the heat back to the outside atmosphere.

3. Absorb the remaining light as heat.

To minimize solar heat gain, the drapery exposed to sunlight should ideally have high reflectance and low transmittance.

Determining Fabric Fenestration Values. Consideration of visible and solar optical properties, shading coefficient, U-value, and airtightness should be included in a determination of fabric fenestration values.

1. Visible properties. Those functions of fabric construction—color and luster—which control the effect of glare and opacity on vision.
   a. Openness factor refers to the percentage of light transmitted through the interstices of the fabric. This factor correlates closely with the reduction of noise from interior sources.
   b. Visible transmittance refers to a numerical value useful in comparing different fabric qualities for glare and opacity.

2. Solar optical properties. Those functions of fabric construction—color and luster—which control the amount of heat energy passed through light.
   a. Solar transmittance refers to the amount of sunlight that passes through the fabric or penetrates through the yarns.
   b. Solar reflection refers to the amount of sunlight that is reflected from the fabric.
   c. Solar absorption refers to the amount of light neither transmitted nor reflected by a fabric, but absorbed as heat.

3. Shading Coefficient. A value derived from the three solar optical properties of a fabric; i.e., the total amount of heat transmitted by a window configuration divided by the total amount of heat transmitted by a single pane of double-strength glass. The *lower* the shading coefficient, the greater the efficiency of the window system. The more efficient systems range from .40 to .60 in shading coefficient; the most effective have shading coefficients below .40. Table 11.2 illustrates a typical fenestration data listing for a particular fabric. The shading coefficient is listed for regular plate glass and heat-absorbing glass. In comparing the visible and solar optical properties, designers will notice that the fabric color has a definite affect on these properties.

Designers will occasionally see charts on which drapery material is characterizd by a "fabric designator," consisting of a roman numeral with a capital letter subscript. The roman numeral refers to the weave and the subscript refers to fabric color or value:

a. I: Open weave
b. II: Semiopen weave
c. III: Closed weave
d. D: Dark
e. M: Medium
f. L: Light

TABLE 11.1   ADVANTAGES AND DISADVANTAGES OF INTERIOR WINDOW COMPONENTS

Component	Advantages	Disadvantages
Venetian blinds	1. Minimal space used to store blinds when open. Stack with minimal obstruction of window area. 2. Can be selectively tilted to direct sunlight to the ceiling or directly on the work surface. 3. Can be partially lowered to eliminate sunlight from only a portion of the room.	1. Difficult to clean. 2. Continued maintenance required to raise and lower, tilt and lift. 3. Maintenance required to replace lifting and tilting hardware, cord replacement. 4. Decreased effectiveness in reducing winter heat loss compared with shades or tight fitting drapery due to the cracks between each slat.
Film shades	1. Reduced summer solar heat gain and winter night losses with a reflective or selective film. 2. Reduced winter heat loss with shade configurations which provide insulating, trapped air spaces. 3. Reduced infiltration provided by obstructing flow of incoming air with a film shade sealed at edges. 4. Increased comfort near windows due to less body heat radiating to the inside film shade than to a cold window. 5. Elimination of ultraviolet radiation, thus less fading of carpets and furniture fabrics. 6. Reduced sky glare. 7. Daytime privacy and night visibility into public buildings for security surveillance.	1. Required management of shades by building occupants. 2. Difficult to install on other-than-right-angle window areas. 3. Lack of glare control from direct sunlight. 4. Lack of privacy at night. 5. Reduced winter solar heat gain through low emissivity film shades installed to reduce heat losses.
Opaque roll shades	1. Reduced solar heat gain in summer. 2. Privacy. 3. Glare control. 4. Self-storing. 5. Inexpensive.	1. Maintenance of spring mechanism. Springs jam with time and need replacement. 2. View out and shading at the same time is impossible. 3. Impeded ventilation from the top opening of double-hung windows when the shade is lowered.
Drapery	1. Improved comfort near windows is possible when the drapery is closed. 2. Glare control. 3. Privacy. 4. Decreased winter heat loss and summer heat gain. 5. Noise absorption. Noise within the room is absorbed by drapery rather than reflected from uncovered glass. Outside noise transmitted through glass is partially absorbed. The denser the weave and heavier the fabric, the more effective it is in reducing noise.	1. Periodic cleaning required. 2. Obstruction of view when closed. 3. Desire for airy, open drapery (casement) conflicts with thermal effectiveness of draperies in both summer and winter. 4. Possible breakage of glass when used in conjunction with heat-absorbing glass. The glass and the way it is set should be designed to withstand the additional heat buildup from sunlight being reflected back at the glass from closed drapery.

TABLE 11.2 FENESTRATION DATA FOR DRAPERY

	Pattern	Fenestration Data			
Width:	48''				
Color:	Flax	Visual properties		Shading coefficients	
Contents:	63% Verel modacrylic, 17% rayon, 10% flax, 10% saran monofilament	Transmittance .38 Openness factor .28		¼'' Regular plate glass .50 ¼'' Heat-absorbing glass .46	
		Solar optical properties			
Inherently fire safe		Transmittance .32 Reflectance .56 Absorption .12			
Color:	White	Visual properties		Shading coefficients	
Contents:	63% Verel modacrylic, 27% rayon, 10% saran monofilament	Transmittance .46 Openness factor .32		¼'' Regular plate glass .49 ¼'' Heat-absorbing glass .46	
		Solar optical properties			
Inherently fire safe		Transmittance .36 Reflectance .60 Absorption .04			
Color:	Bronze	Visual properties		Shading coefficients	
Contents:	63% Verel modacrylic, 27% rayon, 10% saran monofilament	Transmittance .30 Openness factor .24		¼'' Regular plate glass .54 ¼'' Heat-absorbing glass .48	
		Solar optical properties			
Inherently fire safe		Transmittance .32 Reflectance .48 Absorption .20			

Source: Lazarus Fabrics.

TABLE 11.3 FENESTRATION DATA AND FABRIC DESIGNATOR

COLOR	Openness Factor	Visual Transmittance	Solar Transmittance	Solar Reflectance	Solar Absorptance	Shading Coefficient 0°	Shading Coefficient 45°	Yarn Reflectance	Fabric Designator	Shading Coefficient Index Letter
WHITE	0.241	0.583	0.469	0.340	0.191	0.598	0.568	0.448	II$_M$	E
WHITE	0.141	0.566	0.418	0.392	0.190	0.548	0.521	0.456	II$_M$	D
WHITE	0.242	0.649	0.504	0.328	0.168	0.621	0.590	0.433	II$_M$	E
WHITE	0.0646	0.461	0.304	0.458	0.238	0.459	0.436	0.490	III$_M$	B
FLAX	0.131	0.479	0.335	0.422	0.243	0.492	0.468	0.486	II$_M$	C
FLAX	0.0628	0.376	0.277	0.424	0.299	0.463	0.440	0.452	III$_M$	B
WHITE	0.0744	0.411	0.289	0.434	0.277	0.464	0.440	0.469	II$_M$	B
FLAX	0.0529	0.365	0.270	0.402	0.328	0.470	0.447	0.424	III$_M$	C
FLAX	0.0136	0.408	0.289	0.425	0.286	0.468	0.445	0.431	III$_M$	B
FLAX	0.227	0.581	0.445	0.321	0.234	0.595	0.566	0.415	II$_M$	E
FLAX	0.0707	0.377	0.285	0.398	0.317	0.479	0.455	0.428	II$_M$	C
FLAX	0.169	0.582	0.430	0.315	0.255	0.591	0.561	0.379	II$_M$	E
WHITE	0.0563	0.376	0.278	0.475	0.247	0.438	0.416	0.503	III$_L$	B
FLAX	0.115	0.472	0.352	0.387	0.261	0.518	0.492	0.437	II$_M$	C
FLAX	0.122	0.492	0.373	0.355	0.272	0.544	0.517	0.404	II$_M$	D
WHITE	0.131	0.554	0.414	0.380	0.206	0.552	0.524	0.437	II$_M$	D
WHITE	0.140	0.528	0.411	0.341	0.248	0.569	0.541	0.397	II$_M$	D
FLAX	0.00889	0.322	0.255	0.406	0.339	0.461	0.438	0.410	III$_M$	B
WHITE	0.0185	0.473	0.355	0.418	0.227	0.504	0.479	0.426	III$_M$	C
FLAX	0.0106	0.380	0.271	0.464	0.265	0.440	0.418	0.469	III$_M$	B
FLAX	0.0119	0.312	0.263	0.445	0.292	0.445	0.423	0.450	III$_M$	B
WHITE	0.00908	0.365	0.292	0.475	0.233	0.445	0.423	0.479	III$_M$	B
WHITE	0.184	0.620	0.510	0.326	0.164	0.625	0.594	0.400	II$_M$	E
FLAX	0.181	0.591	0.516	0.318	0.166	0.632	0.600	0.388	II$_M$	E
WHITE	0.0204	0.478	0.364	0.430	0.206	0.503	0.478	0.439	III$_M$	C
FLAX	0.00802	0.415	0.319	0.441	0.240	0.475	0.451	0.445	III$_M$	C
FLAX	0.0138	0.253	0.205	0.465	0.330	0.407	0.386	0.472	III$_M$	A
WHITE)										
FLAX)										
WHITE)										
FLAX)										
WHITE)	AVAILABLE UPON REQUEST									
FLAX)										

Reproduced with permission of Contex Fabrics, Los Angeles.

These charts may also contain shading coefficient information in terms of a letter index. These letters range from A to J, with the shading coefficient decreasing from A to J (see Table 11.3).

Using this information, the window heat gain can be calculated by adding the solar heat gain and the conducted heat gain. The solar heat gain equals the amount of solar energy transmitted plus the amount of solar energy absorbed by the window system and dissipated into the building interior. The conducted heat gain equals the U-value multiplied by the inside/outside temperature difference.

4. U-value. The amount of heat conducted from the inside air (or heat conducted from the outside air) through the window configuration. A U-value of 0.65 means 0.65 Btus pass through each square foot of window configuration for every hour and for each Fahrenheit degree difference that exists between the inside and outside temperature. The *lower* the U-value, the greater the efficiency of the window system. For example, if two layers of drapery which are separated by an air space are used, the thermal performance of the window would be improved. A U-value of 0.65 is possible for single glazed windows, assuming the same degree of airtightness for both layers of trapped air. In the event that the two layers of drapery would provide a higher degree of airtightness between the drapery and the window, a much lower U-value of 0.57 could be obtained.[2] If double draperies are used with insulating glass, a U-value of approximately 0.37 is possible.

5. Airtightness. The volume of air passing through an opening. This is measured by the cubic feet of air for a given time period, divided by the crack length. If drapery is installed against the wall or window frame at the sides and allowed to make contact with the floor or window sill, it serves to better insulate the window in the winter and provide shade in the summer. Though drapery can be fairly tight fitting on the sides, it is difficult to obtain an airtight fit at the bottom and still allow for opening and closing the drapery. The manner in which the top is fabricated can aid in energy conservation by preventing conditioned air from circulating between the drapery and the glass. When room air comes in contact with cold glass and cascades back into the room through the bottom of the drapery, the efficiency is greatly impaired.

Additional Guidelines for Window Energy Conservation.
Six more points must be considered for window energy conservation:

1. During the daylight hours in winter, draperies should be kept open for windows that receive direct sunlight, i.e., south-facing windows, east-facing windows in the morning, and west-facing windows in the afternoon. This allows sunlight to penetrate the interior and warm more massive materials and remote surfaces. This heat will then radiate to other interior surfaces rather than back to the glass.

2. In areas with little or no direct sunlight in winter, i.e., north-facing windows, east-facing windows in the afternoon, and west-facing windows in the morning, draperies should be drawn because they will be much closer to room temperature than the glass. During winter nights draperies on all windows should be drawn to reduce heat loss to the exterior. Also, draperies should remain closed as much as possible during summer days to reduce solar heat gains.

3. Drapery should be installed to allow the opened drapery to stack clear of the glass area so that more sunlight can enter the window.

4. Draperies should be designed to prevent conditioned air from blowing between the fabric and the glass. If an air register is directly above or below the window, deflectors may be necessary to direct the air into the room and not between the drapery and the glass.

5. Drapery heading may be designed to fit into a cove or recessed area to prevent air leakage above the drapery top.

6. Thermal liners may be used to promote better heat reflectance, but designers should be cautious about heat buildup which could damage the glass.

DETERMINING WINDOW MEASUREMENT AND HARDWARE INSTALLATION

Accurate measurements must be supplied to the fabricators of the window components for successful installations.

CEILING

WALL

Figure 11.2 Hardware installation.

Drapery

Drapery hardware may be installed inside the window jambs and ceiling- or wall-mounted (see Figure 11.2). Specification of drapery hardware systems is based on the following criteria:

1. System type

2. Operational direction

3. Available lengths (or widths)

4. Drapery headings accommodated

5. Application

6. Bracket supports

7. Maximum fabric weight accommodated

Table 11.4 provides a survey of the characteristics found in typical drapery hardware systems designed for commercial use. Designers should be aware that these systems are made from heavy gauge steel and are engineered to withstand greater drapery weights than those designed for residential use. Calculating the finished weight of drapery is based on the weight per linear yard of the particular fabric. Table 11.5 shows various fabric weights and drapery sizes that could be used to arrive at a total of 32 lb (15.5 kg).[3] Hand-drawn hardware systems are usually installed in shorter widths and therefore accommodate less fabric weight. Some drapery construction makes use of a tape snapping system, which may also limit the weight allowed per drapery unit. Designers should verify weight limitations prior to finalizing fabric selection.

Critical measurement dimensions for drapery hardware involve: (1) the bracket placement and (2) the method of installation. Bracket placement determines the length and width of the drapery, as well as the amount of glass surface that will be exposed when the drapery is fully opened. Figure 11.3 illustrates the dimensions that must be recorded for the installation contractor. Dimension line C is shown 4 in. (10.2 cm) above the glass area to indicate placement of standard pinched pleated drapery. This placement prevents exposing to view the fabrication components (pins and tape). The following formula may be used to calculate bracket placement in order to clear the glass area:

1. Add 12 in. to the total width of the window:

$$100'' + 12'' = 112''$$

2. Divide this total by 6:

$$112'' \div 6 = 18 \ 2/3''$$

(round out to next number, or 19")

3. Extend bracket placement 19 in. on each side of the window, and the fully opened drapery will clear the entire window.

Dimensions that must be recorded on irregularly shaped windows are shown in Figure 11.4. Multiple drapery rods may be used in these installations, or hardware may be custom made or bent to fit the required dimensions.

Drapery hardware designed for ceiling or recessed installation does not require additional support brackets because the rod is usually attached at intervals along the entire length.

TABLE 11.4 COMMERCIAL DRAPERY HARDWARE SYSTEMS

System	Operation	Lengths	Headings	Application	Support Brackets	Maximum Fabric Weights
Draw Cord System: Track is opened and closed by loop cord and tension pulleys	One-way draw Two-way draw Multiple draw	16 to 50' 24 to 60' 32 to 110'	Conventional pleated or snapped tape method	Recessed in coves or acoustic tiles. Ceiling mounted or wall mounted	Only required on wall-mounted hardware systems. Usually placed 48" apart along track	Ranges from 50 to 220 lb
Hand-Drawn System: Track is opened and closed with hand batons which are attached to lead carrier. No pull cords used	One-way draw Two-way draw	20 to 24' Up to 48'	Conventional pleated or snapped tape method	Recessed, ceiling or wall installation	Required on wall-mounted systems	Ranges from 48 to 96 lb

TABLE 11.5 VARIATIONS IN FABRIC WEIGHTS AND DRAPERY SIZES WHICH EQUAL A TOTAL WEIGHT OF 32 LB

Fabric Type	Weight per Linear Yd	Drapery Size 100% Fullness
Sheer or light-weight casement	5 oz	16' wide × 32' long 32' wide × 16' long
Lined sheers or medium-weight fabrics	10 oz	16' wide × 16' long 32' wide × 8' long
Lined medium-weight fabrics or heavy cotton velours and linens	20 oz	16' wide × 8' long

WINDOW MEASUREMENT

A   OUTSIDE LENGTH
B   FLOOR LENGTH
C   INSIDE CASING MOUNTING
D   CASING MOUNTING
E   WALL MOUNTING

Figure 11.3 Critical window dimensions for drapery installation.

FOR BAY WINDOW
FURNISH DIMENSIONS
A, B, X, Y, Z

FOR CURVED WINDOW
FURNISH DIMENSIONS A, B

FOR IRREGULAR CORNER ANGLE
FURNISH DIMENSIONS A, B, X, Y

FOR 90° MITER
FURNISH DIMENSIONS A, B

Figure 11.4 Irregular window shapes. Source: Slim-Line Drapery Systems, Graber Company.

DRAPERY ESTIMATION

After the placement of the hardware has been determined, the designer may proceed to measure for the amount of drapery fabric required and specify the method of fabrication. Standard traverse drapery yardage (without pattern repeat) is calculated in the following manner:

1. *Finished length:* the distance from the top of the rod to the desired bottom of the drapery (allow 1-in. [2.5-cm] clearance at the floor).

2. *Cut length:* the distance from the top of the rod to the desired bottom of the drapery *plus hems and top headings.* These measurements may vary depending on the type of fabric and fabrication. Many designers add 18 in. (45.7 cm) for sheer drapery; 17 in. (43.2 cm) for unlined drapery; 13 in. (33 cm) for lined drapery. Example:

   Finished length = 84″ + 17″ = 101″ cut length

3. *Finished width:* the distance of the rod from bracket to bracket *plus* the number of inches the brackets extend from the wall. This distance is known as the "return." To this measurement add another 6 in. (15.2 cm) for the center overlap (see Figure 11.5). Example: If the rod is 120 in. wide and the brackets extend 3 in. from the wall, the total finished width would be 132 inches:

   120″ + 3″ + 3″ + 6″ = 132″

4. *Number of widths required:* the number of fabric panels needed to span this distance is dependent on the desired fullness. One hundred percent fullness is 2 times the width; 150 percent fullness is 2.5 times the width. Some sheers may require 200 percent fullness, or 3 times the width.

Finished width × 2.5 fullness ÷ width of fabric
= number of widths

Example:

Finished width 132″ × 2.5 = 330″ ÷ 48″ fabric
= 6.87, or 7 panels

The 7 panels would be equally divided into 3½ panels placed on each side of the center draw.

5. *Number of yards required:* the number of panels is multiplied by the cut length to determine the total inches needed. This answer is then transposed into yards (divided by 36 in.). Example:

   7 panels × 101″ = 707″
   707″ ÷ 36″ = 19.63″, or 20 yd

If estimating for a one-way draw wall installation, proceed as follows:

a. Measure the length as in the above example.
b. Measure the width from the bracket to the end of the rod.
c. Add the required inches for bracket projections.
d. Add 3½ in. (8.9 cm) for the return (see Figure 11.6).
e. Proceed as explained above.

Figure 11.5 *Center draw single traverse rod.*

Figure 11.6 *Single one-way draw traverse rod.*

*Figure 11.7
Drapery headings.
Source: Slim-Line
Drapery Systems,
Graber Company.*

STACK PLEATING

ROLL PLEATING

ACCORDIAN PLEATING

PINCH PLEATING

*Figure 11.8
Stack pleating
tape spacing.
Reproduced with
permission of
Slim-Line
Drapery Systems,
Graber Company.*

Pattern Repeats

When the specified fabric has a pattern repeat, the required panel cut lengths and the total yardage will be increased. For example, in step 1 of the estimating procedure for a center draw drapery, the cutting length was calculated to be 101 in. (256.5 cm). If the fabric has a 24-in. (61-cm) repeat, the required cut length would be increased to accommodate matching the 24-in. repeats; i.e., four 24-in. repeats would only total 96 in. (243.8 cm); therefore five 24-in. repeats will be needed per panel (120″ in. [304.8 cm]). The revised panel cutting length would now be 120 in.; therefore

$$120″ \times 7 \text{ panels} = 840″$$

It is suggested that one additional repeat length be added to this total to allow for matching the first panel cut; therefore the total yardage would be determined in this manner:

$$840″ + 24″ = 864″ \div 36″ = 24 \text{ yd}$$

Designers should measure the repeat to verify that the repeat size listed on the sample is accurate.

Institutional Cubicle Curtains

Most institutional cubicle curtains are fabricated to hang 14 to 16 in. (35.6 to 40.6 cm) above the floor. The tracks are either mounted on or suspended from the ceiling. To determine the height of the curtain, designers should measure from the track to the floor and deduct 14 to 16 in. Example:

$$
\begin{aligned}
109″ &= \text{distance from track to floor} \\
- \quad 16″ &= \text{clearance from the bottom of the} \\
&\quad\ \text{curtain to the floor} \\
\hline
93″ &= \text{finished length}
\end{aligned}
$$

The width is determined by measuring the track from left to right and adding 10 percent for fullness. Example:

$$
\begin{aligned}
148″ &= \text{actual track measurement} \\
+ \quad 14″ &= \text{percentage fullness} \\
\hline
162″ &= \text{width}
\end{aligned}
$$

If the top of the curtains is to be fabricated with a mesh for ceiling ventilation, the specification should state that this is included in the finished length.

DRAPERY FABRICATION

There are four major types of drapery construction used in commercial installations. Figure 11.7 illustrates the style of headings employed by these four methods.

Pinch Pleat Systems

Pinch pleat systems are constructed with pleater tape and are attached to side carriers with slip-on or pin-on hooks. This method requires more stacking space than other methods, and the hooks must be removed prior to cleaning. A standard traverse rod is used for installation.

Stack Pleat Systems

Stack pleat systems require one-half the stacking space needed for pinched pleats. Because this system employs a snap-tape fabrication method, the stack-back widths and depths can be varied according to the snap spacings. Tape spacings are available in 7½, 8½, and 10 in. (19.1, 21.6, and 25.4 cm). (See Figure 11.8).

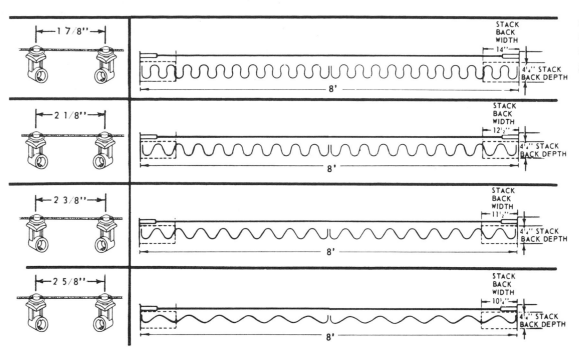

Figure 11.9 Roll pleat snap carrier placement. Reproduced with permission of The Kirsch Company.

1. 7½-in. spacings produce a 14-in. (35.6-cm) stacking which is 3¾ in. (9.5 cm) deep. This tape spacing is recommended for draperies 54 in. (37.2 cm) in length.

2. 8½-in. spacings produce a 12-in. (30.5-cm) stacking which is 4½ in. (11.5 cm) deep. This spacing is recommended for draperies up to 108 in. (274.3 cm) in length.

3. 10-in. spacings produce an 11-in. (27.9 cm) stacking which is 5 in. (12.7 cm) deep. This is recommended for drapery over 108 in. in length or very heavy, bulky fabrics.

This fabrication method requires a special drapery rod which accommodates snap carriers. This and other snap-tape systems reduce installation time, and the tape need not be removed during cleaning.

Roll Pleat Systems[4]

Roll pleat systems provide a pleasing appearance from both the interior and exterior. Headings are fabricated with snap tape and are suspended under the track to prevent sagging. They require little stack space, and the use of a "butt"-type master carrier (instead of a center overlap carrier) eliminates a flat space in the drapery center. Figure 11.9 illustrates the butt-type installation and shows how the snap carriers can be spaced to vary the fullness and stack-back widths. When using 4¼-in. (16.6-cm) snap tape, varied carrier spacing produces the following drapery fullness:

Carrier Spacing	Percentage of Fullness
1⅞ in. (4.7 cm)	120
2⅛ in. (5.4 cm)	100
2⅜ in. (6 cm)	80
2⅝ in. (6.7 cm)	60

Accordion-Type Pleating Systems[5]

Accordion-type pleating systems provide a sharply tailored affect with a uniform exterior and interior appearance. This system is also fabricated with the snap-tape method and requires a rod system that employs the snap carriers. Figure 11.10 illustrates a butt-type center fabrication and shows the stacking width for center draw 88-in. (223.5 cm) wide drapery.

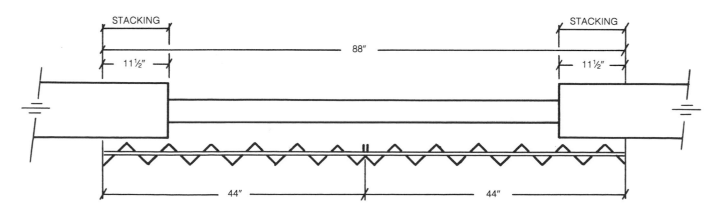

Figure 11.10 Accordian pleating systems: drapery stacking. Source: The Kirsch Company.

Figure 11.11 Drapery measurement sheet.

MEASURE SHEET

Name_____   Phone_____ Store_____

Address_____   Salesman_____

ROOM: FABRIC: LINING:

FABRIC	_____	X_____	_____
LINING	_____	X_____	_____
RODS	_____	X_____	_____
LABOR	_____	X_____	_____
INSTALL	_____	X_____	_____
TRIM	_____	X_____	_____
TRIM LAB.	_____	X_____	_____
	Total	_____	

PIN SETTING:
FINISH WIDTH: FINISH LENGTH: PAIR
PANEL: CUTS: RETURNS:

ROOM: FABRIC: LINING:

FABRIC	_____	X_____	_____
LINING	_____	X_____	_____
RODS	_____	X_____	_____
LABOR	_____	X_____	_____
INSTALL	_____	X_____	_____
TRIM	_____	X_____	_____
TRIM LAB.	_____	X_____	_____
	Total	_____	

PIN SETTING:
FINISH WIDTH: FINISH LENGTH: PAIR
PANEL: CUTS: RETURNS:

ROOM: FABRIC: LINING:

FABRIC	_____	X_____	_____
LINING	_____	X_____	_____
RODS	_____	X_____	_____
LABOR	_____	X_____	_____
INSTALL	_____	X_____	_____
TRIM	_____	X_____	_____
TRIM LAB.	_____	X_____	_____
	Total	_____	

PIN SETTING:
FINISH WIDTH: FINISH LENGTH: PAIR
PANEL: CUTS: RETURNS:

FABRICATION SPECIFICATION

Designers should provide the following information to drapery fabricators:

1. Specified fabric
   Name
   Number (mill number and purchase order number)
   Color
   Width
   Pattern repeat size
   Sample piece to verify correct shipment
   Total yardage required

2. Drapery measurement
   Width
   Stacking width
   Finished width
   Number of fabric widths
   Percentage of fullness
   Finished length
   Hems and headings
   Cutting length

3. Hardware
   Type
   Length of track

Operational method
   One way
   Two way
   Multiple
   Cord operated
   Hand operated
   Motorized

4. Hardware installation
   Ceiling
   Wall
   Distance above casing
   Within casing
   Extension beyond window (inches on each side)

Hardware installation instructions should include a drawing of the window and wall with specific bracket locations clearly marked. Separate drawings should be made for each window and room (see Figure 11.11).

Drapery workrooms advise that designers make their fabric purchase orders as specific as possible, and a sample of the specified fabric should always be attached (see Figure 11.12). Workrooms are advised to inspect the fabric for defects before cutting because many fabrics may have flaws that will require reordering. To avoid costly delays, some designers specify additional yardage.

Figure 11.12 Drapery order form.

SHADES AND BLINDS

Designers may refer to the guide specification for drapery and drapery hardware in Figure 11.18 on page 173 for suggested installation and postinstallation inspection criteria.

Shades

Shades are usually installed within the window jambs. Figure 11.13 illustrates the critical areas to be measured for the installation of spring roller shades. The following measurements must be noted:

Jamb: the width of the window opening into which the shade will be mounted. List this figure as the inside measurement.

Tip to tip: the width from the metal ratchet on the left to the tip of the pin on the right side of the shade roller (⅛ in. [3.2 mm] less than the jamb measurement to allow room for brackets).

Barrel width: the measurement of an existing roller, not including the tips.

Cloth: the measurement of the actual shade surface. The shade length is usually not specified unless the window is exceedingly long.[6]

Horizontal Blinds

Blinds may be mounted within or beyond the window jambs. Since many blinds are custom fitted to the window, it is difficult to alter them if a mistake is made in the measurements. (See Figure 11.14.) Designers should measure accurately to within ⅛ in. (3.2 mm), using a metal or wooden rule. The surface within the casing area (for inside installation) or outside the casing area should be examined for the best location of the bracket supports. Most brackets require a 1-in. (2.5-cm) width. If the installation is to be outside the jamb area, sufficient overlap of the blinds must be provided at the sides and bottom of the window opening. After the bracket position has been determined, the following measurements should be provided to the fabricator:

1. *Width:* the length from jamb to jamb.

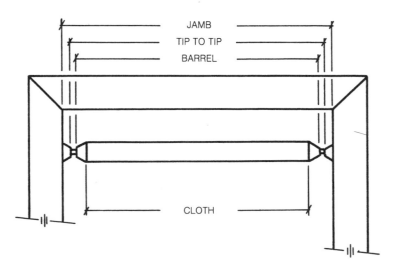

Figure 11.13 Measurement for spring roller shades.

2. *Length:* the exact distance from the inside top of the window to the bottom ledge. If the blind is not to touch the bottom ledge, subtract ½ in. (12.7 mm) from the length measurement. If the blind is to extend to the floor, provide the measurement from the top of the window frame to the floor. On any length, the measurement should include the distance from the floor to the top of the sill. This will allow the fabricator to estimate the required length of the operating controls.

Outside Installation

1. *Width:* the length between the points where the brackets will be located (for privacy, brackets should be located at least 3 in. [7.6 cm] beyond the edge of the window jamb).

2. *Length:* the distance from the top of the bracket location to the point where the blind is to reach. Most fabricators make blinds with a tolerance up to 1 in. (2.5 cm) longer than the given measurement.

Standard horizontal aluminum or wood blinds are manufactured with 1″ (2.54 cm) slats and are hung from a steel head rail 1″ × 1½″ (2.54 × 1.27 cm). Most blinds over 48″ (121.9 cm) wide are supplied with a center support bracket. Unless specially specified, operational equipment is placed in following position:

Wand tilt control	left placement
Lift cord	right placement

Standard wand lengths are as follows:

Blind height (inches and cm)	Wand length (inches and cm)
0″ to 32″ (0–81 cm)	12″ (30 cm)
32″ to 50″ (81–127 cm)	20″ (51 cm)
50″ to 70″ (127–177 cm)	30″ (76 cm)
70″ to 90″ (177–228 cm)	50″ (127 cm)
90″ and over (228+ cm)	60″ (151 cm)

Blind (max. width)	142″ (360.6 cm)
Blind (max. height)	126″ (320 cm)
Blind (minimum width)	10.5″ (26.6 cm)

based on best operation for controls at both left and right sides.

Blind (minimum width)	16″ (40.6 cm)

based on best operation when blind controls are installed on one side.
Cord lengths are factory cut in proportion to blind height, i.e., one half the height, unless specified otherwise.

Measuring Procedure *Outside window mount:* Measure exact width and height of the area to be covered. It is recommended that the blinds overlap the window opening by at least 1.5 inches (3.81 cm) on each side. However, extension brackets may be required if blinds are to be mounted beyond the casing. Finished blind height may have a tolerance of more

Figure 11.14 *Critical dimensions requirements for horizontal blinds.*

than ¾" (19.0 mm) or less than ⅛" (3.0 mm). Finished blind width may have a tolerance of plus or minus ³⁄₁₆" (21.0 mm).

Inside window mount: In order to verify the plumbness of the window framing, measure the width of the window opening at three different places and use the smallest or most narrow dimension. The blind manufacturer usually deducts ½" (1.27 cm) for clearance, unless specified otherwise. Measure the height of the window from the top of the opening to the top of the sill. If the window exceeds 24" (60.9 cm), measure height from both the left and right corner to verify squareness. The minimum recess space required for inside mounting is 1¼" (3.18 cm).

Corner installation: Horizontal blinds can successfully be installed on corner windows. The blades may be overlapped at the corner to provide maximum privacy. See the detail drawings in Figure 11.15. Although the blinds may be installed inside the window frame, the outside mounting is most frequently specified. This installation results in the tilt control on the left with the lift control on the right of each blind. It is recommended that both controls be placed opposite the corner.

Measurements for outside corner or ceiling mounts.
Width

1. For overlapping blinds, measure from the corner to a point not less than 1.5" (3.81 cm) beyond the window opening. Refer to Figure 11.7.

2. For bypass blinds, measure from the corner to a point not less than 1.5" (3.81 cm) beyond the window opening. Manufacturer usually takes corner deduction.

Height
Use the same method shown in Figure 11.6 for installation of standard horizontal blinds.

Figure 11.15 *Corner installation for horizontal blinds.*

TABLE 11.6   STACKING TABLE FOR HORIZONTAL BLINDS

Aluminum Blade length—Stack				Wood Blade length—Stack			
in	cm	in	cm	in	cm	in	cm
22	(56)	2	(5.08)	12	(30)	3½	(8.89)
24	(61)	2½	(6.3)	24	(61)	5¾	(14.6)
36	(91)	3	(7.6)	36	(91)	8·	(20)
48	(122)	3½	(9)	48	(122)	10¼	(26)
60	(152)	4	(11)	48	(152)	12½	(32)
72	(183)	4½	(12)	72	(183)	14¾	(38)
84	(214)	5	(13)	84	(214)	17	(44)
96	(244)	5½	(14)	96	(244)	19¼	(50)

Note: 1½″ (3.81 cm) must be added to the stack height to totally clear glass. (This table based on data provided by Graber Industries, Inc.)

MEASURE AT LEAST 6½″ ABOVE THE DOOR OR TO THE CEILING

OVERALL WIDTH

WIDTH — WIDTH

OVERLAP LENGTH

ALLOW ¾″ CLEARANCE FROM FLOOR

Figure 11.16 Horizontal blind installation for patio glass.

TABLE 11.7   VERTICAL BLINDS ONE-WAY DRAW STACKING

Channel Width	Space Required	Channel Width	Space Required
24″ (70 cm)	6″ (15 cm)	120″ (304 cm)	21½″ (55 cm)
36″ (91 cm)	8″ (20 cm)	132″ (335 cm)	23½″ (60 cm)
48″ (122 cm)	10″ (25 cm)	144″ (365 cm)	25″ (63 cm)
60″ (152 cm)	12″ (30 cm)	156″ (396 cm)	27″ (68 cm)
72″ (182 cm)	13½″ (34 cm)	168″ (426 cm)	29″ (73 cm)
84″ (213 cm)	15½″ (39 cm)	182″ (462 cm)	31″ (79 cm)
96″ (243 cm)	17½″ (44 cm)	192″ (487 cm)	32½″ (80 cm)
108″ (274 cm)	19½″ (49 cm)		

TABLE 11.8   VERTICAL BLINDS

Required Window Depth for Inside Mount Louver Width		Window Frame Depth	
3″	(7.6 cm)	2¾″	(7 cm)
3½″	(9 cm)	2¾″	(7 cm)
4″	(10 cm)	3″	(7.6 cm)
4½″	(11 cm)	3¼″	(8 cm)
5″	(12.7 cm)	3½″	(9 cm)

Patio Sliding Glass Doors. *Installation:* The use of two separate blinds hung from one header track provides the most efficient light and privacy control. The top header should be installed to allow full clearance of the glass. The stacking height is determined by the blade length and material. See Table 11.6.

Measurement: The height is determined by the specified location of the head rail. Standard door height is 84″ (213 cm); therefore, ceiling mounting may be necessary. A minimum of 6-½″ (165 cm) stacking height above the glass will be required for aluminum blinds. Allow 18½″ (47 cm) stacking height for wood blinds. Note that an additional 1½″ (3.81 cm) is added for complete clearance.

VERTICAL BLINDS

Vertical blinds are available in a variety of materials and textures. Laminated fabrics are frequently used for the louvers. Stacking arrangements are a major consideration in the specification of vertical blinds.

Stacking for Vertical Blinds

Vertical blinds are available in the three standard stacking arrangements shown in Figure 11.17. The space required for one-way draws is shown in Table 11.7. For a blind with a center draw, divide the channel width in half and figure each side separately. Example: If a channel width measures 96″, divide this in half.

$$96″ - 2″ = 48″ (244 - 2 = 122 \text{ cm})$$

A 48″ width requires 10″ stacking space. Therefore, 10″ (25 cm) of stacking space is required on each side.

LIFE CYCLE COSTING OF WINDOW SYSTEMS

The initial cost factors plus energy conservation and the expected service life and maintenance are the major elements to consider in cost effectiveness of window systems.

1. Initial costs vary with the specific systems: e.g., material, installation hardware, and labor costs for drapery would be considerably higher than the initial cost of a roller-shade installation.
    a. Materials
        (1) Blinds (vertical and horizontal) are priced by the linear and square foot.
        (2) Drapery fabric is sold by the linear yard.
        (3) Drapery hardware costs are based on the type and length of the system.

    b. Fabrication costs. Drapery workrooms normally base labor charges on the following:
        (1) The number of panels (widths)
        (2) Length of panel (if between 100 and 200 in. [254 and 508 cm] long)
        (3) Amount of handwork involved
        (4) Type of heading
        (5) Hook or pin application, pressing, and folding
        (6) Special fabrications, such as cornices, Austrian shades, or other special treatments
    c. Installation costs. Drapery fabricators will deliver and install completed drapery based on a labor fee per linear foot. Costs for installataion of drapery hardware are based on the size and length of the system.

2. Expected service life. These estimates are based on normal usage and adequate maintenance:

Component	Service Life
Blinds	10 years
Shades	3 to 5 years
Drapery	5 years

3. Maintenance costs. These costs should include regular maintenance, such as vacuuming and periodic professional cleaning. Blinds and shades may also require parts replacement (springs, tapes, and pull cords).

4. Energy conservation. Computing energy savings includes consideration of the following:

a. Initial cost of window system
b. Expected service life
c. Maintenance costs
d. Initial fuel costs savings/unit area. A shading coefficient of .25 for a draped window could, for example, indicate a 75 percent reduction in the solar heat gained through an undraped configuration. Depending on the geographic location and window orientation, this could mean a sizable reduction in the capacity requirement of the heating or air conditioning equipment. The kilowatt hours used per day would be greatly reduced.
e. Expected fuel savings/unit area (including fuel inflation rate) during the expected service life of the window system.

Corner Window Installation
Blinds for windows numbered 1 and 2 that are to be mounted outside the window frame should be specified as *corner* blinds. When center molding makes it necessary to mount blinds inside the frame, the blinds are specified as *standard*. On the window numbered 3, blinds either inside or outside the frame should be specified as *corner* blinds.

Skylight Installation
A top and bottom channel is required on most skylights. To prevent louver sagging, blinds should be constructed of aluminum or other stable material. It is recommended that blinds not exceed 96" in width and 48" in length (244 cm wide by 122 cm long).

Angle Installation
The degree angles shown in drawing B illustrate the steepest window slopes that will permit the blind louvers to rotate without hitting against the top channel. Louvers are to be specified with straight standard hems. Blinds louvers that are to be drawn open should be specified as one-way draw with stacking on the high end. For blinds that will only rotate, it is recommended that controls be specified on the low end of the window.

Drawings should accompany specifications. Provide dimensions and angles indicated on illustration A and B.

Figure 11.17 Vertical blinds specification information.

DESIGNERS' CHECKLIST FOR DEFECTS IN SHADES AND BLINDS

The following checklists for defects in blinds and shades are suggested in federal specifications L-S-001787 (GSA-FSS) and AA-V-00200B (GSA-FSS).

Blinds: Classification of Defects

Examine	Defect
Finish (general)	Not color specified.
	Runs, wrinkles, grit, areas of no film, separation of color, or finish not smooth.
Construction and workmanship	Hardware components not deburred.
Slats	Not shaped as specified.
	Not flexible.
	Corners not rounded.
Rails or channel head	Does not conceal operating mechanism.
	Locking covers not furnished.
	Not U-shaped and size specified.
Bottom	Holddown brackets not furnished when specified.
	Not equipped with end caps.
Ladder tape (Type I)	Spacing of ladders not uniform.
Cords	Too short.
	Equalizer on pull cord not furnished or does not hold cord together.
	Exposed ends of cords not furnished with knots or tassels.
Tilting device	Not attached to left side of head rail (if applicable).
Tilting rod and support	Not secure to other components.
	Does not carry the weight of the blind.
	Does not hold the tape in alignment.
Lifting cord lock	Not furnished.
	Does not hold cord securely at any height.
Installation hardware	Not furnished.
Marking	Omitted, wrong location, incorrect, incomplete, or illegible.

Shades: Classification of Defects

Examine	Defect
Shade cloth	Pinhole (any).
	Cut, hole, or tear.
	Crease or wrinkle (when resulting in doubling or adhesion of surfaces).
	Wavy, rolled, or folded edges.
	Spot, stain, or streak.
	Objectionable odor.
	Color not as specified.
	Color nonuniform, shaded, spotted, or mottled.
	Any tacky areas.
Other material construction and workmanship	Pull with attached eyelet missing (when applicable).
	Pull not a matching color.
	Wood of roller not species required.
	Knot in roller over ¼ in. (6.4 mm) in diameter or clustered knots.
	Hem not as specified.
	Plastic pull (when applicable) poorly constructed and not free of sharp or rough areas.
	Slope of grain in wood or roller exceeds 1 in. (2.5 cm) in 10 in. (25.4 cm).
	Roller not smooth and splinter-free.
	Brackets and screws missing (when specified).
	Metal or combination wood and metal rollers not used on shades over 72 in. (182.9 cm) wide.
	Material and coating of brackets, metal rollers, and ferrules and ends not as required.
	Metal components not free from burrs or rough edges.
	Any evidence of flimsiness (not firm) due to improper roller diameter used.
	Roller barrel extends more than ½ in. (12.7 mm) beyond end of shade cloth when shades are for use between jambs (i.e., inside mounting).
	Roller barrel extends more than ¾ in. (19.1 mm) beyond end of shade cloth when shades are for use on face of window casing.
	Vinyl material not securely fastened to rollers.

Figure 11.18 Guide specification for drapery and drapery hardware.

SECTION 12530

DRAPERY AND DRAPERY HARDWARE

PART 1 GENERAL

1.01   RELATED WORK SPECIFIED ELSEWHERE: _____

1.02   QUALITY ASSURANCE

A. Acceptable Fabricators and Manufacturers:
    1. Minimum of five years experience in drapery fabrication.
    2. Manufacturer to be single source of hardware units including accessories, mounting brackets and fastenings.

B. Requirements of Regulatory Agencies: Install drapery which meets flammability requirements of _____.

C. Fabric Shall be Tested to Provide:
    1. Fenestration data.

D. Fabric Shall be Inspected for Flaws Prior to Fabrication:
    1. Color match to submitted samples.
    2. Pattern alignment.

1.03   SUBMITTALS

A. Samples: Two 12" x 12" fabric samples.

B. Shop Drawings:
    1. Drapery Contractor shall take field measurements to verify openings scheduled to receive drapery.
    2. Where structural form requires cutouts, Contractor is responsible for developing detailed drawings showing special work.
    3. Details of abutments at corners and ceilings.

C. Manufacturer's specifications and installation instructions for drapery hardware.

D. Maintenance Material:
    1. Operation and maintenance of drapery hardware.
    2. Cleaning instructions from fabric mill.

E. Test Reports:
    1. Certification of flame-retardant treatment.
    2. Certification of compliance with regulatory agencies.
    3. Certification of shading coefficient.

1.04   PRODUCT DELIVERY, STORAGE, AND HANDLING

A. Fabricator shall deliver drapery items folded neatly, securely wrapped and clearly marked for size and installation location.

B. Drapery items shall be protected from snagging, soil and other damage. In the event that drapery items suffer damage, the fabricator shall clean, repair or replace at no expense to the Owner or Designer.

C. Drapery items shall be delivered free of loose threads or lint. Drapery items shall not be delivered with horizontal creases.

D. Drapery items or hardware shall not be delivered to job site until the area is ready for installation.

1.05   JOB CONDITIONS

A. Examine substrates and conditions under which units are to be installed. Do not proceed until unsatisfactory conditions have been corrected.

B. Environmental controls shall be in operation 48 hours prior to and after installation of drapery fabric.

1.06   GUARANTEE

A. Drapery fabrication to be unconditionally guaranteed for ____ years against all defects in material or workmanship. All defects are to be replaced or corrected in not more than ____ weeks after notification of said defects, excluding normal wear and tear, without penalty to Owner.

PART 2 PRODUCTS

2.01   DRAPERY HARDWARE

A. Channel Track Section Manufactured by:
    1. Size and Weight:
    2.. Finish:
        (in accordance with Aluminum Association Specification No. AA-C22A 21.)
    3. Permanently Lubricated:

B. Track to be Equipped with Following Components:

```
********************************************************************
Specifier Note: Add or delete nonapplicable provisions.
********************************************************************
```

1. Pulley Sets:

    One-way Draw: Two-way Draw:

2. Master Carriers:

    Butt Carrier: Overlap Carrier:

3. Slides:

    Snap Tabs: Pin Slides:

4. Cord:

    Type:

5. Cord Guide:

    Tension Pulley: Weighted Pull:

6. Baton - Hand Operation:

7. Support Brackets and End Brackets:

8. Provide all end stops, splicers, installation anchorages and other necessary accessories.

2.02   DRAPERY

A. Drapery Fabric Shall Meet the Following Criteria:
    1. Weight (ounces per linear yard):
    2. Weave:
    3. Fiber Content:
    4. Color:
    5. Repeat Size:
    6. Soil-resistant Treatment:
    7. Flame-retardant Treatment:
    8. Shading Coefficient (Configuration):

B. Fabric shall meet or exceed the following Performance standards:
    1. Flammability
        NFPA Test No. 701
        CCC-T-191b(5903)
        CCC-W-408A
    2. Abrasion
        ASTM D-1175-64.T
    3. Colorfastness
        AATCC 16E-1971

2.03   FABRICATION

```
********************************************************************
Specifier Note: Add or delete nonapplicable provisions.
********************************************************************
```

A. Drapery is to be constructed with _____ heading system with _____ percentage of fullness.

B. Drapery shall be constructed of ____ panel widths with (center butt or center overlap) or one-way draw (left or right).

C. Finished Length:

    Cut Length:

    Finished Width:

    Pattern Repeat:

D. Drapery headings to be fabricated with ____ and shall measure ____ inches in depth. Bottom edge of heading is to be stitched through face fabric on sheers with lock stitch machine at 6 to 8 stitches per inch to meet Federal Specification #301.

E. Lined drapery shall have lining securely attached at heading to prevent any roll-up or separating of lining at heading.

F. Pleats are to be securely pinch-tacked with a minimum of 12 stitch tacks of 40/3 thread or equivalent.

G. Bottom hems to be ____ inches full double turned and finished with a "blind stitch" machine at 2 to 1 ratio and not less than 50/3 thread. All bottom hems shall be true and square. Covered lead weights shall be placed in the corner of each panel.

H. Only first quality mercerized cotton, rayon or dacron thread shall be used in the fabrication of the drapery.

Figure 11.18 continued

I. Side hems shall be _____ inches full double turned and finished with blind stitch machine at 2 to 1 ratio on medium drapery and sheers with no rack, roll or wrinkle. Needles shall not exceed #10 for sheer fabrics and #15 for medium-weight fabrics.

J. Sheers shall be selvage edges trimmed and joined with a French seam method or reverse field method at no more than 1/8 inch width at 6 to 8 stitches per inch with 50/3 thread to meet Federal Specification #301.

K. Medium-weight fabrics, such as linens, shall have selvage edges trimmed. Side seams shall have one row of lock stitches; all raw edges shall be overlock stitched at not less than 10 stitches per inch with 50/3 thread. In compliance with Federal Specification #514, the needles shall not be larger than metric size 80.

L. Velours shall be fabricated with an antifriction pressure foot and throat plate on needle feed and bottom feed. Drawn or puckered seams shall not be accepted. Thread shall be 24/4 vat dyed, 100 percent mercerized.

M. Lining fabrics shall have lock stitches for seams at the rate of 6 to 8 stitches per inch. Selvage shall be notched and pressed back ½ inch to relieve pressure on the seams.

PART 3 EXECUTION

3.01 INSPECTION

A. Drapery shall hang in natural draping condition without creases.

B. Drapery Contractor shall steam and hand dress all drapery at job site.

C. Drapery shall hang one inch above the finished floor or _____ inches below the window sill. All other measurements shall conform to drawings.

D. Seams shall be inspected for flatness and lack of puckering.

E. All patterns shall be perfectly aligned vertically and horizontally.

F. No needle holes shall leak light through blackout linings.

3.02 INSTALLATION

A. Install drapery tracks and accessories at locations indicated on the working drawings and in accord with manufacturer's instructions. Install level, plumb and secure. Cooperate with other trades for securing drapery tracks to substrates and finish surfaces.

B. Repair or replace damaged hardware parts as directed by the Designer, at no additional cost to the Owner.

C. Attach drapery to attached tracks installed by others. Fabricator is to add or decrease carriers as required for proper installation of the drapery.

3.03 FIELD QUALITY CONTROL

A. All brackets are mounted to either concrete, wood, or hollow construction and shall be tested to withstand a pull of _____ pounds.

B. All cords and operational components shall operate without application of undue force.

3.04 ADJUST AND CLEAN

A. All debris connected with the installation of the window system shall be collected and disposed of out of the area.

B. All blemishes to surrounding areas that are the result of installation are to be brought to the immediate attention of the Designer.

C. All finger or tool marks or other blemishes are to be corrected and repaired by the Contractor without cost to the Owner.

D. Each room or area that is completed shall be cleaned up in consecutive order and made ready for use in a minimum time span.

3.05 SCHEDULES

****
Specifier Note: Attach applicable schedules or drawings here.
****

END OF SECTION

SPECIFICATION OF COMMERCIAL FURNITURE

In view of increasing safety concerns and the accompanying liability factors involved in the specification of furnishings, it is important that designers maintain quality control through performance evaluation of furniture components. This chapter will classify types of commercial furnishings, survey current performance testing, and provide guidelines for maintenance and life cycle costing.

COMMERCIAL FURNITURE CLASSIFICATION

Furniture manufactured for commercial installation is best classified by use rather than style. Four major categories can be established to include the following: (1) office furniture, such as (a) open office systems, (b) standard office furniture, and (c) executive office furniture; (2) seating; (3) tables; and (4) accessories.

Open Office Systems

Because open office systems entail more precise specification considerations than other types of office furnishings, more detailed information on it is given here. Open office systems are usually based on three methods of component assembly. (1) One system utilizes freestanding vertical screens with conventional office furniture. (2) The second type makes use of panels linked together to become self-stabilizing walls or dividers from which work surfaces and storage components are suspended. The panels vary in size from 30 to 78 in. (76.2 to 198.1 cm) in height and 22 to 48 in. (55.9 to 121.9 cm) in width. (3) A third method employs self-contained solid L-shaped wooden or steel units that serve both as storage components and dividers. The second and third systems' approaches frequently incorporate lighting components. (See Figure 12.1). Each system is usually composed of the following:

Workstations. These are semienclosed areas that may accommodate one or more people. The size of workstations is generally based on the functional needs of the occupant and may be classified as clerical, secretarial, accounting, legal, supervisory, word processing, middle management, and executive. Figure 12.2 shows some general configurations and average sizes of workstations and worksurfaces. It is usually recommended that a percentage of supervisory workstations be provided with a greater measure of privacy to accommodate discussion of confidential matters.

1. Work surfaces, primary and secondary level surfaces
     Panel supported
     Floor supported
   Tilted surfaces
     Panel supported
     Floor supported
   Mobile, pull-out surfaces

2. Storage components
   Filing units
     Panel supported
     Mobile
   Drawer units
   Shelf and overhead storage
   Wardrobes

3. Lighting components
   Integrated
     Ambient
     Task
   Freestanding lighting

4. Utilities
   Internal raceways
   Overhead power connections

SYSTEM TYPE 1   SYSTEM TYPE 2   SYSTEM TYPE 3

Figure 12.1 Types of open office systems.

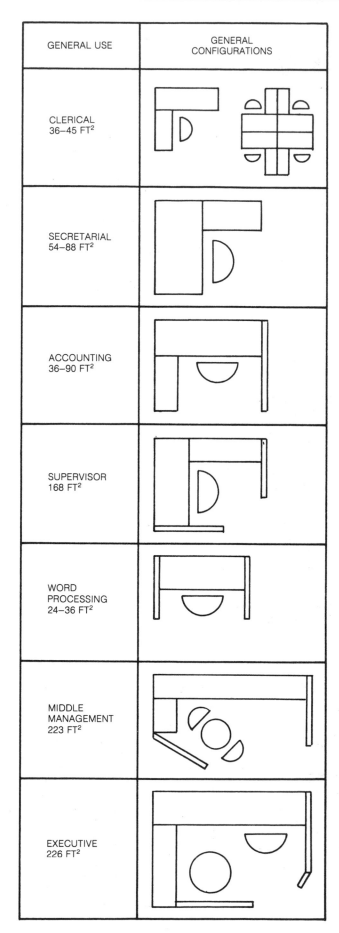

GENERAL USE	GENERAL CONFIGURATIONS
CLERICAL 36–45 FT²	
SECRETARIAL 54–88 FT²	
ACCOUNTING 36–90 FT²	
SUPERVISOR 168 FT²	
WORD PROCESSING 24–36 FT²	
MIDDLE MANAGEMENT 223 FT²	
EXECUTIVE 226 FT²	

Figure 12.2 General classification of workstations.

Floor recessed
Ganged outlet strips

5. Accessories
   Pinup surfaces for display
   Modesty or privacy panels
   Coat racks
   Draw fittings
   Chalk boards

EVALUATING OPEN OFFICE SYSTEMS

In the past several years the abundant production of open office systems has created a perplexing problem for designers. Reaching a decision on which particular system will best meet the needs of a client is often complicated by the complexity of components and similarities between systems. For example, each manufacturer offers variations of the following components:

Workstation configurations

Acoustic controls

Accessories

Lighting components

Methods of integrating utilities

The problem is further complicated by the fact that a system designed by one manufacturer is rarely interchangeable with any other system; i.e., once a commitment is made to a particular system, a client may add to that system, but not mix components from another system. Other than complete reinstallation and certain financial loss, a client is locked into a system for many years. Therefore, designers must give very serious consideration to the evaluation and specification of open office systems.

The performance approach discussed in Chapter 4 would prove very useful in establishing criteria on which to base a final specification decision. The development of a preliminary performance matrix points out major health/safety, durability, maintenance, and functional factors that should be evaluated when *comparing* open office systems (Figure 12.3). It may be necessary to develop a more detailed matrix for the evaluation of lighting and utility components, but designers should be aware that intensive research is being conducted which could make current methods of integrating lighting and electrical wiring obsolete. The flexibility of the electrical wiring system should be considered.

Performance Testing

Early performance testing of open office systems was primarily concentrated in the areas of user satisfaction, increased employee efficiency, ease of relocation, and the conservation of space and energy. Because much of this evaluation has been concerned with general user concepts and acceptance of open office systems, the research methods have involved behavioral observations, interviews, and questionnaires. Actual physical testing with mechanical structure and stability has been conducted on critical components such as vertical panels, work surfaces, panel-hung cabinets and files, and attached storage shelving. Table 12.1 lists tests and minimal test requirements established by American National Standards Institute (ANSI), sponsored by the Business and Institutional Furniture Manufacturer's Association (BIFMA).

The prevention of bodily injury is a major focus of the ANSI/BIFMA X 5.6-1986 Standard for Office Furnishings—Panel Sys-

Open Planned Office Components	Health-Safety							Durability					Maintenance				Function				
	Flammability	Cause falls	Sharp projections	Anthropomorphic fit	Reflectance: glare	Handicapped use		Structurally sound	Positive attachment	Color stability	Lightfastness	Abrasion resistance	Cleanability	Component repair	Component storage	Relocation	Flexibility	Privacy	Color homogeneity	Acoustic control	Energy control
Vertical Panels	•	•	•		•	•		•	•	•	•	•	•	•	•	•	•	•	•	•	
Worksurfaces			•	•	•	•		•	•	•	•	•	•	•	•	•	•		•		
Filing	•	•	•	•		•		•	•	•			•	•	•	•	•		•		
Shelves and Storage		•	•	•	•	•		•	•	•			•	•	•	•	•		•		
Lighting					•	•		•	•	•			•	•	•	•	•				•
Seating	•	•	•	•	•	•		•	•	•	•	•	•	•	•	•	•		•		
Tables		•	•	•	•	•		•	•	•	•	•	•	•	•	•	•		•		
Other																					

Figure 12.3 Performance attributes of open plan office furniture.

TABLE 12.1 PERFORMANCE ATTRIBUTES OF OPEN OFFICE PANELS

Attribute	Tests	Minimal Federal Performance Requirements
1. Flammability		
a. Flame spread	ASTM E-84	Flame spread ≤25 unsprinklered
		Flame spread ≤200 sprinklered
b. Smoke	NBS 708	Specific optical density ≤150
c. Potential heat	Test based on ASTM proceedings Vol. 61, 1961, pp. 1337–47	≤40,000 BTU
2. Acoustics		
a. Airborne sound	PBS-C.1 (Subjective)	SPP ≤60 in open-plan areas
		SPP ≤70 in rooms without doors
	PBS-C.2 (Objective test)	NIC + (NC ≤40) ≤60 in open plan
b. Impact sound	Footfall test IB1-I 1-1965	Mask vertical footfall sounds W/NC ≤40
3. Durability		
a. Abrasion	ASTM E 72-74	Resist abrasion
b. Colorfastness	Fadeometer	No color change after 50 hours at 150° F
c. Chemical resistance	FTM 141 A, Method 6081	Resist staining and damage
4. Stability		
a. Resist horizontal load	ASTM 72–74	Resist load of 50 lb
		Support 40 lb per linear ft of shelving
b. Resist shelf (3) staticproof and functional loads	ASTM/BIFMA × 5.6–86	Resist
		proof load (1) functional load (2)
		A: 5 lb pli 3 lb pli (4)
		B: 8 lb pli 5 lb pli
c. Resist attached storage bin		Resist storage bin (3)
proof load		Inside load top load
size A		5 lb pli 3 lb pli
size B		8 lb pli 5 lb pli
function loads		inside load top load
size A		3 lb pli 2 lb pli
size B		5 lb pli 3 lb pli
d. Resist attached		Resist lateral file (4)
proof load		inside load top load
size A		3 lb pli 3 lb pli
size B		5 lb pli 5 lb pli
function load		inside load top load
size A		2 lb pli 2 lb pli
size B		3 lb pli 3 lb pli
e. File bin tests		
same size as		2 lb pli 3 lb pli
lateral files		3 lb pli 5 lb pli
f. Resist load of work surface (A) with supported loaded drawers		No functional damage
		1. Functional vertical load 200 lb with drawers open for 60 minutes.
		2. Functional horizontal load of 4.5 lb pli for 60 min. open drawers.
		Resist: no failure no injury risk:
		3. Proof load of 7 lb pli along a line 8″ from front edge. 15 min. drawers closed.
g. Resist tipping Resist impact		Resist 50 lb. impact applied 52 inches from floor.
5. Mechanical Strength		
a. Dislodgement of work surface (B)		Resist dislodgement from 130 lb upward force.
b. Dislodgement of storage bin; lateral file (C); shelves		Resist dislodgement from 110 lb upward force.
c. Dislodgement panel-hung lights (D) and clothing hooks. (E)		Resist dislodgement from 110 lb upward force.
6. Panel-mounted components	ASTM/BIFMA × 5.6–86	
a. Roll-out shelves		
1. Retention test		Remain functional.
		Resist 15 lbs applied to front center.
2. Rebound test		Remain functional after 200 open-close cycles loaded 2 lbs pli.
		Resist spring force closure of 40 lbs.
b. Cabinet Receding Doors		
1. Drop test		Remain functional.
		Withstand 10,000 lifts from 60° angle.
2. Cycle test		Remain functional.
		Withstand 10,000 cyclic travel from receded position to extent of horizontal travel and back.
e. Drawers		
1. Retention lateral files only		Remain attached to suspension while open with 15-lb force placed at drawer center.
2. Rebound		No rebound more than 1.5 in. when closed with reasonable force.
3. Cycle center pull		Remain functional without lubrication after 75,000 cycles.
4. Rebound		No rebound more than 1.5 in. when closed with resonable force.
5. Lock		Resist 50-lb pull force with drawers loaded as specified.

Notes: Designers must obtain full copies of test standards from sponsoring agencies prior to specification.
(1) Proof load is the maximum test load applied to a component beyond the functional load.
(2) Functional load is the load equivalent to that expected in normal use.
(3) Shelf and storage bin A: size = 8″ × 16″ deep; B: size = 16″ × 20″ deep.

(4) Pli = per linear inch.
(5) Lateral file/file bin A: size = 18″ deep; B: size = 18″ to 22″ deep.
(A) Storage shelf component typical unmounted weight = 3–10 lbs. (B) Work surface component typical weight = 8–17 lbs. (C) Lateral file component typical unmounted weight = 16–30 lbs. (D) Panel-hung light typical weight = 3–8 lbs. (E) Clothing hooks typical weight = 20–30 lbs.

tems Tests. The tests were designed to be conducted in a prescribed sequence. Every effort is made to test the panels and the components in the configuration suggested by the manufacturer. For example, the Stability or Antitipping Test (Test 4) may be supplemented to take into account the number of panels in a run, the number of doors, and the number of attached files that can increase weight or panel movement.

Panel configurations that are explicitly recommended by the manufacturer are considered when conducting the tests. If the manufacturer recommends that hanging components be secured to one or both sides of a panel, it is understood that all configurations recommended by the manufacturer must be able to meet the test requirements.

The panel configuration shown in Figure 12.1 is similar to those used in the tests discussed above.

Acoustics. Some tests were developed specifically to deal with open office problems; e.g., the acoustics tests PBS C.1 and C.2 evaluate the Speech Privacy Potential (SPP) between any two zones in a typical office area.[1] New terminology has also been developed to establish test parameters.

1. SPP: The voice level for which privacy is required. Through testing, the level was established at ≤60 db for conversation. The Speech Privacy Potential is derived from functional interzone planning criteria which specify the level of speech for which the system in use must provide confidential interzone privacy.

2. ISD: The Integrated Space Divider system which is composed of the following elements:
   a. Open Plan Privacy system (OPP) made up of panels providing privacy to seated people.
   b. OPP upgraded panel systems providing privacy to standing people.
   c. OPP support system (acoustical treatment on exterior walls).
   d. OPP privacy interface system (core walls).
   e. OPP room partitions, ceiling heights, doors.

3. ICB: The Integrated Ceiling and Background system which is composed of five subsystems:
   a. Acoustical materials
   b. Suspended ceiling system
   c. Luminaries
   d. HVAC terminals (air distribution system)
   e. Background noise distribution

4. NC: The background noise generated by the system-in-use condition. It is also considered "electroacoustic" because it includes noise from the luminaries in the ICB system. The NC background must fulfill its masking function without interfering with communication. NC_{40} is the single number rating used to describe the upper limit of background noise. If the NC rating is above 40, conversation will be obstructed.

5. NIC: Noise Isolation Class, which provides an index number for rating a measured set of noise reductions.

The PBS C.1 is considered a "subjective" test because it makes use of a jury of listeners rather than instruments to measure the acoustical quality of an open office space. The test area is made to simulate a typical open office situation with ceilings between 8'10" and 9'10" (2.6 and 3 m) in height, floors carpeted, and a speaker situated 6' (1.8 m) from a panel barrier. The PBS C.2 test is very similar except that the listeners are provided with a background-making sound device which they adjust to attain adequate SPP during the test.

Although most panel systems are currently listed with an NRC rating (refer to Chapter 7 for more information on NRC), designers should question the method used to determine the NRC rating; i.e., does the test method simulate actual use conditions?

Specification for acoustic levels in open office planning should include consideration of all the components of the space, such as the carpet, suspended ceiling, core walls, luminaires, and levels of background noise. The General Services Administration performance specification states the criteria in this manner:

> The subsystem shall not impair the SPP (no less than ≤60) for any two zones in any space in the typical office area. No element in the ICB system shall impair the SPP (no less than ≤60). The ISD shall also perform as noted above. . . .[2]

Furniture-Integrated Lighting. The increased interest in conserving energy during the last decade prompted research into more efficient methods of lighting office environments. Previous theories about lighting had been based on the concept that a high quantity of light resulted in a better quality of light. Sy Shemitz was one of the first lighting engineers to begin working with the idea of localizing light sources directly over the work surface, thus eliminating the need for high levels of general lighting. Integrating task and general (ambient) lighting with the furniture components of a workstation became a viable alternative to the serious energy problems that developed in the midseventies (Figure 12.4). By the late seventies almost every manufacturer of office systems was utilizing the concept of task/ambient lighting. This was prompted, to a great extent, by the publicity surrounding the GSA Energy Conservation Demonstration Project, which was installed in 1977. The GSA performance specification provided a criterion for low level electrical energy consumption through the use of tasklit

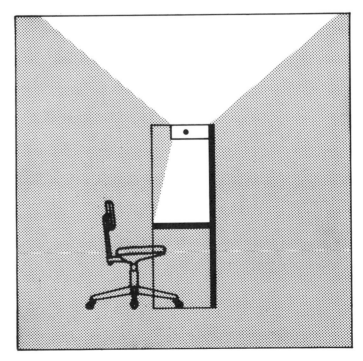

Figure 12.4 Task ambient furniture integrated lighting. Reproduced with permission of Knoll International.

TABLE 12.2   RECOMMENDED ILLUMINATION LEVELS FOR OFFICE TASKS*

Task or Area	Visual Difficulty (VDF)	Design Level (FC)	Average Level Range (FC)
Service or public areas	—	15	12-18
Circulation areas within office space, but not at workstations	—	30	24-36
Normal office work, reading, writing, etc.	1-39	50	40-60
Office work, prolonged, visually difficult or critical in nature	40-59	75	60-90
Office work, prolonged, visually difficult and critical in nature	60 & up	100	80-120

*See Table 12.3 for Visual Difficulty Ratings.

Source: GSA.

TABLE 12.3   VISUAL DIFFICULTY RATING OF TASKS

Task Description	Visual Difficulty Rating
1. Large black object on white background	1
2. Book or magazine, printed matter, 8-point and larger	2
3. Typed original	2
4. Ink writing (script)	3
5. Newspaper text	4
6. Shorthand notes, ink	4
7. Handwriting (script) in no. 2 pencil	5
8. Shorthand notes, no. 3 pencil	6
9. Washed-out copy from copying machine	7
10. Bookkeeping	8
11. Drafting	8
12. Telephone directory	12
13. Typed carbon, fifth copy	15

Source: GSA.

TABLE 12.4   ILLUMINATION LEVELS FOR OTHER AREAS

Areas	Design Level (FC)	Range (FC)
Auditoriums	30	20-40
Cafeteria	30	20-40
Conference rooms	30	25-35
Corridors, lobbies and means of egress	15	10-18
Kitchen (average)	50	30-70
Mechanical rooms (general areas)	10	5-15
Storage areas (general storage)	10	5-15
Storage areas (fine details required)	30	25-35
Toilets	20	15-30

Source: GSA.

systems furniture. The specification established the following requirements:

Provide lighting system with low electrical energy consumption

Criterion: The lighting system's electrical energy consumption shall be less than 2 watts per square foot, for the total number of people within the project's square footage. (Energy per person = EPP.)

Total wattage of all luminaries in service in input watts divided by the net floor area in square feet equals watts per square foot.

$$\frac{\text{Square footage (12,000)}}{\text{Total number of people (68)}} = 176$$

176 × watts per square foot = EPP[3]

Designers not accustomed to the specification of office systems on the basis of energy conservation and watts per square foot have found it increasingly difficult to determine which lighting system should be specified. Aspects of lighting technology, normally handled by lighting engineers, have become the selling tool of furniture manufacturers and their representatives.

Since most systems with integrated lighting have preengineered illumination levels for workstation tasks and offer little or no opportunity for varying those levels, knowledge concerning recommendation illumination levels for various tasks could perhaps aid designers in evaluating various systems.

Table 12.2 lists the illumination levels (in footcandles [FC]) recommended for various office tasks. Designers should be aware that the design criteria are based on the visual difficulty, length of time the task is performed, and the age of the person doing the task. These three factors are considered the Visual Difficulty Factor (VDF) for office tasks and are calculated in the following manner:

$$VDF = R \times T \times F$$

where   VDF = Visual Difficulty Factor

R = Visual Difficulty Rating of Tasks, from Table 12.3

T = Duration of the particular visual tasks for day, hours

F = Multiplying factor for an aged person with uncorrectable eyesight problems. Use F = 1.5 for people over 50 years of age[4]

For a person spending five hours doing bookkeeping and an additional four hours doing shorthand, the Visual Difficulty Factors (Table 12.3) would be determined by multiplying the length of time by the VDF rating. For example:

$$5 \text{ hr} \times 8 + 3 \text{ hr} \times 4 = 52 \text{ VDF}$$

According to Table 12.4, 75 footcandles should be provided. If the person doing the work is over 50 years old, then the VDF should be modified to 52 × 1.5, or 78. This would change the required footcandles from 75 to a total of 100. The multiplying factor (F) cannot usually be applied in the early design phase because the personnel workstation assignments may not be known, but the specified office system should be able to provide for flexibility after installation.

Tables 12.2 and 12.4 also list recommended illumination levels (general lighting) for circulation areas within offices and other areas within an average office building. The last column on these tables gives the range that can be considered equivalent to the design levels when actually measured in the office after installation.

OFFICE ENERGY CONSERVATION

The following twelve principles recommended by GSA for energy conservation through lighting of commercial offices should provide additional design criteria which designers can use in specifying open office systems:

1. Design lighting for the task.
   a. Provide the required illumination for visual tasks in the working areas only and appropriate lower levels in the general areas, such as corridors, storage, and circulation.
   b. Reduce the wattage required for each specific task by a review of user needs and methods of providing illumination (see Table 12.5).
   c. Consider only the amount of illumination required for the specific task, taking into account the duration, character, and user performance required.
   d. Group similar tasks together for optimum conservation of energy per floor.
   e. Consider the use of greater contrast between tasks and background lighting, such as 8 to 1 and 10 to 1.

2. Select proper lighting systems.
   a. Illuminate tasks with fixtures built into furniture and maintain low-intensity lighting elsewhere.
   b. Consider wall washers and special illumination for features such as plants and murals in order to maintain proper contrast ratios without the use of overhead lighting.
   c. For horizontal tasks or duties, consider fixtures whose main lighting component is oblique, and then locate for maximum Equivalent Spherical Illumination (ESI) footcandle on the task. The concept of Equivalent Spherical Illumination was developed to express the effective illumination level on a visual task subject to veiling reflections. The ESI value is highly directional in concept and is very difficult to express without defining the exact angle from which the task is being viewed and the relative positions between the task and the luminaires (Figure 12.5). At present, the only practical method of calculating the true ESI values on the task is by using computer programs. Designers should consult lighting engineers on this matter.
   d. Avoid decorative floodlighting and display lighting.
   e. Use fixtures that give high-contrast rendition at task level.
   f. Reduce lighting requirements for hazards by:
      (1) Use of light fixtures close to and focused on the hazard.
      (2) Increased contrast of hazards; i.e., paint stair treads and risers white with black nosings.
   g. Try to obtain variance from existing codes requiring specific lighting levels by varying the qualitative and quantitative requirements for a specific application.

3. Select the most efficient luminaires.
   a. Consider the use of polarized lenses to improve the quality of lighting at task level.
   b. Consider the use of ballasts which can accommodate different types of High-Intensity Discharge (HID) bulbs.

TABLE 12.5 LIGHTING COSTS USING TASK LIGHTING

Step 1: $1.25 \text{ w/sq ft} \times 10,000 \text{ sq ft} = \dfrac{12,500 \text{ w}}{1000 \text{ w/kw}} = 12.5 \text{ kw}$

Step 2: $12.5 \text{ kw} \times 2600 \text{ bh/y} = 32,500 \text{ kwh}$

Step 3: $32,500 \text{ kwh} \times \$.0775 = \$2518.75$ annual cost of electric energy for lighting

Lighting Cost Using Conventional Ceiling Systems:

The same three-step process can be used by simply changing the 1.25 w/sq ft for task lighting to the 5 w/sq ft normally consumed for ceiling systems. However, since that figure represents the only difference in the equation, ratios can be easily used as follows:

Ratio is 5 to 1.25 = 4

$4 \times 2518.75 = \$10,075$ annual cost of electric energy for lighting

Air Conditioning Costs Related to Task Lighting:

Every watt of electric energy converted to heat = 3.413 BTU

1 ton of air conditioning = 12,000 BTU/year

Tons of air conditioning = $\dfrac{12,500 \text{ w} \times 3413 \text{ BTU}}{12,000} = 3.55$ tons

A/C power (kw) = 3.55×1.2 (factor for kw/ton) or 4.72 kw

Step 2: $4.72 \text{ kw} \times 2600 = 11,092 \text{ kwh}$

Step 3: $11,092 \times .0775 = \$859.65$ annual cost for air conditioning using task lighting

Air Conditioning Cost Related to Ceiling Systems:

$5 \text{ w/sq ft} \times 10,000 = \dfrac{50,000}{1000 \text{ w/kw}} = 50 \text{ kw}$

$\dfrac{50,000 \times 3.413 \text{ BTU}}{12,000 \text{ BTU/ton}} = 14.2$ tons

Step 2: $12 \text{ kw} \times 2600 = 44,369 \text{ kwh/yr}$

Step 3: $44,369 \times .0775 = \$3438.60$ annual cost for air conditioning using ceiling systems

Total Savings for Annual Energy Costs Alone: $10,105.20

Total Savings per Square Foot Is Approximately $1

Source: Knoll International.

Figure 12.5 Nonuniform office lighting with direct luminaries. Source: GSA.

c. Consider the use of high-frequency lighting to reduce wattage per lumen output. Additional benefits are reduced ballast heat loss and longer lamp life.

4. Select the most efficient light sources.
   a. Consider using 250-watt mercury vapor lamps and metal-halide lamps in place of 500-watt incandescent lamps for special applications.
   b. Use lamps with higher lumens per watt input:
      (1) One 8-ft (2.4-m) fluorescent lamp versus two 4-ft (1.2-m) lamps.
      (2) One 4-ft lamp versus two 2-ft (.6-m) lamps.
      (3) U-tube lamps versus two individual lamps.
      (4) Fluorescent lamps in place of all incandescent lamps, except for very close task lighting.

5. Select proper room characteristics.
   a. Consider the use of landscape office planning to improve lighting efficiency. Approximately 25 percent less wattage per footcandle on tasks is possible.
   b. Use light colors for walls, floors, and ceilings to increase reflectance.
   c. Lower the ceiling or mounting height of luminaires to increase the level of illumination with less wattage.
   d. Select furniture and interior appointments that do not have glassy surfaces or give peculiar reflections (see Glossary at the end of this chapter).
   e. Avoid the use of glossy surfaces on the task and its surroundings.
   f. Use high-reflectance finishes on vertical surfaces; 50 to 60 percent reflectance is recommended on matte finished walls; 30 percent for carpet.

6. Provide proper controls for the luminaires.
   a. Install switches for lights near the windows so that lights may be turned off in accordance with the amount of daylight available at any given time.
   b. Luminaires should be selectively switched according to possible groupings of working tasks at different hours.
   c. Use multiple lamp luminaires so that one lamp may be switched off during different times of the day.
   d. Design switch circuits to permit turning off unused or unnecessary lights.
   e. Evaluate the use of low-wattage (24 volts or lower) switching systems to obtain maximum switching capability.
   f. Provide times to turn off lights automatically in remote or seldom-used areas.

7. Utilize daylight.
   a. Use natural illumination in areas when a net energy conservation gain is possible without affecting the heating or cooling loads.
   b. Provide exterior reflectors at windows for more effective internal illumination.

8. Use thermally controlled luminaires.
   If permitted by codes, use luminaires which will allow room air to flow through the lamp compartment.

9. Keep the luminaires in good working condition.
   Use high utilization and maintenance factors in design criteria and instruct users to keep fixtures clean and change lamps frequently.

10. Design electrical wiring to allow for flexibility.
    a. Arrange electrical floor and wall outlets to accommodate relocation of luminaires to suit changing furniture or systems layouts.
    b. Use multilevel ballasts to permit varying lamps that can be added or removed when tasks are changed in location.

11. Optimize all operational procedures.
    Control overtime working hours and schedule maintenance work in various shifts during the working day or immediately following the closure of the offices.

12. In an office without integrated furniture lighting, lay out the luminaires for visual performance rather than uniform space geometry.
    a. Within the limits of the ceiling configuration, locate the luminaires as close to directly over the task as possible without creating excessive reflections.
    b. Locate luminaires just beyond the ends and working edges of the desk. Avoid locating luminaires directly in front of the visual task. Try to avoid a trapezoidal ceiling area projection; i.e., if a line were projected from the working edge of the desk vertically to the ceiling, forming a line 4 ft (1.2 m) long centered on the worker, and a line were projected parallel to and 8 ft (2.4 m) forward of this line, that is, 12 ft (3.6 m) long, the sides of the trapezoid would connect the ends of these two base lines (see Figure 12.5). If luminaires are kept out of this zone, there will be less reflectance on the task surface and more effective use of the illumination.
    c. The use of a checkerboard arrangement with one tube fixture placed every 50 sq ft (4.7 sq m) can result in an energy consumption of 0.92 watts per square foot. The luminaire reflector-baffle assembly could be modified for use near walls to subdue scalloping effects.[5]

LIFE CYCLE COSTING

Aside from providing better lighting and achieving the necessary conservation of energy, task/ambient lighting also combats the rising cost of energy. Calculating the life cycle cost of open planned offices includes the initial cost plus the following factors:

1. Maintenance

2. Space adjustment

3. Energy consumption

4. Luminaire relamping costs

5. Investment tax credits

Maintenance

The maintenance of office systems usually is based on a maintenance contract which can include parts repair and replacement (brackets and fasteners) and surface cleaning of panels and other surfaces. The maintenance calculation should *not* include (1) space adjustment costs; (2) janitorial services (floor cleaning); (3) relamping, reballasting, or cleaning of luminaires. Maintenance can be calculated on a yearly basis and extended to the entire expected service life of the system.

Space Adjustment Costs

Space adjustment costs include the annual cost of space changes based on the following formula:

SAC = area of change $\times$ rate of change $\times$ cost of change

The terms used in the formula are defined below:

Area of change is the estimate of the percentage of typical office space in which an office system will be installed or subject to change.

Rate of change is the estimated annual rate of planning change within the typical office space.

Cost of change includes the labor, material, equipment, and time needed to make the change. Materials or components which are left in position or stored for future use are not included in these figures. Labor costs should be itemized according to the type of assistance needed. For example, special tradespeople such as electricians and telephone installers may be needed to deactivate power and telephones and make changes in the signal outlets. The hours and salary per hour must be included. The amount of time required varies between types of systems, but generally should average about ¼ hr per linear foot for the furniture and panel components. If the change must be made during office hours, the downtime is important in regard to lost working time.[6]

Energy Consumption

The energy cost includes the heating and air conditioning (HVAC) costs and the cost of operating the luminaires. The air-conditioning costs are directly related to the cost of lighting because the heat generated by lighting creates additional air-conditioning costs. For example, for every 1,000 watts of lighting installed, an additional 341 watts of air conditioning is required. It has been estimated that 25 to 30 percent of air conditioning in office areas is consumed to offset heat produced by lamps.

Annual air-conditioning costs

1. Kilowatt hrs. per year = kilowatts × burning hrs. per year

2. Annual air-conditioning costs = kilowatt hrs. × energy cost

Annual lighting costs

1. Kilowatts = watts per square foot × area ÷ 1,000 W/kW

2. Kilowatt hrs. per year = kilowatts × burning hrs. per year

3. Annual lighting costs = kilowatt hrs. × energy rate

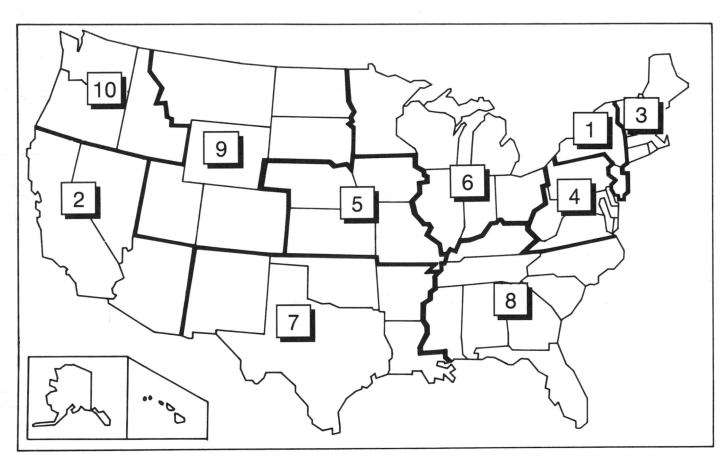

POWER COSTS

Rank	Region	Average Cost Cents/500 WH	Rank	Region	Average Cost Cents/500 WH
1	2 Northeast	10.4	6	5 Midwest	7.9
2	9 Pacific	9.2	7	6 Southwest	7.8
3	1 New England	9.1	8	4 South	7.4
4	3 Mid-Atlantic	8.2	9	8 Rocky Mountain	7.2
5	7 Central Plain	8.2	10	10 Northwest	7.2

Source: Department of Energy

Figure 12.6 Power costs.

Components / Manufacturer	Lighting							Storage				Type				Accessories			
	Raceway, horizontal	Vertical polls	Ganged outlet strips	Task lighting	Ambient lighting	Watts per square feet	UL approved	Files	Shelves	Cabinets: below/above	Racks	Free-standing panels	Panel hung components	Floor-standing comp.	Flame spread	Pin-up surfaces	Drawer fittings	Privacy panels	Coatracks

Figure 12.7 Systems component comparison.

The following case study was provided by Knoll International to illustrate the application of these principles. A hypothetical New York City firm having a typical office space of 10,000 sq ft (950 sq m), operating 12 hours per day (2,600 hours per year), and paying the New York City energy rate of $.104 per kilowatt hour is considering the installation of task/ambient lighting at 1.25 watts per square foot. Table 12.4 shows how the energy saving would be calculated.[7]

GSA predicts, for purposes of life cycle-costing evaluation, a doubling of electrical rates in five years and 5 percent increase per annum thereafter. To factor savings based on these predicted increases, multiply the savings by 1.78. The map in Figure 12.6 illustrates the variances that would occur in different parts of the country based on a difference in energy rates.

To calculate the total initial cost savings for energy-related equipment, the following method could be used:

1. Air-conditioning tonnage savings for _____ square feet = _____

2. Unit initial cost for air conditioning per ton _____

3. Savings on initial cost for air-conditioning equipment _____ (line 1 × line 2)

4. Air-conditioning power reduction equivalent distribution equipment, such as transformers, switchgear, feeders, panel boards, and branch circuits that would be reduced in size. Estimated at $150/kw (this is an approximate figure) = _____

5. Lighting power reduction for _____ sq ft = _____

6. Initial cost savings for electrical distribution equipment (for lighting equipment) that would not be required or could be reduced in size = _____ (line 5 × $150)

7. Grand total (lines 3 + 4 + 6) = _____ initial cost savings.[8]

Luminaire Relamping Cost (LRC)

LRC represents the annual cost of maintaining the performance of the luminaire subsystems.

$$LRC = N \, B/R \, (C + i)$$

where N = Number of lamps

B = Burning hours per year

R = Average rated lamp life (hours)

C = Cost per lamp (in dollars)

i = Labor cost per lamp for replacing lamps individually[9]

SPECIFICATION GUIDELINES FOR OPEN OFFICE SYSTEMS

A matrix may prove the most useful means of comparing the various components provided by systems manufacturers. The example shown in Figure 12.7 may be expanded to include more manufacturers and components.

Figure 12.8 on page 186 is a portion of a performance specification for a secretarial workstation and illustrates aspects of storage that should not be neglected when making specification decisions.[10]

The following checklist can be used when surveying available systems. Fire-safety and barrier-free criteria for open office systems are provided in Chapters 13 and 14.

1. *Panels*
   a. What material is used in the core of the panel?
   b. Was a total panel mockup tested for flammability? How?
   c. For flame spread?
   d. For optical smoke density?
   e. Is the surface material treated with a flame retardant?
   f. What method was used to test the acoustic quality?
   g. Acoustic rating? NRC? NIC?
   h. Base of the panel? Adjustable? Connecting or free-standing?
   i. Are special tools needed to relocate the panels? Estimated time to relocate?
   j. Impact resistance? Test?
   k. Do the panels provide positive attachment for components?
   l. At points of attachment, do panels fully engage without rack or sway?

2. *Work Surfaces*
   a. Are all work surfaces capable of withstanding a vertical load placed at the leading edge and at midpoint between end supports of not less than 250 lb (115 kg)? Panel-suspended work surfaces should not separate from the panel under this weight.
   b. Have all work surfaces been tested to withstand the heat of lighted cigarettes without showing scorch marks?
   c. Are all work surfaces capable of being adjusted within a range of 26 to 31 in. (66 to 78.7 cm) surface height?
   d. Do all work surfaces provide adjustment of clearance between the floor and underside of 24 to 29 in. (61 to 73.7 cm)?
   e. Are work units capable of providing a knee space opening (width) of between 24 and 32 in. (61 to 81.3 cm)?

3. *Integrated Lighting*
   a. Can the illumination level be varied at an individual workstation?
   b. How flexible is the wiring?
   c. Does the system accommodate the use of more than one electrical machine per workstation? How many?
   d. How many workstations are fed off the same circuit?
   e. Are the workstations capable of providing more than one source of power?
   f. Is the secondary work surface provided with enough light? Task or ambient?
   g. Are lenses used on lighting fixtures?
   h. Will the luminaire accommodate varied types of lamps?
   i. Is the quoted wattage per square foot based on gross office space or workstation space?
   j. What is the reflectance levels of workstations components?
   k. What is the height of the ambient lighting sources? Above eye level?
   l. Is the system available without ambient components?
   m. What is the cost difference without ambient components?
   n. Does the task lighting prevent veiling reflections?

*Figure 12.8 General services performance specification for
office workstation. Source: GSA.*

WORKSTATION
TYPE B
SECRETARIAL

SPACE MAXIMUM
88 SQ FT

QUANTITY
7 WORKSTATIONS

All storage
(File, Closed,
Open, Box drawer,
and Pencil drawer)
shall be at
maximum horizontal
or vertical dimen-
sions as space
allows. Values
in the specifica-
tions represent a
functional minimum
requirement

1.00 PRIMARY WORKSURFACE
1.01 Surface shall be a minimum of 1800 square inches.
1.02 Height shall be at task-level not to exceed 29"
      above finished floor.
1.03 Underside must accommodate components attachment.
1.04 Locate contiguous and perpendicular to leading
      edge of secondary worksurface.

2.00 SECONDARY WORKSURFACE
2.01 Surface shall be a minimum of 1,296 square inches.
2.02 Height shall be at machine level not to exceed 27"
      above finished floor.
2.03 Underside must accommodate components attachment.
2.04 Locate contiguous and perpendicular to primary
      worksurface.

3.00 BOX DRAWER STORAGE
3.01 Shall provide capacity of 2,850 +/- 100 cubic
      inches with drawer depth not to exceed 6".
3.02 Locate contiguous to primary worksurface.

4.00 FILE STORAGE
4.01 Shall provide capacity of 180 +/- 15 filing inches
      of which not less than 125 will accommodate both
      letter and legal size.
4.02 Locate contiguous to primary and/or secondary
      worksurface.

5.00 PENCIL STORAGE
5.01 Shall provide 350 +/- 50 cubic inches.
5.02 Locate contiguous to primary worksurface.

6.00 CLOSED STORAGE
6.01 Shall provide capacity of 21,600 +/- 900 cubic
      inches.
6.02 Components shall open to allow full access to
      stored material.
6.03 Locate contiguous to secondary worksurface.

7.00 PAPER ORGANIZER
7.01 Shall provide 35 +/- 5 lineal inches with not less
      than 4 vertical dividers.
7.02 Locate in closed storage component contiguous to
      primary worksurface.

8.00 VERTICAL TACKABLE SURFACE
8.01 Width shall be equal to secondary worksurface.
      Width and height shall be from top of worksurface
      to underside of any component above or to top of
      privacy panel.
8.02 Locate contiguous to secondary worksurface.

9.00 MODESTY PANEL
9.01 Shall be width of worksurface and height shall be
      not less than 15".
9.02 Locate below primary and secondary worksurface.

10.00 PRIVACY PANEL
10.01 Shall provide for visual privacy on one* side of
       workstation. Height shall be not less than 65"
       nor more than 80" above finished floor.

11.00 INTEGRATED POWER AND LIGHTING (See Article 4
       Specific Requirements and Performance Requirement
       Attribute I)
11.01 Shall provide not less than two convenience
       outlets located above and contiguous to secondary
       worksurface.

* Post-use analysis revealed that visual privacy was desirable on three sides.

o. Are switches located within reach of the user?

p. Are all the electrical components approved by the Underwriters Laboratories?

4. *Storage Units*

a. Are all operating hardware and pulls flush or fully recessed to prevent injury?

b. Will hinged door components support a vertical force of more than 100 lb (46 kg) at the outer edge, when open?

c. Do fully loaded drawers travel from the closed position to fully extended position without interfering with a neighboring drawer?

SPECIFICATION OF GENERAL OFFICE FURNITURE

General office furniture is classified as desks, files, tables, credenzas, and other furniture that is not a component of open office systems.

Double Pedestal Desks

These desks are freestanding and usually have at least one file drawer and four storage drawers, and may be equipped to receive an extension that forms a secondary work surface.

Desk heights should be adjustable to accommodate people of different heights. Table 12.6 suggests appropriate height settings.[11]

Desks are not subject to any federal regulation or required testing, but private laboratories have developed methods of testing for structural strength, finish, drawer operation, and desk-top serviceability. Table 12.7 shows test methods frequently used.

Based on many years of testing office equipment, the Buyers Laboratory offers the following suggestions for inspecting a desk:

1. Examine closely all finished surfaces; they should be free of objectional scratches, mars, dents, or blemishes.

2. Check for distortion of the pedestals that sometimes results when a desk is upended in shipping. Such distortion shows up in uneven spacing around the drawer fronts. Apart from appearance, this type of distortion can affect the operation of the drawers.

3. Run a pad of cheesecloth over all surfaces at or near the knee space. Any sharp edge or burred surface that scratches the cheesecloth is a hazard to clothing and skin.

4. Examine the glides at the bottom of the legs to be sure they can be turned without difficulty. On some desks it takes no more than a 6 in. (15.2 cm) drop in handling to bend the glide stems or damage the threads, making height adjustment difficult, if not impossible.

5. Make sure all drawers operate smoothly and with no interference between drawers, especially when they are only partly extended (the top edge of one drawer should not hit the lower edge of another drawer). This check is best made with the drawers loaded (about 50 lb [23 kg] for file drawers and 20 lb [9 kg] for storage drawers).

6. Examine the plastic laminate around the desk top to see that it is securely bonded to the top and edges. Also check for chipping that may have been caused by rough handling.

7. If the desk is equipped with an extension for typing, check the stability and attachment mechanism.

TABLE 12.6 RECOMMENDED DESK HEIGHTS

Height of Occupant	Approximate Desk Height
To 5'4"	28 1/2" (72.4 cm)*
5'4" to 5'9"	29" (73.7 cm)
5'9" to 5'11"	29 1/2" (74.9 cm)
5'11" to 6'1"	30" (76.2 cm)
6'1" and over	30 1/2" (77.5 cm)

*Glides may have to be removed.

TABLE 12.7 PERFORMANCE TESTING OF DESKS

Attribute/Tests	Acceptance Criteria
I. Durability FSAA-D-00191 d	
A. *Sand abrasion*	No finish removal
B. *Metal bending*	No flaking, cracking, or loss of finish adhesion
C. *Cigarette heat*	No scorch marks
D. *Chemicals*	Withstand staining
II. Structural Strength ASTM/ BIFMA × 5.5–83	
A. *Top function load* 300 lbs 1 inch from front edge of the center remain 15 minutes.	Maximum deflection not to exceed 0.001 inch per inch of top length. (60" desk = 0.060 inch max allowed for final measurement.)
B. *Top proof load.* 10 lbs pli along entire length one inch from front edge.	Resist load. No damage that could cause human injury.
C. *Racking test.* For resistance to moving. Desk raised 45° angle on one end for 30 minutes.	Resist damage to drawers and locking system.
D. *Drop test.* Desk raised 100 inches off floor.	Resist damage to drawers. No structural damage.
E. *Leg impact test.* Desk placed upside down. Swinging weight to legs.	Resist structural damage. No damage to drawers.
III. Desk Component Strength and Durability.	
A. *Drawer cycle test.* Loaded drawers opened/ closed to within ¼ inch, 2 cycles per minute.	Resists operational damage. File/ box drawers resist 50,000 cycles. Center drawer resists 20,000 cycles.
B. *Pull test.* Amount of force required to open drawers is measured.	Shall maintain ease of operation. Pull force not to exceed 4½ lbs for large drawer to 3½ lb for center drawer.
C. *Rebound test.* Drawers loaded and spring-type force of 1 lb per lb of drawer load. Five cycles.	Resists rebound in excess of 1½ inches.

Filing Cabinets

Providing storage for paper materials still remains a necessary part of most office planning. The traditional means of storage has involved a vertical file cabinet with either four or five drawers. Five drawer files generally measure 57 to 60 in. (144.8 to 152.4 cm) in height and may present some problems for the user under 5'4" (162.6 cm) or a physically handicapped person. Another type of filing unit is the lateral file which allows side filing; i.e., the storage capacity is measured horizontally and the depth of the file cabinet is usually 15 to 18 in. (38.1 to 45.7 cm). These units can be stacked five high.

Specification of filing cabinets should involve a consideration of the filing needs of the client, available floor space, and the quality of workmanship in individual cabinets. When

DRAWER CYCLING TEST   **ROLL-OUT SHELF TEST**

Figure 12.9 Lateral drawer and shelf cycle test. Source: BIFMA.

Figure 12.10 Stability test (dynamic load/force) lateral file. Source: BIFMA.

comparing vertical and lateral files, the following questions should be considered:

1. Are lateral files more economical than conventional files? Recent cost comparisons show that lateral files cost about $1.60 per linear filing foot while conventional files are $1.10.

2. Do lateral files use less space? Depending on the space needs, lateral files can often fit into areas too narrow to accommodate conventional files. Used in a two-drawer units, the top surfaces may also serve as credenza, and three-drawer units are frequently used as space dividers.

Performance Testing of Lateral Files. The Business and Institutional Furniture Manufacturer's Association (BIFMA) together with the ANSI have developed a voluntary standard. The ANSI/BIFMA X 5.2-1980 Tests for Lateral Files provides manufacturers, designers, and users with a common basis for evaluating the safety, durability, and structural qualities of freestanding lateral files.

This voluntary standard recommends that manufacturers place caution labels on lateral files. These labels should contain operation and safety instructions regarding (1) cabinet leveling procedures, (2) loading techniques, (3) recommendations for weight distribution, and (4) general safety precautions.

The tests employed in this standard involve static functional loads and proof-load applications. Functional loads are those equivalent to normal usage. A proof load is defined as a force that is in excess to maximum or very heavy abusive file use. For example, a proof load of 4 lbs per linear inch is applied to a file top for 10 minutes. The test requires that the file should resist the load with no structural damage to the frame or the drawers. Figure 12.9 illustrates the stability test which is used to determine the stability level of the file in its least stable condition (with the top drawer extended). In this test the drawer is loaded with 2 lb per linear inch (0.91 kg per 25 mm) and a 10 lb (4.6 kg) horizontal force is applied to the normal hand pull location of the extended drawer. Test criteria require that the file withstand the pull force without tipping.

Figures 12.10 and 12.11 illustrate the file strength test which evaluates the ability of the file to support loads to which it will be subjected when in service.

Tables for Conference and Dining Areas

Conference tables are a necessary component in most offices. These tables are usually 30 in. (76.2 cm) in height and have various types of base supports which should not interfere with full capacity seating around the table. The number of people that must be accommodated during conferences is a major factor in the specification of the table size and shape. Because many situations will require very large tables, designers should determine the route by which the table will be delivered into the building; i.e., if the top surface is composed of one piece, check elevators, hallways, doorways, and windows to avoid installation problems.

Figure 12.12 illustrates some of the sizes and shapes used for conference tables.[12] The seating capacity listed for each size table is based on a 23-in. (58.4-cm) wide chair plus 4 in. (10.2 cm) allowance between each chair. When specifying a wider chair, the space should be adjusted accordingly. For example, if a 26-in. (66-cm) wide chair is used, it would be necessary to allow 30 in. for each chair (25" + 4").

Tables specified for dining areas require special performance criteria with respect to (1) top surface construction and

Figure 12.11 Lateral file strength test (static load). Source: BIFMA.

round tops

diameter inches	approximate seating
42	4
48	5
54	6
60	7
66	7
72	8
84	9
96	11
108	12
120	14

square tops

dimensions inches l	w	approximate seating
36	36	4
42	42	4

blunt end oval tops

dimensions inches l	w	approximate seating
44	34	4
55	36	6
82	36 (extension)	8

elliptical tops

dimensions inches l	w	approximate seating
60	30	4
72	34	4
84	42	6
96	48	6
108	48	8
120	48	8
144	48	10

(for conference use, no seating at end)

rounded oval tops

dimensions inches l	w	approximate seating
70	36	4
78	48	6

rectangular tops

l	w	seating	l	w	seating	l	w	seating	l	w	seating
48	24	4	60	30	4	96	36	8	60	48	6
60	24	4	72	30	6	48	42	4	72	48	6
72	24	6	84	30	6	60	42	4	84	48	8
84	24	6	96	30	8	72	42	6	96	48	8
96	24	6	48	36	4	84	42	6	108	48	8
36	30	4	60	36	4	96	42	8	120	48	10
42	30	4	72	36	6	108	42	8	144	48	12
48	30	4	84	36	6	120	42	10			

boat tops

l feet	c inches	e inches	approximate seating
6	36	30	6
7	38	31	6
8	40	32	8
10	44	33	10
12	48	34	12
14	52	35	12
16	56	36	16
18	60	37	16
20	60	38	18
22	60	39	20
24	60	40	22

racetrack tops

l feet	w inches	approximate seating
10	60	12
12	60	12
15	60	16

cross grain racetrack

wedge-end racetrack

cross grain boat

Figure 12.12 Size capacity of conference tables.
Reproduced with permission of Vecta Contract.

finish and (2) the weight and size of the table base. Table tops produced for dining facilities should have level, moisture-resistant surfaces. A well-constructed top is usually composed of three elements: (1) a plastic laminate surface that is highly resistant to burns, scratches, and impact; (2) a core of either plywood (7 to 15 plies) or particle board (1⅛ in. [2.8 cm] thick) that will resist warpage; (3) backing material to prevent warping caused by heat and humidity (kraft paper or additional laminate).

Common problems associated with tables can be avoided through the proper specification of the base weight, size, and construction.[13]

1. Table instability (wobble and shake) is frequently the result of specifying a base size not in proportion to the top size. If the base and connecting column are too small or the gauge of steel used in the legs (spider) or column is not heavy enough, the table will tend to wobble and shake. Wood columns should never be specified for tables having tops larger than 36 in. (91.4 cm) in diameter.

2. Table tipping is a major cause of liability claims. Designers should be aware that many people (especially those who are elderly) use the table top for support when arising from a dining chair. The table will tip if the base leg spread is too narrow and not properly weighted. The table base (at floor level) should never be less than half the size of the table top. Carpet may also cause problems if the table legs do not have glides that can penetrate the carpet pile and form a stable support base. The carpet pile height should determine the length of stem glides used on the table legs (spider bases). Designers should specify compliance with ANSI voluntary standard ANSI/BIFMA X5.5—1983, *Table Stability Test* from "Standard for Office Furnishings—Desk Products."

Seating for Commercial Interiors

Seating is a major source of injuries and liability suits and should therefore be given careful consideration in regard to performance, durability, and stability. Commercial seating may be classified as desk chairs, side chairs, assembly or auxiliary seating, permanent multiple seating, lounge seating, and conference seating, and custom-designed multiple seating.

Desk Chairs.

These may be either posture (tilt seat and back) or fixed seats and back; rotating or nonrotating; with or without arms. These chairs may be partially or fully upholstered and normally have casters for ease of movement. Figure 12.13 illustrates typical secretarial and clerical chairs. It should be noted that secretarial chairs are smaller in size than clerical chairs.

Construction: Swivel Armchairs (Nonposture).   This type of chair is also known as a "fixed-back" chair, in which the seat and back tilt as a unit; in a posture chair, the seam remains horizontal and only the back tilts. The fixed back swivel armchair has two adjustments: one for seat height and the other to control the back tension or force required to tilt the seat and back unit backward. (Posture chairs have as many as four or five adjustments). Figure 12.14 illustrates the major parts that should be considered when specifying a swivel armchair.

1. Chair base is composed of a cross-shaped structure which supports the rest of the chair and to which casters are usually attached.

2. The *spindle* is a part of the structure that passes through the center of the base, supports the seat, and allows the chair to swivel. The spindle is partially enclosed in a *spindle housing* or hub, which is set in the center of the base. The bearing surface in the housing is called the *spindle-bushing*. The height of the chair seat is adjusted by turning the height adjustment *control handwheel* on the spindle thread. The upper end of the spindle is rigidly fastened to the *control iron* or chair control.

3. The *control iron* provides the chair tilting action and consists of three parts: (1) the *chassis* to which the spindle is attached; (2) the tilting mechanism; (3) the "spider arms" which support the seat.

A. SECRETARIAL CHAIR   B. TASK CHAIR   C. CLERICAL CHAIR

Figure 12.13 Secretarial and clerical desk chairs.

Figure 12.14 Construction features of a swivel arm chair. Source: Buyers Laboratory.

Figure 12.15 Swivel arm chair dimensions. Source: Buyers Laboratory.

4. The *tilting mechanism* controls the maximum angle of inclination of the chair seat and back as well as the back tension. Tilting mechanisms generally employ two major types of spring action. One type makes use of torsion bars and the other uses helical springs to control the back tension. Both types of tension mechanisms can be adjusted by the *back tension control.*

5. *Chair seats* usually consist of a steel or plywood *seat pan,* foam rubber or other cushioning material (sometimes springs), and upholstery. In many seats a steel flange is fastened to the outer edge of the seat pan to add rigidity. Seat coverings are often fastened to the outer edge of the seat pan or the steel flange.[14]

Swivel Armchair Dimensions. When specifying chairs that will be used in offices, designers must be aware that individual requirements for seating comfort will vary widely, and therefore chairs engineered to offer the greatest flexibility of adjustment should be specified. The fact that people using the chairs will probably be seated for extended periods of time creates the problem of designing and/or selecting chairs that will prevent fatigue and backache. The following dimensions and flexibility should be considered:

1. Seat height should be adjusted to meet the needs of people with short or long legs; i.e., seat heights should not cause pressure on the underside of the thighs when the feet are placed squarely on the floor. Many office employees are forced to adjust the height of their chairs to accommodate the height of the desk or work surface, instead of adjusting for actual seating comfort. To accommodate the wide range of people who may be using the chair, the seat height adjustment may range from 14½ to 21 in. (36.9 to 53.3 cm). Adjustment to lower than 14½ in. may be necessary for some people. Desk heights should also be adjustable to coordinate work surfaces with seating heights. If a desk cannot be lowered enough for a short person, the seating should be raised, and a footrest may have to be provided to prevent extreme pressure on the underside of the thighs (see Figure 12.15).

2. Backrests and seat-to-back openings are important considerations when specifying office seating. The height of the backrest area should not interfere with ease of movement, but should be high enough to provide adequate back support. The top of the back should be at least 15½ in. (39.4 cm) above the top of the seat to provide adequate support for the back. The space from the seat to the back support is intended to prevent pressure against the lower end of the spine and may range from 4 to 5 in. (10.2 to 15.2 cm).

3. The seat shape should not constrict the movement of the seated person. Movement is essential when a person is seated for extended periods of time; therefore, padded seats that have slightly concave seat pans would be more comfortable than saddle-contoured seat pans, which may constrict movement.

4. Seat cushioning should provide a firm support that would prevent excessive pressure on the bony projections of the buttocks. On unpadded flat seats, pressure may built up to as much as 60 lb psi (28 kg) at pressure points. Good seating should provide an even distribution of body weight over the seating area.

5. Seat depth should be carefully considered in regard to the pressure it will create on the legs. Too deep a seat presses on the legs below the knees and may also cause a person to sit forward and lose contact with the back support area. Recommended seat depths should not exceed 16½ in. (41.9 cm) in depth. Firm padded seats may be more comfortable if the depth is limited to 15 in. (38.1 cm). Some authorities suggest a space of up to 3 in. (7.6 cm) between the rear of the calf and the front edge of the seat to allow adequate space for change of sitting position.

6. Armrests should not be too long or placed too high. The height of the armrest could cause uncomfortable pressure on the shoulder joints and also provide a constant annoyance by bumping into the desk or work surface. The recommended height between the top of the armrest and the seat is between 8 and 10 in. (20.3 and 25.4 cm). Extremely short or tall people may require armrest heights ranging from 6 to 11 in. (15.2 to 27.9 cm).[19]

Dimensions: Secretarial Posture Chairs. The major difference between a nonposture and posture chair is the fact that the backrest on a posture chair can be raised or lowered and the seat does not tilt when the back is tilted. On most posture chairs the back can be flexed and the pressure required to flex the back can be adjusted.

Adjustment Procedures. These are very important in obtaining the full use of a posture chair. The designer should make certain that the client or user is instructed in adjustment procedures. A chair should be adjusted to the particular user initially and again after about two weeks of use if the seating is found to be uncomfortable.

The secretarial posture chair generally has five adjustments: (1) seat height, (2) back height, (3) back angle, (4) back tension, and (5) back position. The seat height is adjustable to permit the user's feet to rest flat on the floor. The height may vary from 16½ to 21 in. (41.9 to 53.3 cm) and is adjustable by turning the height control handwheel on the spindle thread.

The back-top height should be adjustable within a range of 13 to 15 in. (33 to 38.1 cm) above the top of the seat. The height of the bottom of the backrest should range from 4 to 6 in. (10.2 to 15.2 cm) above the seat. The lower edge of the backrest should be set approximately 1 in. (25 mm) below a horizontal line through the top of the hip bone.

The backrest angle or the horizontal position of the chair back should be adjusted to permit the user to lean back about 10 or 15° from a straight/vertical line. The tension control should be set firmly for maximum support.

Side Chairs. These may be rotating or nonrotating; with or without arms; and normally with a nontilt fixed back. They are usually partially upholstered.

Assembly or Auxiliary Seating. This is designed to assemble easily and quickly and later be stored between uses. It is normally light-weight (9½ to 15½ lb [4.3 to 7 kg]) and may have only minimal upholstery. Because these chairs are stacked for storage, they are often constructed of fiberglass or plastic with tubular or rod-type legs of aluminum or other light-weight materials. Welded joints rather than bolted construction are recommended because the heavy use and frequent moving would loosen the bolts and weaken the entire chair structure. Accessories that may be attached to the chairs range from tablet arms and armrests to bookracks and ashtrays. The number

Figure 12.16 Equipment for moving and storing seating. Reproduced with permission of Fixtures Manufacturing Corp., Kansas City, MO.

Figure 12.17 Zermatt cantilever assembly seating. Reproduced with permission of Vecta Contract.

of chairs that may be stacked in one group depends on the design and may vary from 15 to 45 chairs (unupholstered) on dollies, which are designed for storing and transporting the chairs between uses (Figure 12.16). Special ganging devices are often used to interlock these chairs side by side during use because most fire codes require that stacking or folding chairs used in places of assembly be ganged to prevent injury to the occupants. In the event of a fire or other emergency, unattached seating would become disarranged or overturned and destroy aisles and passageways, which would present an obstacle to safe egress of the occupants. The interlocking attachments range from plastic clips to metal hoods welded to the sides of the chairs.

Permanent Multiple Seating. This is primarily designed for use in large public areas such as theaters, transportation terminals, and public lobbies that are subject to heavy use. This seating is permanently joined together, either attached at the base or sides or attached to a long horizontal bar, which results in fewer vertical supports. The latter method of construction provides for greater ease of maintenance in areas that receive constant use. Figure 12.17 illustrates cantilever multiple seating supported by a horizontal bar. In specifying any multiple seating, designers should select units that will resist structural vibrations; i.e., the seating of a person at any point along the unit should not disturb others using the same unit.

Lounge Seating. This is usually upholstered sofas, chairs, and benches which are used in informal commercial or institutional reception and lobby areas that do not receive excessive use. Figure 12.18 shows upholstered lounge seating that is designed with ganging devices that allow the seating to be arranged in free-form arrangements. These units may also incorporate ganged tables and planters.

It is recommended that designers specify testing according to the standard ANSI/BIFMA X5.4—1983, *Standard for Office Furnishings—Lounge Seating Tests*.

Conference Seating. This is designed for use around a conference table, and although these chairs have arms, they are designed to coordinate with the table height. To provide a more relaxed posture, the pitch or tilt of the back is greater than the pitch used in chairs designed for more concentrated tasks.

(Not to scale.)

Figure 12.18 Ganged lounge seating. Reproduced with permission of Tappo Seating System, Vecta Contract.

These chairs often have a sled base or a center pedestal and pronged base that may or may not have casters. Since most conference rooms have carpet installed over padding, casters should be carefully selected to prevent damage to the floor-covering.

Performance Testing of Seating

For many years private industry and independent laboratories have been involved in developing various methods for testing the structural integrity of seating components. These efforts reflect the manufacturers' concern about the increasing rate of product liability claims involving chair-related injuries (see Chapter 2).

Tests to determine the probable performance of office chairs are concerned with durability, structural strength, and stability. Chairs are tested by the application of dynamic and static leads, and all moving parts are evaluated on the basis of endurance or service life.[16]

Durability tests for secretarial posture chairs involve the three primary sources of motion performed by the chair, i.e., the swiveling of the seat, the flexing of the back, and the caster movement.

1. Back-flexing tests mechanically flex the chair back to determine the number of flexes the structure will withstand. Acceptance criteria vary, but some tests require chairs to withstand up to 12,000 flexes. This criteria is based on the assumption that an average secretarial posture chair will recieve about 10 flexes per hour over a six-year use period.

2. Swivel cycling tests often seek to accelerate wear conditions by placing a heavy static (nonmoving) load on the seat of the chair while subjecting the swivel mechanism to an intensive amount of cycling per hour. Well-constructed chairs should withstand up to 200,000 revolutions without showing excessive wear.

3. Caster durability tests are conducted with varying static loads placed in the chair, and casters are normally expected to withstand 100,000 revolutions.

Structural strength tests are conducted to determine any weaknesses that may cause structural failure of the chair and injury to the occupant. Many of these tests are based on the Interim Federal Specifications No. AA-C-00275 (d) for aluminum office chairs and AA-C-00293 (a) for steel office chairs.

1. Back-pull tests require that the chair back be slowly pulled to the rear with a force of 100 lb (46 kg) for steel chairs and 125 lb (56 kg) for aluminum. Acceptance criteria are based on the amount of distortion caused by the test. Permanent distortion should not exceed ¼ in. (6.4 mm).

2. Drop tests for seats are based on the application of a dynamic load to the seat surface. A sandbag weighing 175 lb (80 kg) for aluminum chairs and 225 lb (102 kg) for steel chairs is dropped from a height of 6 in. (15.2 cm) onto the seat. Distortion should not exceed ⅛ in. (3.2 mm) in aluminum chairs and ¼ in. (6.4 mm) in steel chairs. In addition, the chairs should show no signs of fractures or internal or exterior breakage.

Stacking chairs are subjected to the same general types of tests, but the emphasis is on more varied use conditions. Dynamic loads are applied to the front edges of seats, and other tests are conducted to determine the potential hazards presented by the tipping or rocking of lightweight chairs.

In an effort to provide consistent performance and safety standards, the Business and Institutional Furniture Manufacturer's Association (BIFMA) worked with the American National Standards Institute, Inc. (ANSI) to establish voluntary standards. These efforts have produced six standards, two of which deal with seating: ANSI/BIFMA X5.4—1983, *Standard For Office Furnishings—Lounge Seating Tests* and ANSI/BIFMA X5.1—1985, *Standard for Office Furnishings—General Purpose Office Chairs Tests*. The testing machine shown in Figure 12.19 was designed for testing office furniture.

Figure 12.19 Machine for testing office chairs. Reproduced with permission of BIFMA.

MAINTENANCE OF FURNITURE COMPONENTS

Mechanical components of furniture should be maintained on a regular basis to prevent injuries and prolong the service life of the furniture.[17]

Drawer Slides

Metal drawer slides do not usually require lubrication. When drawers receive very heavy wear, a small amount of light oil may be applied to the nylon rollers.

Swiveling or Turning Devices

The swivels and casters on office chairs are usually lubricated permanently, but if additional lubrication is needed, it would be necessary to disassemble the swivel and apply a small amount of light machine oil. Most manufacturers maintain replacement parts, should any difficulty arise.

Desks

Several components parts of the desk may require maintenance checks:

1. Drawers should be removed and cleaned with a flameproof cleaner, such as Carbona.

2. Pedestal channels may be wiped lightly with #10 oil on the roller bearings of large letter drawers. Drawers should be replaced in the same opening from which they were removed. (Number on the bottom to avoid misplacement.)

3. Desk alignment should be checked and corrected if necessary.

Filing Cabinets

1. Remove drawers, clean, and apply #10-weight oil lightly.

2. Tighten loose drawer handles.

3. Check and adjust locks.

4. Large groups or batteries of files should be bolted together to provide alignment. After bolting, the grouping can be shimmed on the floor to obtain evenness and provide square openings for the drawers so they will operate smoothly.

Chairs

Check regularly for loose bolts and weakened joints. If a chair is damaged, it should be removed from use to avoid injury.

LIFE CYCLE COSTING

The question of furniture life cycle costing often arises when a client is moving to a new facility and seeks advice regarding the continued use of currently owned equipment. Before any decision can be made, the designer should conduct a furniture inventory and note the condition of each piece.

Reaching a decision on which furniture should be replaced, repaired, sold, or donated may be dependent on the following factors:

1. Initial cost

2. Maintenance and repair cost

3. Moving cost

After these costs are compared with the cost of total replacement, additional alternatives, such as selling the furnishings at market value or the possibility of receiving a tax deduction by donating the furniture, may be considered.

In the event that new furniture is specified, the designer's choice of furniture finishes and construction will, to a large extent, lengthen the expected service life of furnishings. Assembly seating, such as stacking chairs, requires special life cycle cost consideration. The following equation may be used:

$$I + E + L + S + M = \text{total cost}$$

where
$\quad I = $ initial cost
$\quad E = $ equipment for handling (dollies)
$\quad L = $ labor cost for handling
$\quad S = $ space needed for storage (sq ft)
$\quad M = $ maintenance

The chair design will determine the number of chairs that can be stacked on one dolly. For example, if only ten chairs can be stacked per dolly and the dollies cost $50 each, a 500-chair installation would require 50 dollies. If other chairs were specified that could be stacked 20 per dolly, the client would realize a $1,250 initial cost saving.

Labor cost for handling the chairs can range from 4 to 7 cents per chair. Normally it takes three hours to set up 100 folding chairs and only one hour to set up 100 stacking chairs; therefore stacking chairs could result in sizable savings.

The space needed to store stacking chairs between use must also be considered in the total cost. If 500 chairs can be stacked and stored in 100 sq ft (9.5 sq m) and that commercial space costs $45 per square foot, the total storage cost would be $4,500 per year.

Maintenance costs can vary, depending on the quality of the chair and the design specified. Stacking chairs that are upholstered should have a bumper or other means of preventing damage to the upholstery during handling. Designers should also avoid specifying stacking chairs that are constructed with bolts because these tend to loosen and fall out during constant use.

This example of stacking chairs can also apply to folding or stacking tables or other furniture that has been designed for multiple use.

CUSTOM CASEWORK

Although there are many credenzas, counters, and storage components manufactured for commercial use, designers must often specify custom casework to meet particular design needs. To produce detailed working drawings and specifications that communicate pertinent facts regarding the desired casework, designers should provide the following information:

1. Drawings
   a. Include the location of all counters or cabinets that will be built-in on site.
   b. Each cabinet or counter must be identified by a number or some designation that will correlate to elevations, schedules, and the written specification.
   c. Basic appearance and component arrangement must be clearly delineated in elevations and sections: profile; critical parts; joinery; thickness of material; location and dimensions of drawers, doors, shelves, hardware.
   d. If more than one species of wood is to be used on a particular piece of casework, the location should be shown on the details or on the finish schedule. The same applies to selected grades and finishes.

2. Schedules
   a. Hardware.
   b. Finishes and grade.
   c. Fasteners and adhesives.
   d. Any other items that need clarification.

3. Specification
   a. Definition of exposed, semiexposed, and concealed portions of casework.
   b. Shop assembly of all items.
   c. Hardware must be furnished and applied by the manufacturer or woodworker.
   d. Minimum thickness of all cabinet components and thickness of laminates. (Doors = 1⅜″ [3.4 cm]; case backs and drawer bottoms = ¼″ [6.4 mm]; shelves exceeding 36″ = 1″ [91.4 cm = 2.5 cm].)
   e. Quality of lumber grade and plywood for semiexposed portions.
   f. Gluing performance; types of core, edge treatment, and joint tolerances for high-pressure laminates.
   g. Method of fastening exposed members and tops.
   f. Method of case body joinery.
   i. Edge treatment of all exposed plywood members.
   j. Type of drawer construction (dust panels between drawers are not standard and if desired must be specified).
   k. Required joinery tolerances. (Premium = .007″; Custom = .015″.)
   l. Allowable warp and clearance for casework doors. Gap-flush overlay (premium = .130″); warp (premium = .027″).
   m. Design of casework appearance (flush, lapped, reveal overlay).
   n. Matched grain effect on exposure portions is not required and therefore must be specified (Figure 12.20).[18]

Casework Terminology

Figure 12.21 illustrates the exposed, semiexposed, and concealed portions of casework.

1. Exposed portions include all surfaces visible when doors and drawers are closed. Bottoms of cases more than 4 ft (121.9 cm) above the floor are considered exposed. All areas visible behind glass doors are also considered exposed.

2. Semiexposed portions are those concealed behind opaque doors, e.g., shelves, divisions, case backs, drawer sides, backs, bottoms, and the back side of doors.

3. Concealed portions are those that are not normally seen, such as sleepers, web frames, and dust panels.[19]

PREMIUM GRADE

CUSTOM GRADE

Figure 12.20 Furniture face veneer.

WEB FRAME

EXPOSED OR SHOW END

TOE STRIP

Figure 12.21 Casework construction parts: exposed and semiexposed.

TABLE 12.8 VISUAL TESTS FOR EXPOSED CASEWORK SURFACES

Defects	Premium	Custom
Orange peel — Slight depressions in surface, similar to skin of orange	3'*	6'*
Runs — Running of wet finish film in rivulets	None	None
Sags — Partial slipping of finish film creating a curtain effect	None	3'*
Finish sanding scratches	None	3'*
Blistering — Small swelled areas like a water blister on human skin	None	None
Glue spots	None	None
Checking, crazing or cracking — Crowfoot separation. Irregular line separation.	None	None
Filled nail holes	3'*	6'*

*Not noticeable beyond this distance viewed in the normal light in which casework is intended to be used.

Source: Architectural Woodwork Institute (AWI).

EXPOSED FACE FRAME FLUSH —————

EXPOSED FACE FRAME LIPPED — — — — —

FLUSH OVERLAY

REVEAL OVERLAY

Figure 12.22 Casework design details. Source: Architectural Woodwork Institute.

Casework Hardware

The hardware is usually furnished by the woodwork manufacturer and will be of standard quality unless the designer includes the following in the written specification:

1. Drawer slides _____ (brand and catalog number).

2. Shelf standards and brackets _____ (specify finish and brand name).

3. Sliding door track _____ (specify brand and catalog number).

4. Hinges _____ (specify brand and catalog number).

5. Catches _____ (brand and catalog number).

6. Pulls _____ (brand and catalog number). The desired location must be shown on the drawings.[20]

Table 12.8 explains various defects that are allowed in casework constructed of premium- and custom-grade wood. For more information on wood species and grades, see the AWI Comparative Wood Chart in Chapter 9. See *Interior Graphic and Design Standards* for additional information on Casework Hardware.

Design of Casework Appearance

There are three basic design categories in casework construction:

1. Exposed face frame (Figure 12.22)
   a. *Flush*
      This category is also known as "conventional flush" and is the most basic type. In this style the door and drawer faces are flush with the face frame.
      (1) Advantages: Allows use of different thicknesses of wood for doors and drawer fronts. Heavy-duty and conventional hardware may be used. Recommended for hard service areas because of the superior strength.
      (2) Disadvantages: More expensive because of careful fitting and aligning required for doors and drawers.
   b. *Lipped*
      Very similar in construction to the flush design.
      Advantages: More economical because fitting tolerance of doors and drawers are less critical.

2. Flush overlay (Figure 12.22)
   Provides a very sleek design with only door and drawer fronts visible on the face of the cabinet; permits a matched grain to be used across entire front (can be cut from one panel [Figure 12.8]). Heavy-duty hardware can be used, but the absence of a face frame requires careful alignment.

3. Reveal overlay (Figure 12.22)
   A variation on the flush overlay, it presents a raised panel effect. It does not require a face frame and needs less careful fitting and alignment. The designer may use the "reveal" either vertically or horizontally.

Plastic Laminates

Laminated surfaces have almost become a standard requirement on top surfaces of products specified for commercial use. The standard manufacturing process for general purpose laminates involves impregnating a decorative paper with melamine resins. The decorative paper is then bonded to several kraft phenolic core sheets by heat and pressure (one half ton per square inch at 280° F).

High-pressure decorative laminate (HPDL) is produced with extra thickness to allow the material to be permanently bent and curved around edges (see Figure 12.23).

Industry Labeling: Grades Laminates are classified according to the weight or grade and recommended application. The National Electrical Manufacturers Association (NEMA) Standards Publication No. LD-3-1985 establishes the following grade number and naming system: The number refers to the thickness, which can range from 0.010″ to plus or minus 0.050″. The letters designate use.

I. Standard-Nondimensional
1. *General Purpose* (GP/28±) is the most widely use grade. It may be applied to both vertical or horizontal surfaces.
2. *General Purpose Forming* (GPF/30±) is postformable to permit small radii bending.
3. *Postforming* (PF/42±) is made for both vertical or horizontal use. Specify when inside or outside dimensions require formed radii.

II. Special Purpose Grades
1. *Fire Rated General Purpose* (Grade 50) is for use on vertical or horizontal surfaces that require a flame spread rating (ASTM-84). Note that NEMA tests several grades for radiant heat.
2. *Anti-Static Postforming Grade* is engineered to reduce static buildup.
3. *Chemical Stain Resistant Laboratory Grade* (LGP) is used in medical, industrial, and university laboratories.

Standard Sizes

Widths (inches) 24, 30, 48, and 60
(cm) 70, 76, 122, 152

Lengths (inches) 72, 96, 120, and 144
(cm) 183, 244, 305, 366

Fabrication Specify that fabrication methods comply with the manufacturer's recommendations and those established by the National Association of Plastic Fabricators (NAPF). Also specify compliance with NEMA Publication No. LD3-1980 "Fabrication and Installation of High-Pressure Decorative Laminate" and ANSI-A-161.2-1979 where applicable.

Substrate materials may include plywood, flakeboard wood composition board, inorganic fiberboard, and metal. Specify that the surface be flat and smooth. Excessive moisture inbalance should not exist between laminate and substrate. Forty-eight hours prior to fabrication, the project site and all materials should be maintained at 75° F and 45 percent relative humidity (RH).

Square-cut inside corners should not be specified. All inside corner cutouts should have a minimum of ⅛ in. (3.17 cm) radius to avoid cracking. Require that all edges be rounded smooth.

Installation of Fire Retardant Treated Laminate Fire-retardant laminate must be applied in compliance with requirements outlined in UL listings. Specify that the substrate be fire-rated particle board with a UL rating of 20-15-15 and mineral board. Also consult local code officials.

Postforming Fabrication This process involves the bending of laminated material to conform to the edge of a horizontal

surface or a vertical surface such as stair posts or columns. Surfaces with bends with very close radii, like those found on octagonal and hexagonal tables, require High-Performance Decorative Laminates (HPDL).

Applicable Standards

1. National Electrical Manufacturers Association NEMA Standards Publication No. LD-3-1980. (See Tables 12.9 and 12.10.)

2. Federal Specification GSA-FSS L-P 508 H, "General Purpose and Postforming Grades" Types I and II. Class I.

3. Department of Housing and Urban Development, Federal Register 280.203, "Mobile Home Construction and Safety Standards," Dec. 18, 1975.

4. Department of Transportation
a. Motor Vehicle Safety Standard 302, "Flammability of Interior Materials."

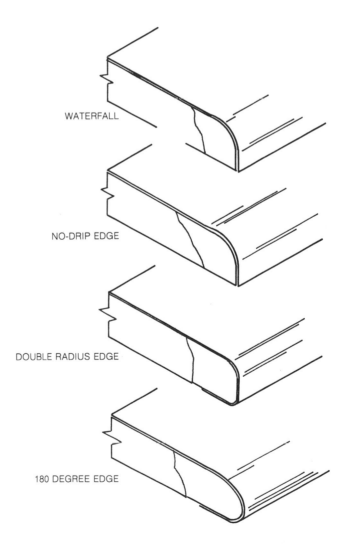

WATERFALL

NO-DRIP EDGE

DOUBLE RADIUS EDGE

180 DEGREE EDGE

Figure 12.23 Postforming horizontal counter and table top applications.

TABLE 12.9   PHYSICAL PROPERTIES OF HIGH-PRESSURE DECORATIVE LAMINATE

Test	NEMA Standard GP28/PF30	NEMA Standard GP50	NEMA Standard PF42
Thickness	0.028″ ± 0.004″ (0.030″ PF30)	0.050″ ± 0.005″	0.042″ ± 0.005″
Surface Wear	200 cycles (min) (300 PF30)	400 cycles (min)	400 cycles (min)
Boiling Water	no effect on face	no effect	no effect
High Temperature	slight effect	slight effect	slight effect
Radiant Heat	80 seconds (min)	125 seconds (min)	100 seconds (min)
Stain (group I) (group II)	no effect moderate effect	no effect moderate effect	no effect moderate effect
Colorfastness	slight change	slight change	slight change
Dimensional Stability (MD) (CD)	0.7% (max) (1.1% PF30) 1.2% (max) (1.4% PF30)	0.50% (max) 0.9% (max)	1.1% (max) 1.4% (max)
Impact	20 inches	50 inches	30 inches
Conductive Heat	no effect	no effect	no effect
Cleanability	25 cycles (max)	25 cycles (max)	25 cycles (max)
Scuffing	no effect	no effect	no effect
Formability	½″ radius	not applicable	⅝″ face
Blistering	40 seconds	not applicable	55 seconds

* It is recommended that the following reagents not be allowed to remain in contact with the decorative material.
1. Hypochlorite bleach (e.g., Hilex, Clorox) except under maintenance provisions, section (7)
2. Hydrogen peroxide solution in any concentration
3. Mineral acids (e.g., hydrochloric, sulfuric, and nitric acids)
4. Lye solution (containing 1 percent or 2 percent lye, e.g., Drano)
5. Sodium bisulfate (e.g., Sani Flush)
6. Potassium permanganate in any concentration
7. Berry juices, such as grape and raspberry
8. Silver nitrate (1 percent concentration)
9. Gentian violet in any concentration
10. Mild silver protein such as 20 percent argyrol
11. Bluing
12. Dye (e.g., Tintex, Rit)
13. Iodine solution (alcohol containing 1 percent iodine)

Source: National Electrical Manufactures Association (NEMA).

TABLE 12.10   TYPICAL FLAME-SPREAD DATA FOR HIGH-PRESSURE DECORATIVE LAMINATE*

Type	Flame	Smoke
Unbonded Sheets		
107	100	35
335	30	30
350	50	40
Bonded W/Contact To Particleboard		
107	190	130
335	165	135
350	170	155

* Based on test results obtained in the ASTM E.84.
Source: NEMA.

b. Transit Systems TSC-75-LFS-6, "Guidelines for Flammability and Smoke Emission Specifications for Transit Systems."

5. Federal Aviation Regulation, Section 25.853 and Appendix F.

6. Federal Aeronautics Authority, Aircraft Interiors, Federal Test Method 191, Part 25,853.

7. National Sanitation Foundation (NSF) #35, "Laminated Plastic for Food Service Equipment."

8. U.S. Coast Guard, Certificate of Approval for Interior Finishes, under 46 CFR 164.012. PRF 1.

9. Military Specifications, GP50-MIL-P-17171 D (SH) Type I. Mil-STD-1623C (SH) for High-Pressure Table Laminates. Mil-P-17171 D (SH), Type IV for PFR 1.

CUSTOM-DESIGNED MULTIPLE SEATING

This is frequently required in public areas, such as lobbies and restaurants. Figure 12.24 illustrates working drawings for restaurant banquettes and booths. Designers should provide detailed drawings containing information on the following:

1. Structural dimensions

2. Construction details

3. Location of springs, cushion components

4. Upholstery detailing (location of tufting, seaming, and welting)

Figure 12.25 on page 203 shows a typical schedule or bill of materials that is required to further clarify the working drawings. This schedule includes:

1. Structural materials (wood, metal, or plastics)

2. Hardware, fasteners, and adhesives

3. Finishes on exposed and semiexposed areas

Figure 12.26 on page 203 illustrates an upholstery schedule that should accompany furniture working drawings. That schedule includes:

1. Frame construction

2. Spring construction

3. Filling materials and liners

4. Fabric direction, construction, and trim

A written specification, shown in Figure 12.27 on page 206, is necessary to assure accurate completion of the work, and should include a description of the following:

1. Quality of materials

2. Fabrication

3. Species of wood and grade required

4. Relationship with the other work in the specifications

Dimensions (not to scale):

	in.	cm
A =	54	137.16
B =	39	99.06
C =	18	45.72
D =	22	55.88
E =	40	101.60
F =	21	53.34
G =	19	48.26
H =	7	17.78
I =	6	15.24
J =	5	12.70
K =	25½	64.77
L =	2¼	5.72
M =	2	5.08
N =	3½	8.89
O =	¾	1.91
P =	½	1.27
Q =	12	30.48
R =	1	2.54
S =	2½	6.35
T =	4	10.16

Notes: Tufting not recommended on the seat area for the following reasons:

1. Cigarette may lodge in space and smolder.

2. Food particles collect.

3. Difficult to slide in seat.

4. Seating friction and stress may pull buttons loose.

Button

Cotton

No sag springs

Welt

Vent holes

Section of custom booth with removable seat

Side elevation

Front   Side

Front elevation of booth & table

Elevation of diamond tufted booth

Recessed

Figure 12.24 Custom upholstered restaurant banquette seating. Reproduced with permission of Selje, Bond, Steward & Romberger, Phoenix and Los Angeles.

Figure 12.24 continued

NAILED ON BACK CUSHION
WITH ¾" FOAM RUBBER

REMOVABLE SEAT CUSHION
ON VELCRO ATTACHMENTS

DECORATIVE NAIL
1" THICK FOAM RUBBER

SEATING

BACK

BACK

SEATING

PLAN OF DOUBLE BOOTH　　6

SECTION DETAIL　　10

REMOVABLE CUSHION

¾" THICK
FOAM
RUBBER

1" THICK
FOAM
RUBBER

FOR A
SINGLE BOOTH

SECTION THROUGH DOUBLE BOOTH　　7

SEAT DETAIL　　11

SHAPED
EDGE
ALL
AROUND

OAK

CONCRETE FLOOR LINE

SIDE ELEVATION OF DOUBLE BOOTH　　8

BILL SHEET OF ONE _____ Booth NO. _____		B. C. SMITH DESIGNERS BILL OF MATERIALS			SHEET _____ OF _____			Date Required _____ Deliver to _____		

Part. No.	Parts per Article	Part Name	Finish			Rough			Species	Molding	Net Rough Footage	Fasteners, Adhesives	Finish and Grade	Remarks
			L	W	T	L	W	T						
1	2	End panel	43	46	3/4	44	47	3/4	Oak	⌐			Transp. Premium	
2	1	Top panel	44	5	3/4	45	6	3/4	Oak	⌐				

Note: Finish dimensions always shown in inches. L = length in direction of wood grain; W = width across the wood grain; T = thickness measurements before sanding; rough measurements = required lumber sizes before cutting; grade = quality of wood (premium, custom, or economy); finish = transparent or opaque (see Chapter 9).

Figure 12.25 Bill of materials for wood furniture construction.

Article No.	Part Name	Frame Construction			Spring/Support			Filling Padding	Liner	Fabric Direction		Trim and Construction				
		Solid	Open	Slip	No Sag	Coil	Other			V	H	Welt	Tuft	Channel	Buttons	Other
Banquette 1	Seat			X				4 lb Neoprene	Heat B.	X		PVC				
Banquette 1	Back	X			X			4 lb Neoprene	Heat B.	X		PVC	X		Brass	

Note: Filling or padding listed by pounds per cubic foot; liner = heat barrier; fabric direction = vertical or horizontal.

Figure 12.26 Upholstery schedule of custom-built seating.

Specification of Upholstery Foam Types

1. *Conventional Foams:* These foams have density ratings ranging from 0.80 to 2.25 lbs per cubic foot. Conventional foams are available in a wide range of comfort ratios, from 1.8 to 2.2. Caution: These foams have no inherent resistance to ignition from smoldering to open flame.

2. *Rebonded Foams:* These are produced by combining scraps and pieces that are bonded together with the addition of urethane. This produces a very high density, which is required in carpet padding; however, the added density cost prohibits the extensive use of rebonded foams in upholstery.

3. *Filler or Loaded Foams:* These products are produced through the addition of inorganic fillers that increase the quality, produce higher support ratios, and decrease the possibility of the foam tearing or splitting. Density ranges

TABLE 12.11 RECOMMENDED UPHOLSTERY FOAM SPECIFICATION

Upholstery Use	Foam Type	Support Ratio
Transportation seats and backs. Medical and institutional seating.	High resilient combustion modified (CMHR)	2.4 to 3.5
Seats in places of assembly.	Filled foams or CMHR.	2.24 to 4.0
Booth backs. Chair backs. Density not critical.	Conventional fire rated	1.8
Seats and backs light to medium use.	Conventional fire rated	2 to 2.5

Note: Consult your manufacturer on the density and support ratio recommended for specific projects. Consult local code officials on necessary flammability requirements.

from 2.25 to 4.0 lbs per cubic foot. Caution: These foams do not resist smoldering and open flame.

4. *High Resilient Foams:* These foams have a very high support ratio. The minimum support usually found in this type of foam is 2.4. This provides for an extended service life.

Performance Criteria

1. *Density.* The quality that provides firmness or softness to foam. Density is measured as the mass per unit volume and expressed in pounds per cubic foot.

2. *Indentation Load Deflection (ILD) and International Indentation Forced Deflection (IFD):* These are the foam industry units of measure for firmness. A sample 4 in. (10 cm) thick and 15 in. (38 cm) square is used in the standard test. A metal plate 8 in. (20.3 cm) in diameter is pushed into the foam sample and a measurement is made the pounds required to compress the foam down to one inch (2.54 cm) or 25 percent of its height. Therefore, an ILD rating of 45 percent means that 45 pounds were required to compress the foam to 25 percent of its height.

3. *Comfort Factor or Support Ratio:* If the designer wishes to specify a very soft feel, the ILD reading should be relatively low, such as 25 percent. If a very firm support is required, specify a higher ILD reading, such as 75 percent. The support ratio is the ratio of the ILD reading to the standard 25 percent ILD. For example, if a designer specified 75 percent ILD, the support ratio would be 3.

25% ILD or less = Soft foam
35–49% ILD = Firm Foam
50% ILD or more = Very Firm Foam

MAINTENANCE OF FURNITURE MATERIALS

Consideration must be given to the maintenance of furniture materials which are specified for commercial interiors. Designers should obtain information from manufacturers about special maintenance requirements, and this information should be used in making specification decisions. For example, knowing that marble is very porous and easily etched by acids contained in wine or fruit juices would make marble a poor choice for a bar surface.

The most common materials used in furniture are metals, woods, plastics, stone, and glass. General maintenance for these materials is listed below.

Aluminum

Aluminum furniture and parts are produced in polished and satin finishes and are usually protected with a coat of clear lacquer. When the lacquer wears off due to prolonged abrasion, the exposed area usually oxidizes in the same color as the original material, and therefore recoating is not necessary.

Baked Enamel Paint on Metal

Many metal desks and files are finished by this process, which fuses the finish to the surface by firing. This produces a very strong and resistive surface, and only soap and water are required for cleaning.

Black Epoxy Finish on Metal

Epoxy enamel is a very tough plastic finish that is baked over a primer for good adhesion. This finish presents few mainte-

nance problems. The sheen of the surface can be restored by polishing and waxing with products designed for automobile finishes. Touch-ups should not be attempted with lacquers because they will not adhere to the finish. An enamel touch-up paint used in auto repair would be more suitable.

Brass with or without Lacquer

Brass is frequently lacquered to prevent oxidation and staining. Cleaning fluids or abrasives should not be applied to lacquered surfaces because they tend to remove the protective coating. A paste wax should be applied every six months to help mainttain the finish and prevent finger markings.

Bronze

This metal corrodes and rusts easily and needs a protective coating of either lemon oil or lacquer. The lemon oil coating must be renewed every six months. The lacquer is usually sprayed on and may be cleaned with a soft dry cloth. If the lacquer needs replacement, it should be professionally removed; the bronze item should then be repolished and relacquered. This is usually necessary every three to five years.

Chromium Plate

Furniture having this plating in either a brushed or a polished finish requires special care. It can be cleaned with automobile cleaners, polished, and waxed with a hard paste wax for protection from the atmosphere and moisture. In areas with high moisture the chromium should be cleaned and waxed frequently to prevent rust.

Pewter Finish on Metal

This process is a hand-antiqued finish which is protected with a clear lacquer. These surfaces should be cleaned with a soft dry cloth to prevent abrasion.

Plastic-Coated Steel

This finish is a cellulose acetate coating that may be cleaned with any soap, detergent, or cleaner. The use of steel wool or other abrasives is not recommended.

Stainless Steel

This is one of the most durable and handsome of all metals. It is rustproof and maintains a high polish without any protective coating. To clean, use automobile polish or ordinary household cleaners. Although small scratches may show on a new surface, they fuse with daily use and are not noticeable after a time.

Woods

Woods may be finished with lacquer, oil, wax, ebony, and numerous other methods to preserve the beauty of the wood.

Ebony Finish on Wood

A standard ebony finish consists of a series of black stain and black lacquer coats. This surface may be maintained in the same manner as lacquered wood except that a clear liquid oil-based polish is recommended. Do not use a paste wax because it will give a gray tone to the open pores. If scratch repairs become necessary, a black wax crayon should be used.

Lacquer Finish on Wood

For best service, lacquer finishes on wood should be protected with a hard wax applied every three to four months during the first year of use. Dirt marks that may show on light woods can be removed with a very fine steel wool (No. 000). More serious scratches can be repaired with a crayon stick, but any really serious repairs must be handled by a professional wood refinisher.

Wax Finish on Wood

This finishing technique usually involves application of wax over a penetrating sealer that gives the wood protection and acts as a base for the wax. Reapplication of an ordinary paste furniture wax will clean and renew the surface.

Natural Cane

Natural cane fiber, which has a hard, glossy outside surface in its natural state, provides its own protective coating. For added protection, cane is frequently lacquered. Cane surfaces can be cleaned in the same manner that lacquered wood is cleaned. Designers will note that cane frequently will show slack or loosening during humid weather and return to its original taut condition as the air dries. Clients should be made aware of this condition prior to installation.

Molded Plastic

For normal cleaning of molded plastic chairs use warm water and soap. After cleaning, the surface may be waxed with a furniture polish. Do not use a strong acid or alkali as a cleaner.

Plastic Laminate

This is frequently used on desk tops, cabinets, and countertops. It is a very durable material that is impervious to many chemicals. It may be cleaned with any household cleaner and waxed. Woodgrain laminates show small scratches less and are almost maintenance free.

Plexiglas

This material has become very popular for table surfaces in the past several years, but designers should be aware that it tends to show scratches. The surface should be dusted with a very soft cloth and washed with a mild soap and lukewarm water. Dry by blotting with a damp cloth or chamois. Do not use window cleaning solutions. The surface may be waxed with a good grade of automobile wax (not a cleaner-wax combination) and buffed with a clean cotton-flannel or jersey cloth. After polishing, wipe with a clean damp cloth to ground any electrostatic charges, which may attract dust particles. Scratches may be removed by sanding with 400-grit wet or dry sandpaper or a fine-grit buffing compound.

Marble

Marble should not be specified for surfaces that will receive excessive wear. The surface may, however, be protected with a coating of clear wax. Marble must be kept very clean with frequent washing. Use clear lukewarm water on a clean cloth and rewax after each washing. Marble may be commercially refinished if the surface becomes deeply etched. To maintain the high luster, apply wax immediately. When specifying marble for a large table, make certain the center area of the marble has substantial support to prevent breakage.

Slate

This surface produces a low luster with a deep black color after being oiled. No artificial colors or lacquers are used. The only maintenance required is the occasional application of mineral or household oil.

Travertine

Follow the instructions for marble. After the application of a sealer, a sealer or buff wax may be used to add luster.

Glass

Commercial spray cleaners may be used to clean the surface. Deep scratches can sometimes be concealed with the use of "plastic glass," which is a synthetic material that hardens clear as glass.

Figure 12.27 Specification guide of upholstered booths.

SECTION 12700

UPHOLSTERED BOOTHS

PART 1 GENERAL

1.01 RELATED WORK SPECIFIED ELSEWHERE:

1.02 NOT FURNISHED, BUT INSTALLED:

1.03 SUBMITTALS

A. Shop Drawings:
1. Submit shop drawings in accord with contract conditions for all wood and upholstered booths, identified with location, quality, grade, type of finish, wood species, fabric, upholstery details.
2. Submit drawing of the installed positions with sections in 3 inch (76.2 mm equal 403.8 mm) scale.
3. The manufacturer shall be responsible for details and dimensions not controlled by job conditions.
4. Show all required field measurements beyond control of the manufacturer.

B. Samples:
1. Submit _____ samples, _____ inches x _____ inches of each species of wood, upholstery fabric, foam, welt cording.
2. Identify each sample -- species, cut, grade, fiber content.

C. Quality Assurance:
1. Compliance with California Upholstery Standard _____.
2. Certificate verifying flame spread, smoke development and density of upholstery fabric and filling material.
3. Certificate verifying type of flame retardant used on fabric and filling material.

D. Maintenance:
Submit complete instructions for recommended repair and maintenance procedures.

1.04 DELIVERY, STORAGE, AND HANDLING

A. Deliver, store, and handle seating units in manner to prevent damage and deterioration.

B. Defer delivery to job until the installation and storage areas are completed and dry of all wet construction.

C. Maintain relative humidity in storage areas not to exceed _____ percent.

D. Protect all surfaces of seating booths subject to damage while in transit.

E. Provide temporary skids under all large or heavy seating booths.

1.05 GUARANTEES

PART 2 PRODUCTS

2.01 QUALITY GRADE
Materials and fabrication: _____ grade for _____ finish in accordance with _____.

2.02 MATERIALS

A. Exposed wood for transparent finish ___(species and cut)___.

B. Solid wood for semi-exposed members ___(species)___.

C. Solid wood for concealed members ___(fill in species or "any")___.

D. Fasteners _____. Adhesives _____.

E. Filling-padding material ___(weight and density - material)___.

F. Spring support ___(type and manufacturer)___.

G. Upholstery fabric ___(weight, fiber content, type of flame and soil retardant) (Manufacturer, style and color number)___.

H. Accessories ___(findings, such as buttons, welt cording or other trim)___.

2.03 FABRICATION

A. All edge grain of exposed and semi-exposed plywood shall be concealed. All upholstery fabric shall be installed in the same direction with all patterns on seat and back areas matching (unless otherwise noted).

B. Welt cording shall be self-covered. Seams of the welt covering shall only appear on the sides or rear of the seating units.

C. The removable seat cushions shall fit securely in frame.

D. All buttons shall be securely attached and anchored with #_____ cord.

PART 3 EXECUTION

3.01 CONDITIONS OF SURFACES

A. Examine all grounds, stripping and blocking to secure seating booths.

B. Do not install until all defects are corrected.

3.02 INSTALLATION

A. Install booths plumb and level without distortion.

B. All booths shall be installed in a rigid manner, shim as necessary.

3.03 ADJUST AND CLEAN

A. All upholstered surfaces shall be free of spots or damage.

B. All exposed wooden areas shall be free from scratches, nicks or other damage.

C. All booths shall be protected from damage until final acceptance.

END OF SECTION

GLOSSARY*

Accelerated life cycle test: See *Cycle testing.*

Acoustical panel: A panel having an acoustical function and rating.

Acceptance level: The performance level required to pass a test.

Acessories: Items not normally furnished with a basic file cabinet, such as trays, suspended file frames, etc.

Adjustable glides: Support devices for leveling and/or stabilizing products. (Alternately referred to as "glides," "levelers," or "height adjusters.")

Ambient lighting fixture: An illuminating device oriented to direct its output toward the ceiling to provide general room illumination. The light source can be incandescent, fluorescent, or high-intensity discharge bulbs.

Anchored: Fastened to a part of the building structure or other stable support in such a way as to secure the cabinet against tipping or displacement.

Antirebound: The feature that ensures that a drawer will stay closed and will not roll out of the compartment opening or recoil from it when closed with normal force.

Antitip device: A mechanism that ensures that a preponderance of the static gross weight of the lateral file and its contents will be confined within the cabinet floor area when a drawer is extended, thus assuring that the lateral file will not accidentally tip over. (Alternately referred to as "antitilt devices," "interlocking devices," and "safety devices.")

Back/back position: The back of each seating position.

Back panel: An integral surface extending across the back of an open kneespace of a desk, table, or workstation.

Base raceway: A device attached to the bottom of a panel to protect and route power and/or communication wires, cables, and their connectors and termination receptacles.

Base trim: A protective and/or aesthetic component along the bottom edge of a panel.

Beginning panel: The first panel in a connected run of panels at an arbitrarily selected end.

Bin (Binder, File, Storage): A panel-supported unit for filing or storage. Can vary in depth and/or width; can be with or without a door.

Binder bin: See *Storage bin.*

Bottom rail: The horizontal structural member of the bottom edge of a panel.

Bracket manager: See *Hanger bracket.*

Butt: That portion of a hinge that is attached to the nonmovable segment of an opening.

*Based on the BIFMA Glossary of Terms.

Cabinet: A case with drawers or shelves to hold or display its contents.

Cantilevered: A method in which a projecting surface or structure is mounted at one end and extends over a space.

Cap size: See *Legal size.*

Card filing: Provision for the storage of cards of various sizes, generally accomplished by the use of "half-height drawers" or of trays in full-height file drawers.

Case: The cabinet shell, including all structural parts but excluding the drawers and shelves.

Caster: See *Hard tread caster* and *Soft tread caster.*

Casting: A part shaped by introducing molten metal (ferrous or nonferrous alloy) into a mold.

Caution label: A label that is affixed to a product and that informs a prospective user about requirements for proper utilization of the product and about any potential hazards.

Chalkboard: A product intended for use as a rigid erasable writing surface selected to accept solid or liquid writing media.

Chalk tray: A product intended to hold the writing instruments for chalkboards.

Clear depth: The dimension from the front to the rear of the unobstructed drawer space, as measured to the front of the follower block, if present, or to the rear of the drawer.

Clear height: The dimension from the support surface for the contents of the drawer or roll-out shelf to the lowest stationary point above the support surface when the drawer or shelf is extended.

Clear width: The inside width of the drawer, roll-out shelf, or fixed shelf.

Compressor: A device, generally consisting of a formed or flat plate, that is used to support the filed material and that usually locks into position. (Alternately referred to as a "follower block.")

Configuration limits: The extremes to which a system is capable of giving safe performance.

Content load: The total weight of the material supported by a drawer, roll-out shelf, or fixed shelf. It does not include the weight of the drawer itself or of suspensions.

Conventional filing: The method of housing filing material that uses folders and index guides that are supported by the bottom of the drawer and oriented from front to rear. This method is in contrast to "suspended filing" and "cross filing."

Corner post: A vertical, integral component used at the intersection, convergence, or change in direction of a panel run.

Counter top: Generally a worksurface located on top of a panel.

Counterweight: Material added to a product to improve stability.

Credenza: Usually a low, wide cabinet containing various combinations of drawers and storage compartments.

Cross-filing: The storage of filing material from side to side in a drawer as opposed to a front-to-rear orientation. This term may be applied to either bottom-supported or suspended filing. Means of support, to accommodate either type, are generally considered as accessory items.

Curved acoustical panel: A panel with its radius about its central vertical axis, having an acoustical function and rating.

Curved end panel: A panel with its radius about its central vertical axis, used to terminate a panel run.

Curved glazed panel: A panel with its radius about its central vertical axis and with a transparent or translucent material as its major surface.

Curved structural panel: A panel with its radius about its central vertical axis and with a rigid or nonacoustical surface.

Curved counter/transaction top: Curved section of worksurface that follows the contour of a curved panel, usually an extension of a countertop.

Curved worksurface: A worksurface that attaches to and follows the contour of a curved panel.

Cycle testing: Repeated dynamic functioning of a product through its designed operation with specified loading for a specified time/cycle period at an accelerated rate.

Deep file drawer: File drawer for storage of larger than standard (letter/legal) forms.

Deep flipper-door unit: A flipper-door unit with height and/or depth dimension(s) for storage of larger than standard (letter/legal) forms.

Deep shelf: A shelf for larger than standard forms.

Deflection: The movement or deviation of a surface or plane from its intended position or location as a result of stress.

Deflection is reasonably stabilized: The deflection is changing at a rate of no more than 5 percent per minute.

Depth: The horizontal dimension from front to rear. This may be applied to either a case or to drawers, so must be specifically identified and described.

Desk: An article of furniture with a flat top for writing and drawer(s) for article storage.

Desk—double pedestal: A worksurface with pedestals attached or mounted, or extending to the floor at both ends of the unit. This arrangement creates a knee space between the pedestals.

Desk—single pedestal: A worksurface with only one pedestal attached or mounted or extending to the floor on either the right or the left side of the unit.

Desk extension: A unit which is generally attached to a single pedestal desk, on the right or left side, to create a worksurface that extends at a 90° (1.57 R) angle to the desk workstation. (Also known as an "extended desk unit.")

Desk product: Freestanding furniture articles tested for acceptability and compliance. Generally, single- and double-pedestal desks, extended desk units, credenzas, and 4-legged or pedestal-type tables.

Display shelf: A panel-supported shelf with a sloping surface and a retaining flange or edge.

Dividers: Plates provided in the drawers, roll-out shelves, or fixed shelves to separate and support the filing contents. (Alternately referred to as "file supports" or "partitions.")

Door
  Receding door: A panel that serves to close off and secure its "compartment." It may recede either into the space above the roll-out shelf or fixed shelf or into the space beneath it.
  Sliding door: A panel which travels horizontally; used primarily in stationary shelving.
  Swing-out door: A door which opens and closes by pivoting on the vertical edge.

Drawer: A typical drawer includes the body, back, and a fixed, full drawer front which closes up the opening. Drawers are extendible.
  Box drawer: A drawer which has an outer head, generally 4–8 in. (101.6–203.2 mm) in height.
  Center drawer: A drawer centrally located under the top of the desk or desk-related product, generally 4 in. (101.6 mm) or less in height.
  File drawer: A drawer which has an outer head, generally 9–17 in. (228.6–431.8 mm) in height.
  Storage drawer: See *Box drawer.*
  Tray drawer: A drawer which has an outer head, generally 4 in. (101.6 mm) or less in height.

Drawer cycle: One complete opening and closing of a drawer.

Drawer slide: See *Suspension.*

Drawer-type lateral bin: See *Lateral file.*

Drop filing: Storage and retrieval of filing material by vertical motion as compared to one horizontal motion required for fixed shelving.

Electrical systems component: Any item used to contain, protect, divide, or distribute electrical power with or without separate provision(s) for communication-transmitting cables and connectors within a panel system.

Edge file: A panel-mounted group of shelves that accept filing material laterally with tabulation devices facing forward. Can have receding door(s) or enclosing surfaces.

Ending panel: The last panel in a connected run at an arbitrarily selected end.

End rail: A vertical structural panel member attached along the edge of a panel. Also see *Side rail; Stile.*

End support panel: (1). A panel mounted at an angle to a panel run to give support to the run. (2) A specific-purpose panel attached perpendicular to a panel run to add stability to the run or loaded section of a run.

Equalizer: A device or arrangement that serves to assure that the extendible element (door, roll-out shelf, or drawer) will move in and out of the case without binding regardless of where on the width of the extendible element the force is applied. This is particularly important in wide, shallow lateral files. (Alternately referred to as "stabilizer" and "motion control device.")

Executive return: A worksurface mounted adjacent to and at right angle to a main surface and at the same height. See *Secretarial return.*

Extended desk unit: See *Desk extension.*

Extra-height drawer: Drawer that is higher than letter and legal size, such as one required for data-processing printouts, etc.

Extra-height opening: An opening that is higher than standard (letter and legal size) as required for data-processing printouts, etc.

File bin: A panel-mounted unit with a movable lid for filing or storage. Can vary in depth and/or width to accommodate letter or legal sizes.

File support: See *Wobble block.*

Filler panel: A panel intended to complete an enclosure that can be adjusted or modified or that is especially fabricated to conform to a space or surface different than that which can be accommodated by a panel available in the normal offering.

Fixed shelf: A shelf that is secured to the cabinet and does not extend. It may be used with or without a door. (Alternately referred to as "open shelf.")

Flexible hinge: A nonrigid integral component used to attach adjacent panels together, when used singly, allowing them to pivot on a vertical axis formed by the joint of identical halves of a hinge.

Flipper door unit: A panel-mounted cabinet with a receding door. See *Storage bin.*

Flush front: The type of cabinet design in which the drawer fronts overlap the case uprights and cross rails, as opposed to the design in which the drawer heads inset in the cabinet openings and expose the cabinet members. (Alternately referred to as "overlapping drawer head" or "contemporary" design.)

Follower block: The adjustable device in the drawer that is used to support the file material. It generally consists of a formed metal plate with some kind of latching means. (Alternately referred to as a "compressor.")

Foot: A support member attached near the bottom edge of a panel to assist or provide stability. See *Panel support leg.*

Force: A vector quantity, expressed in pounds or newtons, that tends to produce an acceleration of a body in the direction of its application. (This term is used primarily in specifications and documentation associated with testing.)

Freestanding panel: A panel that is intended to stand without the support of other panels. Usually used to define area of function, deny visual access, or, if specifically constructed, control or provide acoustical privacy. Also see *Screen panel.*

Freestanding seating: Movable, self-supporting seating, not attached to other structes or furniture.

Full depth: The dimension that denotes the distance from the front to the rear of a cabinet or drawer. For a cabinet it is the maximum overall dimension. For a drawer, it is the distance from the inside head to the opposite surface of the back plate.

Full filing depth of compartment: The dimension from the front edge of the filing area in a roll-out shelf, drawer, or fixed shelf, to its rear vertical surface or front of follower block, if present.

Fully extended: The roll-out shelf or drawer pulled out to the limit of its stops.

Functional load/force: A load/force stress equivalent to that which can be expected in normal use of the component.

Ganging: The arrangement of two or more products secured together in a bank—side to side, opposed, or a combination of both—the purpose being to promote stability.

Glazed panel: A panel with a transparent or translucent material as its major surface.

Glazing panel frame: A panel frame suitable for glazing material.

Glide: A component that rests on the floor with a threaded shank that permits height adjustment.

Glide housing: A component that accepts the threaded shank of a glide.

Guide rod: A rod running from front to back on a drawer bottom to secure index cards.

Half-height drawer: A drawer that is equal in height to one-half an opening.

Half-height end support: The component(s) necessary to join panels of dissimilar heights.

Half-height roll-out shelf: Extendible shelf of a design and dimension to enable two of them to fit into a standard height opening. Used for card filing, etc., and secured by a standard door.

Hanger bracket: A device fastened to any hang-on component that attaches that component to a panel.

Hang-on capability: A panel designed to support the addition of panel-mounted components.

Hang-on component: A product intended to be supported wholly by a panel system.

Hard panel: A panel whose major surface is neither resilient nor glazed.

Hard tread caster: Caster wheels having a tread durometer of higher than 40 on the Shore D Scale.

Height adjuster: See *Adjustable glides.*

High-pressure laminate: Multiple layers of resin-impregnated paper fused under heat and pressure to result in a rigid covering media having long-wearing and dent- and stain-resistant properties. Available in assorted colors and imprinted patterns. It is usually adhered to substrates forming worksurfaces and/or panels.

Hinge: A rigid device attached to a panel and having an external vertical axis allowing the panel to pivot out of alignment of a panel run. See *Flexible hinge.*

Horizontal file: See *Lateral file.*

Impact: An impinging or striking of one body against another. A forceful contact or collision.

Instruction document: Printed reference material supplied by a manufacturer for use by the designer and/or user and his or her installation representative that lists recommendations, limitations, and restrictions on the assembly, configuration, loading, and use of the products. This reference material may be contained in a section of a bound volume containing other information, a specific brochure, or loose-leaf sheets included with the product or in a binder section so entitled.

Interlock: A device that couples two or more drawers together to prevent simultaneous opening. See *Antitip device.*

Kiln-dried lumber: Lumber which has been conditioned (dried) to a specific moisture-level content.

Knocked down: A product shipped in pieces/segments to be assembled at the point of use.

Knockouts: Provisions in the cabinet for accommodating screws, locks, etc., if and when they are added by the customer or dealer. This is accomplished by semi-punching the holes and leaving the slug that is normally ejected in the hole in such a way that it can be "knocked out" when required. In this way, unsightly open holes are avoided.

Label holder: A device for holding marking identifications, usually installed in a pull or on a door or drawer front.

Laminate: The product resulting from bonding two or more layers of materials with adhesive.

Lateral file: A roll-out filing compartment whose major dimension extends horizontally. The depth can vary to accept letter or legal filing matter. The width is generally greater than the depth. (Alternately referred to as "horizontal file.") This device is generally thought of as a freestanding cabinet with two to five compartments.

Lattice or latticework: Intersecting openwork in any type of material.

Leaf: That portion of a hinge attached to the movable segment of an opening.

Leg: The support member of a desk, credenza, or table.

Legal size: The dimensional description for a cabinet that will accommodate 8-½ × 14" (215.9 mm × 355.6 mm) documents. (Sometimes referred to as "cap size.")

Length: The measure of something along its greatest dimension. This may be applied to either the desk product or to the drawers, so must be specifically identified and described.

Letter size: The dimensional description for a cabinet that is limited to 8-½ × 11" (215.9 mm × 279.4 mm) documents.

Leveler: Metal or plastic disc, usually attached to a threaded shank, fastened to a base for stability, straightness, or to prevent leanings. See *Glide.*

Leveling: The process that ensures that products, when fully installed, adopt and maintain a true vertical attitude and do not tilt in any direction. It also implies that the product is stable in that attitude. Leveling may be accomplished by adjustable glides, shimming, or bridging.

Lip drawer: Drawer construction where the drawer front overlaps the case rails.

Load: The weight to which a structure is subjected; a weight or force applied to a product or a portion thereof; force acting on a surface, usually caused by the action of gravity.

Lock: A key- or combination-operated mechanism used to secure a drawer or door.
   Plunger lock: A lock that automatically secures itself when pushed into engagement and requires key action only for unlocking.
   Cam lock: A rotary lock that requires key action for both locking and unlocking.

Locking device: A device that includes all of the parts in the stationary and extendible elements of a lateral file, vertical file, or desk product that are required to secure it, including the keys, all movable adjunct parts, and all fixed parts such as retainers and strikes.

Lock kit: The combination of parts and instructions that is required to change a product from a "no lock" to a "lock" version by the factory, by a dealer, or by the customer.

Loss of serviceability: A failure or a loss of adjustment which results in the normal function being impaired.

Lounge seating: Unassigned, freestanding seating which is intended for use in transient areas, such as waiting, reception, or lounge areas. It is not generally adjustable for personal use.

Modesty panel: See *Back panel.*

Modular system: Collection of related units, some of which are dimensional multiples of others, into various horizontal and/or vertical arrangements, to serve various purposes including storage, display and shelving.

Modulus: Stress, either tension or compression, divided by the elongation per unit of length, within the elastic limit; the modulus of most materials is constant. In wood, it varies greatly with different species and moisture content, even in pieces sawed from the same logs.

Molding: Ornamental or shaped strips, either sunk into or projecting from a surface, used mostly for decoration.

Mounting height: The normal elevation from the floor for task peformance.

Multiple seating: Units which have seating positions provided for more than one person.

Nonwoven fabric: Webs or sheets of textile fibers which have been bonded together by various means at a sufficient number of points to give cohesion to the structure.

Normal use condition: A term used in testing adjustable shelves. Usually the midpoint of a position adjustment range, such as the height.

Open file bin: A filing compartment that is open at the top or front.

Opening: One of the clear spaces in a case, normally bordered by the front uprights and the horizontal members, that will accommodate a drawer, fixed shelf, or roll-out shelf. (Alternately referred to as a "compartment.")

Open shelf: See *Fixed shelf.*

Options: Alternative items or conditions that may be included in, or applied to, the basic unit. *Note:* This term must be used with care because in one instance it may involve choosing from among production items (for example, standard colors or compressor blocks instead of wobble blocks), while in another situation it may involve choosing from among nonproduction items (for example, special colors). Differentiation is sometimes attempted by referring to the first condition as "options" and to the second as "extra options."

Panel: A flat or curved surface that controls and/or defines space; also provides privacy and a means for hanging components. See *Systems.*

Panel connector: The device or collection of devices used to mechanically interconnect two or more panels.

Panel components hanger: An attachment at the sides of each panel for variable height adjustment of panel-mounted components.

Panel-hung light: Light cantilevered from panel surface.

Panel-mounted component: A product intended to be supported wholly by a panel system.

Panel-mounted light: Light mounted to the top of a panel.

Panel run: Two or more panels connected in a straight line.

Panel support leg: A device attached near the base of a panel to provide or assist in maintaining vertical stability. See *Foot.*

Panel systems products: Freestanding non-load-bearing panels, panel-supported systems, modular systems, and various hang-on components used in conjunction with panel systems. See *Systems.*

Particle board: A substrate material manufactured by bonding wood particles with resins under heat and pressure.

Pedestal: A self-contained unit with drawers or doors which may be used to assemble a desk product; a stack-up of interconnected drawers attached to the underside of a work-surface and extending toward, but not necessarily touching, the floor.

Pedestal base: A base which supports a seating unit by a single central structural members such as a spindle.

Pencil drawer: Usually a shallow drawer, three inches or less in depth, with compartments for writing instruments and additional open spaces for small objects.

Permanent set: The attitude of a member when stressed either beyond its elastic limit, or below that limit, but retained in that position for a sufficient length of time for the member to remain in a permanent deformation.

Pigeon holes: Small open compartments, usually in desks and cabinets, to hold letters and small articles.

Pin: That portion of a hinge that allows the hinge leaf to pivot away from the hinge butt.

Pivoting back: A back that rotates on a horizontal axis above the height of the seat.

Plastic: A large group of manmade materials consisting in whole or in part of a carbon compound with oxygen, hydrogen, nitrogen, and other organic and inorganic elements, but excluding rubber. While solid in the finished state, at one time in its manufacture a plastic is liquid and is capable of being formed into various shapes, usually through application of heat or pressure, or both. Some generic divisions are: ABS, acrylic, polypropylene, nylon, polycarbonate, vinyl, styrene, and polyurethane. See *Thermoplastic material* and *Thermoset material.*

Post: Any one of the vertical structural or decorative members.

Posting shelf: An extendible shelf, located between the standard openings in a cabinet, that is used for supporting filing material during the process of storing or retrieval.

Printout height: Compartment/drawer height of the dimension necessary to accommodate data-processing printouts. See *Extra height drawers.*

Proof load: The level of loading in excess of hard use or the response to this load.

Proof load/force: A stress load/force that can be anticipated in the use of the component beyond functional design. Used in proving or testing the maximum abusive loads/forces applied to a component.

Proportionate loading: The amount of load used for service tests in a roll-out shelf or drawer that is proportionate to an established norm. Example: At 2.0 pounds per linear inch (0.91 kilograms per 25 mm) for letter-size filing, the test load in a case 30 in. (762 mm) wide would be approximately 54 pounds (24 kilograms) and, in a case 36 in. (914 mm) wide, approximately 66 pounds (30 kilograms).

Pull: A handle attached to, or depression made into, a panel to open or move the panel; that part of a drawer front that provides the means to physically open a drawer. It may be either a projecting hardware item (alternately referred to as a "handle") or a recessed part (alternately referred to as a "flush" pull). The recessed type of pull may employ a separate hardware item or it may be an integral part of the drawer front.

Rack resistance: Generally refers to the ability of a cabinet to resist stress, such as that developed from an uneven floor, that causes the cabinet to resemble a parallelogram and drawers and doors to become misaligned. The ability of a desk product to resist stresses that tend to make it become misaligned.

Receding door: A compartment closure that pivots to allow access to the compartment, then moves to a storage parallel to the horizontal surface (top or bottom). See *Doors.*

Return panel: See *Stabilizer panel.*

Roll-out shelf: The typical base filing-material support element sometimes referred to as "extendible shelf." ("Roll-out shelf" seems to be the proper term because the shelf does not have a drawer front and is extendible as contrasted to "fixed" or "stationary" shelving. The differentiation between "roll-out shelf," "fixed shelf," and "drawer" thereby becomes not only definite, but also clearly descriptive.)

Roll top: A compartment closure made up of narrow slats adhered to a fabric backing (tambour).

Screen panel: Less than ceiling high, non-load carrying space divider. See *Freestanding panel.*

Seat/seating position: The portion(s) of a unit intended for sitting, approximately 20 inches (508 mm) in width.

Secretarial return: A work surface mounted adjacent to and at right angle to a main surface but at a height to accommodate typing tasks.

Shelf: A flat, usually rectangular structure of a rigid material fixed at right angles to a panel and used to hold or store objects.

Shelf end: The adjacent device that, when fastened to the end of the shelf, allows attachment to, and adjustment on, the panel.

Shelf light: A lighting device depending on some portion of a shelf assembly for attachment or support. See *Task light.*

Shore D scale: A scale for testing caster hardness.

Side rail: A vertical, structural panel member attached along the edge of a panel and slotted to accept hanger brackets.

Signage: A plaque that graphically and/or alphabetically identifies occupant or function of a workstation or area.

Single seating: A unit with one seating position.

Sloped worksurface: An adjustable or fixed inclined surface usually used for drafting or drawing.

Soft tread caster: Caster wheels having a tread durometer of 40 or less on the Shore D Scale.

Stability: The ability of a product to resist tipping under normal loading and use conditions.

Stabilizer panel: A panel mounted perpendicular to the normal panel run. See *End support panel* and *Return panel.*

Stabilizing: A term that describes the means used to provide steady support for a product to avoid rocking. This term, and action, is closely related to "leveling."

Starter panel: A panel attached with mechanical device(s) to a permanent surface of a building from which additional panels can be attached in a regular manner. Not to be confused with a "beginning panel" or a "filler panel."

Stile: An interior vertical member of a frame or panel.

Stops
   In stops: Stops that limit rearward travel. (Alternately referred to as "rear stops.")
   Out stops: Stops that limit extended travel. (Alternately referred to as "front stops.")

Storage bin: A panel-mounted storage unit with or without a door.

Stress: The field quantity generated in a body by an applied force.

Structural breakage/damage: The failure of any structural component that carries load or restricts motion.

Support panel: Panel mounted at an angle to a panel run. See *Return panel* and *Stabilizer panel.*

Suspended filing: The method of housing filing material that utilizes slidable folders that are suspended at their upper corners from continuous rails perpendicular to the folders. This method of filing is in contrast to conventional filing. (Alternately referred to as "hang filing," "drop filing," and "Pendaflex filing" as a generic term.)

Suspension: The system that is used to facilitate the movement of the roll-out shelf or drawer in and out of the case. (Alternately referred to as "drawer slides.")

Systems
   A. *Panel/Screens—Non-load-bearing:* All freestanding screens that provide visual and/or acoustical separations, and are intended to be used to divide space but not to physically support furniture items.
   B. *Panel-supported systems:* Individually connected panels and work surface, filing, storage and shelving components, and accessories receiving their main support from the panels and that, when combined, form complete workstations.

C. Modular systems furniture: Modular furniture made up of independent worksurface and storage units with panels used as end panels or space dividers. Includes all modular furniture components that collectively are required to complete a workstation.

Tackboard: A visual display device with a substrate designed to accept and hold thumbtacks. The visible surface may have a decorative covering such as fabric.

Task light: A lighting device suspended over a worksurface to provide illumination for the immediate area; usually a fluorescent fixture. See *Shelf light.*

Test load: A particular load (weight) placed in or on a component specified by a test procedure and not included in the dead weight of the component.

Test platform: The worksurface, floor, or table to which the unit to be tested is placed during testing.

Thermoplastic material: That family of plastic compounds that become soft and formable when exposed to heat and retain their shape when cooled, such as: ABS, polycarbonate, acrylic, nylon, polyethylene, and polystyrene.

Thermoset material: That family of plastic compounds that become rigid after manufacturing and cannot be reformed by application of heat, such as alkyds, epoxy, melamines, phenolic, silicone, and ureas.

Thumb latch: The device that causes the drawer to interlock with the cabinet structure upon closing.

T-mount: The equipment and devices that allow for the attachment of a panel or run perpendicular to another panel in a run at a point along the face of the second panel, independent of the normal edge or end-of-panel attachment.

Toe plate: A flat plate attached to and extending out from the front bottom of a lateral file. The purpose of the toe plate is to improve the stability of the file.

Tolerance: The total amount by which a specific dimension is permitted to vary.

Uniform load: An evenly distributed weight; the force applied equally along the longitudinal axis of a hang-on component surface and expressed in pounds/foot^2 or kilograms/meter^2. The weight of a typical letter-size or legal-size filing material with which a drawer to be tested is loaded uniformly. The weight shall be 2 pounds per linear inch (0.91 kilograms per 25 mm) for letter-size drawers and 3 pounds per linear inch (1.35 kilograms per 25 mm) for legal-size drawers. The material shall fill the available space in the drawer.

Vertical file: A cabinet containing drawers used for storage and retrieval of documents. The majority of vertical files are of one of two widths, designed to accommodate letter- or legal-size documents, and two to five drawers high. Variations from these basic forms include an assortment of sizes of files to accommodate material from small cards to large drawings. For the purpose of ANSI/BIFMA standards, the definition refers mainly to basic letter- and legal-size files.

Vinyl: The popularized contraction of a thermoplastic material polyvinyl chloride (PVC), fabricated to a range of thickness from 1 to 10 mils, of a solid color, either embossed with a specific texture or pattern, or imprinted (usually with assorted wood grains), and laminated to a substrate that is then used as a structural panel surface or a hang-on component member surface.

Wall mount: A vertical component intended to be attached to an existing building wall to permit attachment of a panel or panel run.

Wardrobe: See *Valet.*

Wire manager: A cable-handling device used to house external wiring.

Wobble block: A device generally consisting of a formed flat plate that is located in a fixed position in a drawer or shelf and that pivots at its bottom point to allow greater access to stored material. (Alternately referred to as "file supports.")

Workstation: A grouping of furniture items and components that when assembled or placed in a location, describes where a person performs his work.

Worksurface: A horizontal surface projecting from the surface on a panel and used to perform tasks and/or as storage space; like a desk top. Does not include sloped surface.

LIFE CYCLE COSTING: VALUE MANAGEMENT

Specification decisions should not be finalized without giving consideration to the concept of value management. The preceding chapters have reviewed methods of quality control through systems classification, performance evaluation, and testing methods. This chapter will examine value management as a method of determining the cost effectiveness of components, specifications, and performance criteria. Life cycle costing (LCC) is used to implement the principles of value management and provide formulas for obtaining the optimum total cost of components.

Since the mid-1960s, federal agencies and some areas of industry have effectively used life cycle costing methods. The publication of the *PBS Building Systems Program and Performance Specification for Office Buildings* by the General Services Administration in 1971 established life cycle costing as a standard of evaluation for interior systems in all federal buildings. In the past two decades, the GSA Design Action Center has shown concern for the total working environment of federal employees by having interior designers serve on federal design teams. Perhaps for many designers this was their first introduction to the concepts of value management and life cycle costing.

The idea of trying to predict cost effectiveness is certainly neither new nor revolutionary. At one time or another everyone makes major decisions based on what is believed to be sound value judgments. Buying an automobile provides an excellent example of how life cycle costing can be effectively employed. When a new car is purchased, the owner is assured that the quality was controlled through performance testing. The warranty states that major expensive repairs will not be the owner's responsibility, at least not for the first several months. However, if soon after the warranty expires, the automobile begins to require expensive and frequent repairs, the owner may decide to replace the automobile for economic reasons. To determine the total ownership cost during the life cycle of the automobile, the following equation might be developed:

$$LCC = (AP_I + L + IN) + OC + PM + CM + R$$

where   LCC = Life cycle cost
     AP_I = Acquisition price plus interest
     L = License
     IN = Insurance
     OC = Regular operating cost, such as oil and gas
     PM = Preventive maintenance, such as tune-ups
     CM = Corrective maintenance: repairs, including parts and labor
     R = Replacement cost which includes depreciation factors; residual value (trade-in)

Once these life cycle costs are established, the owner can determine the return on investment factors (ROI), and this information can also provide a basis for making a decision on the purchase of another automobile.

ADVANTAGES OF USING LIFE CYCLE COSTING

Life cycle costing used as a method of quality control provides an accurate record of initial costs and the logistics of future costs. Obviously this approach can be a very valuable tool for the designer when specifying commercial and institutional installations. Instead of specifying the least expensive office system to meet a proposed budget, a designer would be wise to point out the advantages of life cycle costing to the owner. A client may not be aware of savings that can be realized in operational and maintenance areas. The General Services Administration provides this example of the LCC considerations that would determine federal specification decisions:

	Supplier A (Millions of $)	Supplier B (Millions of $)
BP	$48.00	$45.00
OMP	3.90	3.90
E	29.70	34.00
LRC	.07	.07
SAC	1.30	2.00
AP	**$83.00**	**$85.00**

where   AP = Award price
       BP = Bid, or initial, price
   OMP = Operating and maintenance price
       E = Energy cost
   LRC = Luminaire relamping cost
   SAC = Space adjustment cost

The following formula was used to compute the figures above:

$$AP = BP + OMP + E + LRC + SAC[1]$$

This example illustrates that even though supplier B had the lowest initial cost, the energy and space-adjustment cost factors were greater than those projected by supplier A. Therefore supplier A would be awarded the contract.

PEOPLE COST

Another important aspect that can affect long-range cost is the factor known as "user or people cost." GSA's Public Building Service reports that value management should include user costs over an extended period of time. Research has shown that people cost can account for as much as 92 percent of the total life cost of a facility; operating and maintenance cost for the same period might amount to only 6 percent, and the initial cost spread over the same period, only 2 percent.

The people cost concept is based on the knowledge that working environments do affect human performance. Therefore a design solution that results in improved production and efficient work flow will provide the owner/client with a return on investment. The following equation for projecting people cost was presented by J. T. Malarky at a symposium on "The Performance Concept in Building":

600 people × $5 per hour × 2,100 hours per year × 10 years
= $63,000,000

Based on this hypothetical calculation, the total cost of ownership for an office facility for a 10-year period[2] would include the initial cost, operating cost, and people cost:

Initial cost	$ 4.5 million
Operating cost	4.2 million
People cost	63.0 million
Total cost:	$71.7 million

All design firms are familiar with the process of budget proposal. In some cases, a firm may decide to present an additional comparative cost analysis between the choice of one system as opposed to another, i.e., open office landscaping versus closed office planning. This may prove very helpful to the client in making initial cost decisions, but unless the analysis includes all the life cycle factors, it represents only a partial view of the true ownership cost. Life cycle costing should be employed whenever possible because it adds another dimension to the design effectiveness, in the sense that it allows the designer another means of answering the user's immediate and long-range needs.

ELEMENTS OF LIFE CYCLE COSTING

To understand the actual application of life cycle costing it is important to review the factors that are considered in the process of evaluating components on the basis of total life cost. Figure 13.1 illustrates the major LCC elements and their interrelationships. This portion of the chapter will present more detailed information on each of the LCC elements and provide equations for calculating total costs. These equations were developed by the U.S. Federal Supply Service (FSS) and the General Services Administration for use in federal life cycle costing procurement. The equations are general in scope and designers may add or delete items depending on the circumstances of each particular project. All equations may not apply to every interior component, and designers should be aware that some interior subsystems would not benefit from LCC evaluation. The criteria used in the selection of items for LCC consideration are discussed later in this chapter.

Acquisition or Initial Cost

This involves the immediate known cost elements, such as the number of components needed, discounts for quantity or prompt payment, and shipping expenses. Other factors that could add to the initial cost are the expense of assembly if the components arrive unassembled, storage space if the items arrive prior to the completion of the project, and transportation of the components from the storage facility to the project site. Installation cost, including labor and materials, is added to the initial cost factor. The installation of equipment, such as open office systems, may require a brief training period to acquaint personnel with the optimum use of the system. This training cost would be absorbed into the initial cost factor. In the case of large institutional installations, the owner/client may incur additional administrative expense because of inventory management, i.e., the addition of new items to the inventory due to the new installation. There may be special costs unique to a specific item, such as unusual storage or handling. Inventory

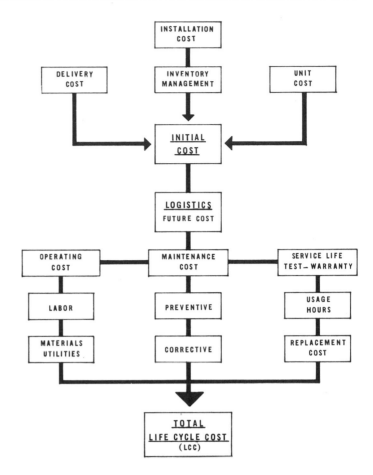

Figure 13.1 Life cycle costing.

management is particularly important in installations such as hotels, motels, schools, hospitals, and nursing homes. A hotel scheduling many meetings and receptions on the same day must maintain an accurate inventory record of tables as well as stacking and folding chairs. Each commercial and institutional project will present different situations and result in different means of arriving at the acquisition cost. The following equations summarize initial cost and inventory management factors.

Initial Cost

$$IC = (P_I \times N_I) + A + I + S - D$$

where   IC = Initial cost
      P_I = Unit price per item
      N_I = Number of items
      A = Assembly
      I = Installation
      S = Shipping
      D = Discount offered

Inventory Management

$$I_{im} = IMCF \times NI$$

where I_{im} = Initial inventory management cost
    IMCF = Initial management cost factor. This cost factor covers the general and administrative cost directly attributable to the addition of new items.
     NI = Number of new items

$$R_{im} = (RMCF \times NI) \times \frac{PIUP}{12}$$

where R_{im} = Recurring item management cost
    RMCF = Recurring management cost factor. This covers the general administrative cost on a yearly basis.
    PIUP = Projected inventory usage period. This is the number of months an item will have to be maintained in inventory.

The Logistics of Future Costs

This represents a most important aspect of the life cycle cost evaluation process. This method of predicting future costs is based on recurring costs, such as operations, maintenance, and inventory management. These records, often provided by industry, are based on previous systems in use. However, records should be carefully analyzed to determine if all the conditions and maintenance factors are similar to those in the proposed use. The performance and expected service life of a component are evaluated and the final cost involved in the removal and replacement of nonrepairable items is also calculated. Although accuracy in logistic cost prediction is preferred, a degree of reasonable accuracy is sufficient. Once the logistics costs are tabulated, a comparison can be made to current dollar values and cost increases.

Service Life

The service life of a component has to do with the reliability, prediction, and verification of how long a particular component will remain in useful service. There are four stages in the service life of a component. The first two stages, development and production, are controlled by the manufacturer who predetermines the reliability factors. After a system is installed, the operational stage becomes the real test of reliability. The

owner aids in continuing the reliability factors by providing appropriate maintenance. The fourth and last stage is reached when the system is no longer repairable and must be discarded.

Prior to specification, a designer must determine if the reliability predicted by the manufacturer can be verified. Reliability verification involves the following procedure:

1. *Definition of System Failure.* If a system has never been used before, the manufacturer will be asked to provide a definition of failure that is applicable to the system. Contract statements regarding failures must be clearly stated in terms of the specific system; i.e., the failure of an office chair may be defined in terms of mechanical parts that malfunction and are beyond repair, such as a swivel joint. The designer or owner may prefer to establish the definition of failure based on previous experience with a particular system.

2. *Prediction of Failure.* The service life rationale is based on the premise that failures are predictable. Components or systems under evaluation are usually classified as "repairable" and "nonrepairable." In the area of interior specifications, office systems and specially constructed institutional furniture would be considered repairable. Many other items specified by designers would be considered nonrepairable or nonreusable. Interior components such as drapery, carpet, wallcoverings, and some types of upholstered seating may be repairable, but in most cases it would be considered uneconomical to do so. Some commercial facilities such as hotels and motels have a third classification that could perhaps be termed "consumables," i.e., items with an extremely high failure rate such as bedding components, dishes, silverware, and glassware. Aside from a high failure rate, these items are also subject to a high theft rate.

When a specification is written for a repairable item, a designer may wish to use an equation known as a "figure of merit" to predict or evaluate the Mean (average) *Time Between* Failures (MTBF). The figure of merit for nonrepairable items is known as the Mean *Time To* Failure (MTTF). The important difference between the two equations is the fact that MTBF, on the one hand, measures the extended service life beyond a first or second failure and also projects the expected usage period. The MTTF equation, on the other hand, measures the total service life of a nonreusable component only to the first failure that terminates its useful life.[3]

   a. *Service Life* (Reliability Prediction)
     (1) Figure of Merit: Nonrepairable components

$$UP = \frac{UL}{MTTF}$$

where   UP = Unit price or unit life cycle cost during the entire useful life of the nonrepairable component.
      UL = Unit logistics cost or all life cycle cost, which would include all cost (operational, maintenance, initial cost, installation, item management, replacement), not on a yearly basis, but for the projected life span.

MTTF = Mean time to failure expressed in units of service life. Example: light bulbs, expressed in hours or lumens of expected life.

(2) Figure of Merit: Repairable components

$$EF = \frac{EU}{MTBF}$$

where
EF = Expected number of failures in projected usage period
EU = Expected usage (hours) of each component
MTBF = Mean time between failures

(3) Expected Usage:

$$EU = PIUP \times H$$

where
EU = Expected usage (hours) of each component
PIUP = Projected inventory usage period (months)
H = Hours operation/months per installed component

3. *Reliability Acceptance Testing.* Essentially the same criteria used in performance testing are applied in reliability acceptance testing. The component is usually tested in a situation simulating the actual use condition. If the component has not previously been in general use, laboratory testing is accepted for evaluation purposes. A specification based on life cycle costing should state which test methods will be acceptable.

4. *Warranties.* It is usually advisable to obtain some form of warranty protection if possible, but it is not absolutely essential. Warranties are not always applicable to all components. There are three major types available:

a. Repair warranties apply to the operational aspects of a component. This type of warranty is usually held by the manufacturer and repair is dependent on the number of hours, months, or years the component has been in use. This warranty may or may not include temporary component replacement while repairs are in progress.

b. Replacement warranties promise to replace defective components at no cost or offer a large discount on the replacement unit.

c. Service function warranties may only apply to one component within the total system. For example, if the paint finish on a piece of office equipment begins to chip or crack, the manufacturer will be responsible for replacing the finish. If this cannot be accomplished, the entire item may be replaced.

Warranties are usually made available through the manufacturer or the supplier/wholesaler. Even though a supplier may be more geographically convenient for repair warranties, the manufacturer may represent a more reliable source for repairs. Every warranty will stipulate certain installation, operational, and maintenance requirements which, if neglected, would invalidate the warranty agreement. The designer may recommend that the client obtain a "service contract," which, for an additional fee, will provide warranty protection, but it should be remembered that this expense should be included as an element in life cycle costing.

To evaluate the feasibility of warranty costs, the following factors should be determined:

1. Determine the price of a component with and without a warranty.

2. Evaluate the relative cost of buying a service contract in comparison with having the repairs done by people on staff (in house).

3. Determine shipping costs involved in returning the component to the manufacturer for repair. If it appears that the cost will be prohibitive, investigate the possibility of a supplier warranty with the stipulation that the supplier post a bond to assure his reliability.

4. Verify that all details of the warranty coverage are clearly defined in the contract.

Life cycle costing logistics include the final cost factors involved in the removal and replacement (R&R) of a system when it has reached the end of its service life. Consideration should be given to any possible residual value that can be obtained from salvageable component parts.

Recurring Operational Costs

It is important to identify what operational cost will be associated with a particular subsystem. Operational costs usually include the number of people required to operate the component, the average hourly wage, the expected service life of the component, and the amount and cost of utilities used in the operation of the system. For example, the operational cost of an ambient task office system would include the electric power consumed and the labor cost to relamp the luminaires. There is also the recurring cost of training new personnel in the use and maintenance of the office system. If a particular system, such as a computer, requires a special form of environmental control, this added expense should be included in the operational cost. The operation of a piece of equipment such as a vacuum cleaner would be calculated as a part of maintenance cost. The following equations explain the process used in calculating operational costs.

Operating Costs

$$MC = W \times N \times OH \times L$$

where
MC = Manpower cost, including any manpower resource involved in the operation or monitoring of the system
W = Average hourly cost of an operator
N = Number of operators
OH = Average number of operating hours per month
L = Operating Life or Projected Inventory Usage Period (PIUP)

$$PEM = E \times C \times OH \times L$$

where
PEM = Power, energy, or material consumed per hour, including the cost of any material consumed in the operation
E = Units of energy, power, or material consumed per hour (watts per hour)
C = Cost of one unit of energy
OH = Average number of operating hours per month
L = Operating Life or Projected Inventory Usage Period (PIUP)

Recurring Maintenance Costs

The calculation of maintenance costs takes into consideration the expected usage of the component (hours per month), expected failures during this usage period, and the required preventive and corrective maintenance that will be necessary to keep the component in working condition.

Preventive maintenance is performed on a regular basis throughout the useful life of a component. Corrective maintenance is performed when a system or component begins to fall below its expected level of performance and needs repair. Carpeting, for example, should receive regular preventive maintenance such as vacuuming and spot cleaning until the level of appearance demands corrective cleaning procedures. The desired maintenance or performance level is based on the owner's requirements and is included in the calculation of maintenance costs. A component may be maintained at a 100 percent perfect level (first), an 85 to 80 percent excellent level (second), or an 80 to 70 percent good level (third). All indications of maintenance level failure which are used in maintenance equation *c* are assumed to be subject to detection, isolation, removal, and replacement ("ith" maintenance level may be used to indicate any desired performance level).

Downtime is a term often associated with maintenance problems. It refers to the period of time involved in making extensive repairs or the time required for complete replacement of a component. The loss of income due to product failure or the added expense of equipment rental is considered as an element of life cycle costing over and above the normal cost of maintenance.

(a) Corrective Maintenance Equation. This equation applies to repairable and nonrepairable components.

$$LC = (LS_R)(LR_1) + \sum_{i=1}^{n} (LS_i)(LR_i)(P_i/100)$$

where
LC = Labor cost per failure
LS_R = Labor standard (hours) to detect, remove, and replace
LS_i = Labor standard (hours) to repair at ith maintenance level
LR_1 = Labor rate at the first maintenance level
LR_i = Labor rate at the ith maintenance level
n = Number of maintenance levels used in components repair
P_i = Percentage of removals repaired at ith maintenance level
i = ith maintenance

Labor standard information should be obtained from records of previous repair work.

(b) Repair Material Cost per Failure

$$MC = \sum_{i=1}^{n} ([MCS_i][P_i/100])$$

where
MC = Material cost per failure
MCS_i = Material Cost at _____ maintenance level
P_i = Percentage of removals to be repaired at _____ maintenance level (owner fills in desired maintenance level)

(c) Transportation Cost per Failure

$$TC = 2W (SPRL + SPMR + [ARS][PW/W])(1 - P_1/100)$$

where
TC = Transportation cost per failure
W = Weight of item
SPLR = Standard packing labor rate
SPMR = Standard packing material rate
ASR = Average shipping rate
P_1 = Percentage of repair actions at _____ maintenance level (owner fills in desired maintenance level)
PW = Packaged weight of item

(d) Preventive Maintenance Equation

$$PMC = (PIUP)(PMH)(PMR)$$

where
PMC = Preventive maintenance cost per item
PIUP = Projected inventory usage period (months)
PMH = Preventive maintenance hours (monthly)
PMR = Preventive maintenance hour rate

(e) Preventive Maintenance Manhours per Month (PMR)

$$PMH = \sum_{i=1}^{m} (F_i)(R_i)$$

where
F_i = Manhours to accomplish preventive maintenance level ith
m = Number of different preventive maintenance actions performed
R_i = Number of times preventive maintenance action performed per month (at ith level)

(f) Total Maintenance Cost per Item

$$TMC = (EF - 1)(LC + MC + TC) + PMC$$

where
TMC = Total maintenance cost
EF = Expected failure rate
LC = Labor cost per failure
MC = Material cost per failure
TC = Transportation cost (item return to factory for repair)
PMC = Preventive maintenance cost

The expression $(EF - 1)$, the expected failure rate, is decreased by one on the assumption that equipment would be junked after the last failure rather than repaired.

APPLICATION OF LIFE CYCLE COSTING

Before deciding if life cycle costing methods will be economically feasible for a particular project, designers are advised to consider the following evaluation checklist.

1. *Initial Cost.* This should be calculated with a degree of accuracy before other logistics are considered. Determine all the elements that will be included in the initial costs:
   _____ Purchase price
   _____ Unit price
   _____ Discount offered
   _____ Shipping/delivery costs
   _____ Unusual handling
   _____ Assembly costs
   _____ Storage costs
   _____ Installation costs

_____ Personnel training
_____ Inventory management
_____ Other

After this list is completed, an individualized equation can be developed for initial cost factors.

2. *Capital Investment.* Having completed the initial cost factors, it is possible to determine which components represent a large capital investment. A listing of these items would indicate which would possibly benefit from an evaluation of return on investment (ROI).

3. *Percentage of Total Cost.* Another means of verifying that a component may benefit from life cycle costing is to consider what percentage of the total project cost it represents:

Component	Percentage of Total Cost

In large institutional projects this evaluation method can be very useful. Hotel installations provide a good example of this concept. The total cost of furnishing one guest room may average $2,000. Of that total cost, furniture may represent 70 percent, carpet 13 percent, drapery 10 percent, and miscellaneous items such as linens, 7 percent. Although it would appear that drapery is only a small percentage of the total cost of the guest room, it should be remembered that this does not reflect the *total project cost.* Total drapery cost is as follows:

$203/room × 300 rooms = $60,900 (TPC)

In all multiple installation situations (including hospitals and nursing homes), the total project costs should not be overlooked.

4. *Logistic Information.* Having narrowed the component list, the designer can now proceed to determine the availability of data that will allow further logistic evaluations. The logistic summary in Table 13.1 indicates where information might be obtained in order to complete LCC evaluations.

5. *Administrative Cost of LCC Applications.* Based on the availability of logistic data, the designer and client must determine if the time and cost involved balance the benefits to be obtained from LCC. Evaluate the following factors:
   a. Importance of LCC factor in obtaining project contract
   b. Research time involved
   c. Administrative staff necessary to conduct and tabulate research
   d. Administrative staff salary rate

6. *Repairable and Nonrepairable Components.* Based on measurable service life (MTBF or MTTF) and reliability testing factors, the designer may further classify the components into two groups: repairable and nonrepairable.
   a. Repairable items: Key LCC factors to consider:
      (1) Projected inventory usage period
      (2) Maintenance factor
      (3) Total life cycle cost

TABLE 13.1 LCC ELEMENT SUMMARY CHECKLIST: SOURCES OF LOGISTIC INFORMATION

	A	B	C	D
1. Purchase price	X			
2. Delivery cost	X			
3. Testing cost	X		X	
4. Installation cost		X		
5. Inventory management cost			X	
6. Personnel training costs	X		X	X
7. Service life and/or MTBF	X		X	X
8. Operating labor	X		X	X
9. Operating materials and utilities	X	X	X	X
10. Preventive maintenance cost	X	X	X	X
11. Corrective maintenance cost	X	X	X	X
12. Desired maintenance level			X	
13. Dismantling cost	X		X	
14. Residual value			X	X
15. Other (list)				

A — Obtain from manufacturer.
B — Contractor should provide.
C — Obtain from client.
D — Documented through designer's past experience.

Note: This table offers only suggestions regarding possible sources of logistic information. Sources may vary in each situation.

    (4) Requirement that manufacturer support proposed values

    (5) Requirements for reliability/maintainability testing

  b. Nonrepairable items: Key LCC factors to consider:

    (1) Statement of minimum acceptable service life

    (2) Formula for computing service life

    (3) Definition of failure

    (4) Requirement that manufacturer support proposed service life

    (5) Determine method of validating claimed service life

7. *Component Selection Matrix.* In order to determine which logistic elements are associated with particular components, a matrix may be developed for each project. For example, inventory management for continued replacement of nonrepairable items in hotel installations may represent a major logistic factor. Furniture and other repairable components may offer larger long-range savings through evaluation of operational and preventive maintenance costs. Figure 13.2 illustrates a component selection matrix based on items most frequently specified for interior use.

COMPONENTS \ LOGISTIC ELEMENTS	Repairable	Non - Reuseable	Item Management	Service Life	Testing Costs	Warranty Costs	Operating Labor Cost	Operating Materials	Preventive Maintenance	Corrective Maintenance	Dismantling Costs	Residual Value	Replacement Cost	Downtime Costs
Office Systems	●		●	●	●	●	●			●	●	●	●	●
Seating – non Uph.	●		●	●	●	●	●			●			●	●
Seating – Uph.	●	●		●	●	●	●	●	●	●			●	●
Desks	●		●	●	●	●				●		●	●	●
Drapery		●	●	●			●	●	●		●		●	●
Carpet		●		●	●	●	●	●	●	●	●	●		●	●
Wall Coverings		●		●	●	●			●		●		●	●
Bedding		●	●	●	●	●	●			●		●		●	●
Luminaires		●	●	●	●	●	●	●	●	●	●	●		●	●
Tables	●		●	●	●				●	●			●	●

Figure 13.2 Component selection matrix.

8. *Equation Application.* After the logistic elements have been matched to the components, the designer may proceed to apply the appropriate equations and complete the life cycle costing of particular components. The following is an example of the process that may be used to calculate maintenance costs for repairable components:

  a. Compute service life equation (Figure of Merit).

$$EF = EU \times MTBF$$

  b. Compute expected usage (in hours).

$$EU = PIUP \times H$$

  c. Compute corrective maintenance equation *a.*

  d. Determine material cost per failure from maintenance equation *b.*

  e. Compute transportation cost per failure if item must be returned to factory for repair, based on maintenance equation *c.*

  f. Determine preventive maintenance, equation *d.*

  g. Compute the preventive maintenance manhours per month, with maintenance equation *e.*

  h. Determine the total maintenance cost per unit by computing maintenance equation *f.*

9. *General Considerations.* Experts on value management and life cycle costing suggest the following general guidelines:

Include: a. Nonrepairable items should be included if they account for an annual expenditure of $100,000.

    b. Repairable components which account for $300,000 annual expense.

    c. Standard commercial components (not custom made).

Exclude: a. Items and components which are one of a kind. No comparative data would be available.

    b. Items for which noncompetitive bidding has been predetermined. Some large firms have prearranged purchasing agreements with manufacturers (hospitals, universities, and hotels).

10. *LCC Summary Cost Equation.* This equation contains three major cost categories:

$$LCC = A + I + R$$

  where A = Acquisition costs: the sum of the unit costs for the component, materials, data, and services

    I = Initial logistics costs: one-time logistic costs which are identifiable and would be incurred

    R = Recurring costs: operation, maintenance, and management of the component, including preventive and corrective maintenance.

SPECIFICATIONS FOR BARRIER-FREE PUBLIC INTERIORS

The material in this chapter is based on standards developed by federal agencies in order to comply with Public Law 90-480 and the American National Standard A 117.1-1980 titled "Specifications for Making Buildings and Facilities Accessible to, and Usable by, the Physically Handicapped."[1]

Due to an increased public awareness about accessibility problems, many buildings, though not government owned or financed, are being planned with barrier-free environments for physically disabled people. During the past decade this concern has been reflected in the numerous state and city codes dealing with barrier-free regulations that have been adopted.

A person confined to a wheelchair is the usual stereotyped image of the "physically disabled" person. The General Services Administration defines a physical disabled person as "any individual who despite a physical disability, can be expected, without assistance from another person, to visit and utilize a building."[2] Another federal agency further expands the definition to include the following categories:

1. Nonambulatory disabilities: those where people are confined to wheelchairs.

2. Semiambulatory disabilities: those which allow a person to walk with difficulty. This includes people who walk with crutches, braces, or walkers.

3. Disabilities of incoordination or palsy: those due to brain or nerve damage.

4. Hearing disabilities: those which impair a person's ability to detect warning signals.

5. Sight disabilities: those which prevent people from perceiving signals or dangerous situations.

6. Temporary disabilities: those due to injury, illness, or pregnancy.

7. General disabilities: those due to aging which reduce a person's mobility, coordination, and perception.[3]

Reviewing this list, designers will agree that "barrier-free" does not merely imply ramps and adequate door widths, but expands to include a whole range of considerations. Aside from the obvious architectural barriers which have limited the free movement of physically disabled people, society is now becoming aware of the *psychological barriers* that physical space imposes upon those who are handicapped. When a handicapped person must enter by a service entrance or ask assistance in opening a door, he or she is made to feel humiliated and helpless. Millions of dollars are spent each year rehabilitating and training physically disabled people to function and contribute to society, but our buildings have made it impossible for them to move about, contribute, and enjoy the same privileges that able-bodied people take for granted. When reduced to the status of second-class citizens, those who are handicapped feel discriminated against.

The design of barrier-free public spaces involves concern for two major categories of users: visitors and employees. The general purpose of the building indicates the type of people who will be using the facility. Theaters, federal buildings (such as post offices), banks, libraries, and restaurants, will require clearly marked exit routes, rest rooms, and other accessibility factors for visitors not familiar with the building. Office buildings will require more detailed planning to accommodate both visitors and employees who are handicapped.

The following guidelines for the specification of barrier-free public interiors are arranged as a checklist for use during the planning phase. Federal requirements are starred (*) and the remaining criteria are recommended. Designers should remember that requirements are minimum; therefore every effort should be made to incorporate the additional recommended guidelines.

GENERAL REQUIREMENTS FOR INTERIOR ACCESSIBILITY

1. Walls and partitions
   * *a. Provide fixed or nonfixed partitions that are sturdy and will withstand a 60-lb (28-kg) force applied from any direction.
   * *b. Mount decorations, hardware, and equipment with the capability of withstanding but not necessarily supporting a 60-lb force applied from any direction.
   * *c. Provide markings at heights of 36 in. (91.4 cm) and 60 in. (152.4 cm) on large expanses of glass.
   * d. Avoid abrasive wall surfaces within 60 in. (152.4 cm) of the floor in heavy traffic areas.
   * e. Avoid hazardous glare in corridors and stairways by specifying matted surfaces, low-glare lighting fixtures, and window coverings.

2. Windows
   * a. Avoid strong contrast between window and wall surface. Provide drapery or window coverings that will eliminate glare in work areas and points of directional decisions, such as lobbies, corridors, and intersection points.
   * b. Provide window coverings that will prevent drafts and reduce radiant heat loss in areas where people will spend extended lengths of time.
   * c. Provide long wand sticks for the manual operation of drapery and blinds.

3. Doors
   * *a. Doors must have a clear opening of at least 32 in. (81.3 cm) when open and must be operable by a single effort. The weight required to open a door should be 5 lbs but should not exceed 8 lbs (2.3 to 3.7 kgs). (Note: two-leaf doors are not recommended unless they open with a single effort or one of the leaves provides a clear opening of 32 in.)
   * *b. The floor on both sides of the door must be level for at least 60 in. (152.4 cm) and the floor must extend at least 12 in. (30.5 cm) beyond each side of the door.

RAMPED THRESHOLD

SLIDING DOOR TRACK

Figure 14.1 Thresholds. Unless otherwise credited, illustrations in this chapter were adapted from Design Criteria: New Public Building Accessibility, *PBS (PCD). DG5.*

Figure 14.2 Vestibule door swing. Source: Department of Health and Human Services, Office of Facilities Engineering.

TRANSITION STRIP

Figure 14.3 Flooring transition strip. Source: Department of Health and Human Services, Office of Facilities Engineering.

*c. Thresholds shall be flush with the floor if possible. When a raised threshold is necessary, it must be beveled or ramped gradually on both sides of the door. (See Figure 14.1.)

*d. Vestibules: the inner and outer doors of a vestibule must be separated by at least 42 in. (106.7 cm) in addition to the door swing. Both doors must swing in the same direction. (See Figure 14.2.)

*e. Handles shall be mounted at a maximum height of 42 in. Panic bars shall be placed 32 in. above the floor. Kickplates at least 16 in. (40.6 cm) high are recommended for all doors. Door closers with a 4- to 6-second time delay are recommended.

f. Vision panels are desirable to all swinging doors. Safety glass should be placed a maximum of 36 in. (91.4 cm) above the floor.

g. Sliding doors should have top-hung self-lubricating tracks and bottom guides. Doors should be easy to operate. Nylon wheels or roller bearings on metal tracks are recommended.

h. Door openings should not be placed directly opposite a stairway.

*i. Provide protection for doors opening into corridors.

*j. Provide outswing doors to storage rooms, closets, and accessible restroom stalls.

4. Hardware

*a. Provide hardware, both latching and nonlatching, operable with a single hand that does not require wrist action or fine finger manipulation.

*b. Position operating hardware between 32 in. (81.3 cm) and 42 in. (106.7 cm) above the floor. A 36-in. (91.4-cm) center line is recommended.

c. Provide a clearance of 1 ¾ to ¼ in. (44.4 to 57.4 mm) between operating hardware and door jambs. (A wider clearance is not recommended.)

d. Provide texture on door hardware for identification.

e. Use lever handles or panic hardware on all side-hung latched doors.

5. Floorcovering

*a. Firmly attach all coverings to base floor.

b. Flush mount floorcovering where it joins another flooring material. (See Figure 14.3.)

*c. Floors must be on a common level throughout a given story or be connected by ramps. Variations no greater than plus or minus ¼ to ⅛ in. (6.4 to 3.2 mm).

*d. Floors must have nonslip surfaces. Friction coefficient: no less than .5 when wet or dry, measured by static means. (See page 88 for the discussion of resilient flooring in Chapter 8.)

e. Floors should withstand a load of 125 psi and deflection shall not exceed ½ in. (12.7 mm).

*f. Carpeting must be heavy-duty contract quality, high-density, tight-weave, low-looped pile. Padding when used should be dense and firm. Broadloom should be tightly stretched and carpet tiles should be securely in place.

*g. Floors of primary circulation paths shall have a hard surface, such as vinyl-asbestos tile, to permit ease of movement for wheelchairs. Travel distance over carpet to reach such a path should not exceed 50 ft (15.2 m).

h. Flooring materials should not produce sharp reflections or glossy surfaces.

i. Select single colors or muted patterns for floorcoverings. Highly contrasting patterns create visual confusion for people with visual impairments.

6. Furniture
   a. Furniture legs or supports should not present a tripping hazard.
   b. Furniture selected for public use should contrast (in value) with the background so it is distinguishable by people with sight disabilities.
   c. Seating depth may vary:
      (1) Lobby: minimum 12 in. (30.5 cm) for short-term seating.
      (2) Assembly seating: minimum 13 to 16 in. (33 to 40.6 cm).
      (3) Short-term seating: maximum 16 in. (40.6 cm) for use with backrest.
   d. Seat widths should be no less than 16 in. (40.6 cm).
   e. Fixed seating should be no less than 15 in. (38.1 cm) from the floor (17 in. [43.2 cm] preferred).
   f. Recommended seating angles vary according to use:
      (1) Backrest to seat angle: 95° to 120°.
      (2) Backrest to vertical angle: 10° to 30° measured from a vertical extended from base of seat. If the back has more than a 30° angle from the vertical line, a headrest should be provided. (See Figure 14.4.)
   g. Upper back support should be provided on lounge chairs and tilted lounge chairs that have more than a 30° angle from the vertical.
   h. Armrest widths should be no less than 2 in. (5.1 cm); 2 ½ to 3 ½ in. (6.4 to 8.9 cm) are preferred widths.
   i. The length of an armrest varies with use:
      (1) Casual seating: full armrest of 11 to 13 in. (27.9 to 33 cm).
      (2) Assembly seating and desk or table seating: short armrests about 8 ½ in. (21.6 cm) long.
   j. The space between the armrests may range between 19 and 22 in. (48.3 and 55.9 cm). Assembly seating should not be wider than 20 ½ in. (52.1 cm).
   k. Height of armrests are usually 8 ½ in. (21.6 cm) above the seat. (See Figure 14.5.)
   l. Padding for upholstered furniture should be firm to prevent bottoming out of the seat area.
   m. Upholstery should be neither rough nor slippery. Material should be porous and of a medium weave. Welt cording should not be placed along the front edge of seat cushions because it may hamper blood circulation.

Communication and Signage for Accessibility

The General Services Administration offers some very effective recommendations for communication or cuing systems to provide directional, emergency, and safety information. Cuing systems make use of changes or contrast in color, texture, and lighting to reinforce communication. An effective communication is based on four criteria: (1) unambiguity: distinct elevator lobbies for various floors; (2) consistency: room numbers and directional signs placed in the same location on each floor; (3) reinforcement of information through coded textural and color cuing: warning danger signals; (4) predictability factors, such as having all room numbers on one side of the corridor.[4]

The following suggestions include areas of concern such as general circulation; emergency safety information; the use of lighting, tactile, and sound cues; and signage design.

1. Circulation
   a. Provide for directional information to accessible areas, such as transportation points; drop-off zones; car parking for people who are handicapped.

Figure 14.4 Built-in seating.

Figure 14.5 Assembly seating armrests.

b. Provide information along accessible routes to the entry; to vertical access (stairs, ramps, elevators). For visitors, provide directions at vertical access to various floors and levels.

c. Signage to accessible interior circulation; to public facilities and conveniences (restrooms, assembly areas, lobbies, offices, and dining facilities).

d. Mark accessibility of conveniences; e.g., indicate the provision of a chairbound water closet on the *exterior* rest room door.

e. Number all rooms including conference rooms and dining rooms.

f. Provide floor numbers at vertical access areas (stairs, elevators, or ramps).

g. Provide warnings if there is a level change in corridors.

2. Emergency safety information

a. Provide both visual and audible alarms when required by local codes. (Flashing light next to exit sign.)

b. Emergency exit signage must be distinct from regular circulation information. Routes to accessible holding areas (for fire emergency) should be clearly marked.

c. Mark areas not recommended for chairbound people during an emergency.

d. Plaques bearing raised letters or numbers shall be used to identify rooms or offices. They shall be placed on the corridor wall on the latch side of the doorway approximately 60 in. (152.4 cm) above the floor. Letters should be ⅝ in. (15.9 mm) in height and should be raised at least ⅟₃₂ in. (.8 mm) above the surface.

e. Doors leading to dangerous areas not normally used by the public, such as mechanical rooms, loading platforms, and fire escapes, should be identified by handles with knurled finish.

3. Signage design

a. Uniform format, color, and wording.

b. Use of short familiar phrases.

c. Simple and clear graphic designs.

d. Use black or dark color background with white or light letters; size will also help the sign be discerned from the surrounding background.

4. Wall graphics

a. When used as directional signage, the graphic should reinforce cues from intersections and level changes.

b. Provide value contrast at junction of walls and flooring. A difference of 20 percent in reflectance value is recommended.

5. Lighting

Use lighting to emphasize important areas or hazards.

6. Tactile and textural cues

a. Handrails should provide a change in texture to indicate approaching vertical level changes, intersections, or doorways.

b. Flooring textures may be used to indicate an approaching level change or doorway.

7. Sound cues

Changes in the floorcovering from soft to hard can be used to warn the blind of an approaching level change.

Horizontal Circulation through Interior Space

Corridors, ramps, and other horizontal passages that accommodate physically disabled people require additional space considerations.

*1. Primary corridors allow for the passage of two wheelchairs side by side. These corridors should measure 60 in. (152.4 cm) in width.

*2. Partial or secondary corridors measure 54 in. to 60 in. (137.2 to 152.4 cm). In a very cramped situation a secondary passage may measure 42 to 44 in. (106.7 to 111.8 cm).

3. A full one-way passage should measure 36 in. (91.4 cm).

*4. Primary corridors are limited to a maximum distance of 100 ft (30.5 m) between rest stops.

*5. Rest stops are alcoves along corridors that are designed to allow parking for wheelchairs and seating. Parking for one wheelchair should measure 48 in. (121.9 cm) in length and 32 in. (81.3 cm) wide. Additional space must also be provided for approach, turning, and backing up. (See Figure 14.6.)

*6. Partial or secondary corridors are limited to a maximum of 50 ft (15.2 m) to a 360° turnaround area (60″ × 60″ [152.4 × 152.4 cm]).

7. One-way passages are limited to a maximum distance of 50 ft (15.2 m) to a 180° wheel-pivot turnaround. Distance to a 180° axle-pivot turn is 25 ft (7.6 m). A one-way passage that requires backing out is limited to 8 ft (243.8 cm).

8. A turn of 360° requires a diameter circle at footrest height. (See Figure 14.7.)

9. 180° turns require 75 in. (190.5 cm) by 64 ½ in. (163.9 cm). (See Figure 14.8.)

10. A 90° turn requires an area 55″ × 66″ × 36″ (139.7 × 167.6 × 91.4 cm). (See Figure 14.9.)

11. Overall lighting should equal 10 footcandles. Major intersections should provide 15 to 20 footcandles.

Vertical Access in Interior Spaces

Means of accessible vertical egress—stairs, elevators—are critical in the event of a fire. The following requirements should be observed:

*1. Provide two types of vertical access at all change levels.

*2. Provide ramped access for level changes from ¼ in. (6.4 mm) to the height of one step.

*3. Cue vertical changes greater than ½ in. (12.7 mm). It is recommended that level changes be avoided in heavy traffic areas. Also avoid level changes of less than three steps.

4. Stairs

*a. Width should be 44 in. (111.8 cm).

b. Risers should not exceed 7 in. (17.8 cm). All risers should be closed on stairs used for primary egress.

c. Tread areas of stairs should not be less than 10 in. (25.4 cm).

Figure 14.6 Corridors with rest stops.

Figure 14.7 Turning requirements: 360° turn.

Figure 14.8 Turning requirements: 180° three-point turn.

Figure 14.9 Turning requirements: 90° turn.

d. Maximum uninterrupted vertical rise should be 9 ft (2.7 m).

e. Approaches and landings should be level and have cuing (color, light, or texture) to warn of approach.

5. Handrails

   *a. Handrails 32 in. (81.3 cm) high measured vertically from the stair noising are required on both sides of the stair. Rails should be round or oval in section and measure between ½ and 2 in. (12.7 to 50.8 mm) in diameter and have a nonslip surface.

   *b. Handrails shall be continuous at landings and extend 12 in. (30.5 cm) beyond the edge of the beginning and final step.

   *c. Treads shall be finished in a nonslip material. Heavily patterned floor surfaces are not recommended on landings.

   *d. Stairs must be adequately lighted at all times. Minimum level of 5 footcandles is recommended.

6. Ramps

   A ramp with a gradient of 5 to 8 percent shall have the following:

   *a. The same width as the walk or corridor it serves—48 in. (121.9 cm) minimum.

   *b. Shall be kept to a maximum gradient of 8.33 percent, or 1-ft (30.5-cm) rise in 12 ft (3.6 m) of run.

   *c. The ramp shall be built of firm, fixed, nonslip materials. The ramp shall also not have grating or other openings.

   *d. Ramp shall be provided with a level platform at the top which shall measure 60" × 60" (152.4 × 152.4 cm) and a straight level clearance of at least 72 in. (182 cm) at the bottom of the ramp.

   *e. A level landing shall be provided at 30-ft (9-m) intervals and at all changes of direction and intersections with other ramps or doors. These landings shall be 60 in. (152.4 cm) in length.

   *f. Ramps shall be provided with handrails on one side (and both sides if possible). The rails must be smooth and extend out from the walls at least 1½ in. (3.8 cm). Rails shall extend beyond the top and bottom of the ramp at least 12 in. (30.5 cm).

   *g. Ramps shall be provided with curbs 2 in. (5.1 cm) high or guard rails or walls at least 32 in. (81.3 cm) high where there is a drop in grade at the edge of the ramp.

   *h. Provide lighting for ramps at all times (5 footcandles minimum recommended).

7. Elevators

   *a. Elevators must be available at the level of the major building entrance which is used by physically disabled people. The elevators must give access to all levels of the building normally used by the public.

   b. Call buttons should be centered at 42 in. (106.7 cm) above the floor. A visible and audible signal indicating direction of travel is required.

   *c. Cab size must allow for movement of a wheelchair. A 180° turning of the wheel is recommended.

   *d. Door opening width must be a minimum of 32 in. (81.3 cm).

   *e. Doors shall be fitted with a door reopening device that is capable of sensing an object in the path of the doors and that does not contact for activation.

   *f. Operation must be automatic and self-leveling within ½ in. (12.7 mm) of floor levels under normal use conditions.

   g. At least one wall of the car should be equipped with a handrail 32 in. (81.3 cm) above the floor.

   *h. All essential controls which are designed for unilateral vertical reach from a wheelchair shall be mounted at a maximum height of 60 in. (152.4 cm). Controls shall be usable by blind people and shall feature raised numerals and symbols.

   *i. An emergency telephone without dial shall be mounted at a maximum height of 48 in. (121.9 cm) above the floor.

8. Entrance lobbies

   a. Provide waiting areas with seating and space for wheelchair parking within the main lobby or adjacent to the main entry. A vestibule area is acceptable, but paths of egress should not be blocked. (See Figure 14.10.)

   b. The space should be provided for parking at least two wheelchairs. This space requires a minimum length of 48 in. (121.9 cm) and a minimum width of 32 in. (81.3 cm). Additional space should be provided for parking, backing, and approaching. Provide at least 24 in. (61 cm) between seating and passageway if seating is facing into the circulation area.

   c. A full primary two-way passage must be provided through the lobby area (60 in. [152.4 cm]). This passage should connect the reception desk, elevators, and public conveniences (drinking fountains, telephones, restrooms) that are located near the lobby.

   d. *Floorcovering* in the immediate entrance area should not be a slick surface that may result in slipping and falling. Avoid the use of terrazzo, polished stone, or hand-crafted ceramic tiles with deeply grouted seams which could make wheelchair movement difficult.

   e. Provide a flush mount between hard-surfaced entry flooring and adjoining carpet. (See Figure 14.10.)

   f. *Furniture* in lobby areas must be designed for use by physically disabled people. Stability of construction in seating furniture is important.

   *g. Information or reception desks (counters) shall not exceed 36 in. (91.4 cm) in height. Exception: Some counters may be built higher if a section (at least 30 in. [76.2 cm] wide) is 36 in. high. If a counter is provided for writing, it should not exceed 34 in. (86.4 cm) in height. (See Figure 14.11.)

   h. Reception counters should be visible from the entrance doors.

   i. *Minimum lighting* levels for lobbies is 10 footcandles. Writing areas should provide 30 footcandles.

9. Exhibit and display areas

   a. Exhibits in lobbies shall not create barriers or obstruct normal passage paths.

   b. Display equipment (structures) should be able to withstand 250 lb (150 kg) of force applied from any direction.

Toilet Facilities

Each floor of a building shall have at least one toilet facility available to physically disabled people of each sex. The following requirements must be provided:

*1. The floor of the toilet room shall be at the same level as the corridor floor.

*2. The layout of entrance foyers, doors, and privacy screens shall allow sufficient clearance for wheelchair passage.

*3. The floor space must contain a clearance of at least 60″ × 60″ (152.4 × 152.4 cm) for wheelchair turning.

4. At least one toilet stall shall be the side-transfer type. (See Figure 14.12.) This type of stall shall have the following measurements:
   a. A minimum width of 66 in. (167.6 cm) and a depth of at least 60 in. (152.4 cm).
   b. A 32-in. (81.3-cm) wide clear opening to one side of the front of the stall with an outswinging door.
   c. One water closet with seat 20 in. (50.8 cm) above the floor and the centerline located 18 in. (45.7 cm) from the side wall on which the grab bar is located and away from the door. If possible, a wall-mounted water closet is preferred.
   d. The wall-mounted bar shall be 1.5 in. (3.8 cm) in diameter and be placed 1.5 in. from the wall. It shall be located 33 in. (83.8 cm) from the floor. When multiple toilet sets are provided, the grab bars and toilets

should be alternated between the left and right sides of stalls.

*5. At least one lavatory shall be wall mounted with a 29-in. (73.7-cm) minimum clearance underneath the apron of the fixture (10 in. [25.4 cm] from the face of the fixture) to provide wheelchair approach. Faucets shall be easily operated with no self-closing fixtures. Single-lever or wrist-blade types that do not require hand grip should be used.

*6. Toilet rooms for men shall have wall-mounted urinals with the rim 19 in. (48.3 cm) above the floor or shall have floor-mounted urinals which are at the same level as the main floor of the toilet room.

*7. Mirrors and shelves shall be mounted above accessible lavatories as low as possible, not exceeding 40 in. (101.6 cm) from the floor. Towel racks, soap dispensers, and all other accessories should be located no higher than 40 in. above the floor.

HARD-SURFACE FLOOR

INFORMATION DESK

VESTIBULE

FLUSH MOUNT DETAIL

24″ (61 CM)

Figure 14.10 Vestibule floor surfacing.

30″ (76.2 CM)

36″ (91.4 CM)

Figure 14.11 Lobby information desk.

32″ (81.3 CM)

1½″ (3.8 CM)

60″ (152.4 CM)

60″ (152.4 CM)

Figure 14.12 Side transfer toilet.

Figure 14.13 Public telephones and drinking fountains.

Drinking Fountains and Public Telephones

At least one telephone and one fountain shall be located at an accessible location on each floor of a building:

*1. The fountain shall be hand operated or hand and foot operated with up-front water and jet controls. A wall-mounted model shall have a 12-in. (30.5-cm) projecting bowl with a rim placed 30 to 36 in. (76.2 to 91.4 cm) above the floor. An alcove is desirable for the location of a fountain in a corridor. (See Figure 14.13.)

*2. Telephone dials, handsets, and coin slots shall be located no higher than 54 in. (137.2 cm) above the floor. Push-button dials are preferred and cords should be 36 in. (91.4 cm) long. Directories should be mounted 30 to 34 in. (76.2 to 86.4 cm) above the floor. At least one telephone should be equipped with an amplifier for use by those with a hearing disability.

Open Office Barrier-Free Criteria

Open offices present special problems for physically disabled people because standard corridors are not established. Therefore accessibility factors require special attention.

1. Locate conference rooms and meeting rooms so that they are convenient to main circulation routes and vertical access.

2. Accessible conference rooms should be within 50 ft (15 m) of accessible rest rooms, drinking fountains, and public telephones. Where application of conference facilities occurs, one room or area of each type should be accessible.

*3. Provide office work areas usable by physically disabled people without segregating them into one area. Allow additional linear wall space and/or floor space for storage usable by those who are handicapped in private office situations.

4. Provide two different means of access to built-up areas and elevated (vertical) computer floors.

5. Workstation access aisles should have a clear width of at least 36 in. (91.4 cm) with a wheelchair turnaround area of at least 60″ × 60″ (152.4 × 152.4 cm) located at 50-ft (15-m) maximum intervals. (See Figure 14.14.)

6. Each workstation, reception area, and storage room should provide space for a wheelchair turn.

7. Provide for several interview spaces beside desks. This space should be large enough for a wheelchair (32″ × 48″ [81.3 × 121.9 cm]). Lightweight furniture may occupy this space when not needed for interviewing handicapped people. (See Figure 14.14.)

8. The distance from an individual workstation to the nearest accessible rest room should not exceed 150 ft (45.7 m).

9. Vertical panels should provide an 8-in. (20.3-cm) open space between the bottom of panel and the floor to permit detection by blind long-cane users.

10. A guide rope or other cue should be provided along vertical panels to aid blind employees. (See Figure 14.15.)

11. Wall panels should not have base supports that extend into a path of egress in an open office plan.

CIRCULATION

PRIMARY 54–60"
(TWO-WAY PASSAGE)

SECONDARY 36–42"
(ONE-WAY PASSAGE)

WHEELCHAIR

HANDICAPPED INTERVIEW
SPACE 32 × 48" MIN.

R   REST AREA

Figure 14.14 Circulation in offices.

GUIDE ROPE OR
WALL CUE FOR CANE

Figure 14.15 Circulation: passage through open office plan.

12. When several panels are connected in a linear assembly, there should be one stabilizing panel attached to the assembly at a 45° to 90° angle for each three panels.

13. The entire open office system, including the carpeting and permanent walls, should provide sufficient color and value contrast to permit identification of components and various means of egress by visually impaired people.

14. Worksurfaces should have a minimum undersurface kneespace width of 32 in. (81.3 cm). A leg room depth of 20 in. (50.8 cm) should also be provided.

15. Worksurfaces, storage units, typing tables, and conference tables should be capable of being adjusted incrementally in height. Other than typing tables, all worksurfaces should have an adjustable height from 25 to 30 in. (63.5 to 76.2 cm) measured from the underside of the worksurface. (See Figure 14.16.)

16. All horizontal worksurfaces should be capable of supporting a 200-lb (90-kg) load at the outer edge without tipping.

17. Worksurfaces should be provided with a nonglare top surface.

18. All edges and corners of furniture components should be rounded with a radius of ⅛ in. (3.2 mm).

19. When overhead storage is used, the worksurface width should not exceed 25 in. (63.5 cm) if kneespace is provided. When kneespace is not provided, the top width should not exceed 20 in. (50.8 cm). The bottom of the overhead shelf should not be higher than 44 in. (111.8 cm) above the floor when a kneespace is provided; without a kneespace, the height should be 46-in. (116.8 cm).

20. All doors and drawers should be operable with one hand. Use side-hung doors if they do not cause obstruction to movement within the space.

21. Provide a variety of file storage that is accessible to disabled people. A seated person may reach a filing system from 10 to 42 in. (25.4 to 106.7 cm) high; a standing person's reach is from 10 to 56 in. (25.4 to 142.2 cm) high. (See Figure 14.17.)

22. All hardware should be flush or recessed. Trim may only protrude ⅛ in. (3.2 mm). Latches and handles to overhead storage should be located at the bottom of the doors. All desk hardware should be located (if possible) at least 18 in. (45.7 cm) from the floor.

23. Hooks and hangers within wardrobes should be adjustable from 48 to 66 in. (121.9 to 167.6 cm).

24. Lighting levels at workstations should average 50 ESI footcandles for task illumination. Overall illumination for general circulation should average 10 footcandles.

25. Locate outlets to prevent potential hazards, such as raised mounts or multiple plug adaptors. Extension cords should not be allowed to run under work surfaces. All electrical power receptacles, switches, and telephone outlets which are housed in the furniture system should be located between 12 and 48 in. (30.5 and 121.9 cm) above the floor.

26. Controls on telephones shall not require wrist action or finger manipulation. Provisions should be made to add receiver volume controls to telephones when needed.

Figure 14.16 Work surfaces.

Figure 14.17 Comparative reach.

Figure 14.18 Food service.

Figure 14.19 Vending machines.

Other handicapped aids should also be made available, such as a teletypewriter, speaker system, and foot controls.

Accessibility to Public Spaces

Dining areas, dormitories, and spectator spaces require the following design considerations:

1. Dining areas
   a. Dining areas should be directly accessible to physically disabled people without having to enter through a service area or kitchen.
   b. Provide a variety of dining choices within the facility. Do not segregate handicapped people in one area.
   c. Access aisles between tables or booths should be at least 36 in. (91.4 cm) wide with wheelchair turning space of no less than 60″ × 60″ (152.4 × 152.4 cm) located at 50-ft (15.2-m) maximum intervals.
   d. *Food service* lines should allow a minimum clear aisle width of 42 in. (106.7 cm) between food service counters (or tray slides) and control railing. Outside rail height of tray slide should not be more than 34 in. (86.4 cm). (See Figure 14.18.)
   e. Vending areas should provide a turning space of no less than 60″ × 60″ (152.4 × 152.4 cm). (See Figure 14.19.)
   f. Undertable clearance should measure 29 to 30 in. (73.7 to 76.2 cm). Minimum clear knee recess width of 32 in. (81.3 cm) and a depth of 20 in. (50.8 cm) should be provided.
   g. Booths, stand-up counters, and other such facilities are permitted when other alternatives are provided for those who are handicapped.
   h. Dispensers for eating utensils, glassware, and drinking water should be available to people not going through the food service line. Drinking glasses should be provided with a support shelf while they are being filled from a tap dispenser.

2. Dormitories
   a. Rooms should be large enough to allow placement of furniture with at least 52 in. (132.1 cm) between major elements. Clearance between the bed and a wall surface should be 38 in. (96.5 cm).
   b. Clothing storage rods should be adjustable to 48 in. (121.9 cm) above the floor. To be fully accessible, closet should allow partial entry of a wheelchair.
   c. Mattress top should be 22 in. (55.9 cm) above the floor.
   d. Rooms should be adequately ventilated in bedrooms where wheelchairs may be recharged.

3. Spectator spaces
   a. Lecture halls, auditoriums, and theaters should have areas set aside for wheelchair users. Wheelchair stations should be level, be out of the traffic zone, and provide good visibility. (See Figure 14.20.)
   b. The number of wheelchair stations varies with the capacity of the assembly space.

Assembly Space	Number of Wheelchair Stations
Up to 75	Minimum 1
76 to 500	Minimum 2
501 to 1000	Minimum 3
1001 to 1500	Minimum 4
Over 1500	Minimum 4 plus 1 for each 400 people over 1500

c. Seating should also be provided for semiambulant people. The amount of seating provided should equal a minimum of 1 percent of the total number of seats. Allow for a choice of seating location.

d. Accessible lounge seating should be provided for a minimum of two people in the entry areas.

*e. All sloping floors must be covered in nonslip materials. Floors that slope more than 1:20 shall be considered ramps. Ramps should be provided at level changes that exceed more than ½ in. (12.7 mm).

f. Where writing surfaces are provided for use in lecture rooms or assembly spaces, the equipment should not prevent ease of sitting or rising.

g. A means of vertical access should be provided to all podia or stages. This may be portable or temporary.

h. A minimum of 10 footcandles should be provided for general circulation areas. Foot lighting should be provided on stairways and aisles.

PROCEDURES FOR COMPLIANCE WITH BARRIER-FREE REQUIREMENTS

Designers involved in the design and specification of interior components for federal buildings or public spaces that must comply with Public Law 90-480 should obtain procedures for compliance from regional offices of the General Services Administration or the Office of Facilities Engineering of the Department of Health and Human Services. Currently these federal agencies employ a checklist for documenting compliances; and after a final inspection to certify that the facilities meet the requirements, a certificate of compliance is issued. State and local governing agencies should also be consulted on compliance procedures.

Exceptions and Waivers

The following exceptions are currently allowed by federal regulations:

1. The design, construction, or alteration of any portion of a building which need not, because of its intended use, be made accessible to, or usable by, the public or by physically disabled people.

2. The alteration of an existing building if the alteration does not involve the installation of, or work on, existing stairs, doors, elevators, toilets, entrances, drinking fountains, floors, telephone location, curbs, parking areas, or any other facilities susceptible of installation or improvements to accommodate physically disabled people.

Figure 14.20 Assembly seating.

24" (61 CM)

18–24" (45.7–61 CM)

SPACE FOR PEOPLE WITH BRACES

BACK-UP SPACE TO LET OTHERS BY

16" (40.6 CM)

3. The alteration of an existing building, or of such portions thereof, to which application of the standard is not structurally possible.

4. The construction or alteration of a building for which plans and specifications were completed or substantially completed on or before September 2, 1969. However, any building constructed under the National Transportation Act of 1960, the National Capital Transportation Act of 1965, or Title III of the Washington Metropolitan Area Transit Regulation Compact shall be designed, constructed, or altered in accordance with ANSI standards regardless of design status or bid solicitation as of date required by law.[5]

All exception and waiver requests submitted for approval shall be fully supported by documentation outlining the conditions which generated the request and the reasons for submittal.

GLOSSARY

Accessible: A means or condition of approach, admittance and use, intended for use by physically handicapped people.

Ambulant disabled: People who have physical disabilities that do not necessarily restrict walking.

Balcony: An interior or exterior portion of seating, circulation, or work space which is raised 4 ft (1.2 m) or more above a floor or ground level.

Barriers: Physical or functional obstructions to the intended use of a space.

Built-up level: An elevation change in floor level of one or more risers not exceeding 4 vertical feet. Note: Less than three risers are not recommended as vertical access to built-up levels.

Chairbound: A person or persons who are confined to a wheelchair during the working day or who elect to use a wheelchair for ease of movement.

Communication and identification system: A standard organization of signs and cuing for purposes of identifying circulation routes, spaces, and hazards to physically handicapped people.

Corridor lobby: A wheelchair turnaround space in corridors; where seating is provided, it qualifies as a rest stop.

Corridor rest stops: Seating and wheelchair parking at specific intervals along a corridor.

Cues or cuing: Materials or components which communicate information by nonliteral means, including textures, color, graphics, and audible signals.

Equipment: Fixed or nonfixed building hardware and accessories. Example: mirrors, dispensers, or lighting fixtures.

Exception: A term indicating an accessible alternative to a requirement.

Flush: Within ⅛ in. (3.2 mm) maximum protrusion from surrounding surfaces.

Governing codes: Any codes applicable to a project, including basic federal criteria documents and state and city codes.

Hazards: Protrusions, obstructions, changes in materials or levels, exposed structural or mechanical components, or the effects of inclement weather which are likely to cause personal injury, confusion, or discomfort.

Leisure run stairs: Stairs having unusually shallow slope or small ruse-to-run ratio.

Loop circulation: Passageway for one-way circulation.

Mounting height: The distance from the floor to the top edge or surface of an object, except as noted.

Physically disabled or handicapped: Any individual who despite a physical disability, can be expected, without assistance from another person, to visit and utilize a building, including its services; the disabled; the handicapped; people with physical disabilities.

Public conveniences: Facilities for public use, such as rest rooms, telephones, and drinking fountains.

Ramping device: A permanent or temporary inclined plane usually ramping a small level change (½ in. [12.7 mm] or less) such as metal plate attached to a threshold.

Required accessible areas: Specified areas which must be physically accessible and functionally usable by physically disabled people.

Semi-ambulant disabled: People with partial mobility impairments, such as difficulty in walking, breathing, strength, stamina, balance, and/or coordination problems.

Shall: A manditory regulation; indicates that an item must conform to a standard.

Should: Recommendations or that which is advised but not required.

Stairway: Three or more risers shall constitute a stairway.

Steps: One to three consecutive treads or risers.

Vertical access: Means of traveling from one floor level to another. Example: ramps, stairs, elevators, and other lifts. Escalators are usually not considered as vertical means of access for physically handicapped people.

Workstation: Floor areas, furniture and/or equipment used by employees for periods of time longer than one-half hour.

Part 3

SPECIFICATION TECHNOLOGY

COORDINATION GUIDELINES FOR CONTRACT DOCUMENTS

Specifications and drawings serve complementary functions, and as such the preparation of both should be pursued concurrently and should be closely coordinated in order to minimize misunderstandings, discrepancies, and oversights. The following claim example indicates the difficulties that could result from inadequate coordination.[1]

Example of Inadequate Coordination

In preparinng a rendering for a college science building, the designers displayed the windows and glass curtain wall as tinted glass. The college authorities were quite pleased with the aesthetic appearance of the structure and commented favorably on the use of the tinted glass. The entire structure, especially the air conditioning system, was designed based on the assumption that tinted glass would be used. The outline specification which included tinted glass was prepared as part of the bidding agreement.

The project was discussed and delayed by the college officials for a period of time before contract documents were prepared. In working up the final contract documents, the designer inadvertently omitted all reference to tinted glass and specified ¼-in. (6.4 mm) plate glass. As a result, ¼-in. clear glass was ordered by the contractor, and by the time the oversight was noted by the designer on a visit to the project site, all the glass had been manufactured and delivered, and a substantial portion had been installed.

The designer suggested several alternate methods of resolving the discrepancy, but the college officials insisted on tinted glass. The total cost to the designer to remedy the situation was $27,827.

This case is a typical example of claims that result from poorly coordinated contract documents. If the drawings and specifications had been prepared with reasonable professional care, the omission that culminated in this claim would probably not have occurred. There was no question about the fact that tinted glass was required from both the functional and aesthetic points of view, but it was not specified simply because of an oversight.

Although drawings, schedules, and specifications are complementary parts of the contract documents, each serves a distinct purpose:

Drawings	Schedules	Specifications
Graphic	Abbreviated Notes	Written
Define QUANTITY	Simplify and CLARIFY	Define QUALITY
Generic materials	Generic materials	Standards of workmanship
Component location, form, and shape	Finishes, colors	Physical requirements
Relationship to space	Room information: ceiling height, columns, casework, trim, doors, windows	Installation methods
Size and structure		Quality of finishes
		Warranty requirements

This brief listing clarifies the fact that drawings contain the graphic means of showing and identifying a material, but drawings should not include a description of the material or component. Drawings show the quantity of components; e.g., the number of chairs to be used, their location, and their size. The schedule further *clarifies* the chair finish or color. The *quality* of construction, finish, and upholstery is described in the written specification document.

COMMON COORDINATION PROBLEMS

The Construction Specifications Institute, Inc. (CSI) points out the following problems that commonly occur in contract documents.[2]

Duplication and Overlapping

Specification experts suggest that the information shown in drawings, schedules, and specifications should not be duplicated; i.e., information need not be repeated more than once in the contract documents. Since each document has been purposely established to cover distinct areas of information, there is no reason for duplication.

The use of trade names on drawings and schedule often accounts for discrepancies. In the event that a product substitution must be made, valuable time is spent changing the drawings and schedules. If an oversight occurs and the trade name is inadvertently left on a drawing, a bidder may interpret the conflicting duplication to mean that he may use either of the two products that are mentioned. When trade names are used, they should appear in the written specifications. All other references should indicate only the generic name of the material, such as resilient tile, paint, or carpet.

Another common source of duplication is the use of written notations on working drawings. Occasional notes may be necessary to identify a component, but the note should give a minimum of information. Too many notes make a drawing difficult to understand and often lead to duplication and confusion.

Omissions and Gaps

The claim regarding tinted glass discussed earlier in this chapter is a perfect example of a situation where the omission of information caused serious problems. Careful attention must be paid to gaps in information that can occur between the contract documents. For example, two types of carpet may be specified for a particular project, but the drawings and schedules neglect to show where the two types of carpet are to be installed.

Inconsistent Terminology

The two most frequent causes of inconsistencies result from improper terminology and graphic symbols. Terms should be defined and clarified in the scope of the specification and their use must be consistent throughout the contract documents. Some common terms that cause confusion are:

Room names: Lounge, rest rooms, ladies room, comfort area
Lobby, foyer, entry
Cocktail area, bar, lounge

Floorcoverings: Rug, carpet, mat, padding, cushion

Window coverings: Drapes, draperies, curtains, blinds, shades

Furnishings: Sofa, lounge, loveseat

Chairs: Executive chair, secretarial chair, clerical chair, posture chair, desk chair, side chair, lounge chair, occasional chair

Casegoods: Desk, work surface, console, credenza, cabinet, end table, lamp table, occasional table, conference table, coffee table, brunch table

Accessories: Wall hanging, relief, sculpture, sculpture relief

Curtains: Casements, sheers, drapery

Hardware: Door, cabinet, furniture, window, drapery, curtain

Windows: Casement, slide, single glazed, louvered, pivot, awning, bay, double hung, triple hung, Palladian, transom, casement bay, projected

Doors: Flush, panel, hollow core, double core, Dutch, French, sliding, pocket, overhead, double acting, fire, exit, revolving, accordion, stacking, bi-fold, by-pass, louver, cafe, sash

The list could go on endlessly, but the importance of using consistent terminology cannot be overemphasized. Figure 15.1 illustrates some inconsistencies that frequently appear on schedules and drawings. On the "Floor Covering Legend," note that item "B—Carpet" would be more accurately termed a "rug." *Carpet* is defined as a floorcovering which is installed (stretched or glued down) wall to wall in a given area. Other inconsistencies appear on the "Paint and Wall Covering Legend." Notice that in some cases the manufacturer, style, and color numbers are mentioned and in other cases they are omitted. Indicating parts of the work to be done by a specific type of contractor or subcontractor should not be placed on the drawings or schedules. The "Drapery Notes" use the improper nomenclature "drapes." Since the directional draw of the drapery was not shown on the drawing, it should have been included in the schedule information.

These examples illustrate just a few of the common inconsistencies, duplications, and omissions that could later be used as evidence that a designer lacked professional competence. For example, in the event that a contractor installed carpet #303—Blue from the Carp Mills, but the color number the designer ordered had previously been changed, the contractor would not be held responsible. If the designer, in the written specfications, had requested and received current color numbers, but neglected to update the schedules, any complaint he or she might make against the contractor would probably be negated by the inconsistency in the schedule. The old belief that specifications have precedence over drawings and schedules is no longer the fact. All contract documents are considered equally legal and binding.

Inconsistent Use of Symbols

Although there is no universal standard for symbols, consistency can be controlled by developing a legend of symbols that will be used in a particular set of working drawings (see

WALL AND PAINT FINISH LEGEND

NO.	MAT'L	MFG'R	NO.	COLOR	REMARKS
1	OAK			STAIN	BY J.J. LEE
2	VINYL	REZ.	461	BLUE	
3	FOIL	COPPER			BRIGHT LITS
4	VINYL	BRITE	33	BROWN	

FLOORCOVERING LEGEND

LET.	MAT'L	MFG'R	NO.	COLOR	
A	WOOD	JONES		WALNUT	PREWAXED
B	CARPET	CARP	303	BLUE	FELT PAD

DRAPERY NOTES
1. ROOM DRAPES
BY T.S.R. MILLS # 463 BROWN

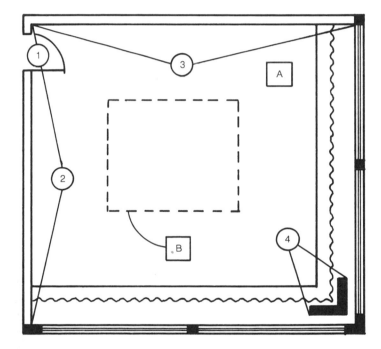

Figure 15.1 Room finish legends.

Figure 15.2). Symbols can be either geometric shapes or number codes, and often a combination of both is used. Symbols are useful when reference is made to a class of material, such as paint, carpet, or furniture. Figure 15.3 illustrates a furniture schedule which lists furniture by general type rather than specific number or trade name. If a symbol refers to a specific type of paint, i.e., semigloss latex, it could become ineffectual and cause revisions each time a specification change was made. Properly used, symbols can aid in avoiding confusing terminology. For example, in Figure 15.4, components have a coded reference note in place of a descriptive note for identification. Instead of labeling "conference chair" on a drawing, a coded reference, such as "317002," could link the chair directly to the specification. The number "31" could indicate chairs, of which several types are specified. The last four numbers indicate the particular conference chair described in the specification. If the designer decided to change the position of the chair or specify another type of chair in its place, he or she could simply remove the last four numbers and insert the proper number corresponding to the new selection.

Aside from avoiding confusing terminology, this method of coding forces the contractor and bidders to read the specifications. An excellent example of the coded reference is provided in Figure 15.5 and the accompanying color schedule.

The finish schedule on the drawing links the coded numbers and letters to the drawing, and the additional written schedule relates the coded numbers and letters to the material. (See Table 15.1.)

INTERIOR ARCHITECTURAL LEGEND DESCRIPTION

SYMBOL	
∿∿∿	DRAPERY
⬡ 9	
◀9▶ 6 5	ELEVATION NUMBER
4 ◆9 2 / 1 / 3	DRAWING NUMBER
7 / A / C	ROOM ELEVATIONS BY WALL NUMBER ROOM NUMBER DOOR NUMBER TYPE OF DOOR A. FULL HT. WALNUT BY MILL
⊨	B.S. BASE DUPLEX OUTLET
– – – –	TELEPHONE CONDUIT
◄	B.S. BASE TELEPHONE OUTLET
●	B.S. FLOOR TELEPHONE OUTLET

Figure 15.2 Interior architectural symbols.

FURNITURE SCHEDULE
1 CURVED SCREEN
2 SECTIONAL SOFA
3 BUNCH TABLE
4 PARSON TABLE
5 LAMP
6 PLANT
7 BUFFET COUNTER
8 SERVICE COUNTER
9 PLANT AND PLANTER
10 DINING CHAIR
11 RECTANGULAR DINING TABLE
12 FLIP-TOP DINING TABLE
13 SQUARE DINING TABLE
14 CASHIER'S COUNTER

Figure 15.3 Furniture schedule. Reproduced with permission of B. Eric Bron & Associates, Phoenix, AZ.

NAU
CENTRAL DINING HALL
"THE BUFFET"

Figure 15.4 Coded furniture schedule. Reproduced with
permission of Architectural Interiors, Inc., Phoenix, AZ.

Figure 15.5 Coded room finish schedule. Reproduced with
permission of B. Eric Bron & Associates, Phoenix, AZ.

TABLE 15.1 FINISH SCHEDULE

1. Base
   R —(rubber) "Burke" #598-P Dark Brown
   Q/T —(quarry tile) "Summitville" Sunglo

2. Floors
   CP —(carpet)
   C/C —(colored concrete) "Davis Colors" Buff #5447
      (substitute if necessary—#5262)
   Q/T —(quarry tile) "Summitville" Sunglo
      Grout color—Flashed Walnut
   C —(concrete) Unfinished
      (vinyl tile)
   V/A—1 "Kentile" pattern: Criterion
      Color: Off-white (ground)

3. Walls
   V/W—(vinyl wallcovering)
   V/W—1 "Vicrtex" pattern: Malmo, color: Arctic Dawn #1517
   V/W—2 "Vicrtex" pattern: Madagaska, color: Jungle Shells #1438
   V/W—3 "Vicrtex" pattern: Madagaska, color: Burnt Orange #1608
   V/W—4 "Vicrtex" pattern: Adagio, color: Crocus #8734
   V/W—5 "Vicrtex" pattern: Adagio, color: Mushroom #8733
   V/W—6 "Vicrtex" pattern: Adagio, color: Topazine #8735
   V/W—7 "Vicrtex" pattern: Adagio, color: Buff #8732
   V/W—8 "Vicrtex" pattern: Studio, color: Tawny Beige #1027
   V/W—9 "Vicrtex" pattern: Studio, color: Ember #5072
   V/W—10 "Vicrtex" pattern: Studio, color: Burnt Orange #1608
   V/W—11 "Vicrtex" pattern: Studio, color: Ginger #1071
   C/T—(ceramic tile)

4. Doors (see floor plans for the designated colors)
   Plochere #73

Source: B. Eric Bron & Associates, Phoenix, Arizona.

Typical Multi-Purpose Room Walls diagram:

```
         P-1
P-7 ◄── CONCRETE DOUBLE T'S ──► P-7
   |  P-7  |  P-7  |  P-7  |
   | WINDOWS |  P-6  | WINDOWS |
   |  P-6   |  P-6  |  P-6   |
   |  P-1   |  P-1  |  P-1   |
```

TYPICAL MULTI-PURPOSE ROOM WALLS
(THIS DRWG. DESIGNATES WHERE COLORS OCCUR)
* REFER TO INTERIOR WRITTEN PORTION OF THE COLOR SCHEDULE TO FIND ABBREVIATIONS.

ROOM FINISH SCHEDULE

NO./RM	ROOM TITLE	FLOOR	BASE	WALLS NORTH	WALLS EAST	WALLS SOUTH	WALLS WEST	WALLS PAINT FIN	CEILING MAT'L	CEILING HGT	CEILING PAINT FIN	RMKS
A 1	CELL	C/C	R	P-4	P-1	P-1	P-1	F/V	C/PL	VARIES	F/V	
A 2	CELL	C/C	R	P-4	P-1	P-1	P-1	F/V	C/PL	VARIES	F/V	
A 3	CELL	C/C	R	P-4	P-1	P-1	P-1	F/V	C/PL	VARIES	F/V	
A 4	CELL	C/C	R	P-1	P-4	P-1	P-1	F/V	C/PL	VARIES	F/V	
A 5	CELL	C/C	R	P-1	P-4	P-1	P-1	F/V	C/PL	VARIES	F/V	
A 6	CELL	C/C	R	P-1	P-4	P-1	P-1	F/V	C/PL	VARIES	F/V	
A 7	CELL	C/C	R	P-1	P-4	P-1	P-1	F/V	C/PL	VARIES	F/V	
A 8	CELL	C/C	R	P-1	P-4	P-1	P-1	F/V	C/PL	VARIES	F/V	
A 9	CELL	C/C	R	P-1	P-1	P-2	P-1	F/V	C/PL	VARIES	F/V	
A 10	CELL	C/C	R	P-1	P-1	P-2	P-1	F/V	C/PL	VARIES	F/V	
A 11	CELL	C/C	R	P-1	P-1	P-2	P-1	F/V	C/PL	VARIES	F/V	
A 12	CELL	C/C	R	P-1	P-1	P-2	P-1	F/V	C/PL	VARIES	F/V	
A 13	CELL	C/C	R	P-1	P-1	P-2	P-1	F/V	C/PL	VARIES	F/V	
A 14	CELL	C/C	R	P-1	P-1	P-1	P-2	F/V	C/PL	VARIES	F/V	
A 15	CELL	C/C	R	P-1	P-1	P-1	P-2	F/V	C/PL	VARIES	F/V	
A 16	CELL	C/C	R	P-1	P-1	P-1	P-2	F/V	C/PL	VARIES	F/V	
A 17	STORAGE	C/C	R	P-1	P-1	P-1	P-1	F/V	C/PL	8'-0"	F/V	
A 18	DAYROOM	C/C	R	P-1	P-1	P-1	P-1	F/V	A/T	9'-0"	□	
A 19	TOILET	Q/T	Q/T	GC-1	GC-3	GC-1	GC-1	□	C/PL	8'-0"	E	
A 20	STORAGE	C/C	R	P-1	P-1	P-1	P-1	F/V	C/PL	8'-0"	F/V	
B 1	CELL	C/C	R	P-3	P-1	P-1	P-1	F/V	C/PL	VARIES	F/V	
B 2	CELL	C/C	R	P-3	P-1	P-1	P-1	F/V	C/PL	VARIES	F/V	
B 3	CELL	C/C	R	P-3	P-1	P-1	P-1	F/V	C/PL	VARIES	F/V	
B 4	CELL	C/C	R	P-1	P-1	P-1	P-3	F/V	C/PL	VARIES	F/V	
B 5	CELL	C/C	R	P-1	P-1	P-1	P-3	F/V	C/PL	VARIES	F/V	
B 6	CELL	C/C	R	P-1	P-1	P-1	P-3	F/V	C/PL	VARIES	F/V	
B 7	CELL	C/C	R	P-1	P-1	P-1	P-3	F/V	C/PL	VARIES	F/V	
B 8	CELL	C/C	R	P-1	P-1	P-1	P-3	F/V	C/PL	VARIES	F/V	
B 9	CELL	C/C	R	P-1	P-1	P-5	P-1	F/V	C/PL	VARIES	F/V	
B 10	CELL	C/C	R	P-1	P-1	P-5	P-1	F/V	C/PL	VARIES	F/V	
B 11	CELL	C/C	R	P-1	P-1	P-5	P-1	F/V	C/PL	VARIES	F/V	
B 12	CELL	C/C	R	P-1	P-1	P-5	P-1	F/V	C/PL	VARIES	F/V	
B 13	CELL	C/C	R	P-1	P-1	P-5	P-1	F/V	C/PL	VARIES	F/V	
B 14	CELL	C/C	R	P-1	P-5	P-1	P-1	F/V	C/PL	VARIES	F/V	
B 15	CELL	C/C	R	P-1	P-5	P-1	P-1	F/V	C/PL	VARIES	F/V	
B 16	CELL	C/C	R	P-1	P-5	P-1	P-1	F/V	C/PL	VARIES	F/V	
B 17	STORAGE	C/C	R	P-1	P-1	P-1	P-1	F/V	C/PL	8'-0"	F/V	
B 18	DAYROOM	C/C	R	P-1	P-1	P-1	P-1	F/V	A/T	9'-0"	□	
B 19	TOILET	Q/T	Q/T	GC-1	GC-1	GC-1	GC-3	□	C/PL	8'-0"	E	
C 1	CELL	C/C	R	P-1	P-1	P-4	P-1	F/V	C/PL	VARIES	F/V	
C 2	CELL	C/C	R	P-1	P-1	P-4	P-1	F/V	C/PL	VARIES	F/V	
C 3	CELL	C/C	R	P-1	P-1	P-4	P-1	F/V	C/PL	VARIES	F/V	
C 4	CELL	C/C	R	P-1	P-1	P-1	P-4	F/V	C/PL	VARIES	F/V	
C 5	CELL	C/C	R	P-1	P-1	P-1	P-4	F/V	C/PL	VARIES	F/V	
C 6	CELL	C/C	R	P-1	P-1	P-1	P-4	F/V	C/PL	VARIES	F/V	
C 7	CELL	C/C	R	P-1	P-1	P-1	P-4	F/V	C/PL	VARIES	F/V	
C 8	CELL	C/C	R	P-1	P-1	P-1	P-4	F/V	C/PL	VARIES	F/V	
C 9	CELL	C/C	R	P-2	P-1	P-1	P-1	F/V	C/PL	VARIES	F/V	
C 10	CELL	C/C	R	P-2	P-1	P-1	P-1	F/V	C/PL	VARIES	F/V	
C 11	CELL	C/C	R	P-2	P-1	P-1	P-1	F/V	C/PL	VARIES	F/V	
C 12	CELL	C/C	R	P-2	P-1	P-1	P-1	F/V	C/PL	VARIES	F/V	
C 13	CELL	C/C	R	P-2	P-1	P-1	P-1	F/V	C/PL	VARIES	F/V	
C 14	CELL	C/C	R	P-1	P-2	P-1	P-1	F/V	C/PL	VARIES	F/V	
C 15	CELL	C/C	R	P-1	P-2	P-1	P-1	F/V	C/PL	VARIES	F/V	
C 16	CELL	C/C	R	P-1	P-2	P-1	P-1	F/V	C/PL	VARIES	F/V	
C 17	STORAGE	C/C	R	P-1	P-1	P-1	P-1	F/V	C/PL	8'-0"	F/V	
C 18	DAYROOM	C/C	R	P-1	P-1	P-1	P-1	F/V	A/T	9'-0"	□	
C 19	TOILET	Q/T	Q/T	GC-1	GC-1	GC-1	GC-3	□	C/PL	8'-0"	E	
D 1	CELL	C/C	R	P-1	P-1	P-3	P-1	F/V	C/PL	VARIES	F/V	
D 2	CELL	C/C	R	P-1	P-1	P-3	P-1	F/V	C/PL	VARIES	F/V	
D 3	CELL	C/C	R	P-1	P-1	P-3	P-1	F/V	C/PL	VARIES	F/V	
D 4	CELL	C/C	R	P-1	P-3	P-1	P-1	F/V	C/PL	VARIES	F/V	
D 5	CELL	C/C	R	P-1	P-3	P-1	P-1	F/V	C/PL	VARIES	F/V	
D 6	CELL	C/C	R	P-1	P-3	P-1	P-1	F/V	C/PL	VARIES	F/V	
D 7	CELL	C/C	R	P-1	P-3	P-1	P-1	F/V	C/PL	VARIES	F/V	
D 8	CELL	C/C	R	P-1	P-3	P-1	P-1	F/V	C/PL	VARIES	F/V	
D 9	CELL	C/C	R	P-5	P-1	P-1	P-1	F/V	C/PL	VARIES	F/V	
D 10	CELL	C/C	R	P-5	P-1	P-1	P-1	F/V	C/PL	VARIES	F/V	
D 11	CELL	C/C	R	P-5	P-1	P-1	P-1	F/V	C/PL	VARIES	F/V	
D 12	CELL	C/C	R	P-5	P-1	P-1	P-1	F/V	C/PL	VARIES	F/V	
D 13	CELL	C/C	R	P-5	P-1	P-1	P-1	F/V	C/PL	VARIES	F/V	
D 14	CELL	C/C	R	P-1	P-1	P-1	P-5	F/V	C/PL	VARIES	F/V	
D 15	CELL	C/C	R	P-1	P-1	P-1	P-5	F/V	C/PL	VARIES	F/V	
D 16	CELL	C/C	R	P-1	P-1	P-1	P-5	F/V	C/PL	VARIES	F/V	
D 17	STORAGE	C/C	R	P-1	P-1	P-1	P-1	F/V	C/PL	8'-0"	F/V	
D 18	DAYROOM	C/C	R	P-1	P-1	P-1	P-1	F/V	A/T	9'-0"	□	
D 19	TOILET	Q/T	Q/T	GC-1	GC-3	GC-1	GC-1	□	C/PL	8'-0"	E	
E 1	MULTI-PURPOSE	C/C	R	*	*	*	*	F/V	C	21'-6"	F/V	(1) *
E 2	TOILET	Q/T	Q/T	P-1	P-3	P-1	P-1	E	C/PL	7'-0"	E	(3)
E 3	MECHANICAL	C		P-1	P-1	P-1	P-1	□	C/PL	8'-0"	□	
E 4	CONTROL	CP-2	R	P-1	P-1	P-1	P-4	F/V	A/T	8'-0"	□	
E 5	CORRIDOR	C/C	R	P-8	P-1	P-1	P-1	F/V	C/PL	8'-0"	F/V	
E 6	CORRIDOR	C/C	R	P-8	P-1	P-1	P-1	F/V	C/PL	8'-0"	F/V	
E 7	COUNSEL	CP-1	R	P-1	P-1	P-1	P-1	F/V	A/T	8'-0"	□	
E 8	STORAGE	C/C	R	P-1	P-1	P-1	P-1	F/V	C/PL	8'-0"	F/V	
E 9-12	MECHANICAL	C	-	C	C	C	C	□	C	VARIES	□	(2)

(1) CEMENT PLASTER FURRED SPACE at PERIPHERY of CEILING.

(2) SEE SHEET 15 for FLOOR PLAN.

(3) FURRED at PLUMBING WALL (EAST).

* LOWER PORTIONS OF WALL DIVIDED BY EXPANSION JOINTS:P-1
UPPER & CENTER PORTION OF WALL DIVIDED BY EXPANSION JOINTS: P-6
SOFFITS OR THAT PORTION OF WALL AT FURRED SPACE:P-7

Figure 15.6 Designation of wall finishes in irregular-shaped rooms.

Symbols used to indicate interior finishes and furnishings require very careful application. The finish schedule shown in the previous example made use of the directional symbols north, south, east, and west. This is very useful on a large project where it would be impossible to show individual rooms. On smaller projects where each room can be shown and in situations where the designer may wish to vary the wall finish within the same room, another symbol system would have to be devised. Often a geometric shape is used, with a letter or number to indicate a particular wall finish. Lines are extended from the geometric symbol to the exact area to which the symbol applies. In the example shown in Figure 15.1, it is easy to determine where finish (2) and (3) are to be applied. The column is clearly marked for another finish number (4).

This symbol method is also very useful in areas having irregular walls and spaces, but the designer must be exact in the placement of the line indicators. The examples shown in Figure 15.6 illustrate the confusion that may result from an inadequate concern for detail. If we compare the three examples, we can readily determine which drawings would result in inconsistencies and inaccuracies.

If a painting contractor tried to determine which areas were to be painted in Exhibit A or B, he would find that some areas have an abundance of lines pointing to walls to show finish material, but other walls, such as the top fireplace walls and the window recesses, have no indication of finish requirements.

Although lines are frequently used to point out a certain detail in drawings, this interior finish symbol was designed to indicate large areas to be finished in the same material. When the line is used as a *pointer* (Exhibit A and B), it does not convey the needed information. In Exhibit C the lines encompass the *entire width* of the area to be finished and therefore offer more precise graphic information. Figure 15.7 illustrates another method of indicating placement of wall finishes. If a wall is to receive two finishes, an elevation may be necessary (see Figure 15.8).

In a drapery symbol, the omission of a line indicating which direction the drapery should draw may result in installation difficulties. If drapery is to be installed over a sliding glass door, the drapery contractor may not be able to determine the slide direction of the door from the drawings, and as a result, the drapery may be made and installed incorrectly.

FINISH MATERIALS LEGEND	
SYM.	**MATERIAL**
A	"DEER-O" ALPINE WHITE
B	"DEER-O" DAWN GRAY
C	"DEER-O" CHARCOAL GRAY
D	"EUROTEX" ACOUSTICORD #587
E	"VICRTEX" TASCO ORIENT GREY 8370
F	"VICRTEX" STIL-L COARSE MOONSTONE 3006
G	"BALMORAL," WALLCOVERING
H	"STAUFFER," STERLING GRAY #1704
I	CERAMIC TILE
J	———
K	WD. PANELING, WALNUT VENEER

Figure 15.7 Room finish materials. Reproduced with permission of Peter A. Lendrum Associates, Architects, Engineers, Planners, Phoenix, AZ.

Figure 15.8 Wall elevations designating multiple finishes. Source: Architectural Interiors, Inc., Phoenix, AZ.

Figure 15.9 Room finish schedule. Reproduced with permission of Selje, Bond, Steward & Romberger, Phoenix and Los Angeles.

ROOM FINISH SCHEDULE/COLOR SCHEDULE

ROOM #	ROOM NAME	FLOOR – CARPET	FLOOR – V.C.T. (EXISTING)	BASE – 4" RUBBER—COVELESS	WALLS – GYP. BD.—PAINTED	WALLS – W.C. "A"	WALLS – W.C. "B"	WALLS – W.C. "C"	CEILING – EXISTING 2×4 SUSPENDED LAY-IN	CEILING – EXISTING GYP. BD.	CLG. HT.	REMARK
201	COMMITTEE ROOM	●		●		●			●			
202	RECEPTION	●		●	●				●			
203	OFFICE #1	●		●	●				●			
204	OFFICE #2	●		●	●				●			
205	OFFICE #3	●		●	●				●			
206	SECRETARY	●		●	●				●			
207	PRESIDENT	●		●			●		●			
208	TOILET		●				●			●		
209	MEN		●							●		
210	WOMEN		●							●		
211	CORRIDOR	●		●	●				●			
212	CORRIDOR	●		●	●				●			
213	BOARDROOM	●		●	●				●			
214	WORK ROOM	●		●	●				●			
215	LUNCH ROOM	●		●	●				●			
216	ADMINISTRATIVE	●		●	●				●			

(FLOOR wall-orientation key: square diagram with N, E, S, W — ● INDICATES WALL)

Figure 15.10 Finish and color schedule. Reproduced with permission of Selje, Bond, Steward & Romberger, Phoenix and Los Angeles.

SCHEDULE EXAMPLES

Schedules are normally made for doors, windows, furniture, room finishes, colors, and any other project components needing clarification that can be provided by a schedule. A Room Finish Schedule would include the assigned room number and room name on smaller scale projects. Categories are established for the floors, bases, walls, ceilings, and trims. Vertical columns are established below these headings, which indicate types of room materials, such as vinyl, carpet, tile, wood, plaster, and any other finishes that may be used. Blank columns are usually left between each category for ease in reading and also to accommodate additional finishes that may be required at a later date. (See Figure 15.9.) A legend is often placed in the upper right-hand corner of the schedule to indicate room materials and finishes. Abbreviations for the materials and finishes should be consistent with those used elsewhere in the documents. A symbol should also be established for "Applicable" and "Not Applicable" situations.

Other columns are established for the ceiling height. This height is stated in feet and inches (meters or centimeters). If a room has varied ceiling heights, the average height should be used, such as 11'0". Another column is needed to indicate the drawing sheet number where the room elevations are to be found. The "Remarks" column is used for providing additional information, such as details concerning custom cabinetwork or columns in the centers of spaces. (See examples in Figure 15.10). The room finish and color schedule combination shown in Figure 15.10 makes use of circles to indicate the location of finishes. Directional symbols (N, S, E, W) are used in the upper left-hand corner. If the circle appears in the center of the square, all four walls are to receive the same finish.

It should be remembered that there is no one correct way to design a schedule. A schedule format that provided the needed information for one project may prove totally inadequate in another situation.

SUMMARY

Contract documents that lack coordination often result in job site confusion that causes faulty construction and installations. Changes of orders and other time delays are frequently directly related to simple oversights that could have been prevented by coordinating the drawings, schedules, and specifications. In addition, a uniform basis for bidding is often impossible to establish when the contract documents are unclear or incomplete.

To prevent some of these problems, a coordination checklist may be helpful.

1. Have all terms and symbols been clearly listed in the general conditions section of the specifications or included in the drawings or a legend?

2. Are components of the same generic type represented with the same symbols?

3. Are all terms consistent on the drawings, schedules, and specifications?

4. If a product substitution has been made in the specification, does it necessitate changes on the drawings or schedules?

5. Is the location of all wall, floor, and ceiling finishes clearly indicated?

6. Would some notes shown on the drawings be better placed in the schedules?

7. Has more than one person checked your drawings and schedules for inconsistencies?

SPECIFICATION FORMAT AND CONTENT

Specifications are used by designers to communicate the project requirements to the contractor. They are written descriptions of a technical nature which deal with materials, equipment, construction systems, standards, and workmanship. Written documents are more readily understood than drawings by persons not commonly associated with the construction industry. Hence, they become a potential source of liability. The courts, among others, often look to the specification to determine the message conveyed by the contract documents to those who must work with them.

POTENTIAL SOURCE OF LIABILITY

Review of numerous liability cases indicates that many of the claims arising out of defective specifications come about for the following major reasons:

1. Ambiguous or inadequate text results in the liability to determine the intended use of specified items.

2. Lack of coordination between the drawings and the specifications. (Overlap or gaps in documenting the design requirements.)

3. Lack of understanding on the part of the specifier about the capabilities of the items specified. (Items specified were not able to meet design or performance requirements.)

Although the professional designer is not legally bound to produce a "perfect" specification, the defective, erroneous, and "impossible" specification is a fairly common basis for legal claims made by contractors against designers.

Defective Specifications
Defective specifications fail to clarify what is expected of the contractor or how the work is to be performed. For example, if the contractor was not informed about a faulty subfloor, the contractor cannot be expected to abide by an original labor estimate for ceramic tile installation.

Defective and Erroneous Specifications
These frequently contain legal errors involving specification of materials that do not comply with fire codes.

Mechanical errors are often written into specifications that require the contractor to consult a drawing. For example, a specification might require that "the contractor shall attach bookshelves to the wall as illustrated on the drawings." The designer, however, neglected to show the bookshelves on the drawing. Functional errors can result from mechanical errors when specifications fail to have an item built according to the concepts of the owner; i.e., bookshelves not speficied to support heavy medical books.

Impossible Specifications
These specifications are defined as those that inadvertently create criteria for an object or process that is beyond the "state of the art," i.e., impossible to fulfill. Specifications may also prove impractical because of exorbitant cost involved in attempting to comply with the specification criteria. If unable to comply, a contractor would not be found guilty of breach of contract. Furthermore, when the court declares a specification "impossible," the court has been known to also rule in favor of compensating the contractor for money expended in the effort to comply.[1] Any design professional who writes specifications would be well advised to place himself in the position of the general contractor's personnel who must use these documents to translate the concept into the accomplished project. Since the specifications set forth those project requirements that are most readily expressed in words, their meaning must be conveyed clearly, adequately, and unambiguously.[13]

TYPES OF SPECIFICATIONS

Specifications may be broadly classified as "closed" or "open." A closed or restrictive specification is one that requires an exact material or product by trade name, style, or color number, thus restricting or eliminating the consideration of any other product. An open or nonrestrictive specification allows consideration of many materials or components through the use of a "modified or equal" clause or the use of performance-required standards. Performance-based specifications state the means necessary to achieve the requirements as well as the end result, but do not refer to any particular material or product. This chapter will discuss the following generic types of specifications:

Proprietary Specifications

Descriptive Specifications

Performance Specifications

Reference Standards Specifications

Closed or Restrictive Specifications
1. Proprietary specifications are those which specify a particular product by trade name. When the specification allows for no substitution of materials, it is known as a "base bid" proprietary specification. The term base bid means that all people who wish to provide materials for the project must base their bid on the product named in the specification. Designers frequently employ this type of specification because of the following advantages:
    a. The designer is able to prepare detailed working drawings based on the component or material which has been selected for use.
    b. Based on these detailed working drawings, the designer is often able to clarify the project details for the client.
    c. Proprietary specifications are shorter in length and easier to write because manufacturers will often supply much of the needed data and installation information.
    d. The designer has full control over the materials and components that will be used on the project.
    e. Because the specification does not allow for multiple selections, competitive price analysis and other bidding procedures are expedited.

2. Manufacturer's guide specifications are written to assist or encourage the specifier or designer in specifying the manufacturer's product. Aside from providing information on the performance attributes and recommended installation methods for the particular product, these specifi-

cations serve to promote a product. Designers may find these specifications useful in making comparative studies of various materials and components. In the event that a particular product is specified, the designer may incorporate all or part of the manufacturer's specification into the final specification.

Nonrestrictive or Open Specifications

The following items should be considered under this category:

1. *Proprietary specifications* may also be used as open specifications with the addition of the "or equal" clause, which allows other products to be considered for bid if the product can be proven equal in all aspects to the product named in the specification. Designers can readily see that there may be certain disadvantages to this method of specification:
   a. Controversy may develop concerning opinions about a product's equal quality.
   b. The designer or specifier becomes involved in a more time-consuming process of evaluating and selecting materials.
   c. This type of specification often results in material selection being diverted from considerations of quality to price comparisons. Because competitive bidding usually results in the lowering of prices, some manufacturers who may have provided reliable warranties and service may withdraw from the bidding.
   d. In order to avoid these difficulties, the Construction Specifications Institute recommends that the following procedures be outlined in the specification:
      (1) "State the requirements and procedures under which proposed substitutions of materials and methods will be considered.
      (2) "State that all proposed substitutions must be submitted in writing before the close of the bid period. (About ten days or so should prove sufficient in most cases.)
      (3) "Inform the bidder that all acceptable substitutions—all 'equals'—will be approved in addenda which will be issued to all bidders."[3]

Another method of controlling "or equal" difficulties is to use a "modified or equal" type of proprietary specifications. This method not only mentions the brand name of a product, but also establishes requirements and standards for the specified materials, thus eliminating opinions as a sole source of material evaluation.

The following clause is suggested for use with the "modified or equal" proprietary specification:

The specified products establish minimum qualities that substitutes must meet to be considered acceptable. To obtain approval of unspecified products under the modified or equal provisions, bidders shall submit written requests at least ten days before the bid date. Requests received after this time will not be considered. Requests must clearly describe the product for which approval is requested, including all data necessary to demonstrate acceptability.[4]

2. *Descriptive specifications* do not employ the name of a particular product and are therefore considered open specifications. This type of specification involves a detailed description of the manner in which the material is to be constructed and the method of installation required. Although this specification is lengthy and more time consuming to produce, it may be necessary when a particular material or component is complex and difficult to show on the drawings. For example, other than indicating the carpet location within the project, it is difficult to indicate carpet construction details on the drawings or schedules. Therefore, it may be necessary to use a descriptive specification for this particular interior component.

A carpet descriptive specification would list the requirements for the following construction features:

Construction type (tufted, woven, or other)
Pile yarn (generic)
Gauge or pitch
Stitches per inch or wires
Pile height or wire height
Coloration method
Yarn size and ply
Width
Pile yarn weight and total weight
Primary and secondary backing

Descriptive specifications may also be written as reference standards; i.e., reference standards, which are also descriptive in character, may be used as a part of the descriptive specification. These standards are listed as additional construction or installation requirements.

American Society for Testing and Materials
ASTM _____ (number)
Federal Standard. FS _____ (number)
(Name of applicable) Building Code (   )

Designers and specifiers should be sure that reference standards do not contradict or duplicate other requirements stated elsewhere in the contract documents. More details on the use of reference standards will be discussed later in this chapter.

To write effective descriptive specifications, the specifier must be knowledgeable in the following areas:
a. Material construction methods and the critical performance factors that will allow the component to function effectively.
b. Minimal acceptable criteria for each type of material to be specified.
c. Procedures for verifying whether a material or component complies with the described requirements. These procedures may include testing methods and established standards.
d. Installation methods that would be suitable for each type of material and component.

Performance specifications establish the performance requirements without dictating the means by which the end results are to be achieved. Any material or system that meets the performance criteria could qualify for use. These specifications contain a qualitative statement regarding the performance requirement, the quantitative criteria, and the test methods that should be used to assure the desired results. For example, for a space divider subsystem, the attribute of "health and safety" is stated as follows:

Requirement: Provide fire safety
Criteria: (a) This subsystem shall have a maximum flame spread of 25. (b) If a fully sprinklered fire protection sprinkler system is provided, the flame-spread rating shall not exceed 200.
Test: Type—Calculation
Method: ASTM-E 84 "Surface Burning Characteristics of Building Materials."[5]

This type of specification does not require that the designer have an extensive knowledge about the generic qualities or construction aspects of any particular materials. *But the ability to establish concise performance requirements and the appropriate testing methods are essential in writing a performance specification.*

The Carpet and Rug Institute has suggested that either a descriptive or performance specification be used when there is to be open bidding on carpet. Because the performance specification tells the manufacturer how the carpet must perform without setting restrictions on how the carpet must be made, the manufacturer is allowed to use the most recent technology and newly developed fibers to meet the performance requirements.

Because material technology is becoming increasingly complex, many designers may choose to use a combination of descriptive and performance specifications to assure that the requirements will be fulfilled by the best materials currently available.

4. *Reference standards* are frequently used in proprietary, descriptive, and performance specifications. Making reference to an established standard serves to clarify material, workmanship, or installation requirements. Though standards originate from reliable sources (see Chapter 3) and are widely known and accepted as a basis for performance evaluation, it should be remembered that many standards represent only minimum levels of performance. Before including a standard in a specification, the designer should become familiar with the entire contents and scope of the particular standard, understand how to incorporate it effectively, and know how to assure compliance with the standard.

The Construction Specifications Institute (CSI) offers the following guidelines for the use of standards in specifications.[6]

a. Make certain that all contractors associated with the project have access to copies of the latest edition of the standards. Copies may either be attached to the specifications or made available through the designer's office.

b. Be aware that some standards may present "hidden choices"; i.e., the material mentioned in the standard may be classed in one or more types, and each type may have different performance criteria.

c. Designers and specifiers should carefully examine the standard for requirements that may conflict with other more stringent requirements listed elsewhere in the specification. If conflicts or duplications are found to exist, a clause may be added to the specification which states that the more stringent requirement shall govern. It is recommended that in all cases of discrepancies between the specification and standards, the requirements of the specification shall remain in effect.

d. To properly incorporate the standard into a specification document, the standard must be listed by the full name and title, as well as the number and the approval date. If a standard is tentative (awaiting final acceptance by standards committees), it may be used as a reference, providing the designer lists it as "tentative" at the time the specifications are written. Contractors should be advised to refer to the latest edition of standards used in the specification.

e. Enforcement of the standard is accomplished through on-site inspections and careful analysis of prepared working drawings, samples, and established performance testing methods. Manufacturers should provide written proof of test results and construction processes required in the standard.

5. *Federal specifications* are developed for use by federal agencies to assure a uniformity throughout the governmental purchasing process. Because these specifications are written by experts in material technology and are frequently revised, they provide an excellent source of information for designers and specifiers. Designers will encounter four major types of governmental specifications: federal, interim federal, military, and departmental. Each type may be amended or revised whenever necessary, and when a federal agency identifies a particular need not covered by a current specification, an interim specification may be written. An Index of Federal Specifications identifies the specifications by letters and numbers.

The portion of the Federal Specifications reproduced in Figure 16.1 illustrates the classification and numbering system used for indexing. The letters and numbers found in the upper-right corner indicate the following:

DDD = The federal procurement group. These letters may appear in single, double, or triple form (the *same* letter is repeated).

   s = Represents the first letter of the item specified (shades).

251 = Serial number refers to the location in the procurement group.

   d = Designates that the specification has been revised four times. Each revision is given a letter symbol in alphabetic order.

The interim specification shown in Figure 16.2 is indexed in the following manner:

AA = Federal procurement group.
 V = First letter of the item specified (Venetian).

"OO" = These are used on all interim specifications. Placed on front of the serial number.

 B = Represents the second revision.

(GSA-FSS) = The agencies issuing the interim specification. (General Services Administration and the Federal Supply Service.)

Examples of proprietary, descriptive, and performance specifications are shown in Figures 16.3 through 16.5 on pages 252, 254, and 255. Tables 16.1 and 16.2 summarize the recommended usage of each specification type.

```
                        DDD-S-251d
                        April 13, 1966

                        SUPERSEDING
                        Fed. Spec. DDD-S-251c
                        July 12, 1962


        FEDERAL SPECIFICATION


   SHADE, ROLLER, WINDOW; ROLLER, SLAT,
        CORD, AND ACCESSORIES


 This specification was approved by the Commissioner,
 Federal Supply Services, General Services Administration,
 for the use of all Federal agencies.
```

Figure 16.1 *Coded indexing numbers on federal specifications. Source: GSA.*

```
                        AA-V-00200B(GSA-FSS)
                        June 5, 1973

                        INTERIM REVISION OF
                        Fed. Spec. AA-V-200A
                        November 6, 1965


   INTERIM FEDERAL SPECIFICATION

        VENETIAN BLINDS
```

Figure 16.2 *Coded indexing of interim federal specifications. Source: GSA.*

TABLE 16.1 RECOMMENDED USAGE OF EACH SPECIFICATION TYPE

Specification	Type		Recommended Use
A. Prescriptive			
	1. Proprietary Base Bid	a.	Used when the designer wishes to have complete control over the product selection.
		b.	Used in remodeling situations where exact colors and materials may have to be matched.
		c.	Recommended when exact dimensions must be used to clarify the design concept to the client.
		d.	Recommended when drawing, specification, and bidding procedures must be expedited due to project deadlines.
	Proprietary "Modified or Equal"	a.	Used when competitive bidding is required.
		b.	Used when designer is prepared to make informed decisions on alternate materials.
		c.	Recommended when adequate control can be placed on bidding periods and submittal requirements.
	2. Descriptive	a.	Used when no trade names are allowed. This is often the case in government building projects.
		b.	Recommended when a component or material is complex and requires detailed descriptive specification. Example: mechanical and electrical systems; carpet.
		c.	Used when performance specification are not feasible.
	3. Reference standards	a.	Recommended for use when the specifier wishes to write a less elaborate document through reference to standards.
		b.	Used when a widely acceptable and familiar reference is needed to expand or implement a descriptive, performance, or proprietary specification.
B. Non-Restrictive			
	1. Performance	a.	Used when trade names are not allowed.
		b.	Used when a designer has a unique design problem that may require an innovative new material or component. Example: ambient task lighting.
		c.	Recommended for use when the desired performance level can be evaluated by valid standards and testing methods.
		d.	Used when it is required that materials be selected on a performance basis.

TABLE 16.2 SPECIFICATION COMPARISONS

Prescriptive—Restrictive				Performance—Nonrestrictive	
Proprietary Base Bid	Proprietary or Equal	Descriptive	Reference Standards	Performance	Performance plus Descriptive
Part 2: Materials *Manufacturer:* Corporation A: Brand Name Style: #245 Cascade Color: 17849 *Base Bid:* When brand names are used no substitute products will be considered.	**Part 2: Materials** *Manufacturers:* Corporation A: Brand name Corporation B: Brand name Corporation C: Brand name *or* *Approved Equal* Proposed substitutions must be given complete consideration, statement of procedure for determining what is "equal" must be included. *or* *Modified or Approved Equal* (1) Required definite prebid deadline for submittal of request. (2) Federal, state or city projects require specifier to include salient characteristics of the item to provide a basis for judging equality.	**Part 2: Materials** *Carpet:* (no brand name) *Construction Type:* Tufted or other *Pile Yarn:* Generic *Gauge or Pitch* *Stitches per inch or Wires* *Pile Height or Wire Height* *Dyeing Method* *Yarn Size and Ply* *Width* *Pile Yarn Weight and Total Weight* *Primary and Secondary Backing* *Detailed Installation Information*	**Part 1: General** *Quality Assurance References:* ANSI A117.1-1986, "Specifications for Making Buildings and Facilities Accessible to, and Usable by, the Physically Handicapped." American National Standards Institute, 1430 Broadway, New York, NY 10018 (A-210, A-5-2.2.4a., A-8-4.5, A-10-1.1.2). NFPA 255-1984, "Standard Method of Test for Critical Radiant Heat Energy Source." National Fire Protection Association, Batterymarch Park, Quincy, MA 02269 (A-12-3.3.2)	**Subsystem: Carpet** *Attribute:* Fire Safety *Requirement:* Provide flame-spread resistance. *Criteria:* This subsystem shall provide a maximum flame-spread rating of 25. *Test: Type*—Calculation method ASTM-E 84, "Surface Burning Characteristics of Building Materials." American Society for Testing and Materials.	**Part 2: Materials** *Carpet Performance and Design Requirements:* Design carpet for the following conditions: 1. Maximum static electricity ... 2.5 Kv 2. Tuft bind to resist ...12 lbs/in. *Carpet Construction* Materials to conform to AATCC 134-1979, Electrostatic Propensity of Carpets. 2.5 Kv at 20% RH and 70° F.
These types of "closed" or restrictive specifications require exact products by brand name, model number, and all important characteristics. Quoted test data is supplied by the manufacturer. Drawings also show dimensions and engineering aspects of the particular product. Examples on pages 105, 107, and 139.	Descriptive: (1) Avoid conflicts with drawings. (2) Research all products. (3) Compare costs vs. performance. (4) State required submittals, including tests and standards. Reference: (1) Know the standard. Have a copy in designers' office files. (2) Avoid use of only minimum standards. (3) Use full names and dates of the referenced standards. (4) Enforce the requirements. Examples on pages 127 and 130.			Performance specifications: (1) Use no manufacturers or trade names. (2) Desired results are stated. (3) Method to achieve end result not included in document. Performance combination: Descriptive and reference standard specifications can produce nonrestrictive specifications. Only essential criteria that will meet intended use are stated. Specifier must ensure that criteria can be met by several manufacturers. See example on page 257.	

Specification concepts from The Construction Specification Institute "Methods of Specifying" MP-1-11, 1980.

SPECIFICATION LANGUAGE

Throughout this chapter specifications have been stressed as a means of communication. The general organization that is accomplished through divisions and sections is important, but if the written text is ambiguous or inadequate, the specification will not communicate.

The clarity of specifications depends on simple, direct statements, concise use of terms, and attention to grammar and punctuation. Specification sentences are usually structured in the indicative or imperative mood; in fact, the indicative mood is the traditional sentence structure found in most specifications. The imperative mood sentence begins with a verb, usually results in shorter sentences, and eliminates the repetitious use of "shall" in every sentence.

Indicative Mood
"The carpet shall be secured to the floor with adhesive."
"All soiled spots shall be removed from the surface."
"Materials shall be stored in an enclosed, dry area."

Imperative Mood
"Secure carpet to the floor with adhesive."
"Remove all soiled spots from the surface."
"Store materials in an enclosed, dry area."

Specification terminology must be carefully evaluated to avoid misunderstanding. Definitions of the following words should be considered:

Shall and Will: Often used incorrectly. "Shall" is used to designate a command; "will" implies a choice.

Either: If the specification states "either side of the column is to be painted," the contractor may assume that a choice may be made between either one side or the other.

Amount: "The amount of fabric." "Amount" is a term used to refer to money.

Quantity: "The quantity of fabric." "Quantity" refers to yardage and volume.

Any: "The Contractor shall assume the responsibility for *any* unacceptable work." This sentence implies that the contractor may select the work that is unacceptable.

All: "The Contractor shall assume the responsibility for *all* unacceptable work." This sentence leaves no doubt about the contractor's responsibility.

And/or: Avoid this word combination in specifications.

Etc.: Meaning: so forth. The implied uncertainty does not belong in a specification.

The Construction Specifications Institute recommends the following guidelines for the use of numerals in specification documents:

1. Numbers less than thirteen, such as twelve, ten, nine, five, one, should be written in words; higher numbers such as 15, 16, 20, should be in numerals.

2. Clock time and dates should be expressed in numerals, e.g., 2:10 P.M. or June 15, 1970.

3. Decimals should be expressed in numerals, e.g., 6.225. (For quantities less than one, a zero should be used before the decimal point.)

4. Numerals should be used for sums of money, e.g., $5.00.[7]

The following words should be capitalized when used in the specification document:

Agreement	Contractor	Client
Architect	Designer	Owner
Article	Engineer	Room Name
Clause	Government	Section
Contract	General Conditions	State

The designer should never underline anything in a specification because underling implies that the remaining material can be ignored.

SPECIFICATION SECTIONS FORMAT

The most widely accepted specification format was developed by the Construction Specifications Institute in 1969. The specification information is organized into a three part document. Part 1, General, describes the scope of the work necessary to accomplish the specification requirements. This part also states the requirements for delivery, job site conditions and so forth. Part 2, Products, provides information on the fabrication or manufacturing of materials and products required to fulfill the specification. Part 3, Execution, states the required quality of work in the preparation and installation of the specified materials and products.

Part 1: General

Description (scope)

Quality Assurance

Submittals

Product Delivery

Storage and Handling

Job Conditions

Alternatives

Guarantee

Part 2: Products

Manufactures

Materials

Mixes

Fabrication

Part 3: Execution

Inspection

Preparation

Installation

Application/Performance

Field Quality Control

Adjust and Clean

Protection

Schedules

*Figure 16.3 Specification
guide outline.*

SECTION

TITLE

PART 1   GENERAL

1.01   WORK INCLUDED

A.   This Article includes the scope of the work and the
     interrelationship between work in this Section and work in other
     Sections. Also includes definitions and options. For example,
     work includes the installation of carpet tiles.

1.02   RELATED WORK

A.   This includes work specified elsewhere in the specification
     documents. Do not include items that are not usually the work of
     this Section.

1.03   DESCRIPTION OF SYSTEM

A.   Only use this Section when specifying something that can be
     considered a system. Systems such as an integrated ceiling system
     or an open office system would qualify.

     ****
     Specifier Note: It is important that each subparagraph contain
     only one specific requirement or action. See A., B., C., below.
     ****

1.04   QUALITY ASSURANCE

A.   Paragraphs used to define qualifications of Contractors,
     Subcontractors, and Consultants.

B.   Standards and test requirements, such as codes that will be
     required in this interior project.

C.   Full size "mock-up" models of items for testing.

1.05   SUBMITTALS

A.   Details and instructions for submitting product samples, dye lot
     samples and other data to the Interior Designer for review. This
     can include warranties, certificates, and product information such
     as installation instructions.

1.06   DELIVERY, STORAGE AND HANDLING

A.   Instructions can include packing, delivery location within the
     project site, temperature control and protection of material after
     delivery.

1.07   PROJECT/SITE CONDITIONS

A.   Describe conditions that are required for the Contractor or
     installation crew to perform the installation. This can include
     temperature and use of necessary utilities. For example, all
     painting should be completed prior to carpet installation.

1.08   SEQUENCING AND SCHEDULING

A.   Use this section when specifying interior finishes or furnishings
     that require careful scheduling.

1.09   ALTERNATES

A.   Acceptable alternates are usually specified in the General
     Requirements of C.S.I. Section 01100. If Specifier is not writing
     a detailed Section, then it is permissible to describe
     alternatives here.

1.10   WARRANTY/GUARANTEE

A.   This Section usually lists warranties that will exceed one year.
     Request that Owner be provided with copies. Establish terms and
     definitions of the guarantee.

PART 2   PRODUCTS

2.01   MANUFACTURERS

A.   Use this section when writing a proprietary specification. List
     approved manufacturers.

B.   Coordinate this statement with Section 01455 that deals with
     Product Options and Substitutions.

2.02   MATERIALS/EQUIPMENT/FURNISHINGS

A.   List the materials to be used in a series of subheadings. When
     writing descriptive or performance specifications include
     performance criteria for materials, equipment or furnishings.

2.03   MIXES

A.   This Section details the proportions of materials that are
     required to mix a certain product on or off the building site.

2.04   FABRICATION

A.   This Section deals with the construction of the item specified.
     Section 2.02 would be used to list the components. For example, a
     carpet specification would state the yarn ply and other materials
     in 2.02.

B.   In this section specify construction details such as density,
     level loop, plush tufted, woven or fusion bonded.

PART 3   EXECUTION

3.01   INSPECTION

A.   Explain what the Contractor must require in the subsurface prior
     to installation. For example, the concrete inspection shall
     determine the appropriate moisture content prior to the
     installation of carpet or resilient flooring.

3.02   PREPARATION

A.   This section specifies the improvements necessary prior to
     installation. For example, concrete dampproofing or patching may
     be required before installation of interior floor finishes.

3.03   INSTALLATION/APPLICATION

A.   Specify the unique requirements of each interior finish or
     equipment.

B.   Specify the quality of work demanded in the installation.

3.04   FIELD QUALITY CONTROL

A.   State the tests and various inspection procedures used to
     determine the quality of the completed work.

3.05   ADJUST AND CLEAN

A.   Specify in detail the cleaning and adjustments that will be
     required. This includes the repair of scratches or marks "left"
     by the workers during installation.

B.   Furniture installation may require adjustments to desks or chairs.

3.06   PROTECTION

A.   This section may be used if the installation requires special
     protection for a length of time, such as a marble tile floor.
     This responsibility for protection from damage usually extends
     until acceptance by the Owner.

3.07   SCHEDULES

     This section may be used if required.

END OF SECTION

****
Specifier Note: Do not use any heading that does not apply.
Although specifications comply with a format, none are identical
in content. Although the same carpet may be specified, the
specification will require information unique to the particular
project environment, as well as the occupancy classification.
****

It is not necessary to list all section heading in each part. If a section such as "mixes" does not apply to an interior component, omit it. On the other hand, a section not shown here may be added. For example, a specifier may a add a section to Part 3 that would provide "Protection after Installation" for a marble floor.

The Specification Guide Outline (Figure 16.3) provides greater detail on the suggested content of each section in the three-part document. Figures 16.4 and 16.5 illustrate a sample specification format.

OFFICE MASTER SPECIFICATIONS

Office master specifications are well organized and comprehensively written. Instead of presenting the specifier with blanks to complete, alternative or optional choices are prewritten. The specification shown in Figure 10.7 illustrates the use of fabrication options. (See Section 2.03.)

Purposes and Advantages of Office Master Specifications

1) Reduce liability because errors and omissions frequently caused by oversights and wrong decisions can be prevented.

2) Increase efficiency and speed the preparation of project specifications.

3) Provide alternatives and options that increase more thoughtful creative material and product.

4) Can provide cost-saving quality assurance guidelines customized to your office standards. For example, special installation procedures based on previously experienced regional weather problems can prevent costly reinstallations.

5) Provide the office with a listing of applicable codes and standards for each generic material.

6) Reduces repetitive office specification work.

Disadvantages of Using Office Master Specifications

1) May foster a false sense of assurance that the specification is suitable for *all projects* without revisions. This, in turn, can expose a firm to liability factors inherent in every project.

2) Failure to update regularly.

3) Failure to correct information that may have caused bidding or installation problems on previous projects.

4) Failure to edit or delete outdated codes and standards.

5) Failure to add adequate data about newly marketed products or materials not known to the specifier. See guidelines for specification of new materials on page 264 in Chapter 17.

SPECIFICATION GUIDES

Specification guides may only contain minimum standards for material and installation quality control. Many are provided by private industry, trade associations, and manufacturers. Guides serve as "shell" outlines that require the knowledgeable specifier to link individual project requirements with detailed quality control. An example may be seen on page 173.

OPERATIONAL AND MAINTENANCE MANUALS

The collection of all technical data on the maintenance and operation of specified components could prevent costly repairs, improper operation, and client dissatisfaction with the entire project.

The specification of open office systems, for example, requires that a training manual be made available to the users of the space. In addition to written material, manufacturers may be required to conduct training sessions with the client and staff involved.

An operations and maintenance manual should include all the warranties or guarantees not covered by the standard contract documents. It should also include the servicing and precautions recommended by the manufacturer in order to keep the guarantees in force.

It is usually the duty of the owner to decide who will be responsible for assembling and writing the manual. The contractor often must supply part of the information, such as parts lists, name of nearest service dealer, and other necessary data. The designer usually assembles and writes the description of the system and sequence of preventive maintenance.

The manual should follow the following order:

Part 1. The general description of the items to be covered in the manual. This should also include names and addresses of the contractors involved, the suppliers, and the dates that use and maintenance will begin. The example given below illustrates how the information may be organized.

Carpet
1. General description:
    a. Approximate area _____
    b. Carpet type _____
    c. Manufacturer _____

2. Construction contractor requirements after acceptance:
    a. Contractor to guarantee installation for a period of one year after work acceptance.

3. Owner begins maintenance:
    a. Anticipated date _____
    b. Actual date _____

4. Names, addresses, and telephone numbers of contractors, suppliers, and installers:
    a. Carpet supplier_____
       Address _____
       Telephone number _____
    b. Installation contractor _____
       Address _____
       Telephone number _____

5. Names, addresses, and telephone numbers of other contacts for advice:
    a. Carpet manufacturer representative _____
       Address _____
       Telephone number _____
    b. Interior designer _____
       Address _____
       Telephone number _____

Part 2. Detailed information on the operation and maintenance of the items contained in the manual.

Figure 16.4 Sample specification format. Reproduced with permission of the Construction Specifications Institute.

Unbound margin ½ inch ————

Top margin minimum ½ inch to ¾ inch

Section (in all capitals) with the appropriate 5-digit number centered on the page

Fully spelled out section title in all capitals centered on page separated from section number by one blank line

Optional indication of master text source document

Separate part designation from section title with two blank lines

Part designation, all capitals, flush left

Separate article heading from part designation with one blank line

Article heading, all capitals, never followed on the same line with text

Separate article heading from paragraph with one blank line

Sublevels of paragraphs stacked with no space between

One paragraph or subparagraph may be submitted under a heading

Separate paragraphs from each other with one blank line

Separate part designation from item above with two blank lines

Bound side margin minimum ¾ inch to 1-¼ inches depending on type of binding

Optional project date on bound edge at page bottom

Bottom margin minimum ½ inch to ¾ inch

5-digit section number with hyphen and sequential section page number

Optional project identification number on unbound edge at page bottom

Optional sequential project manual page number preceded by the word "page" on the unbound edge at page bottom

Begin each section on a right hand page

DEC75   SECTION 06100
                                   ROUGH CARPENTRY

PART 1 - GENERAL

1.01   DESCRIPTION

        A.   Related Work Specified Elsewhere:
             1.   Wood Forms: Section 03110.
             2.   Finish Carpentry: Section 06200.
             3.   Building Insulation: Section 07210.
             4.   Gypsum Wallboard: Section 09250
             5.   Painting: Section 09900.

        B.   Work Installed but Furnished by Others:
             1.   Steel splice plates in Structural Steel: Section 05120.

1.02   QUALITY ASSURANCE

        A.   Lumber grading rules and wood species: U.S. Department of Commerce
             PS 20-70.

        B.   Plywood grading rules: U.S. Department of Commerce PS 1-66.

1.03   SUBMITTALS

        A.   Samples: Two pieces 6 in. in length of wood decking which will be
             exposed in finished work, showing face texture and color of materi-
             al.

        B.   Shop Drawings for trusses only: Indicate framing connection details,
             fastener connections, and dimensions.

PART 2 - PRODUCTS

2.01   STRUCTURAL LIGHT FRAMING

        A.   For studs and plates 2 in. to 4 in. thick, 2 in. to 4 in. wide.

        B.   Allowable extreme stress in bending (Fb): 600 psi.

        C.   Modulus of elasticity (E): 1 400 000 psi.

        D.   Maximum moisture content 19%.

        E.   Dense Douglas Fir, Dense Southern Yellow Pine, or MG (medium grain)
             Southern Yellow Pine.

2.02   STRUCTURAL JOISTS AND PLANKS

        A.   2 in. to 4 in. thick, 6 in. and wider with mill stamp on each piece.

        B.   Allowable extreme stress in bending (Fb): 1350 psi.

10 JUN 75   06100 - 1   7508
                                                                        Page 86

Figure 16.5 Sample specification format. Reproduced with permission of the Construction Specifications Institute.

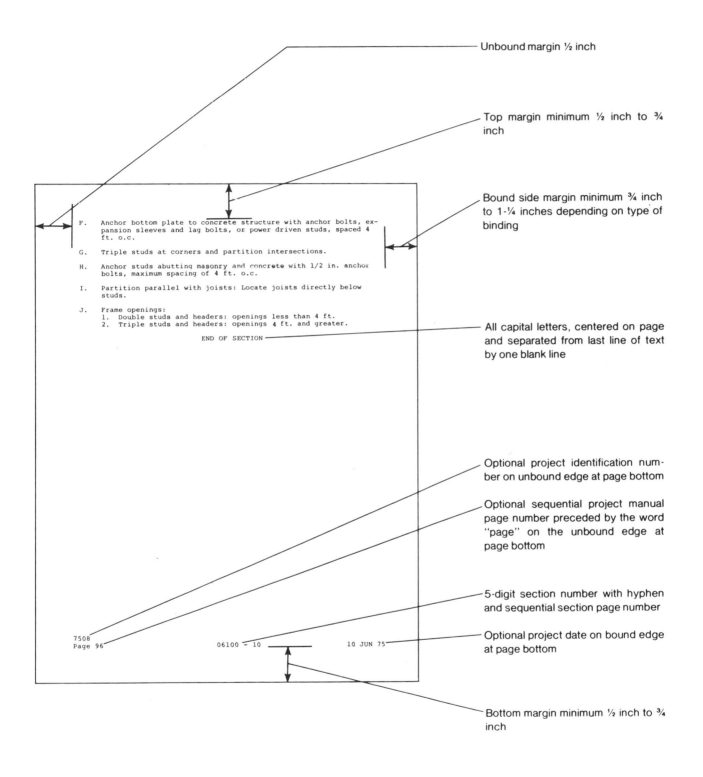

Unbound margin ½ inch

Top margin minimum ½ inch to ¾ inch

Bound side margin minimum ¾ inch to 1-¼ inches depending on type of binding

All capital letters, centered on page and separated from last line of text by one blank line

Optional project identification number on unbound edge at page bottom

Optional sequential project manual page number preceded by the word "page" on the unbound edge at page bottom

5-digit section number with hyphen and sequential section page number

Optional project date on bound edge at page bottom

Bottom margin minimum ½ inch to ¾ inch

SUMMARY AND GENERAL GUIDELINES

The following recommendations may serve as a checklist listing the preparation of specifications:

1. Inform all project personnel concerning the proposed content of the specifications while the project drawings are being prepared. This will improve their understanding about the nature of the specifications and how they relate to the design requirements and the working drawings.

The information contained in the specification must be assembled and coordinated with the drawings early in the design process. As the work on the project proceeds, the designer may use several methods to assemble and organize the material that will later become a part of the specification.

This list may be organized by spatial areas of the project, such as lobby or executive offices, or on the CSI construction filing system, which is explained in Chapter 18.

Specification Checklist (Partial)
Division 6: Wood and Plaster
a. Millwork:
    _____Paneling
    _____Prefinished
    _____Natural hardwood
    _____Paint grade wood
b. Casework (AWI):
    _____Premium grade
    _____Custom grade
    _____Economy grade
    Face Frame:
    _____Lipped
    _____Flush overlay
    _____Reveal overlay

Construction Type:
    _____Exposed face frame
    _____Flush
    _____Exposed

Division 9: Finishes
a. Floor Tile:
    _____Unglazed
    _____Natural clay
    _____Mosaics
    _____Quarry tile
    _____Glazed
b. Resilient Flooring:
    _____ Vinyl asbestos tile
        Thickness: $\frac{1}{16}$" _____$\frac{3}{32}$" _____$\frac{1}{8}$" _____
        Size: 9" × 9" _____12" × 12" _____
    _____ Vinyl coated wood
    _____ Vinyl coated cork
c. Wallcovering
    _____Vinyl, Type I _____Type II _____Type III _____
    _____Fabric
    _____Vinyl-coated paper

2. Coordinate the preparation of the drawings and specifications throughout the construction phase so there will be no gaps in documentation and minimum overlapping of data.

3. *Begin preparing the specifications when work on the drawings is begun. Do not wait until the drawings are virtually complete.*

4. Do not "over" specify or "under" specify. Use just the right amount of text to communicate project requirements to the contractor.

Figure 16.6 Performance specification: GSA space divider subsystem.

E   PERFORMANCE SPECIFICATION
7   SPACE DIVIDER SUBSYSTEM

---

b   SUBSYSTEM ATTRIBUTES

---

c) attribute: ACOUSTICS

REQUIREMENT: (1) Control airborne sound transmission.

Criteria: (a) Provide Speech Privacy Potential (SPP) of no less than 60 in the open plan areas of the Typical Office Space. Utilize 60" height system screens and system carpet.

Test: Type - System Prototype/System Field
Method - PBS-C.1

Criteria: (b) Criterion (a) above shall be met if the sum of the speech privacy Noise Isolation Class (NIC) plus a compatible NC-Background of 40 shall be no less than 60.

Test: Type - System Prototype/System Field
Method - PBS-C.2

Criteria: (c) Provide Speech Privacy Potential (SPP) of no less than 70 between any two adjacent rooms without interconnecting doors. Utilize system carpet and opaque partition (A70).

Test: Type - System Prototype/System Field
Method - PBS-C.1

Criteria: (d) Criterion (c) above shall be met if the sum of the speech privacy Noise Isolation Class (NIC) plus a compatible NC-Background of 35 shall be no less than 70.

Test: Type - System Prototype/System Field
Method - PBS-C.2

Criteria: (e) Provide Speech Privacy Potential (SPP) of no less than 60 between any two adjacent rooms without interconnecting doors. Utilize system carpet and opaque partition (A60).

Test: Type - System Prototype/System Field
Method - PBS-C.1

Criteria: (f) Criterion (e) above shall be met if the sum of the speech privacy Noise Isolation Class (NIC) plus a compatible NC-Background of 35 shall be no less than 60.

REQUIREMENT: (2) Control impact sound transmission.

Criteria: (a) Footstep sounds transmitted to rooms located directly below shall be masked by an NC-Background not greater than 40. The system shall have the capability of masking footfall sounds transmitted to rooms located directly below with an NC-Background not greater than 35.

Test: Type - System Prototype/System Field
Method - Impact Sound Transmission Test by Footfall Method, IBI-1-I, 1965
Modification - The Offerer shall propose modifications to test method for prototype and field application in his Technical Proposal; use male walker with metal-tipped heels in addition to specified female walker.

Criteria: (b) Door slam sounds in this subsystem, transmitted to rooms contiguous vertically and horizontally shall be masked by an NC-Background not greater than 40. A door shall not occur in the partition between the contiguous rooms.

Test: Type - System Prototype/System Field
Method - The Offerer shall submit test in his Technical Proposal. Door slam shall be in accordance with PBS d.1.

REQUIREMENT: (1) Provide resistance to horizontal loads.

Criteria: (a) This subsystem's partitions and screens in use shall resist a uniformly distributed horizontal load of 5 pounds per square foot with no damage to this or any other subsystem. The maximum deflection of a partition under load shall not exceed 0.25 inches. Screens may move horizontally but shall not overturn.

Test: Type - System Prototype
Method - ASTM E 72-68, Section 10
Modification - Apply load to a specimen 5' in length with no abutting partitions. Install and support in the Prototype as in use.

Criteria: (b) This subsystem's partitions in use shall resist a horizontal concentrated load of 50 pounds applied through a 1" diameter disc at the weakest point on the surface on either side, perpendicular to the faces, with the average residual indentation not exceeding 0.030". The average applied concentrated load to produce structural failure of the surface shall be not less than 150 pounds.

Test: Type - System Prototype
Method - ASTM E 72-68, Section 11
Modification - Apply load to a specimen 5 feet in length with no abutting partitions which shall be installed and supported in the prototype as in use. The load shall be applied 3 times. The rate of loading shall be such that the load is attained in not less than 1 minute nor more than 2 minutes.

Criteria: (c) No part of this subsystem or any other subsystem supported by this subsystem shall separate from its supports, fail, or cause failure in a manner that will endanger occupants, when subjected to seismic forces, as specified in the GSA Handbook, "Structural Engineering."

(d) This subsystem, in addition to resisting the seismic forces as specified above in the Project Buildings, shall be capable of resisting seismic forces similarly at any location in the 50 states as specified in the above handbook.

Test: Type - Subsystem
Method - Calculation/Structural Analysis
Modification - The coefficient "Z" shall be 1.5 instead of 1.0 for earthquake zone 3.

Criteria: (e) This subsystem's freestanding screens, in use, with or without bookshelf loading, shall resist an overturning force of 25 pounds perpendicular to its face. Horizontal movement but no overturning shall be allowed.

Test: Type - System Prototype
Method - Apply a horizontal force of 25 pounds perpendicular to the face of a freestanding screen 5'-0" long. Load shall be applied through a 1" diameter disc at one edge of the screen 5'-0" above finished floor. Perform the test 3 times on a screen without bookshelf. Repeat the test 3 times on a screen with a bookshelf attached to one side only loaded with 40 pounds per linear foot. Load shall be applied to face opposite book shelf.

REQUIREMENT: (2) Provide resistance to impact.

Criteria: (a) This subsystem's partitions and screens in use shall resist an impact of 30 foot-pounds with no damage to the surface or other part of this or any other subsystem. Displacement of this subsystem or any other subsystem, when measured immediately after impact, shall not exceed the accepted tolerance limits for that subsystem or any other subsystem. Maximum displacement measured at the time of impact shall not exceed ¼". Screens may overturn but shall not be damaged.

Test: Type - System Prototype
Method - Strength Test of Panels/ASTM E 72-68, Section 13
Modification - Apply impact 5 times to partition specimens 5 and 20 linear feet in length with no abutting partitions and to a specimen 5 linear feet in length abutted at both ends, all of which shall be installed and supported in the prototype as in use, and report all damages in the prototype; apply impact to specimen at lines of supports and half-way between supports. Apply impact 5 times at the center of a free-standing Type B screen 60" long.

Criteria: (b)   No part of this subsystem or any other subsystem shall be damaged or have a displacement measured during and immediately after each door slam exceeding the specified tolerance limits for this subsystem.

Test: Type - System Prototype
Method - Door Slam PBS - d.1
Modification - Slam door located in center of a space divider with none abutting it for at least 30' of its length. Door shall be slammed with a force of 17 foot-pounds. Door shall swing through an angle of 30 degrees.

REQUIREMENT: (3) Provide resistance to point impact.

Criteria: Any component part of this subsystem, one surface of which is exposed to view, shall withstand 9 inch-pounds of impact on its exposed surface without any indentation greater than 1/16 inch measured 24 hours after impact, and without any splitting, cracking, or other permanent damage.

Test: Type - Subsystem
Method - Falling Ball Impact, Fed. Test Method Std. No. 406, Method 1074
Modification - Use ½-pound ball at 18".

Figure 16.6 continued

REQUIREMENT: (4) <u>Provide resistance to racking force.</u>

Criteria: Freestanding screens shall support a concentrated load of 15 pounds applied perpendicular to its face 5'-0" above the finished floor at an end. The screen shall sustain 200 cycles of loading and unloading without delaminating, cracking, taking permanent set, or sustaining other damages.

Test: Type - Subsystem
Method - Load one vertical edge of freestanding screen 5'-0" above finished floor with a 15-pound horizontal force perpendicular to its face. Fix the base of screen to the floor. Repeat load/unload cycle 200 times. Report damage or permanent set.

REQUIREMENT: (5) <u>Provide support for attached loads.</u>

Criteria: This subsystem's screens, in use, shall support the load of 40 pounds per linear foot of shelf imposed on book shelves specified as a capability by this subsystem. Screens shall support loaded shelves on one or both faces of the screen. Any displacement of surface shall be within tolerances specified for this subsystem.

Test: Type - Subsystem
Method - The Offerer shall propose test.

REQUIREMENT: (6) <u>Provide resistance to vertical loading.</u>

Criteria: This subsystem's mechanical unit enclosures shall support without damage a vertical load of 50 pounds per square foot with a 250-pound concentrated load at any point with deflection within this subsystem's specified tolerances.

Test: Type - System Prototype
Method - Load mechanical unit enclosure with 50 pounds per square foot and with a 250-pound concentrated load distributed over an area of one square foot located in the center span. Measure and report deflection.

REQUIREMENT: (7) <u>Control friability.</u>

Criteria: (a) Any component part of this subsystem constructed with acoustically absorbent material shall not lose more than 50% in weight in 10 minutes.

Test: Type - Subsystem
Method - ASTM C 367, Paragraphs 7-12, Strength Properties of Acoustical Materials
Modification - 4 of the specimens tested shall be edge pieces, 10 minutes.

REQUIREMENT: (8) <u>Provide cohesive strength of laminated surfaces.</u>

Criteria: Any component part of this subsystem's partitions and screens shall withstand a tensile force of 2 PSI applied normal to any face or surface with no delamination and no more than 1/8" increase in thickness measured 10 minutes after the force is removed. Surfaces designed to be acoustically absorbent are excepted.

Test: Type - Subsystem
Method - PBS-d.2

REQUIREMENT: (9) <u>Provide cohesion/adhesion of surface coatings.</u>

Criteria: All coatings under 0.005 inches thick on exposed surfaces of this subsystem shall not delaminate.

Test: Type - Subsystem
Method - PBS-d.4

REQUIREMENT: (10) <u>Control surface color stability.</u>

Criteria: (a) The exposed surface of this subsystem, in use, when compared with the reference samples and with any other specimen subjected to this test, shall not differ in color by more than 3 NBS units or by more than color tolerances proposed for the system and approved in the Prototype, whichever is greater. Variegated, irregular, or translucent finishes shall be evaluated visually for acceptability of color change.

(b) The exposed surface of this subsystem in use shall not exhibit any form of cracking, crazing, splitting, spalling, blisters, delaminations, breaks, discontinuities, or other form of surface deterioration when evaluated visually, subject to review by the Contracting Officer.

Test: Type - Subsystem
Method - Colorfastness to Light, Fed. Std. No. 501A, Method 5421
Modification - Exposure time shall be 40 standard fading hours; use 3 samples for each color or texture; samples shall include joints and seams if the design calls for them. Colorimetric evaluation shall be by Fed. Test Method Std. No. 141A, Method 6123; all visual evaluations shall be made from a distance of 36" at any angle, with the sample illuminated as in use, and shall be subject to the approval of the Contracting Officer.

REQUIREMENT: (11) <u>Provide resistance to abrasion.</u>

Criteria: Exposed surfaces of this subsystem shall lose no more than 250 milligrams per 1000 revolutions. If vinyl is proposed, no exposure of the backing material shall occur.

Test: Type - Subsystem
Method - Fed. Test Method No. 406; Method 1091, Abrasion Test for Surfaces Over 1/16" Thick
Modification - Use CS 10 wheel; Paragraph 4.E does not apply.

Method - Fed. Test Method No. 141a; Method 6192, Abrasion Test for Surfaces Less than 1/16" Thick

Modification - Use CS 10 wheel; 1000 gram load, 1000 revolutions.
Method - ASTM-D-1175-71, Abrasion Test for Textile Surfaces; use rotary platform doublehead abraser; 1000 gram load; H 18 wheel; 1000 revolutions.

REQUIREMENT: <u>Provide fire safety.</u>

Criteria: (a) This subsystem shall have a maximum flame-spread rating of 25.

(b) If a fully automatic fire protection sprinkler system is provided as part of the system, as specified in the Structure Subsystem, the flame-spread rating shall not exceed 200.

Test: Type - Subsystem
Method - ASTM E 84, Surface Burning Characteristics of Building Materials

Criteria: (c) The maximum specific optical density shall not exceed 150 when tested under both flaming and nonflaming conditions of burning.

(d) The critical specific optical density of 16 shall not be reached under less than 30 seconds in both flaming and nonflaming conditions of burning.

Test: Type - Subsystem
Method - Interlaboratory Evaluation of Smoke Chamber, National Bureau of Standards Technical Note 708

Criteria: (e) This subsystem shall not have a potential heat of more than 40,000 BTU per linear foot of horizontal projection, except that if a fully automatic fire protection sprinkler system is provided as a part of the system as specified in the Structure Subsystem, there shall be no limitation on the potential heat.

Test: Type - Subsystem
Method - Proceedings of ASTM, Vol. 61, 1961, pp. 1337-1347

REQUIREMENT: (1) <u>Provide stain resistance.</u>

Criteria: (a) Stains of the following types shall not be visually evident on the exposed surface of this system after cleaning. Evaluation shall be subject to the approval of the Contracting Officer.

Pencil or graphite dust
Coffee
Tea
Milk
Cold drinks and carbonated beverages
Chalk
Heel marks
Ten weight motor oil

Criteria: (b) Stains of the following types shall be removed with only a slightly visible trace remaining after cleaning. Evaluation shall be subject to the approval of the Contracting Officer. Surfaces designed to be acoustically absorbent are excepted.

Grease pencil
Ballpoint pen ink
Water-based marker ink

Figure 16.6 continued

Test: Type - Subsystem
         Method - PBS-F.2
         Modification - Stains shall be removed using methods and
         agents proposed by the Offerer.

REQUIREMENT: (2) Provide chemical resistance.

Criteria: (a) The exposed surface of this subsystem in use when
compared with the reference samples and with any other
specimen subjected to this test shall not differ in color
by more than 3 NBS units. Variegated, irregular, or
translucent finishes shall be evaluated visually for
acceptability of color change. Surfaces designed to be
acoustically absorbent are excepted.

Criteria: (b) The exposed surface of this subsystem in use shall not
exhibit any form of cracking, crazing, splitting, spalling,
blisters, delaminations, breaks, discontinuities, or other
form of surface deterioration when evaluated visually,
subject to review by the Contracting Officer.

(c) The component parts of this subsystem, the surface of
which is exposed in use, shall not change in dimension
sufficiently to impair the specified performance of the
system in use.

Test: Type - Subsystem
Method - Spotting Resistance, Federal Test Method Std. No.
141A, Method 6081
Modifications - Use 60-minute exposure time; apply over
joints, if applicable. Use the following reagents in
accordance with ASTM D 543-67: distilled water (15),
detergent solution (12), soap solution (37), and any
additional cleaning agents specified in the maintenance
manual. Colorimetric evaluation shall be Fed. Test Method
Std. No 141A, Method 6123; all visual evaluations shall be
made from a distance of 36" at any angle, with the sample
illuminated as in use, and shall be subject to the approval
of the Contracting Officer.

CONCEPTS OF PERFORMANCE EVALUATION

After a review of the various liability factors, codes, regulations, and standards that are a vital part of professional practice today, the importance of knowing more about material performance and specification becomes increasingly evident. As professional designers, we are obligated to research, assimilate, and apply current material evaluation methods. Keeping pace with advances in material technology involves understanding human behavioral and physical needs, energy conservation, health and safety factors, economic feasibility, and functional effectiveness.

During the past decade, design education has primarily stressed the programming and developmental stages of the design process while often neglecting to provide the information necessary to transform design concepts into reality through *knowledgeable specification of material components.* As a result many designers are facing the increasingly difficult task of material quality control with little training in the area of material technology. This fact was verified in a survey conducted by the Cooper-Hewitt Museum. In order to determine the feasibility of a design data bank, researchers asked practicing designers what information they most frequently needed. The results showed that material and product information were the two highest ranking concerns.

Architects	Building materials	74.3%
	Product information	72.1%
Interior designers/ space planners	Product information	98.7%
	Materials systems	73.2%

In many design offices, material selection and evaluation are often based on past experience with a particular material component. Information from trade journals, manufacturers' representatives, and advertisements also serve as another basis for selection. On other occasions, decisions may be based on minimum performance requirements set forth in local codes and standards. All these methods have some degree of validity, but represent a disorganized approach to a very serious aspect of the design process. Moreover, none of these methods provides a basis for evaluating new materials or subsystems that are constantly being produced.

SPECIFICATION OF NEW MATERIAL: LIABILITIES

The Office of Professional Liability Research, a division of Victor O. Schinnerer & Company, cited the following claim as an example of the consequences that can occur when specifications are prepared by a design professional who does not fully comprehend the characteristics of the material which he or she specified. Acting on a recommendation from the school district for which he was designing a school and gymnasium, a designer contacted a floor products company and received information in the form of advertising literature describing a particular sealant and finish for the gym floor. He also received a list of "satisfied customers." Since the school district had successfully used this particular product to refinish old gymnasium floors, the designer did not investigate any further into the properties of the finish or its compatibility with new floors,

but relied on the experience of the school district and the advertising literature in specifying the same sealant and finish for the new gym floor.

Several months after the sealant had been applied, the gymnasium floor began to buckle and crack. A subsequent investigation by a testing company and an expert on wood technology and utilization revealed that the specified finish possessed a peculiar adhesive effect, which had caused the wood strips to become glued together. In the process of shrinking, the individual strips acted in the aggregate, causing rupture and buckling at those joints which were the weakest. The conclusion was that while the sealant and finish were an excellent choice for older gym floors which had settled and shrunk, it should have never been used on new floors. The entire gymnasium floor had to be replaced at a cost of $34,000. If the specifier had adequately researched and fully understood the characteristics of the material he had specified, the claim probably would not have resulted.

An article by attorney John S. Martel that appeared in *Guidelines for Improved Practice* further advises that "whenever a designer abandons a proven product in favor of a new product [see Glossary, at the end of this chapter], however justified the reason, the designer may be exposing himself to potential claims and lawsuits if the new product fails.

"When claims do arise from the failure of new products, the injured party may, and usually does, seek relief from the person who specified the product, the person who installed the product (the general contractor or subcontractor, or both), and the manufacturer of the product. If the injured party is the owner, he falls back on his own inexperience in construction matters and stresses his reliance on the expertise of his design professional. The contractor typically defends against such a claim by contending that he was never very enthusiastic about the specification, but nevertheless faithfully followed the plans and specifications provided by the designer in accordance with his contractual obligation. The manufacturer predictably contends that the product was not intended to be used in the manner specified by the design professional or that the new product must not have been applied as specified.

"Thus embattled on three fronts, the design professional is challenged with two basic allegations: (1) that he negligently selected or specified the new product, and (2) that he negligently 'supervised' the contractor's application of the new product."[1] Recommendations regarding procedures for the specification of new products will be found in Chapter 16.

Legally, the design professional is expected to use reasonable diligence and be informed about the latest developments in the profession. A designer's reliance on previous specifications would not constitute "reasonable diligence" under the applicable standard of "professional care," i.e., failure to "use the care ordinarily exercised in like cases by reputable members of his profession . . . and to use reasonable diligence and his best judgment in the exercise of his skill and the application of his learning, in an effort to accomplish the purpose for which he is employed."[2]

In order to avoid charges of negligence in the selection of material components, a rational and systematic method of accumulating information is badly needed. The approach employed should provide not only a basis for predicting material *performance*, but also a method of *documenting* a designer's "diligence" in accumulating information.

THE PERFORMANCE SYSTEMS APPROACH

A possible solution to the complicated problem of material evaluation and the need for a systematic approach to quality control was addressed at a 1972 international symposium jointly sponsored by the International Union of Testing and Research for Materials and Structures (RILEM), The American Society for Testing and Materials (ASTM), and the International Council for Building Research Studies and Documentation (CIB). The conference theme was "The Performance Concept in Buildings," and participants explored the areas of user requirements, design procedures, and methods of evaluating materials through performance requirements. Prior to and since this conference there has been much written about performance and systems concepts in relation to the design process.

Before evaluating the usefulness of these concepts in regard to material selection and specification, it is important to clarify their distinct differences and examine the advantages and disadvantages of their use. John Vilett, an architect and participant in the 1972 conference, pointed out that the widespread interest in the application of these concepts had resulted in some semantic confusion, and in common usage the performance and systems concepts are often considered inseparable or even synonymous.

We often refer to the performance of a single component or the performance of an entire system, which perhaps results in some confusion in terminology. Vilett cited this example: "One can speak of the performance of the entire building industry in terms of production rates, environmental quality, and provision of employment or one can also speak of the performance of a nail in terms of withdrawal resistance, shear strength, and corrosive resistance. The systems concept, however, is usually applied only to the larger scale of reference. Thus, the entire building industry can and should be viewed as a system, whereas a nail, although certainly a component of many building systems is not itself a system in any meaningful sense."[3]

The systems concept, on the one hand, emphasizes the whole rather than the parts. Emphasis is placed on the *interaction* between the components within the total system. *System analysis* is used to measure, identify, and control various kinds of interaction within the whole. The performance concept, on the other hand, is relevant to problems associated with *individual components* which have measurable physical properties and which have a direct influence on the users' environment. The emphasis is placed on the characteristics that a certain product or component must have, without making reference to how these characteristics are to be produced.

There may be situations and problems which call for the use of both the performance and systems approaches. For example, one might consider carpet a system made up of components such as yarn, latex, primary and secondary backing. An individual component of this carpet system could be evaluated in terms of performance; i.e., a careful analysis could be made of measurable qualities such as the physical strength, moisture retention, and abrasion resistance of the yarn. However, when the carpet is installed in a building it becomes a subsystem, or component, of the building and may require an additional systems analysis. If an evaluation of the acoustic performance of the installed carpet is required, one would have to identify, control, and measure the various kinds of acoustic interaction between the carpet, walls, and ceiling surfaces that are involved in shaping the total acoustic environment. (See Chapter 7.)

This example illustrates the fact that the performance and systems concepts actually complement each other and are often used in combination.

Although the performance concept was evolved for use in industry, its application to the areas of building and design has provided some useful means of informational processing for the designer. Designers are familiar with performance codes, standards, performance specifications, the last of which are treated in this book in Chapter 16. In addition, most designers are currently using some of the preliminary phases of the performance approach in their daily practice. The definition of the design problem and the analysis of user requirements are methods used in most design approaches. To further implement and expand the designer's ability to evaluate materials, the performance approach offers additional methods of evaluation and documentation such as (1) establishment of performance attributes, (2) determination of material performance requirements, and (3) verification of material performance through various testing methods.

Phase 1: User Requirements and Performance Attributes

The first and most important consideration in the development of performance requirements for materials is the determination of the user needs. The performance requirement takes the form of a qualitative statement which identifies user needs through investigative methods based on the following questions:

Who is the user?

What are the user's needs?

Where do the needs exist?

When and for how long do the needs exist?

Performance attributes, or criteria, define the required health/safety, economic, and functional levels of performance which relate to the user's requirements. The performance attributes (Table 17.1) summarize the major areas of performance criteria that frequently result from a study of user requirements. Note that the criteria state the desired performance without establishing constraints on the methods used to accomplish the desired result.

Health/Safety Attributes. The major concern of the health/safety criteria is to provide protection from personal injury or death. These attributes impose the following component requirements:

1. Provide protection through the specification of materials that will not contribute to the spread of fire.

2. Provide surfaces that will not result in falls or injury from sharp projections.

3. Provide materials that possess azotic properties which will not produce or retain odors nor be subject to verminal and organic deterioration. The material shall not support the growth of organism. (This is particularly important in health-care and food-service facilities.)

4. Provide furnishings designed for human dimensions (anthropomorphic fit) and not impair use by humans.

5. Provide illumination that will not produce glare on work surfaces and work areas.

TABLE 17.1   PERFORMANCE ATTRIBUTES*

| Health/Safety | Economic Effectiveness | | Functional Effectiveness |
	Durability/Stability	Maintenance	

1. Provide protection from personal injury and death:
  a. Fire
  b. Falls
  c. Azotic properties
  d. Sharp projections
 	
2. Provide anthropomorphic fit
 	
3. Provide glare-free illumination of worksurfaces and work area
 	
4. Provide acceptable reflectance levels
 	
5. Provide for use and make accessible to physically handicapped people
	1. Provide structurally sound components
	
	2. Provide resistance to tipping
	
	3. Provide resistance to damage
	
	4. Provide positive attachment of components
	  a. Resist vibration
	
	5. Provide color stability
	  a. Lightfastness
	  b. Crockfastness
		1. Provide ease of maintenance and cleanability; stain resistance
		
		2. Provide ease of component replacement
		  a. Upholstery
		  b. Luminaires
		  c. Telephones
		
		3. Provide for east of component storage and assembly
		
		4. Relocation does not impair performance of system
			1. Provide for flexibility of modification
			
			2. Provide components that meet modular tolerances of the space
			
			3. Provide components that address *psychological* and *aesthetic* needs of the user:
			  a. Privacy
			  b. Sense of place
			  c. Color homogeneity
			  d. Visual compatibility
			  e. Appearance control
			
			4. Provide acoustical control
			  a. Airborne sound
			  b. Speech privacy potential
			  c. Impact sound transmission
			  d. Control sound generation
			
			5. Provide thermal control
			  a. Energy conservation

* These attributes are general in scope and do not represent any particular project.

6. Provide components that will have acceptable reflectance levels. This includes walls, floors, and furniture surfaces.

7. Provide components that allow accessibility to all physically disabled people (see Chapter 14 for more details on specification requirements for handicapped or physically disabled people).

Economic Feasibility Attributes.   Economic considerations include (1) durability and stability and (2) operational and maintenance factors that represent the user's intermediate and long-range requirements.

Durability and stability:

1. Provide components that are structurally sound.

2. Provide furnishings and wall dividers that will resist tipping.

3. Provide positive and firm attachment of components that will prevent vibration.

4. Provide components that will maintain color stability and resist fading, crocking, and abrasion.

Operational and maintenance factors:

1. Provide components that will permit ease of maintenance.

2. Provide components that will not involve costly operational methods. This includes replacement of upholstery, luminaries, and relocation of office systems.

3. Provide components that will not involve costly storage and reassembly problems.

4. Provide components that can meet requirements of relocation without impairing performance. This is particularly important in furniture systems.

Functional Effectiveness Attributes.   This category includes some criteria that could possibly be included in the category of health and safety. For example, acoustic control of the environment may be considered vital to health as well as a functional requirement.

1. Provide components that allow flexible modification.

2. Provide components that meet modular tolerance of the space and are capable of interfacing with other components. Many commercial spaces are designed on modular grids, and components should be adaptable in size and scale.

3. Provide components that address psychological and aesthetic needs of the users. Components should provide a degree of privacy and allow the user to establish personal identity within the space—a sense of place. Components should also provide for appearance control when interfacing with other components through color homogeneity and visual and geometric compatibility.

4. Provide components that will aid in controlling impact and airborne sound. Components should control sound generation and provide speech privacy potential in open and closed spaces.

5. Provide components that include thermal control and energy conservation.

Phase 2: Determining Material Performance Requirements

After the performance attributes have been established for a particular project, the designer may proceed to evaluate individual materials and components in relation to the established user requirements. A sample matrix of components and performance attributes is shown in Figure 17.1. The matrix provides a simple systematic method for accomplishing this evaluation. The process of selecting materials and components to be included on the matrix is usually based on the following factors:

1. Components that make up a large percentage of the project cost may benefit from a thorough, careful performance evaluation.

2. Components that present the potential for technical improvement may be included.

3. Components that have a direct impact on the user's working environment in terms of his or her ability to be comfortable and productive. For interior specification purposes this means interior surfaces, finishes, and furnishing components that *directly interface* with the user.

The sample matrix (Figure 17.1) illustrates that a performance requirement is established each time a component and attribute intercept (see Glossary at the end of this chapter) on the matrix. For example, it becomes clear that almost all the components are required to provide fire safety, but the performance requirement for storage primarily involves furnishings.

The designer considering a component for specification now has a more systematic and rational basis for evaluating performance and establishing preliminary performance and specification checklists.

Phase 3: Proof of Material Performance

At the completion of phase 2 the designer may decide to evaluate two or more particular components in relation to the established performance requirements. If it appears that one of the components meets the necessary criteria, then the problem of verifying the performance claims made by the manufacturer must be considered. The designer can require special performance tests (see Glossary at the end of this chapter) or use those that are standard in the industry. Millions of dollars are spent each year evaluating performance test methods. Areas of special concern, such as fire safety, may require the use of several test methods in order to fully understand how a material will function in a fire situation. It is, therefore, important that a designer specify exactly *how* and *where* a component will interface with other components. When requesting technical data from a manufacturer, the designer should state the intended use of the material in *written* form. This will document efforts to obtain complete information on the material performance and/or limitations.

DOCUMENTING MATERIAL EVALUATION

Legal authorities strongly advise that efforts to acquire information about material performance be transacted in writing. Matrix forms and checklists can also serve as evidence of a conscientious effort to investigate the product's reliability. The designer's prospects for success in establishing compliance with standards governing professional liability will be in almost direct relationship to the *quantity* and *quality* of the documentation of professional concern.

The development of a performance checklist can be very useful in summarizing all the information accumulated through the performance evaluation process. The checklist shown in Table 17.2 lists components that intercepted with fire safety on the component and performance matrix (Figure 17.1). Items such as carpet, drapery, wallcovering, seating, desks, and space dividers can be listed with the necessary fire safety requirements and test methods. Information contained in column B, Requirements, would be determined by the designer under prescribed federal regulations or local codes. Column C contains the test methods that would be prescribed by codes, standards, regulations, or special tests required by the designer. Performance test methods for each component subsystem were explained in Part 1. It should be noted that the installation location of some components is important because many code requirements vary with the proposed use of the material. (See the NFPA Safety Code 101 in Chapter 5.)

Performance Attributes / Components	Health-Safety							Durability					Maintenance				Function				
	Fire	Falls	Sharp projections	Azotic	Anthropomorphic fit	Glare free	Handicapped use	Structurally sound	Positive attachment	Color stability	Crockfastness	Light fastness	Cleanability	Component repair	Component storage	Relocation ability	Flexibility	Privacy	Color homogeneity	Acoustical control	Thermal control
Carpet	•	•		•			•	•	•	•	•	•	•	•					•	•	
Resilient tile		•				•		•	•	•		•	•	•					•	•	
Drapery	•			•				•	•	•	•	•	•	•		•		•	•	•	•
Wallcovering	•			•		•		•	•	•	•	•	•	•				•	•	•	•
Seating	•	•	•	•	•	•		•	•	•	•	•	•	•	•	•	•		•		
Desks	•		•		•	•	•	•	•	•			•	•	•	•	•	•	•		
Space dividers	•		•	•				•	•	•		•	•	•	•	•	•	•	•	•	•
Others:																					

*Where a component intercepts (•) with a performance attribute a performance requirement is established.

Figure 17.1 Matrix of components and performance attributes.

**TABLE 17.2 PERFORMANCE CHECKLIST
FOR FIRE SAFETY Criteria: Health/Fire Safety**

**Fire Performance Requirements
for Job Project No. _____**

Component	Requirements	Test Method	Approved Yes/No	Comments
Carpet: Location in project*	Surface ignition	FF 1-70	X	
___ Corridor	Radiant flux .22 w/cm²	NFPA 255	X	
___ Public area	Smoke density ≤150	NBS 708	X	
___ Semipublic area	Flame spread ≤25 unsprinklered	ASTM E-84	X	
___ Other	Flame spread ≤200 sprinklered	ASTM E-84		
Wallcovering:				
___ Corridor				
___ Public area	(Column B)	(Column C)	(Column D)	
___ Semipublic area				
___ Other				
Drapery:				

* Consult the NFPA Life Safety Code for Interior Finishes. Note variances in finish location.
Column B—List required federal regulations, local codes, or requirements of the designer.
Column C—List test method required by federal or local codes and/or by designer.
Column D—Result of test to be provided by manufacturer or test laboratory.

Other checklists could be devised that would serve to measure individual components against all the performance requirement categories, i.e., health and safety, maintenance, durability, and functional effectiveness. The example shown in Table 17.3 is based on a performance test plan used by the General Services Administration.

It is obvious that these forms can aid the designer in evaluating particular components that are being considered for use. They can also provide an accurate record of performance requirements for each design project, and as the project proceeds these checklists could prevent oversights in relation to compliance with various code requirements. In addition, these checklists can form the basis for developing specification outline guides, which is discussed in Chapter 16.

In order to verify professional concern, designers should consider use of the following guidelines.

Application Guidelines

1. Seek out and use the latest information on all materials. Reliance on previous experience with a material may not always prove beneficial because the product may have been improved or altered in some way since the last time you specified it for a project.

2. Carefully research and analyze all items before specification, particularly if you are not familiar with them through previous experience.

3. Document all evidence of your evaluation process.

4. Avoid using dimensions of components on *preliminary* drawings. The use of schematic-type drawings can prevent the use of too much detail that could cause potential conflict with specification requirements developed later.

5. Start component evaluation early in the design process. The phases discussed in this chapter are summarized in Table 17.4.

TABLE 17.3   PERFORMANCE TEST PLAN—CARPET

Project Number_____

Date Carpet Submitted_____

Matrix Yes/No	Carpet Requirement/Criteria*	Test		Test Results	Approved Yes/No
		As Spec.	Alt.		
	Airborne sound:				
	SPP $\geq$ 60 in open planned areas				
	NIC' + (NC $\leq$ 40) $\geq$ 60 in open planned areas				
	SPP $\geq$ 70 in rooms				
	NIC' + (NC $\leq$ 35) $\geq$ 70 in rooms				
	Mask vertical footfall sounds with NC $\leq$ 40				
	Fiber type, weight, density and relationship				
	Resistance to forces:				
	Tuft bind $\geq$ 7#				
	Pill resistance $\geq$ 4.0				
	Resist 2#/" width strip force				
	Horizontal adhesive strength $\geq$ 40 psf				
	Vertical adhesive strength $\geq$ vacuum cleaner force				
	Support wheel load of 1500#				
	Resist 100 psi static load				
	Resist shrinkage — no joint opening				
	Colorfastness:				
	Crock rating $\geq$ 4.0				
	Wet cleaning rating $\geq$ "good"				
	Colorfastness to light rating $\geq$ 4.0				
	Fire safety:				
	Flame spread $\leq$ 75 unsprinklered				
	Flame spread $\leq$ 200 sprinklered				
	Specific optical density of smoke $\leq$ 450				
	Critical specific optical density $\leq$ 16 in 30 seconds				
	Meet DOC standards for surface flammability				

*This chart may be extended to include all the requirements of a project.

TABLE 17.4   SUMMARY OF DESIGN PHASES

Phase	Design Process	Component Evaluation
1	Schematic design	Develop performance attributes based on user requirements.
2	Design development	Based on attributes, develop matrix and establish material performance requirements. Develop checklists.
3	Contract document	Select specification methods.

SPECIFICATION OF NEW MATERIALS

Once the designer is satisfied that a certain new product justifies selection over other, more standard products, steps must be taken to assure that it is properly specified and installed.

1. Commit the manufacturer to an appropriate specification, either by having him or her personally prepare the specification (which should later be checked and approved by the general contractor) or by obtaining his or her written approval of a specification prepared by you. In either case, provide the manufacturer with as much information as you can concerning the intended use of the product, including, where possible, copies of all relevant working drawings. This helps to establish express warranties of fitness of the product for the intended use. If you should fail to provide relevant data and a problem develops, the manufacturer will claim that he or she would not have made the recommendation or given approval had the omitted data had been provided. For the same reason, it is important to submit any pertinent subsequent changes in drawings or specifications to the manufacturer and to obtain his or her assurance that the changes do not affect the appropriateness of the approved specification.

2. When a project involves the use of a new material or product, require the manufacturer to provide the following:
   a. Shop drawings
   b. A field representative to observe or supervise the installation.
   c. Certification by the representative that the product has been installed according to manufacturer's recommendations.
   d. Written certification from the installing contractor as a condition to your own certification that the product was installed according to recommended procedure.

3. The general or supporting conditions should contain provisions requiring contractors to thoroughly familiarize themselves with all specified products relating to their work and to submit written objections prior to bidding if they object to the proposed use of any product.

4. The specifications should require installing contractors to adhere strictly to drawings and specifications in the installation of all products unless written authorization for deviation is obtained from the designer, in which case the designer should obtain written approval from the manufacturer's field representative.

5. Finally, if proper installation of the new product is critical, the designer should arrange to make at least one visit to the site during installation to personally verify proper installation procedures.[4]

GLOSSARY

Attributes: A list of qualities or properties that a subsystem or a component must have if it is to function according to the owner's needs.

Building system: A set of coordinated subsystems suitable for many building types, performing the major function of a building. Though it runs contrary to common usage, "system" refers to the whole building, not the major integrated components, which are termed "subsystems."

In-system: All the parts that go to make a subsystem or the building system itself.

Intercept: A term used to define the point at which two items intersect on the vertical and horizontal lines of a matrix.

New product: May refer to a time-tested product which (a) has not previously been used in a particular geographic area or (b) is being used in a new way.

Performance criteria: The set of detailed statements of verifiable requirements that must be met in order to fulfill user needs.

Product: The basic unit of construction, whether it be a material or an item of equipment; the usual level at which prescriptive specifying is carried on. Performance criteria can be introduced in specifying a product, but performance specifying is more effectively carried on at a level of subsystem.

Standards: Criteria that have been formulated and published and against which subsystems or products have been tested. Though subsystems or products may be tested to check their conformity to standards, it is sometimes deemed sufficient for the manufacturer responsible to certify that standards have been met.

Subsystem: An assembly of products manufactured to perform as specified, designed to fit the building system as a whole and the other subsystems. Ideally, a subsystem is designed, manufactured, tested, and installed as a unit. Example: a ceiling/lighting subsystem; an office subsystem.

Systems building: Design and construction which uses highly organized subsystems or assemblies of products, suitable for many building types, designed to provide universal fit and to generate economies in overall building time and cost.

Test: A check of a component for conformity to performance criteria (including standards). Testing may be performed in a prototype stage, during manufacture, at the site during and after installation, and after project completion, or at any combination of these. Testing may also be specified on either a sampling or one-by-one basis. Testing may be performed by the design professional, the owner, a testing consultant, public agencies, or the manufacturer (with appropriate certification).

DESIGN DATA MANAGEMENT

The efficient management of product and material data is a major factor in the success or failure of a design firm. Not only must the data be easily accessible, it must also coordinate with widely used professional systems.

For three decades the data management system developed by the Construction Specifications Institute has been used for filing construction data, organizing project manuals, and listing specifications. The Masterformat system is based on sixteen divisions that encompass the entire spectrum of the building, engineering, and design fields. Although the majority of the divisions deal with areas beyond the scope of interior design work, several divisions deal with concerns of the interiors specialist (note the italicized divisions with asterisks below).

CSI Masterformat Divisions

Division 1: General Requirements

Division 2: Sitework

Division 3: Concrete

Division 4: Masonry

Division 5: Metals

Division 6: *Wood and Plastics**

Division 7: Thermal and Moisture Protection

Division 8: *Doors and Windows**

Division 9: *Finishes**

Division 10: *Specialties**

Division 11: *Equipment**

Division 12: *Furnishings**

Division 13: *Special Construction**

Division 14: Conveying Systems

Division 15: Mechanical

Division 16: Electrical

The sixteen divisions are identified by a *fixed* number and *title*. In Figure 18.1, on pages 268 and 269, the divisions are extended onto a five-digit reference system. For example, Division 9, Finishes, is expanded into numerous "broadscope," "mediumscope," and "narrowscope" sections.*

Division 9: Finishes

09680 Carpet (broadscope section)

−685 Tufted Broadloom (mediumscope)

−690 Woven Carpet (mediumscope)

.1 Axminster (narrowscope)

.2 Wilton (narrowscope)

COORDINATION WITH SPECIFICATION DOCUMENTS

The placement of the CSI *division* or *section* number above the specification title further clarifies the content. For example, a document number "Section 09690" states that the content deals with the general subject of woven carpet. However, if the document is numbered "Section 09690.1," the subject is limited to details about Axminster woven carpet.

Interior specifications developed for large commercial projects are incorporated into the general building project manual. This manual may have a table of contents similar to the one shown in Figure 18.2. In order to preserve continuity of the data system, all divisions are listed in the table of contents regardless of inclusion in the manual.

In summary, the Masterformat Data System relates to specifications in the following ways:

1. It identifies the specification scope and subject of the specification.

2. It identifies the specification placement within the contract manual.

3. It identifies the source of the specification data within the design-office filing system.

Requirements, Forms, Conditions
Instructions to Bidders
Form of Proposal
Form of Agreement between Owner and Contractor
Standard General Conditions
Division 1: General Requirements
a. Scope
b. Submittals
c. Testing
d. Delivery and Storage
e. Alternatives
f. Guarantees
Division 2: Sitework
Division 3: Concrete
Division 4: Masonry
Division 5: Metals
Division 6: Wood and Plastics
a. Millwork
b. Paneling
Division 7: Thermal and Moisture Protection
Division 8: Doors and Windows
a. Hardware
Division 9: Finishes
a. Resilient Flooring
b. Painting
c. Vinyl Wallcovering
d. Carpeting
Division 10: Specialties
Division 11: Equipment
Division 12: Furnishing
a. Drapery
b. Artwork
c. Furniture (casegoods)
d. Seating
Division 13: Special Construction
Division 14: Conveying Systems
Division 15: Mechanical
Division 16: Electrical

Figure 18.2 Project manual table of contents. Project: Saint Charles Hotel, June 10, 1990.

Figure 18.1 CSI format. Reproduced with permission of the Construction Specifications Institute.

BIDDING REQUIREMENTS, CONTRACT FORMS, AND CONDITIONS OF THE CONTRACT

00010   PRE-BID INFORMATION
00100   INSTRUCTIONS TO BIDDERS
00200   INFORMATION AVAILABLE TO BIDDERS
00300   BID FORMS
00400   SUPPLEMENTS TO BID FORMS
00500   AGREEMENT FORMS
00600   BONDS AND CERTIFICATES
00700   GENERAL CONDITIONS
00800   SUPPLEMENTARY CONDITIONS
00900   ADDENDA

Note: The items listed above are not specification sections and are referred to as "Documents" rather than "Sections" in the master list of section titles and numbers.

SPECIFICATIONS

DIVISION 1—GENERAL REQUIREMENTS

01010   SUMMARY OF WORK
01020   ALLOWANCES
01025   MEASUREMENT AND PAYMENT
01030   ALTERNATES/ALTERNATIVES
01035   MODIFICATION PROCEDURES
01040   COORDINATION
01050   FIELD ENGINEERING
01060   REGULATORY REQUIREMENTS
01070   IDENTIFICATION SYSTEMS
01090   REFERENCES
01100   SPECIAL PROJECT PROCEDURES
01200   PROJECT MEETINGS
01300   SUBMITTALS
01400   QUALITY CONTROL
01500   CONSTRUCTION FACILITIES AND TEMPORARY CONTROLS
01600   MATERIAL AND EQUIPMENT
01650   FACILITY STARTUP/COMMISSIONING
01700   CONTRACT CLOSEOUT
01800   MAINTENANCE

DIVISION 2—SITEWORK

02010   SUBSURFACE INVESTIGATION
02050   DEMOLITION
02100   SITE PREPARATION
02140   DEWATERING
02150   SHORING AND UNDERPINNING
02160   EXCAVATION SUPPORT SYSTEMS
02170   COFFERDAMS
02200   EARTHWORK
02300   TUNNELING
02350   PILES AND CAISSONS
02450   RAILROAD WORK
02480   MARINE WORK
02500   PAVING AND SURFACING
02600   UTILITY PIPING MATERIALS
02660   WATER DISTRIBUTION
02680   FUEL AND STEAM DISTRIBUTION
02700   SEWERAGE AND DRAINAGE
02760   RESTORATION OF UNDERGROUND PIPE
02770   PONDS AND RESERVOIRS
02780   POWER AND COMMUNICATIONS
02800   SITE IMPROVEMENTS
02900   LANDSCAPING

DIVISION 3—CONCRETE

03100   CONCRETE FORMWORK
03200   CONCRETE REINFORCEMENT
03250   CONCRETE ACCESSORIES
03300   CAST-IN-PLACE CONCRETE
03370   CONCRETE CURING
03400   PRECAST CONCRETE
03500   CEMENTITIOUS DECKS AND TOPPINGS
03600   GROUT
03700   CONCRETE RESTORATION AND CLEANING
03800   MASS CONCRETE

DIVISION 4—MASONRY

04100   MORTAR AND MASONRY GROUT
04150   MASONRY ACCESSORIES
04200   UNIT MASONRY
04400   STONE
04500   MASONRY RESTORATION AND CLEANING
04550   REFRACTORIES
04600   CORROSION RESISTANT MASONRY
04700   SIMULATED MASONRY

DIVISION 5—METALS

05010   METAL MATERIALS
05030   METAL COATINGS
05050   METAL FASTENING
05100   STRUCTURAL METAL FRAMING
05200   METAL JOISTS
05300   METAL DECKING
05400   COLD FORMED METAL FRAMING
05500   METAL FABRICATIONS
05580   SHEET METAL FABRICATIONS
05700   ORNAMENTAL METAL
05800   EXPANSION CONTROL
05900   HYDRAULIC STRUCTURES

DIVISION 6—WOOD AND PLASTICS

06050   FASTENERS AND ADHESIVES
06100   ROUGH CARPENTRY
06130   HEAVY TIMBER CONSTRUCTION
06150   WOOD AND METAL SYSTEMS
06170   PREFABRICATED STRUCTURAL WOOD
06200   FINISH CARPENTRY
06300   WOOD TREATMENT
06400   ARCHITECTURAL WOODWORK
06500   STRUCTURAL PLASTICS
06600   PLASTIC FABRICATIONS
06650   SOLID POLYMER FABRICATIONS

DIVISION 7—THERMAL AND MOISTURE PROTECTION

07100   WATERPROOFING
07150   DAMPPROOFING
07180   WATER REPELLENTS
07190   VAPOR RETARDERS
07195   AIR BARRIERS
07200   INSULATION
07240   EXTERIOR INSULATION AND FINISH SYSTEMS
07250   FIREPROOFING
07270   FIRESTOPPING
07300   SHINGLES AND ROOFING TILES
07400   MANUFACTURED ROOFING AND SIDING
07480   EXTERIOR WALL ASSEMBLIES
07500   MEMBRANE ROOFING
07570   TRAFFIC COATINGS
07600   FLASHING AND SHEET METAL
07700   ROOF SPECIALTIES AND ACCESSORIES
07800   SKYLIGHTS
07900   JOINT SEALERS

DIVISION 8—DOORS AND WINDOWS

08100   METAL DOORS AND FRAMES
08200   WOOD AND PLASTIC DOORS
08250   DOOR OPENING ASSEMBLIES
08300   SPECIAL DOORS
08400   ENTRANCES AND STOREFRONTS
08500   METAL WINDOWS
08600   WOOD AND PLASTIC WINDOWS
08650   SPECIAL WINDOWS
08700   HARDWARE
08800   GLAZING
08900   GLAZED CURTAIN WALLS

DIVISION 9—FINISHES

09100   METAL SUPPORT SYSTEMS
09200   LATH AND PLASTER

09250	GYPSUM BOARD
09300	TILE
09400	TERRAZZO
09450	STONE FACING (New)
09500	ACOUSTICAL TREATMENT
09540	SPECIAL WALL SURFACES
09545	SPECIAL CEILING SURFACES
09550	WOOD FLOORING
09600	STONE FLOORING
09630	UNIT MASONRY FLOORING
09650	RESILIENT FLOORING
09680	CARPET
09700	SPECIAL FLOORING
09780	FLOOR TREATMENT
09800	SPECIAL COATINGS
09900	PAINTING
09950	WALL COVERINGS

DIVISION 10—SPECIALTIES

10100	VISUAL DISPLAY BOARDS
10150	COMPARTMENTS AND CUBICLES
10200	LOUVERS AND VENTS
10240	GRILLES AND SCREENS
10250	SERVICE WALL SYSTEMS
10260	WALL AND CORNER GUARDS
10270	ACCESS FLOORING
10290	PEST CONTROL
10300	FIREPLACES AND STOVES
10340	MANUFACTURED EXTERIOR SPECIALTIES
10350	FLAGPOLES
10400	IDENTIFYING DEVICES
10450	PEDESTRIAN CONTROL DEVICES
10500	LOCKERS
10520	FIRE PROTECTION SPECIALTIES
10530	PROTECTIVE COVERS
10550	POSTAL SPECIALTIES
10600	PARTITIONS
10650	OPERABLE PARTITIONS
10670	STORAGE SHELVING
10700	EXTERIOR PROTECTION DEVICES FOR OPENINGS
10750	TELEPHONE SPECIALTIES
10800	TOILET AND BATH ACCESSORIES
10880	SCALES
10900	WARDROBE AND CLOSED SPECIALTIES

DIVISION 11—EQUIPMENT

11010	MAINTENANCE EQUIPMENT
11020	SECURITY AND VAULT EQUIPMENT
11030	TELLER AND SERVICE EQUIPMENT
11040	ECCLESIASTICAL EQUIPMENT
11050	LIBRARY EQUIPMENT
11060	THEATER AND STAGE EQUIPMENT
11070	INSTRUMENTAL EQUIPMENT
11080	REGISTRATION EQUIPMENT
11100	MERCANTILE EQUIPMENT
11090	CHECKROOM EQUIPMENT
11110	COMMERCIAL LAUNDRY AND DRY CLEANING EQUIPMENT
11120	VENDING EQUIPMENT
11130	AUDIO-VISUAL EQUIPMENT
11140	VEHICLE SERVICE EQUIPMENT
11150	PARKING CONTROL EQUIPMENT
11160	LOADING DOCK EQUIPMENT
11170	SOLID WASTE HANDLING EQUIPMENT
11190	DETENTION EQUIPMENT
11200	WATER SUPPLY AND TREATMENT EQUIPMENT
11280	HYDRAULIC GATES AND VALVES
11300	FLUID WASTE TREATMENT AND DISPOSAL EQUIPMENT
11400	FOOD SERVICE EQUIPMENT
11450	RESIDENTIAL EQUIPMENT
11460	UNIT KITCHENS
11470	DARKROOM EQUIPMENT
11480	ATHLETIC, RECREATIONAL, AND THERAPEUTIC EQUIPMENT
11500	INDUSTRIAL AND PROCESS EQUIPMENT
11600	LABORATORY EQUIPMENT
11650	PLANETARIUM EQUIPMENT
11660	OBSERVATORY EQUIPMENT
11680	OFFICE EQUIPMENT
11700	MEDICAL EQUIPMENT
11780	MORTUARY EQUIPMENT

11850	NAVIGATION EQUIPMENT
11870	AGRICULTURAL EQUIPMENT

DIVISION 12—FURNISHINGS

12050	FABRICS
12100	ARTWORK
12300	MANUFACTURED CASEWORK
12500	WINDOW TREATMENT
12600	FURNITURE AND ACCESSORIES
12670	RUGS AND MATS
12700	MULTIPLE SEATING
12800	INTERIOR PLANTS AND PLANTERS

DIVISION 13—SPECIAL CONSTRUCTION

13010	AIR SUPPORTED STRUCTURES
13020	INTEGRATED ASSEMBLIES
13030	SPECIAL PURPOSE ROOMS
13080	SOUND, VIBRATION, AND SEISMIC CONTROL
13090	RADIATION PROTECTION
13100	NUCLEAR REACTORS
13120	PRE-ENGINEERED STRUCTURES
13150	AQUATIC FACILITIES
13175	ICE RINKS
13180	SITE CONSTRUCTED INCINERATORS
13185	KENNELS AND ANIMAL SHELTERS
13200	LIQUID AND GAS STORAGE TANKS
13220	FILTER UNDERDRAINS AND MEDIA
13230	DIGESTER COVERS AND APPURTENANCES
13240	OXYGENATION SYSTEMS
13260	SLUDGE CONDITIONING SYSTEMS
13300	UTILITY CONTROL SYSTEMS
13400	INDUSTRIAL AND PROCESS CONTROL SYSTEMS
13500	RECORDING INSTRUMENTATION
13550	TRANSPORTATION CONTROL INSTRUMENTATION
13600	SOLAR ENERGY SYSTEMS
13700	WIND ENERGY SYSTEMS
13750	COGENERATION SYSTEMS—New
13800	BUILDING AUTOMATION SYSTEMS
13900	FIRE SUPPRESSION AND SUPERVISORY SYSTEMS
13950	SPECIAL SECURITY CONSTRUCTION

DIVISION 14—CONVEYING SYSTEMS

14100	DUMBWAITERS
14200	ELEVATORS
14300	ESCALATORS AND MOVING WALKS
14400	LIFTS
14500	MATERIAL HANDLING SYSTEMS
14600	HOISTS AND CRANES
14700	TURNTABLES
14800	SCAFFOLDING
14900	TRANSPORTATION SYSTEMS

DIVISION 15—MECHANICAL

15050	BASIC MECHANICAL MATERIALS AND METHODS
15250	MECHANICAL INSULATION
15300	FIRE PROTECTION
15400	PLUMBING
15500	HEATING, VENTILATING, AND AIR CONDITIONING
15550	HEAT GENERATION
15650	REFRIGERATION
15750	HEAT TRANSFER
15850	AIR HANDLING
15880	AIR DISTRIBUTION
15950	CONTROLS
15990	TESTING, ADJUSTING, AND BALANCING

DIVISION 16—ELECTRICAL

16050	BASIC ELECTRICAL MATERIALS AND METHODS
16200	POWER GENERATION—BUILT-UP SYSTEMS
16300	MEDIUM VOLTAGE DISTRIBUTION
16400	SERVICE AND DISTRIBUTION
16500	LIGHTING
16600	SPECIAL SYSTEMS
16700	COMMUNICATIONS
16850	ELECTRIC RESISTANCE HEATING
16900	CONTROLS
16950	TESTING

Numbering Flexibility

It should be noted that broadscope numbers range from 100 to 1000. The CSI Masterformat has been designed so the user can insert additional broadscope items as needed. However, these additions should only be assigned unused numbers within groupings that contain similar products or materials. For example, the addition of "Contract Carpet" could be placed as a narrowscope section under either 09685, "Tufted Broadloom," or 98690, "Woven Carpet". Also note that there are many mediumscope numbers left open under each subject. "Tufted Broadloom" could have been placed anywhere between 09681 and 09699. Although it is helpful in data retrieval, narrowscope sections are not required to be numbered or alphabetized.

A block of numbers, either 01 to 09 or 01 to 99, is left open for general data at the beginning of each division.

Interior Design Use and Application

Designers not familiar with this system frequently ask questions such as the following:

1. *Question:* May we create a Division 17, "Historic Furnishings"?

    Answer: No, that would not be possible under this system because there is already a preestablished Division 12, Furnishings. Broadscope Section 12600, "Furniture and Accessories," would be the appropriate place to add a mediumscope section dealing with historic furnishings.

    Example:

    12600—FURNITURE AND ACCESSORIES
    —632   Historic Furnishings and Accessories
       .1   Italian [narrowscope]
         a.   Accessories
           1.   Clocks
         b.   Rugs
         c.   Textiles
         d.   Doors
         e.   Lighting fixtures
         [Plus others]
       .2   Spanish
       .3   French
         a.   Louis XV
         b.   Louis XVI
         [Others as needed]
       .4   English
       .5   American
       .6   Chinese
       .7   Japanese
       .8   Near Eastern
       .9   Russian

    You would then locate data on Italian rugs in the *computer* or *standard* office file under 12632.1b. and data on Louis XV tables under 12632.3.a. When an antique dealer or manufacturer is the source of more than one period or style, simply cross-reference.

2. *Question:* Why is "Stone" listed in two Divisions (4—Masonry, and 9—Finishes)?

    Answer: Based on the concept of "prevalent use," CSI allows material placement based on use. As an example, look at the CSI key word listings for "Stone" and "Marble." Note: the key word index *is* alphabetized.

    Example 1: Stone
      04400—STONE
        Natural or manufactured stone.
        Related Work:
          Stone pavers: Section 02500.

Stone faced architectural precast concrete: Section 09600.
Stone Flooring: Section 09600.

Note:

Mortar procedures, accessories, and cleaning may be specified in this section.
Furnishing of stone for facing of composite precast panels may be specified in this section.

stone	04400
anchor	04150
carvings	12100
cast	04400
crushed	02500
	02700
	02900
	03300
	03400
	07500
curbs	02500
cut	04400
flag	02500
	04400
flooring	09600
manufactured	02800
	04400
mosaics	12100
paving units	02500
rubble	04400
sculpture	12100
simulated	02800
	04400
	09800
surfacing, decorative	02900
surfacing, roof	07300
	07500
tablets & plaques	10400
tiles	04400
toilet compartments	10150
veneer, natural	04400

Example 2: Marble

marble	04400
aggregates, roofing	07500
aggregates, terrazzo	09400
chip-epoxy flooring	09700
compartments	10150
countertops	04400
flooring	09600
thresholds	04400
veneer stone	04400

Other subjects that illustrate multiple listings include adhesives and hardware.

Example 3: Adhesives

adhesives	ALSO SEE SPECIFIC ITEMS
acoustical tile	09500
bonding agents, concrete	03300
bonding agents, plaster	09200
carpeting	09680
ceramic tile	09300
fasteners &	06050
gypsum board	09250
insulation	07200
	15250
millwork	06400
resilient tile	09650
special flooring	09700
stone	04400

wallcovering 09950
wood 06170

Example 4: Hardware
08700—HARDWARE
Operating hardware for doors and windows not specifically supplied as part of the manufactured item.
Weatherstripping and thresholds for doors and weatherstripping for windows not specifically supplied as
a part of the manufactured item.

Related Work:
*Cabinet hardware: Sections 06200, 06400,
12300, etc.*
Curtain and drapery hardware: Section 12500.
Security system: Sections 13800 or 16700.

Note:
*Hardware integral with manufactured items is in-
cluded in other sections as appropriate.*
*Hardware for entrance doors may be specified
with the doors in Section 08400.*
*Coordinate electrical items with Divisions 13 and
16.*

hardware, finish 08700
  cabinet 06200
  coiling partitions 10650
  compartment & cubicle 10150
  cubicle 10150
  curtain 12500
  demountable partition 10600
  door 08250
                                            08700
  drapery 12500
  flexible door 08300
                                            08700
  folding gates 08700
                                            10600
  folding partition 10650
  hangar door 08300
                                            08375
  mesh partition 10600
  overhead door 08300
                                            08700
  partition system 10600

revolving door 08470
                                            08700
sliding glass door 08300
                                            08700
sliding metal firedoor 08300
                                            08700
tempered glass door 08300
                                            08700
window 08600
                                            08700

3. *Question:* Can the 12050 Fabrics broadscope section be
    expanded?

    Answer: YES. The section can be expanded either by *use,*
    fabric *name,* or any other method most suited to the design
    office use.
      Example: File by use
        Section 12060 Upholstery fabrics
        Section 12070 Drapery fabrics
        Section 12075 Casement fabrics
      Example: File by name
        Section 12060 Damask
        Section 12070 Chintz

4. *Question:* Where should data on fire retardant and soil re-
    sistant treatments for fabrics be placed?

    Answer: In both cases data about these treatments would
    be filed with specific use. For example, fire-retardant paint
    would be listed under mediumscope Section 09900. Data
    on fabric fire retardant or soil treatments would be filed
    under Section 12050. Designers may create narrowscope
    Section 12053, Fabric Treatments.

5. *Question:* Is there a section for people such as consult-
    ants, installers, drapery fabricators, and upholsterers?

    Answer: Yes. Division 01900, References, can accom-
    modate a listing.
      Section—921 Consultants
      Section—922 Fabricators
      Section—923 Craftspersons
      Section—924 Installers

Answers to further questions may be determined through the
use of the system and the subject listings keyed to broadscope
section numbers (see Figures 18.3 and 18.4).

Figure 18.3 CSI Masterformat Broadscopes. Reproduced with permission of the Construction Specifications Institute.

DIVISION 9 - FINISHES

Section Number	Title	Broadscope Explanation

09100   **METAL SUPPORT SYSTEMS**

    -110   Non-load Bearing Wall Framing Systems
    -120   Ceiling Suspension Systems
    -130   Acoustical Suspension Systems

09100—METAL SUPPORT SYSTEMS

Metal non-load bearing framing systems and ceiling suspension systems. Includes furring systems.

> ***Related Sections:***
> > Section 05100 - Structural Metal Framing: Load bearing metal framing systems.
> > Section 05400 - Cold Formed Metal Framing: Metal framing systems subjected to continuous lateral and vertical loads.
> > Section 09200 - Lath and Plaster.
> > Section 09250 - Gypsum Board.
> > Section 09500 - Acoustical Treatment.
> > Section 09540 - Special Wall Surfaces: Non-acoustical surfaces.
> > Section 09545 - Special Ceiling Surfaces.
> > Section 13020 - Integrated Assemblies: Integrated ceilings.
> > Section 13120 - Pre-Engineered Structures: Metal support components for pre-engineered structures.

> ***Notes:*** Support systems may be specified in this section or in Sections 09200, 09250, 09500, 09540, and 09545.
>
>   Metal framing components of composite curtain wall panels or systems are usually specified in Sections 05400 - Cold Formed Metal Framing and 07400 - Manufactured Roofing and Siding.

09200   **LATH AND PLASTER**

    -205   Furring and Lathing
            Gypsum Lath
            Metal Lath
            Veneer Plaster Base
            Plaster Accessories
    -210   Gypsum Plaster
            Acoustical Plaster
            Fireproofing Plaster
    -215   Veneer Plaster
    -220   Portland Cement Plaster
    -225   Adobe Finish
    -230   Plaster Fabrications

09200—LATH AND PLASTER

Lathing including accessories and trim. Exterior and interior plaster including veneer plaster, acoustical plaster, plaster partitions, and plaster fireproofing systems.

> ***Related Sections:***
> > Section 05400 - Cold Formed Metal Framing.
> > Section 06100 - Rough Carpentry: Wood support systems.
> > Section 07240 - Exterior Insulation and Finish System: Composite insulation and finish systems.
> > Section 07250 - Fireproofing.
> > Section 09100 - Metal Support Systems.
> > Section 09540 - Special Wall Surfaces: Aggregate coatings.
> > Section 13090 - Radiation Protection: Lead lined lath.

> ***Notes:*** Metal support systems may be specified in this section or in Sections 05400 and 09100.
>
>   Acoustical insulation and sealants for plaster systems are usually specified in this section.

09250   **GYPSUM BOARD**

    -260   Gypsum Board Systems
    -270   Gypsum Board Accessories

09250—GYPSUM BOARD

Unfinished and prefinished gypsum board on wood and metal framing and on solid substrates; laminated solid, and semi-solid partition systems; gypsum backing board for other finishes; accessories and trim; and joint taping and finishing.

> ***Related Sections:***
> > Section 05400 - Cold Formed Metal Framing.
> > Section 06100 - Rough Carpentry: Wood support systems and gypsum sheathing on wood.
> > Section 07250 - Fireproofing.
> > Section 09100 - Metal Support Systems.
> > Section 10600 - Partitions: Demountable gypsum board partitions.

> ***Notes:*** Metal support systems to receive gypsum board may be specified in this section or in Sections 05400 and 09100.
>
>   Acoustical insulation and sealants for gypsum board systems are usually specified in this section.
>
>   Gypsum sheathing on metal framing is usually specified in this section.

09300	**TILE**
-310	Ceramic Tile
	Ceramic Mosaics
	Conductive Tile
-320	Thin Brick Tile
-330	Quarry Tile
	Chemical Resistant Quarry Tile
-340	Paver Tile
-350	Glass Mosaics
-360	Plastic Tile
-370	Metal Tile
-380	Cut Natural Stone Tile

09400	**TERRAZZO**
-410	Portland Cement Terrazzo
-420	Precast Terrazzo
-430	Conductive Terrazzo
-440	Plastic Matrix Terrazzo

09450	**STONE FACING**

09500	**ACOUSTICAL TREATMENT**
-510	Acoustical Ceilings
	Acoustical Panel Ceilings
	Acoustical Tile Ceilings
	Acoustical Metal Pan Ceilings
-520	Acoustical Wall Treatment
-525	Acoustical Space Units
-530	Acoustical Insulation and Barriers

09540	**SPECIAL WALL SURFACES**
	Fiber Reinforced Plastic Coated Panels
	Reinforced Gypsum Units
	Aggregate Coatings

09300—TILE

Manufactured surfacing units of impervious, vitreous, semivitreous, and non-vitreous materials; glazed, unglazed, conductive, abrasive, and textured surfaces.

Related Sections:
Section 02500 - Paving and Surfacing: Exterior unit pavers.
Section 03400 - Precast Concrete: Tile faced architectural precast concrete.
Section 07300 - Shingles and Roofing Tiles: Clay roofing tiles.
Section 07400 - Manufactured Roofing and Siding: Tile faced composite building panels.
Section 09450 - Stone Facing.
Section 09600 - Stone Flooring.
Section 09630 - Unit Masonry Flooring.

Notes: Furnishing of tile for facing of composite or precast concrete panels may be specified in this section.

Ceramic tile towel bar holders, toilet paper roll holders, soap dishes, and other ceramic tile toilet room accessories are usually specified here rather than in Section 10800 - Toilet and Bath Accessories.

09400—TERRAZZO

Cast-in-place, sand-cushion, monolithic, bonded and adhesively-bonded portland cement terrazzo; poured-in-place epoxy, polyester, and conductive plastic matrix terrazzo; and precast terrazzo. Includes accessories and finish sealers.

09450—STONE FACING

Natural stone two inches or less in thickness, with polished or matte finish applied as an exterior and interior veneer surface.

Related Sections:
Section 02500 - Paving and Surfacing: Stone pavers.
Section 04400 - Stone: Stone masonry.
Section 09300 - Tile: Cut natural stone tile.

09500—ACOUSTICAL TREATMENT

Acoustical tiles and panels, perforated metal pan ceiling systems, sound absorbing wall and ceiling units, acoustical wall systems, and sound barrier boards and blankets.

Related Sections:
Section 04200 - Unit Masonry: Sound absorbing masonry.
Section 05300 - Metal Decking: Sound absorbing metal decks.
Section 09100 - Metal Support Systems: Ceiling suspension systems.
Section 09200 - Lath and Plaster: Acoustical plaster.
Section 12600 - Furniture and Accessories: Open office sound absorbing partitions.
Section 13020 - Integrated Assemblies: Acoustic panels and tiles for integrated ceilings.
Section 13030 - Special Purpose Rooms: Sound conditioned rooms.
Section 13080 - Sound Vibration, and Seismic Control: Sound and vibration control.
Section 15050 - Basic Mechanical Materials and Methods: Sound and vibration control.

Notes: Acoustical ceiling suspension systems may be specified in this section or in Section 09100.

Acoustical insulation in plaster and gypsum board systems is usually specified in Sections 09200 and 09250.

09540—SPECIAL WALL SURFACES

Wall surfaces and panels of materials other than plaster and gypsum board.
Includes hand and machine applied aggregate over base coats of portland cement, epoxy, and other synthetic base coats.

Related Sections:
Section 07240 - Exterior Insulation and Finish Systems: Composite insulation and finish systems.
Section 07400 - Manufactured Roofing and Siding: Manufactured panels with aggregate facing.
Section 09800 - Special Coatings.

Notes: If a product is used for both wall and ceiling applications, it is usually specified in this section.

Figure 18.3 continued

09545   **SPECIAL CEILING SURFACES**

    Linear Metal Ceilings
    Mirror Panel Ceilings
    Textured Metal Ceiling Panels
    Textured Gypsum Ceiling Panel
    Linear Wood Ceilings
    Suspended Decorative Grids

09550   **WOOD FLOORING**

-560   Wood Strip Flooring
-565   Wood Block Flooring
-570   Wood Parquet Flooring
    Acrylic Impregnated Wood Parquet Flooring
    Vinyl Bonded Wood Parquet Flooring
-580   Wood Composition Flooring
-590   Resilient Wood Flooring Systems
    Cushioned Wood Flooring
    Mastic Set Wood Flooring
    Spring Supported Wood Flooring
    Steel Channel Wood Flooring
    Steel Splined Wood Flooring

09600   **STONE FLOORING**

-610   Flagstone Flooring
-615   Marble Flooring
-620   Granite Flooring
-625   Slate Flooring

09630   **UNIT MASONRY FLOORING**

-635   Brick Flooring
    Chemical Resistant Brick Flooring
    Industrial Brick Flooring
-640   Pressed Concrete Unit Flooring

09650   **RESILIENT FLOORING**

-660   Resilient Tile Flooring
-665   Resilient Sheet Flooring
-670   Fluid-Applied Resilient Flooring
-675   Static Control Resilient Flooring
    Static Resistant Resilient Flooring
    Conductive Resilient Flooring
    Static Dissipative Resilient Flooring
-678   Resilient Base and Accessories

09680   **CARPET**

-682   Carpet Cushion
-685   Sheet Carpet
-690   Carpet Tile
-695   Wall Carpet
-698   Indoor/Outdoor Carpet

09545—SPECIAL CEILING SURFACES

Special ceiling panels, units, and materials manufactured as finished ceiling surfaces. Acoustical provisions, if any, are of secondary consideration.

    Related Sections:
        Section 09100 - Metal Support Systems.
        Section 09500 - Acoustical Treatment: Acoustical tiles,
           panels, and ceiling systems.
        Section 13020 - Integrated Assemblies: Integrated ceiling
           systems.

    Notes: *Special surface suspension systems are usually*
        specified in this section.

09550—WOOD FLOORING

Strip, parquet, block, and composition wood flooring. Includes resilient wood flooring systems, stage flooring, and gymnasium flooring.

    Related Sections:
        Section 06100 - Rough Carpentry: Wood decking.
        Section 06170 - Prefabricated Structural Wood: Glued-
           laminated decking.

    Notes: *Finish sealers, coatings, and waxes are usually*
        included in this section.

09600—STONE FLOORING

Flooring of natural, simulated, and cast stone.

    Related Sections:
        Section 02500 - Paving and Surfacing: Stone pavers.
        Section 04400 - Stone: Stone masonry.
        Section 04700 - Simulated Masonry: Simulated and cast
           stone masonry.
        Section 09300 - Tile: Cut natural stone tile.

09630—UNIT MASONRY FLOORING

Fired clay unit masonry and pressed concrete unit masonry flooring.

    Related Section:
        Section 02500 - Paving and Surfacing: Exterior brick and
           concrete unit paving.
        Section 04200 - Unit Masonry: Brick and concrete unit
           masonry.
        Section 04600 - Corrosion Resistant Masonry: Chemical
           resistant brick and vitrified clay liner plates.

09650—RESILIENT FLOORING

Resilient tile and sheet flooring, conductive resilient flooring, and fluid-applied resilient flooring. Includes resilient base, resilient stair treads and risers, resilient stair nosings, resilient edging and transitions for carpet, and resilient athletic flooring.

    Related Sections:
        Section 03500 - Cementitious Decks and Toppings: Self-
           leveling floor fills.
        Section 12670 - Rugs and Mats: Floor mats and entrance
           tiles.

    Notes: *Athletic surfacing for exterior use is specified in*
        Section 02500 - Paving and Surfacing. Interior resilient
        athletic flooring is specified in this section.

09680—CARPET

Carpet materials including cushions and accessories.

    Related Sections:
        Section 02500 - Paving and Surfacing: Synthetic grass.
        Section 09650 - Resilient Flooring: Resilient base.
        Section 12670 - Rugs and Mats.

09700	**SPECIAL FLOORING**
-705	Resinous Flooring
-710	Magnesium Oxychloride Flooring
-720	Epoxy-Marble Chip Flooring
-725	Seamless Quartz Flooring
-730	Elastomeric Liquid Flooring
	Conductive Elastomeric Liquid Flooring
-750	Mastic Fills
-755	Plastic Laminate Flooring
-760	Asphalt Plank Flooring

09780	**FLOOR TREATMENT**
-785	Metallic-Type Static Disseminating and
	Spark Resistant Finish
-790	Slip Resistant Finishes

09800	**SPECIAL COATINGS**
-810	Abrasion Resistant Coatings
-815	High Build Glazed Coatings
-820	Cementitious Coatings
-830	Elastomeric Coatings
-835	Textured Plastic Coatings
-840	Fire Resistant Paints
-845	Intumescent Paints
-850	Chemical Resistant Coatings
-860	Graffiti Resistant Coatings
-870	Coating Systems for Steel
	Exterior Coating System for Steel Storage Tanks
	Interior Coating System for Steel Storage Tanks
	Coating System for Steel Piping
-880	Protective Coatings for Concrete

09900	**PAINTING**
-910	Exterior Painting
-920	Interior Painting
-930	Transparent Finishes

09950	**WALL COVERINGS**

09700—SPECIAL FLOORING

Heavy duty and other special flooring.

> ***Related Sections:***
> Section 03300 - Cast-in-Place Concrete: Heavy-duty concrete floor finish.
> Section 07570 - Traffic Coatings: Pedestrian and vehicular traffic coatings.
> Section 09650 - Resilient Flooring: Fluid-applied resilient flooring.
> Section 09780 - Floor Treatment.
> Section 09800 - Special Coatings.

09780—FLOOR TREATMENT

Static disseminating and spark resistant finishes.

> ***Related Sections:***
> Section 03300 - Cast-in-Place Concrete: Concrete sealers and heavy-duty concrete floor finishes. Section 07570 - Traffic Coating.
> Section 09550 - Wood Flooring: Wood floor finishes and waxes.
> Section 09700 - Special Flooring.

09800—SPECIAL COATINGS

High-performance, glazed resinous coatings, including epoxy polyester, or polyurethane, interior and exterior cementitious coatings; heavy industrial coatings, including chlorinated rubber, heat resistant, elastomeric, and zinc-rich primers; and fire retardant paint. Includes storage tank coating systems.

> ***Related Sections:***
> Section 02760 - Restoration of Underground Pipe: Relining existing underground pipelines.
> Section 06300 - Wood Treatment: Fire retardant treated lumber.
> Section 07180 - Water Repellents.
> Section 07250 - Fireproofing: Fire resistant mastic and applied fireproofing.
> Section 09540 - Special Wall Surfaces: Aggregate coatings.
> Section 09700 - Special Flooring.
> Section 13200 - Liquid and Gas Storage Tanks.

09900—PAINTING

Exterior and interior painting with transparent and opaque finishes. Includes stains, varnishes, lacquers, primers, fillers, paint removers, and waxes, and preparation of surfaces.

> ***Related Sections:***
> Section 09550 - Wood Flooring: Wood floor finishes and waxes.
> Section 09800 - Special Coatings: Fire resistant paints.
> Section 15050 - Basic Mechanical Materials and Methods: Mechanical identification systems.
> Section 16050 - Basic Electrical Materials and Methods: Electrical identification systems.

> ***Notes:*** Pavement marking may be specified in this section or in Section 02500 - Paving and Surfacing.
>
> Painted mechanical and electrical identification may be specified in this section or in Sections 15050 and 16050.

09950—WALL COVERINGS

Wall coverings applied over solid substrates. Includes vinyl-coated fabric backed for light, medium, and heavy usage; unsupported vinyl and cork wall coverings; wallpapers; wall fabrics; and flexible wood sheets.

> ***Related Sections:***
> Section 06200 - Finish Carpentry: Wood paneling.
> Section 06400 - Architectural Woodwork: Wood and plastic laminate paneling.
> Section 09250 - Gypsum Board: Prefinished gypsum board.
> Section 09500 - Acoustical Treatment: Fabric covered acoustical wall and ceiling panels.
> Section 09680 - Carpet: Carpet wall covering.
> Section 10260 - Wall and Corner Guards: Impact resistant **wall** protection.

Figure 18.3 continued

DIVISION 10 - SPECIALTIES

Section Number	Title	Broadscope Explanation

10100 **VISUAL DISPLAY BOARDS**

-110 Chalkboards
-115 Markerboards
-120 Tackboards
-130 Operable Board Units
-140 Display Track System
-145 Visual Aid Board Units

10100—VISUAL DISPLAY BOARDS

Chalk and marker writing surfaces manufactured of slate, painted composition board, porcelain-enameled steel, and aluminum. Mounting surfaces of cork, composition board, and fabric covered material. Includes framing systems and accessories, and manual and motor operated units with integral projection screens.

> *Related Sections:*
> *Section 10400 - Identifying Devices: Bulletin boards and directories.*
> *Section 12300 - Manufactured Casework: Display cases.*
> *Section 12600 - Furniture and Accessories: Chalkboards and tackboards integral with landscape partition systems.*

10150 **COMPARTMENTS AND CUBICLES**

-160 Metal Toilet Compartments
-165 Plastic Laminate Toilet Compartments
-170 Plastic Toilet Compartments
-175 Particleboard Toilet Compartments
-180 Stone Toilet Compartments
-185 Shower and Dressing Compartments
-190 Cubicles
    Cubicle Curtains
    Cubicle Track and Hardware

10150—COMPARTMENTS AND CUBICLES

Enclosures, dividers, screens, and curtains for toilets, urinals, showers, dressing compartments, and hospital cubicles including hardware and accessories. Includes ceiling hung, floor supported, and wall supported types.

> *Related Sections:*
> *Section 10800 - Toilet and Bath Accessories: Grab bars, toilet tissue dispensers, and seat cover dispensers.*

> *Notes:* *Precast and preformed shower receptors and shower cabinets may be specified in Section 15400 - Plumbing.*

10200 **LOUVERS AND VENTS**

-210 Metal Wall Louvers
    Operable Metal Wall Louvers
    Stationary Metal Wall Louvers
    Motorized Metal Wall Louvers
-220 Louvered Equipment Enclosures
-225 Metal Door Louvers
-230 Metal Vents
    Metal Soffit Vents
    Metal Wall Vents

10200—LOUVERS AND VENTS

Louver, vents, and other items for ventilation which are not an integral part of the mechanical system.

> *Related Sections:*
> *Section 06400 - Architectural Woodwork: Screens and louvers.*
> *Section 07400 - Manufactured Roofing and Siding: Louvers fabricated integrally with siding.*
> *Section 07700 - Roof Specialties and Accessories: Louvered penthouse vents, ridge vents, roof vents.*
> *Section 08100 - Metal Doors and Frames: Louvers fabricated integrally with metal frames.*
> *Section 08200 - Wood and Plastic Doors: Wood louvers.*
> *Section 08900 - Glazed Curtain Walls: Louvers fabricated integrally with curtain walls.*
> *Section 15880 - Air Distribution: Louvers and vents integral with ductwork and operable dampers.*

> *Notes:* *Door louvers may be specified with doors in Sections 08100 and 08200. Louvers in fire-rated wood doors should be specified with the doors.*
>
> *Air intake louvers for HVAC terminal units are usually specified with the units in Section 15750 - Heat Transfer.*

10240 **GRILLES AND SCREENS**

10240—GRILLES AND SCREENS

Exterior and interior grilles and screens of wood, metal, plastic, and other materials. Used for a variety of functions and not limited to ventilation purposes.

> *Related Sections:*
> *Section 06400 - Architectural Woodwork: Wood screens*
> *Section 15880 - Air Distribution: Grilles and screens integral with ductwork.*

> *Notes:* *Sight screens also used for sun control may be specified in Section 10700 - Exterior Protection Devices for Openings.*

10250 **SERVICE WALL SYSTEMS**

10250—SERVICE WALL SYSTEMS

Wall systems and wall mounted units incorporating services such as drinking fountains, clocks, fire hose, extinguisher cabinets, telephones, and waste receptacles.

> *Related Sections:*
> *Section 11460 - Unit Kitchens: Manufactured units with kitchen fixtures and appliances.*
> *Section 15300 - Fire Protection.*
> *Section 15400 - Plumbing: Mechanical connections.*
> *Section 16050 - Basic Electrical Materials and Methods: Electrical connections.*

10260	**WALL AND CORNER GUARDS**
	Corner Guards
	Bumper Guards
	Impact Resistant Wall Protection

10260—WALL AND CORNER GUARDS

Protective devices such as corner guards and bumper rails of metal, plastic, rubber, and other finish materials.

> **Notes:** *Corner guards fabricated from rolled metal sections and bent plate are specified under Section 05500 - Metal Fabrications.*

10270	**ACCESS FLOORING**
-272	Rigid Grid Access Floor Systems
-274	Snap-on Stringer Access Floor Systems
-276	Stringerless Access Floor Systems

10270—ACCESS FLOORING

Free-standing, accessible floor assembly of modular panels and elevated support systems forming an underfloor cavity for mechanical and electrical services distribution.

> **Related Sections:**
> *Section 15880 - Air Distribution: Floor air outlets and inlets.*
>
> **Notes:** *Floor air outlets and inlets integral with floor panels are usually specified in this section.*
>
> *Loose-laid or glued-down carpet tile may be specified under Section 09680 - Carpet.*

10290	**PEST CONTROL**
-292	Rodent Control
-294	Insect Control
-296	Bird Control

10290—PEST CONTROL

Mechanical, electrical, physical, and chemical pest repellent systems and protective devices.

> **Related Sections:**
> *Section 01500 - Construction Facilities and Temporary Controls: Temporary pest and rodent control during construction.*
> *Section 02200 - Earthwork: Pest control treatments.*

10300	**FIREPLACES AND STOVES**
-305	Manufactured Fireplaces
	Manufactured Fireplace Chimneys
	Manufactured Fireplace Forms
-310	Fireplace Specialties and Accessories
	Fireplace Dampers
	Fireplace Water Heaters
	Fireplace Screens and Doors
	Fireplace Inserts
-320	Stoves

10300—FIREPLACES AND STOVES

Manufactured fireplaces, stoves, chimneys, dampers, and specialties for use in construction of fireplaces and stove units.

> **Related Sections:**
> *Section 04200 - Unit Masonry: Brick, and concrete unit masonry.*
> *Section 04400 - Stone.*
> *Section 04550 - Refractories: Firebrick and flue liners.*
> *Section 13180 - Site Constructed Incinerators.*
> *Section 15550 - Heat Generation: Breechings, chimneys, and stacks.*

10340	**MANUFACTURED EXTERIOR SPECIALTIES**
-342	Steeples
-344	Spires
-346	Cupolas
-348	Weathervanes

10340—MANUFACTURED EXTERIOR SPECIALTIES

Stock and custom designed, steeples, spires, cupolas, weathervanes, and other similar exterior specialties.

> **Related Requirements and Sections:**
> *Divisions 5, 6, and 7: On-site fabricated steeples, spires and cupolas.*
> *Section 16600 - Special Systems: Lightning protection.*

10350	**FLAGPOLES**
-352	Ground Set Flagpoles
-354	Wall Mounted Flagpoles
-356	Automatic Flagpoles
-358	Nautical Flagpoles

10350—FLAGPOLES

Complete flagpole fabrications of metal, wood, and fiberglass, including all accessories and appurtenances.

10400	**IDENTIFYING DEVICES**
-410	Directories
	Electronic Directories
-415	Bulletin Boards
-420	Plaques
-430	Exterior Signs
	Dimensional Letter Signs
	Illuminated Exterior Signs
	Non-illuminated Exterior Signs
	Post and Panel/Pylon Exterior Signs
	Electronic Message Signs
-440	Interior Signs
	Dimensional Letters
	Door Signs
	Engraved Signs
	Illuminated Interior Signs
	Non-Illuminated Interior Signs
	Electronic Message Signs

10400—IDENTIFYING DEVICES

Directories, bulletin boards, directional items, letters, signs, and plaques of various materials used in establishing identity and communication. Includes integral lighted units, neon signs, computerized directories, electronic message boards, and other types of electronic signs.

> **Related Sections:**
> *Section 01080 - Identification Systems: For equipment and systems.*
> *Section 01500 - Construction Facilities and Temporary Controls: Project sign.*
> *Section 02800 - Site Improvements: Site signs.*
> *Section 09900 - Painting: Painted signs.*
> *Section 10100 - Visual Display Boards.*
> *Section 11480 - Athletic, Recreational, and Therapeutic Equipment: Score boards.*
> *Section 15050 - Basic Mechanical Materials and Methods: Mechanical Identification.*
> *Section 16050 - Basic Electrical Materials and Methods: Electrical Identification.*
> *Section 16500 - Lighting.*

Figure 18.3 continued

10450	**PEDESTRIAN CONTROL DEVICES**
-452	Portable Posts and Railings
-454	Rotary Gates
-456	Turnstiles
-458	Detection Specialties

10450—PEDESTRIAN CONTROL DEVICES

Portable posts and railings, rotary gates, turnstiles, electronic detection and counting systems, restrictive guides used to limit access, and temporary enclosures for pedestrian traffic.

> *Related Sections:*
> *Section 02800 - Site Improvements: Traffic signals.*
> *Section 11150 - Parking Control Equipment.*
> *Section 13800 - Building Automation systems: Security, monitoring and alarm systems.*

> *Notes:* *Electronic detection systems may be specified in Section 16700 - Communications.*

10500	**LOCKERS**
-505	Metal Lockers
-510	Wood Lockers
	Plastic Laminate Faced Lockers
-515	Coin-Operated Lockers
-518	Glass Lockers

10500—LOCKERS

Storage facilities providing temporary security of contents. Includes tenant storage lockers, benches, and related hardware.

> *Related Sections:*
> *Section 06400 - Architectural Woodwork: Custom casework.*
> *Section 10900 - Wardrobe and Closet Specialties.*
> *Section 11480 - Athletic, Recreational, and Therapeutic Equipment.*
> *Section 12300 - Manufactured Casework.*
> *Section 12600 - Furniture and Accessories.*

10520	**FIRE PROTECTION SPECIALTIES**
-522	Fire Extinguishers, Cabinets, and Accessories
	Fire Extinguishers
	Fire Extinguisher Cabinets
-526	Fire Blankets and Cabinets
-528	Wheeled Fire Extinguisher Units

10520—FIRE PROTECTION SPECIALTIES

Fire fighting devices and storage cabinets, not including items or devices physically connected to a fire protection system.

> *Related Sections:*
> *Section 10250 - Service Wall Systems.*
> *Section 15300 - Fire Protection: Fire hose connections and related cabinets and accessories.*

10530	**PROTECTIVE COVERS**
-532	Walkway Covers
-534	Car Shelters
-536	Awnings
-538	Canopies

10530—PROTECTIVE COVERS

Manufactured awnings, canopies, marquees, covered walkways, bus stops, and car shelters of various materials.

> *Related Sections:*
> *Section 10700 - Exterior Protection Devices for Openings: Sun control devices.*
> *Section 13120 - Pre-Engineered Structures.*

10550	**POSTAL SPECIALTIES**
-551	Mail Chutes
-552	Mail Boxes
-554	Collection Boxes
-556	Central Mail Delivery Boxes

10550—POSTAL SPECIALTIES

Mail chutes, collection boxes, letter boxes, letter slots, view windows, and other postal service facilities and devices.

> *Related Sections:*
> *Section 14500 - Material Handling Systems: Mail handling equipment.*

10600	**PARTITIONS**
-605	Wire Mesh Partitions
-610	Folding Gates
-615	Demountable Partitions
	Demountable Gypsum Board Partitions
	Demountable Metal Partitions
	Demountable Wood Partitions
-630	Portable Partitions, Screens, and Panels

10600—PARTITIONS

Enclosures, dividers, screens, and partitions which may be fixed or demounted and relocated with a minimum of labor. Partitions can be free standing post and panel, ceiling hung, wall mounted, and pressure locked between floor and ceiling. Also, includes partitions of an open nature, such as wire mesh partitions.

> *Related Sections:*
> *Section 08300 - Special Doors: Folding doors.*
> *Section 10650 - Operable Partitions: Folding partitions.*

> *Notes:* *Landscape partitions integral with open plan furniture may be specified in 12600 - Furniture and Accessories.*

10650	**OPERABLE PARTITIONS**
-652	Folding Panel Partitions
-655	Accordion Folding Partitions
-660	Sliding Partitions
-665	Coiling Partitions

10650—OPERABLE PARTITIONS

Track-supported, operable panels and partitions, top hung and floor supported, manually and power operated. Includes gymnasium and auditorium partitions and dividers.

> *Notes:* *Folding and accordion folding partitions are differentiated from folding doors under Section 08300 - Special Doors, because of size and construction.*

10670	**STORAGE SHELVING**
-675	Metal Storage Shelving
-680	Storage and Shelving Systems
-683	Mobile Storage Systems
	Motorized Mobile Storage Systems
	Manual Mobile Storage Systems
-685	Wire Shelving
-688	Prefabricated Wood Storage Shelving

10670—STORAGE SHELVING

Open, manufactured shelving for general storage, as opposed to specific items. Includes manual and motorized mobile and compact storage systems.

> *Related Sections:*
> *Section 10900 - Wardrobe and Closet Specialties.*
> *Section 11050 - Library Equipment: Library stack systems.*
> *Section 12300 - Manufactured Casework: Library casework shelving.*

> *Notes:* *Wire shelving for food service may be specified in Section 11400 - Food Service Equipment.*

10700	**EXTERIOR PROTECTION DEVICES FOR OPENINGS**
-705	Exterior Sun Control Devices
-710	Exterior Shutters
-715	Storm Panels

10700—EXTERIOR PROTECTION DEVICES FOR OPENINGS

Manufactured items such as louvers, fins, shutters, demountable panels, and sun screens to provide sun control, privacy, security, insulation, and storm protection on exterior of windows, skylights, and entrances. Includes fixed and movable, manually and electrically operated, and automatically controlled devices.

> *Related Sections:*
> *Section 10530 - Protective Covers: Awnings.*
> *Section 12500 - Window Treatment: Interior window treatment and sun control film.*

> *Notes:* *Items covered in Sections 10530 and 12500 may also function as sun control devices.*

10750	**TELEPHONE SPECIALTIES**
-755	Telephone Enclosures
-760	Telephone Directory Units
-765	Telephone Shelves

10750—TELEPHONE SPECIALTIES

Manufactured enclosures, stalls, booths, and alcoves for installation of telephones. Includes accessories.

> *Related Sections:*
> *Section 10250 - Service Wall Systems.*
> *Section 16700 - Communications: Telephone connections.*

10800	**TOILET AND BATH ACCESSORIES**
-810	Toilet Accessories
	Commercial Toilet Accessories
	Detention Toilet Accessories
	Hospital Toilet Accessories
-820	Bath Accessories
	Residential Bath Accessories
	Shower and Tub Doors

10800—TOILET AND BATH ACCESSORIES

Manufactured items for use in conjunction with toilets and baths.

> *Related Sections:*
> *Section 08800 - Glazing: Mirror glass.*
> *Section 10150 - Compartments and Cubicles: Toilet and shower enclosures.*
> *Section 10250 - Service Wall Systems.*
> *Section 12300 - Manufactured Casework.*

> *Notes:* *For consistency in materials finish and quality, grab bars for disabled persons and other accessories mounted on compartments should be specified in this section.*
>
> *Integral accessories for ceramic tile walls are specified in Section 09300 - Tile.*
>
> *Detention toilet facilities are often specified in Section 11190 - Detention Equipment.*

10880	**SCALES**

10880—SCALES

Weighing devices, usually of a fixed nature.

10900	**WARDROBE AND CLOSET SPECIALTIES**

10900—WARDROBE AND CLOSET SPECIALTIES

Manufactured hat and coat racks, and other specialties for storage of clothing.

> *Related Sections:*
> *Section 10500 - Lockers.*
> *Section 10670 - Storge Shelving: General storage shelving.*
> *Section 11090 - Checkroom Equipment.*

Figure 18.3 continued

DIVISION 11 - EQUIPMENT

Section Number	Title	Broadscope Explanation

11010 | **MAINTENANCE EQUIPMENT**

-012 Vacuum Cleaning Systems
-014 Window Washing Systems
-016 Floor and Wall Cleaning Equipment
-018 Housekeeping Carts

11010—MAINTENANCE EQUIPMENT

Built-in and freestanding equipment for building maintenance.

> ***Related Sections:***
> *Section 14800 - Scaffolding: Powered scaffolding.*

11020 | **SECURITY AND VAULT EQUIPMENT**

-022 Vault Doors and Day Gates
-024 Security and Emergency Systems
-026 Safes
-028 Safe Deposit Boxes

11020—SECURITY AND VAULT EQUIPMENT

Built-in and freestanding equipment specifically designed for money or valuable material storage, including vault ventilators and specialized security systems.

> ***Related Sections:***
> *Section 01650 - Facility Startup/Commissioning: Administrative procedures for starting, testing, adjusting, and demonstrating systems.*
> *Section 11030 - Teller and Service Equipment.*
> *Section 12300 - Manufactured Casework: Bank fixtures and casework.*
> *Section 13030 - Special Purpose Rooms: Vaults.*
> *Section 13800 - Building Automation Systems: Security controls integrating the entire building.*
> *Section 13950 - Special Security Construction.*
> *Section 16700 - Communications: Security access systems.*

11030 | **TELLER AND SERVICE EQUIPMENT**

-032 Service and Teller Window Units
-034 Package Transfer Units
-036 Automatic Banking Systems
-038 Teller Equipment Systems

11030—TELLER AND SERVICE EQUIPMENT

Built-in and freestanding equipment specifically designed for handling and transfer of money and other high security items.

> ***Related Sections:***
> *Section 01650 - Facility Startup/Commissioning: Administrative procedures for starting, testing, adjusting, balancing, and demonstrating systems.*
> *Section 11020 - Security and Vault Equipment.*
> *Section 12300 - Manufactured Casework: Bank fixtures and casework.*
> *Section 13030 - Special Purpose Rooms: Vaults.*
> *Section 13800 - Building Automation Systems: Security controls integrating the entire building.*
> *Section 13950 - Special Security Construction.*
> *Section 16700 - Communications: Security access systems.*

11040 | **ECCLESIASTICAL EQUIPMENT**

-042 Baptisteries
-044 Chancel Fittings

11040—ECCLESIASTICAL EQUIPMENT

Built-in, and freestanding church-related equipment, including baptistery and chancel fittings.

> ***Related Sections:***
> *Section 12300 - Manufactured Casework: Ecclesiastical woodwork and casework.*
> *Section 12700 - Multiple Seating: Pews.*

11050 | **LIBRARY EQUIPMENT**

-052 Book Theft Protection Equipment
-054 Library Stack Systems
-056 Study Carrels
-058 Book Depositories
    Automated Book Storage and Retrieval Systems

11050—LIBRARY EQUIPMENT

Equipment related to libraries including book storage and retrieval systems.

> ***Related Sections:***
> *Section 10670 - Storage Shelving: Movable compact storage systems.*
> *Section 12300 - Manufactured Casework: Library casework and shelving.*
> *Section 12600 - Furniture and Accessories: Library furniture.*

11060 | **THEATER AND STAGE EQUIPMENT**

-062 Stage Curtains
-064 Rigging Systems and Controls
-066 Acoustical Shell Systems
-068 Folding and Portable Stages

11060—THEATER AND STAGE EQUIPMENT

Equipment designed, engineered, and field assembled for use in the support of theatrical, instrumental, and voice programs.

> ***Related Sections:***
> *Section 12700 - Multiple Seating: Theater seating.*
> *Section 14400 - Lifts: Stage and orchestra lifts.*
> *Section 16500 - Lighting: Stage and theater lighting.*
> *Section 16700 - Communications: Public address, music, and sound systems.*
> *Section 16900 - Controls: Controls for electrical systems.*

> ***Notes:*** *Stage lighting instruments, systems, and controls are usually specified in this section but may be specified in Sections 16500 - Lighting, and 16900 - Controls.*

11070	INSTRUMENTAL EQUIPMENT
-072	Organs
-074	Carillons
-076	Bells

11070—INSTRUMENTAL EQUIPMENT

Musical instruments, including field assembled and built-in instruments.

11080	REGISTRATION EQUIPMENT

11080—REGISTRATION EQUIPMENT

Custom and stock designed, manufactured, and field assembled specialized equipment for the purpose for registering, admitting, and controlling rooms at hotels, motels, hospitals, and other similar installations.

> *Related Sections:*
> *Section 06200 - Finish Carpentry: Site built casework.*
> *Section 06400 - Architectural Woodwork: Shop built casework.*
> *Section 12300 - Manufactured Casework: Stock designed, manufactured casework.*

11090	CHECKROOM EQUIPMENT

11090—CHECKROOM EQUIPMENT

Manual and automated equipment used where wearing apparel and luggage are checked and stored on a temporary basis.

> *Related Sections:*
> *Section 10500 - Lockers: Coin operated and other storage lockers.*
> *Section 10900 - Wardrobe and Closet Specialties: Hat and coat racks.*

11100	MERCANTILE EQUIPMENT
-102	Barber and Beauty Shop Equipment
-104	Cash Registers and Checking Equipment
-106	Display Cases
	Refrigerated Display Cases
-108	Food Processing Equipment
	Food Weighing and Wrapping Equipment

11100—MERCANTILE EQUIPMENT

Built-in and freestanding equipment used in retail and service stores.

> *Related Sections:*
> *Section 06200 - Finish Carpentry: Site-built display casework.*
> *Section 06400 - Architectural Woodwork: Shop-built display casework.*
> *Section 12300 - Manufactured Casework: Stock designed, manufactured display casework.*

> *Notes:* *Display cases which include equipment are included in this section. Display casework without equipment is included in Sections 06200 - Finish Carpentry, 06400 - Architectural Woodwork, or 12300 - Manufactured Casework.*

11110	COMMERCIAL LAUNDRY AND DRY CLEANING EQUIPMENT
-112	Washers and Extractors
-114	Dry Cleaning Equipment
-116	Drying and Conditioning Equipment
-118	Finishing Equipment
	Ironers and Accessories

11110—COMMERCIAL LAUNDRY AND DRY CLEANING EQUIPMENT

Manufactured equipment for commercial laundry and dry cleaning operations including coin-operated equipment.

> *Related Sections:*
> *Section 11450 - Residential Equipment: Residential laundry equipment.*
> *Section 14500 - Material Handling Systems: Laundry conveyors.*

11120	VENDING EQUIPMENT
-122	Money Changing Machines
-124	Vending Machines
	Beverage Vending Machines
	Candy Vending Machines
	Cigarette Vending Machines
	Food Vending Machines
	Stamp Vending Machines
	Sundry Vending Machines

11120—VENDING EQUIPMENT

Coin-operated equipment for dispensing various foods, drinks, stamps, and miscellaneous salable items. Includes money changing machines.

> *Related Sections:*
> *Section 11110 - Commercial Laundry and Dry Cleaning Equipment: Coin-operated laundry equipment.*

11130	AUDIOVISUAL EQUIPMENT
-132	'Projection Screens
-134	Projectors
-136	Learning Laboratories

11130—AUDIOVISUAL EQUIPMENT

Movie, slide, overhead, and opaque projectors; fixed, portable and rear projection screens; players and recorders. Includes learning laboratories.

> *Related Sections:*
> *Section 11050 - Library Equipment: Study carrels.*
> *Section 16700 - Communications: Voice, data, public address, music, and television systems.*

Figure 18.3 continued

11140	**VEHICLE SERVICE EQUIPMENT**	

11140—VEHICLE SERVICE EQUIPMENT

-142 Vehicle Washing Equipment
-144 Fuel Dispensing Equipment
-146 Lubrication Equipment

Equipment normally associated with vehicular service facilities. Includes washing, fuel-dispensing, tire-changing, air-systems, and lubrication equipment.

> *Related Sections:*
> *Section 01650 - Facility Startup/Commissioning: Administrative procedures for starting, testing, adjusting, and demonstrating systems.*
> *Section 14400 - Lifts: Vehicle lifts.*

> *Notes: Fuel dispensing systems and related storage tanks are usually specified in this section but may be specified in Section 15400 - Plumbing.*

11150   PARKING CONTROL EQUIPMENT

11150—PARKING CONTROL EQUIPMENT

-152 Parking Gates
-154 Ticket Dispensers
-156 Key and Card Control Units
-158 Coin Machine Units

Equipment for parking control, including meters, gates, ticket dispensers, and related accessories.

> *Related Sections:*
> *Section 02800 - Site improvements: Traffic signals. Precast concrete parking bumpers and barriers:*
> *Section 10450 - Pedestrian Control Devices.*
> *Section 16700 - Communications: Security access systems.*

11160   LOADING DOCK EQUIPMENT

11160—LOADING DOCK EQUIPMENT

-161 Dock Levelers
-162 Dock Lifts
-163 Portable Ramps, Bridges, and Platforms
-164 Dock Seals and Shelters
-165 Dock Bumpers

Equipment and material for the protection of service docks and for the loading and unloading of service vehicles.

> *Related Sections:*
> *Section 14400 - Lifts: Vehicle lifts.*

11170   SOLID WASTE HANDLING EQUIPMENT

11170—SOLID WASTE HANDLING EQUIPMENT

-171 Packaged Incinerators
-172 Waste Compactors
-173 Bins
-174 Pulping Machines and Systems
-175 Chutes and Collectors
-176 Pneumatic Waste Systems

Packaged equipment involving the collection, shredding, compaction, removal and incineration of trash and other solid waste.

> *Related Sections:*
> *Section 01650 - Facility Startup/Commissioning: Administrative procedures for starting, testing, and demonstrating systems.*
> *Section 13180 - Site Constructed Incinerators.*
> *Section 14500 - Material Handling Systems: Chutes, conveyers, and feeder equipment for transfer of bulk materials.*

11190   DETENTION EQUIPMENT

11190—DETENTION EQUIPMENT

Custom-designed, manufactured, field-assembled detention enclosures and equipment including detention furnishings and fittings.

> *Related Sections:*
> *Section 08300 - Special Doors: Security doors.*
> *Section 08650 - Special Windows: Security windows and screens.*
> *Section 08700 - Hardware: Electrical locking systems.*

> *Notes: Detention windows, doors, hardware, accessories and electronic controls are usually included in this section, but may be specified in other sections.*

11200   WATER SUPPLY AND TREATMENT EQUIPMENT

11200—WATER SUPPLY AND TREATMENT EQUIPMENT

-210 Pumps
  Axial Flow Pumps
  Centrifugal Pumps
  Deepwell Turbine Pumps
  Mixed Flow Pumps
  Vertical Turbine Pumps
-220 Mixers and Flocculators
-225 Clarifiers
-230 Water Aeration Equipment
-240 Chemical Feeding Equipment
  Coagulant Feed Equipment
-250 Water Softening Equipment
  Base-Exchange or Zeolite Equipment
  Lime-Soda Process Equipment
-260 Disinfectant Feed Equipment
  Chlorination Equipment
  pH Equipment
-270 Fluoridation Equipment

Various equipment used in water supply and treatment.

> *Related Sections:*
> *Section 01650 - Facility Startup/Commissioning: Administrative procedures for starting, testing, adjusting, and demonstrating systems.*
> *Section 02660 - Water Distribution: Wells and water transmission systems.*
> *Section 02770 - Ponds and Reservoirs.*
> *Section 13200 - Liquid and Gas Storage Tanks: Ground, elevated, and underground storage tanks.*
> *Section 13220 - Filter Underdrains and Media.*
> *Section 13300 - Utility Control Systems: Water supply plant operating and monitoring systems.*
> *Section 15400 - Plumbing: Plumbing within structures.*

11280	**HYDRAULIC GATES AND VALVES**
-285	Hydraulic Gates
	Bulkhead Gates
	High Pressure Gates
	Hinged Leaf Gates
	Radial Gates
	Slide Gates
	Sluice Gates
	Spillway Crest Gates
	Vertical Lift Gates
-295	Hydraulic Valves
	Butterfly Valves
	Regulating Valves

11280—HYDRAULIC GATES AND VALVES

Large gates and valves for dams, hydroelectric, and irrigation projects; as required for equipment such as penstocks, turbine intakes, and manifolds.

> *Related Sections:*
> *Section 01650 - Facility Startup/Commissioning: Administrative procedures for starting, testing, adjusting, and demonstrating systems.*
> *Section 05900 - Hydraulic Structures: Penstocks, bulkheads, and manifolds.*

11300	**FLUID WASTE TREATMENT AND DISPOSAL EQUIPMENT**
-302	Oil/Water Separators
-304	Sewage Ejectors
-306	Packaged Pump Stations
-310	Sewage and Sludge Pumps
-320	Grit Collecting Equipment
-330	Screening and Grinding Equipment
-335	Sedimentation Tank Equipment
-340	Scum Removal Equipment
-345	Chemical Equipment
-350	Sludge Handling and Treatment Equipment
-360	Filter Press Equipment
-365	Trickling Filter Equipment
-370	Compressors
-375	Aeration Equipment
-380	Sludge Digestion Equipment
-385	Digester Mixing Equipment
-390	Package Sewage Treatment Plants

11300—FLUID WASTE TREATMENT AND DISPOSAL EQUIPMENT

Various equipment used in fluid waste treatment and disposal.

> *Related Sections:*
> *Section 01650 - Facility Startup/Commissioning: Administrative procedures for starting, testing, adjusting, and demonstrating systems.*
> *Section 02700 - Sewerage and Drainage: Storm and sanitary sewerage and septic systems.*
> *Section 02770 - Ponds and Reservoirs: Sewage lagoons.*
> *Section 13220 - Filter Underdrains and Media.*
> *Section 13230 - Digester Covers and Appurtenances.*
> *Section 13240 - Oxygenation Systems.*
> *Section 13260 - Sludge Conditioning Systems.*
> *Section 13300 - Utility Control Systems: Wastewater treatment plant operating and monitoring systems.*
> *Section 15400 - Plumbing.*

11400	**FOOD SERVICE EQUIPMENT**
-405	Food Storage Equipment
-410	Food Preparation Equipment
-415	Food Delivery Carts and Conveyors
-420	Food Cooking Equipment
-425	Hood and Ventilation Systems
	Surface Fire Protection Systems
-430	Food Dispensing Equipment
-435	Ice machines
-440	Cleaning and Disposal Equipment
-445	Bar and Soda Fountain Equipment

11400—FOOD SERVICE EQUIPMENT

Manufactured and field assembled, built-in and freestanding equipment, used for liquid and solid food storage, preparation, display, serving, and cleanup in commercial and institutional kitchens, and bars. Includes cooking equipment, dishwashing equipment, garbage disposers, refrigerated cases, serving line equipment, and bar and soda fountain equipment.

> *Related Sections:*
> *Section 01650 - Facility Startup/Commissioning: Administrative procedures for starting, testing, adjusting, and demonstrating systems.*
> *Section 11450 - Residential Equipment: Residential appliances.*
> *Section 11460 - Unit Kitchens.*
> *Section 12300 - Manufactured Casework: Restaurant and cafeteria casework.*
> *Section 15300 - Fire Protection: Hood fire protection systems.*
> *Section 15400 - Plumbing.*
> *Section 15850 - Air Handling: Make up air and exhaust system.*

> **Notes:** *Prefabricated walk-in coolers and freezers are included in Section 13030 - Special Purpose Rooms, but are often specified in this section.*

11450	**RESIDENTIAL EQUIPMENT**
-452	Residential Appliances
-454	Built-In Ironing Boards
-458	Disappearing Stairs

11450—RESIDENTIAL EQUIPMENT

Built-in and freestanding appliances and other components specifically for residential use.

> *Related Sections:*
> *Section 06200 - Finish Carpentry: Site built cabinets and counters.*
> *Section 06400 - Architectural Woodwork: Shop built cabinets and counters.*
> *Section 10300 - Fireplaces and Stoves.*
> *Section 11010 - Maintenance Equipment: Vacuum cleaning systems.*
> *Section 11460 - Unit Kitchens.*
> *Section 12300 - Manufactured Casework: Stock designed residential casework.*

Figure 18.3 continued

11460	**UNIT KITCHENS**

11460—UNIT KITCHENS

Manufactured units incorporating kitchen fixtures and appliances.

> **Related Sections:**
> Section 11450 - Residential Equipment: Residential appliances.
> Section 12300 - Manufactured Casework: Kitchen casework.

11470	**DARKROOM EQUIPMENT**
-472	Transfer Cabinets
-474	Darkroom Processing Equipment
-476	Revolving Darkroom Doors

11470—DARKROOM EQUIPMENT

Manufactured built-in, and freestanding photographic film processing equipment and other products for darkroom use.

> **Related Sections:**
> Section 12300 - Manufactured Casework: Labortory casework.
> Section 18500 - Lighting: Darkroom lighting.

11480	**ATHLETIC, RECREATIONAL, AND THERAPEUTIC EQUIPMENT**
-482	Scoreboards
-484	Backstops
-486	Gym Dividers
-488	Bowling Alleys
-490	Gymnasium Equipment
-492	Exercise Equipment
-494	Therapy Equipment
-496	Shooting Ranges

11480—ATHLETIC, RECREATIONAL AND THERAPEUTIC EQUIPMENT

Manufactured, preassembled, and field-assembled, built-in, and freestanding equipment for athletic, recreational, and therapeutic use.

> **Related Sections:**
> Section 12700 - Multiple Seating: Telescoping bleachers and chair platforms.
> Section 13030 - Special Purpose Rooms: Athletic rooms.
> Section 13120 - Pre-engineered Structures: Grandstands and bleachers.
> Section 13150 - Aquatic Facilities: Swimming pools.

11500	**INDUSTRIAL AND PROCESS EQUIPMENT**

11500—INDUSTRIAL AND PROCESS EQUIPMENT

Specialized equipment for manufacturing, processing, and assembly plants. Includes vocational shop equipment and tools.

> **Related Sections:**
> Section 01650 - Facility Startup/Commissioning: Administrative procedures for starting, testing, adjusting, and demonstrating systems.
> Section 13200 - Liquid and Gas Storage Tanks.
> Section 13400 - Industrial and Process Control Systems.
> Section 15400 - Plumbing; Special piping systems.

11600	**LABORATORY EQUIPMENT**

11600—LABORATORY EQUIPMENT

Manufactured, preassembled, and field-assembled equipment for scientific use; including service fittings and accessories, fume hoods, incubators, sterilizers, refrigerators, and emergency safety appliances especially designed for laboratories.

> **Related Sections:**
> Section 01650 - Facility Startup/Commissioning; Administrative procedures for starting, testing, adjusting, and demonstrating systems.
> Section 12300 - Manufactured Casework: Laboratory casework, laboratory tops, and sinks, and service fixtures mounted on counter tops.
> Section 15400 - Plumbing.
> Section 15850 - Air Handling: Fume hood exhaust systems.

11650	**PLANETARIUM EQUIPMENT**

11650—PLANETARIUM EQUIPMENT

Projectors and related equipment unique to planetariums.

> **Related Sections:**
> Section 01650 - Facility Startup/Commissioning: Administrative procedures for starting, testing, adjusting, and demonstrating systems.
> Section 13030 - Special Purpose Rooms: Planetariums.

> **Notes:** This section relates to equipment while Section 13030 - Special Purpose Rooms relates to structures.

11660	OBSERVATORY EQUIPMENT

11660—OBSERVATORY EQUIPMENT

Telescopes and related equipment unique to observatories.

Related Sections:
Section 01650 - Facility Startup/Commissioning:
Administrative procedures for starting, testing,
adjusting, and demonstrating systems.
Section 13120 - Pre-engineered Structures: Observatories.

Notes: This section relates to equipment while Section 13120
- Pre-Engineered Structures relates to structures.

11680	OFFICE EQUIPMENT

11680—OFFICE EQUIPMENT

Computers, printers, word processors, copiers, drafting equipment, plotters, carto-stereographs, and other equipment items typically used in offices.

Related Sections:
Section 12600 - Furniture and Accessories: Office furniture
including open office systems.

11700	MEDICAL EQUIPMENT
-710	Medical Sterilizing Equipment
-720	Examination and Treatment Equipment
-730	Patient Care Equipment
-740	Dental Equipment
-750	Optical Equipment
-760	Operating Room Equipment
-770	Radiology Equipment

11700—MEDICAL EQUIPMENT

Specialized equipment for health care facilities for humans and animals.

Related Sections:
Section 01650 - Facility Startup/Commissioning:
Administrative procedures for starting, testing,
adjusting, and demonstrating systems.
Section 12300 - Manufactured Casework: Dental
Casework. Hospital casework. Medical casework.
Section 13090 - Radiation Protection: Radiation shielding
components and structures.
Section 16500 - Lighting: Hospital operating room and
other medical lighting.

11780	MORTUARY EQUIPMENT

11780—MORTUARY EQUIPMENT

Specialized equipment for handling and preparation of cadavers, including refrigerators, crematorium equipment, and lifts.

Related Sections:
Section 12300 - Manufactured Casework: Laboratory
casework.
Section 13030 - Special Purpose Rooms: Walk-in
refrigerators.

11850	NAVIGATION EQUIPMENT

11850—NAVIGATION EQUIPMENT

Unique, permanently mounted navigation equipment for airports, canals, rivers, and harbors.

Related Sections:
Section 01650 - Facility Startup/Commissioning:
Administrative procedures for starting, testing,
adjusting, and demonstrating systems.
Section 02480 - Marine Work.

Notes: This section does not include equipment on moving
carriers.

11870	AGRICULTURAL EQUIPMENT

11870—AGRICULTURAL EQUIPMENT

Milkers, stock feeders, stock waterers, and waste cleanup equipment.

Related Sections:
Section 02800 - Site Improvements: Fences and gates.

Figure 18.3 continued

DIVISION 12 - FURNISHINGS

Section Number	Title	Broadscope Explanation

12050   **FABRICS**

12050—FABRICS

Fabrics, leathers, and furs for upholstery and window applications and general information on fabric fibers and treatments.

> ***Notes:*** *This section is used for filing information on fabric fibers and treatment. These materials are usually specified in the sections where used.*

12100   **ARTWORK**

-110   Murals
    Photo Murals
-120   Wall Decorations
    Paintings
    Prints
    Tapestries
    Wall Hangings
-140   Sculpture
    Carved Sculpture
    Cast Sculpture
    Constructed Sculpture
    Relief Artwork
-160   Ecclesiastical Artwork
-170   Stained Glass Work

12100—ARTWORK

Interior and exterior art objects such as murals, paintings, sculpture, and stained glass.

> ***Related Sections:***
>   *Section 05700 - Ornamental Metal: Ornamental metal castings and pressed or stamped metal moldings and sheets.*
>   *Section 06400 - Architectural Woodwork: Moldings, columns, capitals, and other ornamental wood items.*
>   *Section 06600 - Plastic Fabrications: Glass fiber, resin, and cast plastic moldings and other decorative items.*
>   *Section 09200 - Lath and Plaster: Cast plaster ornamentation.*
>   *Section 11040 - Ecclesiastical Equipment: Standard manufactured ecclesiastical fittings.*

> ***Notes:*** *Depending on method of execution, sculptured brick panels and murals may be specified in this section or in Section 04200 - Unit Masonry.*
>
> *Depending on method of execution, ceramic tile murals may be specified in this section or in Section 09300 - Tile.*

12300   **MANUFACTURED CASEWORK**

-301   Metal Casework
-302   Wood Casework
-304   Plastic Laminate Faced Casework
-345   Laboratory Casework
    Laboratory Countertops, Sinks, and Accessories
-350   Medical Casework
    Dental Casework
    Hospital Casework
    Nurse Station Casework
    Optical Casework
    Veterinary Casework
-360   Educational Casework
    Library Casework
-370   Residential Casework
    Bath Casework
    Kitchen Casework
-380   Specialty Casework
    Bank Casework
    Display Casework
    Dormitory Casework
    Ecclesiastical Casework
    Hotel and Motel Casework
    Restaurant Casework

12300—MANUFACTURED CASEWORK

Stock design cabinets and other casework units manufactured from steel, wood, and plastic laminate for a variety of uses. Includes laboratory countertops with integral sinks, and fixtures and accessories mounted on countertops.

> ***Related Sections:***
>   *Section 06200 - Finish Carpentry: Custom built casework.*
>   *Section 06400 - Architectural Woodwork: Custom built casework requiring expert craftsmanship and joinery.*
>   *Section 10500 - Lockers: Storage lockers of a variety of materials.*
>   *Section 10670 - Storage Shelving: Open manufactured general storage shelving including movable compact storage systems.*
>   *Section 11050 - Library Equipment: Library stack systems and study carrels.*
>   *Section 11100 - Mercantile Equipment: Refrigerated and other display cases which include specialized equipment.*
>   *Section 11460 - Unit Kitchens: Manufactured units incorporating kitchen fixtures, appliances, cabinets, and countertops.*
>   *Section 12600 - Furniture and Accessories: Open office landscape furniture with cabinet components and other movable furniture items.*

> ***Notes:*** *Casework with integral specialized equipment, such as refrigerated display cases, laboratory fume hoods, and unit kitchens are specified in Division 11.*
>
> *Sinks integral with countertops, such as resin type corrosion resistant sinks, are specified in this section. Stainless steel and other types of sinks field inserted in countertops are specified in Section 15400 - Plumbing.*
>
> *Sections 12301, 12302, and 12304 may be used for data filing or for specifying casework manufactured for multiple uses.*

12500	**WINDOW TREATMENT**
-510	Blinds
	Horizontal Louver Blinds
	Vertical Louver Blinds
-515	Interior Shutters
-520	Shades
	Insulating Shades
	Lightproof Shades
	Translucent Shades
	Woven Wood Shades
-525	Solar Control Film
-530	Curtain Hardware
	Curtain Track
-540	Curtains
	Draperies
	Fabric Curtains
	Lightproof Curtains
	Vertical Louver Curtains
	Woven Wood Curtains

12500—WINDOW TREATMENT

Interior window coverings such as blinds, shades, shutters, draperies, and curtains, including hardware and controls.

> ***Related Sections:***
> *Section 08650 - Special Windows: Windows with integral louver blinds and shutters applied to exterior of windows to provide privacy, security, storm protection, insulation, and sun control.*
> *Section 10700 - Exterior Protection Devices for Openings: Exterior louver, blinds, sunscreens, and shutters for sun control at windows.*

12600	**FURNITURE AND ACCESSORIES**
-605	Portable Screens
-610	Open Office Furniture
	Open Office Partitions
	Open Office Work Surfaces
	Open Office Storage Units
	Open Office Shelving
	Open Office Light Fixtures
-620	Furniture
	Classroom Furniture
	Dormitory Furniture
	Ecclesiastical Furniture
	Hotel and Motel Furniture
	Laboratory Furniture
	Library Furniture
	Lounge Furniture
	Medical Furniture
	Office Furniture
	Restaurant Furniture
	Residential Furniture
	Specialized Furniture
-640	Furniture Systems
	Integrated Work Units
-650	Furniture Accessories
	Ash Receptacles
	Clocks
	Desk Accessories
	Lamps
	Waste Receptacles

12600—FURNITURE AND ACCESSORIES

Items of movable furniture and furnishing accessories.

> ***Related Sections:***
> *Section 02800 - Site Improvements: Seating, tables, and other site and street furnishings, typically fixed.*
> *Section 10600 - Partitions: Freestanding, portable partitions.*
> *Section 10670 - Storage Shelving: Manufactured general storage shelving.*
> *Section 12700 - Multiple Seating: Interlocking, folding, stacking, and other chairs for public assembly.*

> ***Notes:*** *Permanently installed site and street furniture is specified in Section 02800 - Site Improvements, while movable exterior furniture may be specified in this section or in Section 02800 - Site Improvements.*

12670	**RUGS AND MATS**
-675	Rugs
-680	Foot Grilles
-690	Floor Mats and Frames
	Chair Pads
	Entrance Tiles
	Floor Mats
	Floor Runners
	Mat Frames

12670—RUGS AND MATS

Loose rugs and pads; foot grilles, gratings, and floor grid systems; entrance mats; recessed and surface mat frames; floor runners; and entrance tile. Constructed of a variety of materials including rubber, vinyl, carpet, tire fabric, cocoa fiber, aluminum, and stainless steel.

> ***Related Sections:***
> *Section 09680 - Carpet: Carpet and carpet tile.*

> ***Notes:*** *Loose laid tile designed specifically for entrances is specified in this section. Standard adhesive mounted tile is specified in Sections 09650 - Resilient Flooring.*

12700	**MULTIPLE SEATING**
-705	Portable Audience Seating
	Folding Chairs
	Interlocking Chairs
	Stacking Chairs
-710	Fixed Audience Seating
-730	Stadium and Arena Seating
-740	Booths and Tables
-750	Multiple Use Fixed Seating
-760	Telescoping Stands
	Telescoping Bleachers
	Telescoping Chair Platforms
-770	Pews and Benches
-775	Seat and Table Systems
	Pedestal Tablet Arm Chairs

12700—MULTIPLE SEATING

Portable, fixed, and telescoping seating for theatres, auditoriums, lecture halls, stadiums, arenas, gymnasiums, churches, restaurants, and other facilities where multiple seating is required. Includes fixed booths and fixed combination seat and table modules for restaurants and classrooms.

> ***Related Sections:***
> *Section 11060 - Theater and Stage Equipment: Theater equipment other than seating.*
> *Section 11480 - Athletic, Recreational, and Therapeutic Equipment: Gymnasium equipment other than seating.*
> *Section 12600 - Furniture and Accessories: Portable chairs for other than assembly activities and audience functions. Movable tables for classrooms and restaurants.*
> *Section 13120 - Pre-Engineered Structures: Pre-engineered grandstands and bleachers with fixed rather than telescoping seating.*

Figure 18.3 continued

12800	**INTERIOR PLANTS AND PLANTERS**
-810	Interior Plants
-815	Artificial Plants
-820	Interior Planters
-825	Interior Landscape Accessories
-830	Interior Plant Maintenance

12800—INTERIOR PLANTS AND PLANTERS

Live and artificial plants, planters, accessories, soil, fertilizer, and plant maintenance for interior planting.

Related Sections:
Section 01800 - Maintenance: General procedures for maintenance after completion of the facility.
Section 02900 - Landscaping: Exterior planting.

Notes: Irrigation systems for interior planters may be specified in this section or combined with exterior irrigation systems in

Figure 18.4 Key word index.

KEY WORD INDEX

	CSI Broadscope Number		CSI Broadscope Number
A-frame shelving	10150	Appliances:	11400
Abacus	06400	commercial kitchens:	11400
Abbreviations and symbols:		appliance symbols	11400
architectural	01070	dishwashing, automated	11400
door hardware	08250	equipment schedule	11400
electrical	16500	refrigerators and freezers	11400
exercise equipment	11480	salad bars and sandwich bars	11400
fire extinguishers	10520	residential checklist	11450
fire rating	08300	dryers	11450
lumber	06100	freezers	11450
plywood	06200	gas ranges	11460
signage	10400		11450
store fixtures	11100	hoods	11450
Access doors	08300		15850
Accessibility:		microwave ovens	11400
banking facilities	12631		11160
ceilings	09500	refrigerators	11450
drinking fountains	15400	trash compactors	11450
entrance doors	08350	washers	11450
floor assemblies	10270	Aquariums	13150
folding stairs	11450	Architectural abbreviations	01090
kitchen counter and cabinet frontage	11450	Architectural material symbols	01090
pressurized stairs	13130	Architectural millwork and interior trim	06050
public telephones	10750	Architectural ornamentation (historic)	06200
ramps	01060	Architectural symbols	01090
retail spaces	11100	Architectural woodwork glossary	06400
stairs	01060	Architrave	06400
vending machines	11120	Art glass	12100
Accessories:		Artificial lighting. *See* Lighting	
aquariums	13150	Asbestos abatement	02080
banking	12631	Assembly seating:	12710
bedding yardages	12600	aisle requirements	12710
clocks	12632	codes	01090
closet and wardrobe	12300	continental	12710
lamps (floor and table)	16501.1	folding tables	12710
public washrooms	10800	ganging devices	12705
racks and screens	12300	movable pedestal	12710
residential baths	12300	riser or floor mounted	12710
retail stores	11100	stacking chairs and dolly	12705
Accordian folding doors	08350	with writing arms	12710
Accordian folding partitions	01650	Associations (industry):	00960
Accordian folding window shutters	12500	interior finishes	00960
Acoustical ceilings	09100	interior furnishings	01090
Acoustical interior materials	09250	walls, partitions, and doors	00960
Acoustical walls	09250	windows, skylights, glass, and glazing	00960
Actuating doors	08700	wood	00960
Actuation devices. *See* Automated devices		Astragals	08700
Adam style	12632.4	Athletic equipment	
Adult measurements:	01090	exercise equipment	11480
closet storage		health club	11480
easy-reach height		playground equipment	02800
eye level		Atlas case. *See* Library equipment	
wheelchair dimensions	01090	Attic stairs	11450
Aggregates (terrazzo)	09400	Audio-visual equipment:	
Air conditioning in integrated ceilings	15850	custom television screen installation	12636
Airborne sound control	09500	media storage custom millwork	12636
Alkali. *See* Paint, primers		projection booths	16700
Alkyd. *See* Paint, primers		projection screens specifications	16700
All-glass entrances	08400	security installation for television sets	12600
Altars	11040	security monitor custom systems	12636
Ambient lighting	16500	stereo custom cabinet	12636
Amperages of commonly used items	16594.1	teleconferencing rooms	11800
Anthropometric data		television (orthodontics waiting room custom installation)	12355
See also Barrier-free entries	12300	video equipment space requirements	12600
Antiques reproductions. *See* Furniture, historic		Auditorium lighting requirements	16592
Apartments:		Auditorium seating. *See* Assembly seating	12700
combined spaces	12600	Automated devices:	15950
for elderly	01090	computer tables and desks	12642.2
furnishings for	12600	door-activated mats	08400
minimum space	12600	door closers (smoke activated)	08700
types of	12600	drafting tables	11100

Figure 18.4 continued

KEY WORD INDEX

KEY WORD INDEX

Figure 18.4 continued

KEY WORD INDEX

Figure 18.4 continued

KEY WORD INDEX

Figure 18.4 continued

KEY WORD INDEX

Figure 18.4 continued

KEY WORD INDEX

	CSI Broadscope Number		CSI Broadscope Number
Sizes of office files	12631	Studs (wood and steel)	05400
Skylights:			06100
barrel vaults	07800	Study carrels. *See* Library equipment	
ceiling domes	07800	Suede estimating by sq. ft.	10250
construction methods	07800	Sun-control window systems	12500
structural details	07800	Supports and anchors	09250
types	07800	Suspension ceilings	15850
Slate	09625	Swings (playground)	02800
Slides (drawer hardware)	08700	Swivel chairs	12710
Sliding doors	08300	Symbols and abbreviations. *See* Abbreviations and symbols	
Sliding partitions	10600	Systems furniture. *See* Open office furnishings	
Sliding windows	08300		
Slipperiness factor	09650	Table hardware. *See* Hardware, table	
Snack bar equipment	12300	Tables:	
Soap dispensers for public washrooms	10800	arrangement for elderly	12600
Sofa bed for public lounge	12633	banquet placement for safe exit	12700
Sofas	12629	bases	12630
Soffit details	06100	cocktail (custom)	06410
Solid core doors (exterior)	08250	conference (custom)	12642.1
Sound control	09250	conference teleconferencing	16500
Spas	13050	dining (custom)	12635
Spanish furniture	12632.2	height from booth top	12700
Special service windows	11030	rectangular banquet when cross aisles required	12700
Species of woods	06100	seating capacity	12631
Spiral stairs	05700	top construction	06410
Spline joint (wood)	06400	top sizes	12630
Spring hinge for double-action door	08700	Tambour	12636
Springs. *See* Upholstery		Task lighting. *See* Lighting	
Sprinkler systems	15340	Telecommunication space and equipment	11800
Stack units (washer and dryer)	11450	Telephone booths	10750
Stacking chairs	12705	Television set custom installation	12636
Stacks (books). *See* Library		Television set security mounting	12600
Stage lighting	16500	Television set sizes	15300
Stains (wood)	09900	Teller counters. *See* Banks	
Stair lifts	14400	Teller windows. *See* Banks	
Stair rails (metal)	05500	Terrazzo	09400
Stair rails (wood)	06200	Textiles. *See* Fabrics	
Stairs:		Thresholds	08400
disappearing	11450	Tile bathtub enclosures	09300
fire safety	03100	Tile (ceramic)	09300
monumental	06400	Toilet and bath accessories	10800
spiral	05700	Toilet tissue dispensers	10800
wood (custom)	06400	Tongue-and-grove construction	06400
Standard abbreviations and symbols. *See* Abbreviations and symbols		Towel bars and holders	10800
Standard showcase cabinets. *See* Retail stores		Track lighting. *See* Lighting	
Standards and references. *See* Codes and standards		Tracks and hardware for doors	08300
Steam room ceramic tile wall	09300	Traditional furnishings. *See* Furniture, historic	
Steel stud systems	05400	Trash compactors. *See* Kitchens, appliances	
Stone:		Traverse rods (drapery)	12350
installation	04465	Tray conveyors (food)	11400
	09400	Treads of stairs	01060
standards	04400	Trestle tables	12632
terminology	04465	Trundle beds	12633
uses and finishes	04400	Tubs. *See* Bath fixtures	
Storage:		Turnstiles	10450
bar	11400	Turntable, (phonograph, custom)	12636
clothing:			
hanging garments	12300	Uniform wall lighting. *See* Lighting	
shoes	12635	Unit kitchens	11460
commercial kitchens	11450	Upholstery:	
kitchen	11450	booth (rigid coil springs)	12051
merchandise	11100	booths (custom, specification)	12700
office	12642	chair construction	12051
residential	12635	leather and suede square footage	12051
residential bath	12300	pitch and crown	12051
restaurant (wine and glasses)	11450	railroading fabric application	12050
women's retail clothing store	11100	spring numbers and positions	12051
Store fixtures. *See* Retail stores		yardage requirements	12050
Storefronts	08400	Upright office files	12631
Stoves (heating)	10300	Urinals	10800
Studio couches	12633	Utility room (janitor)	13030

KEY WORD INDEX

APPENDIXES

A. CONVERSION TABLE: ENGLISH TO METRIC UNIT MEASUREMENT*

ENGLISH MEASUREMENT	ACTUAL METRIC CONVERSION	SUGGESTED METRIC SIZE*
1/8″	3.18 mm	3.0 mm
1/4″	6.35	6.0
9/32″	7.14	7.0
5/16″	7.94	8.0
11/32″	8.73	9.0
3/8″	9.53	10.0
7/16″	11.11	11.0
15/32″	11.91	12.0
1/2″	12.70	13.0
9/16″	14.29	14.0
19/32″	15.08	15.0
5/8″	15.88	16.0
21/32″	16.67	17.0
11/16″	17.46	17.0
23/32″	18.26	18.0
3/4″	19.05	19.0
25/32″	19.84	20.0
13/16″	20.64	21.0
7/8″	22.23	22.0
1″	25.40	25.0
1-5/32″	29.39	29.0
1-1/4″	31.75	32.0
1-5/16″	33.34	33.0
1-13/32″	35.72	36.0
1-1/2″	38.10	38.0
1-9/16″	39.69	40.0
1-3/4″	44.45	44.0
2″	50.80	51.0
2-1/8″	53.98	54.0
2-1/4″	57.25	57.0
2-1/2″	63.50	64.0
3″	76.20	76.0
3-1/4″	82.55	83.0
3-1/2″	88.90	89.0
3-9/16″	90.49	90.0
3-3/4″	95.25	95.0
4-1/4″	107.95	108.0
4-1/2″	114.30	114.0
4-9/16″	115.89	116.0
4-3/4″	120.65	121.0
5-1/2″	139.70	140.0
5-3/4″	146.05	145.0

*Reproduced with permission of the Wood Molding and Millwork Producers.

B. PART 1632: STANDARD FOR THE FLAMMABILITY OF MATTRESSES (AND MATTRESS PADS) (FF $—72)*

AUTHORITY: Sec. 4, 67 Stat. 112, as amended, 81 Stat. 569-70; 15 U.S.C. 1193, unless otherwise noted.

SOURCE: 40 FR 59940, Dec. 30, 1975, unless otherwise noted.

Subpart A—The Standard

§ 1632.1 Definitions.

In addition to the definitions given in section 2 of the Flammable Fabrics Act as amended (sec. 1, 81 Stat. 568; 15 U.S.C. 1191) and the procedures under that act for setting standards (16 CFR Part 1607), the following definitions apply for the purpose of this standard.

(a) "Mattress" means a ticking filled with a resilient material used alone or in combination with other products and intended or promoted for sleeping upon. This definition includes, but is not limited to, mattress pads, adult mattresses, youth mattresses, crib mattresses including portable crib mattresses, bunk bed mattresses, convertible sofa bed mattresses, corner group mattresses, daybed mattresses, roll-a-way bed mattresses, high risers, and trundle bed mattresses. This definition excludes sleeping bags, pillows, mattress foundations such as box springs, liquid and gaseous filled tickings such as water beds and air mattresses, upholstered furniture such as chaise lounges, drop-arm love seats, press-back lounges, push-back sofas, sleep lounges, sofa beds (including jackknife sofa beds), sofa lounges (including glide-outs), studio couches, and studio divans (including twin studio divans and studio beds), and juvenile product pads such as car bed pads, carriage pads, basket pads, infant carrier and lounge pads, dressing table pads, stroller pads, crib bumpers, and playpen pads. See § 1632.6, Glossary of terms, for definition of the above.

(b) "Ticking" means the outermost layer of fabric or related material that encloses the mattress core and upholstery materials.

(c) "Core" means the main support system that may be present in a mattress, such as springs, foam, or hair block.

(d) "Upholstery material" means all material, either loose or attached, between the ticking or between the ticking and the core of the mattress, if a core is present.

(e) "Tape edge" (edge) means the seam or border edge of a mattress.

(f) "Quilted" means stitched through the ticking and one or more layers of upholstery material.

(g) "Tufted" means buttoned or laced through the ticking and upholstery material and/or core.

(h) "Mattress prototype" means mattresses of a particular design, sharing all materials and methods of assembly, but excluding differences in mattress size. If it has been shown as a result of prototype qualification testing that a material has not influenced the ignition resistance of the mattress prototype, substitution of another material for such material shall not be deemed a difference in materials for purposes of prototype definition. If it is determined or suspected that a material has influenced the ignition resistance of the mattress prototype, a dimensional or other change in that material shall be deemed a difference in materials for purposes of prototype definition unless it is previously shown to the satisfaction of the Consumer Product Safety Commission that such dimensional or other change will not reduce the ignition resistance of the mattress prototype.

(i) "Mattress type" means mattresses sharing a method of assembly, such as tufted, multineedle continuous quilt, deep panel quilt, and smooth top, and all materials affecting cigarette ignition, but excluding differences in mattress size. More than one mattress prototype may be included in a single mattress type, provided each prototype has the same method of assembly.

(j) "Production unit" (unit) means a quantity of mattresses of one mattress type. This quantity is predetermined by the mattress manufacturer subject to the maximum number specified in the applicable parts of § 1632.4(b) *Specimen and Sampling*. No mattress completed while other mattresses of the same type are in production shall be excluded from the production unit to which such other mattresses are assigned.

(k) "Surface" means one side of a mattress which is intended for sleeping upon and which can be tested.

§ 1632.2 Scope and application.

(a) This standard provides a test method to determine the ignition resistance of a mattress when exposed to a lighted cigarette.

(b) All mattresses, as defined in § 1632.1(a), are subject to the requirements of this standard.

(c) Mattresses which are subject to the coverage of the Motor Vehicle Safety Standard, No. 302, subject: "Flammability of Interior Materials—Passenger Cars, Multipurpose Passenger Vehicles, Trucks, and Buses" (36 FR 290), issued by the National Highway Traffic Safety Administration, are excluded from coverage under this standard, unless also intended or promoted for uses included in § 1632.1(a).

(d) One of a kind mattresses, such as nonstandard sizes or shapes, may be excluded from testing under this standard pursuant to rules and regulations established by the Consumer Product Safety Commission.

§ 1632.3 General requirements.

(a) *Summary of test method.* The method involves the exposure of the mattress surface to lighted cigarettes as the standard igniting source in a draft-protected environment and the measurement of the ignition resistance of the mattress. These exposures include smooth, tape edge, and quilted or tufted locations, if they exist on the mattress surface. Two-sheet tests are also conducted on similar surface locations. In the latter test, the burning cigarettes are placed between the sheets.

(b) *Test criterion.* Testing the mattress surface in accordance with the testing procedure set forth in § 1632.4 *test procedure*, individual cigarette test locations pass the test if the char length on the mattress surface is not

---

* *Reproduced with permission from the Code of Federal Regulations, Title 16, Part 1000 to End, Revised as of January 1, 1976.*

more than 5.1 cm (2 in) in any direction from the nearest point of the cigarette. In the interest of safety, the test operator should discontinue the test and record a failure before reaching the 2 in. char length if, in his opinion, an obvious ignition has occurred.

§ 1632.4 Test procedure.

(a) *Apparatus*—(1) *Testroom.* The testroom shall be large enough to accommodate a full-scale mattress in a horizontal position and to allow for free movement of personnel and air around the test mattress. The room shall be equipped with a support system (platform, bench, etc.) upon which a mattress may be placed flat in a horizontal position at a reasonable height for making observations. For thin, flexible mattresses and mattress pads, the top surface of the support system shall be nonmetallic. The test area shall be draft-protected and equipped with a suitable system for exhausting smoke and/or noxious gases produced by testing. The testroom atmospheric conditions shall be greater than 18° C (65° F) and at less than 55 percent relative humidity, except for production testing.

(2) *Ignition source.* The ignition source shall be cigarettes without filter tips made from natural tobacco, 85 ± 2 mm long with a tobacco packing density of 0.270 ± 0.020 g/cm^3 and a total weight of 1.1 ± 0.1 gm.

(3) *Fire extinguisher.* A pressurized water fire extinguisher, or other suitable fire extinguishing equipment, shall be immediately available.

– (4) *Water bottle.* A water bottle fitted with a spray nozzle shall be used to extinguish the ignited portions of the mattress.

(5) *Scale.* A linear scale graduated in millimeters, 0.1 inch, or ¹⁄₁₆-inch divisions shall be used to measure char length.

(6) *Other apparatus.* In addition to the above, a thermometer, a relative humidity measuring instrument, a knife or scissors, and tongs are required to carry out the testing.

(b) *Specimen and sampling*—(1) *General.* The test criterion of section 1632.3(b) shall be used in conjunction with the following mattress sampling plan, or any other approved by the Consumer Product Safety Commission that provides at least the equivalent level of fire safety to the consumer (see Subpart B of this Part). Alternate Sampling plans submitted for approval shall have operating characteristics such that the probability of unit acceptance at any percentage defective does not exceed the corresponding probability of unit acceptance of the following sampling plan in the region of the latter's operating characteristic curves that lies between 5 and 95 percent acceptance probability. If such alternate sampling plan involves testing of components of mattresses or materials used in mattresses, its submittal shall be supported by clear evidence of the necessary correlation of the results of such testing with those results from testing as prescribed hereunder.

(2) *Mattress sampling.* The basic mattress sampling plan is made up of two parts: (1) Prototype qualification and (2) production testing. In addition, a batch sampling plan is given which may be used for small production quantities, when shipping requirements prohibit the use of the basic plan, or for other reasons at the discretion of the manufacturer.

(i) *Basic sampling plan.* A production unit in the basic sampling plan shall consist of not more than 500 mattresses of a mattress type or the quantity produced in 3 consecutive calendar months, whichever is smaller. This unit size may be increased to the quantity produced in 3 consecutive calendar months or less: *Provided,* That it is either documented that each of the materials contributing to the cigarette ignition characteristics of all the mattresses in the unit came from a single manufacturing lot of such material or 50 consecutive production units, at least 20,000 mattresses, have all been accepted in production testing as set forth in § 1632.4(b)(2)(i)(B).

(A) *Prototype qualification.* (1) For prototype qualification, the term "manufacturer" shall mean (a) with respect to a company having one manufacturing facility, that company, (b) with respect to a company having two or more manufacturing facilities, either that company or one or more of its manufacturing facilities as it elects, or (c) with respect to a company that is part of a group of companies that have elected to share in a prototype design, either that group of companies or a portion of that group or (a) or (b) above, as that company elects.

(2) Each "manufacturer" shall select enough of each mattress prototype from preproduction or current production to provide six surfaces for test (three mattresses if both sides can be tested or six mattresses if only one side can be tested). Test each of the six surfaces according to § 1632.4(d) *Testing.* If all the cigarette test locations on all six surfaces satisfy the test criterion of § 1632.3(b), accept the mattress prototype. If one or more of the cigarette test locations on the six surfaces fail the test criterion of § 1632.3(b), reject the mattress prototype.

(3) If it has been elected to include more than one company and/or more than one manufacturing facility in the term "manufacturer" for purposes of prototype qualification, each such company and each such manufacturing facility shall select enough additional prototype mattresses from its own preproduction or current production to provide two surfaces for test. Test each of the two surfaces according to § 1632.4(d) *Testing.* If all cigarette test locations on both surfaces satisfy the test criterion of § 1632.3(b), accept the mattress prototype for that company or manufactur-

ing facility. If one or more of the cigarette test locations on the two surfaces fail the test criterion of § 1632.3(b), reject the mattress prototype for that company or manufacturing facility.

(4) Mattress prototype qualification may be repeated after the manufacturer has taken action to improve the resistance of the mattress prototype to ignition by cigarettes through mattress design, production, or materials selection. When mattress prototype qualification is repeated as a result of prototype rejection by the "manufacturer", such qualification shall be conducted as if it were an original qualification. When the mattress prototype qualification is repeated as a result of prototype rejection under the provisions of the preceding paragraph or as a result of production unit rejection, such qualification shall be performed as if the producer of the failing mattress were a company having one manufacturing facility.

(5) Each mattress prototype must be accepted in prototype qualification prior to shipping any mattresses to customers and prior to producing significant quantities of mattresses. If the "manufacturer" is one manufacturing facility, the first production unit manufactured immediately after successful prototype qualification or the production unit from which the mattresses were selected for the successful prototype qualification not to exceed 500 mattresses, may be accepted and shipped to customers without further testing if all mattresses in the production unit are the same as the prototype except for size.

(B) *Production testing.* For production testing, the term "manufacturer" shall mean each manufacturing facility. Random selection for production testing shall be accomplished by use of random number tables or equivalent means as determined by the Consumer Product Safety Commission. If it is desired to use only mattresses of a specified size (e.g., "twin") for testing, the drawing may be repeated until sufficient mattresses of that size have been selected. A production unit, except for the first production unit following successful prototype qualification as specified in § 1632.4(b)(2)(i)(A), is either accepted or rejected according to the following plan:

(1) *Normal sampling.* From each unit, randomly select enough mattresses to provide two surfaces for test (one mattress if both sides can be tested or two mattresses if only one side can be tested). Test each of the two surfaces according to § 1632.4(d) *Testing.* If all the cigarette test locations on both surfaces meet the test criterion of § 1632.3(b), accept the unit. If two or more individual cigarette test locations fail the test criterion of § 1632.3(b), reject the unit. If only one individual cigarette test location fails the test criterion of § 1632.3(b), select enough additional mattresses to provide four additional surfaces for test. Test each of the four

additional surfaces according to § 1632.4(d) *Testing.* If all the cigarette test locations on the four additional surfaces meet the test criterion of § 1632.3(b), accept the unit. If one or more of the individual cigarette test locations on the four additional surfaces fail the test criterion of § 1632.3(b), reject the unit. Unit rejection shall include all mattresses in the particular unit under test. Unit rejection also results in the loss of prototype qualification for all prototypes included in the unit under test. The loss of prototype qualification applies only to the company or manufacturing facility that produced the rejected unit.

(2) *Reduced sampling.* (i) The level of sampling required for mattress production acceptance may be reduced provided the preceding 15 consecutive units of mattresses, at least 500 mattresses, have all been accepted using the normal sampling plan. In this case, the production quantity for reduced sampling may be increased to up to two units, still not to exceed the production of 3 consecutive calendar months.

(ii) From this production quantity, randomly select enough mattresses to provide two surfaces for test. Test each of the two surfaces according to § 1632.4(d) *Testing.* If all the cigarette test locations on both surfaces meet the test criterion of § 1632.3(b), accept this production quantity. If two or more individual cigarette test locations fail the test criterion of § 1632.3(b), reject this production quantity. If only one individual cigarette test location fails the test criterion of § 1632.3(b), accept this production quantity.

(iii) Rejection shall include all mattresses in the production quantity under test. Rejection also results in the loss of prototype qualification for all prototypes included in the production quantity under test. The loss of prototype qualification applies only to the company or manufacturing facility that produced the rejected unit.

(ii) *Batch sampling plan.* (A) *General (1)* For the batch sampling plan, the term "manufacturer" shall mean each manufacturing facility.

(2) A production unit in the batch sampling plan shall consist of not more than 250 mattresses or the quantity produced in one period of 30 consecutive calendar days, whichever is smaller.

(B) *Batch unit qualification and acceptance (1)* Select enough mattresses from the initial production of the unit to provide four surfaces for test (two mattresses if both sides can be tested or four mattresses if only one side can be tested). Test each of the four surfaces according to § 1632.4(d) *Testing.* If all the cigarette test locations on the four surfaces meet the test criterion of § 1632.3(b), accept the unit. If one or more of the cigarette test locations on the four surfaces fail the test criterion of § 1632.3(b), reject the unit.

(2) After rejection, unit qualification and acceptance under this batch sampling plan may be repeated after the resistance of the mattress to ignition by cigarettes is improved by the manufacturer taking corrective action in mattress design, production, or materials selection.

(3) Acceptance of any production unit under this batch sampling plan shall not have any effect on prototype qualification or unit acceptance of any other production unit.

(3) *Disposition of rejected units.* Rejected units shall not be retested, offered for sale, sold, or promoted for use as a mattress as defined in § 1632.1(a) except after reworking to improve the resistance to ignition by cigarettes and subsequent retesting in accordance with the procedures set forth in § 1632.4(b)(2)(i) *Basic Sampling Plan.*

(4) *Records.* Records of all unit sizes, test results, and the disposition of rejected units shall be maintained by the manufacturer, in accordance with rules and regulations established by the Consumer Product Safety Commission.

(5) *Preparation of mattress samples.* The mattress surface shall be divided laterally into two sections (see fig. 1), one section for the bare mattress tests and the other for the two-sheet tests.

(6) *Sheet selection.* The sheets shall be white, 100 percent combed cotton percale, not treated with a chemical finish which imparts a characteristic such as permanent press or flame resistance, with 170-200 threads per square inch and fabric weight of 115 ± 14 gm/m^2 (3.4 ± 0.4 oz/yd^2), or of another type approved by the Consumer Product Safety Commission. Size of sheet shall be appropriate for the mattress being tested.

(7) *Sheet preparation.* The sheets shall be laundered once before use in an automatic home washer using the hot water setting and longest normal cycle with the manufacturer's recommended quantity of a commercial detergent, and dried in an automatic home tumble dryer. The sheet shall be cut across the width into two equal parts after washing.

(8) *Cigarettes.* Unopened packages of cigarettes shall be selected for each series of tests.

(9) *Compliance marketing sampling plans.* Sampling plans for use in market testing of items covered by this standard may be issued by the Consumer Product Safety Commission. Such plans shall define noncompliance of a production unit to exist only when it is shown, with a high level of statistical confidence, those production units represented by tested items which fail such plans will, in fact, fail this standard. Production units found to be noncomplying under these provisions shall be deemed not to conform to this standard. The Consumer Product Safety Commission will publish such plans in the FEDERAL REGISTER for public comment prior to

their enactment.

(10) *Postponement of production testing.* Temporary suspension of production testing may be granted on a case-by-case basis by the Consumer Product Safety Commission in those instances where an individual manufacturer proves, under rules prescribed by CPSC, that he cannot acquire access to either in-house or independent testing facilities for production testing. In the event of such a suspension, the manufacturer would still be obligated to produce a mattress which meets all other requirements of the standard.

(c) *Conditioning—(1) Prototype and batch.* The mattresses, washed sheets, and cigarettes shall be conditioned in air at a temperature greater than 18° C (65° F) and a relative humidity less than 55 percent for at least 48 hours prior to test. The mattresses, washed sheets, and cigarettes shall be removed from any packaging and supported in a suitable manner to permit free movement of air around them during conditioning. The mattress meets this conditioning requirement if the mattress and/or all its component materials, except the metallic core, have been exposed only to the above temperature and humidity conditions for at least 48 hours prior to testing the mattress.

(2) *Production.* Mattresses to be tested according to § 1632.4(b)(2)(i)(B) *Production testing* shall be exempt from conditioning as specified in § 1632.4(c)(1). However, the mattresses shall not be exposed to any environmental conditions which promote resistance to cigarette ignition. Sheets and cigarettes in their normally used condition (dry) shall be used.

(d) *Testing—(1) General.* Mattress specimens selected for testing in prototype and batch sampling shall be tested in a testroom with atmospheric conditions of a temperature greater than 18° C (65° F) and a relative humidity less than 55 percent. If the test is not performed in the conditioning room, the mattress shall be tested within 1 hour after removal from the conditioning room.

(i) Light and place one cigarette at a time on the mattress surface. (If previous experience with the same type of mattress has indicated that ignition is not likely, the number of cigarettes which may be lighted and placed on the mattress at one time is left to the test operator's judgment. The number of cigarettes must be carefully considered because a smoldering or burning mattress is extremely hazardous and difficult to extinguish.) If more than one cigarette is burning at one time, the cigarettes must be positioned no less than 6 inches apart on the mattress surface. Each cigarette used as an ignition source shall be well lighted but not burned more than 4 mm (0.16 in) when placed on the mattress. (Fire extinguishing equipment must be readily available at all times.)

(ii) If a cigarette extinguishes before

burning its full length, the test must be repeated with a freshly lit cigarette on a different portion of the same type of location on the mattress surface until either (a) the number of cigarettes specified in § 1632.4(d)(1)(iii) have burned their full lengths, (b) the number of cigarettes specified has extinguished before burning their full lengths, or (c) the number of cigarettes specified have resulted in failures according to § 1632.3(b) *Test criterion.*

(iii) At least 18 cigarettes shall be burned on each mattress test surface, 9 in the bare mattress tests and 9 in the 2-sheet tests. If three or more mattress surface locations (smooth surface, tape edge, quilted, or tufted areas) exists in the particular mattress surface under test, three cigarettes shall be burned on each different surface location. If only two mattress surface locations exist in the particular mattress surface under test (tape edge and smooth surface), four cigarettes shall be burned on the smooth surface and five cigarettes shall be burned on the tape edge.

(2) *Bare mattress tests*—(i) *Smooth surfaces.* Each burning cigarette shall be placed directly on a smooth surface location on the test surface on the half reserved for bare mattress tests. The cigarettes should burn their full lengths on a smooth surface without burning across a tuft, or stitching of a quilted area. However, if this is not possible because of mattress design, then the cigarettes shall be positioned on the mattress in a manner which will allow as much of the butt ends as possible to burn on smooth surfaces. Report results for each cigarette as pass or fail as defined in the test criterion.

CAUTION: Even under the most carefully observed conditions, smoldering combustion can progress to the point where it cannot be readily extinguished. It is imperative that a test be discontinued as soon as ignition has definitely occurred. Immediately wet the exposed area with a water spray (from water bottle), cut around the burning material with a knife or scissors and pull the material out of the mattress with tongs. Make sure that all charred or burned material is removed. Ventilate the room.

(ii) *Tape edge.* Each burning cigarette shall be placed in the depression between the mattress top surface and the tape edge, parallel to the tape edge on the half of the test surface reserved for bare mattress tests. If there is no depression at the edge, support the cigarettes in place along the edge and parallel to the edge with straight pins. Three straight pins may be inserted through the edge at a 45° angle such that one pin supports the cigarette at the burning end, one at the center, and one at the butt. The heads of the pins must be below the upper surface of the cigarette (see fig. 2). Report results for each cigarette as pass or fail as defined in the test criterion.

MATTRESS PREPARATION

FIGURE 1

CIGARETTE LOCATION

FIGURE 2

(iii) *Quilted location.* If quilting exists on the test surface, each burning cigarette shall be placed on quilted locations of the test surface. The cigarettes shall be positioned directly over the thread in the depression created by the quilting process on the half of the test surface reserved for bare mattress tests. If the quilt design is such that the cigarettes cannot burn their full lengths over the thread, then the cigarettes shall be positioned in a manner which will allow as much of the butt ends as possible to burn on the thread. Report results for each cigarette as pass or fail as defined in the test criterion.

(iv) *Tufted location.* If tufting exists on the test surface, each burning cigarette shall be placed on tufted locations of the test surface. The cigarettes shall be positioned so that they burn down into the depression caused by the tufts and so that the butt ends of the cigarettes burn out over the buttons or laces used in the tufts on the half of the test surface reserved for bare mattress tests. Report results for each cigarette as pass or fail as defined in the test criterion.

(3) *Two-sheet tests.* Spread a section of sheet smoothly over the mattress surface and tuck under the mattress

on the second half of the test surface, which has been reserved for the two-sheet test. Care must be taken that hems or any other portion of the sheet which is more than one fabric thickness, is neither directly under nor directly over the test cigarette in the two-sheet test.

(i) *Smooth surfaces.* Each burning cigarette shall be placed directly on the sheet covered mattress in a smooth surface location as defined in the bare mattress test. Immediately cover the first sheet and the burning cigarettes loosely with a second, or top sheet (see fig. 2). Do not raise or lift the top sheet during testing unless obvious ignition has occurred or until the cigarette has burned out. (The extinguishment of the cigarette may be determined by holding the hand near the surface of the top sheet over the test location. If neither heat is felt nor smoke observed, the cigarette has burned out.) If ignition occurs, immediately remove the sheets and cigarette and follow the cautionary procedures outlined in the bare mattress test. Report results for each cigarette as pass or fail as defined in the test criterion.

(ii) *Tape edge.* (A) Each burning cigarette shall be placed in the depression between the top surface and the tape edge on top of the sheet, and immediately covered with a second sheet. It is important that the air space be eliminated, as much as possible, between the mattress and the bottom sheet at the test location before testing. Depress the bottom sheet into the depression using a thin rod or other suitable instrument.

(B) In most cases, the cigarettes will remain in place throughout the test; however, if the cigarettes show a marked tendency to roll off the tape edge location, they may be supported with straight pins. Three straight pins may be inserted through the bottom sheet and tape at a 45° angle such that one pin supports the cigarette at the burning end, one at the center, and one at the butt. The heads of the pins must be below the upper surface of the cigarette (see fig. 2). Report results for each cigarette as pass or fail as defined in the test criterion.

(iii) *Quilted locations.* If quilting exists on the test surface, each burning cigarette shall be placed in a depression caused by quilting, directly over the thread and on the bottom sheet, and immediately covered with the top sheet. It is important that the air space be eliminated, as much as possible, between the mattress and the bottom sheet at the test location before testing. Depress the bottom sheet into the depression using a thin rod or other suitable instrument. If the quilt design is such that the cigarettes cannot burn their full lengths over the thread, then the cigarettes shall be positioned in a manner which will allow as much of the butt ends as possible to burn on the thread. Report results for each cigarette as pass or fail as defined in the test criterion.

(iv) *Tufted locations.* If tufting exists on the test surface, each burning cigarette shall be placed in the depression caused by tufting, directly over the tuft and on the bottom sheet, and immediately covered with the top sheet. It is important that the air space be eliminated, as much as possible, between the mattress and the bottom sheet at the test location before testing. Depress the bottom sheet into the depression using a thin rod or other suitable instrument. The cigarettes shall be positioned so that they burn down into the depression caused by the tuft and so that the butt ends of the cigarettes burn out over the buttons or laces used in the tufts. Report results for each cigarette as pass or fail as defined in the test criterion.

§ 1632.5 **Mattress pads.**

(a) *Testing.* Mattress pads shall be tested in the same manner as mattresses according to § 1632.4 *Test procedure* except for laundering.

(b) *Laundering.* (1) Mattress pads which have had a chemical fire retardant treatment or contain any chemically fire retardant treated components, shall be tested in accordance with § 1632.4 *Test procedure* in the condition in which they are intended to be sold, and after they have been washed and dried 10 times according to the procedure prescribed in method 124-1969 of the American Association of Textile Chemists and Colorists washing procedure 6.2 (III), with a water temperature of 60°±2.8° C (140°±5° F), and drying procedure 6.3.2(B). Maximum load shall be 3.46 kg (8 lb) and may consist of any combination of test items and dummy pieces. Alternately, a different number of times under another washing and drying procedure may be specified and used, if that procedure has previously been found to be equivalent by the Consumer Product Safety Commission.

(2) Such laundering is not required of mattress pads which are not intended to be laundered, as determined by the Consumer Product Safety Commission.

(3) Mattress pads which are not susceptible to being laundered and are labeled "dryclean only" shall be drycleaned by a procedure which has previously been found acceptable by the Consumer Product Safety Commission.

(c) *Labeling.* (1) *Treatment label.* If a mattress pad has had a chemical fire retardant treatment or contains any fire retardant treated components, it shall be labeled with the letter "T" pursuant to rules and regulations established by the Consumer Product Safety Commission.

(2) *Care label.* All mattress pads which have had a chemical fire retardant treatment or contain any fire re-

tardant treated components shall be labeled with precautionary instructions to protect the pads from agents or treatments which are known to cause deterioration of their flame resistance. Such labels shall be permanent and otherwise in accordance with rules and regulations established by the Consumer Product Safety Commission.

(3) *Temporary requirement for noncomplying mattresses.* (i) Mattresses which do not comply with all the provisions of this standard and are manufactured during the 6 months following the effective date of this standard shall, prior to introduction into commerce, be prominently and conspicuously labeled with the following statement:

WARNING: This mattress does not meet the Consumer Product Safety Commission Flammability Standard for Mattresses (FF 4-72, as amended). It may be subject to ignition and hazardous smoldering from cigarettes.

(ii) Such label must be affixed to the mattress in such a manner so as to remain on or affixed thereto until its sale or delivery to the ultimate consumer. The label must be displayed on the mattress at the place of retail sale and the statement on the label must be prominently and conspicuously displayed on the invoice or other sales papers that accompany the mattress through commerce from the manufacturer to the final point of sale to a consumer.

(iii) This label must be at least 250 cm² (approximately 40 in²) with no linear dimension less than 12.5 cm (approximately 5 in). The wording of such label shall appear on a contrasting background with the letters in the heading WARNING no less than 1.2 cm (approximately ½ in) in height.

§ 1632.6 **Glossary of terms.**

(a) *Basket pad.* Cushion for use in an infant basket.

(b) *Box spring.* A bedspring that consists of springs attached to a foundation and enclosed in a cloth covered, upholstered frame.

(c) *Bunk beds.* A tier of beds, usually two or three, in a high frame complete with mattresses (see fig. 3).

(d) *Car bed.* Portable bed used to carry a baby in an automobile.

(e) *Carriage pad.* Cushion to go into a baby carriage.

(f) *Chaise lounge.* An upholstered couch chair or a couch with a chair back. It has a permanent back rest, no arms, and sleeps one (see fig. 3).

(g) *Convertible sofa.* An upholstered sofa that converts into an adult sized bed. Mattress unfolds out and up from under the seat cushioning (see fig. 3).

(h) *Corner groups.* Two twin size bedding sets on frames, usually slipcovered, and abutted to a corner table. They also usually have loose bolsters slipcovered (see fig. 3).

(i) *Crib bumper.* Padded cushion which goes around three or four sides inside a crib to protect the baby. Can

also be used in a playpen.

(j) *Daybed.* Daybed has foundation, usually supported by coil or flat springs, mounted between arms on which mattress is placed. It has permanent arms, no backrest, and sleeps one (see fig. 3).

(k) *Dressing table pad.* Pad to cushion a baby on top of a dressing table.

(l) *Drop-arm loveseat.* When side arms are in vertical position, this piece is a loveseat. The adjustable arms can be lowered to one of four positions for a chaise lounge effect or a single sleeper. The vertical back support always remains upright and stationary (see fig. 3).

(m) *High riser.* This is a frame of sofa seating height with two equal size mattresses without a backrest. The frame slides out with the lower bed and rises to form a double or two single beds (see fig. 3).

(n) *Infant carrier and lounge pad.* Pad to cushion a baby in an infant carrier.

(o) *Mattress foundation.* Consists of any surface upon which a mattress is placed to lend it support for use in sleeping upon.

(p) *Mattress pad.* A thin, flat, mat or cushion for use on top of a mattress.

(q) *Pillow.* Cloth bag filled with resilient material such as feathers, down, sponge rubber, urethane, or fiber used as the support for the head of a person.

(r) *Playpen pad.* Cushion used on the bottom of a playpen.

(s) *Portable crib.* Smaller size than a conventional crib. Can usually be converted into a playpen.

(t) *Press-back lounges.* Longer and wider than conventional sofa beds. When the lounge seat is pressed lightly, it levels off to form, with the seat, a flat sleeping surface. The seat slopes, in the sitting position, for added comfort (see fig. 3).

(u) *Push-back sofa.* When you push on the back of the sofa, it becomes a bed. Lift the back and it is a sofa again. Styled in tight or loose cushions (see fig. 3).

(v) *Roll-a-way bed.* Portable bed which has frame which folds in half with the mattress for compact storage.

(w) *Sleep lounge.* Upholstered seating section is mounted on a sturdy frame. May have bolster pillows along the wall as backrests or may have attached headrests (see fig. 3).

(x) *Stroller pad.* Cushion used in a baby stroller.

(y) *Sofa bed.* These are pieces in which the back of the sofa swings down flat with the seat to form the sleeping surface. All upholstered. Some sofa beds have bedding boxes for storage of bedding. There are two types: the one-piece, where the back and seat are upholstered as a unit, supplying an unbroken sleeping surface; and the two-piece, where back and seat are upholstered separately (see fig. 3).

(z) *Sofa lounge—(includes glideouts).* Upholstered seating section is mounted on springs and in a special frame that permits it to be pulled out for sleeping. Has upholstered backrest bedding box that is hinged. Glideouts are single sleepers with sloping seats and backrests. Seat pulls out from beneath back and evens up to supply level sleeping surface (see fig. 3).

(aa) *Studio couch.* Consists of upholstered seating section on upholstered foundation. Many types convert to twin beds (see fig. 3).

(bb) *Studio divan.* Twin size upholstered seating section with foundation is mounted on metal bed frame. Has no arms or backrest, and sleeps one (see fig. 3).

(cc) *Trundle bed.* A low bed which is rolled under a larger bed. In some lines, the lower bed springs up to form a double or two single beds as in a high riser (see fig. 3).

(dd) *Twin studio divan.* Frames which glide out (but not up) and use seat cushions, in addition to upholstered foundation to sleep two. Has neither arms nor back rest (see fig. 3).

FIGURE 3

C. CONSUMER PRODUCT SAFETY ACT REGULATIONS*

PART 1105—SUBMISSION OF EXISTING STANDARDS; OFFERS TO DEVELOP STANDARDS; AND THE DEVELOPMENT OF STANDARDS

AUTHORITY: Secs. 7 and 9, Pub. L. 92–573, as amended Pub. L. 94–284, 86 Stat. 1212–15, as amended 90 Stat. 505–506; 15 U.S.C. 2056, 2058.

SOURCE: 39 FR 16213, May 7, 1974, unless otherwise noted.

§ 1105.1 General policy considerations.

(a) The general policy under which the procedures in this Part 1105 are issued is that the interest and participation of the public is vital for carrying out the functions of the Consumer Product Safety Commission. Commission activities and deliberations are open to the public and afford any interested person the opportunity to participate and be heard. Accordingly, standards development activities by offerors will be open to the public and will afford the opportunity for any interested person to participate in the development of standards.

(b) The major objective of the Consumer Product Safety Act ("act") is to reduce unreasonable risks of injury associated with the use of consumer products. This objective may be achieved through the development and promulgation of mandatory "consumer product safety standards" where they are considered necessary to eliminate or reduce the risk of injury. A consumer product safety standard is a standard which will consist of (1) requirements as to performance, composition, contents, design, construction, finish, or packaging, or (2) requirements that a consumer product be marked with or accompanied by clear and adequate warnings or instructions, or requirements respecting the form of warnings or instructions, or (3) any combination of (1) and (2). Requirements other than those relating to labeling, warnings, or instructions, shall whenever feasible be expressed in terms of performance requirements.

(c) Under the act, consumer product safety standards may originate in three ways. First, the Commission, after publishing a "notice of proceeding" in the FEDERAL REGISTER, is authorized to publish as a proposed standard an existing standard which has been previously issued or adopted by a qualified public or private agency or organization. Second, the Commission is authorized to accept offers from one or more persons or organizations to develop a standard. Third, the Commission may under certain circumstances independently develop a standard.

(d) Since safety standards are intended to eliminate or reduce unreasonable risks of injury associated with consumer products, the Commission, in issuing this Part 1105, seeks the involvement of all interested persons, the general public, and especially ultimate consumers. Ultimate consumers and their representatives, as well as all other interested persons, are invited and encouraged to become involved by submitting offers to develop standards and by participating in the development of standards by other offerors.

(e) Persons who are not members of an established organization may form a group for the express purpose of submitting offers and developing standards; such groups are referred to in these rules as "ad hoc associations."

(f) Public involvement will be encouraged through the use of extensive public notice. In addition to providing notice in the FEDERAL REGISTER, the Commission will issue a press release at the initiation of a proceeding. This release will invite any person to either submit an existing standard or offer to develop a standard. A press release will also be issued at the time an offer is accepted. This second press release will invite all interested persons to participate in the development of a standard and will describe the method by which interested persons, including ultimate consumers, may participate.

(g) The Commission will maintain a list of all persons and organizations that have expressed an interest in either being offerors or in participating in the development of standards. Copies of the FEDERAL REGISTER notice of proceeding, press release, and/or other relevant documents will be transmitted by the Commission to appropriate persons and organizations on the list that have expressed an interest in being offerors. Copies of the FEDERAL REGISTER notice of proceeding and the notice of acceptance of any offers will be transmitted by the Commission to appropriate persons and organizations on the list that have expressed an interest in participating in the development of standards.

(h) The act enables the Commission to contribute to the offeror's cost in developing a standard in any case in which the Commission determines that a contribution is likely to result in a more satisfactory standard. The Commission views this provision of the act as a means by which a variety of organizations will be able to develop standards. The Commission also views this provision as a means by which Commission can assist a cross section of interested persons, including consumers, to participate in the development of standards.

(i) The act provides that the invitation for the submission of offers to develop a standard shall state the period of time during which the standard is to be developed. Congress anticipated that this period would normally end 150 days after the publication of the invitation. The act also provides that the Commission may extend or shorten the period for development if it finds for good cause that a different period of time is appropriate either at the time of the invitation or at a later time. The Commission expects to receive standards that will, if adopted, appropriately reduce the unreasonable risks of injury to the public. The Commission will adopt a reasonable approach to determining the amount of time necessary to develop standards. The Commission believes, however, that as a general rule the public interest is best served by the development of standards in the shortest possible time commensurate with the objectives of the act and in conformance with the requirements contained in this Part 1105.

[39 FR 16213, May 7, 1974, as amended at 42 FR 58400, Nov. 9, 1977]

§ 1105.2 Summary of time sequence for the development of standards.

The notice of proceeding inviting the submission of existing standards and the submission of offers to develop standards will specify a period of time during which the standard is to be developed and submitted to the Commission. The act specifies that this period will end 150 days after the publication of the notice in the FEDERAL REGISTER, unless the Commission for good cause finds, and includes such finding in the notice, that a different period is appropriate. Under the act, persons must submit existing standards or offers to develop standards to the Commission within 30 days after the date of publication of the notice of

* Reproduced with permission from the Code of Federal Regulations, Title 16, Part 1000 to End, Revised as of January 1, 1976.

proceeding in the FEDERAL REGISTER. The Commission will evaluate the submissions and publish a summary of the terms of any accepted offer or offers as soon as possible, usually within 60 days after the date of publication of the notice of proceeding. In submitting an offer to develop a standard, each offeror is required to include a realistic estimate of the time required to develop the standard, including a detailed schedule for each phase of the development period. In accepting an offer and publishing a notice of the summary of the terms of each accepted offer, the Commission will either reaffirm the original period of time for the development of the standard, or, for good cause stated, establish and publicize a new period of time for the development of the standard. The standard, with all required accompanying information, must then be submitted to the Commission within the specified time, unless the Commission grants an extension and publishes a notice in the FEDERAL REGISTER stating its reasons for the extension.

[39 FR 16213, May 7, 1974, as amended at 42 FR 58400, Nov. 9, 1977]

§ 1105.3 Commencement of proceedings.

(a) A proceeding for the development of a consumer product safety standard shall be commenced by the publication of a "notice of proceeding" in the FEDERAL REGISTER which shall:

(1) Identify the product and clearly describe the nature of the risks of injury associated with the product;

(2) State the Commission's determination that a consumer product safety standard is necessary to eliminate or reduce the specified unreasonable risks of injury associated with the product;

(3) Include information with respect to any existing domestic, foreign, or international standard known to the Commission which may be relevant to the proceeding, including information as to any deficiencies that the Commission recognizes in each identified standard that may make it not totally acceptable as a proposed rule;

(4) Provide information concerning the availability of Commission material relating to: (i) The specific nature of the risks of injury associated with the product, (ii) the basis for the Commission's determination concerning the need for a mandatory standard, and (iii) additional information relating to the development of a mandatory standard which may be helpful to potential offerors;

(5) Include an invitation for any standards-writing organization, trade association, consumer organization, professional or technical society, testing laboratory, university or college department, wholesale or retail organization, Federal, State, or local government agency, engineering or research and development establishment, ad hoc association, or any company or person, within 30 days after the date of FEDERAL REGISTER publication of the notice:

(i) To submit to the Commission an existing standard as the proposed consumer product safety standard; or

(ii) To offer to develop a proposed consumer product safety standard;

(6) Include, to the extent known at the time the notice of proceeding is published, any requirement for additional information which is to be submitted to the Commission with either an existing standard or a standard to be developed by an offeror; and

(7) Specify the period of time during which the standard is to be developed and submitted to the Commission.

(b) The Commission will, for the purpose of providing greater public awareness of its actions, issue a press release concerning the initiation of the proceeding. The press release will summarize the information contained in the FEDERAL REGISTER notice, including the invitation to any interested organization or person to submit an existing standard or to offer to develop a proposed consumer product safety standard.

(c) The Commission will transmit a copy of the FEDERAL REGISTER notice, press release, and/or other relevant documents to appropriate persons and organizations, on a list maintained by the Commission, that have expressed an interest in being offerors for one or more standards.

§ 1105.4 Submission of existing standards.

(a) Any standards-writing organization, trade association, consumer organization, professional or technical society, testing laboratory, university or college department, wholesale or retail organization, Federal, State, or local government agency, engineering or research and development establishment, ad hoc association, or any company or person may submit a standard previously issued or adopted by any private or public organization or agency, domestic or foreign, or any international standards organization, that contains safety-related requirements which the person believes would be adequate to prevent or reduce the unreasonable risks of injury associated with the product identified by the Commission.

(b) Any submission of an existing standard should:

(1) To the extent possible, meet the requirements for standards developed by offerors contained in § 1105.8 as specified in each notice of proceeding;

(2) Identify the specific portions which are appropriate for inclusion in the proposed rule; and

(3) Be accompanied, to the extent that such information is available, by a description of the procedures used to develop the standard and a listing of the persons and organizations that participated in the development and approval of the standard.

(c) If the Commission determines that (1) there exists a standard which has been issued or adopted by any Federal agency or by any other qualified agency, organization, or institu-

tion, and (2) such standard if promulgated under the act would eliminate or reduce the unreasonable risks of injury associated with the product, then the Commission may, in lieu of accepting an offer to develop a standard under § 1105.6, publish the existing standard as a proposed consumer product safety standard.

§ 1105.5 Submission of offers.

(a) Any standards-writing organization, trade association, consumer organization, technical or professional society, testing laboratory, university or college department, wholesale or retail organization, Federal, State, or local government agency, engineering or research and development establishment, ad hoc association, or any company or person may submit an offer to develop a proposed consumer product safety standard. Each offer shall include a detailed description of the procedure the offeror will utilize in developing the standard. Each offer shall also include:

(1) A description of the plan the offeror will use to give adequate and reasonable notice to interested persons (including individual consumers, manufacturers, distributors, retailers, importers, trade associations, professional and technical societies, testing laboratories, Federal and State agencies, educational institutions, and consumer organizations) of their right and opportunity to participate in the development of the standard;

(2) A description of the method whereby interested persons who have responded to the notice may participate, either in person or through correspondence, in the development of the standard; and

(3) A realistic estimate of the time required to develop the standard, including a detailed schedule for each phase of the standard development period.

(b) Each offeror shall submit with the offer the following information to supplement the description of the standard development procedure:

(1) A statement listing the number and experience of the personnel, including voluntary participants, the offeror intends to utilize in developing the standard. This list should distinguish between (i) persons directly employed by the offeror, (ii) persons who have made a commitment to participate, (iii) organizaions that have made commitments to provide a specific number of personnel and (iv) other persons to be utilized, although unidentified and uncommitted at the time of the submission. The educational and experience qualifications of these personnel relevant to the development of the standard should also be included in the statement. This list should include only those persons who will be directly involved in person in the development of the standard; and

(2) A statement describing the type of facilities or equipment which the offeror plans to utilize in developing

the standard and how the offeror plans to gain access to the facilities or equipment.

(c) Persons who are not members of an established organization may form a group for the express purpose of submitting offers and developing standards. These groups are referred to as "ad hoc associations." An offer by an ad hoc association may be submitted by an individual member if the offer states that it is submitted on behalf of the members of the association. The individual member submitting the offer shall submit to the Commission a notarized copy of a power of attorney from each member of the association authorizing the individual member to submit an offer on behalf of each other member.

[39 FR 16213, May 7, 1974; 39 FR 18093, May 23, 1974]

§ 1105.6 Acceptance of offers.

(a)(1) If the Commission (i) does not decide to publish an existing standard as a proposed consumer product safety standard or (ii) decides to publish an existing standard as a proposed consumer product safety standard which does not address all of the specified unreasonable risks of injury associated with the product, the Commission will as soon as possible, usually within 60 days of the date of publication of the notice of proceeding in the FEDERAL REGISTER, accept one or more offers to develop a proposed consumer product safety standard.

(2) Acceptance of an offer will be based on a determination by the Commission that an offeror is technically competent, is likely to develop an appropriate standard within the period specified in the notice of proceeding or within the period determined by the Commission to be necessary and appropriate for the development of the standard, and will comply with all of the requirements of the Commission for the development of the standard.

(3) An offeror will be considered to have technical competence if the offer submitted indicates to the satisfaction of the Commission (i) that the offeror has demonstrated a thorough understanding of the problem, (ii) that the offeror has provided a rational approach to the solution of that problem, and (iii) that persons with appropriate technical expertise or experience will be utilized in the development of the standard either as employees, consultants, or volunteers.

(b) Prior to accepting an offer to develop a standard, the Commission may require minor modifications of the offer as a condition of acceptance.

(c) The Commission shall publish in the FEDERAL REGISTER the name, address, and organizational affiliation of each person whose offer it accepts and a summary of the terms of each accepted offer including the date established for the submission of the standard.

(d) The Commission, at or near the time of the FEDERAL REGISTER acceptance notice, will issue a press release which:

(1) Identifies each person (name, address, and organizational affiliation) whose offer has been accepted;

(2) Summarizes the terms of each accepted offer including the date established for the submission of the standard; and

(3) Invites all interested persons to participate in the development of the standard and informs them of how they may participate.

(e) The Commission will transmit to appropriate persons and organizations, on a list maintained by the Commission, that have expressed an interest in participating in the development of one or more standards a copy of the FEDERAL REGISTER notice of proceeding as well as the notice of the acceptance of any offers.

(f) All persons submitting offers to develop standards whose offers have not been accepted will be notified in writing by the Commission. If requested by an offeror, the reasons for the nonacceptance of the offer will be supplied.

(g) If the Commission does not accept an offer to develop a proposed consumer product safety standard, the Commission may independently develop a proposed consumer product safety standard. Notice of this decision will be published in the FEDERAL REGISTER.

(h) In any case in which the sole offeror whose offer is accepted is a manufacturer, distributor, or retailer of the consumer product proposed to be regulated by the consumer product safety standard, the Commission may independently proceed to develop a proposed standard during the development period.

§ 1105.7 Development of recommended consumer product safety standards.

(a) The offeror shall comply with all Commission requirements for the development of standards and with all terms of the acceptance and shall cooperate with Commission liaison personnel assigned to monitor the development of the standard.

(b) In developing a standard, the offeror shall use the method agreed upon for interested persons to participate in the development of the standard and shall fully consider all of the suggestions and contributions of the respective participants. The offeror, after considering all suggestions and contributions, shall draft a standard. The draft standard shall be sent to all participants for their review and concurrence or nonconcurrence. Unanimity among all participants shall not be a prerequisite to the submission by the offeror to the Commission of a standard which, in the offeror's judgment, optimally meets the terms of the offer accepted by the Commission.

(c) The offeror shall maintain complete written records of the development of the standard. These records shall include:

(1) The names, addresses, and titles if any, of all persons contacting the offeror for the purpose of participating in the development of the standard;

(2) All written comments and any other information submitted by any person in connection with the development of the standard, including the dissenting views of participants and comments and information with respect to the need for the standard;

(3) A discussion describing the base for resolution by the offeror of all of the substantive issues raised during the development of the standard;

(4) A statement of the economic and environmental factors considered during the development of the standard; and

(5) Records of all other matters relevant to the development and evaluation of the standard. These records shall be submitted to the Commission at the termination of the development period. The Commission will make these records available for public inspection and will supply copies upon request, subject to the provisions of the Freedom of Information Act (5 U.S.C. 552), section 6 of the Consumer Product Safety Act (15 U.S.C. 2055), and regulations relating to the availability of Commission records.

(d) The offeror shall provide monthly progress reports containing a summary of progress made, the work under way, the significant problems encountered and the work remaining to be accomplished. These reports shall be transmitted to the Technical Analysis Division, Office of Standards Coordination and Appraisal, Consumer Product Safety Commission, Washington, D.C. 20207. The offeror shall cooperate fully with the Commission and permit the inspection of its facilities and development activities by duly authorized representatives of the Commission for the purpose of determining whether satisfactory progress is being made toward the completion of the standard. The offeror shall be considered to be making satisfactory progress if the Commission concludes that the standard may reasonably be expected to be completed in accordance with the provisions of the accepted offer by the end of the development period.

(e)(1) If it appears to the Commission that an offeror is not making satisfactory progress, the offeror will be given the opportunity (i) to demonstrate ability and willingness to complete the development of the standard by the end of the development period, or (ii) to justify the need for an extension of the development period.

(2) The Commission, after consideration and due notice, may (i) terminate the offeror's role in the development process and require the offeror to submit to the Commission all information, records, and documents which pertain to the development of the standard, or (ii) extend the development period and publish notice of

such extension in the FEDERAL REGISTER, with the justification for the extension. If the Commission terminates the offeror's role in the development process, the offeror shall remit all funds contributed by the Commission which have not been expended.

(f) If the Commission determines that no offeror whose offer was accepted is making satisfactory progress, the Commission may terminate the development proceeding, publish a notice of the decision to terminate in the FEDERAL REGISTER, and independently develop a proposed standard.

(g) The offeror shall submit with the standard, test instruments or devices constructed or acquired to perform compliance tests if the Commission determines that these instruments or devices are necessary for the evaluation of the standard. In such a case, the instrument or device shall be sold to the Commission at the offeror's cost or loaned to the Commission for the evaluation of the standard. Further, the offeror shall in any circumstance submit detailed descriptions or plans and specifications for the acquisition or construction of these instruments or devices.

§ 1105.8 Recommended consumer product safety standards developed by offerors.

(a) Recommended standards must be suitable for promulgation under the act. To be considered suitable, a standard shall be written in a manner appropriate for use as a Federal mandatory standard as specified in the format established by the Commission. The format for each standard will be made available by the Commission on or before the acceptance of an offer. Recommended standards shall be supported by test data or other documents or materials which the Commission requires. Recommended standards shall also, if the Commission considers it to be appropriate, contain suitable test methods and reasonable testing programs. Test methods for the measurement of compliance with proposed standards shall be reasonably capable of being performed by the Commission and by persons subject to the act or by private testing facilities. Testing programs shall, if the Commission considers it to be appropriate and so states in the FEDERAL REGISTER notice of the acceptance of the offer, include sampling plans.

(b) Recommended standards shall consist of:

(1) Requirements as to performance, composition, contents, design, construction, finish, or packaging; or

(2) Requirements that a consumer product be marked with or accompanied by clear and adequate warnings or instructions or requirements respecting the form of warnings or instructions; or

(3) Any combination of (1) and (2).

(c) A recommended standard shall be supported by:

(1) An analysis demonstrating that each of the requirements is reasonably

necessary to prevent or reduce the unreasonable risks of injury identified in the notice of proceeding; and

(2) An analysis explaining why the recommended standard is in the public interest.

(3) An analysis of the extent to which elderly and handicaped persons may be adversely affected by the recommended standard.

(d) Each requirement of a standard, other than requirements relating to labeling, warnings, or instructions, shall whenever feasible be expressed in terms of performance. Whenever the requirements are not expressed in terms of performance, an explanation shall be provided to support the use of the nonperformance requirements.

(e) The offeror shall, in submitting a recommended standard, include data and information to demonstrate that compliance with the standard would be technologically practicable. The offeror shall also submit, to the extent that it can reasonably be obtained by the offeror, data and information on the potential economic effect of the standard, including the potential effect on small business and international trade. The economic information should include data indicating (1) the types and classes as well as the approximate number of consumer products which would be subject to the standard; (2) the probable effect of the standard on the utility, cost, and availability of the products; (3) any potential adverse effects of the standard on competition; and (4) the standard's potential disruption or dislocation, if any, of manufacturing and other commercial practices. Further, the offeror shall include information, to the extent that it can reasonably be obtained by the offeror, concerning the potential environmental impact of the standard.

[39 FR 16213, May 7, 1974, as amended at 42 FR 58400, Nov. 9, 1977]

§ 1105.9 Contributions to the offeror's cost.

(a) The Commission may, in accepting an offer, agree to contribute to the offeror's cost in developing a proposed consumer product safety standard in any case in which the Commission determines:

(1) That a contribution is likely to result in a more satisfactory standard than would be developed without a contribution; and

(2) That the offeror is financially responsible.

(b) In order to be eligible to receive a financial contribution, the offeror, in addition to furnishing the information required under § 1105.5, must submit:

(1) A request for a specific contribution with an explanation as to why the contribution is likely to result in a more satisfactory standard than would be developed without a contribution;

(2) A statement asserting that the offeror will employ an adequate accounting system (one in accordance

with generally accepted accounting principles) to record standard development costs and expenditures; and

(3) A request for an advance payment of funds if necessary to enable the offeror to meet operating expenses during the development period.

(c) The Commission, in publishing the terms of the accepted offer, shall include a statement of the purpose and amount of the Commission's contribution.

(d) The offeror whose offer has been accepted shall, for a period of three years after final payment under the development agreement, maintain records which fully disclose the total cost and expenditures for the project and such other records which will facilitate an effective audit. The Commission and the Comptroller General of the United States, or any of their duly authorized representatives, shall have access, for the purpose of audit and examination, to any books, documents, papers, and records relevant to the development of the standard.

(e) The Commission, based upon a finding after an informal hearing that all or part of the Commission's contribution has been or is being misused, may seek reimbursement of that part of the contribution which has been or is being misused and shall have the right, after providing due notice, to terminate the development agreement and to discontinue payments towards the contribution. For the purpose of this Part 1105, "misuse of a contribution" means a use other than that agreed upon in writing by the parties.

(f) The items of cost toward which the Commission may contribute are those allowable direct and indirect costs allocable to the development project (as set forth in the applicable subparts of Part 1-15 of the Federal Procurement Regulations (41 CFR Part 1-15)). The Commission may contribute to the costs of assuring adequate consumer participation in the development of the standard. The Commission may make its contribution in advance and without regard to 31 U.S.C. 529.

(g) The items of cost toward which the Commission will not contribute include:

(1) Costs for the acquisition of any interest in land or buildings; however, the Commission may contribute toward the lease or rental of land or buildings;

(2) Costs for the payment of salaries in excess of the salaries paid by the offeror to individuals at the time immediately preceding the offer, except for longevity and other routine increases which may accrue during the development of the standard;

(3) Costs for the payment of items in excess of the offeror's actual cost;

(4) Costs for items having a usable lifespan in excess of the development period, except that a contribution may be made toward the proportionate

value of the item during the development period determined by subtracting the item's estimated market value at the termination of the development period from the actual acquisition cost (the cost of items purchased by the Commission under § 1105.7(g) cannot be included in the Commission's contribution); and

(5) Costs determined not to be allowable under generally accepted accounting principles and practices or Part 1-15, Federal Procurement Regulations (41 CFR Part 1-15).

(h) Offerors who have received contributions from the Commission shall submit to the Commission a full accounting of these contributions and shall remit all amounts not expended within 60 calendar days after the offeror submits the standard.

[39 FR 16213, May 7, 1974, as amended at 42 FR 58400, Nov. 9, 1977]

NOTES

INTRODUCTION

1. Harry Anderson, "The Corporate Image," *Interior Design* 32, no. 10 (October 1961): 141.

2. Sherman R. Emery, "Contract Design: A Study in Growth," *Interior Design* 36, no. 10 (October 1965): 161. Italics indicated by S. C. Reznikoff.

CHAPTER 1

1. Reprinted with permission from Justin Sweet's *Legal Aspects of Architecture, Engineering and the Construction Process*, copyrighted © 1977 by West Publishing Co., St. Paul, p. 739.

2. American Society of Interior Designers, "Instruction Sheet for Interior Design Services Agreement" (New York, 1978, Document B 171a), p. 2, paragraph 1.4.

3. Orto v. Jackson, Ind. App. 413 N.E. 2nd 273, 278 (1980).

4. Reprinted with permission from *Guidelines for Improving Practice* (Washington, D.C.: Victor O. Schinnerer and Co., 1978).

5. Ibid.

CHAPTER 2

1. "The Cynical Consumers," *Human Behavior Magazine*, August 1977, p. 49. Copyright © 1977. Reprinted with permission.

2. U.S. Department of Commerce, *Interagency Task Force on Product Liability*, vol. 1 (Washington: 1977), pp. 2–10.

3. Norman Polsky, "Report to Business and Institutional Furniture Manufacturers Association on MAAC II," 1977.

CHAPTER 3

1. *Fire Protection Handbook*, 14th ed. (Boston: National Fire Protection Association, 1976), Appendix D, A-30, 31.

CHAPTER 4

1. *Fire Protection Handbook*, 14 ed. (Boston: National Fire Protection Association, 1976), p. 46.

2. Ibid.

3. "Flammability Testing for Carpeting," National Bureau of Standards, NBS Report NBSIR 78-1436, April 1978.

4. See the NIST report for more details on the fuel contribution and smoke temperatures.

5. Drawing by Ib Ohlsson, *Newsweek* magazine, June 13, 1944, p. 24.

6. Anderson, R. C. and Y. C. Alarie, "Approaches to the Evaluation of the Toxicity of Decomposition Products of Polymeric Materials Under Thermal Stress," *Journal of Combustion Toxicology* 5 (May 1978): 214–21.

CHAPTER 5

1. "Design Approach to Fire Safety in Buildings," *Progressive Architecture*. Copyrighted by the Reinhold Publishing Company. Reprinted from the April 1974 issue.

2. Belles, Donald W., Fred L. Fisher, and Dr. Robert B. Williamson, "How Well Does the ASTM E-84 Predict Fire Performance of Textiles and Wallcoverings?", *Fire Journal*, January-February 1988.

3. H. J. Roux, "The Scope and Limitations of Fire Testing," unpublished paper presented at the Fifth International Fire, Security and Safety Exhibition and Conference, London, England, 1978, pp. 5–7.

4. U.S. Department of Housing and Urban Development, Office of Policy Development and Research, "Fire Safety Systems Analysis for Residential Occupancies," vol. 1 (March 1977), pp. 48–50.

CHAPTER 6

1. Consumer Product Safety Act, Commission Organization and Functions, 16 CRF, Section 1000.1, The Commission, paragraph a, Washington, D.C., 1978.

2. *Arizona Republic*, Phoenix, Arizona, January 16, 1979, p. A-10.

3. Fire and Thermal Burn Program Staff, "Briefing Paper on Upholstered Furniture Flammability Standard" (Washington, D.C.: Consumer Product Safety Commission, October 1978).

4. Ibid.

5. Consumer Product Safety Act Regulations, Subchapter B, Part 1105.1, paragraph c. *Code of Federal Regulations*, 1009.3, revised January 1, 1978.

6. Gottlieb and Beck, 1959.

7. Neily, "Technical Update."

8. Nester B. Knoephfler and Julius P. Neumeyer, "Summary of Presentation to CPSC Staff Concerning Mythyborate Vapor Phase Process" (New Orleans, La.: Southern Regional Research Center, 1978), pp. 1–2.

9. Margaret Neily, "Technical Update, Technical Practicability, Proposed Standard for the Flammability (Cigarette Ignition Resistance) of Upholstered Furniture" (Washington, D.C.: Consumer Product Safety Commission, October 1978.)

10. Ibid.

11. Produced for upholstery liners and carpet liners.

12. Marketed under the trade name "Vonar," produced by The E.I. du Pont de Nemours and Company, Inc., Wilmington, Del.

13. NBS Laboratory Tests on UFAC Welt Cord and Foam Test Methods, August 1978.

14. Damant and Young, "Smoldering Characteristics of Fabric Used as Upholstered Furniture Coverings," Laboratory Report Number SP 77-1, State of California, Bureau of Home Furnishings, January 1977.

15. Federal Trade Commission, Docket Number C-2596, Washington, D.C., Nov. 4, 1974, p. 11.

16. Chester J. Barecki, *Ignition of Bus Seats*, paper presented at a meeting of NFPA, May 1976; and *Theater Chair Burn Test: A Technical Report*, E. I. du Pont de Nemours & Company, Inc., Wilmington, Del.

17. Neily, "Technical Update."

CHAPTER 7

1. *Standard for the Surface Flammability of Small Carpets and Rugs*, FF 2-70 (Washington, D.C.: U.S. Government Printing Office,) Section 1631.34, paragraph a.

2. Ibid., Section 1631.62, paragraph c.

3. Reprinted by permission of Allied Chemical Company.

4. William G. Klein, "Static Electricity: Problems and Solutions in Computer Facilities," unpublished paper, United Technical Products, Inc., Westwood, Mass., 1978, pp. 1–8.

5. "Why Use Carpet in Hospitals," J & J Industries, Inc., 1976.

6. *Carpet Specifier's Handbook*, 2nd ed. (Dalton, Ga.: Carpet and Rug Institute, 1977), p. 18.

7. Carpet Cushion Council, "The Supporting Facts about Carpet Cushion," 1977.

8. Housing and Urban Development, *Standard for Detached Carpet Cushion*, UM 72, 1979.

9. Burlington Carpet Division, Burlington Industries, Inc., Technical Services Department, "Measuring and Estimating Made Easy."

10. Ibid.

11. Ibid.

12. Ibid.

13. Burlington Carpet Division, Burlington Industries, Inc., Technical Services Department, "Carpet Workroom and Installation Manual," p. 8.

14. Burlington Carpet Division, Burlington Industries, Inc., Technical Services Department, "Installation Instructions for Direct Gluedown of Conventional Back Fabrics."

15. "Carpet Workroom and Installation Manual," pp. 12–14.

16. *Carpet Specifier's Handbook: Specification, Selection, Installation, Maintenance*, J & J Industries, Inc., revised May 1978, pp. 24–26.

17. "20-Day Maintenance Plan," Racine Industrial Plant, Racine, Wisc., 1978.

18. *Carpet Specifier's Handbook*.

CHAPTER 8

1. A. Philips Cramp, et al., "Preliminary Study of the Slipperiness of Flooring," NBS, COM-75-10059, Washington, D.C., July 1974, p. 1.

2. *The PBS Building Systems Program and Performance Specification for Office Buildings*, 3rd ed. (Washington, D.C.: General Services Administration, 1975).

3. "Resilient Flooring," CSI Monograph, Puget Sound CSI Chapter, Specification Series 09650, 1971.

14. "Maintenance of Vinyl Asbestos and Asphalt Tile Floors for Commercial, Institutional and Industrial Buildings" (Washington, D.C.: Resilient Floor Covering Institute, 1975).

5. Richard Perrell, FCSI, "The PAGS System of Architectural Guide Specifications," Scottsdale, Arizona.

6. "Technical Article: Specifying Acrylic/Wood Flooring," *Contract Interiors*, June 1975, pp. 98–99.

7. Radiation Technology, Incorporated, Bulletin RV 1073, Rockaway, N.J.

CHAPTER 9

1. Richard C. Perrel, FCSI, *The PAGS System of Architectural Guide Specifications*, Scottsdale, Arizona, 1977.

2. "Guide to Measuring for Wallcovering," Wallcovering Manufacturers Association, Springfield, N.J.

CHAPTER 10

1. "Comparative Table of Wood Species." Reprinted with permission of the Architectural Woodwork Institute, Arlington, Va.

2. "Installation of Hardwood Plywood," *How to Sell Hardwood Plywood* (Arlington, Va.: Hardwood Plywood Manufacturers Association, 1975).

3. "Architectural Woodwork Interiors, Wall and Ceiling Treatments." Reprinted by permission of the Architectural Woodwork Institute, Arlington, Virginia, 1975, pp. 22–23.

4. Ibid., p. 19.

CHAPTER 11

1. S. Robert Hastings and Richard W. Crenshaw, "Window Design Strategies to Conserve Energy," NBS Building Science Series, NBS-BSS-104, Washington, D.C., 1977.

2. "Woven Woods and Window Shades by Graber," Graber Form No. 3219-00, p. 8.

3. "Kirsch Compact Architrac with Accordian-Fold Snap on Tape and Carrier System," Kirsch Company, Sturgis, Mich., 1976, p. 5.

4. These headings are also known as "Ripplefold," manufactured by The Kirsch Co.

5. Trade names "Neat Pleat" by Graber and "Archifold" by The Kirsch Co.

6. "Woven Woods and Window Shades by Graber," Garber Form No. 3219-00, p. 8.

CHAPTER 12

1. *The PBS Building Systems Program and Performance Specifications for Office Buildings*, 3rd ed. (Washington, D.C.: GSA, PBS, 1975), pp. F1–3.

2. Ibid., p. F4.

3. *Task-Lit Systems Furniture Energy Conservation Demonstration Project*, PCB-IPD-76-02-DHUD (Washington, D.C.: General Services Administration, Public Services, June 18, 1976), p. 66.

4. *Energy Conservation Design Guidelines for Existing Office Buildings*, 2nd ed. (Washington, D.C.: General Services Administration, Public Building Service, 1977), pp. 4–13, 4–16.

5. General Services Administration, Design Action Center.

6. *The PBS Building Systems Program and Performance Specifications for Office Buildings*, p. G5.3.

7. Knoll International, Inc., "Economics of Task Lighting," *Knoll Task Lighting*, 1976, pp. 12–15.

8. Ibid.

9. *The PBS Building Systems Program and Performance Specifications for Office Buildings*, p. D40.

10. *Task-Lit Systems Furniture Energy Conservation Demonstration Project*, pp. 39–40.

11. *Guide to Office Products, Furniture: Introductory Notes* (Hackensack, N.J.: Buyers Laboratory, Inc., 1977).

12. Vecta Contract, Dallas, Tex.

13. Fixtures Mfg., Corporation, Kansas City, Mo.

14. *Guide to Office Products, Furniture: Introductory Notes.*

15. Ibid.

16. Ibid.

17. Ibid.

18. *Architectural Casework Details* (Arlington, Va.: Architectural Woodwork Institute, 1969), pp. 2–3.

19. *Factory Finishing of Architectural Woodwork* (Arlington, Va.: Architectural Woodwork Institute, 1970), p. 8.

20. *Specifying Wood Cabinets: Unfinished*, CSI Specification Series, 06411, The Construction Specifications Institute, 1970.

CHAPTER 13

1. *Office Building by System: The PBS Building System Program*, General Services Administration, Public Building Service, Washington, DC, 1977, p. 17.

2. This period of time may be extended to forty years, which is considered the average life span of a building.

3. *Life Cycle Costing Workbook: A Guide for the Implementation of Life Cycle Costing in the Federal Supply Service* (Washington, D.C.: General Services Administration, Value Management Division, 1977), pp. vi–25.

CHAPTER 14

1. *Design Criteria: New Public Building Accessibility*, General Services Administration and the Public Buildings Service, May 1977; and *Technical Handbook for Facilities Engineering and Construction Manual*, Part 4, Facilities Design and Construction, Section 4.12, Design of Barrier Free Facilities, Department of Health, Education, and Welfare, August 1978.

2. Ibid., p. 7.

3. Ibid., pp. 1, 2.

4. Ibid., p. 55.

5. Public Law 90-480, Subpart 101-19.604 "Exceptions," paragraphs a-d, as amended 1968.

CHAPTER 15

1. Victor O. Schinnerer and Co., Washington, D.C.

2. *Project Manual: Procedures and Techniques*, vol. 1, CSI Manual of Practice (Washington, D.C.: Construction Specifications Institute, 1975).

CHAPTER 16

1. United States v. Spearin, Supreme Court of the United States, 1918. 248 U.S. 132, 29 S. Ct. 59, 63. L. Ed. 166.

2. Victor O. Schinnerer and Co., Washington, D.C.

CHAPTER 17

1.   John S. Martel, "Safeguards in Specifying New Products," *Guidelines for Improved Practice* (Washington, D.C.: Victor O. Schinnerer & Company, 1971.

2.   *Paxton v. Alameda County*, 259 Pac. 934. 938 (1953).

3.   John Vilett, "The Relationship between the Performance Concept and the Systems Concept," *Performance Concept in Building*, NBS Special Publication 361, vol. 1, 1972, p. 208.

4.   *Guidelines for Improving Practice* (Washington, D.C.: Victor O. Schinnerer and Co., 1978).

CHAPTER 18

1.   Terms developed by the Construction Specifications Institute.

3.   *Project Manual: Procedures and Techniques*, vol. 1, CSI Manual of Practice (Washington, D.C.: Construction Specifications Institute, 1975), chap. 11, p. 6.

4.   Ibid.

5.   *The PBS Building Systems Program and Performance Specifications for Office Buildings*, 3rd ed. (Washington, D.C.: General Services Administration and Public Building Service, 1975), Section A.

6.   *Project Manual: Procedures and Techniques*, chap. 11, pp. 12–13.

7.   Ibid.

8.   See performance checklist in Chapter 4.

INDEX